INTRODUCTION

1. Management and Organizational Behavior: An Overview
2. History of Management and Organizational Behavior
3. The Manager's Environment
4. Social Responsibility and Business Ethics

THE MANAGEMENT PROCESS

5. The Planning Process
6. Strategic Planning
7. Managerial Decision Making
8. The Organizing Process
9. Organizing Structure

10. Staffing the Organization
11. The Controlling Process
12. Controlling Techniques
13. Communication and the Influencing Process

MANAGEMENT AND INDIVIDUAL BEHAVIOR

14. Perception and Attribution
15. Motivation
16. Individual Differences, Development, and Stress

MANAGEMENT AND GROUP BEHAVIOR

17. Group Performance, Intergroup Behavior, and Conflict
18. Leadership
19. Power and Organizational Politics

MANAGEMENT AND BEHAVIOR AT THE ORGANIZATIONAL LEVEL

20. Corporate Culture, Change, and Development
21. Managing the Multinational Enterprise
22. Management Information Systems

Judith R. Gordon
Boston College

Management and Organizational Behavior

R. Wayne Mondy
McNeese State University

Arthur Sharplin
McNeese State University

Shane R. Premeaux
McNeese State University

Allyn and Bacon
Boston • London • Sydney • Toronto

Series Editor: Jack Peters
Developmental Editor: Judith Fifer
Senior Editorial Assistant: Carol Alper
Cover Administrator: Linda K. Dickinson
Composition Buyer: Linda Cox
Manufacturing Buyer: Tamara McCracken
Production Administrator: Rowena Dores
Editorial-Production Service: Karen Mason
Text Designer: Karen Mason
Photo Researcher: Susan Carlson

Library of Congress Cataloging-in-Publication Data

Management and Organizational Behavior / R. Wayne Mondy . . . [et al.],
      p.   cm.
   Includes bibliographies and index.
   ISBN 0-205-12056-3
   1. Organizational behavior. 2. Management. I. Mondy, R. Wayne
   HD 58.7.M35 1989   89–1507
   658.4—dc20   CIP

ISBN 0–205–12056–3
ISBN 0–205–12409–7 (International)

Printed in the United States of America

10 9 8 7 6 5 4 3 2 1   95 94 93 92 91 90

■ PHOTO CREDITS FOR CHAPTER OPENERS

CHAPTER 1—© 1987 Marvin Lewiton/Adams-Russell, All rights reserved.
CHAPTER 2—© Jon Feingersh 1987/Stock, Boston, Inc., All rights reserved.
CHAPTER 3—Stock Boston/© Rick Browne
CHAPTER 4—Mark Godfrey/Courtesy of Aluminum Company of America
CHAPTER 5—Janeart Ltd./The Image Bank
CHAPTER 6—Jon Feingersh/Stock, Boston, Inc.
CHAPTER 7—William Taufic/Courtesy of Air Products and Chemicals, Inc.
CHAPTER 8—Joseph Nettis/Stock, Boston, Inc.
CHAPTER 9—Jon Feingersh/Stock, Boston, Inc.

CHAPTER 10—Michael Stuckey/COMSTOCK, Inc.
CHAPTER 11—COMSTOCK, Inc.
CHAPTER 12—Courtesy of Air Products and Chemicals, Inc.
CHAPTER 13—COMSTOCK, Inc.
CHAPTER 14—Michael Stuckey/COMSTOCK, Inc.
CHAPTER 15—Courtesy of Burndy Corporation
CHAPTER 16—COMSTOCK, Inc.
CHAPTER 17—George Haling/Photo Researchers, Inc.
CHAPTER 18—COMSTOCK, Inc.
CHAPTER 19—COMSTOCK, Inc.
CHAPTER 20—COMSTOCK, Inc.
CHAPTER 21—Courtesy of The Dow Chemical Company
CHAPTER 22—Mike and Carol Werner/COMSTOCK, Inc.

To Judy Bandy Mondy,
my wife, my friend, and strongest supporter.
R. Wayne Mondy

To Steve, Brian, Laurie, and Michael,
whose enthusiasm, encouragement, and love
are the mainstays of my career.
Judith R. Gordon

To Daniel Sharplin,
a young management practioner currently
adding value at Lone Star Steel, Inc.
Arthur Sharplin

To Sonya,
my new wife and the source of my inspiration.
Shane R. Premeaux

Brief Contents

Contents

PART THREE ■
MANAGEMENT AND
INDIVIDUAL BEHAVIOR

14 Understanding Perception, Attribution,
and Learning   393

15 Motivation   421

16 Individual Differences, Development,
and Stress   467

PART FOUR ■ MANAGEMENT
AND GROUP BEHAVIOR

17 Group Performance, Intergroup
Behavior, and Conflict   505

Preface

Effective management is critical for every firm's success. In order to be effective, managers must successfully practice the management functions of planning, organizing, influencing, and controlling. And they must accomplish these tasks in view of how individuals, groups, and the entire organization are affected. Students will learn to properly apply the management functions and utilize the organizational behavior aspects of management to achieve organizational objectives. This book is written for an audience that desires management theory to be linked with organizational behavior. It takes a functional approach to the study of management, but provides organizational behavior emphasis where appropriate. In discussing traditional organizational behavior topics a management flavor is incorporated. *It is truly a management and organizational behavior book which recognizes the extreme importance of both topics.*

■ FEATURES OF THE CHAPTERS

• An introductory chapter which shows how both management and organizational behavior topics will be integrated throughout the book to develop an effective management approach. Utilizing this approach allows a manager to accomplish organizational objectives regardless of whether the problem encountered is related to the function of management or the practice of organizational behavior.

• A management and organizational history chapter which is both informative and interesting to read. Mistakes of the past are prone to be repeated, and therefore students of management must understand and appreciate the history of management and organizational behavior so they have a better frame of reference with which to make critical decisions.

• A manager's environment chapter which shows the many environmental factors that impact top-level managers. It also stresses that the environment of lower-level managers in the organization is different from that of upper-level managers.

• A social responsibility and business ethics chapter is included at the beginning of the book in order to permit the discussion of ethics throughout the text.

• A strategic planning chapter which includes current topics in the field and the organizational aspects that impact strategic planning. Strategy implementation is also discussed, along with the organizational behavior changes required for effective implementation including leadership, organization structure, information and control systems, human resources, and production technology.

• A managerial decision-making chapter which has an organizational behavior flavor. An understanding of participation and the decision-making process and the advantages and disadvantages of group decision making are incorporated into this chapter to allow a comprehensive appreciation of managerial decision making.

• Two organizing chapters are toned to organizational behavior. Departmentation, organizational differentiation, the informal organization, and committees are discussed to create an appreciation of the organizational behavior aspects of organizing.

• A separate chapter covering staffing the organization.

• A communication chapter which introduces the next three sections of individual behavior, group behavior, and behavior at the organizational level. A discussion of intergroup communication is included to illustrate how the various aspects of communication develop in group situations.

• Three management and individual behavior chapters in which such topics as perception, attribution, learning, motivation, individual differences, development, and stress are discussed as they relate to management and organizational behavior.

• Three management and group behavior chapters in which group performance, intergroup behavior, conflict, leadership, power, and politics are discussed as they relate to management and organizational behavior.

• A definitive chapter on corporate culture, change, and development as it relates to individuals, groups, and organizations is included.

• A chapter focusing on managing the multinational enterprise as it relates to individuals, groups, and organizations is also included.

■ FEATURES OF THE BOOK

The following features are included to promote the readability and understanding of important management and organizational behavior concepts:

• A case study involving management and organizational behavior is provided at the beginning of each chapter to set the tone for a discussion of the major topics included within the chapter.

• An "Ethical Dilemma" is provided in Chapters 3–22. These Ethical Dilemmas provide instructors with an opportunity to allow students to experience some realistic dilemmas in a classroom setting.

• "CNN Business Briefs," which relate directly to CNN business reports drawn from such sources as "Pinnacle" and "Inside Business," are provided. A brief recap of the video segment (to be provided to adopters) will be included in fifteen chapters of the text. Professors can briefly discuss the CNN Business Brief scenario and then show the video segment. Those who prefer can use the CNN Business Brief as another current example related directly to the text material.

• Two case studies involving management and organizational behavior are provided at the end of each chapter to highlight material covered in the chapter.

• A comprehensive "Experiential Exercise" is provided at the end of each chapter. These exercises provide for considerable class participation and group involvement.

• Learning objectives are listed at the beginning of each chapter to highlight the general purpose and key concepts of the chapter.

• Review questions appear at the end of each chapter to test the student's understanding of the material.

• Key terms are listed at the end of each chapter. In addition, a key term is presented, in the margin, in bold print the first time it is defined or described in the chapter.

• A glossary of all key terms appears at the end of the book.

• A subject index, name index, and company index are provided at the end of the book.

• Finally, a comprehensive list of references is provided at the end of each chapter to permit additional in-depth study of selected topics.

We sincerely hope that students of management and organizational behavior derive as much pleasure from reading the book as we did in writing it.

▬ ACKNOWLEDGMENTS

The assistance and encouragement of many people is normally required in the writing of any book. It is especially true in the writing of *Management and Organizational Behavior.* Although it would be virtually impossible to list each person who assisted in this project, we feel that certain people must be credited because of the magnitude of their contribution.

Our sincere thanks go to the many members of the faculty and staff at our universities. A special note of thanks goes to Professor Don White of the University of Arkansas who provided one of the authors with considerable encouragement during the early stages of his career.

Two special, competent, and professional individuals—Marthanne Lamansky and Debbie Clark VanNetta—were always available to ensure that our deadlines were met. They are very special people.

We would also like to acknowledge the many contributions of the staff at Allyn and Bacon for their thoughtfulness and assistance throughout the project: Judy Fifer, Developmental Editor, Carolyn Harris, Marketing Manager, Carol Alper, Editorial Assistant, Robin Tiano, Administrative Assistant, and Jack Peters, Senior Editor. We would also like to thank our reviewers for their excellent suggestions during the preparation of the manuscript:

Gabriel Buntzman
Western Kentucky University

Frank Barone
Ohio University

Laura Lynn Beauvair
University of Rhode Island

Al Bluedorn
University of Missouri—Columbia

Timothy Matherly
Florida State University

Jeffrey Pinto
University of Maine—Orono

Joseph Weiss
Bentley College

Bruce Kemelgor
University of Louisville

CHAPTER

1

Chapter Outline

Management and Organizational Behavior: An Overview

Learning Objectives

After completing this chapter students should be able to

1. Define **management** and **organizational behavior** and explain the importance of both.
2. Explain the management functions of planning, organizing, influencing, and controlling.
3. Describe the work of managers at different organizational levels.
4. Discuss the importance of conceptual, technical, and human managerial skills.
5. Explain how management and organizational behavior interrelate.
6. Define **productivity** and state why it is important to managers.

WHEN LEE IACOCCA assumed the presidency of Chrysler in 1979, the company had just suffered its worst one-quarter loss in history. The United States auto industry was beset by foreign competition. The country was entering a lengthy recession. Interest rates were at all-time highs, depressing demand for autos and other durable consumer goods. Actual and threatened auto industry layoffs, along with wage and benefit cuts, had produced a difficult labor-relations climate. Iacocca had his work cut out for him.

Iacocca brought with him impressive credentials. As a Ford Motor Company executive, he had been credited with developing the Mustang and had risen rapidly through the ranks to become second in command to Henry Ford II. Many thought Iacocca had an uncanny knack for sensing market needs and creating products to meet those needs. He had a reputation for getting the most out of his subordinates, for creating enthusiasm, for making difficult decisions, and for working harder than anyone around him. He also brought along a number of able lieutenants, most former Ford executives.

At Chrysler, Iacocca tried to live up to his billing. He visited factories, jawboned the union, made television commercials, and at all times maintained the appearance of a vibrant, forceful, in-charge—though kindly—executive.

Behind the glamour, however, Iacocca had to make hard decisions and take great personal risks. He cut Chrysler's factory employment in half. He closed one-third of the company's plants. He had a number of Chrysler's cars redesigned to reuse parts of older models and to use fewer parts overall.

Dissatisfaction with Iacocca's actions was immediate, while the benefits were significantly delayed. In 1981 the company was still losing hundreds of millions of dollars, but Chrysler was on its way to recovery. Market share increased from 7.8 percent in 1980 to 12.5 percent in 1984. Chrysler moved up eight rungs on the Fortune 500 list of companies to No. 21. Government-guaranteed loans, made to help Chrysler survive, were completely repaid. And Chrysler's break-even point, the number of cars that the company must sell to keep from losing money, was reduced from 2.3 million units to less than half that figure.

The improvement was not just a flash in the pan. At Chrysler's 1987 model preview, held in Texas Stadium near Dallas, Iacocca forecasted a 15-percent share of the United States auto market by the 1990s. By early 1987 Chrysler stock was trading around $42 a share, up from $2 at the depth of the 1982 recession.

As so often happens, benefits of effective management were widely distributed at Chrysler. Stockholders saw their share prices escalate. The management team that led Chrysler through its crisis received millions of dollars in bonuses. And the employees, who had agreed to wage and benefit cuts at the beginning of the crisis, ended up substantial owners of the corporation because of shares contributed to their retirement plan.[1] ■

W HAT ACCOUNTS FOR Chrysler's remarkable success? Most would agree that effective management and the proper application of organizational behavior techniques played a major part in Chrysler's comeback. This book is about management and organizational behavior. These topics are not simple ones. At Chrysler, management was involved in negotiations with government and with unions. The management process required laying off employees, closing plants, and forecasting future opportunities and preparing to take advantage of them. An executive team had to be developed. Through the application of such organizational behavior techniques as motivation and leadership, the company's 80,000 men and women were given a boost, and made to pull together toward common, or at least compatible, goals. A complex organization, involving a dozen levels of management, had to be administered and improved.

Most managerial situations are not as exciting as the one Iacocca faced. And not all business adventures end in success. Half of all new businesses fail within the first two years of operation, and 70 percent fail within five years. In over 90 percent of such cases, the cause of failure is said to be ineffective management. Despite Iacocca's reputation, few gave him much chance of salvaging Chrysler, let alone making it a real competitor. The costs of poor management to individuals and to society are great. Not only are financial and physical resources wasted, but individuals often suffer psychological damage from a business failure. Many business failures can be avoided through good management and organizational behavior practices.

We live in a society of large and small organizations. Within these organizations people work together to accomplish goals that are too challenging to be achieved by a single individual. Throughout life each person has experiences with a variety of organizations—hospitals, schools, churches, the military, businesses, colleges, government agencies, and other types of institutions. More and more it is being recognized that the most significant factor in determining the performance and success of any organization is the quality of its management.

The job of managing is likely to become even more challenging. Foreign competition, coupled with the large number of corporate takeovers and restructurings, has resulted in the new "lean and mean" organizations. As Chrysler did earlier, USX Corporation (formerly U.S. Steel), BankAmerica, and General Electric cut out layers of managers and made greater demands on those who remained. Similar efficiency measures were necessary at thousands of smaller firms. Cotton's, a bakery in Monroe, Louisiana, and the Vermont Apple Company near Montpelier were forced to retrench when national firms opened branches to compete with them. *Fortune* magazine's Peter Nulty forecasted "downsizing" and "flattening of the pyramid" for many companies, both large and small. No longer, Nulty wrote, will managers succeed because they "master the bureaucracy," but only if they add real value to their organization.[2]

Why are some managers successful and others not? The reasons are as diverse as individual personalities. This book is concerned with providing students with information about the concepts and techniques used by good managers such as Iacocca. Ideas, concepts, and practices that can serve as aids to effective management will be presented. Additionally, the study of human behavior in organizations is given major emphasis. The primary focus of the text is on for-profit businesses; however, not-for-profit examples are included since most of what may be said about one applies to the other.

In this first chapter the concept of management is discussed, and the four management functions are described. Decision making is then presented as a topic that relates to all of them. The manner in which management differs at various levels in the organization and the skills managers need are described. An overview of organizational behavior is presented and, finally, the productivity challenge management faces is addressed.

■ WHAT IS MANAGEMENT?

Unless you inherit a fortune, you will probably choose to be employed by some type of organization. Many of you will become managers, and those who do not are likely to be professional and technical personnel such as engineers, salespersons, systems analysts, accountants, marketing researchers, and computer programmers. In any case, all of you will be managed and manage others at various times in your lives. Thus, it is important to address the question, What is management?

Management is the process of getting things done through the efforts of other people. This often involves the allocation and control of money and physical resources. Iacocca's position gave him extraordinary power over those with whom he worked. He could hire and fire managers and employees; fund or not fund the activities his subordinates favored; shut down plants, replace workers with robots, and carry out his purposes at Chrysler in dozens of other ways. The definition of management includes all of these activities. What is excluded is the action of an individual working alone. A person is not a manager unless involved in the process of getting things done through others. H. Ross Perot, founder of the highly successful Electronic Data Systems Corporation (EDS), recognizes that management success is people success. After selling EDS to the General Motors Corporation (GM) and assuming a position on the GM board, Perot became openly critical of the management at GM for ignoring the people component of the organization. In his well-publicized comments directed at the GM board chairman, Roger B. Smith, Perot repeatedly warned that management's lack of concern for the employees at GM threatened the future of the company.

In order to function properly as a manager, an individual must also understand, and be capable of applying, the organizational behavioral concepts that facilitate the management of people. **Organizational behavior** is the field of study that analyzes individuals, groups, and structure to determine the effects they have on behavior within an organization. These concepts are essential to a manager who desires to maximize the efforts of others and thereby accomplish organizational objectives. An overview of organizational behavior is provided later in this chapter to orient the student to the interrelationship between management and organizational behavior.

■ THE MANAGEMENT FUNCTIONS

A **function** is a type of work activity that can be identified and distinguished from other work. By general agreement, the management process is thought of as consisting of four functions: planning, organizing, influencing, and controlling (see Figure 1.1).

Management
The process of getting things done through the efforts of other people.

Organizational behavior
The field of study that analyzes individuals, groups, and structure to determine the effects they have on behavior within an organization.

Function
A type of work activity that can be identified and distinguished from other work.

FIGURE 1.1 ■
The Management Process

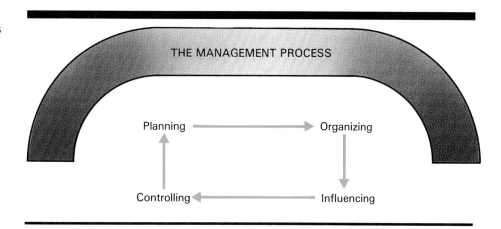

Planning

Planning
The process of determining in advance what should be accomplished and how it should be realized.

Planning, both short- and long-term, is the process of determining in advance what should be accomplished and how it should be realized. In the United States long-term planning may apply to a time frame as short as five years, whereas overseas it may extend to 100 years or more. Ideally, plans should be stated in specific terms in order to provide clear guidance for managers and workers. For example, when Chrysler Corporation sought to gain market share by developing new products, management had to make specific decisions about both the types of new cars and the numbers to make, and also about the market share improvement to seek. Partly as a result of introduction of the K-car and the minivan, the company's market share climbed by more than 30 percent. The Chrysler example is one of strategic planning—the determination of overall organizational purposes and objectives and how they are to be achieved.

The Chrysler story is a well-known example of top-level planning, but the planning process is similar at all levels of an organization. For example, suppose at the first of the week a supervisor is given a production list for completion by Friday. Since the list tells the supervisor what should be accomplished, part of the planning has already occurred. The supervisor, however, still has to determine how the required production can be completed on time. After analyzing all available information, the supervisor will schedule one-fifth of the output for Monday, one-fifth for Tuesday, and so forth. Analyzing all information available and making decisions are major aspects of the planning process.

Planning frequently requires updating and sometimes means abandoning many aspects of the overall plan in order to accomplish the mission of the organization. For example, when Frederick W. Smith, founder of Federal Express Corporation, went international with his business, he ran head-on into entrenched overseas rivals and onerous foreign regulations. The result over a three-year period was a loss of approximately $74 million. Smith's mission remained the same, to become a successful multinational, but his plans changed. Smith purchased Tiger International Inc., and with it bought the rights to the delivery routes Tiger had acquired over 40 years. Tiger's routes and planes have provided a much-needed boost for Federal's express package delivery service, helping Smith toward his ultimate goal of making Federal "the largest and best transportation company in the world."[3] Planning, a complex and constantly changing aspect of management, is covered in greater detail in both Chapters 5 and 6.

Organizing

Organizing
The process of prescribing formal relationships among people and resources to accomplish goals.

Organizing is the process of prescribing formal relationships among people and resources to accomplish goals. For Chrysler Corporation in 1979, organizing required determining the new relationships that would exist among thousands of workers and managers. It also required determining work flows among the remaining plants. At lower levels, workers were assigned to different supervisors, assembly lines were rearranged, and many activities previously performed by Chrysler employees were contracted out.

During the 1980s, organizing required companies to do as Xerox has done and rethink their plans. A decade earlier Xerox watched as its near monopoly in the lucrative copier business was overrun by smaller, cheaper, and better machines from Japan. Xerox has regained some lost ground, and has further reorganized to make additional gains. On January 31, 1989, the company announced that it would lay off 2,000 of its 100,000 employees and take a $275 million pretax write-off to dump nonperforming assets.[4] Xerox is reorganizing into a no-nonsense copier company.

Chapters 8 and 9 discuss organizing as a formal process. Of course, the formal organization must take into account the informal organization, which is the set of evolving relationships and patterns of human interaction within the organization that are not officially prescribed. The informal organization is discussed in greater detail in Chapter 8 and in other portions of the text.

Influencing

Influencing
The process of determining or affecting the behavior of others.
Motivation
The willingness to put forth effort in the pursuit of goals.

Influencing is the process of determining or affecting the behavior of others. This involves motivation, leadership, and communication, all aspects of organizational behavior. **Motivation** is the willingness to put forth effort in the pursuit of goals. Motivating workers often means simply creating an environment that makes them want to work. H. Ross Perot places a high premium on creating such an environment for his employees. Whether he is going to Iran to rescue his employees being held hostage, or taking on General Motors because, as a board member at GM, he believed management was ignoring the people component of the organization, he serves as an extremely positive and motivating influence.

Essential in this environment is the direction provided by the manager. Each worker may require a different means of motivation, and no manager can motivate a worker to produce if the worker chooses not to respond. Thus the manager's challenge is to create a situation in which workers will want to produce more (be motivated), as Lee Iacocca did at Chrysler.

Leadership
Getting others to do what the leader wants them to do.

Leadership is getting others to do what the leader wants them to do. A good leader is one who gets others to put forth their best efforts. Many leaders depend in part on charisma and other personal attributes for their effectiveness. For example, many observers believe that much of Lee Iacocca's success is his ability

A manager influences others through motivation, leadership, and communication. (© Lou Jones/The Image Bank)

to inspire others. Good leadership, however, more often results from learning what motivates individual workers and using this knowledge to direct their activities. The leadership style that works best varies depending on the characteristics of the leader, the led, and the situation. As one president of a top Fortune 500 firm said, "A leader must *lead,* not drive. People are unpredictable, different from one another, often irascible, frequently petty, sometimes vain, but always magnificent if they are properly motivated."

In 1988, the five best-managed companies in the United States were Apple Computer, Merck & Company, Rubbermaid, Wal-Mart Stores, and the Washington Post Company.[5] These companies had one thing in common: all had chief executives who thoroughly understood their businesses and their people. These leaders continually inspire their employees to follow them and to willingly exert the extra effort necessary to achieve collective success.[6]

Communication

The transfer of information, ideas, understanding, or feelings among people.

Communication is the transfer of information, ideas, understanding, or feelings among people. Much of a manager's day is spent communicating. Supervisors, for example, tell workers what needs to be done. They also report to upper-level management, summarizing their unit's activities, seeking support and guidance, and representing subordinates. Lack of good communication skills can severely hurt an organization's productivity. Communication is discussed extensively in Chapter 13.

The way in which managers motivate and lead workers and communicate with superiors and subordinates affects, and is affected by, corporate culture, the system of shared values, beliefs, and habits within an organization. The culture can be one of openness and support, as Thomas Peters and Robert Waterman, in their landmark book *In Search of Excellence,* said is the case at IBM and Xerox. It also may be one of autocracy and fear, which some say exists at Manville Corporation, the huge asbestos maker that obtained bankruptcy court protection in 1982 from thousands of asbestos victims who sought recompense. Corporate culture is discussed in Chapter 20.

Controlling

Controlling is the process of comparing actual performance with standards and taking any necessary corrective action. Controls are established to ensure proper performance in accordance with plans. If performance is unsatisfactory, corrective action can be taken. For instance, if a company's costs for producing a product are higher than planned, management must have some means of recognizing the problem and taking the appropriate action to correct the situation. Control can be applied when performance is satisfactory. For example, when sales of Chrysler's minivans exceeded expectations in 1982, shifts were added at existing plants to meet the demand, and plans were made to reopen a factory that had been closed. One aspect of the controlling function that relates uniquely to the human resource is disciplinary action. This action is taken to correct undesirable behavior and can range from a verbal warning to outright dismissal. Controlling is discussed in Chapters 11 and 12.

■ DECISION MAKING AND THE MANAGEMENT FUNCTIONS

As may be seen in Figure 1.2, each management function involves **decision making.** This is the process of generating and evaluating alternatives and making choices among them. The ability to make decisions is the attribute that most frequently distinguishes the excellent manager from a mediocre one.

Lee Iacocca has repeatedly proved himself to be an effective decision maker. When he arrived at Chrysler, he found an unmotivated, listless work force. Decisions had to be made about how a new, more flexible organization at Chrysler might function. Iacocca made a hard decision to give substantial Chrysler stock to the employee stock-ownership trust. He determined with his management team the kinds of controls to impose, placing special emphasis on quality control because of the threat presented by high-quality Japanese and European imports.

F I G U R E 1.2 ■
Decision Making and the
Management Functions

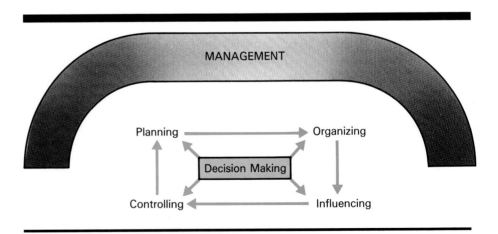

August Busch III is another corporate executive who is considered to be an effective decision maker, and one who governs in unlikely ways. As chairman of Anheuser-Busch, the United States' largest brewer, Busch employs an unusual means for arriving at answers to tough, meaty, complicated decisions: he arranges debates in which managers are assigned opposing positions. Each manager is given staff support and several weeks to prepare. After listening to the debate, Busch makes the final decision. Decision making is the topic of Chapter 7.

■ MANAGEMENT AT DIFFERENT LEVELS

Sometimes managers are only thought of as being top-level individuals within large organizations. Certainly Chrysler's Lee Iacocca is a manager. But most managers do not have responsibility for an entire company. Although the distinctions are by no means clear, it is useful to think of managers as being divided into three levels, as shown in Figure 1.3.

Supervisory managers directly oversee the efforts of those who actually perform the work. Most supervisory managers have titles like supervisor, foreman, leadman, or office manager. Department heads at universities are typically

Supervisory managers
Persons who directly oversee the efforts of those who actually perform the work.

FIGURE 1.3 ■
Managerial Levels

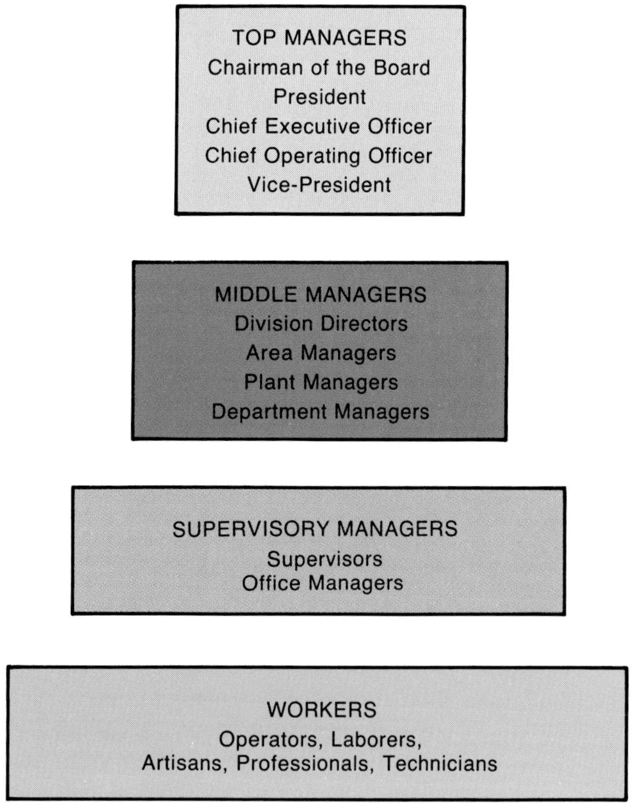

TOP MANAGERS
Chairman of the Board
President
Chief Executive Officer
Chief Operating Officer
Vice-President

MIDDLE MANAGERS
Division Directors
Area Managers
Plant Managers
Department Managers

SUPERVISORY MANAGERS
Supervisors
Office Managers

WORKERS
Operators, Laborers,
Artisans, Professionals, Technicians

**BUSINESS
BRIEFS**

Middle managers
Managers above the supervisory level but subordinate to the firm's most senior executives.

Top managers
The organization's most senior executives.

considered to be supervisory managers because they oversee the activities of professors, who actually do the jobs of research and teaching.

Middle managers are above the supervisory level but subordinate to the firm's most senior executives. These persons might be department managers, division directors, area managers, or plant managers. Chrysler has several levels of middle managers.

Top managers are the organization's most senior executives. They usually include the chairman of the board and the president, along with vice presidents who are responsible for major subdivisions of the organization. Top managers are responsible for providing the overall direction of the firm. Certainly, Iacocca is a top manager.

In summary, a manager is anyone, at any level of the organization, who directs the efforts of other people. Wherever a group of people work together to achieve results, a manager is usually present. School principals, meat market supervisors, and service station operators are managers, as are the presidents of Porsche, Prudential Insurance, and Bank of America. The president of the United States is a manager, too, along with government agency heads and college deans. A manager is the catalyst who makes things happen. He or she establishes goals, plans operations, organizes various resources—personnel, materials, equipment, capital—leads and motivates people to perform, evaluates actual results against the goals, and develops people for the organization.

Unfortunately, in many organizations a manager is judged exclusively on short-run output, being considered effective if a unit is earning a profit, reducing costs, or increasing the market share for the company's products. Naturally, these accomplishments are very important to a business organization; however, a major added challenge and obligation of all managers is the development of subordinates. More than any other single variable, it is perhaps the quality of a manager's subordinates that ultimately determines the long-term success and effectiveness of that manager.

■ MANAGERIAL SKILLS

To be effective, a manager must possess and continually develop several essential skills. Figure 1.4 illustrates three categories of necessary skills and their relative significance at each level of management. The best managers recognize that they must develop and practice each of the managerial skills to be effective in accomplishing organizational and personal goals. They dare not concentrate their efforts on only one of these skills, even though it may be the most important one at their level in the organization. It is the combination of skills that is vital to managerial success. With this clearly in mind, let us now consider the three categories of skills separately.

Conceptual Skill

Conceptual skill
The ability to comprehend abstract or general ideas and apply them to specific situations.

The ability to comprehend abstract or general ideas and apply them to specific situations is **conceptual skill.** By exercising conceptual skills managers understand the complexities of the overall organization, including how each subunit contributes to the accomplishment of the firm's purposes. These skills are crucial to the success of top-level executives who must be concerned with the big picture. Failure to assess opportunities and decide how to take advantage of them can mean disaster. For example, General Motors Corporation apparently has yet to apply appropriate conceptual skills to resolving the problems of its domestic automobile operations. The cars GM has been producing have thus far not appealed to American drivers. Because of this lack of direction, most of GM's profit gains for 1988 were from its European vehicle sales and from nonauto business.[7]

The farther down in the organization one looks, the less vital conceptual skills are. Middle managers need moderate conceptual skills but not as much as top managers. Supervisors typically have the least need for these skills because they usually are given fairly specific guidelines. They are primarily concerned

FIGURE 1.4 ■■
Skills at Various Levels of
Management

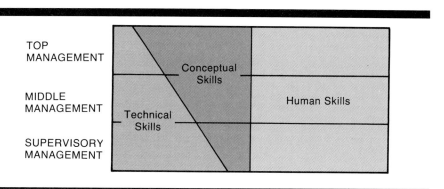

Managers work with individuals and groups within the structure of the organization to accomplish their goals. (© 1987 Bob Hahn/Air Products and Chemicals, Inc.)

with their own and other closely related departments, and these relationships and functions are more clearly defined.

Technical Skill

Technical skill
The ability to use specific knowledge, methods, and techniques in performing work.

Technical skill is the ability to use specific knowledge, methods, and techniques in performing work. This category is very important to job success for supervisors, who must use technical skills to train new workers and monitor daily work activities. If corrections are needed, the technically skilled supervisor is much better qualified to make them.

As one moves to higher levels of management within the organization, the importance of technical skills usually diminishes because managers at those levels have less direct contact with day-to-day problems and activities. Top management has perhaps the least need for technical skills. Many upper-level managers have technical backgrounds, but, unlike supervisors, they seldom use their technical skills on a daily basis. For instance, the president of an engineering firm, although trained as an engineer, is not likely to design a new machine personally. However, some chief executives, including Chrysler's Lee Iacocca, are highly respected by subordinates for their technical expertise. This undoubtedly makes them better managers, even though their primary organizational mission is not technical.

Human Skill

Human skill
The ability to understand, motivate, and get along with other people.

The ability to understand, motivate, and get along with other people is **human skill.** Human skills are about equally important at all levels of management. Activities requiring human skills include such organizational behavior techniques as communication, leadership, and motivation. For example, supervisors must interact with their workers. Similarly, company presidents must communicate with and influence other executives and directors, as well as persons outside the organization, such as investment bankers.

■ WHAT IS ORGANIZATIONAL BEHAVIOR?

As is noted throughout the book, considerable overlap exists between the study of management and the study of organizational behavior. As previously defined, organizational behavior is the analysis of the effect that individuals, groups, and structure have on behavior within an organization. Remember that the definition of management is the process of getting things done through the efforts of other people. Managers must work with individuals and groups and within the structure of the organization if their goals are to be accomplished. As illustrated in Figure 1.5, an understanding of the concepts of organizational behavior is essential in every function of management: planning, organizing, influencing, and controlling.

Planning is a task that all effective managers must accomplish. But it cannot be accomplished in a vacuum. Individuals and groups are affected by plans, and even a well-conceived plan may experience failure if the people affected by the plan are unable or unwilling to carry it out.

Implicit within the definition of organizing, is the idea that managers arrange both individuals and groups in a way that will best accomplish goals. When this occurs, old relationships are necessarily disturbed and new ones made. As will be established later, changes in these relationships can have either a positive or a negative impact on productivity.

The influencing function of management is thoroughly integrated with the concepts of organizational behavior. Consider, for instance, the effect a manager's leadership style has on individuals and groups. Likewise, a manager's ability to motivate and communicate effectively has impact throughout all levels of an organization.

Controlling has consequences beyond the money and materials that are targets for adjustment in this process. Individuals and groups are also affected, as when deviations from standards occur and disciplinary action is required.

FIGURE 1.5 ■
Management and
Organizational Behavior

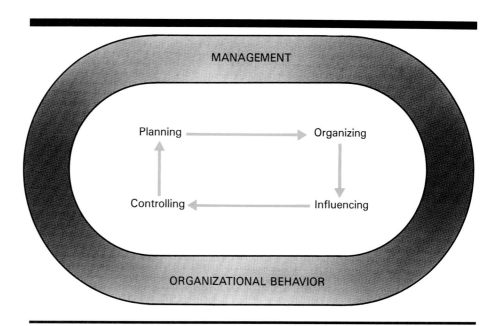

▦ THE PRODUCTIVITY CHALLENGE

Efficiency
The proportional relationship between the quality and quantity of inputs, and the quality and quantity of outputs produced.

Effectiveness
The degree to which the process produces the intended outputs.

Understanding management and organizational behavior is not an end in itself. This knowledge is useless unless it is applied to increase the quality and quantity of goods and services produced in the economy. The proportional relationship between the quality and quantity of inputs, and the quality and quantity of outputs produced is referred to as **efficiency.** The degree to which the process produces the intended outputs is called **effectiveness.** For society, and for the individual, high standards of living are obtained by producing goods and services efficiently. Historically, the United States has had the highest levels of productivity of all major countries. **Productivity** is a measure of the relationship between inputs (labor, capital, natural resources, energy, and so forth) and the quality

F I G U R E   1.6   ▦▦   Relative Levels in Real Gross Domestic Product per Employed Person for Selected Countries and Years

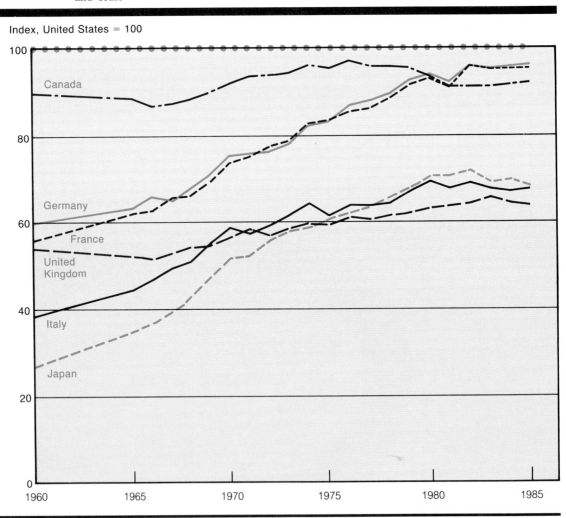

Source: Bureau of Labor Statistics

Productivity
A measure of the relationship between inputs (labor, capital, natural resources, energy, and so forth) and the quality and quantity of outputs (goods and services).

and quantity of outputs (goods and services). Note from this definition that outputs must be measured in terms of both quality and quantity. For example, although the Chevrolet Vega was produced in the United States at a cost approximating that of the Toyota Corolla, which was made in Japan, the United States auto industry's productivity may not have been as high as that of Japan. The output in terms of quantity may have been the same, but the Corolla was clearly superior in terms of quality.

Productivity is usually expressed only in terms of output per person-hour or output per employed person. What causes it to be high or low? Productivity is a result not only of the capability and motivation of workers but also of technology, capital investment, capacity utilization, scale of production, and many other factors.

How does productivity in the United States compare with that in other countries? Figure 1.6 shows the relative levels of productivity in terms of output per employed person in the major industrial countries over more than two decades. Note that although the United States has a commanding lead over most of these other countries, that lead is narrowing in a relative sense. Even in 1985, however, the United States held a productivity advantage over its nearest competitor nation.

In the 1980s there was much concern in the United States because its *rate of growth* in productivity was less than that for other industrial nations. Table 1.1 lists the rate of growth for some of the countries represented in Figure 1.6. Remember, Table 1.1 does not show productivity levels but the *rates of growth* in productivity. Note that productivity grew more slowly in the United States than in any of the other countries; however, the difference narrowed during the second period. This difference exists in part because the United States started from a higher base. For example, in 1960, when Japanese productivity was less than one-fourth that of the United States, an increase in productivity by the same absolute amount for both countries would have been four times as high a percentage increase for Japan. Still, the major challenge facing management in the United States is to attain levels of productivity growth that will ensure that the United States remains the most productive major industrialized nation in the world. This

TABLE 1.1 ■ Rates of Growth in Productivity
(average annual percent change)

Country	Real gross domestic product per employed person	
	1965–1977	1980–1985
United States	1.04	1.6
Canada	1.48	1.7
France	3.72	2.3
Germany	3.60	1.9
Japan	6.08	5.2
United Kingdom	2.44	2.8

Source: U.S. Department of Commerce

can be accomplished through improvements in all of the factors of production. If management has a single societal goal, it is to increase productivity.

Several authorities—such as John Naisbitt, who wrote *Megatrends,* and Peters and Waterman, authors of *In Search of Excellence*—have noted the shift in the United States from an industrial economy to one of service and information. As this occurs, productivity becomes more difficult to measure. For example, it is harder to calculate the output of a computer programmer or a financial adviser than that of a person who works on an assembly line at Ford Motor Company. Nevertheless, productivity remains the control objective of organized human activity.

F I G U R E 1.7 ■■ Organization of the Book

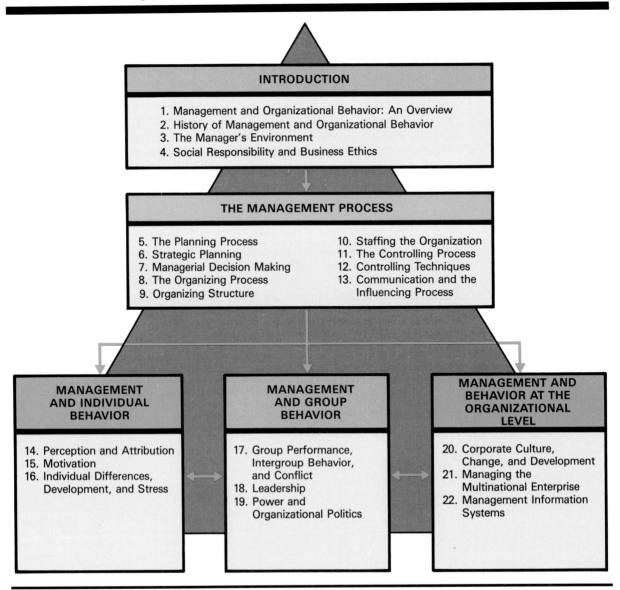

■ PURPOSES AND ORGANIZATION OF THIS TEXT

Effective management is critical for every firm's success. To be effective, managers must successfully practice the management functions of planning, organizing, influencing, and controlling, always keeping in mind how individuals, groups, and the entire organization are affected. Basically, managers must understand the management concepts, properly apply the management functions, and utilize the organizational behavior aspects of management to achieve organizational goals. This book is designed to provide students with the following:

- A greater knowledge of, and insight into, the responsibilities of managing people and other resources
- A better understanding of the problems of operating a business organization
- An opportunity to learn the skills essential to effective managerial decision making
- An understanding of basic principles of management
- A knowledge of how individual behavior affects the job of a manager
- A realization of how group behavior affects tasks that managers perform
- An appreciation of how behavior at the organizational level affects managers

This book is organized into five parts (outlined in Figure 1.7) to provide students with an appreciation of the importance of both management and organizational behavior.

SUMMARY

Management is defined as the process of getting things done through the efforts of other people. This often involves the allocation and control of money and physical resources. To function properly as a manager, an individual must also understand and be capable of applying the organizational behavioral concepts that facilitate the management of people. Organizational behavior is the field of study that analyzes individuals, groups, and structure to determine the effect they have on behavior within an organization.

The management process consists of four functions: planning, organizing, influencing, and controlling. Planning is the process of determining in advance what should be accomplished and how to do it. Organizing is the process of prescribing formal relationships among people and resources to accomplish goals. Influencing is the process of determining or affecting the behavior of others. This involves the organizational behavioral topics of motivation, leadership, and communication. Controlling is the process of comparing actual performance with standards and taking any necessary corrective action. Each management function involves and is affected by decision making, the process of generating and evaluating alternatives and making choices among them.

At all three managerial levels, from supervisory to top management, managers must motivate and lead workers and communicate with superiors and subordinates. Their methods affect, and are affected by, corporate culture, the system of shared values, beliefs, and habits within an organization.

To be effective, a manager must possess and continually develop several essential skills. Comprehending abstract or general ideas and applying them to specific situations are conceptual skills. Technical skill is the ability to use specific knowledge, methods, or techniques in performing work. Understanding, motivating, and getting along with other people are human skills.

There is considerable overlap between the study of management and the study of organizational behavior. Managers must work with individuals and groups and within the structure of the organization if their goals are to be accomplished.

Managerial skills are developed for the purpose of increasing the quality and quantity of goods and services produced in the economy. Historically, the United States has had the highest levels of productivity of all major countries. Productivity is a measure of the relationship between inputs (labor, capital, natural resources, energy, and so forth) and the quality and quantity of outputs (goods and services). Productivity is usually expressed only in terms of output per person-hour or output per employed person. The major challenge facing American management is to attain levels of productivity growth that will ensure that the United States remains the most productive major industrialized nation in the world.

REVIEW QUESTIONS

1. Define management. Why does the definition exclude the action of an individual working alone?
2. List and briefly describe the functions of management.
3. Distinguish by definition and example among supervisory managers, middle managers, and top managers.
4. List and briefly define the types of skills important to managerial effectiveness.
5. Describe the relationship between management and organizational behavior.
6. Define productivity. How does the United States rank among industrial nations with regard to levels of productivity? Productivity growth?

KEY TERMS

management	leadership	conceptual skill
organizational behavior	communication	technical skill
function	controlling	human skill
planning	decision making	efficiency
organizing	supervisory managers	effectiveness
influencing	middle managers	productivity
motivation	top managers	

CASE STUDY

FROM OPERATOR TO MANAGER

BRENDA SIDOLI HAD been working as a machine operator at Parma Cycle Company's Cleveland, Ohio, plant for three years when she got her chance to become a manager. When the supervisor in the frame-painting department quit, Brenda applied for and got the job. The promotion did not mean a pay raise, but Brenda saw it as an opportunity to advance. She thought she was selected primarily because of her good record. She had one of the highest records of quality and quantity in the plant. Brenda's supervisor had always marked her "excellent" in cooperativeness on her performance evaluations. Also, she missed only one day in attendance in the last two years.

Brenda expected to receive a few days of training in her new position, but the former supervisor was already gone when she reported for work that first day, and her new boss, the assistant plant manager, was away on a week-long trip.

Brenda went to see the plant manager and asked him what she was to do. He said, "Just move into your office, study the procedures manuals for the paint department, and try to get to know your people." The plant manager seemed to be in a rush, so Brenda did not take any more of his time. Her office was an eight-foot-square room next to the frame-painting line with windows from about waist high to the ceiling. Brenda located the procedures manuals and began to look through them while watching the operators on the paint line.

QUESTIONS
1. Discuss the pros and cons of Brenda's accepting the job as a manager.
2. Explain how Brenda might expect to be involved in performance of the four management functions. How will this differ from the way the plant manager is involved?

CASE STUDY

THE NEW PRESIDENT

AS GLORIA PHILLIPS seated herself behind her new executive desk on her first day as president of Wharton Products Company, she decided to allow herself a moment of nostalgia. She had come to work early that morning with the intention of getting a running start at the day. But she was a full two hours early and thought that she could afford a few minutes of relaxation.

Wharton Products is a New Brunswick, New Jersey, maker of high-quality control mechanisms for the petrochemical industry. Gloria had known that she was the likely choice for president when the previous president resigned. She had worked hard over the years and was respected for her competence in the field and for her ability to work with employees at all levels. As she sipped her coffee that morning, her thoughts raced back over the twenty years she had been with Wharton.

Gloria had come to Wharton as a young college graduate with a degree in industrial management but no business experience. She was hired as an assistant supervisor and was immediately placed on the production line. "I don't see how I got by," she thought. "I knew so little about the operations and even less about management. It seemed that every day was filled with one brush fire after another." Thanks to procedures manuals and a patient superior, Gloria was able to stay out of trouble. In fact, she was soon competent to handle the supervisor's job alone.

She did not get to do that, though. After just six months on the job, she had a chance to become production manager, and the supervisor who had been her boss became one of her subordinates. As a supervisor, Gloria had been primarily concerned with daily operations. As production manager, she found it necessary to plan weeks and even months in advance. She also had to complete more reports and attend more meetings, and she found herself with less time for the technical responsibilities she had enjoyed carrying out as a supervisor.

She chuckled as she thought about the time, just after she took over as production manager, she discovered that the operating procedures manuals were grossly out of date and inadequate. Several new machines had been installed, and one whole production line had been added since the last revision to the manuals. It took Gloria more than a year to put them in order. In the process, she learned a lot about how the production division fit into the overall plant operations. She also visited several other plants and discovered a number of new and better ways of doing things, which she incorporated into the procedures manuals.

Because the company was growing and changes in the manufacturing technology Wharton used occurred frequently, the procedures manuals had to be modified often. Soon Gloria was able to turn this work over to an assistant and spend more time on planning and assisting her subordinates in doing their jobs better. She also spent much time in meetings and discussions with superiors and in reviewing and completing reports.

When Gloria was twenty-eight, just five years after she had become production manager, Wharton lost its vice president for planning to a competitor. Gloria applied for the job and, in competition with five other well-qualified applicants, got the promotion. Gloria had thought she was well qualified, but the complexities of her new position were overwhelming at first. It was difficult enough to forecast production requirements a year in advance, but the typical lead time for a new plant or even a new production line was several years. Also, in the new job, Gloria had to consider the interrelationships among marketing, finance, personnel, and production. The higher Gloria rose in the organization, the less she was able to depend on standard operating procedures.

From the planning job, Gloria was promoted to senior vice president for manufacturing, and later to chief operating officer before her advancement to president.

"Surely," thought Gloria, "at some point one begins to feel fully competent to handle any situation that might arise." Gloria knew that she had not reached that point, however; she felt nervous and apprehensive about how things would go over the next few months.

QUESTIONS

1. What specific skills will be most important to Gloria's success as president of Wharton Products? Do you feel that she possesses these skills? Explain.
2. How do managerial responsibilities change as one progresses up the hierarchy in an organization?

EXPERIENTIAL EXERCISE

Managers have to get things done through the efforts of other people. Therefore, managers who have a clear understanding of the people being managed have a decided edge in enhancing productivity. Managers should first gain a clear understanding of themselves, however, since their attitudes and values affect the way they deal with others. Self-understanding is by no means easy, because individuals often have difficulty admitting their true attitudes and values, especially to themselves. The purpose of this exercise is to assist you in gaining a better understanding of how you would manage people. After completing the exercise, you should be better aware of some of your attitudes and values. The exercise will not answer all of your questions, but it should provide some valuable insight. Self-awareness assessment is the method applied here to impart a clearer picture of the manager's true makeup.

Self-Awareness Assessment

Complete each of the following twenty sentence fragments. Be honest and the self-assessment will pay off. When doing a self-assessment, individuals are sometimes required to complete sentence fragments such as the twenty included below. If an individual honestly completes the fragments, a useful self-assessment is possible.

1. I feel best when people . . .
2. Many people don't agree with me about . . .
3. Some people seem to want just to . . .
4. I am best at . . .
5. Those with whom I work the closest are . . .
6. In a group I am . . .
7. The kind of person who always asks the boss for directions is . . .
8. When people depend on me, I . . .
9. I get angry when . . .
10. People who expect a lot from me make me feel . . .
11. If I feel I can't get something across to another person . . .
12. I have difficulty trying to deal with . . .
13. When I see someone always agreeing with the boss . . .
14. When heated arguments arise in a meeting, I . . .
15. People who work for me think I am . . .
16. I feel most productive when . . .
17. I trust those who . . .
18. I have never liked . . .
19. What I want most out of my job is . . .
20. I need to improve most in . . .

NOTES

1. This case is a composite of a number of published accounts, among them: Jill Bettner, "What's Good for GM Isn't Good for the Country," *Forbes,* 7 November 1983; "Blue Collars in the Board Room," *Time,* 19 May 1980; "Cooperation, UAW-Style," *Business Week,* 21 November 1983; Edwin Diamond, "Driving Ambition: A Man with the Pedal to the Floor," *Family Weekly,* 27 May 1984, 4–9; John Hoerr, "Auto Workers Inch Toward the Driver's Seat," *Business Week,* 9 February 1981; Michael Moritz and Barrett Seaman, *Going for Broke: The Chrysler Story* (Garden City, N.Y.: Doubleday, 1981); James K. Glassman, "The Iacocca Mystique," *New Republic,* 23 July 1984, 20–23; numerous articles in *The Wall Street Journal;* and Chrysler Corporation, *Annual Reports* (various years).
2. Peter Nulty, "How Managers Will Manage," *Fortune,* 2 February 1987, 47.
3. "Mr. Smith Goes Global," *Business Week,* 13 February, 1989, 66.
4. "Xerox Rethinks Itself—and This Could Be the Last Time," *Business Week,* 13 February 1989, 90–91.
5. "The Five Best," *Business Month,* December 1988, 31.
6. "Five Best," 30–31.
7. "GM's Bumpy Ride on the Long Road Back," *Business Week,* 13 February 1989, 74.

REFERENCES

Bahrami, Bahman. "Productivity Improvement Through Cooperation of Employees and Employers." *Labor Law Journal* 39 (March 1988): 167–178.

Boc, Ann. "Networking: Management's New Contact Sport." *Manage* 39 (July 1986): 15–17.

Carrol, Stephen J., and Dennis J. Gillen. "Are the Classical Management Functions Useful in Describing Managerial Work?" *Academy of Management Review* 12, no. 1 (January 1987).

Cetron, Marvin, and Thomas O'Toole. *Encounters with the Future: A Forecast of Life into the 21st Century.* New York: McGraw-Hill, 1982.

Drucker, Peter F. *Management: Tasks, Responsibilities and Practices.* New York: Harper & Row, 1974.

Hornaday, Robert W., and Walter J. Wheatley. "Managerial Characteristics and the Financial Performance of Small Business." *Journal of Small Business Management* 24, no. 2 (April 1986): 1–7.

Kantrow, Alen M. "Why Read Peter Drucker?" *Harvard Business Review* 58, no. 1 (January–February 1980): 74–83.

Naisbitt, John. *Megatrends.* New York: Warner Books, 1982.

Newman, William H., ed. *Managers for the Year 2000.* Englewood Cliffs, N.J.: Prentice-Hall, 1978.

Oliva, Terence A., and Christel M. Capdevielle. "Can Systems Really Be Taught? (A Socratic Dialogue)." *Academy of Management Review* 5, no. 2 (April 1980): 277–281.

Peters, Thomas J. "Facing Up to the Need for a Management Revolution." *California Management Review* 30 (Winter 1988): 7–38.

Peters, Thomas J., and Robert H. Waterman, Jr. *In Search of Excellence.* New York: Harper & Row, 1982.

Roskies, Ethel, Jeffrey K. Liker, and David B. Roitman. "Winners and Losers: Employee Perceptions of Their Company's Technological Transformation." *Journal of Organizational Behavior Management* 9 (April 1988): 123–147.

Shaffer, James C. "Mission Statements: Why Have Them? (Corporate Mission Statements)." *Communication World* 4 (June 1987): 14–16.

C H A P T E R

2

Chapter Outline

History
of
Management
and
Organizational
Behavior

Learning Objectives

After completing this chapter students should be able to

1. Explain the structural perspectives of management and organizational behavior.
2. Describe the human perspectives of management and organizational behavior.
3. Explain the integrative perspectives of management and organizational behavior.

PAUL CARNEY MANAGES the main, downtown ticket office in Dallas, Texas, for Continental Airlines. Originally, he supervised ten agents who worked five eight-hour shifts from 8 A.M. to 8 P.M., Monday through Saturday. Continental recently expanded its service into the airport, requiring a doubling of the number of sales agents at the office to meet the increased demand for tickets and information. Paul now has to manage an increased number of agents, including some who have not completed their training at the central headquarters.

When the office had only ten employees, Paul gave the agents great discretion in determining their schedules. He repeatedly told them, "We are a team; you will determine whether we succeed in this city." Agents frequently and voluntarily worked overtime, absences were rare, and there was a feeling of camaraderie and worker satisfaction. The employees willingly covered for others who had to change their schedules, and the more experienced agents helped the new hires until they felt comfortable in their jobs. When a problem arose at the agency, all the agents met on a Sunday morning to discuss it and work together to solve it. The agents frequently suggested ideas for sales campaigns, which Paul forwarded to the corporate headquarters, and a number of these ideas were implemented. The agents took pride in serving their customers quickly and efficiently. In fact, the number of customers serviced per agent at that office was the highest in Continental's system, and the number of complaints received was the lowest.

With the significant increase in the number of employees, Paul felt the need to standardize office procedures. He instituted fixed work shifts and nonnegotiable schedules for each agent; promoted one agent to supervise each shift, and introduced new procedures for queueing customers as they arrived in the office. He felt that twenty agents could not easily communicate on an "as-needed" basis and discouraged the group approach to decision making that he had previously encouraged.

During the three months after these changes were implemented, Paul noticed a change in the spirit and performance of the office. The workers seemed less enthusiastic about their jobs, and absenteeism and tardiness increased. Overall, the office's performance declined during the three-month period, as reflected by companywide measures of agent effectiveness. A survey of the office indicated that most agents expressed dissatisfaction with numerous aspects of their jobs. In addition, customer complaints increased.

Paul often overheard the more experienced agents blaming poor perfor- mance on the newly hired employees, claiming they did not pull their share of the work load. The new employees said that the experienced agents refused to share important information. When Paul suggested that all the agents meet on Sunday morning to solve the problem, every agent but one refused to work overtime, even though they had repeatedly done so in the past. ▪

MISTAKES OF THE PAST are likely to be repeated. Virtually everyone has heard this statement, but many unfortunately ignore its message. It is vitally important that managers like Paul Carney understand and appreciate the history of management and organizational behavior in order to gain a better frame of reference within which to make critical decisions. Paul ignored many aspects of that history when he designed a new management system to cope with the changing work environment at the Dallas office. If he had taken his cues from the historical perspectives of management and organizational behavior, his agents might still be supporting him and excelling.

■■■ THE HISTORICAL PERSPECTIVES

The first step to understanding and identifying the key issues in particular organizational situations is to review the historical perspectives that dominated management and organizational thought during this century. Many aspects of earlier viewpoints, philosophies, and schools of thought remain relevant today and can provide the careful observer with valuable insight into present-day organizational situations.

Since 1900 each of a dozen major schools of thought have fallen within one of three areas, or historical perspectives, of management and organizational thought: The structural perspective, generally held at the turn of the century, evolved from that time to encompass the theory of scientific management, classical theory, bureaucracy, and decision theory. The human perspective, which first appeared in the 1920s, eventually included schools of thought focused on human relations, group dynamics, and leadership research. Since the 1960s, however, the schools of thought that have prevailed have each integrated the human perspectives with the structural perspectives to form the third major area of organizational thought, integrative perspectives.

Adam Smith's writings on the division of labor helped to lay the foundation for the concept of the assembly line. (© Farrell Grehan/Photo Researchers, Inc.)

TABLE 2.1 ■ Schools of Organizational Thought and Their Components by Decade

School	Decade	Perspective	Description
Organizational theory prior to 1900	Before 1900	Structural	Emphasized the division of labor and the importance of machinery to facilitate labor
Scientific management	1910s	Structural	Described management as a science with employees having specific but different responsibilities; encouraged the scientific selection, training, and development of workers and the equal division of work between workers and management
Classical	1910s	Structural	Listed the duties of a manager as planning, organizing, commanding employees, coordinating activities, and controlling performance; basic principles called for specialization of work, unity of command, scalar chain of command, and coordination of activities
Human relations	1920s	Human	Focused on the importance of the attitudes and feelings of workers; informal roles and norms influenced performance
Group dynamics	1940s	Human	Encouraged individual participation in decision making; noted the impact of the work group on performance
Bureaucracy	1940s	Structural	Emphasized order, system, rationality, uniformity, and consistency in management; led to equitable treatment for all employees by management
Leadership	1950s	Human	Stressed the importance of groups having both social and task leaders; differentiated between theory X and theory Y management
Decision theory	1960s	Structural	Suggested that individuals "satisfice" when they make decisions
Sociotechnical	1960s	Integrative	Called for considering technology and work groups when understanding a work system
Systems theory	1970s	Integrative	Represented organizations as open systems with inputs, transformations, outputs, and feedback; systems strive for equilibrium and experience equifinality
Management roles	1970s	Integrative	Emphasized that managerial work encompasses ten roles and three focuses; interpersonal contact, informational processing, and decision making
Contingency theory	1980s	Integrative	Emphasized the fit between organizational processes and characteristics of the situation; called for fitting the organization's structure to various contingencies

This chapter will examine these three perspectives and their major schools of thought to determine how understanding them may help managers better analyze problem situations such as the one Paul Carney faced at the downtown ticket office of Continental Airlines. Table 2.1 groups schools of organizational thought into three historical perspectives and provides a brief description of the thinking that characterized each school.

▥ STRUCTURAL PERSPECTIVES

The earliest theorists primarily expressed concern for the structuring and design of work within the organization.

Organizational Theory Prior to 1900

The emphasis in this book is on the current state of management and organizational behavior. However, just as political science students cannot fail to consider the history of government, management students must have at least a moderate familiarity with what has gone before in the field. This history obviously extends several thousand years into the past. Moses, for example, is credited with having employed the first management consultant (his father-in-law) to help design the organization through which Moses governed the Hebrews. Before the turn of this century, however, very little formal theorizing took place. Few industrial organizations of the types that exist today were around during that time, and the basic organizational models were the military and the Roman Catholic Church.

Despite a lack of formal theory, economists such as Adam Smith sowed the seeds of later theory. In his book *An Inquiry into the Nature and Cause of the Wealth of Nations,*[1] Smith included a chapter on the division of labor that laid the groundwork for the later introduction of assembly-line processes. Smith spoke approvingly of a pin manufacturer who divided the work into a number of "branches," causing the separation of pin making into eighteen different operations. This separation of operations permitted workers to concentrate on only one task, and thus radically increased the quantity of pins that could be manufactured in a day. Smith also emphasized the importance of proper machinery to facilitate labor.

Scientific Management

Not until the early twentieth century did management emerge as a field of study per se. Frederick Taylor, who made major contributions to management thinking around the turn of this century, is often called the father of scientific management. Supported in his efforts by Henry Gantt, Frank and Lillian Gilbreth, and Harrington Emerson, all of whom became famous in their own rights, Taylor is credited with revolutionizing management thinking.

Scientific management
The name given to the principles and practices that grew out of the work of Frederick Taylor and his followers and that are characterized by concern for efficiency and systematization in management.

Scientific management is the name given to the principles and practices that grew out of the work of Taylor and his followers and that are characterized by concern for efficiency and systematization in management. Taylor was convinced that the scientific method which provides a logical framework for the analysis of problems, could be applied to the management process. The method consists of defining the problem, gathering data, analyzing the data, developing alternatives, and selecting the best alternative. Taylor believed that use of the scientific method would direct the manager to the most efficient way work could be performed. Thus, instead of abdicating responsibility for establishing standards, for example, management could scientifically study all facets of an operation and carefully set a logical and rational standard. Instead of guessing or relying solely on trial and error, management could go through the logical, though time-consuming, process

TABLE 2.2 ■■ Taylor's Philosophy of Management
• Apply the scientific method to the practice of management to find the "one best way" to perform work
• Use scientific approaches to select employees best suited to perform a given job
• Provide employees with scientific education, training, and development
• Encourage friendly interaction and cooperation between management and employees, but with a clear separation of duties between managers and workers
• Take charge of all work for which management is better prepared than the workers, ending the pattern of placing most of the work and the greater part of the responsibility on the workers[2]

of scientific research to develop answers to business problems. Taylor's philosophy is summarized in Table 2.2.

Taylor sincerely believed that scientific management practices would benefit not only the employer through increased output but the workers as well, who would receive more income. But he stressed that scientific management would require both manager and employees to undergo a revolution in thinking.

The greater part of Taylor's work was oriented toward improving management of production operations. The classic case of the pig iron experiment at the Bethlehem Steel Company illustrates his approach.[3] Laborers would pick up ninety-two-pound pigs (chunks of iron) from a storage yard, walk up a plank onto a railroad car, and place the pigs in the car. In a group of seventy-five laborers, Taylor determined the average output was about 12.5 tons per man per day. By applying the scientific method, he developed (1) an improved method of work, (2) a prescribed amount of rest on the job, (3) a specific standard of output, and (4) payment by the unit of output. After Taylor's recommendations were implemented, the average output per worker rose to 48 tons per day, and daily pay rose from $1.15 to $1.85 under the incentive system.

Taylor's dedication to systematic planning and study of processes of all kinds pervaded his life. With a specially designed tennis racket, he played on a national doubles tennis championship team. When playing golf, he used clubs he designed individually to achieve a predictable lie; his friends reportedly refused to play with him when he used a particular putter because of its accuracy. Legend has it that Taylor died of pneumonia in a hospital with his stopwatch in his hand.

Frank and Lillian Gilbreth concentrated on motion study to develop more efficient ways to pour concrete, lay bricks, and perform many other repetitive tasks. After Frank's death, Lillian continued their work alone, eventually becoming a professor of management at Purdue University. Until her death in 1972 she was considered the first lady of management.

H. L. Gantt developed a control chart that is used to this day in production operations. The Gantt chart is considered by many to have been the forerunner of modern PERT (program evaluation and review technique) analysis.

Harrington Emerson set forth "twelve principles of efficiency" in his 1913 book of that title. Certain of Emerson's principles state that a manager should carefully define objectives, use the scientific method of analysis, develop and use standardized procedures, and reward employees for good work. His book remains a recognized management classic.

Perhaps the application of scientific management principles to the jobs of the ticket agents would improve the situation at Continental Airlines. The training of workers might be changed to more systematically prepare them for their jobs. Or Paul Carney might analyze the tasks being carried out in the office and change the work process to maximize performance. He might, for example, give the new agents only a fraction of the types of work the more experienced agents perform.

General Management Theory: The Classical School

In contrast to the proponents of scientific management, Henri Fayol and Chester I. Barnard developed a broader theory of general management that is identified today as the *classical* view of organizational theory. Henri Fayol was a French manager who wrote at about the same time as Taylor, although his works were not widely available in English translation until 1930. Fayol's major contribution to management literature, *General and Industrial Management,* was not translated into English until long after Taylor and Fayol had died. Once translated, however, it became very popular in the United States. Fayol's view of management theory complemented Taylor's scientific approach in many ways.[4] Fayol listed the duties of a manager as planning, organizing, commanding employees, coordinating activities, and controlling performance. He also specified the fourteen principles of management shown in Table 2.3.[5]

TABLE 2.3 ■■ Fayol's Principles of Management

1. **Division of work**—the specialization of work
2. **Authority**—"the right to give orders, and power to exact obedience"
3. **Discipline**—"obedience, application, energy, behavior, and outward marks of respect"
4. **Unity of command**—"an employee should receive orders from one superior only"
5. **Unity of direction**—"one head and one plan for a group of activities having the same objective"
6. **Subordination of individual interests to the general interest**—the interest of an individual or group should not supercede the organization's concerns
7. **Remuneration**—fair payment for services
8. **Centralization**—degree of consolidation of the management functions
9. **Scalar chain (line of authority)**—"the chain of superiors ranging from the ultimate authority to the lower ranks"
10. **Order**—all materials and people should be in an appointed place
11. **Equity**—equality of treatment
12. **Stability of tenure of personnel**—limited turnover of personnel
13. **Initiative**—"thinking out a plan and ensuring its success"
14. **Esprit de corps**—"harmony, union among the personnel of a concern"

Source: Adapted and excerpted from H. Fayol, *General and Industrial Management,* Trans. C. Storrs, London: Pitman, 1949.

Chester I. Barnard's ideas, expressed in his 1938 book *The Functions of the Executive,* have significantly influenced the theory and practice of management for more than half a century.[6] Barnard, who for years was president of New Jersey Bell Telephone, believed that the most important function of a manager is to promote cooperative effort toward the goals of the organization. He believed that cooperation depends on effective communications and a balance between rewards to, and contributions by, each employee.

Other proponents of general management, or classical, theory have identified four features of organizations that are similar to the elements and principles Fayol and Barnard espoused.[7] First, organizations should *specialize,* meaning workers should be organized according to logical groupings such as client, place of work, product, expertise, or functional area. At Continental Airlines, for example, all ticket agents who service the downtown area are located in a single office. Second, *unity of command* dictates that each organizational member should have exactly one supervisor. At the Continental ticket office, therefore, the agents should report directly to either the newly appointed supervisor or to Paul Carney, but not to both. Third, the *scalar chain of command,* or the reporting relationships, should be clearly defined within a formal organizational structure, beginning with the chief administrator and extending to the least skilled employee. The scalar chain at the downtown ticket office begins with Paul Carney, the office manager, and continues through the newly appointed supervisors to the ticket agents. Fourth and finally, managers should *coordinate activities* using mechanisms that will ensure good communication among specialized groups. For example, Paul Carney should introduce new rules and procedures that will guarantee the efficient implementation and coordination of activities in the ticket office.

Bureaucracy

Bureaucracy
A prototype form of organization that emphasizes order, system, rationality, uniformity, and consistency.

Max Weber, a German sociologist, addressed the issue of organizational administration in a somewhat different fashion. He studied European organization during the late 1800s and described a prototype form of organization that emphasizes order, system, rationality, uniformity, and consistency—a **bureaucracy.** Weber's writings were not widely read in the United States, however, until their English translation was published in 1947.[8]

For many people the term bureaucracy conjures up an image of massive red tape and endless unneeded details. Weber, on the other hand, felt a bureaucracy led to equitable treatment for all employees by management.[9] To the extent that bureaucratic organizations are impersonal and have strict rules, Weber saw these characteristics as ensuring fairness to all workers.[10]

In a bureaucracy each employee has specified and official areas of responsibility that are assigned on the basis of competence and expertise. Applying this approach to Continental, Paul Carney would first assess whether the agents are competent to handle their roles. His introduction of new rules to govern the jobs of the agents might then be viewed as an attempt to increase the fairness and quality of performance in that situation.

Like the classical schools, bureaucracy calls for an orderly system of supervision and subordination, a unity of command that specifies for each subordinate a single supervisor. Managers in a bureaucracy use written documents extensively in managing employees. Not only do rules and regulations exist, but they are translated into detailed employment manuals; office managers or other work groups receive extensive training in their job requirements. Within this system management must use rules that are consistent, complete, and can be learned.

Does Paul Carney operate according to classical and bureaucratic principles? Although specialization surely exists within Continental Airlines, it apparently does not exist within the downtown ticket office. Likewise, unity of command is intended, but it may not be fully implemented. A scalar chain of authority does exist; and some, but possibly insufficient, coordination of activities takes place among ticket agents. Fayol might suggest, in addition, that there are problems with the remuneration, equity of treatment, and stability of tenure of personnel. Weber would likely note that lack of specified areas of responsibility, absence of a clearly ordered system of supervision, limited use of written documents, insufficient expert training, lack of management dedication and devotion to the job, and failure to establish general rules explain the problems experienced at the downtown ticket agency.

Decision Theory

In the 1950s Herbert Simon and James March introduced the decision-making framework for understanding organizational behavior.[11] They elaborated on the bureaucratic model by emphasizing that individuals who work in rational organizations behave rationally. But their model (for which Simon won the Nobel Memorial Prize for Economics) added a new dimension: the idea that a human being's rationality is limited. The model suggests that individuals generally make decisions by examining a limited set of possible alternatives rather than all available options. Moreover, they do so by drawing on the rules and experience they have at hand. For example, in deciding the best way to ticket customers, the experienced agents might use certain rules of thumb, while the newly hired agents might follow different rules and programs, thereby creating conflict in the office.

The model states further that individuals "satisfice"; that is, they choose adequate solutions to problems rather than seeking optimal choices. Thus, Paul Carney might implement a work schedule that is good enough to be acceptable to most agents but not the best for all. The decision-making analyst would ask Paul whether he generates alternative solutions to problems, how he chooses his solution, and whether he optimizes or satisfices.

■ HUMAN PERSPECTIVES

When the structural perspectives of scientific management, classical, bureaucratic, and decision theory are applied to the downtown ticket office, many organizational problems can be solved, but much of the workers' dissatisfaction and resistance to change is not addressed by these theories. Seeking answers to the remaining problems, researchers began to focus on the *human* side of organizations, specifically on human relations, group dynamics, and leadership theory.

Human Relations School

Beginning in 1924 the Western Electric Company, in conjunction with the National Academy of Sciences, performed five studies of various work groups at Western

Electric's Hawthorne plant.[12] The first study looked at the effects of lighting on the productivity of workers in different departments of the company. In the tradition of scientific management, the study considered whether various illumination levels affected output positively or adversely. Researchers first increased the lighting to an extreme brightness and then decreased the light until the work area was so dim that assembly material could hardly be seen. Results showed that the workers maintained or even exceeded their normal output regardless of whether illumination was increased or decreased. But what explains this behavior?

Subsequent studies by Elton Mayo, Fritz Roethlisberger, William Dickson, and their colleagues examined the impact of rest pauses, shorter working days and weeks, wage incentives, and the nature of supervision on output.[13] They speculated that something other than the physical work environment was responsible for improved productivity among workers. By observing and interviewing the employees, researchers discovered that the employees, by participating in the experiments, felt that someone cared about them. Their morale improved and they produced more. This influence that behavioral researchers can have on the people they study became known as the **Hawthorne effect,** marking the first dramatic indication that the attitudes and feelings of workers could significantly influence productivity.

Hawthorne effect
The influence of behavioral researchers on the people they study.

Based on these findings, Western Electric instituted a program in which interviewers questioned workers regarding their feelings about work. Results of the interviews suggested even more strongly the close relationship between morale and the quality of supervision and led to the creation of a new training program for supervisors.

In the final experiments of the Hawthorne series, researchers identified one other human feature of organizations: the tendency for workers to develop informal groups among themselves. When the researchers observed a group from the bank-wiring room, they found that the workers established informal roles and norms (expected standards of behavior) among themselves through which they controlled and restricted their productivity level. For example, workers could be

The human side of organizations includes informal work groups as well as groups that are formally created by the organization.
(©Richard Hutchings/Photo Researchers, Inc.)

Rate-busters
Individuals who produce more than the level acceptable to the leaders.

identified as leaders or followers; **rate-busters**—those who produced more than the level acceptable to the leaders—were ostracized by the group, as were those who produced too little.

Group Dynamics

Because of a shortage of meat during World War II, Kurt Lewin, a social psychologist at the University of Iowa, was asked to study methods of changing housewives' dietary habits to decrease meat consumption.[14] Lewin believed that the women were expected by their families, parents, and other housewives not to serve other kinds of food; this norm created a significant barrier to change. He suggested that the way to break down this barrier was to give the housewives the opportunity to discuss and make decisions themselves about the types of foods to serve. The results of the experiments conducted by Lewin and his associates supported his ideas about participation: housewives who joined in group discussions were ten times more likely to change their food habits than were housewives who received lectures on the subject.[15]

Lewin's associates later extended these experiments to industrial settings. For example, Lester Coch and John R. P. French found that employees at the Harwood pajama plant in Marion, Virginia, were much more likely to learn new work methods if given the opportunity to discuss the methods and have some influence on how to apply them to their jobs.[16] Studies such as these led to a greatly expanded awareness of the impact of the work group and spawned research on the relationship between organizational effectiveness and group formation, development, behavior, and attitudes.[17]

Leadership

The 1950s marked the beginning of concentrated research in the area of leadership as theorists such as Bales and McGregor examined the roles of managers and leaders in organizations.[18] Bales postulated the importance of groups having both task and social leaders. The **task leader** helps the group achieve its goals by clarifying and summarizing member comments and focusing on the group's tasks. The **social leader** maintains the group and helps it develop cohesiveness and collaboration by encouraging group members' involvement.

Task leader
Individual who helps the group achieve its goals by clarifying and summarizing member comments and focusing on the group's tasks.

Social leader
Individual who maintains the group and helps it develop cohesiveness and collaboration by encouraging group members' involvement.

McGregor described two types of managers.[19] Those who adhere to theory X believe that workers have an inherent dislike of work, must be controlled and threatened with punishment if they are to put forth adequate effort, and prefer to avoid responsibility. Managers who believe theory Y, on the other hand, believe that employees feel work is as natural as play or rest, will exercise self-direction toward objectives to which they are committed (requiring less strict control), and can learn to seek responsibility. McGregor, together with other researchers, postulated that the assumptions managers hold affect the way they treat their employees and thus affect employees' productivity.

The question can be asked whether or not the agents at Continental's downtown ticket office include both task and social leaders. What assumptions did Paul Carney have regarding the agents in his office? Did his leadership style fit the situation?

The importance of the group to the agents' performance can be analyzed from a human perspective. When Paul emphasized their participation in decision making, their performance and satisfaction were considerably higher than when he decreased their involvement. Further, the newly hired employees were not integrated into the group of experienced workers. Researchers in the group-dynamics tradition might attribute the problems to the decreased involvement of the agents in discussions and decision making about their jobs.

■■ INTEGRATIVE PERSPECTIVES

Organizational thought in the past few decades has emphasized the integration of structural and human perspectives. More recently, contingency theory has added an emphasis on fitting organizational features to the work situation.

Sociotechnical School

Sociotechnical school
A school of management thought which is based on the premise that managers could exclude neither technology (representing organizational structure) nor work groups (reflecting human relations) when trying to understand a work system.

In the 1950s several theorists began studying technology and its interaction with functioning work groups. The **sociotechnical school** assumed that managers could exclude neither technology (representing organizational structure) nor work groups (reflecting human relations) when trying to understand a work system. The most notable members of the sociotechnical school were Trist, Bamforth, Rice, and Emery.[20]

Trist and Bamforth described a change in technology in a British coal mine in which workers were used to working independently in small, self-contained units in which they organized the work themselves.[21] When the technology for mining coal improved, management was required to increase job specialization and decrease the workers' participation in job assignments. According to scientific management and classical management traditions, greater job specialization should have increased productivity. But the coal miners hated the specialization; they much preferred working closely with each other and performing a variety of tasks.

Trist and Bamforth compared the performance of work groups whose jobs had become specialized to that of work groups that retained their original social structure when the new technology was introduced. They found that absenteeism was several times greater and productivity much lower in the specialized groups. Researchers concluded after a number of such studies, that technological changes must be made in conjunction with a strong social system: both social *and* technical aspects of jobs must be considered simultaneously.

How would sociotechnical researchers assess the problems at Continental Airlines? Did the introduction of new technology influence the performance of the agents? What effect does the work process have on the agents' performance and attitudes? Is more automation required or less? Did Paul Carney consider the social implications of the procedural changes he introduced? Did the addition of a large number of new hires influence the group orientation of the more experienced workers? Certainly consideration of both structural and human issues at the downtown ticket office should provide a more complete diagnosis of the situation.

Systems Theory

According to Harold Koontz, "The systems approach requires that the physical, human, and capital resources be interrelated and coordinated within the external and internal environment of an organization."[22] Systems theory, which offers an integrated and comprehensive view of organizational functioning, evolved from economic, sociological, psychological, and natural-science theories and includes human, structural, environmental, technological, and other concerns. The general systems model described by Katz and Kahn, among others, represents an organization as an open system, one that interacts with environmental forces and factors, much like physical systems such as the human body, a microscopic organism, or a cell.[23] First, a system consists of a number of interdependent and interrelated subsystems; second, the organization is open and dynamic; third, it strives for equilibrium; and fourth, it has multiple purposes, objectives, and functions, some of which are in conflict.

Subsystems vary in size from an individual cell to a major division of an organization. Typical subsystems include individual employees, work teams, departments, and management groups. To trace subsystems in organizations, the observer generally must specify significant individuals and groups and examine their interdependence. The downtown ticket office is a subsystem of Continental Airlines, as is each individual agent, the two groups of experienced agents and newly hired agents, and the management of the office—the newly appointed supervisors and Paul Carney. How are the two groups of agents interdependent and interrelated? How is the downtown ticket office related to the rest of Continental Airlines—to the marketing department, the operations department, or the finance department?

An organization as a system is also open and dynamic; that is, it continually receives new energy in the form of resources (people, materials, and money) or information (concerning strategy, environment, and history) from the environment. This new energy, called *inputs*, is then *transformed* into new *outputs*. The key organizational components that change inputs into outputs are **transformation processes.** In the downtown ticket office, for example, newly hired workers are inputs, and Paul Carney's leadership and the team development of all employees are transformations that change these new employees into productive organizational members.

Transformation processes include the interactions between the tasks, individuals, formal organizational arrangements, and the informal organization.[24] The transformation of inputs creates changes in individual, group, and organizational behaviors and attitudes. For example, the new policies and procedures introduced at the downtown ticket office created changes in the agents' behavior and attitudes. Changes in performance, satisfaction, morale, turnover, and absenteeism, as well as other indicators of functioning or other outputs, may also occur.

When organizations receive new inputs or experience certain transformations, they simultaneously seek balance or equilibrium. When organizations become unbalanced or experience disequilibrium, such as when changes in the environment make current staffing inadequate, they attempt to return to a steady state, which may mirror or significantly differ from the original state of equilibrium. They use information about their outputs, called *feedback,* to modify their inputs or transformations to result in more desirable outcomes and equilibrium, as shown in Figure 2.1. Assume, for example, as in the case of Continental Airlines,

Transformation processes
Key organizational components that change inputs into outputs.

F I G U R E 2.1 ■■
The Basic Systems Model

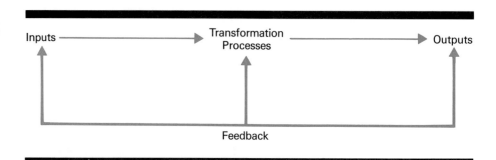

that worker performance has declined significantly. This information cues the organization to examine the nature of its inputs and transformations for a cause. The feedback may subsequently pinpoint changes in employee training or reward systems as causes.

Feedback may also indicate which subsystems within an organization have similar, and which have different, goals. For example, Paul Carney might aim for consistency among work assignments, whereas workers might aspire to jobs that respond to their unique needs and talents. What goals does the management of the downtown ticket office have? What goals does Paul Carney have? What goals do the agents have? Which goals are the same? Which are different? How similar are the goals of the managers and employees?

Finally, organizations as open systems demonstrate equifinality. Equifinality suggests that organizations may employ a variety of means to achieve their desired objectives. For example, the McDonald's Corporation achieves its objectives of growth and profitability by employing a highly specialized system for producing its hamburgers. Apple Computer, on the other hand, employs less structure in operations to achieve the same objective. No single structure results in a predetermined set of inputs, outputs, and transformations. Introducing a more open and participatory structure does not necessarily result in increased productivity; increasing the level of individual involvement in decision making does not necessarily change worker attitudes. Thus, organizations that survive *adapt* to a particular situation. They respond to changes in the environment with appropriate changes in the system. Paul Carney responded with certain changes that were not effective; he must now respond with different adjustments.

Now consider the downtown ticket office from the systems perspective. Figure 2.2 presents the different systems components that can be determined from the case. The inputs described in the case center on the company's addition of new staff members, but the inputs are not limited to the workers. Other inputs include the current employees, the raw materials, management's goals, and the feedback the company receives about the workers' performance. The interaction of the individuals, task characteristics, organizational arrangements, and informal organization transform these inputs into outputs.

The case tells us little about the *individuals,* with the exception of Paul Carney. Nothing is known about their age, education, personality, sex, or background. The case does, however, provide limited information about their tasks: they write airline tickets, plan travel routes, and give information to potential customers. The agents primarily work independently, although they rely on other agents for information and back up when they become too busy.

F I G U R E 2.2 ■ Systems Components of the Downtown Ticket Office

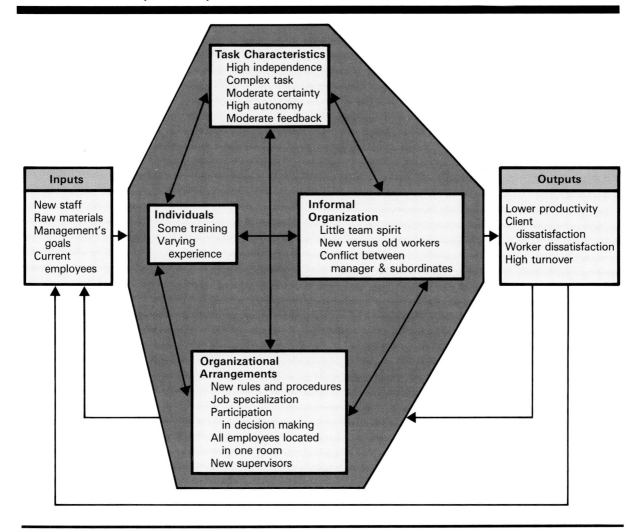

Among the *organizational arrangements* are the new rules and procedures introduced by Paul Carney. Paul also added a new level to the supervisory hierarchy. The training provided to the new hires, as well as the reward system, also influences worker outcomes.

Finally, the cohesive *informal organization* that existed prior to the increase in staff has deteriorated. Attempts to integrate the new workers with the more experienced employees have failed. The new organizational arrangements seem to interfere with the group dynamics that existed previously.

The arrows in Figure 2.2 suggest that the different systems, components—individuals, task characteristics, organizational arrangements, and informal organization—are interacting and interdependent, and should fit with each other for maximum organizational effectiveness. However, these different components may or may not fit. For example, a task may be too simple for highly skilled workers; or, as in the downtown ticket agency, the introduction of formal rules and regulations may conflict with the informal, team-focused organization that existed before.

The relatively poor performance of those in the office indicates that some mismatches exist among the different systems components. The description of the situation in the downtown ticket office suggests where some misfits may exist; but Paul Carney, when using the systems model, must pinpoint and verify the location of the poor fits.

Contingency Theory

Contingency theory
A management theory which refers to a manager's ability to adapt to meet particular circumstances and restraints a firm may encounter.

Contingency theory refers to a manager's ability to adapt to meet particular circumstances and restraints an organization may encounter.[25] It emphasizes the fit between organizational processes and characteristics of the situation.

Early contingency research looked at the fit between an organization's structure and its environment. Burns and Stalker described two radically different types of management systems: mechanistic (machinelike) and organic (living, human, and flexible).[26] Mechanistic systems have characteristics such as those described in the scientific and classical management traditions. Organic systems are much more flexible and loosely structured and allow more employee influence over decisions. With regard to the changes Paul Carney initiated in the downtown ticket office, it may be noted that he seems to have shifted the mechanistic systems as appropriate to stable environmental conditions and organic systems as appropriate to changing organizations. Did he choose the appropriate structure for the changing conditions?

Woodward found that the type of structure an organization develops (and should develop) is influenced by the organization's technology, whether the technology is unit, mass production, or a continuous process.[27] She suggested that a mechanistic type of organization fits best with mass production technology—producing pins, lifting pig iron, or manufacturing heavy equipment. A more organic form of organization responds best to a unit (craft) or continuous process (e.g., gas refinery) technology. Is the technology in the downtown ticket office increasingly automated and sophisticated? Is the lack of fit between technology and structure of the problem? Paul Carney's introduction of a more mechanistic structure seems to fit well with the increasingly automated technology (computerization of the travel industry) faced by his agents, but it does not fit well with the dynamic environment of the office.

Recent thinking in organization design has reemphasized the importance of fitting organizational structure to various contingencies. Thus contingency theory has also extended to leadership, group dynamics, power relations, and work design.[28]

Management Roles Approach

Henry Mintzberg, in studying what managers actually do, observed that managerial work encompasses ten roles: three focus on *interpersonal* contact—(1) figurehead, (2) leader, (3) liaison; three involve mainly *information processing*—(1) monitor, (2) disseminator, (3) spokesperson; and four relate to *decision making*—(1) entrepreneur, (2) disturbance handler, (3) resource allocator, and (4) negotiator.[29]

The three roles that focus on *interpersonal* contact are:

1. **Figurehead.** The manager, acting as a symbol or representative of the organization, performs diverse ceremonial duties. By attending chamber of commerce meetings, heading the local United Way drive, or representing the president of the firm at an awards banquet, a manager performs the figurehead role.

2. **Leader.** The manager, interacting with subordinates, motivates and develops them. The supervisor who conducts quarterly performance interviews or selects training opportunities for subordinates performs this role.

3. **Liaison.** The manager establishes a network of contacts to gather information for the organization. Belonging to professional associations or meeting over lunch with peers in other organizations helps the manager perform the liaison role.

The three roles that involve mainly *information processing* are:

1. **Monitor.** The manager gathers information from the environment inside and outside the organization. The manager may attend meetings with subordinates, scan company publications, or participate in companywide committees as a way of performing this role.

2. **Disseminator.** The manager transmits both factual and value information to subordinates. Managers may conduct staff meetings, send memoranda to staff, or meet informally with them on a one-to-one basis to discuss current and future projects.

3. **Spokesperson.** The manager gives information to people outside the organization about its performance and policies. The manager who oversees preparation of the annual report, prepares advertising copy, or speaks at community and professional meetings fulfills this role.

The four roles related to *decision making* are:

1. **Entrepreneur.** The manager designs and initiates change in the organization. The supervisor who redesigns the job of subordinates, introduces flextime to the workplace, or brings new technology to a job performs this role.

2. **Disturbance handler.** The manager deals with problems that arise when organizational operations break down. A person who finds a new supplier on short notice for an out-of-stock part, replaces unexpectedly absent employees, or deals with machine breakdowns performs this role.

3. **Resource allocator.** The manager controls the allocation of people, money, materials, and time by scheduling his or her own time, programming subordinates' work effort, and authorizing all significant decisions. Preparation of a budget is a major aspect of this role.

4. **Negotiator.** The manager participates in negotiation activities. A manager who hires a new employee may negotiate work assignments or compensation with that person.

TABLE 2.4 ■ Eight Management Job Types

Managerial Job Type	Key Roles	Examples
Contact person	Liaison, figurehead	Sales managers, chief executives in service industries
Political manager	Spokesperson, negotiator	Top government, hospital, university managers
Entrepreneur	Entrepreneur, negotiator	Owner of small, young business; CEO of rapidly changing, large organization
Insider	Resource allocator	Middle or senior production or operations manager, manager rebuilding after crisis
Real-time manager	Disturbance handler	Foreman; head of organization in crisis; head of small, one-manager business
Team manager	Leader	Hockey coach, head of R&D group
Expert manager	Monitor, spokesperson	Head of specialist group
New manager	Liaison, monitor	Manager in a new job

Source: Excerpt and table from *The Nature of Managerial Work* by Henry Mintzberg. Copyright © 1973 by Henry Mintzberg. Reprinted by permission of Harper & Row Publishers, Inc.

Not all managers perform every role listed here, but some diversity of role performance always occurs. Table 2.4 shows the roles most frequently played by a variety of managers. The choice of roles depends on the manager's specific job description and the situation in question. An examination of the manager's work role suggests that leadership is only one of many roles, but one that is essential to effective management.

Mintzberg's view of managerial behavior offers a perspective that complements those of various organizational behavior topics, including perception, attribution, motivation, communication, personal development, group dynamics, and leadership theory. The roles he identified emphasize the individual and motivation (interpersonal roles), communication (information roles), and leadership and decision making (decisional roles).

SUMMARY

Many aspects of earlier viewpoints, philosophies, and schools of organizational thought remain relevant today and can provide useful management insight. Prior to 1900 little formal management or organizational theorizing took place. Few industrial organizations of the types known today existed then, and the basic organizational models were the military and the Roman Catholic Church.

Since 1900 each of a dozen major schools of thought have fallen within one of three historical perspectives: *structural,* which dominated early thinking in the field; *human,* which first appeared in the 1920s; and *integrative,* which since the 1960s have focused on the integration of structural and human perspectives to achieve a more comprehensive understanding of organizational behavior.

Structural perspectives: When management began to emerge as a field of study early in the twentieth century, theorists first expressed concern for the structuring and design of work within the organization. Frederick Taylor, with his followers, Henry Gantt, Frank and Lillian Gilbreth, and Harrington Emerson, pioneered the field of *scientific management* by employing the scientific method to promote efficiency and systematization in management operations. Henri Fayol and Chester I. Barnard developed a broader theory of *general,* or *classical, management* that established principles of management and identified the duties of managers. Max Weber espoused a *bureaucracy* as an effective organizational structure because of its emphasis on order, system, rationality, uniformity, and consistency, which he felt led to equitable treatment for all employees by management. Herbert Simon and James March, in their model of *decision theory,* expanded on the bureaucratic model by adding rationality as a component. They went further to suggest that because a human being's rationality is limited, an individual, when asked to make a decision, will "satisfice," or make an adequate choice from a limited set of alternatives, rather than seeking optimal choices.

Human perspectives: Theorists who felt the problems of worker dissatisfaction and resistance to change could not be answered from a structural viewpoint began to examine the human side of organizations. Researchers from the *human relations* school studied work groups at the Western Electric Company's Hawthorne plant and demonstrated that employees who participated in the experiments produced more and had better morale than workers who didn't. This provided the first dramatic indication that the attitudes and feelings of workers might significantly influence productivity. From this work the Hawthorne effect—the influence of behavioral researchers on the people they study—was identified. Later work by Kurt Lewin and his associates led to greater understanding of the impact interactions within a work group, or *group dynamics,* can have on employee performance. By the 1950s research began to concentrate on the area of *leadership,* with theorists such as Bales and McGregor examining the roles managers and leaders play in organizations.

Integrative perspectives: Organizational thought in recent decades has emphasized the integration of structural and human perspectives. Trist, Bamforth, Rice, and Emery, members of the *sociotechnical school,* held that neither technology nor work groups could be excluded when trying to understand a work system. *Systems theory,* as originally portrayed by the model of Katz and Kahn, represents the organization as an open system, consisting of a number of interdependent and interrelated subsystems, that interacts with environmental forces and factors, much like physical systems. *Contingency theory* in recent years has placed emphasis on fitting the organizational features to the work situation. Burns and Stalker described two radically different types of management systems: mechanistic and organic; and Woodward found that the type of structure an organization develops is influenced by its technology. Current thinking in organization design reemphasizes the importance of fitting organizational structure to various contingencies, thus extending contingency theory to leadership, group dynamics, power relations, and work design.

Henry Mintzberg observed that managerial work encompasses ten distinct roles within three general areas of *interpersonal contact, information processing,* and *decision making.* Leadership, while only one of many roles, is essential to effective management.

REVIEW QUESTIONS

1. What was the emphasis of organizational theory prior to 1900?
2. Define scientific management. Briefly describe the work of Frederick Taylor, Henry Gantt, Frank and Lillian Gilbreth, and Harrington Emerson.
3. What were the duties of a manager as described by Henri Fayol?
4. Distinguish between bureaucracy as described by Max Weber and "satisficing" as described by Simon and March.
5. What is the Hawthorne effect?
6. Briefly describe the focus of the following schools of thought:
   a. sociotechnical
   b. systems theory
   c. contingency theory
7. List and briefly describe the management roles as described by Henry Mintzberg.

KEY TERMS

scientific management	rate-busters	sociotechnical school
bureaucracy	task leader	transformation processes
Hawthorne effect	social leader	contingency theory

CASE STUDY ■■■■ A SECOND CHANCE

DWAYNE LONDON groggily reached for the phone as it rang for about the tenth time. The voice on the other end said, "This is Joe Davis, with the sheriff's patrol. I just found your Center Street store unlocked."

Immediately wide awake, Dwayne asked, "Has it been broken into? What does it look like?"

Officer Davis told Dwayne that the store seemed to have been left open, that there was no sign of a forced entry. Dwayne asked him to keep an eye on the store. "I'll be there in ten minutes," he said.

Dwayne was the Dallas area supervisor for Quik-Shop, a chain of convenience stores. He had full responsibility for managing the seven Quik-Shop stores in the Dallas area. Each store operated with only one person on duty at a time. Although several of the stores stayed open all night, the Center Street store was open only from 6:00 A.M. to 10:00 P.M.

After finding that nothing seemed to be missing, Dwayne thought about what he should do. The company had a policy that anyone leaving a store unlocked would be fired on the spot. Bill Catron had worked the night shift at the Center Street store and had been responsible for locking up. Dwayne decided to wait until the next day when Bill reported to work before deciding what to do.

As Dwayne drove up to the Center Street store the next day at 2:30 P.M., he saw Bill at work inside the U-shaped counter. There were no customers in the store so Dwayne decided to get it over with. "Hello, Bill," he said, "I need to talk to you."

Obviously concerned, Bill asked, "What's wrong, Dwayne? You look worried."

"You left the store open last night, and you know what the company policy is," Dwayne said.

Bill became very upset. "I really need this job," he exclaimed. "With the new baby and all the medical expenses we have had this winter, I sure can't stand to be out of a job."

"But you knew about the policy, Bill," said Dwayne.

"Yes, I did," said Bill, "and I really don't have any excuse. If you don't fire me, though, I promise you that I'll be the best store manager you've got."

While Bill waited on the customer who came in, Dwayne called his boss at the home office in Houston. After receiving his boss's approval, Dwayne decided not to fire Bill.

Recalling the incident six months later, Dwayne was glad that he had given Bill a second chance. Bill was indeed his best store manager. He was conscientious about every part of the job. He was early for work every day and stayed a few minutes late each night to ensure that the store was properly secured. Dwayne noticed, too, that the Center Street store was kept cleaner than any of the others. Four months after the incident Bill developed a system for keeping up with the perishable stock, such as meats and milk, that was adopted for all of the stores. Consequently, he received a $1,200 cost-reduction award and a certificate of commendation from the company president.

QUESTIONS
1. From a historical perspective, which management philosophy was Dwayne exhibiting? Discuss.
2. In terms of Mintzberg's management roles, which roles was Dwayne using? Discuss.

CASE STUDY ■■■■ A NEW ROLE

JERRY SHARPLIN eagerly drove his new company pickup onto the construction site. He had just been assigned by his employer, Lurgi-Knost Construction Company, to supervise a crew of sixteen equipment operators, oilers, and mechanics. This was the first unionized crew Jerry

had supervised. As he approached his work area, he noticed one of the cherry pickers (a type of mobile crane with an extendable boom) standing idle with the operator beside it. Jerry pulled up beside the operator and said, "What's going on here?"

"Out of gas," the operator said.

"Well, go and get some," Jerry said.

The operator reached to get his thermos jug out of the tool box on the side of the crane and said, "The oiler's on break right now, but he will be back in a few minutes."

Jerry remembered that he had a five-gallon can of gasoline in the back of his pickup. So he quickly got the gasoline, climbed onto the cherry picker, and started to pour it into the gas tank. As he did, he heard the other machines shutting down in unison. He looked around and saw all the other operators climbing down from their equipment and standing to watch him pour the gasoline. A moment later he saw the union steward approaching.

QUESTIONS

1. From the viewpoint of Henry Mintzberg, which managerial roles was Jerry attempting to accomplish?
2. From a historical standpoint, which managerial perspective was Jerry following?

EXPERIENTIAL EXERCISE

In every organization, managers work with many individuals and groups. Cooperation is a must if the tasks involved are to be accomplished effectively. The Blue-Green Exercise provides an excellent experience in the value of cooperation. This exercise is a good icebreaker and discussion stimulator. Specifically, this exercise provides students with the opportunity to experience some of the interrelationships which occur in a structured setting, such as an organization or work group.

The Blue-Green Exercise is one of the best exercises to use with a relatively large group. In fact, it is not recommended for groups of less than twelve. It has been successfully used in groups as large as forty. This exercise works equally well with groups of people who have been working together for some time and with heterogeneous groups who barely know one another. Its impact, however, is probably greater when dealing with people who are *supposed* to work together. The language used by the person in charge of conducting the exercise is extremely important, so participants should listen carefully to the rules.

This exercise is usually quite enlightening to those who participate and has therefore been repeated many times over the years. The total group will be divided into four subgroups of as nearly equal size as possible. These subgroups will be called teams and designated as Team A-1, Team A-2, Team B-1, and Team B-2. Your instructor will provide the participants with the additional information necessary to participate. Enjoy the classic Blue-Green Exercise, the second of the experiential exercises provided to expand your educational horizons.

NOTES

1. Adam Smith, *An Inquiry into the Nature and Cause of the Wealth of Nations* (1776).
2. F. W. Taylor, *The Principles of Scientific Management* (New York: Harper and Brothers, 1911), 36–37.
3. Taylor, *Scientific Management*, 41–47.
4. H. Fayol, *General and Industrial Management*, trans. C. Storrs (London: Pitman, 1949).
5. Fayol, *Management*.
6. L. Gulick and L. Urwick, eds., *Papers on the Science of Administration* (New York: Columbia University Institute of Public Administration, 1937) and J. D. Mooney and A. C. Reiley, *Onward Industry* (New York: Harper, 1931) offered complementary views of management.
7. Chester I. Barnard, *The Functions of the Executive* (Cambridge: Harvard University Press, 1938).
8. M. Weber, *The Theory of Social and Economic Organization,* ed. and trans. A. M. Henderson and T. Parsons (New York: Oxford University Press, 1947).
9. R. M. Weiss, "Weber on Bureaucracy: Management Consultant or Political Theorist?" *Academy of Management Review* 8 (1983): 242–248, argues that Weber was not concerned with prescribing the characteristics of an efficient organization but rather was solely offering political theory.

10. M. Weber, *Essays on Sociology,* ed. and trans. H. H. Gerth and C.W. Mills (New York: Oxford University Press, 1947), 196–198.

11. H. Simon, *Administrative Behavior,* 2d ed. (New York: Macmillan Co., 1957); J. G. March and H. A. Simon, *Organizations* (New York: John Wiley & Sons, 1958).

12. C. E. Snow, "A Discussion of the Relation of Illumination Intensity to Productive Efficiency," *The Tech Engineering News* (November 1927), cited in E. J. Roethlisberger and W. J. Dickson, *Management and the Worker* (Cambridge: Harvard University Press, 1939).

13. Roethlisberger and Dickson, *Management.*

14. K. Lewin, "Forces Behind Food Habits and Methods of Change," *Bulletin of the National Research Council* 108 (1943): 35–65.

15. M. Radke and D. Klisurich, "Experiments in Changing Food Habits," *Journal of the American Dietetics Association* 23 (1947): 403–409.

16. L. Cosh and J. R. P. French, Jr., "Overcoming Resistance to Change," *Human Relations* 1 (1948): 512–533.

17. See C. S. Bartlem and E. A. Locke, "The Coch and French Study: A Critique and Reinterpretation," *Human Relations* 34 (1981): 555–566, for another view of the significance of research about participation.

18. R. F. Bales, "Task Roles and Social Roles in Problem Solving Groups," in *Readings in Social Psychology,* 3d ed., ed. E. Maccoby, T. M. Newcomb, and E. L. Hartley (New York: Holt, Rinehart, and Winston, 1958), 437–447; D. McGregor, *The Human Side of Enterprise* (New York: McGraw-Hill, 1960).

19. McGregor, *Human Side;* E. H. Schein, "The Hawthorne Group Studies Revisited: A Defense of Theory Y," (Cambridge, Mass.: M.I.T. Sloan School of Management Working Paper #756-74, December 1974).

20. E. K. Trist and K. W. Bamforth, "Some Social and Psychological Consequences of the Long Wall Method of Coal Getting," *Human Relations* 4 (1951): 3–38; A. K. Rice, *The Enterprise and Its Environment* (London: Tavistock, 1963); F. E. Emery and I. L. Trist, "Socio-technical systems," in *Management Science: Models and Techniques,* vol. 2 (London: Pergamon, 1960).

21. Trist and Bamforth, "Consequences," 3–38.

22. Harold Koontz, "The Management Theory Jungle Revisited," *Academy of Management Review* 5 (April 1980).

23. D. Katz and R. L. Kahn, *The Social Psychology of Organizations,* 2d ed. (New York: John Wiley & Sons, 1978).

24. D. A. Nadler and M. L. Tushman, "A Diagnostic Model for Organizational Behavior," in *Perspectives on Behavior in Organizations,* ed. J. R. Hackman, L. W. Porter, and E. E. Lawler III (New York: McGraw-Hill, 1977).

25. Koontz, "Management Theory."

26. T. Burns and G. M. Stalker, *The Management of Innovation* (London: Tavistock, 1961).

27. J. Woodward, *Industrial Organization: Theory and Practice* (London: Oxford University Press, 1965); P. Lawrence and J. Lorsch, *Organization and Environment* (Boston: Harvard University Graduate School of Business, Division of Research, 1967).

28. H. Mintzberg, *Structure in Fives: Designing Effective Organizations* (Englewood Cliffs, N.J.: Prentice-Hall, 1983), summarizes the fit between structure and the contingencies of technology, environment, goals, work force, age, and size of the organization.

29. See Chapters 17, 18, and 19 for a discussion of these areas.

30. H. Mintzberg, *The Nature of Managerial Work,* 2d ed. (Englewood Cliffs, N.J.: Prentice-Hall, 1979).

REFERENCES

Burns, T., and G. M. Stalker. *The Management of Innovation.* London: Tavistock, 1961.

Emerson, Harrington. *The Twelve Principles of Efficiency.* New York: The Engineering Magazine Co., 1913.

Emery, F. E., and I. L. Trist. "Socio-Technical Systems." In *Management Science: Models and Techniques,* vol. 2. London: Pergamon, 1960.

Fayol, Henri. *General and Industrial Management.* New York: Pitman, 1949.

Franke, R. H., and J. D. Kaul. "The Hawthorne Experiments: First Statistical Interpretation." *American Sociological Review* 43 (1978): 623–643.

Henderson, A. M., and T. Parsons. *The Theory of Social and Economic Organization.* Edited and translated by M. Weber. New York: Oxford University Press, 1947.

Katz, D., and R. L. Kahn. *The Social Psychology of Organizations.* 2d ed. New York: John Wiley & Sons, 1978.

Kieehel, Walter, III. "The Ages of a Manager; Each Decade of Life Brings an Executive New Abilities." *Fortune* 115 (11 May 1987): 170–173.

Koontz, Harold. "The Management Theory Jungle Revisited." *Academy of Management Review* 5, no. 2 (April 1980): 175–189.

Lawrence, P., and J. Lorsch. *Organization and Environment.* Boston: Harvard University Graduate School of Business, Division of Research, 1967.

Locke, E. A. "The Ideas of Frederick W. Taylor: An Evaluation." *Academy of Management Review* 7 (1982): 14–24.

McGregor, Douglas. *The Professional Manager.* New York: McGraw-Hill, 1967.

March, J. G., and H. A. Simon. *Organizations.* New York: John Wiley & Sons, 1958.

Mintzberg, Henry. *Structure in Fives: Designing Effective Organizations.* Englewood Cliffs, N.J.: Prentice-Hall, 1983.

————. "The Manager's Job: Folklore and Fact." *Harvard Business Review* (July–August 1975): 49–61.

Oliva, Terence A., and Christel M. Capdevielle. "Can Systems Really Be Taught? (A Socratic Dialogue)." *Academy of Management Review* 5, no. 2 (April 1980): 277–281.

Peters, Thomas J. "Facing Up to the Need for a Management Revolution." *California Management Review* 30 (Winter 1988): 7–38.

Rice, A. K. *The Enterprise and Its Environment.* London: Tavistock, 1963.

Roethlisberger, F. J., and W. J. Dickson. *Management and the Worker: An Account of a Research Program Conducted by the Western Electric Company Hawthorne Works, Chicago.* Cambridge: Harvard University Press, 1939.

Shaffer, James C. "Mission Statements: Why Have Them? (Corporate Mission Statements)." *Communication World* 4 (June 1987): 14–16.

Simon, H. *Administrative Behavior.* 2d ed. New York: Macmillan, 1957.

Smith, Adam. *An Inquiry into the Nature and Cause of the Wealth of Nations.* 1776.

Taylor, F. W. *The Principles of Scientific Management.* New York: Harper and Brothers, 1911.

Trist, E. K., and K. W. Bamforth. "Some Social and Psychological Consequences of the Long Wall Method of Coal Getting." *Human Relations* 4 (1951): 3–38.

Wilmet, Robb W. "Change in Management and the Management of Change." *Long Range Planning* 20 (December 1987): 23–28.

Woodward, J. *Industrial Organization: Theory and Practice.* London: Oxford University Press, 1965.

Wrege, C. D., and A. G. Perroni. "Taylor's Pig-Tale: A Historical Analysis of Frederick W. Taylor's Pig-Iron Experiments." *Academy of Management Journal* 17 (1974): 6–17.

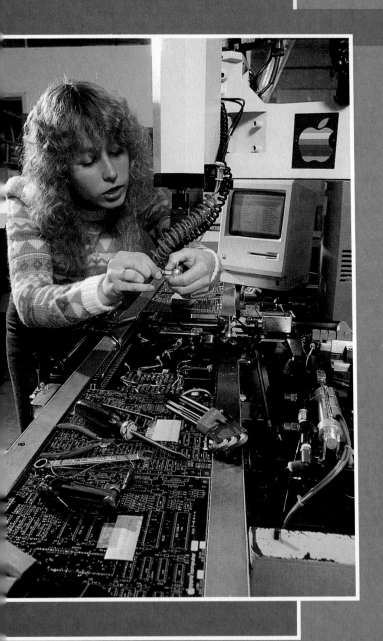

CHAPTER

3

Chapter Outline

The Manager's Environment

Learning Objectives

After completing this chapter students should be able to

1. Describe the major factors in the external environment that can affect an organization.
2. Describe the major factors in the internal environment that can affect an organization.
3. Describe the basic transformation process that may occur in any organization.

AS THE LARGEST employer in Ouachita County, Arkansas, International Forest Products Company (IFP) is an important part of the local economy. IFP employs almost ten percent of the work force in this rural area of south-central Arkansas, and few alternative job opportunities are available.

Scott Wheeler, the personnel director at IFP, tells of a difficult decision he had to make in December 1982:

Everything was going along pretty well despite the economic recession, but I knew that sooner or later we would be affected. I got the word at a private meeting with the president, Mr. Deason, that we would have to cut employment by thirty percent on a crash basis. I was to get back to him within a week with a suggested plan. I knew that my plan would not be the final one since the move was so major. But I knew that Mr. Deason was depending on me to provide at least a workable approach.

First of all, I thought about how the union would react. Certainly, workers would have to be let go in order of seniority. The union would try to protect as many jobs as possible. I also knew that all management's actions during this period would be intensely scrutinized by the union, so we had to make sure we had our act together.

Then there was the matter of the effect the cuts would have on the surrounding community. The impact on the individual workers to be laid off was bad enough. But the economy of Ouachita County had not been in good shape recently, and I knew our cutbacks would further depress the area's economy. I knew that a number of government officials and civic leaders would want to know how we were trying to minimize the harm done to the public in that area.

I believe we really had no choice but to make the cuts. I personally had no choice because my boss said IFP was going to do it. But I had recently read a news account that one of our competitors, Johns Manville Corporation in West Monroe, Louisiana, had laid off several hundred workers in a cost-cutting move. The wood products market is very competitive, and a cost advantage of even two or three percent would allow a competitor to take many of our customers. So, to keep our sales from being further depressed, we had to ensure that our costs were just as low as those of our competition.

Another reason I was sure the cutbacks were inevitable was management's concern for our shareholders. The shareholders are aware of social responsibility—a few years ago a shareholder group disrupted an annual meeting to insist that IFP make certain antipollution changes—but, in general, they seem to be more concerned with the return on their investment. Mr. Deason reminded me at our meeting that, just like every other manager in the company, I should place the shareholders' interest foremost. I really was quite overwhelmed as I began to work on a personnel plan that would balance all of the conflicting interests I knew about. ■

AS IS EVIDENCED from the above case, the external environment has a major impact on the operations of International Forest Products. This chapter begins with an overview of the components of a business system. Next, some of the major external environmental factors will be described, followed by a discussion of the internal environment. Finally, the transformation process in which inputs are converted to outputs within the business system will be described.

THE BUSINESS SYSTEM: AN OVERVIEW

The IFP story illustrates the importance management must place on understanding the interrelationships between the firm and its environment. The systems approach—the viewing of any organization or entity as an arrangement of interrelated parts that interact in ways that can be specified and to some extent predicted—provides a rational means for examining these interactions. Use of the systems approach inevitably leads one to conclude that every organization, indeed every system, is an open system. An open system is an organization or assemblage of things that affects and is affected by outside events.

Figure 3.1 illustrates the business system. Note that the organization is affected by a number of forces, both external and internal. Top management has perhaps the greatest concern for the external forces, while management at all levels must be concerned with the forces of the internal environment. Managers at lower levels of the organization, however, confront an internal environment that is markedly different from that encountered by management at more senior levels. Within these complex external and internal environments, the business system operates: inputs are converted to outputs through a transformation process directed and controlled by managers. Figure 3.1, therefore, provides the framework for our discussion of the manager's environment.

THE EXTERNAL ENVIRONMENT

The manager's job cannot be accomplished in a vacuum within the organization. Many interacting external factors can affect managerial performance. The external environment consists of those factors that affect a firm from outside the organizational boundaries. As illustrated in Figure 3.2, the external factors include: the labor force, legal considerations, society, unions, stockholders, competition, customers, and technology. Each of these factors, separately or in combination, can result in constraints on the manager's job; thus, the impact of such factors must always be considered.

Frederick W. Smith, founder of Federal Express Corporation, realized how important the external environment could be when he went international with his business and ran headlong into entrenched overseas rivals and onerous foreign regulations. The lesson Smith learned about the importance of the external environment was a costly one: his company lost approximately $74 million dollars over a three-year period. Smith remained undaunted, however, and purchased Tiger International airline to secure rights to the delivery routes Tiger had acquired over forty years. This acquisition may help Smith cope with the external environment he encountered.[1]

Systems approach
The viewing of any organization or entity as an arrangement of interrelated parts that interact in ways that can be specified and to some extent predicted.

Open system
An organization or assemblage of things that affects and is affected by outside events.

External environment
Those factors that affect a firm from outside the organization's boundaries.

53

F I G U R E 3.1 ■■ The Business System

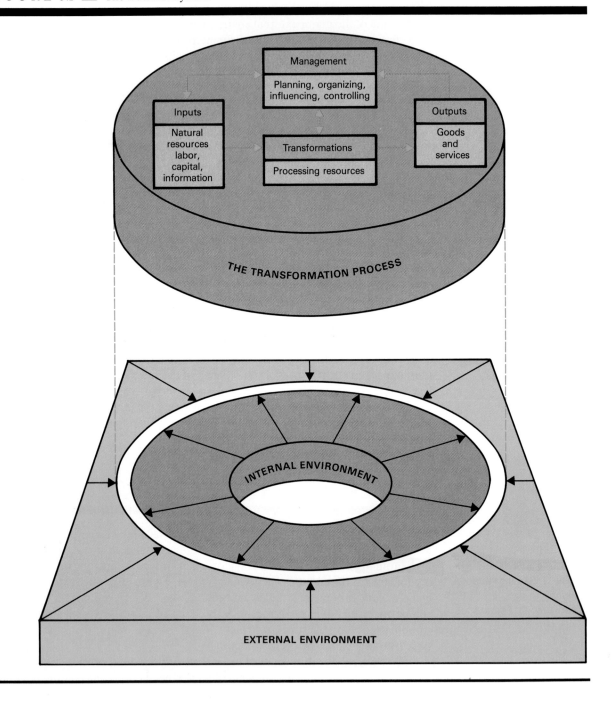

The Labor Force

The capabilities of a firm's employees determines to a large extent how well the organization can perform its mission. Since an organization obtains its workers

BUSINESS BRIEFS

INSIDE BUSINESS

Coping with the Business's External Environment

THE MANAGER'S EXTERNAL environment is comprised of those factors that affect a firm from outside the organization's boundaries. The external factors commonly include the labor force, legal considerations, society, unions, stockholders, competition, customers, and technology. Mr. Bernard Fauber, Chairman of K mart Corporation, has a keen awareness of many of these factors that impact his organization. Competitively, K mart is number two to Sears, and Wal-Mart is closing in rapidly. In terms of modernization and technology, they appear to be playing catch-up ball. Questions arise such as, should they increase the percentage of goods they purchase overseas, and what about the new tax laws that have just come into play? Fauber's ability to cope with, and capitalize on, these and other external factors will set the future course and possibly the ultimate destiny of the K mart Corporation. Fauber's approach for dealing with these and other external factors are expanded on in an interview conducted by CNN's Kandel, *Business Week*'s Sturm, and Hagedorn of *The Wall Street Journal*.

from a pool of individuals external to the firm, the labor force is considered an external environmental factor. Moreover, the labor force is an ever-changing component, which, to some degree, causes changes in the work force of an organization. In turn, changes in individuals within an organization affect the

F I G U R E 3.2 ▬▬ The External Environment

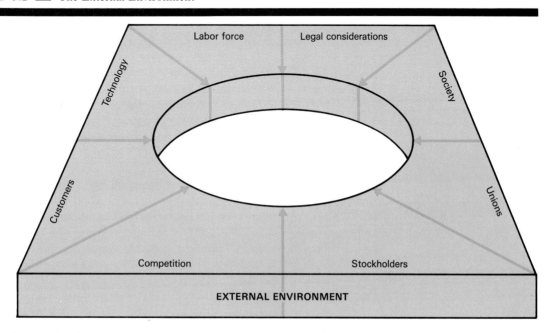

FIGURE 3.3 ■ Labor-Force Growth Rate

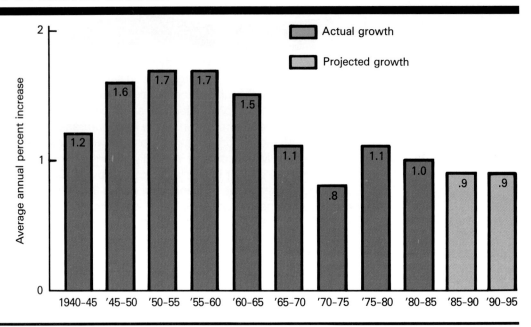

Source: Bureau of Census

way management must deal with its work force. In short, changes in the country's labor force create a dynamic situation within an organization.

By 1995 the United States' labor force is projected to be about 129 million people, representing an increase of about 14 percent from the 1984 level of 114 million. Figure 3.3 shows actual and expected labor-force growth rates through 1995. Size alone, however, does not tell the entire story. The labor force now includes more working women and older persons. Many companies hire part-time workers, and the use of temporary and leased employees is increasing. Handicapped employees are being included in increasing numbers; and many immigrants from developing areas, especially Southeast Asia and Latin America, are joining the labor force. New entrants in the labor force between 1985 and the year 2000 are expected to be 15 percent U.S.-born white males, 42 percent U.S.-born white females, 7 percent U.S.-born nonwhite males, 13 percent U.S.-born nonwhite females, 13 percent immigrant males, and 10 percent immigrant females.[2]

WOMEN IN THE WORK FORCE

Through the mid-1990s, the chief cause of labor-force growth will be the continued, though slower, rise in the number and proportion of women who seek jobs. Women will account for more than three-fifths of labor-force growth during the period from 1984 to 1995 (see Figure 3.4). As the number of women entering the work force increases, the problems they experience become of greater concern to management.

OLDER WORKERS

The United States population grew older through the 1980s, a trend which will continue at least through the year 2000. Life expectancies continue to

FIGURE 3.4 ■
Women as a Percent of
Labor-Force Growth

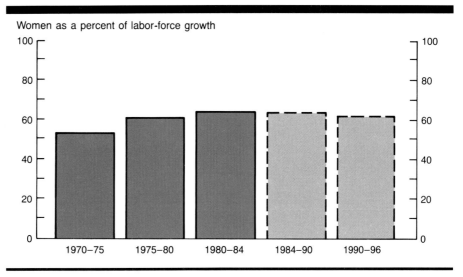

Women as a percent of labor-force growth

Source: Bureau of Labor Statistics

increase; and the baby-boom generation, born from the end of World War II through 1964, has had only half as many children as their parents did. The trend toward earlier retirement reversed itself in the mid-1980s, perhaps caused by the 1986 amendment to the Age Discrimination In Employment Act of 1967, which prohibited discrimination above age 40. Now firms cannot force a worker to retire at seventy or at any age. Many older persons do not want to retire or even slow down. Some favor a less demanding, although full-time, job; others choose semi-retirement; and still others prefer part-time work.

PART-TIME WORKERS

More and more companies employ part-time workers. In fact, it has been estimated that part-time workers were the fastest growing segment of the work force after 1980.[3] Managers who employ part-time workers must relate to, and communicate with, different people performing the same job, thus increasing the complexity of the situation. Nevertheless, it is vitally important that managers treat part-time workers as fairly as possible in order to engage their sense of responsibility and satisfy their need to feel worthwhile. Overcoming the disadvantages of part-time employees requires that managers exercise extraordinary leadership. Some problems are eased if company policy gives part-time workers the first opportunity to fill full-time job openings. Another creative option for part-time workers is **job sharing,** or the filling of a job by two or more part-time employees, each working part of a regular work week and sharing the benefits of one full-time worker.

TEMPORARY AND LEASED EMPLOYEES

The need for traditional temporary employees increased after the mid-1980s, in part because more women, and a few men, were taking parental leave. Additionally, the corporate-takeover fervor late in the decade caused many firms

Job sharing
The filling of a job by two or more part-time employees, each working part of a regular work week and sharing the benefits of one full-time worker.

to cut work forces to the bare minimum, making it necessary for gaps to be filled with temporaries.

A special type of temporary assignment can be filled by **leased employees,** that is, by individuals provided by an outside firm at a fixed hourly rate, similar to a rental fee, often for extended periods. Managers of temporary or leased workers generally find them to be well qualified and eager to please, although their ties to the firm are not as strong as those of traditional employees.

Leased employees
Individuals provided by an outside firm at a fixed hourly rate, similar to a rental fee, often for extended periods.

PERSONS WITH DISABILITIES

According to one estimation, approximately 36 million disabled persons are employed in the United States, not including mentally handicapped persons.[4] A handicap, or disability, is a disadvantage which limits the amount or kind of work a person can do or makes achievement unusually difficult. Laws pertaining to handicapped workers generally define handicap or disability quite broadly. Among the more common disabilities are limited hearing or sight, limited mobility, mental or emotional deficiencies, and various nerve disorders. Recent studies indicate that handicapped workers can do as well as unimpaired workers in areas such as productivity, attendance, and average tenure.[5] In fact, in certain high-turnover occupations handicapped workers were found to have lower turnover rates.

IMMIGRANTS FROM DEVELOPING AREAS

Large numbers of immigrants from developing areas, such as Southeast Asia and Latin America, have settled in many parts of the United States bringing with

Disabled individuals comprise an important segment of the labor force. (© Charles Gupton/Stock, Boston, Inc.)

them attitudes, values, and mores particular to their home-country cultures. As corporations employ more foreign nationals in this country, effective managers must work to understand the different cultures and languages of their employees.

YOUNG PERSONS WITH LIMITED EDUCATION OR SKILLS

Each year thousands of young, unskilled workers are hired, especially during peak periods such as holiday buying seasons. These workers generally have limited education, sometimes even less than a high school diploma. Those who have completed high school often find that their education hardly fits the work they are expected to do. Most, for example, lack familiarity with computers. Many of these young adults and teenagers have poor work habits; they tend to be tardy or absent more often than experienced or better educated workers.

Although the negative attributes of these workers at times seem to outweigh the positives, more young workers with limited skills and education will be needed in the future. Since a chronic shortage of qualified workers is predicted, managers should avoid stereotyping young workers in favor of viewing each as a potential long-term employee.

Legal Considerations

Another significant external force affecting management relates to federal, state, and local legislation and the many court decisions interpreting this legislation. Table 3.1 lists some of the federal laws that affect virtually the entire spectrum of management policies. Note from the table that a number of the laws that have had the greatest impact on business date from the 1930s and before. This includes the Social Security Act (1935), the National Labor Relations Act (1935), the Pure Food and Drug Act (1906), and the Sherman Act (1890). Among the laws that have been passed in recent decades, the Civil Rights Act of 1964, as amended, has perhaps affected business managers most extensively. This act has been largely responsible for bringing many more women and minorities into the work force and for giving them opportunities for advancement.

Laws continue to be passed that seriously limit the actions a firm may take. In 1988, for example, the Employee Polygraph Protection Action went into effect, prohibiting employers from requiring employees or prospective employees to submit to lie detector tests. Firms who previously made extensive use of the polygraph in employee selection now must make such selections using other criteria. The Plant Closing/Layoff Act, also passed in 1988, requires employers with one hundred or more workers to give sixty-days' notice to employees and local government officials when a plant closing or layoff affecting fifty or more employees for a ninety-day period is planned. Today's managers must be alert to the ever-changing legal environment in the United States. Likewise, when a firm's operations extend into other countries, the laws and regulations of those countries must be taken into account.

Society

Members of society may also exert pressure on management. The public no longer accepts the actions of the business community without question, and they have

TABLE 3.1 ■ Sample of Federal Laws Affecting Business

Laws	Major Provisions
Sherman Act of 1890	The federal government's first large-scale intervention in private business; aimed at controlling trusts and preventing monopolies
Pure Food and Drug Act of 1906 as amended	Designed to protect consumers by requiring inspection of food and drug products
Clayton Act and the Federal Trade Commission Act of 1914	Clayton Act made tying contracts, exclusive trading, and price discrimination illegal; Federal Trade Commission Act established the Federal Trade Commission to enforce the Clayton Act
Security Exchange Commission Act of 1934	Protects investors from fraud and swindles and regulates securities markets
National Labor Relations Act of 1935	Protects rights of employees to form unions and levies bargaining responsibilities on management
Social Security Act of 1935 as amended	Established a federal insurance program to provide retirement and survivor benefits, disability payments, medicare, and unemployment insurance
Fair Labor Standards Act of 1938	Requires firms to pay minimum wages and extra compensation for overtime
Air Pollution Control Act of 1962 as amended by the Clean Air Acts of 1970 and 1977	Established air quality standards to promote the public health and welfare and the productive capacity of the nation
Equal Pay Act of 1963	Requires that males and females on the same job get equal pay
Civil Rights Act of 1964 as amended in 1972 by the Equal Employment Opportunity Act	Prohibits discrimination in hiring, training, promotion, and pay on the basis of race, color, religion, nationality, and sex
Age Discrimination Act of 1967 as amended in 1978, 1986	Prohibits age discrimination
Occupational Safety and Health Act of 1970	Sets safety and health standards and enforces them through surprise inspections and fines
Consumer Products Safety Act of 1972	Sets safety standards for consumer products and bans products that create undue risk of injury
Employee Retirement Income Security Act of 1974	Protects employee rights in private pension plans

learned that change can be brought about through their voices and votes. The large number of regulatory laws that have been passed since the early 1960s is testimony to the public's influence. The firm that is to remain acceptable to the general public must accomplish its mission within the range of societal norms.

Management should consider that the firm's employees are part of the society the firm must accommodate. For instance, an organization employing ten thousand people has influence over a far larger number of people who are not connected with the firm, as each employee communicates with family members and friends. Management is therefore well served when it maintains clear and honest communications with its employees, who, in turn, can effectively articulate the firm's position.

Because the public's attitude and beliefs often directly affect a firm's profitability, those attitudes and beliefs can significantly alter that firm's behavior. When a corporation behaves as if it has a conscience, it is said to be socially

Social responsibility
The implied, enforced, or felt obligation of managers, acting in their official capacities, to serve or protect the interests of groups other than themselves.

Ethics
The discipline dealing with what is good and bad, or right and wrong, or with moral duty and obligation.

Union
A group of employees who have joined together for the purpose of dealing with their employer.

responsible. **Social responsibility** is the implied, enforced, or felt obligation of managers, acting in their official capacities, to serve or protect the interests of groups other than themselves.[6] Many companies develop patterns of concern for moral issues variously through policy statements, practices over time, or the leadership of morally strong employees and managers. Open-door policies, grievance procedures, and employee-benefit programs often stem as much from desire to do what is right as from concern for productivity and avoidance of strife.[7]

If the goal of a business is to make a profit and grow, some may ask, Why should a firm be concerned with the welfare of society? That a business must make a profit in the long run to survive is obvious, but a basic point should also be remembered: if the needs of society are not satisfied, a firm will ultimately cease to exist because a firm operates by public consent to satisfy society's needs. The business is a member of the community in which it operates; and, just as citizens may work to improve the quality of life in their community, the firm should also respect and work with the other members of its community. For instance, a high unemployment rate of a certain minority group may exist in the region in which a firm is based. The firm, in order to be socially responsible, may adjust its policy and hire workers who are capable of being trained, as opposed to hiring only trained applicants. This change in policy would likely ease the unemployment in the area; it no doubt would enhance the firm's image in the community; and in the long run it may actually improve the firm's profitability.

Social responsibility is closely related to **ethics,** the discipline dealing with what is good and bad or right and wrong or with moral duty and obligation. In order for students to gain greater appreciation of the difficulties involved when considering ethics, an ethical dilemma is presented in the ethics box. Social responsibility and ethics are the topics of the next chapter.

Unions

Wage levels, benefits, and working conditions for millions of employees now reflect decisions made jointly by unions and management. A **union** is a group of

ETHICAL DILEMMA

SUPPOSE FOR A MOMENT that you have a goal that is critically important to you. Your friends are very supportive and are determined to assist you in the accomplishment of your goal. You later attain your goal, and find out still later that your friends did some illegal things they believed would help you reach your goal. You just found out about their activities. Although their illegal activities did not help you attain your goal, your friends thought it might. No one was hurt by your friends' illegal activities, but they did break the law. You have two options: you can cover for your friends and possibly get caught; or you can turn your friends in and allow them to suffer the consequences of their actions.

Let's further assume that you are President of the United States Richard M. Nixon, and your friends are the Watergate burglars.
What would you do?

employees who have joined together for the purpose of dealing with their employer. Unions are treated as an environmental factor because, essentially, they become a third party when dealing with the company. In a unionized organization it is the union rather than the individual employee that negotiates an agreement with the firm. In the case that opened the chapter, Scott Wheeler no doubt knew the layoffs at IFP would be made in order of seniority because that is what the labor/management agreement likely specified.

Although unions remain a fairly powerful force, union membership as a percentage of the nonagricultural work force slipped from 33 percent in 1955 to about 17 percent in 1987.[8] Between 1980 and 1984 alone, organized labor lost 2.7 million members.[9] Organized labor's share of the work force is expected to continue to decline to the point of representing only 13 percent of all nonfarm workers by the year 2000. As the percentage of nonunion workers increases, the courts and state legislatures are becoming the *most effective champions of employee rights*. The emphasis in future years will likely shift to a management system that deals directly with the individual worker to satisfy his or her needs.

In many other countries union power is also decreasing. In Germany more and more union members are starting to realize that they can make excellent gains without union representation. Also, when union members in Korea struck in 1987, the labor minister, Lee Hun Ki, made it perfectly clear that government authorities would take legal action if demands by workers became unreasonable and labor strikes spread beyond control. Regardless of the relative strength of the local unions, managers whose firms compete in the national or global markets must adjust and operate effectively with the unionized environment in the particular markets with which they deal.

Stockholders

Stockholders
The owners of a corporation.

The owners of a corporation, called **stockholders,** have significant influence on management. Remember in the case of International Forest Products that a major reason for the cutbacks was protection of the interests of the company's shareholders. Because stockholders have a monetary investment in the firm, they may at times challenge programs considered by management to be beneficial to the organization. Managers may be forced to justify the merits of a particular program in terms of how it will affect future costs, projects, and revenues. For instance, a recommendation that $50 thousand be spent to implement a management development program may require more justification to the stockholders than the statement that "managers should become more open and adaptive to the needs of employees." Management must be prepared to explain how such an expenditure will increase revenues or decrease costs, while at the same time benefiting the organization as a whole. Another means by which stockholders can influence a company is through stockholder activism. Prior to the 1960s, such activism was virtually unheard of, but management has since then been forced to become extremely sensitive to its public image. The last thing most corporations want is criticism of the firm's performance on the front page of a major newspaper. Management, therefore, is often very sensitive to stockholder pressure.[10]

Competition

Unless an organization is in the unusual position of monopolizing the market it serves, other firms will be producing similar products or services. For a firm to succeed, grow, and prosper, it must maintain a supply of competent employees. But other organizations are also striving toward that same objective. A major task of management, therefore, is to ensure that the firm obtains and retains a sufficient number of employees in various career fields to allow the firm to compete effectively.

The competitive nature of many businesses causes many managers to feel under considerable pressure to improve their compensation system. A bidding war often results when competitors attempt to fill certain critical positions in their firms. On the other hand, the strategic nature of a firm's needs sometimes forces managers to resort to unusual means to recruit and retain critical employees. Increasingly, firms are not only improving salaries but emphasizing other forms of reward as well to meet this challenge. Today the effective manager views the overall quality of the work environment as part of the compensation program the firm is promoting to prospective employees.

When a firm competes in the global markets, the posture of the governments in which the firm operates must be taken into account. A good example of the importance of government support, or the lack of it, is provided by the superconductivity industry, which by the year 2000 is expected to represent a $20 billion-a-year industry. In February of 1987 a researcher at the University of Houston discovered a ceramic that would superconduct at −195 degrees centigrade, a much higher temperature than previously known to be possible. This discovery set off a furor worldwide.

Today, organizations must deal with competition that arises from a global economy.
(Courtesy of Air Products and Chemicals, Inc.)

In the United States bills to supplement superconductivity research wove their way through Congress during 1987, but the profit motives of individual private companies provided the primary impetus for pursuing this research. Dozens of research labs in the United States, mostly corporate research and development divisions, sprang into action. New developments were closely guarded, with each research team aware of the proprietary nature of their work and therefore unwilling to share their results with others. Apparent early leaders

in the race were IBM, which had actually abandoned research on superconducting chips in 1983, and AT&T. No single government agency coordinated the development effort.

In Japan, on the other hand, the Ministry of International Trade and Industry (MITI) jumped into action once the University of Houston discovery was announced. A forty-member superconductivity research team was formed; and a superconductivity advisory group, made up of executives from Toshiba, Hitachi, and several other companies in the electronics, telecommunications, and electric power fields, helped steer MITI policy. The effort quickly became the central focus of MITI's Office of Basic Technologies for Future Industries. But, as the composition of the advisory group suggests, the work did not rely solely on government initiative for its direction. The Japanese effort instead combined the research strength of private industry with that of the government to advance the technology more rapidly. As a result, Japanese industry did make several quick advances: Toshiba produced wire, and NEC Corporation developed a new computer chip using the new ceramic superconductor discovered in Houston. Commenting on the combined business-government effort, one reporter termed Japan's work in superconductivity "a national obsession." Against this level of coordination and cooperation, private industry in the United States seems to be unable to adequately compete with Japan.

Customers

The people who actually use a firm's products and services must also be considered a part of the external environment. Because sales are critical to the firm's survival, management must take care that the company's practices do not antagonize the members of the market it serves. For example, if a certain minority or ethnic group purchases a large share of the firm's products, it surely is in the best interest of the organization to have a representative proportion of this group included within its work force. When organizations have limited the number of minorities they employ, consumer boycotts have in some instances been effective and damaging to the image of the firm.

Customers constantly demand high-quality products and improved service, and a firm must always strive to maintain a work force capable of meeting this demand. Fluctuations in sales often result from variations in product quality, which in turn is directly related to the skills, qualifications, and motivations of the organization's employees.

Technology

Change is occurring at an ever-increasing pace, and few firms operate today as they did even a decade ago. Of major concern to management is the effect that technological or state-of-the-art changes have had and will continue to have on businesses. Products not envisioned only a few years ago are now being mass-produced, and new skills are continually needed to meet new technological demands. Since new skills are typically not held by many in the work force, recruiting qualified individuals in these developing areas is extremely difficult.

At the same time, the advance of technology renders certain other skills no longer necessary, requiring periodic retraining of the current work force. It has

FIGURE 3.5 ■
Projected Growth of
Service- versus Goods-
Producing Industries

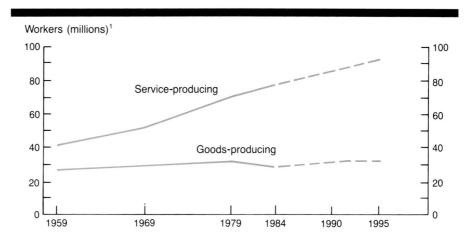

Workers (millions)[1]

¹Includes wage and salary workers, the self-employed, and unpaid family workers

Source: Bureau of Labor Statistics

been estimated that more than half of all existing jobs will be changed within the next decades, with thirty percent of them being eliminated as a result of technological advances.[11] The advent of word processing, for instance, has substantially changed the traditional role of the secretary. Many managers now generate and print their own letters using a word processor instead of writing or dictating letters to the secretary. A major portion of Chapter 22 is devoted to technological advances affecting management.

At times the need for new technology is generated by other environmental factors. Fast-foods chains, for example, have turned to technology to find ways to reduce the number of workers needed because of the difficulty many have in obtaining reliable help. For instance, self-service drink dispensing machines are being installed to eliminate the need to have employees pour soft drinks.[12] Research is also being conducted into the preparation of such items as self-service hamburgers and other fast foods to reduce the number of employees needed.

Technological change will have a long-range effect on the industries that will be hiring new employees over the next few years. Figure 3.5 shows that employment in service-producing industries has been increasing faster than employment in goods-producing industries. As incomes and living standards have risen, people's desire for services has grown more rapidly than their desire for goods. Service-producing industries, in fact, are projected to account for approximately nine out of ten new jobs generated between 1984 and 1995. Employment in these industries is expected to increase by 18 percent from 77.2 million in 1984 to 91.3 million in 1995.

Proactive response
The anticipation of what is occurring in the external environment and making decisions based on these conclusions.

Responding to the External Environment: Proactive versus Reactive

Managers respond to the external environment in two ways—proactive and reactive. A **proactive response** is the anticipation of what is occurring in the external environment and making decisions based on these conclusions. A **reactive response** is the action by managers based on forces impacting the firm from the external environment. For example, prior to the passage of the Occupational Safety and Health Act (OSHA) of 1970, many organizations made a concerted effort to create a safe and healthy work environment for their employees. These firms would be considered proactive with regard to health and safety. Other firms that had not been as concerned with providing a safe and healthy work environment suddenly were required to become so by the enactment of OSHA. These firms would be considered reactive with regard to health and safety because they only implemented health and safety guidelines when faced with a legal requirement to do so.

Organizations exhibit varying degrees of proactive and reactive behavior. Again with regard to the enactment of OSHA, some firms responded by adhering strictly to that interpretation regarding health and safety. Other firms, however, went far beyond that interpretation and have truly attempted to develop a total environment that promotes health and safety in all respects. By making the extra effort, these firms have moved from a reactive to a proactive stance.

Much the same situation occurred with the passage of Title VII of the Civil Rights Act of 1964. Prior to 1964 a large majority of firms would likely have been considered reactive with regard to equal employment opportunity. Since 1964, however, many of these same firms have become proactive; that is, they have gone beyond the strict requirements of the law in promoting equal opportunity and have recognized that individuals of all races, creed, and sex have the potential to become competent employees.

A firm may be either reactive or proactive with regard to issues other than legal considerations. For example, if a firm wishes to remain union-free, it might be reactive and only begin to consider the welfare of its employees when these workers attempt to form a union. Such efforts often come too late, and the firm becomes unionized. Another organization might concentrate its efforts on creating an environment where its workers are happy and do not feel the need to be represented by a union. Such a firm would be considered proactive since it took action before external forces caused the firm to respond.

Whether a firm is reactive or proactive depends largely on the philosophy and attitudes of top management. In both instances management must ultimately confront the external environment. Proactive managers, however, tend to be best able to adapt to environmental constraints as they are presented.

■■ THE INTERNAL ENVIRONMENT

The internal environment of an organization, as shown in Figure 3.6, is really quite different from that of the external environment. The **internal environment** consists of those factors that affect a firm from inside the organization's boundaries. Top level managers, although heavily influenced by external environmental factors, must nevertheless pay careful attention to the internal environment, as must managers at all levels.

Mission

Mission is the organization's continuing purpose or reason for being. Each management level in the organization should conduct its operation with a clear

---

Reactive response
The action by managers based on forces impacting the firm from the external environment.   *or internal*

usually not as effective

Internal environment
Those factors that affect a firm from inside the organization's boundaries.

Mission
The organization's continuing purpose or reason for being.

F I G U R E 3.6 ██
The Internal Environment

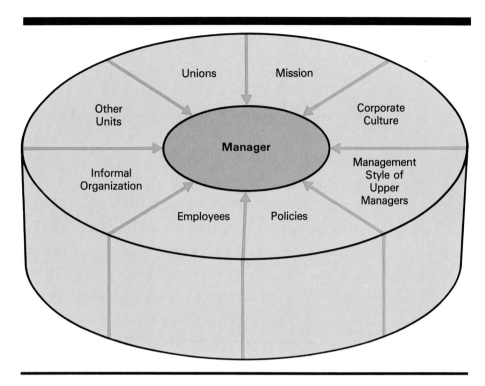

FIGURE 3.6 ██
The Internal Environment

understanding of the overall mission of the firm. In fact, each unit in the organization (division, plant, department) should have clearly articulated objectives that coincide with the organizational mission.

Corporate Culture

Corporate culture
The system of shared values, beliefs, and habits within an organization that interacts with the formal structure to produce behavioral norms.

Corporate culture—the system of shared values, beliefs, and habits within an organization that interacts with the formal structure to produce behavioral norms[13]—refers to the firm's social and psychological climate. An infinite number of possible cultures could exist, and they might best be discussed as parts of a spectrum.

At one extreme is a closed and threatening culture. In this type of culture decisions tend to be made higher up in the organization; managers tend to lack trust and confidence in subordinates; secrecy abounds throughout the firm; and workers are not encouraged to be creative and engage in problem-solving activities. At the other end of the spectrum is an open culture in which decisions tend to be made at lower levels in the organization; management has a high degree of trust and confidence in subordinates; open communication is advocated; and workers are encouraged to be creative and to solve problems with other team members. In all likelihood, the corporate culture of any given firm will fall somewhere in between these two extremes. Identification of the type of culture that exists within a firm is important to management since it can affect job performance throughout the organization and ultimately profitability. Corporate culture will be discussed in considerable detail in Chapter 20.

Management Style of Upper Managers

Closely related to corporate culture is the way in which the attitudes and preferences of one's superior affects how a job is accomplished. This deserves special emphasis here because of the problems that can result if the managerial style of upper level managers differs significantly from that of lower level managers. If, for example, a superior believes in giving orders and having them followed while the supervisor prefers to involve employees in decision making and give them a greater degree of freedom, conflict likely will result. This is especially true if the superior perceives the supervisor's approach as stemming from a lack of decisiveness. Even the company president must deal with the management style and attitudes of his or her superiors, the board of directors of the firm. The president may be a risk taker and want to be more aggressive in the marketplace, and the board may desire a more conservative approach; thus, the potential for conflict exists.

Policies

Policy
A predetermined guide established to provide direction in decision making.

A **policy** is a predetermined guide established to provide direction in decision making. Policies establish parameters that assist people in the organization as they go about accomplishing their jobs. Policies are also flexible since some interpretation and judgment is generally required in their use. Managers can be influenced significantly by the existence of policies, as in the case of firms having an open door policy. This policy permits employees to bypass their immediate supervisor and take problems to the next higher level in the organizational hierarchy. Knowing that their subordinates can speak to a higher level, managers may encourage supervisors to try harder to resolve problems with subordinates.

Employees

Employees differ in capabilities, attitudes, personal goals, and personalities, among many other ways. As a result, behavior a manager finds effective with one worker may not be effective with another. In extreme cases employees can be so different that it is virtually impossible for them to be managed as a group. The manager therefore, in order to be effective, must consider both individual and group differences. A supervisor directing experienced workers, for instance, may choose to pay less attention to the technical details of the job and more attention to encouraging group cooperation, while another supervisor directing a group of inexperienced workers may elect to focus on the technical aspects of the task.

Informal Organization

Informal organization
The set of evolving relationships and patterns of human interaction within an organization that are not officially prescribed.

Managers quickly learn that there are two organizations within any firm—the formal and the informal. The formal organization can be visualized: everyone has a job description, knows to whom to report, and can see his or her place in the company's organizational chart.

Yet existing within every formal organization is an informal one, which is often quite powerful but which can't be seen. The **informal organization** is the set of evolving relationships and patterns of human interaction within an organization that are not officially prescribed. Such informal relationships can significantly affect a manager's ability to perform adequately. Assume, for instance, that top management is fully committed to equal employment opportunity. While the initial commitment is made by upper management, the supervisors are responsible for promoting the ideal of equal employment on a day-to-day basis. One supervisor may have a group of male employees who believe the woman's place is in the home. When a female is hired into this group, its members may offer her no support in becoming adjusted to the work place. The supervisor is thus caught between the dictates of upper management and the actions of the informal organization, in this case, the male work group. Successful managers understand the informal system and work with it to better accomplish their jobs.

Other Units

Managers must be keenly aware of interrelationships that exist among divisions or departments and should use such relationships to best advantage. Some of the possible relationships among departments are presented in Figure 3.7. The personnel department helps maintain a competent work force; the purchasing department buys materials and parts. Because one department precedes another in the flow of work, that department's output becomes the other department's input. Most managers soon discover that cooperation with other departments is necessary if the job is to get done efficiently. Managers who make enemies of other managers may jeopardize the productivity of several departments.

Unions

Upper management typically negotiates labor-management agreements, but managers throughout the organization must implement the terms of the agreements. In most instances agreements place restrictions on the manager's actions.

FIGURE 3.7 ■
Possible Relationships with
Other Departments

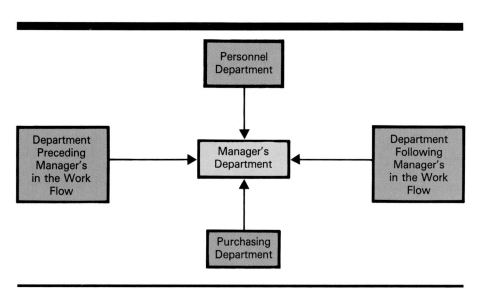

For example, a manager may want to shift a maintenance worker to an operator's job temporarily; but if the labor-management agreement specifies the tasks that can and cannot be performed in each job, the supervisor may not be able to make the temporary assignment.

■ THE TRANSFORMATION PROCESS

In any organization, management's job is to use resources (inputs) in an efficient manner to produce desirable products and/or services (outputs). Management's role in transforming inputs to outputs is illustrated in Figure 3.8.

Inputs

Just as humans cannot live long without food and water, a dynamic business system cannot survive without resources to sustain it. Managers must assure that the inputs needed to complete the transformation process exist in sufficient quality and quantity. These inputs—categorized as natural resources, labor, capital and information—will vary according to the type of business the firm conducts and its particular goals. For example, the manufacturer of Rolex Oyster Perpetual watches emphasizes high-quality watches; the inputs needed, therefore, are likely to be highly trained craftspeople and quality equipment and materials. A manufacturer of low-price watches may need different inputs, including perhaps, equipment capable of mass production and less-skilled employees.

FIGURE 3.8 ■
The Transformation
Process

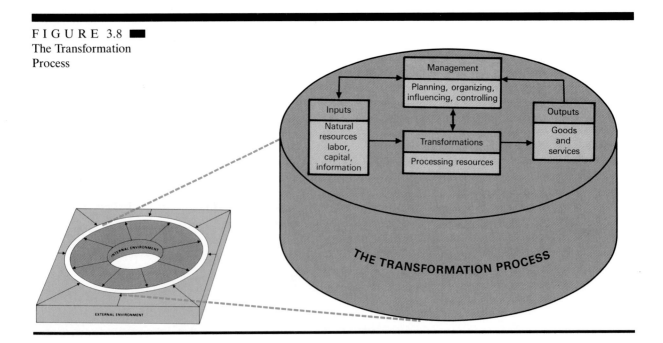

Processing Resources

Managers are responsible for assuring that resources are properly processed. Resources (inputs) are processed (transformed) within the organization to create desired outputs in the form of goods or services according to one of three kinds of production operations. Inputs may be *combined* to form significantly different outputs, as when sand, gravel, and Portland cement are mixed in a concrete plant to make concrete. Or, inputs may undergo a process of *extraction* to create something that is useful, an example being the iron smeltering process whereby usable iron is removed from natural iron ore. The third type of production process, *changing the form* of inputs, is the operation that results in iron being rolled into sheets, logs being cut into boards, and glass being spun into fiberglass.

The process for service industries is more difficult to observe than that for manufacturing industries because service firms do not produce a tangible product. Rather, they create, produce, and distribute services. The growing importance of the service industry is illustrated by the fact that approximately two of every three working Americans are employed in the service area in such industries as banking, insurance, transportation, real estate, medical care, beauty, education, and government agencies. The fundamental process that service industries follow, however, is the same as that for manufacturing industries: hospitals convert ill patients into healthy ones; schools turn uninformed students into knowledgeable ones; and beauty salons transform individuals into more attractive ones.

Outputs

Goods and services are the end result of the transformation process. Once inputs are converted to outputs, the products are returned to the environment. The output of IBM is largely information processing, whereas Consolidated Edison produces energy. Once again, however, the fundamental process of transformation is carried out by each.

As mentioned in Chapter 1, the proportional relationship between the quality and quantity of inputs and the quality and quantity of outputs produced is referred to as efficiency. The degree to which the process produces the intended outputs is called effectiveness. The overall objective of the manager in managing the transformation process is to obtain high effectiveness and to do so efficiently.

Management

The operation of the transformation process shown in Figure 3.8 is the responsibility of management, who must plan, organize, influence, and control. As the arrows indicate, management receives feedback from the output of the production process and monitors the inputs and the process itself. Inputs are then controlled or changed and the production process adjusted to provide the desired results in the form of outputs.

SUMMARY

The systems approach—the viewing of any organization or entity as an arrangement of interrelated parts that interact in ways that can be specified and to some extent predicted—provides a rational means for examining these interactions. Use of the systems approach inevitably leads one to conclude that every organization, indeed every system, is an open system. An open system is an organization or assemblage of things that affects and is affected by outside events.

The business system is affected by many forces, both external and internal. Top management has perhaps the greatest concern for the external forces, while management at all levels must be concerned with the forces of the internal environment. Managers at lower levels of the organization, however, confront an internal environment that is markedly different from that encountered by management at more senior levels. Within these complex external and internal environments, the business system operates: inputs are converted to outputs through a transformation process directed and controlled by managers.

Factors that management must consider in the external environment include: the labor force, legal considerations, society, unions, stockholders, the competition, customers, and technology. Factors to be considered in the internal environment include: the firm's mission, corporate culture, the management style of upper managers, policies, employees, the informal organization, other units, and unions.

Management's job is to direct the transformation of resources (inputs) in an efficient manner to produce desirable goods and/or services (outputs). In the course of this process, managers plan, organize, influence, and control. They monitor the input and the actual transformation process and, upon analyzing feedback from the output, make the adjustments necessary in the production process to obtain the desired results.

REVIEW QUESTIONS

1. Define a system. Why does a manager need to understand the systems approach?
2. Identify and describe the major external environmental factors that can affect top managers.
3. How is the work force expected to change by the year 1995?
4. What are the major internal environmental factors that can affect the jobs that managers do?
5. What are the components of an organization's transformation process?

KEY TERMS

systems approach	ethics	internal environment
open system	union	mission
external environment	stockholders	corporate culture
job sharing	proactive response	policy
leased employees	reactive response	informal organization
social responsibility		

CASE STUDY

GETTING BY ON A SHOESTRING

AS THE PERSONNEL director for KBH Stores in St. Louis, Missouri, Virginia Knickerbocker knew that she had her work cut out for her. Company management had just announced a goal of opening ten new stores during the next twelve months. KBH employed 480 people in the thirty-five stores already in operation. Virginia knew that staffing the new stores would require hiring and training about 150 people. She felt that her own small office was inadequately funded and staffed to handle such an increase in operations.

Virginia learned of the expansion plans from a friend who knew the president's secretary. Although she didn't like being kept in the dark, Virginia was not surprised that she had not been told. Glenn Sullivan, the president of KBH, was noted for his autocratic leadership style. He tended to tell subordinates only what he wanted them to know. He expected everyone who worked for him to follow orders without question. He wasn't an unkind person, though, and Virginia had always gotten along with him pretty well. She had never confronted Mr. Sullivan about anything, so it was with some concern that she approached his office that day.

"Mr. Sullivan," she began, "I hear that we are going to be opening ten new stores next year."

"That's right, Virginia," said Mr. Sullivan. "We've already arranged the credit lines and have picked out several of the sites."

"What about staffing?" asked Virginia.

"Well, I presume that you will take care of that, Virginia, when we get to that point," replied Mr. Sullivan.

"What about my own staff?" asked Virginia. "I think I am going to need at least three or four more people. And we are already crowded, so I hope you're planning to expand the personnel office."

"Not really," said Mr. Sullivan. "You will have to get by with what you have for at least a year or so. It's going to be hard enough to afford the new stores and the people we need to staff them."

QUESTIONS
1. How does the environment Virginia faces differ from that confronting top executives?
2. How does the internal environment affect Virginia's ability to do her job?

CASE STUDY

BILLY OSBON'S NEW BUSINESS

BILLY OSBON HAD worked for the J. C. Penney Company for eighteen years when he decided to go into business for himself. Billy was forty-seven years old. He and his wife, Joyce, had two grown sons and another one fifteen years old. Billy knew the kind of business he wanted to be in—furniture and appliances. He was the general merchandise manager for the J. C. Penney store in Charleston, West Virginia. Before Penney's discontinued its furniture and appliances in 1983, he had managed that department in another, larger Penney store.

Billy felt that he was well qualified to run his own business. He had worked for years as a commissioned salesman. At the same time, he had managed other salespersons and had been responsible for product displays, inventory turnover, credit approvals, and many other aspects of business management.

Billy and Joyce had saved nearly $10 thousand in cash. Their home was nearly paid for. Billy also had 300 shares of J. C. Penney stock, valued at $52 a share.

Billy and Joyce had been actively looking for a business to buy for about three months when they learned of Garvan Appliance Company. Garvan Appliance was owned by Andrew Garvan, who was sixty-eight years old and had decided to retire.

Andrew was offering his business for sale for only $25 thousand, although monthly sales averaged about $30 thousand.

The business was in a rented store in a small shopping center on the outskirts of Charleston. When Billy talked with Mr. Garvan, he found that the furniture inventory of about $80 thousand was financed with a local bank, and the appliance inventory was floor planned by General Electric. Under the floor-planning arrangement, General Electric finances the appliances in full and charges no interest as long as the inventory is turned over every ninety days. Billy knew that what he would really be purchasing with the $25 thousand was a small amount of office equipment, a three-year-old delivery truck, and the company's good will.

After going over the financial statements for Garvan Appliance with his accountant, Billy decided that the business was probably a good deal. It was exactly what he and Joyce had been looking for. Joyce could keep the books and help out part-time, and he could be the main salesman. Mr. Garvan had said he would stay and help four hours a day until Billy felt that he could get along without him.

QUESTIONS
1. What external environmental factors might Billy be expected to confront?
2. How would you recommend that they prepare to handle the problems that may occur?

EXPERIENTIAL EXERCISE

This is an exercise involving Jesse Heard, the human resource manager at Parma Cycle Company; Gene Wilson, the corporate planner; and Edmont Fitzgerald, the controller. Parma Cycle Company is one of only three companies that actually manufacture complete bicycles in the United States. Most of Parma's competitors import parts from other countries and simply assemble bicycles here. Parma Cycle currently employs about 800 workers at wages well above the average wage levels in the area. Most of these workers are machine operators and assemblers. Parma Cycle Company is experiencing severe difficulties competing with lower cost bicycles, and the time has come to lower costs.

Jesse Heard is faced with a dilemma. He feels obligated to find the best quality labor at the best available price, but he is also concerned about the workers, some of whom have been with Parma Cycle for many years. Even though the highly favorable labor market allows replacement of many of them with lower paid workers, he hesitates to do so. Yesterday Jesse received an angry call from the president, Mr. Burgess, who told him to meet with the corporate planner and the controller to come up with a unified recommendation for taking advantage of the improved labor market.

Gene Wilson never really had much power at Parma Cycle, although his title sounds impressive enough. Primarily, he maintains a chart room and keeps track of various trends. He basically agrees that Parma Cycle Company is headed downhill because of depressed markets and an inability on the part of company managers to decrease unit costs. In his opinion, the most important asset that Parma Cycle has is a trained and loyal work force. While many of the workers could be replaced with lower paid workers, he is afraid that this would destroy the team spirit that now exists at Parma Cycle. He believes that workers are more likely than ever to respond to financial incentives, such as some kind of piece-rate program or bonus system.

Edmont Fitzgerald, an Ohio State University graduate in finance, believes that, above all, the corporation is an economic entity. He believes that market forces will take care of those workers who really wish to contribute to the economy. He believes in purchasing all resources, including labor, at the lowest possible price. He views the current situation as an opportunity to decrease costs radically. The union is weak, jobs are scarce, and there is a surplus of skilled workers in the Cleveland area.

Three students will participate: one to serve as Jesse Heard, the human resource manager; one to serve as Gene Wilson, the corporate planner; and one to serve as Edmont Fitzgerald, the controller. All students not participating in the exercise should carefully observe the behavior of the participants. Your instructor will provide the participants with additional information necessary to participate.

NOTES

1. "Mr. Smith Goes Global," *Business Week,* 13 February 1989, 66.
2. Bruce Nussbaum, "Needed: Human Capital," *Business Week,* 19 September 1988, 103.
3. Harry Bacas, "Desperately Seeking Workers," *Nation's Business* (February 1988): 20.
4. Susan Goff Condon, "Hiring the Handicapped Confronts Cultural Uneasiness," *Personnel Journal* (April 1987): 28.
5. Condon, "Hiring the Handicapped," 28.
6. R. Wayne Mondy, Arthur Sharplin, and Edwin B. Flippo, *Management: Concepts and Practices,* 4th ed. (Boston: Allyn & Bacon, 1988), 632.
7. Kenneth E. Goodpaster and John B. Matthews, Jr., "Can a Corporation Have a Conscience?" *Harvard Business Review* 60 (January–February 1982): 132–141.
8. Larry T. Adams, "Union Membership of Wage and Salary Employees in 1987," in *Current Wage Developments* (U.S. Department of Labor, Bureau of Labor Statistics, February 1988), 4.
9. Shane R. Premeaux, R. Wayne Mondy, and Art Bethke, "Decertification: Fulfilling Unions' Destiny?" *Personnel Journal* 66 (June 1987): 144.
10. David Vogel, "Ralph Nader's All Over the Place: Citizens vs. the Corporation," *Across the Board* 1 (April 1979): 26–31.
11. Eric G. Flanholtz, Yvonne Randle, and Sonja Sackmann, "Personnel Management: The Tenor of Today," *Personnel Journal* 66 (June 1987): 64.
12. "Help Wanted," *Business Week,* 10 August 1987.
13. Arthur Sharplin, *Strategic Management* (New York: McGraw-Hill, 1985), 102.

REFERENCES

Dugan, Terry M. "Helping Disabled Older People Find Jobs." *Aging* (July 1985): 31–32.
Gartrell, Kenneth D., and Thom Yantek. "The Political Climate and Corporate Mergers: When Politics Affects Economics." *Western Political Quarterly* 41 (June 1988): 309–322.
Glassman, Edward. "Leadership Style's Effect on the Creativity of Employees." *Management Solutions* 31 (November 1986): 18–25.
Haley, Michael. "The Economic Dynamics of Work." *Strategic Management Journal* 7 (September–October 1986): 459–472.
Herzberg, Frederick. "Overcoming the Betrayals of the '80s." *Industry Week* 231 (13 July 1987): 72.
Kieehel, Walter, III. "The Ages of a Manager; Each Decade of Life Brings an Executive New Abilities." *Fortune* 115 (11 May 1987): 170–173.
Kleinman, Dan. "What to Look for in Tomorrow's Employee." *Personnel Journal* 66 (October 1987): 192–206.
Kleinschrod, Walter A. "Where Have All the Workers Gone?" *Administrative Management* 48 (February 1987): 45.
Lewis, John C. "Issues Concerning High Technology Managers from Multiple Cultural Backgrounds." *Journal of Management Development* 6 (Fall 1987): 73–86.
Nardone, Thomas. "Decline in Youth Population Does Not Lead to Lower Jobless Rates." *Monthly Labor Review* 110 (June 1987): 37–42.
Nelson-Horchler, Joani. "Still No Way to the Top?" *Industry Week* 231 (13 July 1987): 57–58.
Nitcoki, Joseph Z. "In Search of Sense in Common Sense Management." *Journal of Business Ethics* 6 (November 1987): 639–647.

Norwood, Janet L. "The Labor Force of the Future." *Business Economics* 22 (July 1987): 9–14.

O'Donnell, Joseph. "The Creative-Rational Manager." *Manage* 10 (July 1988): 1–3.

Oliva, Terence A., and Christel M. Capdevielle. "Can Systems Really Be Taught? (A Socratic Dialogue)." *Academy of Management Review* 5, no. 2 (April 1980): 277–281.

Peters, Thomas J. "Facing Up to the Need for a Management Revolution." *California Management Review* 30 (Winter 1988): 7–38.

Pryor, Austin K., and William K. Foster. "The Strategic Management of Innovation." *Journal of Business Strategy* 7 (Summer 1986): 38–42.

Saad, Henry N. "AIDS Discrimination in the Workplace." *Small Business Report* 12 (March 1987): 79.

Scelsi, Paul. "Middle Manager Woes?" *Management World* 16 (April–May 1987): 20–21.

Schoenberger, Barbara A. "Managing Multiple Personalities." *Management World* 16 (February–March 1987): 10–11.

Silver, P. G., and Craig Jurgenson. "The Disabled Employee: A Supervisory Challenge." *Thrust: Journal for Employment & Training Professionals* 7 (Fall–Winter 1986): 65–70.

Smith, Harold Ivan. "Singles in the Workplace." *Personnel Administrator* 33 (February 1988): 76–81.

Solomon, Jeffrey R. "How to Work with the Rehabilitated Mentally Ill." *Supervisory Management* 31 (January 1986): 32.

Standing, Guy. "Unemployment and the Recomposition of Labor Reserves." *Annals of the American Academy of Political and Social Science* 492 (July 1987): 80–96.

Tabatabai, Cheryl. "Staff Productivity: The Other Side of Cost Cutting." *Healthcare Financial Management* 11 (May 1987): 12–14.

Taylor, Alex, Jr. "Why Women Managers Are Bailing Out." *Fortune* 114 (18 August 1986): 16–23.

Turbett, Peggy. "To Balance a Job and Motherhood." *American Banker* 152 (6 February 1987): 16–17.

Wheelock, Keith. "A Tough Job Market Ahead, Especially for Working Mothers." *Personnel Administrator* 31 (April 1986): 119–128.

CHAPTER

4

Social
Responsibility
and
Business
Ethics

Learning Objectives

After completing this chapter students should be able to

1. Describe the concept of corporate social responsibility.
2. Explain what is meant by stakeholder analysis and the social contract.
3. Describe the changing values toward social responsibility and the business-government interface.
4. Explain the concepts of ethics, business ethics, and the social audit.

CYANIDE IS A deadly poison. Even a minute amount can cause instant death. When the substance found its way into a few bottles of Extra-Strength Tylenol capsules in Chicago in September 1982 the results were disastrous: seven people died. With more than 30 million bottles on store shelves all over the world, and many millions more in home medicine cabinets, the fatalities raised an unthinkable specter: If just 1 percent of the bottles were poisoned, thousands of people could die.

Tylenol is manufactured by McNeil Consumer Products, a subsidiary of Johnson & Johnson, a $5.4 billion giant in the health care industry. "Are you sure this isn't a hoax?" asked Arthur Quitty, a member of J & J's executive committee, when the news first broke. When the story hit the international news wires, calls began to come in from television and radio stations, pharmacies, doctors, poison control centers, and hundreds of panic-stricken consumers. In the confusion of those first hours, thousands reported suspected poisonings. Practically all of the reports turned out to be false. "It looked like the plague," recalls McNeil's public relations chief, David Collins.

Within hours, J & J had determined that the cyanide was probably placed in the capsules after they left the McNeil plant. Nevertheless, the plant was closed. An investigation quickly revealed that all of the poisoned Tylenol capsules had been purchased on Chicago's West Side, and all seemed to have come from one lot. J & J had every reason to believe that the danger could be eliminated by recalling that one lot from the relatively few retailers to whom it had gone.

But the company's credo, displayed for all to see at J & J's red brick headquarters, declared that J & J's "first responsibility" is to those who "use our products and services." Chairman James Burke prepared to recall all Extra-Strength Tylenol capsules. Burke says the FBI opposed the recall "because that would say to whomever did this, 'Hey, I'm winning. I can bring a major corporation to its knees.' " The Food and Drug Administration argued, "It might cause more public anxiety than it would relieve." Still, the campaign to get back $100 million worth of Extra-Strength Tylenol capsules was initiated immediately. At its own expense, J & J took out advertisements, sent thousands of letters to doctors and pharmacists, and orchestrated a major media campaign. The company took no chance that anyone else would be harmed. In an omission that many found remarkable for a major corporation, J & J spent almost no effort in publicizing a defense or disclaiming responsibility. But no expense was spared in protecting the public.

Within weeks the fear subsided, and J & J recaptured 95 percent of its earlier market share for a nonaspirin, extra-strength pain reliever. But the near monopoly that J & J had was broken, and several other drug manufacturers began national promotion of similar products.

Although the company suffered tens of millions of dollars in losses, its reputation was not hurt. In a *Fortune* magazine survey, J & J was among the top five U.S. "most-admired corporations." In the area of community and environmental responsibility, J & J ranked number one.

After another person was poisoned by cyanide-laced Tylenol capsules in 1986, the company discontinued making the product, substituting "caplets." A *Business Week* editorial, which lauded the company's actions in this and the earlier case, was titled "Johnson and Johnson's Class Act."[1] ■

J OHNSON & JOHNSON'S positive image clearly springs in large measure from its handling of the Tylenol scare. There seems to be general agreement that J & J did as much as it should have done, and possibly even more. Most questions of corporate social responsibility are not so clear-cut. There are no simple right or wrong answers. Rather, management must juggle the claims of various groups. It must produce profits for stockholders, preserve jobs for employees, comply with government regulations, and provide a product to consumers at a price they will pay.

In this chapter, a number of basic issues of corporate social responsibility and business ethics are examined. First, the concept of corporate social responsibility is discussed. This is followed by a discussion of stakeholder analysis and the social contract that exists between the organization and other elements of society. Then, traditional and modern views concerning the social responsibilities of business are described. The next three sections of the chapter discuss the business-government interface, present a model of ethics, and address the specific topic of business ethics. The last topic covered in the chapter is the social audit, whereby companies can evaluate their social performance.

▨ CORPORATE SOCIAL RESPONSIBILITY

Social responsibility
The implied, enforced, or felt obligation of managers, acting in their official capacities, to serve or protect the interests of groups other than themselves.

When a corporation behaves as if it had a conscience, it is said to be socially responsible. **Social responsibility** is the implied, enforced, or felt obligation of managers, acting in their official capacities, to serve or protect the interests of groups other than themselves. When Johnson & Johnson chose to protect the public interest by destroying millions of containers of Tylenol, the company surely suffered, at least in the short run. Such decisions are the domain of a corporation's top executives.[2]

Many companies develop patterns of concern for moral issues. This is done through policy statements, practices over time, and the leadership of morally strong individuals. Some companies have programs of community involvement for their employees and managers. They cooperate with fund drives such as the United Way. Open-door policies, grievance procedures, and employee-benefit programs often stem as much from a desire to do what is right as from a concern for productivity and the avoidance of strife. In fact, some argue that a corporation itself can have a conscience.[3] Certainly most Americans believe that J & J does, because of the way it handled the Tylenol issue.

It appears that the larger the number of stockholders a corporation has, the more committed management is to a sense of social responsibility. For example, the Environment Service Department at Allied Chemical is concerned with air and water pollution control, occupational health, and product safety. The manager of that department reports directly to the company president. Koppers Company has established two committees of directors outside the company, one concerned with the environment and the other with human resources. At least twice a year company management must account to these two committees concerning the company's efforts in the areas of social responsibility.

Others feel that a sense of social responsibility cannot be segmented and compartmentalized into departments and committees but should pervade all levels of the company. When Coca-Cola's treatment of migrant field-workers made national headlines due to an investigative reporter's articles, a special project was established at the direction of the president of Coca-Cola's food division. Expenditures on housing, education, and health services for migrant workers have now been integrated into the company's regular activities.

Economic and social values can at times be co-aligned, even in the short run. Dow Chemical invested $20 million in pollution control in a plant in Michigan. The yearly cost to run the pollution control equipment was $10.5 million. Dow claims to have recovered its costs through reduced corrosion on cooling towers and by the saving of valuable chemicals previously pumped out as waste. In three years' time over $6 million was saved in recovery of these wasted chemicals alone. Although this attempt at pollution control was quite successful, Dow still has serious air and water pollution problems to be solved in other plants it owns.

Several years ago, International Business Machines Corporation (IBM) located a new plant in the Bedford-Stuyvesant neighborhood of Brooklyn, an area that probably had the largest concentration of hard-core unemployed in the United States. Although the plant became profitable within two years, it had a financially disastrous beginning, which probably wouldn't have happened if it had been located elsewhere. Corporate decision makers were affected by a felt responsibility to provide jobs where they were most needed.

Most Americans would not have predicted the kind of socially responsible actions described above. During the 1980s, managers and the corporations they worked for were subjected to considerable criticism and received low levels of approval from the public. Hardly a week passed without news headlines of corporate misconduct. In 1987 Chrysler Motors Corporation was indicted on charges it had disconnected the odometers of more than 60,000 vehicles, which had been driven by company managers, before selling them as new automobiles. On Wall Street, insider trading scandals have done much to lower the trust of the general public in the stock market. Similarly, public mistrust of business and business executives is revealed by surveys of public opinion. In a 1985 survey by Opinion Research Corporation, 75 percent of the public agreed that business neglects the problems of society, and 65 percent believed that business executives "do everything they can to make a profit, even if it means ignoring the public's needs."[4] Clearly, the public's confidence in business has declined.

Other surveys have revealed that the public's estimate of the profits of business is considerably out of line with reality. For example, the public's estimate of the level of after-tax profits per dollar of sales for the typical business is between twenty-five and thirty cents; the actual amount was about four cents in 1984.

Socially responsible decision makers within corporations consider both the economic and the social impact of their decisions, as well as the impact the firm's operations have on various groups in society. Noted authority Keith Davis believes that, in meeting its responsibilities to society, a firm must be concerned with more than narrow technical and legal requirements.[5] It should recognize that an obligation exists to protect and enhance the interests and welfare of society, as well as the interests and welfare of the corporation.

In today's environment, business organizations are expected to assume broader and more diverse responsibilities to the various groups within society. However, critics argue that there is more lip service than action, more public relations programs than concrete social responsibility activities. Nevertheless, social responsibility is an area on which the modern business firm must take a stance, accompanied by appropriate policies and activities. Social responsibility can be understood in terms of the social contract that exists between a firm and its environment.

■■ STAKEHOLDER ANALYSIS AND THE SOCIAL CONTRACT

All business and nonprofit organizations have a large number of stakeholders, some of whom are recognized by the company as constituents and some of whom are not. An **organizational stakeholder** is an individual or group whose interests are affected by organizational activities. Remember that, although the interests of all stakeholders are affected by the corporation, managers may not acknowledge responsibility to them. Some of the stakeholders for Crown Metal Products, a small manufacturer of metal furniture near Boise, Idaho, are shown in Figure 4.1, but only a few, identified by bold arrows, are viewed as constituencies by Crown management.

The actions of many corporate executives are designed to serve interests other than those of the common shareholder. For example, a number of corporate managements have recently placed large amounts of company stock in employee stock ownership trusts for the purpose of avoiding takeover attempts that were clearly in the interests of the common shareholders. This benefited the employees, of course, but it also helped the managers keep their jobs. Major companies that have taken these kinds of actions to avoid takeovers include Walt Disney Productions and Martin Marietta Corporation. Other companies make gifts of company resources, often cash, to universities, churches, clubs, and so forth, knowing that any possible benefit to shareholders is remote. Some authorities suggest that members of the public should be placed on the boards of directors of major corporations to protect the interests of nonowner stakeholders.[6]

Protecting such a diversity of interests would require answering questions such as the following: During an economic downturn, should employees be afforded continuous employment, even when this is not in the best interest of the owners of the corporation and is not in accord with their preferences? Should managers be concerned about whether suppliers receive a reasonable profit on the items purchased from them, or should management simply buy the best inputs at the lowest price possible?

Answering such questions as these is what we term "stakeholder analysis." One method of stakeholder analysis involves consideration of the social contract. The **social contract** is the set of rules and assumptions about behavior patterns among the various elements of society. Much of the social contract is embedded in the customs of society. For example, in integrating minorities into the work force, society has come to expect companies to do more than the law requires. When a company like Johnson & Johnson behaves in an especially commendable way, its actions tend to increase the expectations society has concerning other companies.

Some of the "contract provisions" result from practices between parties. Like a legal contract, the social contract often involves a quid pro quo (something for something) exchange. One party to the contract behaves in a certain way and expects a predictable pattern of behavior from the other. For example, a relationship of trust may have developed between a manufacturer and the community in which it operates. Because of this, each will inform the other well

Organizational stakeholder
An individual or group whose interests are affected by organizational activities.

Social contract
The set of rules and assumptions about behavior patterns among the various elements of society.

FIGURE 4.1 ■ Stakeholders of Crown Metal Products

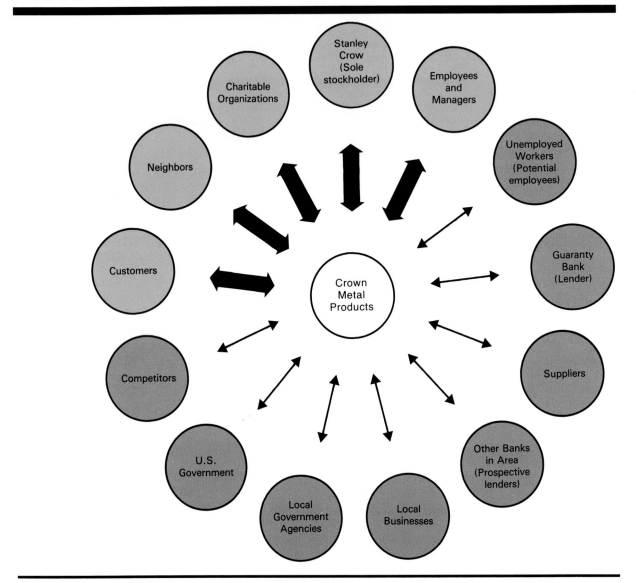

in advance of any planned action that might cause harm, such as the closing of the plant by the company. Obviously many firms were not attempting to develop this trust relationship because the Plant Closure Act was passed in 1988, which required firms to give sixty-days' notice prior to closure.

The social contract concerns relationships with individuals, government, other organizations, and society in general. This is illustrated in Figure 4.2. Each of these relationships will be considered individually in the following sections, to instill in the reader a true appreciation of each aspect of the social contract.

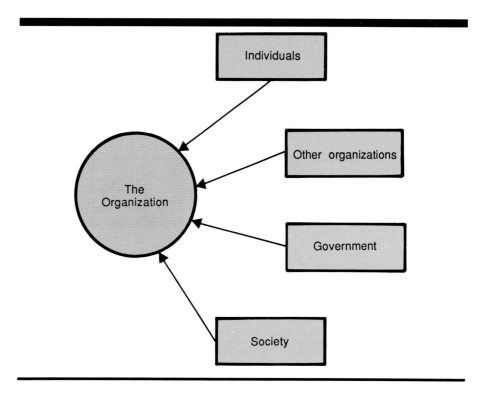

Obligations to Individuals

Individuals often find healthy outlets for their energies through joining organizations. From the church, they expect guidance, ministerial services, and fellowship, and they devote time and money to its sustenance. From their employers, they expect a fair day's pay for a fair day's work—and perhaps much more. Many expect to be paid for time off to vote, perform jury service, and so forth. Clubs and associations provide opportunities for fellowship and for community service. Customers expect to be catered to. To some degree, most of society still subscribes to the notion that the customer is king. To the extent that these expectations are acknowledged as responsibilities by the organization, they become part of the social contract.

Obligations to Other Organizations

Managers must be concerned with relationships involving other organizations, both organizations that are like their own—such as competitors—and organizations that are quite different from their own. Commercial businesses are expected to compete with one another on an honorable basis, without subterfuge or reckless unconcern for their mutual rights. Charities such as the United Way expect support from businesses, support that often includes loaning executives and help with annual fund drives. At the same time, such institutions are expected to come hat in hand, requesting rather than demanding assistance.

In the traditional view of social responsibility, which we discuss later on in the chapter, business best meets its obligations through pursuit of its own self-interests. For example, the policy of FMC Corporation, a major diversified manufacturer, is based on a firm criteria concerning how it will direct its contributions. Contributions must help areas around company facilities or areas where its employees live, and gifts must improve the corporation's business environment.[7] FMC might contribute to a business college in an area where it has a plant, but it would not make gifts to distant universities.

Obligations to Government

Government is an important party to the social contract for every kind of organization. Under the auspices of government, companies have a license to do business, along with patent rights, trademarks, and so forth. Churches are often incorporated under state laws and given nonprofit status. Many quasi-governmental agencies, such as the Federal Deposit Insurance Corporation, regional planning commissions, and levee boards, have been given special missions by government.

In addition, organizations are expected to recognize the need for order rather than anarchy and to accept some government intervention in organizational affairs. For example, even though the law no longer gives the Occupational Safety and Health Administration (OSHA) inspector the right to come into an organization without permission, it is usual for organizations to accept such visits. Johnson & Johnson must deal with the Food and Drug Administration (FDA) on a daily basis. In the case at the beginning of the chapter, J & J went well beyond what the FDA requires.

Obligations to Society in General

The traditional responsibility of the business firm is to produce and distribute goods and services in return for a profit. Businesses have performed this function effectively. Largely as a result of our economic system and the important contributions of business firms, the United States enjoys one of the highest overall standards of living in the world. Rising standards of living in the United States have enabled a high percentage of the population to have their basic needs for food, clothing, shelter, health, and education reasonably well satisfied. Businesses can take pride in these accomplishments because they had a great deal to do with making the higher standards of living possible.

Business has been able to make significant contributions to the rising living standards primarily because of the manner in which the free enterprise economic system operates. The profit motive provides incentive to business to produce products and services efficiently. Practically every business firm tries to curb costs in order to keep the low prices required to attract customers and still allow for profit. However, some feel that quality improvement is thus often neglected as a competitive tool.[8] By earning profits, the successful firm pays taxes to the government and makes donations to provide financial support for charitable causes. Because of the efficient operations of business firms, an ever-increasing number of people have increasing means and leisure time.

Businesses operate by public consent with the basic purpose of satisfying the needs of society. Despite significant improvements in standards of living in recent years, society has begun expecting—even demanding—more of all of its institutions, particularly large business firms. Goals, values, and attitudes in society are changing to reflect a greater concern for improvements in the quality of life. An indication of this greater concern is seen in such goals as the following:

- Eliminate poverty and provide quality health care
- Preserve the environment by reducing the level of pollution
- Provide a sufficient number of jobs and career opportunities for all members of society
- Improve the quality of working life of employees
- Provide safe, livable communities with good housing and efficient transportation[9]

As responsible corporate citizens, businesses should follow the spirit of the law as well as the letter. Many companies that created huge hazardous waste dumps throughout the country now defend themselves by saying that the dumps were "legal" when created. But the fact is that the laws and regulations controlling hazardous waste dumping were meant to protect the public health, and the dumping of certain concentrations of substances was actually prohibited. In many cases, such as the notorious Love Canal incident involving Hooker Chemical, dangerous but unregulated substances and harmful (though legal) concentrations of other substances were dumped over an extended period of years. The result is that the public health in those areas has been endangered. It is clear that society now considers this unacceptable.

Many believe that "managerial self-interest" is in the best interests of the public as well.[10] They would no doubt agree with Sir Thomas More, who in the sixteenth century said, "Common sense would make us good, and greed would make us saintly." But in the United States today the consensus is clear. Corporate strategists must consider other groups, even when doing so conflicts with managerial self-interest or with the interests of stockholders.

As the discussion indicates, society's expectations of business have broadened considerably in recent years to encompass more than the traditional economic function. This is illustrated in Figure 4.3. The inner circle, Level I, represents the traditional economic functions of business. The economic function is the primary responsibility of businesses to society. In performing the economic function, businesses produce needed goods and services, provide employment, contribute to economic growth, and earn a profit. Level II represents the responsibility of business to perform the economic functions but with an awareness of changing social goals, values, and demands. Management must be aware of such concerns as the efficient utilization of resources, the reduction of environmental pollution, the employment and development of disadvantaged minorities and females, and the provision of safe products and a safe working environment. The actions of Hershey Chocolate Company following the Three Mile Island nuclear incident provide an example of Level II concern. Located near the nuclear plant, Hershey immediately instituted a careful testing program for milk received from within seventy-five miles of Three Mile Island and isolated all milk coming from within ten miles. A Hershey executive said, "While we have no indication

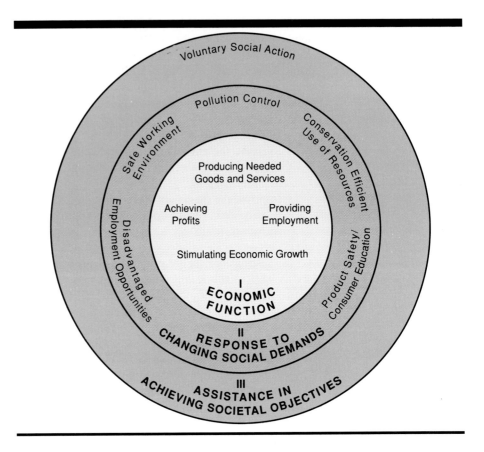

of anything wrong with any product, if we are going to err, we want to err on the safe side."[11]

Level III, the outer circle, is concerned with the corporation's responsibility for assisting society in achieving such broad goals as the elimination of poverty and urban decay through a partnership of business, government agencies, and

Voluntary social action programs, such as the career counseling conducted by this business executive, are encouraged by many organizations. (© Daemmrich/Stock, Boston, Inc.)

other private institutions. Although the responsibilities in Level III are not primary obligations of business, business has shown increasing interest in voluntary social action programs. In its handling of the Tylenol incident, J & J, with "an awareness of changing social goals, values, and demands," went beyond simply carrying out economic functions. This is an example of Level III concern.

■■■ CHANGING VALUES AND SOCIAL RESPONSIBILITY

Numerous associations and groups of respected business leaders, including the American Management Association and the Committee for Economic Development, have encouraged corporations and managers to become involved in socially responsible activities. In a climate of changing social values, these groups have stressed such programs as providing better jobs and promotion opportunities to minorities and women, financial support for education, financial and managerial support for improving health and medical care, a safer working environment, leadership and financial support for urban renewal, and means to reduce environmental pollution.

Iron law of responsibility In the long run, those who do not use power in a manner in which society considers responsible will tend to lose it.

The major arguments for the acceptance of social responsibility by business may be seen in Table 4.1. Keith Davis summarizes these arguments in what he terms the **iron law of responsibility,** in which he states that "in the long run, those who do not use power in a manner in which society considers responsible will tend to lose it." Thus, if business firms are to retain their social power and role, they must be responsive to society's needs.[12]

The Traditional View of Social Responsibility

In 1776 Adam Smith published *The Wealth of Nations,* sometimes called the "Capitalist Manifesto." In it he described a system in which individuals and businesses pursued their own self-interests and government played a limited role. This system became the model for capitalism in the United States. Adam Smith wrote:

TABLE 4.1 ■ Arguments for the Acceptance of Social Responsibility

1. People expect businesses and other institutions to be socially responsible.
2. It is in the best interest of the business to pursue socially responsible programs.
3. It improves the image of the firm.
4. Business should be involved in social projects because it has the resources.
5. Corporations must be concerned about society's interests and needs because society, in effect, sanctions business operations.
6. If the business is not responsive to society's needs, the public will press for more governmental regulation requiring more socially responsible behavior.
7. Socially responsible actions may increase profits in the long run.

> [An individual or business] generally, indeed, neither intends to promote
> the public interest, nor knows how much he is promoting it. . . . He
> intends only his own gains, and he is in this, as in many other cases, led by
> an invisible hand to promote an end which was no part of his intention,
> nor is it always the worse for society that it was no part of it. By pursuing
> his own interest he frequently promotes that of the society more effectively
> than when he really intends to promote it.[13]

This idea—that capitalism allows the serving of the public interest by individuals and businesses who seek maximization of satisfaction or profit—is the foundation of the U.S. economic system. Traditionally, companies were not expected to serve social goals, except indirectly. For example, until the mid-1930s it was illegal for a U.S. corporation to make charitable contributions. This was based on a precedent set in an 1883 lawsuit in Great Britain, *Hutton* v. *West Cork Railway Corporation*. The court in that case ruled that the corporation should be concerned only with the equitable distribution of its earnings to its owners. This could not include corporate philanthropy.[14]

In 1935 a revision of the Federal Revenue Act made provisions for tax deductibility of corporate charitable contributions. Under that revision, corporations could deduct up to 5 percent of net income for charitable purposes. By 1953, the right of businesses to make extensive charitable gifts was clearly established. That year, in *A.P. Smith Manufacturing Company* v. *Barlow et al.*, the New Jersey Supreme Court concluded that business support of higher education is in society's best interest.[15]

Nobel laureate economist Milton Friedman called the idea of corporate social responsibility a "fundamentally subversive doctrine." Friedman said, "There is one and only one social responsibility of business—to use its resources and engage in activities designed to increase its profits so long as it stays within the rules of the game, which is to say engages in open and free competition without deception or fraud."[16]

Friedman's statement is often quoted as an example of a radical view. Far from being a radical, however, Dr. Friedman simply subscribes to the idea that, in the long run, the public interests are served by individuals and businesses pursuing their own best interests, primarily financial well-being, through participation in a relatively free economy. Friedman sets a rather high standard, when he suggests that businesses should operate within the "rules of the game," practicing neither deception nor fraud. The rules of the game obviously include, in addition to accepted ethical practices, international, national, and other laws. How many corporations actually are willing to tell the absolute truth in their advertisements and to engage in open and fair competition, avoiding collusion, price fixing, and so forth? The general public would be greatly surprised if STP Corporation were to admit that the lubricating oil additive has no real value, as has been shown.[17] However, there is some evidence that few subscribe to Friedman's hard-line views, and therefore it is important to look at how values concerning social responsibility are changing.

Trend toward Social Responsibility

More and more U.S. corporate executives see themselves as legitimate servants of a variety of constituencies. In a political sense, constituency means a body of

Organizational constituency
Any identifiable group that organizational managers either have or acknowledge a responsibility to represent.

citizens or voters who are entitled to elect a representative to a legislative or other public body. An **organizational constituency** is any identifiable group that organizational managers either have or acknowledge a responsibility to represent. The intention of political constituents is that they will be represented by the person they elect. Unlike political constituents, constituents of corporate managers may or may not have the power to elect those managers.

For some executives, the common shareholder is only one of many constituencies to be served—and not even the primary one. For example, at Lincoln Electric Company, the world's largest producer of arc welding products, corporate executives see the customer as their primary constituency. Employees are in second place, with stockholders a distant third. James Lincoln, the company's founder and president until his death in 1965, said, "The last group to be considered is the stockholders, who own stock because they think it will be more profitable than investing money in any other way."[18]

■■ THE BUSINESS-GOVERNMENT INTERFACE

The influence of business firms and other private organizations on government is understandably a matter of concern to the general public. However, the pervasive involvement of government in business activities is of even greater concern to most managers. The trend today is toward lessening regulation and reducing government interference in both business and private activities. The airline, trucking, and banking industries are now largely deregulated. It is ironic that it is the deregulated industries that tend to be the most vehement opponents of deregulation. Once companies have adapted to a regulated environment they apparently are not sure they will be able to compete in a freely competitive one.

Recently there has been a fear that political contributions, causing elected officials to serve the interests of those groups that make the contributions rather than the interests of their constituents, will likely subvert governmental processes. This is especially true for contributions made by PACs, political action committees.

Political action committees
Tax-favored organizations formed by special interest groups representing U.S. industries to accept contributions and influence governmental action favoring those industries.

In a business sense, **political action committees** (PACs) are tax-favored organizations formed by special interest groups representing U.S. industries to accept contributions and influence governmental action favoring those industries. The growth of PACs has created an avenue through which corporations can contribute hundreds of millions of dollars to political candidates. Much of the money is obviously aimed at serving the special interests of those corporations. Billions of dollars in subsidies and price supports have been approved for the dairy industry, and even the tobacco industry after PACs representing those industries made large contributions to key legislators.

■■ A MODEL OF ETHICS

Ethics
The discipline dealing with what is good and bad, or right and wrong, or with moral duty and obligation.

Closely related to social responsibility, but not identical to it, is the concept of ethics. **Ethics** is the discipline dealing with what is good and bad, or right and wrong, or with moral duty and obligation. Everyone makes ethical (or unethical)

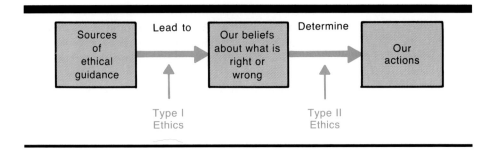

decisions every day. Should a person tell the clerk that he or she received too much change? What should a student do if the professor, in calculating the student's grade, makes a mistake in the student's favor?

A model of ethics is presented in Figure 4.4. It can be seen that ethics consists mainly of two relationships, indicated by the bold horizontal arrows in the figure. A person or organization is ethical if these relationships are strong and positive. There are a number of sources that one might use to determine what is right or wrong or good or bad or moral or immoral behavior. These include the Bible, the Koran, and a number of other holy books. They also include that "still small voice" that many refer to as conscience. Millions believe that conscience is a gift of God, or the voice of God. Others see it as a developed response based on the internalization of societal mores.

Another source of ethical guidance is the behavior and advice of those whom psychologists call "significant others"—our parents, friends, role models, and members of our churches, clubs, and associations. For organized professionals especially, there are often codes of ethics that proscribe behavior. Any type of act sufficiently hurtful to others is often prohibited by law. Thus, enacted laws offer guides to ethical behavior. If a certain behavior is illegal, most would consider it to be unethical as well. There are exceptions, of course. For example, through the 1950s, laws in most southern states relegated black persons to the back of the bus and otherwise assigned them inferior status. Today, many consider the actions of Martin Luther King, who opposed such laws and in fact disobeyed them, to have been highly moral ones.

Notice in Figure 4.4 that the sources of ethical guidance should lead to appropriate beliefs or convictions about what is right or wrong. Most would agree that persons have a responsibility to avail themselves of these sources of ethical guidance. In short, individuals should care about what is right and wrong and not just be concerned with what is expedient. The strength of the relationship between what an individual or an organization believes to be moral and correct and what available sources of guidance suggest is morally correct is **Type I ethics.** For example, suppose a student believes it is acceptable to copy another student's exam paper, despite the fact that almost everyone condemns this practice. This student is unethical, but only in a Type I sense.

Simply having strong beliefs about what is right and wrong and basing them on the proper sources does not make one ethical. Figure 4.4 illustrates that behavior should conform with what a person believes about right and wrong. **Type II ethics** is the strength of the relationship between what one believes and how one behaves. Everyone would agree that to do what one believes is wrong is unethical. For example, if a student knows that it is wrong to look on another's

Type I ethics
The strength of the relationship between what an individual or an organization believes to be moral and correct and what available sources of guidance suggest is morally correct.

Type II ethics
The strength of the relationship between what one believes and how one behaves.

examination answer sheet but does so anyway, the student has been unethical in a Type II sense. Generally, a person is not considered ethical unless he or she possesses both types of ethics. If a business manager knows that it is wrong to damage the environment yet dumps poisonous waste in a nearby stream, this behavior is unethical also.

■■ BUSINESS ETHICS

Business ethics
The application of ethical principles to business relationships and activities.

One can usually provoke a lively discussion by simply mentioning the two words, "business ethics." **Business ethics** is the application of ethical principles to business relationships and activities. Reading the newspaper or watching the evening news provides ample illustration of illegal and/or unethical practices of individuals within large corporations. Particularly ethical practices seldom make the news. When Southland Corporation executives were accused of bribing New York State tax officials in 1984, the story made every major newspaper. Yet the company's support of Olympic athletes was barely noted.

Deciding what is ethical is often difficult. The following are examples of activities usually perceived as unethical:

- Falsifying information on an application blank
- Illegal insider trading on the stock market
- Padding expense accounts to obtain reimbursement for questionable business expenses
- Divulging confidential information or trade secrets
- Availing oneself of company property or materials for personal use

BUSINESS BRIEFS

INSIDE BUSINESS

Creating a "Culture of Compliance" on Wall Street

BUSINESS ETHICS IS the application of ethical principles to business relationships and activities. Business ethics has come into sharp focus during the decade of the eighties. Nowhere has unethical and illegal behavior been more apparent than on Wall Street. U.S. Attorney Rudolph Giuliani has been waging a remarkably successful fight to curb Wall Street's unethical and illegal practices. He is the man who brought down Mr. Ivan Boesky. Of the fifty-three cases of insider trading he has investigated, forty-six resulted in convictions, one in acquittal, three in dismissals, and one person awaiting trial. Two individuals are currently fugitives from justice. Giuliani's goal is to create a "culture of compliance," in which the ethical climate of Wall Street, and business in general, will be an important counterweight to the drive for profit. Giuliani believes that a "culture of compliance" could lead to integrity being more important than profits. CNN correspondent Lou Dobbs discusses these, and other issues, with Mr. Giuliani.

ETHICAL DILEMMA

THE U.S. SURGEON GENERAL, admitting his position is mainly advisory and informational, called for a "smoke-free society" by the year 2000. By 1987, smoking was banned in many federal government work places, and forty-two states had passed laws restricting public smoking. Dozens of bills were introduced in Congress to protect non-smokers against smokers—and smokers against themselves, according to some opponents of the bills. Ahron Leichtman, president of Citizens Against Tobacco Smoke, said airlines "are the next big battleground in the whole anti-smoking movement." And in August 1987 the U.S. House of Representatives passed a bill banning smoking on flights shorter than two hours. U.S. cigarette sales have been declining, and the entire industry is clearly in decline. You are a recent college graduate and you have been working for the second largest cigarette marketer in the United States for two years. Your boss just gave you your first major assignment. You are going overseas to help sell and promote cigarettes with sales and promotional methods long ago banned in the United States. According to your boss, "we don't have to really worry about the Surgeon General overseas, our purpose is to sell as many packs as possible."

You know that cigarette smoking is harmful, but you always believed that since people were constantly told it was bad, if they kept smoking it was their fault. You are now given the goal to maximize overseas sales and to forget the warnings. You have two options: You can follow your orders, sell what you believe is a harmful product, and not bother to continually warn the overseas consumer, or you can refuse the assignment and possibly sacrifice your career.

What would you do?

- Giving or receiving gifts in return for favors
- Firing an employee for whistle-blowing
- Terminating employment without giving sufficient notice, either to the employee or the employer
- Stealing from the company
- Receiving or offering kickbacks

Many industries and individual companies have formal, written codes of ethics, which provide specific guidelines for managers and other employees. The key question in this regard is whether individuals within organizations are truly governed by these codes of ethics or simply give lip service to the guidelines. Another issue is whether the company or industry enforces the code if individuals or companies violate it. In any event, these codes of ethics define or clarify the ethical issues and allow the individual to make the final decision.

Many companies have developed specific codes of ethics. Texas Instruments provides an excellent example. Texas Instruments published a handbook entitled "Ethics in the Business of T.I."[19] The company summarizes its overall philosophy of business as follows:

It is fundamental to TI's philosophy that good ethics and good business are synonymous when viewed from moral, legal and practical standpoints. The trust and respect of all people—fellow workers, customers, consumers, stockholders, government employees, elected officials, suppliers, competitors, neighbors, friends, the press, and the general public—are assets that cannot be purchased. They must be earned. This is why all of the business of TI must be conducted according to the highest ethical standards.

In the handbook, TI has statements establishing guidelines for ethical decision making in business. Areas covered include: truthfulness in advertising, gifts and entertainment, improper use of corporate assets, political contributions, payments in connection with business transactions, conflicts of interest, trade secrets and proprietary information, and other matters.

There are advantages for organizations to form industry associations to develop and promote improved codes of ethics. It is difficult for a single firm to pioneer ethical practices if its competitors undercut them by taking advantage of unethical shortcuts. For example, U.S. companies must comply with the Foreign Corrupt Practices Act with respect to bribes of foreign government officials or business executives. Obviously this law does not prevent foreign competitors from bribing government or business officials to achieve business.[20] Perhaps the best hope would be for the major multinational enterprises to agree jointly to such a prohibition. When codes are not voluntarily followed, a society usually resorts to specific laws and penalties. In the case of international bribes, there is no international law. Should the United States declare the practice illegal, its multinational companies may find it difficult to compete with firms based in nations that do not disapprove. In this case, a voluntary code adopted by the leading firms of the world is likely to be the most effective method of handling the situation.

The concern for ethics in business appears to be increasing. According to one researcher, "Business behavior is more ethical than it was in 1961, but the expectations of a better educated and ethically sensitized public have risen more rapidly than the behavior." The study also found that respondents thought that they were more ethical than the average manager and that their department and company were more ethical than others. The respondents suggested that a written code of ethics would help to improve business practices.[21]

Apparently the use of formalized corporate codes of ethics is increasing in U.S. businesses. A survey of 611 companies found that 77 percent of the firms had a code of conduct. Of the largest companies (those with $400 million or more in sales), 97 percent had corporate codes of conduct.

■■ THE SOCIAL AUDIT

Many firms acknowledge their responsibilities to various segments of society, and some even set specific objectives in social areas. Over the last two decades or so, a number of organizations and individuals have recommended that firms measure the degree to which they contribute to the welfare of various elements of society

An organization may choose to become involved in selected community projects, such as the annual Walk for Hunger in Boston.
(The Jet Commercial Photographers, courtesy of Bank of Boston)

Social audit
Measuring the degree to which firms contribute to the welfare of various elements of society and to that of society as a whole.

and to that of society as a whole. When this effort is formalized, it is called a **social audit.** This is a systematic assessment of a company's activities in terms of social impact. Despite the efforts of the American Institute of Certified Public Accountants and a number of management societies, it has not been possible to apply the rigor of financial auditing in social areas. As may be seen in Table 4.2, there are a number of possible reasons for this failure.

Although few companies have ever attempted to conduct a rigorous social audit, most make efforts to respond to the public's desire to know how they are doing in social areas. A survey of the annual reports of 500 large companies in the United States showed that over 90 percent of them contained social responsibility disclosures.[22] Four possible types of audits are currently being utilized: (1) a simple inventory of activities, (2) compilation of socially relevant expenditures, (3) specific program management, and (4) determination of social

---

TABLE 4.2 ■■ Reasons for Not Applying Financial Auditing in Social Areas

1. The company may not have specific objectives in social areas.
2. Specific criteria or units of measurement may not be agreed upon.
3. It may be difficult to determine how an action today might affect society's interests tomorrow.
4. The business system, which previously had focused on economic variables, may not have control points or measurement techniques appropriate to measuring social variables.
5. Auditing implies the collection of complete, objective, and accurate data, not usually available in social areas.

impact. The inventory is generally the place where one would start. It would consist of a simple listing of activities undertaken by the firm over and above what is required. For example, firms have itemized the following types of social activities: (1) minority employment and training, (2) support of minority enterprises, (3) pollution control, (4) corporate giving, (5) involvement in selected community projects by firm executives, and (6) a hard-core unemployment program. The ideal social audit would involve determination of the true *benefits* to society of any socially oriented business activity.

SUMMARY

Social responsibility is the implied, enforced, or felt obligation of managers, acting in their official capacities, to serve or protect the interests of groups other than themselves. In a sense, organizations and society enter into a contract. This social contract is the set of rules and assumptions about behavior patterns among the various elements of society. The contract concerns relationships with individuals, government, other organizations, and society in general. Society's expectations of business have broadened considerably in recent years to encompass more than the traditional economic function. As noted in Figure 4.3, inner circle I represents the traditional economic functions of business. The economic function is the primary responsibility of businesses to society. Level II represents the responsibility of business to perform the economic functions with an awareness of changing social goals, values, and demands. In Level III, the outer circle is concerned with the corporation's responsibility for assisting society in achieving such broad goals as the elimination of poverty and urban decay through a partnership of business, government agencies, and other private institutions.

The iron law of responsibility states that in the long run, those who do not use power in a manner society considers responsible will tend to lose it. Thus, if business firms are to retain their social power and role, they must be responsive to society's needs. Traditionally, companies were not expected to serve social goals, except indirectly. Nobel laureate economist Milton Friedman called the idea of corporate social responsibility a "fundamentally subversive doctrine."

More and more U.S. corporate executives see themselves as legitimate servants of a variety of constituencies. In a political sense, constituency means a body of citizens or voters that is entitled to elect a representative to a legislative or other public body. An organizational constituency is any identifiable group that organizational managers either have or acknowledge a responsibility to represent. The intention of political constituents is that they will be represented by the person they elect. Unlike political constituents, those of corporate managers may or may not have the power to elect those managers.

Every business or other organization has a large number of stakeholders, some of whom are recognized as constituents and some of whom are not. An organizational stakeholder is an individual or group whose interests are affected by organizational activities. Remember that, although the interests of all stakeholders are affected by the corporation, managers may not acknowledge any responsibility to them. The actions of many corporate executives are not designed to serve simply the common shareholder's interests.

Closely related to social responsibility, but not identical to it, is the concept of ethics. Ethics is the discipline dealing with what is good and bad, or right and wrong, or with moral duty and obligation. The strength of the relationship between what an individual or an organization believes to be moral and correct and what available sources of guidance suggest is morally correct is Type I ethics. Simply having strong beliefs about what is right and wrong and basing them on the proper sources does not make one ethical. Type II ethics is the strength of the relationship between what one believes and how one behaves. Generally, a person is not considered ethical unless he or she possesses both types of ethics. Business ethics is the application of ethical principles to business relationships and activities.

Many firms acknowledge their responsibilities to various segments of society, and some even set specific objectives in social areas. Over the last two decades or so, a number of organizations and individuals have recommended that firms measure the degree to which they contribute to the welfare of various elements of society and to that of society as a whole. When this effort is formalized, it is called a social audit. This is a systematic assessment of a company's activities in terms of social impact.

REVIEW QUESTIONS

1. Define social responsibility. In general, how is U.S. business viewed by the general public?
2. What is the social contract? Describe the various relationships involved with the social contract.
3. Contrast the traditional view of social responsibility to the recent trend concerning social responsibility.
4. What are political action committees?
5. What are ethics? Distinguish between Type I and Type II ethics.
6. Are the ethics of business and its managers changing? Discuss.
7. What is the purpose of the social audit?

KEY TERMS

social responsibility	organizational	Type I ethics
organizational	constituency	Type II ethics
stakeholder	political action	business ethics
social contract	committees	social audit
iron law of responsibility	ethics	

CASE STUDY — FIRING TOM SERINSKY

As NORMAN BLANKENSHIP came into the mine office at Consolidation Coal Company's Rowland mine, near Clear Creek, West Virginia, he told the mine dispatcher not to tell anyone of his presence. Norman was the general superintendent over the Rowland operation. He had been with Consolidation for over twenty-three years, having started out as a coal digger.

Norman had heard that one of his section bosses, Tom Serinsky, had been sleeping on the job. Tom had been hired two months earlier and assigned to the Rowland mine by the regional personnel office. He went to work as section boss, working the midnight to 8:00 A.M. shift. Because of his age and experience, he was the senior person in the mine on his shift.

Norman took one of the battery-operated jeeps used to transport personnel and supplies in and out of the mine and proceeded to the area where Tom was assigned. Upon arriving, he saw Tom lying on an emergency stretcher. Norman stopped his jeep a few yards away from where Tom was sleeping and approached him. "Hey, you asleep?" Norman asked. Tom awakened with a start and said, "No, I wasn't sleeping."

Norman waited a moment for Tom to collect his senses and then said, "I could tell that you were sleeping. But that's beside the point. You weren't at your work station. You know that I have no choice but to fire you." After Tom had left, Norman called his mine foreman, who had accompanied him to the dispatcher's office, and asked him to complete the remainder of Tom's shift.

The next morning, Norman had the mine personnel officer officially terminate Tom. As part of the standard procedure, the mine personnel officer notified the regional personnel director that Tom had been fired and gave the reasons for firing him. The regional personnel director asked the personnel officer to get Norman on the line. When he did so, Norman was told, "You know that Tom is the brother-in-law of our regional vice president, Eustus Frederick?" "No, I didn't know that," replied Norman, "but it doesn't matter. The rules are clear. I wouldn't care if he was the regional vice-president's son."

The next day, the regional personnel director showed up at the mine just as Norman was getting ready to make a routine tour of the mine. "I guess you know what I'm here for," said the personnel director. "Yeah, you're here to take away my authority," replied Norman. "No, I'm just here to investigate," said the personnel director.

By the time Norman returned to the mine office after his tour, the personnel director had finished his interviews. He told Norman, "I think we're going to have to put Tom back to work. If we decide to do that, can you let him work for you?" "No, absolutely not," said Norman. "In fact, if he works here, I go." A week later, Norman learned that Tom had gone to work as section boss at another Consolidation coal mine in the region.

QUESTIONS
1. What would you do now if you were Norman?
2. Do you believe the personnel director handled the matter in an ethical manner? Explain.

CASE STUDY — THE HIRING OF A FRIEND'S DAUGHTER

MARCIE SWEENEY HAD recently graduated from college with a degree in general business. Marcie was quite bright, although her grades might lead a person to think otherwise. She had thoroughly enjoyed school—dating, tennis, swimming, and some equally stimulating academic events. When she graduated, she could not find a job. Her dad was extremely upset when he discovered this, and he took it on himself to see that Marcie became employed.

Her father, Allen Sweeney, was executive vice-president of a medium-sized manufacturing firm. One of the people he contacted in seeking employment for Marcie was Bill Garbo, the president of another firm in the area. Mr. Sweeney purchased many of his firm's supplies from

Garbo's company. On telling Bill his problem, Allen was told to send Marcie to Bill's office for an interview. Marcie did as instructed by her father and was surprised that before she left that day she had a job in the accounting department. Marcie may have been lazy but she certainly was not stupid. She realized that this job was obtained because of the hope of future business from her father's company. Although the work was not challenging, it paid better than the other jobs in the accounting department.

It did not take long for the employees in the department to discover the reason she had been hired—Marcie told them. When a difficult job was assigned to Marcie, she normally got one of the other employees to do it, implying that Mr. Garbo would be pleased with them if they helped her out.

She developed a pattern of coming in late, taking long lunch breaks, and leaving early. When the department manager attempted to reprimand her for these unorthodox activities, Marcie mentioned the close relationship that her father had with the president of the firm. The department manager was furious but did not know what to do.

QUESTIONS

1. From an ethical standpoint, how would you evaluate the merits of Mr. Garbo's employing Marcie? Discuss.
2. Now that she is employed, how would you suggest that the situation be resolved?
3. Do you feel that a firm should have policies regarding such practices? Discuss.

EXPERIENTIAL EXERCISE

A major task that all managers are involved in is decision making. At times the decision involves ethics. This exercise places the manager in a position to determine just how ethical he or she is. Leroy Hasty was faced with a dilemma. He was being transferred to a new assignment with the company, and his boss had just asked him to nominate one of his subordinates as a replacement. Leroy had always felt that, as a matter of fairness, the best qualified person should always be the one promoted. He had to decide whether to recommend Carlos Chavez, a Mexican-American who was highly qualified, or James Mitchell, who, though not as well qualified, would be better accepted by the workers.

Leroy supervised twelve process technicians at the Indestro chemical plant in El Dorado, Arkansas. He knew that his workers were prejudiced against Mexican-Americans. Therefore, he thought that if Carlos were given the promotion, he would have difficulties, no matter what his qualifications. Carlos was a very intelligent twenty-four-year-old technician. He had just earned his bachelor's degree in management by attending night school at nearby Arkansas State University. He had done an excellent job on every assignment Leroy had given him. Carlos had all the qualifications Leroy felt a good supervisor should have. He was punctual, diligent, mature, and intelligent.

James, on the other hand, was a twenty-five-year-old high school graduate. He was a hard worker and was liked and respected by the others, including Carlos. Like Carlos, he had made it clear that he wanted to move into management.

Leroy asked himself, "If Carlos were white, would I have any hesitation about recommending him for this job?" The answer was clearly no. Carlos was without any doubt the better qualified person. Leroy had also struggled with the question, "How will productivity and worker attitudes be affected if Carlos is given the job?" Leroy knew that Carlos would not be easily accepted as the new supervisor, and that morale and productivity would probably plunge for a time.

As Leroy labored over the decision, he thought about how unfair it would be to Carlos if his race were to keep him from getting a deserved promotion. At the same time, Leroy felt that his primary responsibility should be to maintain the productivity of the work unit. The existing prejudice was a fact of life. Leroy could not eliminate it. As Leroy had these thoughts, he realized that it would be very easy to rationalize either decision. He could recommend Carlos on the basis of fairness, or James on the basis of maintaining group morale.

Leroy knew that the way he handled this question might substantially affect his future with Indestro. If his division fell apart after his departure, it would hurt his reputation. More importantly, though, Leroy believed that he would face even more difficult ethical decisions in his new job. If he stood by his principles in this case, he thought it would make those future ethical decisions easier.

NOTES

1. This story is a composite taken from a number of published sources, including: Thomas Moore, "The Fight to Save Tylenol," *Fortune,* 29 November 1982, 44–49; Michelle Osborn, "Tylenol Crisis Tests Public Relations Staff," *Editor & Publisher,* 23 October 1982, 15; "Salvaging Tylenol," *Dun's Business Month,* November 1982, 14–19; "The

Battering of a Best-Selling Brand," *Fortune,* 1 November 1982, 7; "A Death Blow for Tylenol?" *Business Week,* 18 October 1982, 151; Nancy Giges, "Tylenol Tablets Lead Rebound," *Advertising Age,* 13 December 1982, 1; Nancy J. Perry, "America's Most Admired Corporations," *Fortune,* 9 January 1984, 50–56; "Johnson and Johnson's Class Act," *Business Week,* 3 March 1986, 134; and numerous articles from *The Wall Street Journal.*

2. Keith B. Murray and John R. Montanari, "Strategic Management of the Socially Responsible Firm: Integrating Management and Marketing Theory," *Academy of Management Review* 11, no. 4 (October 1986): 816.

3. Kenneth E. Goodpaster and John B. Matthews, Jr., "Can a Corporation Have a Conscience?" *Harvard Business Review* 60, no. 1 (January–February 1982): 132–141.

4. Edward L. Hennesy, Jr., "Business Ethics: Is It a Priority for Corporate America?" *FE* (formerly *Financial Executive*) 2 (October 1986): 14–15.

5. Keith Davis, "The Case For and Against Business Assumption of Social Responsibilities," *Academy of Management Journal* (June 1973): 39.

6. Thomas M. Jones and Leonard D. Goldberg, "Governing the Large Corporation: More Arguments for Public Directors," *Academy of Management Review* 7, no. 4 (October 1982): 603–605.

7. Louis F. Boone and David L. Kurtz, *Principles of Management,* 2d ed. (New York: Random House, 1984), 547.

8. Robert Luchs, "Successful Businesses Compete on Quality—Not Costs," *Long Range Planning* 19, no. 1 (February 1986): 12.

9. Adapted from the Committee for Economic Development and from Sandra L. Holmes, "Corporate Social Performance and Present Areas of Commitment," *Academy of Management Journal* 20 (1977): 435.

10. William J. Byron, "In Defense of Social Responsibility," *Journal of Economics and Business* 34, no. 2 (1982): 190.

11. Dennis Montgomery, "Candy Firm Monitoring Atomic Risk," *Detroit News,* 2 April 1979, 3A, 6A.

12. Davis, "Case For and Against," 36.

13. Adam Smith, *The Wealth of Nations* (1776; reprint, New York: Modern Library), 423.

14. Daniel Wren, *The Evolution of Management Thought,* 2d ed. (New York: John Wiley & Sons, 1979), 109.

15. Wren, *Evolution,* 453.

16. Milton Friedman, *Capitalism and Freedom* (Chicago: University of Chicago Press, 1962), 133; *see also* Theodore Leavitt, "The Dangers of Social Responsibility," *Harvard Business Review* 36, no. 5 (September–October 1958).

17. Robert F. Hartley, *Marketing Mistakes,* 2d ed. (Columbus, Ohio: Grid Publishing, 1981).

18. James F. Lincoln, *A New Approach to Industrial Economics* (New York: Devin Adair, 1961), 38, 122.

19. "Ethics in the Business of T.I." (Dallas: Texas Instruments, 1977).

20. Bernard J. White and B. Ruth Montgomery, "Corporate Codes of Conduct," *California Management Review* 22, no. 2 (Winter 1980): 80.

21. Steven N. Brenner and Earl A. Molander, "Is the Ethics of Business Changing?" *Harvard Business Review* (January–February 1977): 60.

22. *Social Responsibility Disclosure: 1977 Survey of Fortune 500 Annual Reports* (Ernst and Ernst, 1300 Union Commerce Building, Cleveland, Ohio 44115).

REFERENCES

Armandi, B. R., and F. Tuzzolino. "Need Hierarchy Framework for Assessing Corporation Social Responsibility." *Academy of Management Review* 6 (January 1981): 21–28.

Baoard, Andre. "Why Be Ethical Amongst Villains?" *Humanist* 15 (January–February 1985): 32–33.

Boone, Louis F., and David L. Keirtz. *Principles of Management.* 2d ed. New York: Random House, 1984.

Byron, William J. "In Defense of Social Responsibility." *Journal of Economics and Business* 34, no. 2 (1982): 189–192.

Chattopadhyay, Amitave, and Joseph W. Alba. "The Situational Importance of Recall and Inference in Consumer Decision Making." *Journal of Consumer Research* 15 (June 1988): 1–12.

Clutterback, D. "Blowing the Whistle on Corporate Misconduct." *International Management* 35 (January 1980): 14–16.

Drory, Amos, and Uri M. Gluskinos. "Machiavellianism and Leadership." *Journal of Applied Psychology* 64, no. 1 (February 1980): 81–86.

Fombrum, Charles, and W. Graham Astley. "Beyond Corporate Strategy." *Journal of Business Strategy* 3, no. 4 (Spring 1983): 47–54.

Fox, J. Ronald. "Breaking the Regulatory Deadlock." *Harvard Business Review* 59, no. 5 (September–October 1981): 97–105.

Friedman, Hershey H., and Linda W. Friedman. "Ethics: Everybody's Business." *Collegiate News and Views* 35, no. 2 (Winter 1981–1982): 11–13.

Friedman, Milton. *Capitalism and Freedom.* Chicago: University of Chicago Press, 1962.

Galant, Debbie. "Coping with Activists." *Institutional Investor* 22 (June 1988): 127–129.

Gini, A. R., and T. Sullivan. "Work: The Process and the Person." *Journal of Business Ethics* 6 (November 1987): 649–655.

Goodpaster, Kenneth E., and John B. Matthews, Jr. "Can a Corporation Have a Conscience?" *Harvard Business Review* 60, no. 1 (January–February 1982): 132–141.

Greenough, William Croan. "Keeping Corporate Governance in the Private Sector." *Business Horizons* 23, no. 1 (February 1980): 71–81.

Hartley, Robert F. *Marketing Mistakes.* 2d ed. Columbus, Ohio: Grid Publishing, 1981.

"How Business Treats Its Environment." *Business and Society Review* 33 (Spring 1980): 56–65.

Jones, T. M. "Corporate Social Responsibility Revisited, Redefined." *California Management Review* 22 (Spring 1980): 59–67.

Jones, Thomas M., and Leonard D. Goldberg. "Governing the Large Corporation: More Arguments for Public Directors." *Academy of Management Review* 7, no. 4 (October 1982): 603–611.

Kesner, Idalene F., Bart Victor, and Bruce T. Lamont. "Board Composition and the Commission of Illegal Acts: An Investigation of *Fortune 500* Companies." *Academy of Management Journal* 29 (December 1986): 789–799.

Lippin, P. "When Business and the Community Cooperate." *Administrative Management* 42 (February 1981): 34–35.

Luchs, Robert. "Successful Businesses Compete on Quality—Not Costs." *Long Range Planning* 19, no. 1 (February 1986): 12–17.

Murray, Keith B., and John R. Montanari. "Strategic Management of the Socially Responsible Firm: Integrating Management and Marketing Theory." *Academy of Management Review* 11, no. 4 (October 1986): 811–827.

Nitcoki, Joseph Z. "In Search of Sense in Common Sense Management." *Journal of Business Ethics* 6 (November 1987): 639–647.

"Privacy Issue Arouses Concern about Ethics in Marketing Research." *Sales and Marketing Management* (8 December 1980): 88–89.

Reich, Robert B. "Why the U.S. Needs an Industrial Policy." *Harvard Business Review* 60, no. 1 (January–February 1982): 74–81.

Shapiro, I. S. "Accountability and Power: Whither Corporate Governance in a Free Society?" *Management Review* 69 (February 1980): 29–31.

Tang, Ming-Je. "An Economic Perspective on Escalating Commitment." *Strategic Management Journal* 9 (Special Issue: Strategy Content Research, Summer 1988): 79–92.

White, B. J., and B. R. Montgomery. "Corporate Codes of Conduct." *California Management Review* 22 (Winter 1980): 80–87.

CHAPTER
5

The
Planning
Process

Learning Objectives

After completing this chapter students should be able to

1. Describe the planning process and explain the function of a mission statement.
2. Define the term **objective,** identify the characteristics of good objectives, describe the main types of objectives, and state some problems encountered in establishing objectives.
3. Identify the questions that planning should answer, distinguish among a policy, a procedure, and a rule, and explain contingency planning.
4. Describe management by objectives (MBO), explain the essential elements of the MBO process, and list and briefly describe the primary benefits and potential problems of MBO programs.

BUFORD COENEN, PRESIDENT and owner of Peach Growers International, was up early that June morning, when the sun began to peek over the horizon. Even though Buford is the head of the largest peach growing and processing operation in the United States, he was already at his local peach orchard thinking about how to accomplish the day's work. Within an hour, he would have thirty workers in the field picking his bumper crop of peaches. Buford needed to be there early to think about how the pickers were to be kept supplied with baskets, and how to efficiently schedule his trucks to deliver the peaches to the broker's warehouse with a minimum of handling.

There were many other matters to attend to. The pickers were paid according to the amount they picked, so careful records had to be kept. The peaches had to be picked at just the right ripeness or Buford would be docked a certain percentage when the peaches were inspected at the warehouse. Even simple details like not having drinking water available to the pickers could significantly slow down the harvest.

Buford thought about how complicated peach farming was. He and his father had planted the trees twelve years earlier. They had spent what then seemed to be a lot of extra money to get the finest strain of hybrid trees available. These trees produced 50 percent more than ordinary peach trees and had a longer bearing life. It was necessary to prune and spray the trees every year, to irrigate them during the dry periods, and to cultivate and fertilize the area covered by the irrigation systems. It was also useful to treat the ground to eliminate bore worms and to supply "blossom fast" liquid to each tree to decrease the likelihood that it would shed its blooms before the fruit buds were properly formed.

Buford was the third generation of Coenens to be in the peach farming business, and this orchard was the best ever. It would not be the best for long, though. The previous fall Buford had planted 300 acres with a new type of tree that was expected to do even better. Buford had become moderately wealthy raising peaches, but he knew his success had not happened by accident. He hoped to pass on to his son, then twelve, not only the finest peach orchard in Georgia but also a legacy of scientific farming and disciplined hard work.

Even as the first pickers were arriving that morning, Buford was looking forward to the fall. He thought of how he would prune and trim his peach trees so that they could withstand a cold winter, in case one occurred, and produce an even larger crop the following year. ∎

P LANNING IS ESSENTIAL to the success of any company and many endeavors such as peach farming. As the above story suggests, planning involves far more than just deciding what to do on a given day. Buford has a clear picture of the peach farming business, and of what he intends to accomplish in that business. Specific objectives are established in a wide range of areas. Because objectives and plans are specific and well thought out, Buford is justified in being confident of success.

This chapter begins with a brief overview of the planning process. Next, the elements of the planning process—mission, objectives, and plans—are discussed in detail. The remainder of the chapter is devoted to discussion of the following planning topics: standing plans, contingency planning, and management by objectives. This chapter is intended to instill in readers an appreciation of the importance of effective planning, regardless of whether the planner is a company president, a supervisor, or a manager of a small business.

▓ THE PLANNING PROCESS

Planning

The process of determining in advance what should be accomplished and how it should be realized.

Planning is the process of determining in advance what should be accomplished and how it should be realized. Figure 5.1 illustrates the planning process and serves as a guide for planning. This process applies to planning done by managers at all levels. As the figure indicates, planning begins with an understanding of the organizational mission. From the mission statement specific objectives (or goals) can be established, then plans can be developed to accomplish those objectives. The planning process is a dynamic one and should be continuously evaluated and adapted to conform to the unfolding situation the organization confronts. Prior to a discussion of the three main elements in the planning model, the necessity of effective planning must be appreciated.

FIGURE 5.1 ■
The Planning Process

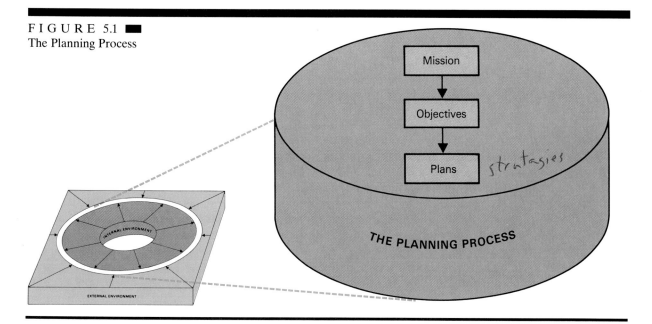

107

Effective planning can have a major impact on individual, group, and organizational productivity. As the United States reeled under record trade deficits in the 1980s, major U.S. companies sought ways to become more competitive internationally. Foreign competitors, especially Japan, were chipping away at domestic markets—in automobiles, in electronics, in steel, and even in computer chips, where the United States had long retained dominance. Plans had to be made to improve productivity so that American firms could keep their markets. However, according to Dataquest Inc., in its 1988 rankings of the world's chip producers, the Japanese grabbed 50 percent of the world's open market for chips, as much as the United States and Europe combined. Only in the captive chip-making operations does the U.S. still retain a slight edge, largely because of their IBM market.[1] It is quite possible that the planning process for U.S. chip producers is deficient. Of course, purely domestic firms must also plan. Competitors are constantly changing in competence and character, and planning must be tailored to cope with such changes.

The other elements of the organization's environment, as shown in Figure 5.1, are also dynamic. For example, the Boston city government decided to dismantle an old elevated railway (called "The El") in 1987. Underneath the railway, traffic was being disrupted during the project, and the merchants along the street had to make plans to remain in business. A fish market owner planned to take out a loan so that the business could survive with lower profits for a time. And the manager of a grocery store rearranged his store so that a side entrance could be used.

Even for small businesses, such as Buford Coenen's peach farming operation, planning is improved by following a systematic approach. For Buford, systematic planning was important to a successful business. Even as the first pickers were arriving in early summer, he was looking forward to the fall. He thought of how he would prune and trim his peach trees so that they could withstand a cold winter, in case one occurred, and produce an even larger crop the following year. He also planted 300 acres with a new type of tree that was expected to do even better than the trees he already had. Buford was successful, and systematic planning in all likelihood contributed to that success.

■ MISSION

Mission
The organization's continuing purpose or reason for being.

According to one dictionary authority for U.S. usage, *mission* is "a continuing task or responsibility that one is destined or fitted to do or specially called on to undertake: like work, vocation." In a military sense, the term is defined this way: "A major continuing duty assigned to a military service or command as part of its function in the national military establishment." Mission is often thought of as the raison d'être, or reason for existence. In this text, **mission** is defined as the organization's continuing purpose or reason for being. For example, the pharmaceutical company Merck is number one in the world, but that means a market share of only 4.4 percent. Dr. P. Roy Vagelos, Merck's chairman and CEO, will not allow his managers to rest until the company doubles its current market share.[2] Merck's mission, its continuing purpose, is to be the untouchable number one pharmaceutical company in the world.

ETHICAL DILEMMA

Y OUR FIRM IS one of the largest subcontractors in the toy assembly business. Your operation is located in South Florida, where older, well-qualified workers are willing to provide you with excellent labor for minimum wages and no benefits. When you selected the area, you promised its residents that if they could locate another 150 workers who were willing to work for no benefits and minimum wages, you would give them permanent jobs and good working conditions. Each of these retirees would be able to substantially increase their standard of living by moving to this area. Your work force grew to 250 employees. After nineteen months, all of your employees from other areas had sold their homes and moved to Florida. They were enjoying the location, their jobs, and their increased incomes.

You have just received some bad news from your business advisor. Congress is about to pass a wage and benefits act that will increase the minimum wage by thirty cents per hour and require each employer with over 100 workers to offer a benefits package to each employee. If you provide such a pay and benefits package your profits will be reduced by approximately 68 percent. You are advised by your advisor that the bill will pass. She recommends that you purchase a new sub-assembly machine that will allow you to eliminate the need for all but seventy-five employees. You can either take a chance and hope the bill does not pass, or you can purchase the new machinery and cut your staff.

What would you do?

The published mission statements of most companies relate to service of customers. But every company must be concerned with service to a number of constituent groups. A return must be earned for stockholders. Employees should be assured of continuing, profitable employment under conditions conducive to good health and personal growth. And the right of society to have good corporate citizens—who obey the laws, produce economic output efficiently, and sustain the environment—must not be neglected.

a real mission is a continuing purpose occurs day in and day out

A clear statement of mission serves to guide individuals, groups, and managers throughout the organization. The mission need not be published externally but should be clearly understood by managers at all levels. In fact, each unit within the organization (division, plant, department) may find it useful to clearly state a unit mission, and its corresponding objectives, that conforms to the broader organizational mission and objectives.

■ OBJECTIVES

Objectives
The desired end results of any activity.

Specific objectives, or goals, can be established once the mission is understood. **Objectives** are the desired end results of any activity. Objectives should be set at each managerial level in the organization; however, lower-level objectives should be consistent with upper-level objectives (see Figure 5.2).

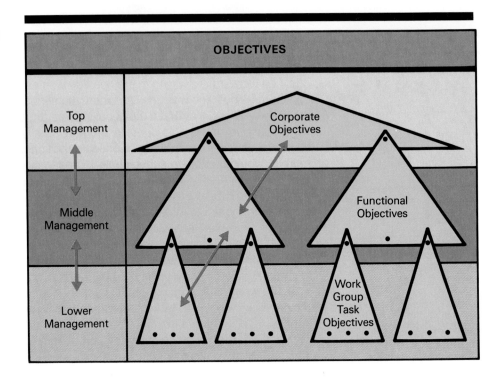

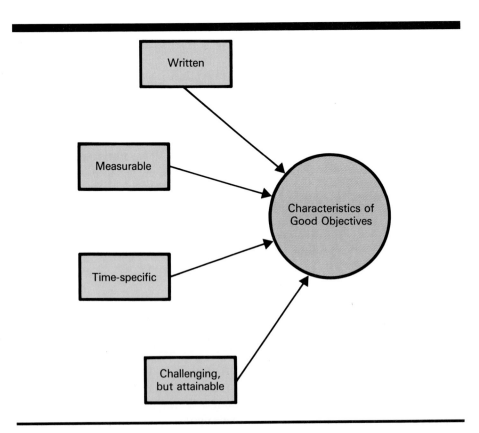

quantify wherever possible
increase profits
less confusion

Characteristics of Good Objectives

Objectives should have four basic characteristics: (1) They should be expressed in writing, (2) they should be measurable, (3) they should be specific as to time, and (4) they should be challenging but attainable (see Figure 5.3). Placing the objectives in written form increases understanding and commitment. Confusion as to what the objectives actually are is less likely to occur when they are written.

Measurability suggests that the objectives should be quantified whenever possible. It would be much better to have an objective of "increasing profits by 10 percent" during a certain period than to merely say, "We want to increase profits." A 1-percent increase would meet the latter objective.

Objectives should be specific as to time. Individuals need and want to know when an objective should be accomplished. Also, an objective that is set without a time limit cannot be challenging. In the example above, are the profits to be increased by 10 percent this year or by the end of the century?

Finally, an objective that is too easily accomplished provides little satisfaction when completed. On the other hand, an unattainable objective is more likely to frustrate workers than to encourage them. The corporate objectives for Robertshaw Controls are shown in Table 5.1.

Objectives are established at each level of management. Objectives set by top management should be consistent with the overall mission of the firm. And

TABLE 5.1 ■ Robertshaw Controls Company Corporate Objectives

1. Minimize historical trends in sales and profits.
   (*Objective:* 10 percent profit before tax is necessary to assure adequate stockholder return and reinvestment in corporate growth.)

2. Increase Robertshaw's sales and profits in the international market.
   (*Objective:* 10 percent minimum annual profit growth assures compounding profitability and established a positive trend line.)

3. Increase utilization of stockholders' equity through return on assets and return on investment justification.
   (*Objective:* 10–15 percent annual sales growth is required to double the sales of the corporation every five to eight years.)

4. Review all product lines and products that cannot justify continuance.
   (*Objective:* Within the broad parameters of sensors and associated controls, Robertshaw can develop adequate diversification and maximize in-house abilities and expertise.)

5. Establish corporate and divisional financial standards.
   (*Objective:* To evaluate and justify investments in new or old areas of opportunity to verify the potential for the corporation to achieve an industry position of no less than third.)

6. Develop improved consumer awareness and recognition of Robertshaw.
   (*Objective:* The criteria for growth must include favorable corporate identity at the consumer and investor levels.)

Source: Y. K. Shetty, "New Look at Corporate Goals." Copyright © 1979 by The Regents of the University of California. Reprinted from the *California Management Review* 22, no. 2: 72. By permission of The Regents.

Specific and measurable objectives should be set at each managerial level in the organization. (© Mark Solomon/The Image Bank)

objectives of lower-level management should be in line with those of upper-level management.

The persons charged with the responsibility of establishing corporate objectives vary from business to business. At times, the president or chairman of the board provides the major thrust in objective creation. At other times, a group of top-level executives are consulted. Whatever the source, these objectives provide the course along which future energies of the firm will be directed and set the tone for objective setting throughout the organization.

Types of Objectives

The creation of specific organizational and subunit objectives is no simple task. Numerous external factors exert their influence on a firm. An organization usually has a number of objectives, and the emphasis each receives may change depending on the impact of a particular environmental factor or group of factors. At least three main types of objectives can be identified:

- *Economic*—survival, profit, and growth.
- *Service*—creation of benefit for society.
- *Personal*—objectives of individuals and groups within the organization.

Wal-Mart stores are enormously successful, and one reason may be that the company continually attempts to achieve all three types of objectives.

ECONOMIC OBJECTIVES

Survival is a basic objective of all organizations. Wal-Mart stores are a prime example of an economically successful company that is a survivor. If Wall Street is to be believed, Wal-Mart will double sales and push past Sears, Roebuck and K mart to become the nation's largest retailer in the next five years.[3] Whether an organization is producing a desired economic value or not seems to take second place to just staying alive. It is difficult for a firm to take into account higher social objectives when it is not known whether the next payroll can be met. As an anonymous statesman once said, "It is extremely difficult to think that your initial objective was to drain the swamp when you are up to your knees in alligators."

In order to survive, a firm must at least break even—that is, it must generate enough revenues to cover costs. But business firms want more than mere survival; they are in business to make a profit. Profit provides a vital incentive for the continued, successful operation of the business enterprise. An adequate profit primarily depends on the industry and the specific needs of an organization. For many companies, it depends on how much profit is possible.

Growth—in sales, number of employees, or number of facilities—may also be a major objective of a firm. Growth may set the stage for long-term survival. A company may seek unrestricted growth, and sometimes this growth can become an end in itself. When this happens, the company may fail to give proper emphasis to profitability. There are, of course, certain economic advantages that come with size, and many companies see growth as a way of competing more effectively.

SERVICE OBJECTIVES

Profit alone is often viewed as the primary motive for being in business. Although it is true a firm cannot survive for long without making a profit, many managers recognize an obligation to society. Even those who feel no such responsibility know that, if a firm cannot consistently create economic value for society, it will not stay in business long enough to make a profit. As with few other retail outlets, Wal-Mart stores continually strive to offer their customers the "best for less." In fact, the company is "consistently on the cutting edge of low-markup mass merchandising."[4] Subsequently, Wal-Mart consistently creates economic value for society. Many firms went out of existence when they ceased producing goods and services desired by society. For instance, Manville Corporation, the well-known maker of asbestos, became unprofitable for a period of time after the public learned of the dangers of asbestos.

PERSONAL OBJECTIVES

Organizations are made up of people who have different personalities, backgrounds, experiences, and objectives. Personal objectives are seldom identical to the objectives of the organization. However, the management of Wal-Mart stores places a high value on their employees' involvement and personal objectives. Wal-Mart's highly motivated employees are the envy of competitors. Management keeps employees closely informed about company plans and practices and includes them in corporate decision making. Employee suggestions are made on a weekly basis and are taken very seriously at headquarters.[5] Because of Japan's communal heritage, many employees are likely to more closely mirror corporate objectives in Japan than in the United States. If personal and organizational objectives are incompatible, the employee concerned may choose to withdraw from the firm. But an employee may not feel financially able to leave the firm. A conflict between the employee's objectives and the organization's objectives can result in minimum work effort, absenteeism, and even sabotage. A conflict between group objectives and the organization's objectives can have the same negative effects. Employees are not the only ones whose objectives, when they differ from those of the organization, can affect that organization. For instance, a stockholder whose

Groups	Possible Objectives
	TABLE 5.2 ■■ Possible Objectives of the Organization and Related Groups
Organization	Maximize profits
Management	Promotions, higher salaries, or bonuses
Employees	Increased wages and bonuses
Government	Adherence of firm to all government legislation, laws, and regulations
Competition	Attain a greater share of the market
Customers	Quality product at lowest price
Stockholders/owners	Higher dividends
Society	Protection of the environment
Unions	Greater influence for union members

goals conflict with the goals of the organization could cease to provide support for the organization by selling stock.

Personal objectives also include the objectives of groups. If an organization is to survive, grow, and earn a profit, it must provide a reasonable match between its objectives and the objectives of powerful groups. Table 5.2 shows how the objectives of a business might differ from those of stakeholders. It is not unusual for stakeholders to experience actual or imagined conflict between their personal objectives and the objectives of the organization. For instance, some customers may believe that higher wages will make the price of products higher, whereas the union may believe that stockholders' profits are too high. Management has the difficult task of reconciling these conflicts, whether or not they are based on factual information.

Problems Encountered in Establishing Objectives

Objective conflict can result from many sources. Three potential causes are the existence of real objectives that are different from the stated ones, the use of multiple objectives, and the application of quantitative and nonquantitative objectives.

REAL VERSUS STATED OBJECTIVES

The *real* objectives may be at odds with the *stated* objectives. Objectives are often the result of power plays and pressures that come from circumstances in the marketplace or from internal tensions. The personal objectives of the board of directors, outside creditors, lower-level managers, employees, stockholders, and labor unions are bound to be different. Stated objectives are often significantly altered by individuals and groups who seek to adapt the organization to their narrower purposes. Because of these differences, the stated objectives are at times different from the actual objectives.

To determine the real objectives, one must look at the actual decisions and actions that occur from day to day. A manager's actions speak louder than words. For example, Japanese corporations are normally polite, collective-rule companies. However, those who work for the Kyocera Corporation realize that the company founder and president Kazuo Inamori does not believe in shared leadership through quality circles. His actions in the recent past have shown him to be a military-style disciplinarian. Employees at this company would do well to carefully evaluate objectives, not in the traditional way, but rather by questioning the real objectives of the company.

Other clues to the actual direction of the organization may be discovered by asking these questions: What functions or groups actually receive the major share of the resources? What type of behavior is accorded the greatest rewards by management? If the administration of a prison, for example, specifies its major objectives as rehabilitation of prisoners, but has only two counselors on its payroll whereas it employs 500 guards, the facts contradict the stated objective.

MULTIPLE OBJECTIVES

All organizations have multiple objectives that must be recognized by management. For instance, what is the major objective of a university? Is it to provide education for students, to conduct research to advance the state of knowledge, or to provide community service? In some universities, research is given the first priority in money, personnel, and privilege. In others, the teaching objective is dominant. In still others, an attempt is made to be all things to all people. Given limited funds, however, priorities must be established. One can debate the priority of objectives for such institutions as a mental hospital (therapy or confinement), a church (religion or social relationships), a prison (rehabilitation or confinement), a vocational high school (skill development, general education, or keeping young people off the streets), a medical school (training medical students for clinical practice, basic research, or academic medicine), and an aerospace firm (research information or usable hardware). Seemingly conflicting objectives may not be mutually exclusive, but choices must be made as to how much emphasis each is to receive.

QUANTITATIVE VERSUS NONQUANTITATIVE OBJECTIVES

In general, the more quantitative an objective, the greater the attention and pressure for its accomplishment. The feasibility of quantifying objectives varies throughout the organization. Production managers, for example, often have specific quotas and schedules. It is easy to tell if either quantity or quality declines. Personnel managers, on the other hand, often have more subjective objectives. The fact that the personnel manager's objectives are more subjective does not mean that they are less important.

If the most important objective is also the most measurable, such as the objective of winning for a professional sports team, then little distortion will take place. But when important objectives are not so easily measured, organizations are likely to be pushed in the direction of the more quantitative, but perhaps less important, objectives. For example, in universities, research and publication are far easier to measure precisely than excellence in teaching. Thus, the primary objective, excellence in education, may be replaced with the research emphasis.

~~PLANS~~ Strategies

~~Plans~~ Strategy
Statements of how
objectives are to be
accomplished.

Objectives are concerned with the end results desired. ~~Plans~~ *Strategies* are statements of how objectives are to be accomplished. When Mr. Frederick W. Smith, founder of Federal Express Corporation, went international with his business, he soon realized how important plans were. His plan was to attack the competition directly, as he had done domestically, but he ran head-on into entrenched overseas rivals and foreign regulations. His plan had to be restructured, and he ultimately competed by purchasing Tiger International Inc. to secure rights to the delivery routes it had acquired over forty years.[6] Planning is a task that every manager, whether a top-level executive or a first-line supervisor, must perform. Stating an objective does not guarantee its accomplishment. A plan must be developed to inform people what to do in order to fulfill the objective. There are usually more ways than one to accomplish an objective. The plan states which approach is to be taken. Specifically, planning should answer the following questions:

1. What activities are required to accomplish the objectives? *Strategies*
2. When should these activities be carried out? *implementation of the strategy*
3. Who is responsible for doing what?
4. Where should the activities be carried out?
5. When should the action be completed?

When Michael Dukakis decided to challenge George Bush for the presidency in the 1988 election, he had to answer each of these questions. His intermediate objective was to get a majority of the delegates at the Democratic convention. First, though, he had to build a campaign organization in each state, obtain funds, and win caucuses, presidential preference primaries, and other kinds of elections.

This could not all be done at once, nor could it be done in random order. So it was necessary to determine a time schedule. Some of the times when things had to be accomplished were determined by election dates and other factors over which Dukakis had no control. With regard to other scheduling questions, however, he had flexibility. Responsibilities had to be assigned to members of the campaign organization. Dukakis had to appoint a chairman and assign responsibility to many others further down in the campaign organization.

The question of where the activities should be carried out was a dominant one throughout the campaign. Emphasis had to shift to California, for example, when that large state was approaching its election. And the candidate himself had to plan to be in certain states at opportune times.

Finally, Dukakis wanted to lock up the nomination early in the campaign, so an objective was set to sweep the early primaries and convince everyone that he was the choice. It did not work out that way; other challengers won several of the early primaries, and Michael Dukakis had to modify his objective. It was not until the results were in on the later primaries, in May 1988, that Michael Dukakis could say with authority that he was the nominee. Then he looked toward a later objective, winning the general elections by beating George Bush at the polls. This required new plans, plans that would prove unsuccessful.

■ STANDING PLANS

Standing plans
Plans that remain roughly the same for long periods of time.

Plans that remain roughly the same for long periods of time are referred to as **standing plans.** The most common kinds of standing plans are policies, procedures, and rules.

Policies

Policy
A predetermined guide established to provide direction in decision making.

A **policy** is a predetermined guide established to provide direction in decision making. As such, policies should be based on a thorough analysis of corporate objectives. Separate policies cover the important areas of a firm such as personnel, marketing, research and development, production, and finance.

To formulate policies, the manager must have knowledge and skill in the area for which the policy is being created; however, there are certain generalizations that apply to the establishment of policies. The most important has already been stated: Policies must be based on a thorough analysis of objectives. Several other general principles can help the manager create appropriate policies:

1. *Policies should be based on factual information.*
2. *Subordinate and superior policies should be complementary, not contradictory.*
3. *Policies of different divisions or departments should be coordinated.* They should be directed toward overall organizational optimization instead of optimizing a particular department such as sales, engineering, purchasing, or production, to the detriment of the whole.
4. *Policies should be definite, understandable, and preferably in writing.* If a policy is to guide actions, persons concerned must be aware of its existence, and this requires creating understandable directives in a definitive written form. In effect, policies are the memory of the organization, which it uses to help cope with future events.
5. *Policies should be flexible and stable.* The requirements of policy stability and flexibility are not contradictory; one is a prerequisite to the other. Stable policies change only in response to fundamental and basic changes in conditions. Government regulations can represent such a basic change in conditions and therefore have a major impact on a firm's employment policies. The higher the organizational level, the more stable the policy must be. Changing the direction of the enterprise is a much more complex and time-consuming task than changing the direction of a department or section. The higher the organizational level, the more policy resembles principle. Armco Inc. provides an excellent example of a firm whose policies have been remarkably stable. First formulated in 1919, these policies, outlined in Table 5.3, are still applicable today.
6. *Policies should be reasonably comprehensive in scope.* Policies conserve the executive's time by making available a previously determined decision. The manager should organize the work in such a way that subordinate personnel can handle the routine and predictable work in

TABLE 5.3 ■ Armco Inc. Policies	
Ethics	To do business guided and governed by the highest standards of conduct so the end result of action taken makes a good reputation an invaluable and permanent asset.
Square deal	To insist on a square deal always. To make sure people are listened to and treated fairly, so that men and women really do right for right's sake and not just to achieve a desired result. For everyone to go beyond narrowness, littleness, and selfishness in order to get the job done.
Organization	To develop and maintain an efficient, loyal, aggressive organization who believe in their company, to whom work is a challenge and to whom extraordinary accomplishment is a personal goal.
Working conditions	To create and maintain good working conditions . . . to provide the best possible equipment and facilities . . . and plants and offices that are clean, orderly, and safe.
Quality and service	To adopt "Quality and Service" as an everyday practice. Quality will be the highest attainable in products, organization, plant, property, and equipment. Service will be the best possible to customers, to shareholders, to city, state, and nation.
Opportunity	To employ people without regard to race, sex, religion, or national origin. To encourage employees to improve their skills by participating in available educational or training programs. To provide every possible opportunity for advancement so that each individual may reach his or her highest potential.
Compensation	To provide not only fair remuneration, but the best compensation for services rendered that it is possible to pay under the changing economic, commercial, and other competitive conditions that exist from time to time. It is Armco's ambition to develop an organization of such spirit, loyalty, and efficiency that can and will secure results which will make it possible for individual members to earn and receive better compensation than would be possible if performing a similar service in other fields of effort.
Incentive	To provide realistic and practical incentives as a means of encouraging the highest standard of individual performance and to assure increased quantity and quality of performance.
Cooperation	To recognize cooperation as the medium through which great accomplishments are attained. Success depends more on a spirit of helpful cooperation than on any other one factor.
Objectivity	To always consider what is right and best for the business as a whole, rather than what may be expedient in dealing with a single, separate situation.
Conflict of interest	To prohibit employees from becoming financially interested in any company with which Armco does business, if such financial interest might possibly influence decisions employees must make in their areas of responsibility. The above policy does not apply to ownership in publicly owned companies. This is not considered a conflict of interest but, rather, is encouraged as part of the free enterprise system.
Citizenship	To create and maintain a working partnership between industry and community in this country and throughout the world. To support constructive agencies in communities where Armco people live and work in an effort to create civic conditions that respond to the highest needs of the citizens.

Source: Used with permission from Armco Inc.

conformity with established policies while the manager's time is devoted to exceptional events and problems. If the body of policies is reasonably comprehensive, few cases arise that are not covered by policy.

Procedures and Rules

Procedures and rules might be thought of as further restrictions on the actions of lower-level personnel. They are usually established to ensure adherence to a particular policy.

Procedure
A series of steps for the accomplishment of some specific project or endeavor.

Standard operating procedures (SOP)
The stable body of procedures, written and unwritten, that govern an organization.

Rule
A specific and detailed guide to action set up to direct or restrict action in a fairly narrow manner.

PROCEDURES

A **procedure** is a series of steps for the accomplishment of some specific project or endeavor. Many organizations have extensive procedures manuals and instructions designed to provide guidelines for those managers and workers lower in the organization. The stable body of procedures, written and unwritten, that govern an organization is called **standard operating procedures (SOP).** For most policies, there are accompanying procedures to indicate how that policy should be carried out.

RULES

A **rule** is a specific and detailed guide to action set up to direct or restrict action in a fairly narrow manner. There may be a rule that requires that hard hats be worn in a certain work area, for example.

The differences among policies, procedures, and rules are shown in Table 5.4. As may be seen from the illustration, procedures and rules may overlap as a definition. Taken out of sequence, a step in a procedure may actually become a rule.

Policies, procedures, and rules are designed to direct action toward the accomplishment of objectives. If assurances were absolute that persons doing the work are thoroughly in agreement with and completely understand basic objectives, there would be less need for policies, procedures, and rules. However, it is apparent that objectives at times are unclear and even controversial. Thus, all organizations have a need for policies, procedures, and rules. They should be more definitive and understandable than the objectives on which they are based.

■ LEVELS OF PLANNING

Planning occurs at every level in the organization. At the top-management level, the primary concern is with strategic planning, relating to overall organizational purposes (see Figure 5.4). This is the subject of Chapter 6. Strategic plans are designed to implement or carry out the broader-based plans of top management. Strategic plans must be broken down into less generalized operating or **tactical plans** which are plans designed to implement or carry out the strategic plans of top management. They often relate to limited functional areas such as sales, finance, production, and personnel. Tactical plans also encompass a shorter time frame than strategic plans. The managers who are responsible for implementing tactical plans tend to be middle and lower managers, rather than top managers.

Tactical plans
Plans designed to implement or carry out the strategic plans of top management.

TABLE 5.4 ■ Examples of Policies, Procedures, and Rules

Policy: It is the policy of the company that every employee is entitled to a safe and healthful place in which to work, and to prevent accidents from occuring in any phase of its operation. Toward this end the full cooperation of all employees will be required.

Management will view neglect of safety policy or program as just cause for disciplinary action.

Procedure: The purpose of this procedure is to prevent injury to personnel or damage to equipment by inadvertent starting, energizing, or pressurizing equipment that has been shut down for maintenance, overhaul, lubrication, or setup.

1. Maintenance persons assigned to work on a job will lock out the machine at the proper disconnect with their own safety lock and keep the key in their possession.

2. If the job is not finished before shift change, the maintenance person will remove the lock and put a seal on the disconnect. A danger tag will be hung on the control station stating why the equipment is shut down.

3. The maintenance person who will be coming on the following shift will place his or her lock on the disconnect along with a seal.

4. Upon completion of the repairs, the area supervisor will be notified by maintenance that work is completed.

5. The supervisor and the maintenance person will check the equipment to see that all guards and safety devices are securely in place and operable. Then the supervisor will break the seal and remove the danger tag from the machine.

Rules: The following rules are intended to promote employee safety.

1. The company and each employee are required to comply with provisions of the Occupational Safety and Health Act (OSHA). You will be informed by your supervisor on specific OSHA rules not covered here that apply to your job or area.

2. Report all accidents promptly that occur on the job or on company premises—this should be done whether or not any injury or damage resulted from the incident.

3. Horseplay, practical jokes, wrestling, throwing things, running in the plant, and similar actions will not be tolerated as they can cause serious accidents.

4. Observe all warning signs, such as "No Smoking," "Stop," etc. They are there for your protection.

5. Keep your mind on the work being performed.

6. Familiarize yourself with the specific safety rules and precautions that relate to your work area.

7. Approved eye protection must be worn in all factory and research lab areas during scheduled working hours or at any other time work is being performed.

8. Hearing protection is required when the noise level in an area reaches limits established by OSHA.

9. Adequate hand protection should be worn while working with solvents or other materials that might be harmful to hands.

10. Wearing rings or other jewelry that could cause injury is not allowed for persons performing work in the factory area.

11. Good housekeeping is important to accident prevention. Keep your immediate work area, machinery, and equipment clean. Keep tools and materials neatly and securely stored so that they will not cause injury to you or others.

12. Aisles, fire equipment access, and other designated "clear" areas must not be blocked.

13. Learn the correct way to lift. Get help if the material to be lifted is too heavy to be lifted alone. Avoid an effort that is likely to injure you.

TABLE 5.4 ■ Examples of Policies, Procedures, and Rules (*continued*)

14. Only authorized employees are allowed to operate forklifts and company vehicles. Passengers are not allowed on lift equipment or other material-handling equipment except as required in the performance of a job.

15. Learn the right way to do your job. If you are not sure you thoroughly understand a job, ask for assistance. This will often contribute to your job performance as well as your job safety.

16. Observe safe and courteous driving habits in the parking lot.

■ CONTINGENCY PLANNING

Robert Burns's line, "The best laid plans of mice and men often go astray," is certainly applicable in today's business world. Events can occur so rapidly that plans may become useless before they can be fully implemented. External and internal disturbances resulting in the need for a change in plans often occur. **Contingency planning** is the development of different plans to be placed in effect if certain events occur (see Figure 5.4). In the vignette at the beginning of the chapter, Buford had already worked out a contingency plan involving the pruning and trimming of his peach trees so that they could withstand a cold winter, in case one occurred.

Contingency planning
The development of different plans to be placed in effect if certain events occur.

F I G U R E 5.4 ■
Contingency Planning
and the Levels
of Management

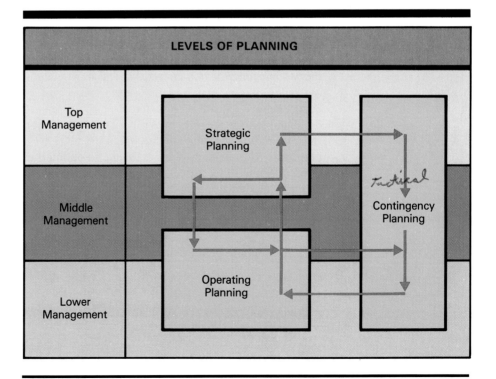

Contingency planning enables individuals in an organization to react to changes in the environment.
(© Jay Freis/The Image Bank)

Clearly contingency planning entails a recognition that unforeseen events can, and will, occur to alter the results of initial plans. Contingency planning makes it unnecessary for a firm to wait for a situation to occur before it prepares to respond. Naturally not all situations can be anticipated, but the manager who tries to anticipate reasonably probable occurrences will stand a much better chance of coping with future events. Separate plans cannot be made for even the situations that are reasonably probable. They are too numerous. So it is often useful to categorize events and link each category to fairly generalized plans.[7]

A disaster recovery plan for a computer installation is a common example of a contingency plan. Organizations that use computers become very dependent on them. This is true for practically every modern company. But what happens when the system fails? Sabotage and vandalism are human-made disasters to which computer systems may be vulnerable. Fires, floods, rainstorms, tornadoes, and hurricanes are natural threats that often disable computer systems.

The plan for recovery typically involves provisions for backups (not only for the information contained in the computer, but also for the functions the computer performs). Contingency plans are made to obtain these files if and when they are needed. Some other aspects of a data-processing contingency plan might be site evacuation, damage assessment, emergency processing, and methods to keep system users informed about restoration efforts. Reciprocal emergency processing agreements and pacts between firms are often the subject of contingency plans. Because of the ever-changing external and internal conditions of many of today's businesses, contingency planning is becoming increasingly important.

▬ PLANNING THROUGH MANAGEMENT BY OBJECTIVES (MBO)

During the past two decades, few other developments in the theory and practice of management have received as much attention and application as MBO.

Management by objectives (MBO)
A philosophy of management that emphasizes the setting of agreed-on objectives by superior and subordinate managers and the use of these objectives as the primary bases of motivation, evaluation, and control efforts.

Effective management practice concentrates on establishing and attaining measurable objectives. **Management by objectives (MBO)** is a philosophy of management that emphasizes the setting of agreed-on objectives by superior and subordinate managers and the use of these objectives as the primary bases of motivation, evaluation, and control efforts. Above all else, MBO represents a way of thinking that concentrates on achieving results. It forces management to plan explicitly, as opposed to simply responding or reacting on the basis of guesses or hunches. It provides a more systematic and rational approach to management and helps prevent "management by crisis," "firefighting," or "seat-of-the-pants" methods. MBO emphasizes measurable achievements and results and may lead to improvements in organizational, group, and individual effectiveness.[8] MBO depends heavily on active participation in objective setting at all levels of management.

■ BACKGROUND AND EVALUATION OF MBO

Peter Drucker first described management by objectives in 1954 in *The Practice of Management.*[9] According to Drucker, management's primary responsibility is to balance conflicting demands in all areas where performance and results directly affect the survival, profits, and growth of the business. Drucker stated that specific objectives should be established in the following areas:

- Market standing
- Innovation
- Productivity
- Worker performance and attitude
- Physical and financial resources
- Profitability
- Managerial performance and development
- Public responsibility

Drucker argued that the first requirement of managing any enterprise is "management by objectives and self-control." As originally described, an MBO system was designed to satisfy three managerial needs.

First, *MBO should provide a basis for more effective planning.* Drucker had in mind what might be called the systems approach to planning—that of integrating objectives and plans for every level within the organization. The basic concept of planning should consist of *making it happen* as opposed to *just letting things happen.* According to Drucker, MBO is a planning system requiring individual managers to be involved in the total planning process by participating in establishing the objectives for their departments and for higher levels in the organization.

Second, *MBO improves communications within the firm by requiring that managers and employees discuss and reach agreement on performance objectives.* In the process, there is frequent review and discussion of the objectives and plans of action at all levels within the firm.

Finally, Drucker thought that *the implementation of an MBO system would encourage the acceptance of a behavioral or more participative approach to*

Activity trap
The tendency described by
George Odiorne of some
managers and employees
to become so enmeshed in
carrying out activities that
they lose sight of the
reasons for what they are
doing.

management. By participating in the process of setting objectives, managers and employees develop a better understanding of the broader objectives of the organization and how their objectives relate to those of the total organization.[10]

One of the foremost advocates of MBO contends that special efforts must be undertaken to avoid the **activity trap,**[11] the tendency described by George Odiorne of some managers and employees to become so enmeshed in carrying out activities that they lose sight of the reasons for what they are doing. As a result, such persons often justify their existence by the energy and sweat expended and avoid questioning whether they have accomplished any result necessary for organizational effectiveness.

■■■ THE MBO PROCESS

The dynamics of an MBO system are illustrated in Figure 5.5. Notice that MBO requires top management support and commitment and involves five steps. These aspects of MBO are each discussed in the following paragraphs.

Top Management's Support and Commitment

An effective MBO program requires the enthusiastic support of top management. It is because of the lack of top-level commitment that many MBO programs fail. For MBO to be effective, the philosophy of top management must be consistent with its principles. MBO relies on the participative approach to management, requiring the active involvement of managers at all levels. The chief executive should trust subordinates and be personally committed to a participative style of management. Top management cannot introduce MBO by simply giving an order or a directive. Lower-level managers, too, must be convinced of the merits of the system and desire meaningful participation in the process.

Establish Long-Range Objectives and Plans

A vital element of MBO is the development of long-range objectives and plans. Long-range objectives and plans established through strategic planning are essential to the success of the organization. Long-term plans are developed through thoughtful consideration of the basic purpose or mission of the organization.

Establish Specific Shorter-Term Organizational Objectives

After long-range objectives and plans are established, management must be concerned with determining specific objectives to be attained within a shorter time period. These objectives must be supportive of the overall purpose as well as the long-range objectives and plans. Usually shorter-term objectives are expressed as specific and quantifiable targets covering such areas as productivity, marketing, and profitability.

FIGURE 5.5 ■
The MBO Process

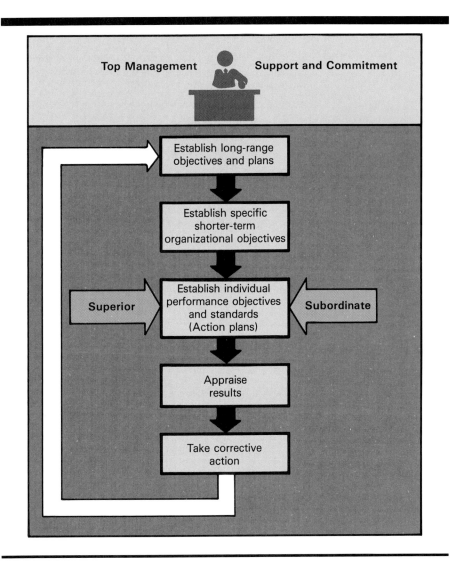

Top Management   Support and Commitment

Establish long-range
objectives and plans

Establish specific
shorter-term
organizational objectives

Superior → Establish individual
performance objectives
and standards
(Action plans) ← Subordinate

Appraise
results

Take corrective
action

Establish Individual Performance
Objectives and Standards (Action Plans)

Action planning
The establishment of
performance objectives
and standards for
individuals.

The establishment of performance objectives and standards for individuals is known as **action planning.** This crucial phase of the MBO process requires that challenging but attainable objectives and standards be established through an interaction with superiors and subordinates. Action plans require clear delineation of *what* specifically is to be accomplished and *when* it is to be completed. For example, if a sales manager has an individual performance objective of increasing sales in his or her area by 38 percent next year the action plan might include the employment of three experienced salespersons, six calls a week by the sales manager on major customers, and assignment of appropriate sales quotas to all the salespersons.

Appraise Results

The next step in the MBO process is to measure and evaluate the actual performance, based on progress toward objective attainment. Having specific performance objectives provides management with an objective basis for comparison. When objectives are agreed on by the manager and the subordinate, self-evaluation and control become possible. In fact, with MBO, performance appraisal can be a joint effort based on mutual agreement.

Take Corrective Action

Although an MBO system provides a good management framework, it is left up to the managers themselves to take corrective action when results are not as planned. Such action may take the form of changes in personnel, changes in the organization, or even changes in the objectives. Other forms of corrective action may include providing additional training and development of individual managers or employees to enable them to better achieve the desired results. Corrective action should not necessarily have negative connotations. Under MBO, objectives can be renegotiated downward without any penalty or fear of loss of job.

Use of the MBO Concept at Monsanto Company[12]

Utilizing many MBO concepts, the Monsanto Company has implemented its management by results (MBR) program throughout the company. While the initial direction came from top-level management, program implementation has since been decentralized, and MBR has become part of the fabric of Monsanto's management process. Its purpose is to motivate people, assist them in setting personal and unit directions, evaluate performance, provide equitable compensation, and ensure development for employees throughout the firm.

Management by results ensures that plans of individuals are properly integrated with those of their reporting unit and that involvement and cooperation are encouraged as the unit seeks to achieve group objectives. In addition, Monsanto's MBR system permits flexibility by focusing not on subordinates' specific and immediate activities, but rather on their progress on a broader and longer-term basis. By emphasizing results for one year or longer, employees are encouraged to avoid short-term gains at the expense of longer-term results.

■■■ CHARACTERISTICS OF PERFORMANCE OBJECTIVES FOR THE INDIVIDUAL

In order for MBO to achieve maximum results, the performance objectives for each individual should be carefully developed. They should be limited in number, highly specific, challenging, and attainable. The number of objectives for each manager should range from four to eight. Each objective should be assigned a priority, perhaps ranging from 1 to 3. Should time and resources prove to be more limited than anticipated, this ranking gives the individual a basis for deciding which objective to pursue.

Perhaps the most important characteristic of good performance objectives is that they should be stated in specific terms. In most instances, this means quantification. For example, objectives may have little impact when stated in such terms as "improve the effectiveness of the unit," "keep costs to a minimum," or "be alert to market changes." At the performance review, one should be able to answer definitely the question, "Did I do it or not?" An objective stating that production will be increased by 1,000 units during a given period is clear. Thus, in writing performance objectives, a special attempt should be made to state them in such terms as volume, costs, frequency, ratios, percentages, indexes, degrees, and phases. It is particularly important to place time limits on each objective. In ten of eleven studies that examined the impact of such specific objectives on performance, evidence supported the contention that specifically stated objectives will increase the level of accomplishment.[13]

Developing challenging and attainable objectives requires a delicate balance. Obviously supervisors want objectives to be set at levels that require special efforts on the part of subordinates. In attaining objectives, promotion and salary are and should be related to success. However, as some researchers have pointed out, in attempting a participatory approach to goal attainment, a subordinate may well be constructing a "do-it-yourself hangman's kit."[14] For instance, Dean Bishop, a hospital supply sales representative, might optimistically indicate to his sales manager that he plans to sell $1 million in surgical instruments and supplies during the next three months. However, no one else in the company had ever accomplished this level of sales in a three-month period, and Dean sold only $1 million in supplies the previous year, it is highly unlikely that he will attain his objective. It is much more likely that Dean has just hung himself, because his objective is unrealistic and probably unattainable.

In the initial phases of new MBO programs, one of the more common errors is the establishment of objectives that are unattainable. This is particularly the case if the time period for review is six months to a year. Anything seems possible with that much time. The superior must not allow excessively high objectives to be set. Specific attention must be given to obstacles that affect accomplishment, particularly the availability of resources. The impact of other personnel on the subordinate's performance must be recognized and discussed.

Research indicates that challenging objectives lead to greater accomplishment only if the subordinate truly accepts the objectives as reasonable, and only if objective accomplishment actually leads to rewards. Challenging objectives with a history of past success will lead to continued success. A series of failures creates a mental set that makes attainment increasingly less likely. Subordinates' assessment of the probability of success should be that they at least have a fifty-fifty chance of achieving each objective.

■ CHARACTERISTICS OF TEAM OBJECTIVES

The accomplishment of most objectives requires that individuals cooperate as a team. As may be seen in Figure 5.6, many factors can affect the attainment of group or team objectives. For instance, it should be apparent that if the sales manager sets a specific objective of selling 50,000 units by March 1, the objective cannot be met if production does not manufacture that number of units. One of

FIGURE 5.6 MBO Team Approach Sequence

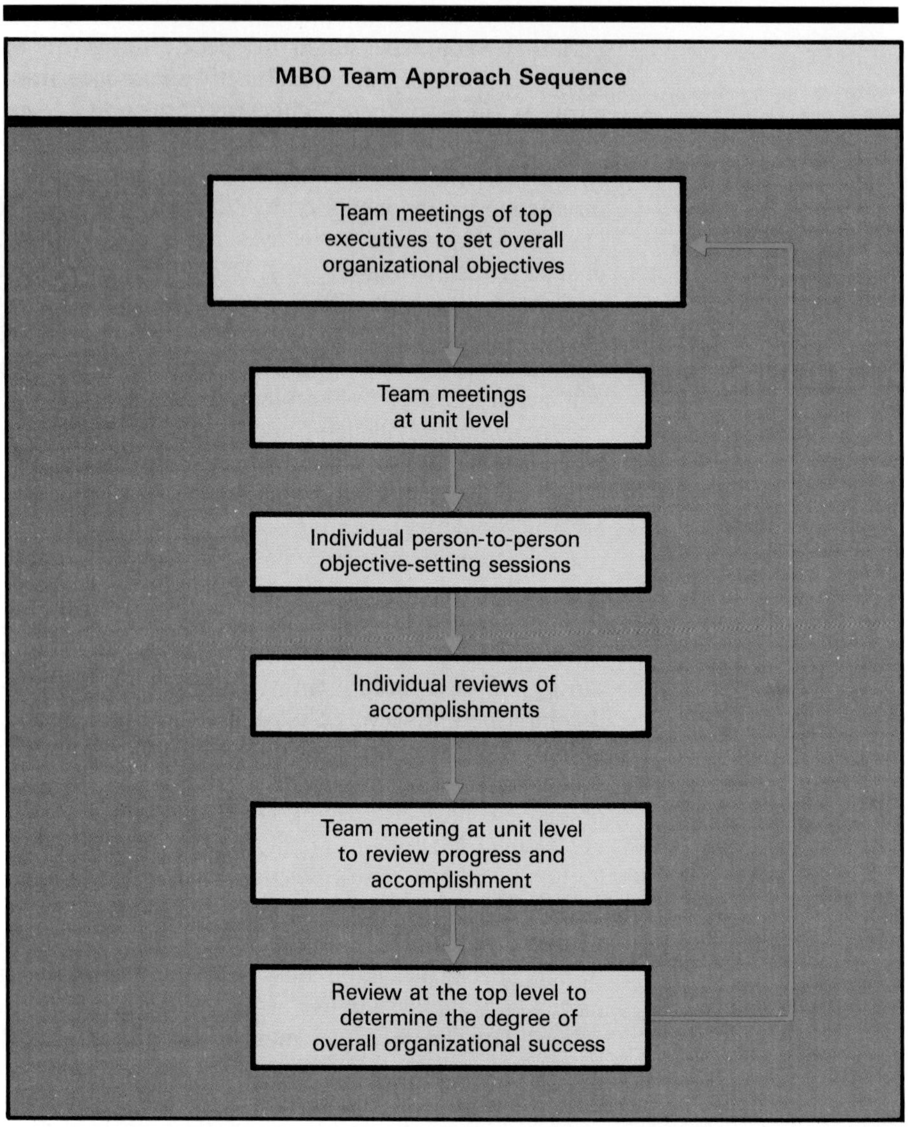

the recommended approaches to overall objective setting involves team meetings to establish group objectives. Team objective setting requires an open and supportive organizational climate. The following, as illustrated in Figure 5.6, is a suggested sequence in an MBO team approach: (1) team meetings of top executives to set overall organizational objectives, (2) team meetings at unit level, (3) individual person-to-person objective-setting sessions, (4) individual reviews of accomplishments, (5) team meetings at unit level to review progress and accomplishment, and (6) review at the top level to determine the degree of overall organizational success.[15]

In one instance, "a medium-size service company experimented with the team approach and decided to ignore individual objectives altogether, reasoning that too much interlinking support and cooperation are required to blame or reward any individual for the production of any single end result."[16] If team objective-setting sessions are to be used, some training in group processes most likely is necessary. It is difficult enough for a manager to establish an open and participatory climate with an employee, but it is far more complex and challenging to try the same thing in a group. Programs of training directed toward this end go under the title of *organizational development*.

■■ BENEFITS OF MBO PROGRAMS

Proponents of MBO have claimed the following benefits:

1. *Results in better overall management and the achievement of higher performance levels.* MBO systems encourage a results-oriented philosophy of management that requires managers to do specific planning. Managers are required to develop action plans and consider the resources needed.
2. *Provides an effective overall planning system.* MBO helps the manager avoid management-by-crisis and firefighting.
3. *Forces managers to establish priorities and measurable targets or standards of performance.* MBO programs sharpen the planning process. Rather than just saying "do your best" or "give it your best shot," specific objectives tend to force specific planning. Such planning is typically more realistic, because the program calls for a scheduled review at a designated future date. Subordinates make sure that they can obtain the resources necessary for objective accomplishment and that obstacles to performance are discussed and removed. MBO forces planning a logical sequence of activities before action begins.
4. *Clarifies the specific role, responsibilities, and authority of personnel.* Objectives must be set in key areas, and individuals responsible must be given adequate authority to accomplish them. A production plant superintendent who has an objective of producing 10,000 units a day must be given the authority to organize and direct resources to achieve the desired level of production.
5. *Encourages the participation of individual employees and managers in establishing objectives.* If the process of MBO has been undertaken on a joint and participatory basis, the chances are that increased commitment will be obtained. *MBO facilitates the process of control.* Periodic reviews of performance results are scheduled, and information collected is classified by specific objectives. Subordinates are forced to report what was accomplished rather than concentrate on descriptions of what they did or how hard they worked. MBO also stimulates improvement in the performance of superiors, who are forced to clarify their own thinking and to communicate this to subordinates.
6. *MBO provides a golden opportunity for career development for managers and employees.* Personal development objectives are often part of the set of objectives developed in joint sessions. MBO results identify

the areas where employees need additional training. Establishment of priorities provides realistic guides for effort, as well as enabling the concrete demonstration of objective accomplishment. This, in turn, makes possible a more realistic and specific annual performance review, which is crucial in deciding on promotions, pay increases, and other organizational rewards.

7. *Other specific strengths of an MBO system* might be that it—
   a. Lets individuals know what is expected of them.
   b. Provides a more objective and tangible basis for performance appraisal and salary decisions.
   c. Improves communications within the organization.
   d. Helps identify promotable managers and employees.
   e. Facilitates the enterprise's ability to change.
   f. Increases motivation and commitment to employees.[17]

■■■ MBO: ASSESSING ITS OVERALL EFFECTIVENESS

In a review of 185 studies, Jack N. Kondrasuk found that there are numerous arguments relating to the pros and cons of the effectiveness of MBO.[18] Many organizations have adopted MBO on faith, often as a result of questionable case studies or unsubstantiated testimonies. One researcher concluded, "There is relatively little empirical evidence to demonstrate the impact of MBO on any aspect of organizational or individual behavior, including job performance."[19] As illustrated in Table 5.5, MBO did achieve positive results in 153 organizations— a ratio of 9:1, positive to not positive. Case studies and surveys show a much higher level of effectiveness for MBO than do experiments. "Positive results" does not necessarily mean that respondents thought MBO to be worth the effort. According to Kondrasuk, "There are tendencies for MBO to be more effective in the short term [less than two years], in the private sector, and in organizations removed from direct contacts with the customer. Basically, MBO can be effective, but questions remain about the circumstances under which it is effective."

TABLE 5.5 ■ MBO Effectiveness as Applied in 185 Organizations

Research Approach	Positive	Mixed	Not Positive	Ratio Positive: Not Positive
Case studies	123	8	10	12:1
Surveys	9	2	1	9:1
Quasi-experiments	20	3	4	5:1
True experiments	1	2	2	1:2
Totals/average	153	15	17	9:1

Source: From Jack N. Kondrasuk, "Studies in MBO Effectiveness," *Academy of Management Review* 6, no. 3 (1981): 425. Used with permission.

■■ POTENTIAL PROBLEMS WITH MBO

Although there are numerous benefits attributed to MBO, certain problems may be encountered, such as the following:

1. MBO programs often lack the support and commitment of top management.
2. Objectives are often difficult to establish.
3. The implementation of an MBO system can create excessive paperwork if it is not closely monitored. *Computer has helped*
4. There is a tendency to concentrate too much on the short run at the expense of long-range planning.
5. Some managers believe that MBO programs may be excessively time-consuming.

Although there is strong evidence that MBO has not generally worked out well as a complete system, it still provides a good model for planning. The central principles of MBO have been incorporated into all kinds of organizations and continue to have a major impact. These principles include specific, verifiable objectives, evaluation of performance on the basis of objective accomplishment, and integration of individual objectives with organizational objectives. When established as part of a rigid MBO structure, these principles tend not to work out too successfully, but taken individually they have proven to be sound concepts.

SUMMARY

Planning is the process of determining in advance what should be accomplished and how it should be realized. Planning begins with an understanding of the organizational mission. From the mission statement specific objectives (or goals) can be established, then plans can be developed to accomplish those objectives. The planning process is a dynamic one and should be continuously evaluated and adapted to conform to the unfolding situation the organization confronts.

Objectives are the desired end results of any activity and should be set at each managerial level in the organization. Plans are statements of how objectives are to be accomplished; those that remain roughly the same for long periods of time are referred to as standing plans. The most common kinds of standing plans are policies, procedures, and rules, all designed to direct action toward the accomplishment of objectives.

Planning occurs at every level in the organization. Strategic plans, relating to overall organizational purposes, are designed to implement the broader-based plans of top management. Tactical plans encompass a shorter time frame than strategic plans; those responsible for implementing tactical plans tend to be middle and lower managers. Contingency planning is the development of different plans to be placed in effect if certain events occur to alter the results of initial plans.

Management by objectives (MBO) is a philosophy of management that emphasizes the setting of agreed-on objectives by superior and subordinate managers and the use of these objectives as the primary bases of motivation, evaluation, and control efforts. Above all else, MBO represents a way of thinking that concentrates on achieving results.

A vital element of MBO is the development of long-range objectives and plans established through strategic planning. These are essential to the success of the organization, as is the enthusiastic support of top management. The accomplishment of most objectives requires that individuals cooperate as a team. Many factors can affect the attainment of group or team objectives. Team objective setting requires an open and supportive organizational climate.

REVIEW QUESTIONS

1. What are the steps involved in the planning process?
2. What is the purpose of a mission statement?
3. Describe the characteristics of good objectives. What are the three main types of objectives?
4. What are the specific questions that planning should answer?
5. Distinguish by definition and example among policies, procedures, and rules.
6. What is meant by the term **contingency planning**?
7. What is management by objectives (MBO)? Describe the basic steps in the MBO process.
8. Briefly discuss the benefits of, and problems with, MBO.

KEY TERMS

planning	procedure	contingency planning
mission	standard operating	management by
objectives	procedures (SOP)	objectives (MBO)
plans	rule	activity trap
standing plans	tactical plans	action planning
policy		

CERTIFIED DEPARTMENT STORES' MBO PROGRAM

PARKER NEILSON WAS irritated and confused after his meeting with Dale Simpson. Parker was the manager of the Kansas City Certified store, and Dale, the district manager for the company, was in charge of stores in Missouri, Kansas, and Oklahoma. Three weeks earlier, Parker had received a letter from Dale explaining that top management had decided on an MBO program to help Certified Stores in improving efficiency and increasing profit contributions. In that letter Dale had said that the objectives established would be used to measure performance of store managers and that salary increases and promotion would be directly related to performance. The accompanying instructions required managers to list the objectives they felt were appropriate for their store and then stand by for the district manager's review visit.

Parker had done just what he was instructed to do. In a meeting with his five department managers, Parker had chosen objectives that they all agreed were appropriate. All of the objectives represented performance levels that were improvements over the past year and reasonably attainable. The objectives they established were to

- Increase selling efficiency, as measured by the ratio of salaries to sales by 10 percent
- Reduce inventory losses to 2 percent of sales
- Reduce cash register shortages to 0.05 percent of sales
- Improve customer service to the extent that 20 percent fewer complaint letters will be mailed to the home office

Dale arrived late for the MBO review visit and stressed that there was little time. He quickly scanned the written statement of objectives Parker gave him, then explained that profit improvement was really what the home office was interested in, rather than trying to monitor multiple objectives from each store. Senior management had decided that a 12-percent increase in profit would be a reasonable objective for Parker's store. This single objective, Dale said, would facilitate the monitoring of performance by the home office and would also reduce the amount of information the store would have to submit. This visit was cut short because the district manager had to attend a meeting on the advertising budget back at the home office.

QUESTIONS
1. Did the MBO system at Certified meet the criteria for an effective program as discussed in the chapter? Why or why not?
2. Evaluate Parker's approach to objective setting.
3. If you were Parker, what would be your approach to Certified's MBO program? Defend your answer.

A BUSY DAY

DAVE JOHNSON, Human Resource Manager for Eagle Aircraft, had just returned from a brief vacation in Cozumel, Mexico. Eagle is a Wichita, Kansas, maker of small commercial aircraft. Eagle's work force in 1989 totaled 236. Dave's friend Carl Edwards, vice-president of marketing, stopped by to ask Dave to lunch, as he often did. In the course of their conversation, Carl asked Dave's opinion on the president's announcement concerning expansion. "What announcement?" was Dave's response.

Carl explained that there had been a special meeting of the executive council to announce a major expansion, involving a new plant to be built near St. Louis, Missouri. He continued, "Everyone at the meeting seemed to be completely behind the president. Joe Davis, the controller, stressed our independent financial position; the production manager had done a complete work-up on the equipment we are going to need, including availability and cost information. And I have been pushing for this expansion for some time. So I was ready. I think it will be good for you too, Dave. The president said he expects employment to double in the next year."

As Carl left, Rex Schearer, a production supervisor, arrived. "Dave," said Rex, "the production manager jumped on me Friday because maintenance doesn't have anybody qualified to work on the new digital lathe they are installing." "He's right," Dave replied. "Maintenance sent me a requisition last week. We'd better get hot and see if we can find someone." Dave knew that it was going to be another busy Monday.

QUESTIONS

1. What are the possible repercussions of keeping Dave in the dark about the expansion? Discuss.
2. Discuss the planning problems highlighted by the case and tell what should be done to solve them.

EXPERIENTIAL EXERCISE

Patsy Olson is the controller for Multifoods International, and three supervisors of various specialties report directly to her. Today she must meet with her supervisors in order to put in place management's latest directive—Management by Objectives (MBO). As Patsy prepares for her meeting, she thinks, "I am sure that not every supervisor is in total agreement as to the appropriateness of MBO. I've got to tell them exactly how to apply MBO, as much in line with their management styles as possible. I have been in various management positions for the past twenty years, and I have seen management policies and practices come and go. Now I must make sure that each of the supervisors involved understands how to apply the new system. I wonder how Nita, Robert, and Doug will react."

Nita Dickey has been in various management positions for the past fifteen years, and she has also seen management policies and practices come and go. She is ready to find out exactly how to implement management's latest miracle—MBO. Nita is sure that this is just another experiment in futility, but she will go along. After all, what is the harm of letting the people upstairs experiment as long as the experiment is a short one?

Robert Zackery has been out of college for six years, and he is eager to see how MBO actually works in practice. He is anxious to get this experiment under way. This could be just the way to make some sorely needed changes.

Doug Warner has a degree in industrial psychology and is very excited about MBO. He believes that the primary emphasis of an organization should be on the employee. Doug is eager to get this organizational change under way. For some time he has been bothered by the lack of emphasis on the human element shown by some of the less progressive supervisors.

Once these supervisors get together, the result will probably be less than total agreement. If you like that kind of thing, volunteer. This exercise will require four of you, so raise your hands quickly, to assure that you can actively participate. Those of you who are not lucky enough to participate should observe carefully. Additional instructions will be provided by the instructor.

NOTES

1. "Developments to Watch," *Business Week,* 13 February 1989, 100.
2. "Merck & Company Sheer Energy," *Business Month,* December 1988, 36.
3. Thomas J. Murry, "Wal-Mart Stores Penny Wise," *Business Month,* December 1988, 42.
4. Murry, "Wal-Mart Stores Penny Wise," 42.
5. Murry, "Wal-Mart Stores Penny Wise," 42.
6. "Mr. Smith Goes Global," *Business Week,* 13 February 1989, 66.
7. Jane E. Dutton and Susan E. Jackson, "Categorizing Strategic Issues: Links to Organizational Action," *Academy of Management Journal* 12, no. 1 (January 1987): 76.
8. Anthony P. Raia, *Managing by Objectives* (Glenview, Ill.: Scott Foresman, 1974), 10–12.

9. Peter F. Drucker, *The Practice of Management* (New York: Harper, 1954).
10. *Management: Tasks, Responsibilities, Practices* (New York: Harper, 1954).
11. See George S. Odiorne, *Management by Objectives* (Belmont, Calif.: Pitman, 1965); and *Management Decisions* (Englewood Cliffs, N.J.: Prentice-Hall, 1969).
12. R. Wayne Mondy and Robert M. Noe, III, *Personnel: The Management of Human Resources,* 3rd ed. (Boston: Allyn and Bacon, 1987), 316.
13. Anthony P. Raia, *Managing,* 14–15.
14. Gary P. Latham and Gary A. Yuki, "A Review of Research on the Application of Goal Setting in Organizations," *Academy of Management Journal* 18, no. 4 (December 1975): 829.
15. Richard E. Byrd and John Cowan, "MBO: A Behavioral Science Approach," *Personnel* 51, no. 2 (March–April 1974): 48.
16. W. J. Reddin, *Effective Management by Objectives* (New York: McGraw-Hill, 1971), 16.
17. Harold Koontz, "Making MBO Effective," *California Management Review* 20 (Fall 1977): 5–7.
18. Jack N. Kondrasuk, "Studies in MBO Effectiveness," *Academy of Management Review* 6, no. 3 (1981): 419–430.
19. Kondrasuk, "MBO Effectiveness," 419–430.

REFERENCES

Allen, L. A. "Managerial Planning: Back to the Basics." *Management Review* 70 (April 1981): 15–20.

Blair, John. "Not Again! The Messy Business of Planning." *Computerworld* 21 (30 November 1987): 69–73.

Bologna, J. "Why MBO Programs Don't Meet Their Goals." *Management Review* 69 (December 1980): 32.

Camillus, John C., and John H. Grant. "Operational Planning: The Integration of Programming and Budgeting." *Academy of Management Review* 5 (July 1980): 369–379.

Cross, Richard Hunter, III. "Strategic Planning: What It Can and Can't Do." *SAM Advanced Management Journal* 52 (Winter 1987): 13–16.

Duncan, Jack W. "When Necessity Becomes a Virtue: Don't Act Too Cynical about Strategy." *Journal of General Management* 13 (Winter 1987): 28–43.

Durack, Elmer, II. "Corporate Business and Human Resources Planning Practices: Strategic Issues and Concerns." *Organizational Dynamics* 15 (Summer 1986): 73–87.

Dutton, Jane E., and Susan E. Jackson. "Categorizing Strategic Issues: Links to Organizational Action." *Academy of Management Journal* 12, no. 1 (January 1987): 76–90.

Ford, R. C., et al. "Ten Questions about MBO." *California Management Review* 23 (Winter 1980): 48–55.

Galbraith, John Kenneth. "The New, Improved Industrial State: The Genius of the Modern Corporation Is Not in Its Command but in Its Combination of Diverse Intelligence for Decisions Far Beyond the Reach of Any Individual." *Business Month* 131 (January 1988): 38–40.

Goldstein, S. G. Mike. "Involving Managers in System-Improvement Planning." *Long Range Planning* 14 (February 1981): 93–99.

Jackson, J. H. "Using Management by Objectives: Case Studies of Four Attempts." *Personnel Administrator* 26 (February 1981): 78–81.

Kahalas, Harvey. "Planning Types and Approaches: A Necessary Function." *Managerial Planning* 28 (May–June 1980): 22–27.

Kelly, Charles M. "Remedial MBO." *Business Horizons* (September–October 1983): 62–67.

Koehler, Kenneth G. "Link Budget to Overall Plan." *CMA—The Management Accounting Magazine* 61 (May–June 1987): 17.

Linsay, W. M., and L. W. Rue. "Impact of the Organization Environment on the Long-Range Planning Process: A Contingency View." *Academy of Management Journal* 23 (September 1980): 385–404.

Lopata, R. "Key Indicators: Simpler Way to Manage." *Iron Age* (26 January 1981): 41–44.

Michael, Steven R. "Feedforward versus Feedback Controls in Planning." *Managerial Planning* 29 (November–December 1980): 34–38.

———. "Tailor-Made Planning: Making Planning Fit the Firm." *Long Range Planning* 13 (December 1980): 74–79.

Morrisey, George L. "Who Needs a Mission Statement? You Do." *Training and Development Journal* 42 (March 1988): 50–52.

Pekar, Peter P. "Planning: A Guide to Implementation." *Managerial Planning* 29 (July–August 1980): 3–6.

Ratcliffe, Thomas A., and D. J. Logsdon. "Business Planning Process—A Behavioral Perspective." *Managerial Planning* 28 (March 1980): 32–38.

Schaeffer, Dorothy. "MBO Pitfalls." *Supervision* (August 1983): 9–10.

Shaffer, James C. "Mission Statements: Why Have Them? (Corporate Mission Statements)." *Communication World* 4 (June 1987): 14–16.

Simmons, William W. "Future of Planning." *Managerial Planning* 29 (January–February 1981): 2–3.

Snyder, N., and W. F. Glueck. "How Managers Plan the Analysis of Manager's Activities." *Long Range Planning* 18 (February 1980): 70–76.

Thackray, John. "The Fall of Corporate Planning." *Management Today* (July 1986): 17.

Word, E. Peter. "Focussing Innovative Effort Through a Convergent Dialogue." *Long Range Planning* 13 (December 1980): 32–41.

Wright, Phillip C. "Management by Objectives—One More Time." *Supervision* (January 1984): 3–5.

CHAPTER

6

Chapter Outline

Strategic Planning

Learning Objectives

After completing this chapter students should be able to

1. Describe the various levels of strategic planning and explain who are the organizational strategists.
2. Explain the strategic planning and implementation processes.
3. Describe the means of formulating corporate-level strategy.
4. Explain the means of formulating business-level and functional-level strategy.

GENERAL ELECTRIC IS primarily identified with major appliances, electric motors, and lighting. But the company also makes jet engines, electronics items, and medical equipment, and even provides financial services. In 1987 GE was engaged in about forty businesses.

When Jack Welch took over as chairman and chief executive officer of GE in 1981, he identified this diversity as a major problem. He reasoned that it was impossible for a company to be a leader in so many different kinds of activities.

Sixteen of the businesses accounted for 92 percent of GE's profit and 87 percent of sales. In each of these businesses, GE was one of the dominant competitors. In the other twenty or so business areas, GE was not dominant, although some were growing rapidly.

Top managers of the laggard businesses were put on notice: either become a dominant player or be sold or closed. Jack Welch's plan was to strip the corporation of its low performers and concentrate management talent and financial resources on the others. By 1984 the small appliance division and the subunit that made central air-conditioning systems had been sold. A number of unrelated businesses, such as broadcasting, were up for sale.

Within the individual businesses, Welch and his staff were trying to make sure resources were applied where they would do the most good. New plant investment was at $1.9 billion in 1983, up 20 percent from the year before, and the company spent a whopping $2 billion on research and development.

Largely because of its divestitures, GE began 1984 with $3 billion in cash and expected that to grow to $5 billion by year end. But with interest rates near record levels, there was no rush to reinvest the cash in plant and equipment. Although GE continues to look for companies to buy, it is interested only if they are exceptional bargains. And once in the GE family, they will be subject to the same mandate to performance that guides GE's existing businesses.

In 1984, Jack Welch, forty-eight, had been at the helm for three years. He claimed to have accomplished only 15 percent of what he intended to do at GE. Welch stated the company goal this way: "We were a company that was identified with safety. Now it is safety with upside potential."

Welch's "grand design" became clearer by 1987. GE continued to shore up the manufacturing divisions that met Welch's rigid performance standards and to prune those that did not. But there was then a pronounced movement by the company toward service and technology areas. For example, GE had bought RCA Corporation in June 1986, later selling off RCA's record division. And Kidder, Peabody, and Company, a major financial services firm, had become part of the GE family that year.

Welch subordinate, Michael Carpenter, said GE would do a "lot of divesting" within the ensuing year or so. But GE announced intentions to keep the RCA defense, semiconductor, and electronics-repair businesses. GE expected to save millions of dollars in overhead by combining its existing and acquired service businesses. Carpenter said that strong earnings and money from divestments would give GE "a lot of cash" again within three or four years.[1] ■

Strategic planning
The determination of overall organizational purposes and objectives and how they are to be achieved.

T HE PLANNING PROCESS remains essentially the same at each of the levels of organizations such as GE; however, managers today have access to a number of concepts and techniques that relate specifically to strategic planning. **Strategic planning** is the determination of overall organizational purposes and objectives and how they are to be achieved. *strategies*

General Electric has long been a leader in strategic planning. Jack Welch recognizes that GE's common stock has typically been considered a safe investment, but one with little upside potential. He expects to improve the common shareholders' opportunity for gain without decreasing the security of the stock. Part of his strategic plan for doing this is to concentrate on those businesses where GE is a market leader and to eliminate weak divisions. He also has embarked on a program of expansion into technology and service areas.

In this chapter, the discussion begins with the levels of strategic planning, identification of the organizational strategists, and a brief description of the strategic planning and implementation processes. This is followed by a discussion of the formulation of corporate-level strategies, portfolio strategies, business-level strategies, and functional-level strategies.

▦ SBUs AND THE LEVELS OF STRATEGIC PLANNING

Corporate-level strategic planning
The process of defining the overall character and purpose of the organization, the businesses it will enter and leave, and how resources will be distributed among those businesses.

It is important to consider strategic planning according to the organizational levels at which it occurs, particularly in light of the growth in recent decades of such complex organizations as General Electric, United Technologies, Allied Corporation, and Textron. Figure 6.1 illustrates the organizational levels of a typical complex corporation along with the corresponding levels of strategic planning. Since each level has its own distinctive characteristics, the tools and processes that are useful to formulate strategy at the three levels differ.

Corporate-level strategic planning is the process of defining the overall character and purpose of the organization, the businesses it will enter and leave,

The CEO and other high-level executives of an organization are responsible for defining and communicating the character and purpose of the organization.
(COMSTOCK, Inc.)

FIGURE 6.1 ■
The Levels of
Strategic Planning

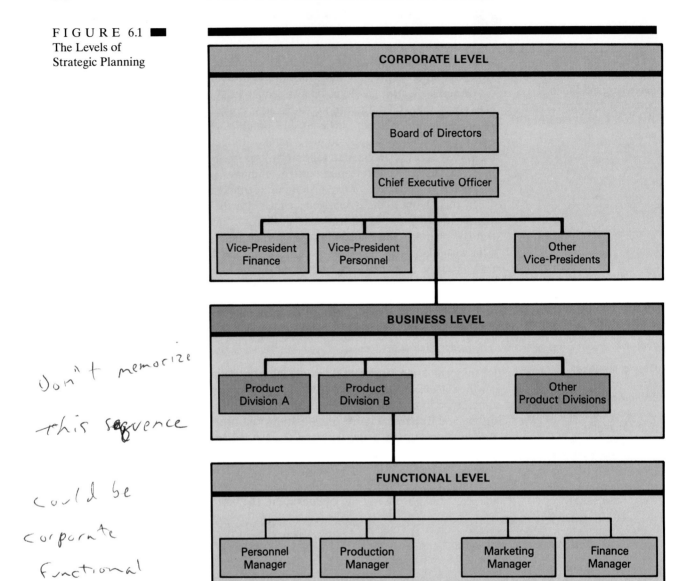

Don't memorize this sequence

could be corporate functional business

and how resources will be distributed among those businesses. Corporate-level strategy typically concerns the mix and utilization of business divisions called strategic business units (SBUs). These divisions are meant to facilitate management of large organizations. A **strategic business unit,** then, is any part of a business organization that is treated separately for strategic planning purposes. For example, AT&T is expected to be selected as the joint venture partner for Italy's state-owned Italtel telecommunication equipment manufacturer. If this partnership goes through, the Italian arm of AT&T may become a separate strategic business unit.[2] One SBU has a unique mission, product line, competitors,

Strategic business unit
Any part of a business organization that is treated separately for strategic planning purposes.

and markets relative to other SBUs in the corporation.[3] Referring again to Figure 6.1, corporate-level strategic planning is primarily the responsibility of the organization's top executives, like Jack Welch and his immediate subordinates at GE. The major focus here is on formulating strategies to accomplish the organization's mission.

Organizational mission is the organization's continuing purposes—in short, what is to be accomplished for whom. For example, AT&T's visionary mission some eighty years ago was described by a former chairman: "A dream of good, cheap, fast, worldwide telephone service . . . is not a speculation. It is a perfectly clear statement that you are going to do something."[4] In line with that mission, AT&T has recently signed joint-venture contracts with Philips, a Dutch telecommunications company, to bid together on the installation of large telephone systems in Europe, Asia, and the Middle East. In light of this, and the expected contract with Italtel, AT&T's eighty-year-old mission to expand into the international market appears to be still on course.

Basically, executives in charge of the entire corporation generally define an overall strategic direction—called a grand strategy—and then bring together a portfolio of strategic business units to carry it out, referred to as a portfolio strategy, which will be discussed later in the chapter. Many companies set up SBUs as separate profit centers, sometimes giving them virtual autonomy. Other companies have tight control over their SBUs, enforcing corporate policies and standards down to very low levels in the organization. In general, SBU-level strategic planning is the responsibility of vice-presidents or division heads. In single-SBU organizations, senior executives have both corporate-level and SBU-level responsibilities.

Business-level strategic planning is primarily concerned with how to compete; it takes place within the strategic business units. **Functional-level strategic planning** is the process of determining policies and procedures for relatively narrow areas of activity that are critical to the success of the organization. Practically every large organization is divided into functional subdivisions, usually production, marketing, finance, and personnel. Military installations have supply, police, and maintenance departments, among others. Churches have preaching, education, and music ministries. Each of these functional subdivisions is typically vital to the success of the organization.

■■■ THE ORGANIZATIONAL STRATEGISTS

For most organizations, it is difficult to identify the organizational strategists. In ancient Greece, where the concept of strategy originated, perhaps strategy was determined by the general. For some companies today, strategy clearly comes from the top. For example, Lee Iacocca, chairman of Chrysler Corporation, and Robert Goizueta, president and chief executive officer of Coca-Cola, seem to call the shots. Many companies use in-house **strategic planning staff specialists.** These specialists assist and advise managers in strategic planning. Strategic management involves planning and doing. Staff strategic management specialists are especially involved in planning. At GE, the corporate planning staff includes over 100 persons.

Organizational mission
The organization's continuing purposes—in short, what is to be accomplished for whom.

pg 66 + 108

Business-level strategic planning
The process concerned with how to compete; it takes place within the strategic business units.

Functional-level strategic planning
The process of determining policies and procedures for relatively narrow areas of activity that are critical to the success of the organization.

Strategic planning staff specialists
Specialists who assist and advise managers in strategic planning.

Many organizations retain consultants to assist in designing and implementing strategy. Consultants are particularly useful in that they conduct marketing and other kinds of research that provides an important informational base for strategic decisions. Consultants can play an effective part in strategic planning, even for small firms.[5] In fact, most small firms cannot afford full-time staff specialists. For these companies, using consultants may be the most economical approach to strategic planning.

At least to a limited extent, every manager is an organizational strategist.[6] This is because every manager is responsible for activities related to continuing business operations and achieving vital corporate objectives. It should be recognized, however, that what may be an overwhelming matter to the personnel director, for example—the size of the annual personnel department budget—may be a relatively incidental one from the standpoint of the total organization. Whether or not a matter is important to any one individual has nothing to do with whether or not it is strategic. Strategic matters are determined by answers to the question, "How important is it to the organization as a whole, and to what degree does it have continuing significance?" So **organizational strategists** are generally considered to be those persons who spend a large portion of their time on matters of vital or far-ranging importance to the organization as a whole. In general, they include the top two levels of management, in-house staff specialists in strategic management, and retained consultants who are experts in the areas in which strategic decisions must be made.

Organizational strategists
Individuals who spend a large portion of their time on matters of vital or far-ranging importance to the organization as a whole.

■ THE STRATEGIC PLANNING AND IMPLEMENTATION PROCESSES

Strategic planning at all levels of the organization can be divided into four steps: (1) determination of the organizational mission, (2) assessment of the organization and its environment, (3) setting of specific objectives or direction, and (4) determination of strategies to accomplish those objectives (see Figure 6.2).[7] The strategic planning process described here is basically a derivative of the SWOT (strengths, weaknesses, opportunities, threats) framework, which affects organizational performance but is less structured. This step-by-step approach, we feel, does a better job of guiding understanding of the strategic planning process. Once the strategic plan is developed, the next step is to implement the plan. Basically, strategic implementation is the process of doing what has been planned. Since effective planning cannot occur without considering how to implement plans, planning and implementation will be considered together in this section of the chapter. In Figure 6.2 Strategy Implementation is below the dashed line, illustrating that it is not part of the strategic planning process but an extension of that process.

In real-world strategic planning, of course, steps overlap, are repeated, and occur out of order or at the same time. Emphasis, however, is on the mission of the organization as a whole and environmental considerations. Emphasis at GE, for example, may be on analyzing the environment. This does not mean that organizational strategists like Jack Welch can avoid considering the company's existing objectives and possible changes to them. Strategic planning at all levels

FIGURE 6.2 ■
The Strategic
Planning Process

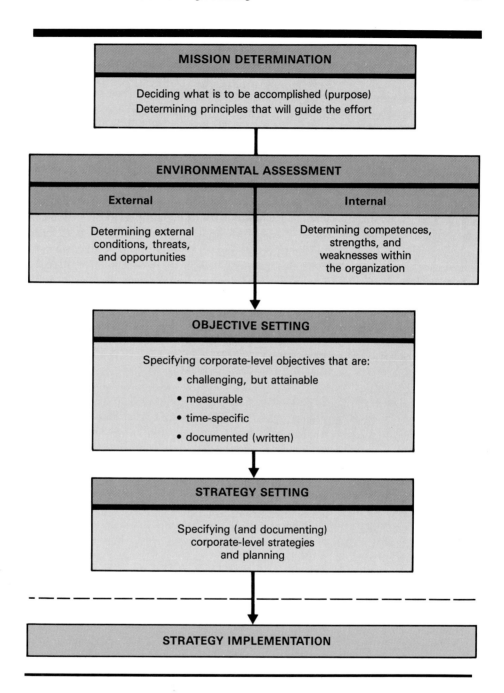

has always been important. However, with the intense concern for international competitiveness that exists today in the United States and many other Western countries, it has new significance. This is especially true in high-technology areas.[8]

Despite its complexity, it is useful to think of strategic planning as a sequential process. By reviewing the four steps of the strategic planning process and the final step of strategy implementation individually, we bring into focus in the following sections the desirability of a systematic approach to strategic planning and implementation.

Mission Determination

The first step of the strategic planning process is to determine the corporate mission. The corporate mission is the sum total of the organization's continuing purpose. Arriving at a mission statement should involve answering the question, "What are we, in management, attempting to do for whom?" Should we maximize profit so that shareholders can receive higher dividends or so that share price will increase? Or should we emphasize stability of earnings so that employees remain secure? Remember that GE had previously emphasized what CEO Jack Welch called "safety" but now is more concerned with growth in earnings. There are many other possibilities. Mission determination also requires deciding the principles on which management decisions will be based. Will the corporation be honorable or dishonorable, ruthless or considerate, devious or forthright, in dealing with its various publics? The answers to these questions, once arrived at, tend to become embedded in corporate culture, and determine the organizational mission.

Environmental Assessment

Once the mission has been determined, the organization must be assessed for strengths and weaknesses, and the threats and opportunities in the external environment must be evaluated. Specific objectives can be established and strategies developed for accomplishing those objectives. For example, through environmental assessment BIC Corporation discovered an opportunity during the early 1980s to market disposable safety razors. Assessment within the organization revealed that BIC had greater capability to mass produce small, plastic-based items than almost any other U.S. company. The company set sales, production, and profit objectives, designed strategies, and quickly became the world's leading marketer of disposable safety razors.

Making strategic plans involves information flows from both the internal and external environments. From inside comes information about organizational competencies, strengths, and weaknesses. Scanning the external environment allows the organizational strategists to identify threats and opportunities, as well as constraints. In brief, the job in the planning phase is to develop strategies that take advantage of the company's strengths and minimize its weaknesses in order to grasp opportunities and avoid threats. One of the opportunities BIC identified was that of employing John McEnroe, the "bad boy" of tennis, to promote its twenty-nine-cent razors. The resulting ads were highly successful.

Objective Setting

Explicitly stating objectives and directing all activities toward their attainment is not the only approach to strategic management; it may not even be the best approach for some organizations at certain times. However, since Peter Drucker coined the term "management by objectives" in the 1950s, it has been generally accepted that the use of objectives improves the process of management. This is no less true at the corporate level of strategic management than it is for the miler who wishes to better the existing world record.

CHARACTERISTICS OF STRATEGIC OBJECTIVES

Objectives should be challenging but attainable. If the miler mentioned above were capable of running near world-record speed, yet set an objective of a five-minute mile, the objective could be easily achieved, but the miler would probably not run at maximum speed. On the other hand, if the objective were set at three minutes, no one in the world could come close. Anyone who attempted it would be frustrated. Corporate goals, too, should offer a reasonable opportunity for accomplishment. To avoid frustration, the probability of accomplishment should not be zero, and to avoid suboptimum performance, it should not be nearly 100 percent.

Remember, too, that objectives should be specific, preferably quantifiable, and measurable. An objective to "maximize profits" offers little specific guidance. To earn $1.2 million in profits or to increase profits by 5 percent over last year's level is specific. The more specific objectives are, the more definite can be the strategies designed to accomplish them.

SATISFICING

Herbert Simon has suggested that managers in general do not attempt to optimize or maximize corporate results.[9] He believes that the term "satisficing" more correctly describes what managers do. According to Simon's theory, managers typically accept the first satisfactory outcome they are offered. For example, one who believes that 10 percent is a reasonable return on invested funds is likely to approve any ROI (return on investment) objective that exceeds that amount.

If Simon is right, many corporate strategists may be more concerned with establishing direction than with setting specific objectives. As long as this year's sales and profits are above last year's, that may be acceptable because the direction is upward. Many effective organizations have never set specific objectives. In fact, some have only a vague understanding of the direction in which they are headed. It appears likely, however, that any organization can improve its performance by setting objectives that are challenging, but attainable and specific, preferably quantified.

Strategy Setting

Once objectives are established or direction is determined, strategies can be formulated. The acquisition strategy at GE is to maintain large cash balances so that the company can take advantage of exceptional bargains immediately rather than having to go into the financial markets, a time-consuming process. It is important that this strategy be understood by the financial vice-president and other managers so that everyone will cooperate to generate the needed funds and so that funds may be kept in reserve and not committed to other purposes.

In contrast to GE, many organizations limit their written strategic plans to financial budgets. And some do not even have budgets. Most authorities, however, consider it worthwhile to put strategies in writing. Whether strategies are written or not, it is the task of organizational strategists to clearly communicate how the organization intends to accomplish its goals.

Strategy Implementation

Once the strategic planning process is complete, the strategy must be implemented. Some people argue that strategy implementation is the most difficult and important part of strategic management.[10] No matter how creative and well formulated the strategic plan, the organization will not benefit if it is incorrectly implemented. Strategy implementation involves several dimensions of the organization, as illustrated in Figure 6.3. It requires changes in the organization's

FIGURE 6.3 ■
Organizational Dimensions for Strategy Implementation

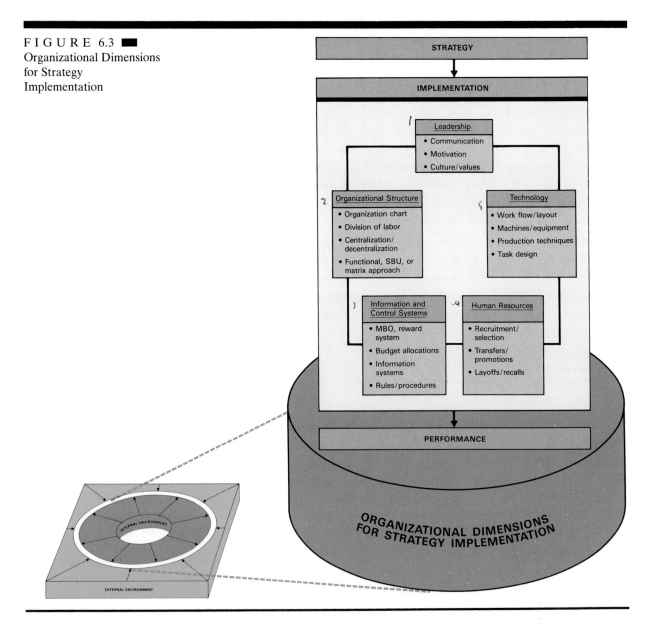

Source: Adapted from Jay R. Galbraith and Robert K. Kazanjian, *Strategy Implementation: Structure, Systems and Process,* 2d ed. (St. Paul, Minn.: West, 1986), 115. Used with permission.

behavior, which can be brought about by changing one or more dimensions, including management's leadership ability, organizational structure, information and control systems, human resources, and production technology.[11]

LEADERSHIP

Leadership is getting others to do what the leader wants them to do. Managers must influence organizational members to adopt the behaviors needed for strategy implementation. Leadership includes communication and motivation as well as changes in corporate values and culture. Managers seeking to implement a new strategy may find it useful to build coalitions and persuade middle managers to go along with the strategic plan and its implementation. If leaders involve other managers during strategy formulation, implementation will be easier because managers and employees will better understand, and be more fully committed to, the new strategy. Basically, leadership is used to encourage employees to adopt supportive behaviors and, when necessary, to accept the required new values and attitudes. For example, normally, Japanese companies are polite, collective-rule companies, where leaders assist employees in accomplishing the organizational goals. In fact, the normal distinctions between leaders and followers, such as large offices and dress differences, are often blurred in Japanese companies. However, as we saw in Chapter 5, those who work for the Kyocera Corporation realize that the company founder and president, Kazuo Inamori, does not believe in shared leadership through quality circles. Traditional Japanese employees will probably have severe problems following him. Inamori will probably be unable to build supportive coalitions among Japanese employees with his current leadership style.

ORGANIZATIONAL STRUCTURE

Organizational structure is typically illustrated in the organization chart. This structure indicates individual managers' responsibilities and degree of authority and incorporates jobs into departments. Structure also pertains to the degree of centralization and whether a functional, divisional, or matrix approach will be utilized. One of the earliest studies of organizational structure examined historical changes in General Motors, Du Pont, Standard Oil of New Jersey, and Sears, Roebuck. As these companies grew large and prosperous, they altered their structures to reflect new strategies.[12]

INFORMATION AND CONTROL SYSTEMS

Information and control systems include reward systems, incentives, management-by-objective types of systems, budgets for allocating resources, information systems, and the organization's rules, policies, and implementation. A proper mix of information and control systems must be developed to support the implementation of the strategic plan. Managers and employees must be rewarded for adhering to the new strategy and making it a success, or the intensity of implementation will be reduced substantially.[13]

HUMAN RESOURCES

The human resources of the organization are its employees. The human resource function involves recruitment, selection, training, transfers, promotion, and layoffs of employees to properly implement the strategic plan. In certain

staffing the
organizational structure

situations, employees simply are incompatible with a new strategy and may have to be replaced with new people. New strategy may foster resentment and resistance among both managers and employees, and this is a matter that must be resolved quickly or it may hinder strategy implementation. In essence, a proper balance of human resources must be developed to support strategy implementation.

TECHNOLOGY

Technology relates to the knowledge, tools, and equipment used to accomplish an organization's assignments. If an organization adopts a strategy of producing a new product, managers must often redesign jobs and construct new buildings and facilities. New technology, because of its efficiency, may also be required for implementing a low-cost strategy. As with other aspects of strategy implementation, the appropriate level of technology must be found for proper implementation of the strategic plan.

Finance is another step

■■■ FORMULATING CORPORATE-LEVEL STRATEGY

Corporate-level strategy typically concerns the mix and utilization of strategic business units. As stated earlier in the chapter in the section on SBUs and the Levels of Strategic Planning, executives generally define an overall strategic direction, a grand strategy, and then develop a portfolio of strategic business units to carry it out.

BUSINESS BRIEFS

INSIDE BUSINESS

Corporate-Level Strategic Planning

CORPORATE-LEVEL STRATEGIC planning is the process of defining the overall character and purpose of the organization, the businesses it will enter and leave, and how resources will be distributed among those businesses. According to Mr. Wayne Calloway, the Chairman and CEO of PepsiCo, the company's mission has been, and will continue to be, only to do what they can best do. They are no longer in the transportation business, and they have gotten out of the sporting goods business. PepsiCo is now one third beverages, one third snacks, and one third restaurants. They are number one in the chicken category, number one in the Mexican category, and number one in the pizza category. They aren't in the hamburger business because they couldn't buy McDonald's, so they couldn't be number one in this category. Calloway's strategic planning vision, in terms of both the domestic and the international business scene, came into full view when he was interviewed by the CNN business news team of Kandel, Hartley, and Perry.

COLGATE-PALMOLIVE COMPANY'S Asian market was solidified by the purchase of 50 percent of Hawley & Hazel Company. Hawley & Hazel Company markets an extremely popular toothpaste called *Darkie*. Darkie toothpaste bears the logo of a smiling, top-hatted blackface. American critics were quick to charge the company with racism, especially the Interfaith Center for Corporate Responsibility, a nonprofit New York organization of more than 240 church groups. However, according to Colgate research, Asians don't find Darkie brand toothpaste offensive. In fact, Darkie is a big seller in all of the Asian markets.* Subsequently, Colgate has decided to stick with the brand. You work for Colgate-Palmolive Co. and you have just been transferred overseas to oversee their Asian toothpaste merchandising operation. Your wife is a member of one of the churches affiliated with the Interfaith Center for Corporate Responsibility. She had expressed concern that your company continued to sell the Darkie brand overseas. You were also bothered by Colgate's insistence to sell toothpaste with a *logo of a smiling, top-hatted black-face,* but you kept your feelings to yourself. You can either refuse the assignment and jeopardize your career, or you can take the overseas assignment.
What would you do?

*Ann Hagedorn, "Colgate Still Seeking to Placate Critics of Its Darkie Brand," *The Wall Street Journal,* 18 April 1988, 36–37.

Several Grand Strategies

The nature of the strategic planning process has been discussed thus far in general terms. Strategic planning at the corporate level will now be considered in terms of several grand or master strategies that often grow out of the strategic planning process.

INTEGRATION

Integration
The unified control of a number of successive or similar operations.

A commonly used term among organizational strategists is **integration,** the unified control of a number of successive or similar operations. When companies combine, this is integration. Integration also includes a company's taking over a portion of the industrial or commercial process that previously was accomplished by other firms. Frank Lorenzo, chairman of Texas Air, jolted the competition when he took over Continental and Eastern, a move, according to some, calculated to make Lorenzo the King of the Air. Integration need not involve ownership, only control. Thus, supply and marketing contracts are forms of integration. Integration toward the final users of a company's product or service, as when Tandy Corporation opened its Radio Shack stores, is **forward integration.** A company's taking control of any of the sources of its inputs, including raw materials and labor, is **backward integration.** Southland Corporation's 1983 purchase of a petroleum refinery that supplies gasoline to the company's 7-Eleven stores is an example of backward integration. Buying or taking control of

Forward integration
Integration toward the final users of a company's product or service.
Backward integration
A company's taking control of any of the sources of its inputs, including raw materials and labor.

Integration may involve taking another company over. (© Marvin Lewiton/Adams-Russell Electronics Company, Inc.)

Horizontal integration
Buying or taking control of competitors at the same level in the production and marketing process.

competitors at the same level in the production and marketing process is **horizontal integration.** For example, when Firestone, already in the auto service business, took over J. C. Penney's auto service centers, horizontal integration occurred.

Integration can extend beyond the boundaries of the United States, as in the case of AT&T mentioned earlier in the chapter. AT&T's expected joint venture with Italtel, an example of backward integration, will establish AT&T as a major player in the European telecom market.[14]

While recognizing its possible disadvantages, Harrigan lists the following competitive advantages of integration:[15]

• Improved marketing and technological intelligence
• Superior control of the firm's economic environment
• Product differentiation advantages

Each type of integration can be a strategy for accomplishing a different objective. For example, if the objective is to decrease costs of inputs, one possible way to do this would be to buy out suppliers that earn profits producing the inputs, an example of backward integration. If the strategic objective is to obtain additional market share, horizontal integration might be attempted. This was done when 7-Eleven parent Southland Corporation bought the Pak-A-Sak convenience store chain. Southland Corporation provides an example of a single company that was involved in both backward and horizontal integration.

Backward and forward integration are usually designed to accomplish one or both of two purposes: capturing additional profits and obtaining better control. Backward integration does this for the supply channels. Forward integration does this for distribution channels. Obviously, if either a supplier or an intermediate customer is making exorbitant profits, vertical integration may be justified on this basis alone. Vertical integration may also be justified when a company believes it can perform the functions of suppliers or intermediate customers effectively and efficiently. But if better control of sources of supply or distribution channels is the *only* objective, it may be better not to buy the business. There may be better ways to ensure control, such as making franchise agreements with intermediate customers and long-term supply agreements with suppliers. Taking over customers or suppliers is costly, and it often involves a company in businesses with which its managers are unfamiliar.

DIVERSIFICATION

Diversification is increasing the variety of products or services made or sold. Diversification may be conglomerate or concentric. **Conglomerate diversification** simply means the development of businesses unrelated to the firm's current businesses. **Concentric diversification** means the development of businesses related to the firm's current businesses.[16] As a grand strategy, diversification usually has reduction of risk as its purpose. A company that is involved in a number of different businesses avoids having all its eggs in one basket. Ideally, when some of a conglomerate firm's businesses decline, others will be on the increase. Some conglomerate firms are countercyclical, that is, they tend to see increasing sales when the economy in general is declining. Such businesses are hard to find. The do-it-yourselfer hand-tool market is one of the rare exceptions. When times are tough, people tend to repair their own automobiles, for example, and they need tools in order to accomplish tasks such as this.

About the best a conglomerate firm can hope for, in general, is a group of SBUs whose valleys and peaks occur at different times in the business cycle. Of course, diversification into related businesses may not appear to serve the risk-reduction objective as well as conglomerate diversification; however, concentric diversification tends to be more successful in improving profitability.[17] This is probably because the managers of concentrically diversifying firms know something about the businesses they are buying.

Diversification often occurs as a by-product of bargain hunting by corporate strategists. Even if the preference is for a related merger candidate, corporate-level strategists may opt for acquiring an SBU in an entirely different business because it is deemed to be greatly underpriced. Diversification can also be a product of a desire for growth. During the growth fever of the 1970s, many companies, including Textron, Beatrice Foods, and United Technologies, acquired unrelated, though rapidly growing, subsidiaries.

RETRENCHMENT

Another grand strategy, usually applied only when failure is imminent, is retrenchment. **Retrenchment** means the reduction of the size or scope of a firm's activities. Most corporate managements resist this strategy. Although growth is often an objective, retrenchment seldom is. When a retrenchment strategy is followed, the goal is often survival.

When Sanford Sigoloff took over Wickes Corporation in 1981, it was in dire straits. Sigoloff immediately began to sell off unproductive assets, lay off employees, and guide the company through a lengthy retrenchment process. In 1982, Wickes filed for bankruptcy court protection to help in the retrenchment. By 1984 Wickes had again become a profitable though somewhat smaller company, and in January 1985 it emerged from bankruptcy. The company embarked upon renewed expansion efforts in 1986 and 1987, acquiring units of Gulf + Western, Inc. Wickes also earned large profits in attempts to take over National Gypsum Company and Owens-Corning Fiberglas Corporation. The Wickes example

---

Diversification
Increasing the variety of products or services made or sold.

Conglomerate diversification
The development of businesses unrelated to the firm's current businesses.

Concentric diversification
The development of businesses related to the firm's current businesses.

horizontal diversification

same as conglomerate diversification except it's for current customers.

Sell more to present customers

Retrenchment
The reduction of the size or scope of a firm's activities.

also called downsizing

For new customers

Divestiture - you sell
off part of your business

Liquidation - selling off assets
of business, usually done
when business fails

suggests that retrenchment, as a grand strategy, should be considered as viable an option for growth as integration or diversification.

Prompt elimination of losing businesses has been the hallmark of a number of successful managers of large corporations. Of course, smaller companies also often find themselves involved in activities that are unprofitable and that appear likely to remain so. For example, Superior Printing Company, a small printing operation in Columbus, Ohio, was losing money producing standard business forms. When Superior Printing stopped doing the unprofitable work and sold the related equipment, profits improved markedly. In addition, the owner, Jeffrey Shuman, could then pay attention to what he really knew best, limited orders for custom-printed items such as fine letterhead and direct mail circulars.

Portfolio Strategy

Portfolio strategy
The process of
determining how an SBU
will compete in a particular
line of business.
Specifically it pertains to
the mix of business units
and product lines that fit
together in a logical way to
provide maximum
competitive advantage for
the corporation.

Once the grand strategy has been determined, that is, the organization has established the major action by which it intends to achieve its long-term objectives, a portfolio strategy is developed. **Portfolio strategy** is the process of determining how an SBU will compete in a particular line of business. Specifically, portfolio strategy pertains to the mix of business units and product lines that fit together in a logical way to provide maximum competitive advantage for the corporation.[18] For example, an individual may wish to diversify in an investment portfolio with some high-risk stocks, some low-risk stocks, some growth stocks, and perhaps a few income bonds. In much the same way, corporations like to have a balanced mix of SBUs. In general, however, an SBU engages in just one line of business. The BCG matrix is probably the most popular portfolio strategy.

The BCG Matrix

During the 1970s there were a number of attempts to make sense of the process of corporate-level strategic management. Recent research shows that half or more of America's largest corporations practice some kind of formal business portfolio planning.[19] Most of them use a two-dimensional model to display various attributes of a diversified corporation's group of businesses (or SBUs) in a concise way. The best-known way of doing this was developed by the Boston Consulting Group (BCG). The BCG matrix is illustrated in Figure 6.4. Each circle on the BCG matrix represents a different SBU. Although the BCG matrix greatly simplifies the strategic planning process, to show the SBUs of a complex company like General Mills (forty SBUs) would still produce a rather cluttered diagram.

your market share / market share of biggest competitor

PLACING SBUs ON THE BCG MATRIX

The matrix shows three things about each SBU. First, the area of each circle is proportional to the sales revenue of the respective business. For example, SBU-A is the largest in sales among those illustrated. SBU-E has the lowest contribution to the firm's total sales.

Second, the relative position of a circle along the horizontal axis is determined by the respective SBU's market share as compared to that of the largest rival firm. For example, in the personal computer business, Apple is very large, having sold over 500,000 units. As compared to IBM, its major competitor, however, Apple sells fewer than half as many PCs. So IBM would place its personal

FIGURE 6.4 ■
The BCG Matrix

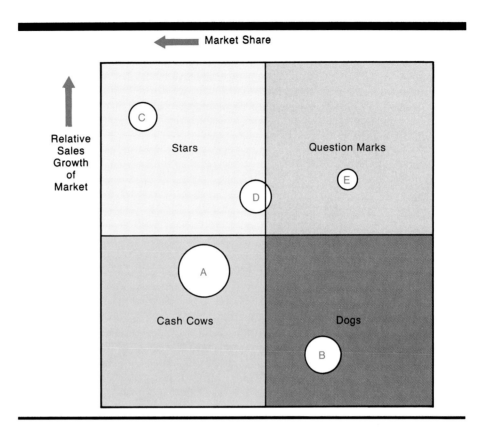

computer business at the extreme left of the BCG matrix, with Apple shown farther to the right.

Third, the vertical axis of the BCG matrix measures the market growth rate of the industry, not the growth rate in sales of the individual business. A business that is gaining market share will show a higher growth rate than the market in general—for example, the growth rate of IBM's personal computer business has recently exceeded 20 percent a year, which is higher than the 10-percent growth rate of the personal computer industry in general. On the BCG matrix, IBM's vertical placement would be according to the lower growth rate of the PC industry in general, not the higher growth rate of its SBU.

STARS, QUESTION MARKS, COWS, AND DOGS

An implicit assumption of the BCG analysis is that, in a given business, market share signifies strength and market growth rate signifies opportunity. This is why GE demands that each division of the company be, or become, dominant in its field on these two dimensions. Referring again to Figure 6.4, businesses with high market shares that are also in high-growth-rate industries are given the favorable designation "Stars." Theoretically, Stars offer the best profit and growth opportunities for the company. SBUs with low market shares in low-growth industries are called "Dogs," because their market shares suggest competitive weakness and because the slow industry growth rates suggest approaching market saturation. The steel industry, for example, is considered by many to be saturated.

The major focus of the BCG analysis is on cash flows. SBUs that hold high market shares in low-growth-rate industries should not be expanding investment rapidly (because there are better investments available). Still, these high-market-share SBUs should be allowed to earn profits, and research suggests that the profitability of such companies depends mostly on employee productivity, capital utilization, and pricing policies, but not added investment.[20] Because there is no need for added investment in the business, the profits can be used to finance the corporation's other businesses, particularly Stars. These high-market, low-growth-rate businesses plot in the lower left-hand quadrant of the BCG matrix and are called "Cash Cows."

Usually when a company enters a new business it will at first have a low market share. If the new business segment is part of a rapidly growing industry, such as the home computer industry, as a new entry into the market it faces an uncertain future. So low-market-share businesses in high-growth industries are called "Question Marks" on the BCG matrix. Typically it requires large amounts of cash to develop them into Stars. Sometimes, however, a Question Mark business is growing so rapidly and is so profitable it can generate the cash flows it requires for its own growth.

IMPLICATIONS OF THE BCG ANALYSIS

The corporate-level strategist who uses the BCG approach must ask, "What are the strategic implications for the corporation as a whole? What does BCG analysis say about resource allocation and about disposition of the various SBUs?" First, BCG proponents argue, the corporation's overall cash flow must be balanced. There should be enough Cash Cows in the business portfolio to fund the cash needs of the Stars and Question Marks, which offer the greatest promise. Second, BCG clearly feels that positions on the BCG matrix imply certain strategies. Sale or liquidation is recommended for Dogs and perhaps weak Cash Cows. Growth is the right path for Question Marks and Stars. Efforts should be made to get back the funds invested by drawing surpluses from Cash Cows.

Some researchers feel that resource allocation is an important but often ignored use of the BCG matrix.[21] In other words, BCG analysis, they feel, should not be limited to buy-sell and invest-disinvest decisions but should also be used to distribute funds within the corporation.

■■ FORMULATING BUSINESS-LEVEL STRATEGY

Strategy formulation at the business level, that is, within the strategic business units, is primarily concerned with how to compete. The three strategies of growth, stability, and retrenchment apply at the business level as well as the corporate level, but they are accomplished through competitive actions rather than by the acquisition or divestment of other business. The three frameworks in which business units formulate strategy are the adaptive strategy typology, Porter's competitive strategies, and the product life cycle.

Adaptive Strategy Typology

The adaptive strategy typology is based on the study of business strategies by Raymond Miles and Charles Snow.[22] The basic idea is that business-level managers

TABLE 6.1 ■ Miles and Snow's Adaptive Strategy Typology

	Strategy	External Environment	Organizational Characteristics
Prospector	Innovate. Find new market opportunities. Grow. Take risks.	Dynamic, growing	Creative, innovative, flexible, decentralized
Defender	Protect turf. Retrench, hold current market.	Stable	Tight control, centralized, production efficiency, low overhead
Analyzer	Maintain current market plus moderate innovation.	Moderate change	Tight control and flexibility, efficient production, creativity
Reactor	No clear strategy. React to specific conditions. Drift.	Any condition	No clear organizational approach; depends on current needs

Source: Based on Raymond E. Miles, Charles C. Snow, Alan D. Meyer, and Henry L. Coleman, Jr., "Organizational Strategy, Structure, and Process," *Academy of Management Review* 3 (1978), pp. 546–562.

seek to formulate strategies that will adapt to, that is, be harmonious with the external environment. Organizations strive to achieve a fit among internal characteristics, strategy, and environmental characteristics. Such strategies allow organizations to successfully adapt to the environment. The four strategies that can be adopted based on the environment are the prospector, defender, analyzer, and reactor strategies. These strategies, their environments, and their internal characteristics are summarized in Table 6.1.

PROSPECTOR

Prospector strategy
A strategy involving innovation, by seeking out new opportunities, taking risks, and expanding.

The **prospector strategy** is to be innovative, by seeking out new opportunities, taking risks, and expanding. The prospector strategy is well suited to a dynamic, growing environment, where creativity is more important than efficiency. The internal organization is flexible and decentralized to facilitate desired innovation. One example of prospector strategy is United Parcel Service, which innovated in both services and production techniques in the rapidly changing overnight mail industry.

DEFENDER

Defender strategy
A strategy that seeks to maintain current market share by holding on to current customers.

The defender strategy is almost the opposite of the prospector in that it is concerned with stability or retrenchment rather than growth. The **defender strategy** seeks to maintain current market share by holding on to current customers. The goal is neither to innovate nor to grow. The defender is concerned with internal efficiency and control to produce reliable products for regular customers. Defenders can be successful, especially when they exist in a declining industry or a stable environment.[23] An example of a defender strategy is PPG (formerly Pittsburgh Plate Glass), which is a very efficient producer in the stable, commodity-analogous chemical industry.

ANALYZER

Analyzer strategy
A strategy that attempts to maintain a stable business while innovating on the fringe.

Analyzers are considered to lie midway between prospectors and defenders. The **analyzer strategy** is to maintain a stable business while innovating on the fringe. Some products are targeted toward stable environments, in which an efficiency strategy designed to retain current customers is employed. Others are targeted toward new, more dynamic environments, where growth is possible. The analyzer attempts to balance efficient production for current line along with the creative development of new product lines. One example is Anheuser-Busch, with its stable beer line and innovation of snack foods as a complementary line.

REACTOR

skip

The reactor has no strategy whatsoever. Rather than defining a strategy to suit a specific environment, reactors respond to environmental threats and opportunities in ad hoc fashion. Reactors take whatever actions seem likely to meet their immediate needs and have no long-term plan for congruence with the external environment. Reactors exist in any environment, but the company may have no strategy or internal characteristics suited to that environment. A reactor strategy seems almost random, because top management has not defined a plan or given the organization an explicit direction. Consequently, failing companies are often the result of reactor strategies. For instance, Schlitz Brewing Company suffered a period during which it dropped from first to seventh in the brewing industry, due to poor strategic decisions.

Porter's Competitive Strategies

Michael E. Porter studied a number of business organizations and proposed three effective business-level strategies: differentiation, cost leadership, and focus.[24] The organizational characteristics associated with each strategy are summarized in Table 6.2.

Differentiation strategy
A strategy that involves an attempt to distinguish the firm's products or services from others in the industry.

DIFFERENTIATION

The **differentiation strategy** involves an attempt to distinguish the firm's products or services from others in the industry. The organization may use such

---

TABLE 6.2 ■ Organizational Characteristics for Porter's Competitive Strategies

Strategy	Commonly Required Skills and Resources	Common Organizational Requirements
Differentiation	Strong marketing abilities Product engineering Creative flair Strong capability in basic research Corporate reputation for quality or technological leadership	Strong coordination among functions in R&D, product development, and marketing Subjective measurement and incentives instead of quantitative measures Amenities to attract highly skilled labor, scientists, or creative people
Cost leadership	Sustained capital investment and access to capital Process engineering skills Intense supervision of labor Products designed for ease in manufacture Low-cost distribution system	Tight cost control Frequent, detailed control reports Structured organization and responsibilities Incentives based on meeting strict quantitative targets
Focus	Combination of the above policies directed at the particular strategic target	Combination of the above policies directed at the regular strategic target

Source: Reprinted with permission of The Free Press, a division of Macmillan, Inc., from COMPETITIVE STRATEGY: Techniques for Analyzing Industries and Competitors by Michael E. Porter. Copyright © 1980 by The Free Press.

cheap generic products undermine these strategies sometimes

skills and resources as advertising, distinctive product features, exceptional service, and technology to achieve a product that could be perceived as unique. Successful differentiation strategy is often profitable because customers will usually be loyal and will pay high prices for the product. Examples of products that have benefited from a differentiation strategy include Porsche automobiles, Maytag appliances, and Ralph Lauren Polo clothing, all of which are perceived as distinctive in their markets.

COST LEADERSHIP

Cost leadership strategy
A strategy in which the organization aggressively seeks efficient facilities, pursues cost reductions, and uses tight cost controls to produce products more efficiently than competitors.

Focus strategy
A strategy in which the organization concentrates on a specific regional market, product line, or buyer group.

Cost leadership strategy means that the organization aggressively seeks efficient facilities, pursues cost reductions, and uses tight cost controls to produce products more efficiently than competitors. A low-cost position means that the company can undercut competitors' prices and still offer comparable quality and earn a reasonable profit. Quality Inns is a low-priced alternative to lodging outlets such as Holiday Inns and Ramada Inns.

FOCUS

In the **focus strategy,** the organization concentrates on a specific regional market, product line, or buyer group. When focusing on a single market segment, the company may use either a differentiation or a low-cost approach, but only for that narrow market. The company may be seeking either a competitive cost advantage or a perceived differentiation in the target segment.

Porter found that many businesses did not consciously adopt one of these three strategies and therefore were stuck in the middle of the pack with no strategic advantage. Without a strategic advantage, these businesses earned below-average profits compared to those that used differentiation, cost leadership, or focus strategies and therefore were not in a position to compete successfully. There is some similarity between Porter's strategies and Miles and Snow's adaptive typology. The differentiation strategy is similar to the prospector, the low-cost strategy is similar to the defender, and the focus strategy is similar to the analyzer, which adopts a focus strategy appropriate for each product line. The reactor strategy, which is really not a strategy at all, is similar to that adopted by those middle-of-the-pack organizations that could not attain strategic advantage.

Product Life Cycle

Product life cycle
The pattern of sales volume that all products follow and that includes the stages of introduction, growth, maturity, and decline.

The pattern of sales volume that all products follow and that includes the stages of introduction, growth, maturity, and decline is referred to as **product life cycle.** Corporate strategists who value stability in sales and earnings will tend to diversify among businesses, of course. But to gain maximum benefit from diversification, they will also tend to promote a balance of products and services across product life cycle stages. Figure 6.5 illustrates the product life cycle curve. Certainly every product must go through the life cycle stages; however, some products get a new lease on life. For example, a few years ago, Arm & Hammer baking soda, well into the decline phase of the product life cycle, saw renewed growth in response to a national advertising campaign touting its multiple uses.

Still, for most products, the cycle is rather consistent, with variation only in the length of the various stages and the amount of sales and profits earned in each stage. Because of this, many companies, especially consumer goods

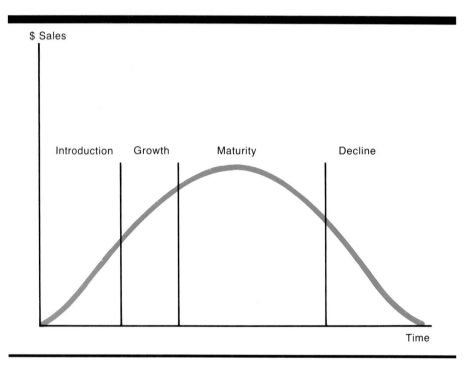

companies such as Procter & Gamble, try to have a certain number of products or services in each stage of the product life cycle at all times. As one product goes into the decline stage, another is experiencing sales growth, and the company has a stable source of profits from those products in the mature stage.

■ FORMULATING FUNCTIONAL-LEVEL STRATEGY

Functional-level strategies are the action plans adopted by the major functional departments to support the execution of a business-level strategy. Major organizational functions include marketing, production, finance, personnel, and research and development. For example, strategic planning for the finance function at GE involves establishing budgeting, accounting, and investment policies and the allocation of SBU cash flows. In the personnel area, policies for compensation, hiring and firing, training, and personnel planning are of strategic concern. Strategic planning is not concerned with day-to-day supervision; it mainly involves providing general, longer-range direction and guidance. Many more corporations are expanding their strategic planning range beyond the domestic front to the international arena. Coca-Cola, Kentucky Fried Chicken, Bausch & Lomb, Johnson & Johnson, RJR Nabisco, Seagram, and Procter & Gamble have established strategic joint partnerships with the Chinese. Increasingly, companies are seeking potential overseas markets and making this goal part of their organizational mission. Senior managers in these departments adopt strategies that are coordinated with the business-level strategy to achieve the organization's strategic goals.[25]

Consider a company that has adopted a prospector strategy and is introducing new products that are expected to experience rapid growth in the early stages of the life cycle. The personnel department should adopt a strategy appropriate for growth, which would mean recruiting additional personnel and training middle managers for movement into new positions. The marketing department should undertake test marketing, aggressive advertising campaigns, and induce product trials by consumers. The finance department should adopt plans to borrow money, handle large cash investments, and authorize construction of new production facilities.

A company with mature products or an analyzer strategy will have different functional strategies. The personnel department should develop strategies for retaining and developing a stable work force, including transfers, advancements, and incentives for efficiency and safety. Marketing should stress brand loyalty and the development of established, reliable distribution channels. Production should maintain long production runs, routinization, and cost reduction. Finance should focus on net cash flows and positive cash balances. Basically, functional-level strategies should support the execution of business-level strategies by developing an effective mix of the major organizational functions.

SUMMARY

Strategic planning is the determination of overall organizational purposes and objectives and how they are to be achieved. Corporate-level strategic planning is the process of defining the overall character and purpose of the organization, the businesses it will enter and leave, and how resources will be distributed among those businesses. Strategy formulation within the strategic business units, at the business level, is primarily concerned with how to compete. Strategy at the functional level is the action plans adopted by the major functional departments to support the execution of business-level strategy. Many companies use in-house organizational strategists to assist and advise managers in strategic planning.

The strategic planning process is a structured technique comprised of four steps. Basically it is a derivative of the SWOT—strengths, weaknesses, opportunities, and threats—framework, which affects organizational performance. Once the strategic plan is developed, the next step is to implement the plan.

Corporate-level strategy typically concerns the mix and utilization of business divisions called strategic business units (SBUs). One SBU has a unique mission, product line, competitors, and markets relative to other SBUs in the corporation. Executives in charge of the entire corporation generally define an overall strategic direction—called a grand strategy—and then develop a portfolio of strategic business units to carry out the grand strategy.

Portfolio strategy is the process of determining how an SBU will compete in a particular line of business. Specifically, portfolio strategy pertains to the mix of business units and product lines that fit together in a logical way to provide maximum competitive advantage for the corporation. Half or more of America's largest corporations practice some kind of formal business portfolio planning. Most of them use a two-dimensional model to display various attributes of a diversified corporation's group of businesses (or SBUs) in a concise way. The best-known is the matrix developed by the Boston Consulting Group (BCG).

The three frameworks in which business units formulate strategy are the adaptive typology, Porter's competitive strategies, and the product life cycle. Functional-level strategies are the action plans adopted by major functional departments to support the execution of business-level strategy. Senior managers adopt strategies that are coordinated with the business-level strategy to achieve the organization's strategic goals.

REVIEW QUESTIONS

1. Define strategic planning. What is a strategic business unit?
2. Distinguish among corporate-level strategic planning, business-level strategic planning, and functional-level strategic planning.
3. Who are the organizational strategists?
4. List and briefly describe each step in the strategic planning process.
5. Describe the concept of satisficing as suggested by Herbert Simon.
6. Identify and briefly describe the grand or master strategies that grow out of the strategic planning process.
7. Briefly describe the following business-level strategies:
   a. Adaptive strategy typology
   b. Porter's competitive strategy
   c. Product life cycle

KEY TERMS

strategic planning
corporate-level strategic
   planning
strategic business unit
organizational mission
business-level strategic
   planning
functional-level strategic
   planning
strategic planning staff
   specialists

organizational strategists
integration
forward integration
backward integration
horizontal integration
diversification
conglomerate
   diversification
concentric diversification

retrenchment
portfolio strategy
prospector strategy
defender strategy
analyzer strategy
differentiation strategy
cost leadership strategy
focus strategy
product life cycle

CASE STUDY — MASTER HARDWARE

MASTER HARDWARE STORES is a chain of twelve retail outlets located in small towns in northern Kentucky and southern Ohio. The parent corporation, Master Merchandisers, Inc., is a Kentucky corporation owned by the Booker family of Louisville. The Bookers, led by Beatrice, who was eighty-five years old in 1987, have steadfastly refused to vary from the plan that Beatrice found successful when the first Master Hardware stores were opened during the 1940s. The plan is simple: Only one store is opened in each town, and the towns must be between 8,000 and 15,000 population at the time. Inventories are tightly controlled, and no item is stocked unless it turns at least four times a year. Each store is managed by a carefully selected local citizen who is paid 50 percent of the profits the store generates. All purchasing is done by the central office in Louisville, although most items are shipped directly from hardware wholesalers and manufacturers to the individual stores. The store buildings are rented. After an initial infusion of capital, each store is required to pay its own way. If it does not, it is closed.

Master Merchandisers had opened no new stores for several years, although the existing stores were quite profitable. The company had never done much borrowing, so the high profits resulted in increasing cash balances, even after paying family members director's fees, salaries, and so forth.

Until 1984, the excess funds were invested in U.S. Treasury securities, which are safe but yield low returns. That year, Beatrice Booker agreed with the board of directors—made up of two of her

sons, a nephew, and a niece—that the company should go into the restaurant business. The Bookers decided that Master Merchandisers would invest $3 million and build at least five new seafood restaurants. They would feature pond-raised catfish and would be located in towns similar to those where the Master Hardware stores were.

The restaurant business was separately incorporated as Catfish Master Restaurants, Inc. By mid-1985 three Catfish Master Restaurants were opened. The system was patterned as much as possible after the Master Hardware chain. Restaurant managers were paid on a percentage of the profit basis. Purchasing was done centrally, and each restaurant was required to support itself after the initial investment. It became clear within a year, however, that the first two restaurants would have to be closed unless additional funds were provided. The Bookers put up an additional $50,000 to help those two restaurants stay open, but both were still unprofitable two years later.

QUESTIONS

1. As clearly as you can, state what you believe to be the corporate mission of Master Merchandisers, Inc.
2. List the strategies discussed in the case that you would consider SBU-level strategies and the ones that are corporate-level strategies. Explain your answer.
3. What kind of integration occurred when Master Merchandisers went into the restaurant business? Discuss.
4. Do you believe that the Booker family is likely to be successful in the restaurant business? Why or why not?

CASE STUDY — A STRATEGIC MANAGEMENT CONSULTANT

ON A LATE EVENING FLIGHT from Seattle to Phoenix, I had the good fortune of sitting beside a gentleman who introduced himself as "a management consultant who helps companies develop strategies for overcoming personnel problems." His name was Joe Zuber. Joe said that most of his clients were banks, although he had

been employed by businesses as diverse as hospitals, contractors, and computer firms.

I asked him to describe a typical consulting situation for me. He said that he was a member of a three-person firm headquartered in Denver, which advertised nationally in *The Wall Street Journal* and several other business publications.

When his office in Denver was contacted by a potential client, one of the three principals would make an initial sales pitch by telephone.

In a recent case, Joe had worked with a large savings and loan company in Phoenix. In fact, he was on his way back there at the time to submit his final report. What he had done for the bank was conduct a series of interviews with the bank's fourteen managers, starting with the chief executive and working on down. Each manager was asked to identify any problems or opportunities and to suggest how the company might go about addressing them.

Before talking to anyone other than the chief executive, Joe asked that a memorandum be prepared saying that he had been retained to help the company seek ways to improve its operations. After an initial series of interviews, each one taking about an hour, Joe prepared an interim report. With the president's permission, he met with the managers as a group and discussed the conflicts and frustrations that had been mentioned without identifying the managers involved. He also discussed each opportunity that had been stated by as many as two of the managers.

I asked Joe to give me an example of an opportunity and a problem. He said, "The major problem which came up time and again, was that the chief executive was too involved in the details of the operation and didn't give his subordinates as much authority as their abilities justified." There was no consensus about the opportunities. Four of the fifteen managers said that they should move into commercial banking, that is, short- and

intermediate-term business loans and business checking accounts. The banking industry had recently been deregulated, and banks and savings and loan companies were often crossing over onto one another's turf.

Joe said that after the initial series of interviews and the interim report, he visited again with several of the managers whom he considered to be especially well informed. They again went over the problems and opportunities that had received some agreement. After that, he had gone back to the main office in Denver to prepare his final report. His intention, he said, was to clear the report with the chief executive and then ask for another meeting of all the managers. This meeting would preferably be held in the evening, and a meal would be served. He expected the meeting to last for several hours.

There was much more that I wanted to ask Joe, but we were interrupted by the flight attendant telling us we were about to land in Phoenix. It was not until then that Joe asked me what my business was. Upon learning that I was a management professor, he asked if we might keep in touch. I assured him that I would like that.

QUESTIONS
1. Explain why you think a bank might hire a consultant like Joe Zuber when it has fifteen managers on the permanent payroll.
2. What do you believe is likely to happen when the chief executive receives the final report highlighting his own tendency to get too much involved in detail and to withhold authority from his subordinates?

EXPERIENTIAL EXERCISE

This exercise is designed to give participants experience in dealing with some of the planning requirements faced by a typical manager. Students will also be exposed to some of the activities that managers confront on a daily basis. The old axiom, "plan your work and work your plan," will probably have new meaning after this exercise.

You are the manager of operations at a large canning plant. Your plant produces several lines of canned food products, which are shipped to wholesale distributors nationwide. Your responsibilities are involved with the planning and scheduling of plant operations.

It is Monday morning, August 30. You have just returned from a week-long corporate executives' meeting at the home office. The meeting was attended by all operations managers from every one of the company's plants. You returned with notes from the meeting and other materials you were given concerning the company's goals and plans for the next six months. When you arrive at your office (an hour early), you find your in-basket full of notes, messages, and other correspondence.

The material provided to participants represents your notes and information from the meeting, plus what was in your in-basket. You must go through these and be prepared for the meeting the plant manager has scheduled for 8:00 A.M. It is now 7:30 A.M. Remember, you need to deal with some items immediately, some later today, and some tomorrow or later in the week, or some other time. You will need to sort, prioritize, and set up your plan of activities. Participants will sort the material and information according to some priority in order to properly sequence handling. After sorting, participants can address each item concerning the action they plan to take. The participants will do the following on each item:

1. Note when it is to be handled.
2. Note who is to handle it, if not themselves.
3. Note what is to be done or who is to be informed.
4. If a meeting is to be called, set up an agenda.
5. If a memo or notice is to be sent out, write it out.

Your instructor will provide the participants with the additional information necessary to participate.

NOTES

1. This discussion is a composite from a number of popular articles appearing in 1983 and 1984, among them: Howard Banks, "General Electric—Going with the Winners," *Forbes,* 26 March 1984, 97–106; N. Nelson-Horchtes, "GE Builds a High-Tech Arsenal," *Industry Week,* 3 October 1983, 49–50; N. Snyderman, "GE Is Doing the Things the U.S. Must Do to Be Competitive," *Electronic News,* suppl. B, 3 October 1983; and "A New P/E for the New GE," *Fortune,* 9 January 1984, 114.

2. Harris Collingwood, "AT&T Gets Its Toe in the Boot," *Business Week,* 13 February 1989.

3. Frederick W. Gluck, "A Fresh Look at Strategic Management," *Journal of Business Strategy* 6 (Fall 1985), 4–19.

4. Quoted in Charles H. Granger, "The Hierarchy of Objectives," *Harvard Business Review* 42, no. 3 (May–June 1964): 63–74.

5. Richard B. Robinson, Jr., "The Importance of 'Outsiders' in Small Firm Strategic Planning," *Academy of Management Journal* 25 (March 1982): 80–93.

6. James J. Polyczynski and Jason Leniski, "Inviting Front-Line Managers into the Strategic-Planning and Decision-Making Process," *Appalachian Business Review* 9 (1982): 2–5.

7. Ian Wilson, "The Strategic Management Technology: Corporate Fad of Strategic Necessity," *Long-Range Planning* 19, no. 2 (April 1986): 21–22.

8. Frederick Gluck, Stephen Kaufman, and A. Steven Walleck, "The Four Phases of Strategic Management," *Journal of Business Strategy* 2 (Winter 1982): 11–12.

9. Herbert A. Simon, *The New Science of Management Decision* (New York: Harper & Row, 1960).

10. L. J. Bourgeois III and David R. Brodwin, "Strategic Implementation: Five Approaches to an Elusive Phenomenon," *Strategic Management Journal* 5 (1984):241–264; and Anil K. Gupta and V. Govindarajan, "Business Unit Strategy, Managerial Characteristics, and Business Unit Effectiveness at Strategy Implementation," *Academy of Management Journal* (1984): 25–41.

11. Jay R. Galbraith and Robert K. Kazanjian, *Strategy Implementation: Structure, Systems and Process,* 2d ed. (St. Paul, Minn.: West, 1986).

12. Alfred V. Chandler, *Strategies and Structures* (Cambridge, Mass.: MIT Press, 1962).

13. Gupta and Govindarajan, "Business Unit Strategy," and Bourgeois and Brodwin, "Strategic Implementation."

14. Harris Collingwood, "In Business This Week," *Business Week,* 13 February 1989, 38.

15. Kathryn Rudie Harrigan, "A Framework for Looking at Vertical Integration," *Journal of Business Strategy* 3 (Winter 1983): 30–37.

16. In a technical sense, the term *related diversification* is better than *concentric diversification,* but the latter has found more widespread use.

17. Richard A. Bettis, "Performance Differences in Related and Unrelated Diversified Firms," *Strategic Management Journal* 2 (October–December 1981): 379–393.

18. Richard L. Daft, *Management* (New York: The Dryden Press, 1988), 140.

19. Philippe Haspeslagh, "Portfolio Planning: Uses and Limits," *Harvard Business Review* 60 (January–February 1982): 58–73.

20. Ian C. MacMillan, Donald C. Hambrick, and Diana L. Day, "The Product Portfolio and Profitability: A PIMS-Based Analysis of Industrial-Product Businesses," *Academy of Management Journal* 25 (December 1982): 733–755.

21. Frederick Gluck, "The Dilemmas of Resource Allocation," *Journal of Business Strategy* (Fall 1981), 67–71; and Philippe Haspeslagh, "Portfolio Planning," 58–73.

22. Raymond E. Miles and Charles C. Snow, *Organizational Strategy, Structure, and Process* (New York: McGraw-Hill, 1978).

23. Donald C. Hambrick, "Some Tests of the Effectiveness and Functional Attributes of Miles and Snow's Strategic Types," *Academy of Management Journal* 26 (1983): 5–26.
24. Michael E. Porter, *Competitive Strategy* (New York: Free Press, 1980), 36–46.
25. Harold W. Fox, "A Framework for Functional Coordination," *Atlanta Economic Review* (now *Business Magazine*) (November–December 1973).

REFERENCES

Athos, Anthony G., and Richard T. Pascale. *The Art of Japanese Management: Applications for American Executives.* New York: Simon & Schuster, 1981.

Bettis, Richard A. "Performance Differences in Related and Unrelated Diversified Firms." *Strategic Management Journal* 2 (October–December 1981): 379–393.

Bowman, Edward H. "Risk/Return Paradox for Strategic Management." *Sloan Management Review* 21 (Spring 1980): 17–31.

Bracker, J. S., and J. N. Nelson. "Planning and Financial Performance of Small, Mature Firms." *Strategic Management Journal* 7, no. 6 (December 1986): 503–522.

Cross, Richard Hunter, III. "Strategic Planning: What It Can and Can't Do." *SAM Advanced Management Journal* 52 (Winter 1987): 13–16.

Duncan, Jack W. "When Necessity Becomes a Virtue: Don't Get Too Cynical about Strategy." *Journal of General Management* 13 (Winter 1987): 28–45.

Durack, Elmer, II. "Corporate Business and Human Resources Planning Practices: Strategic Issues and Concerns." *Organizational Dynamics* 15 (Summer 1986): 73–87.

Edelhart, Mike. "Brushing Up on Strategic Systems." *PC Week* 5 (7 June 1988): 815–816.

Fiegenbaum, Avi, John McGee, and Howard Thomas. "Exploring the Linkage Between Strategic Groups and Competitive Strategy." *International Studies of Management & Organization* 18 (Spring 1988): 6–25.

Fox, H. W. "Frontiers of Strategic Planning: Intuition or Formal Models." *Management Review* 70 (April 1981): 44–50.

Galbraith, John Kenneth. "The New, Improved Industrial State: The Genius of the Modern Corporation Is Not in Its Command But in Its Combination of Diverse Intelligence for Decisions Far Beyond the Reach of Any Individual." *Business Month* 131 (January 1988): 38–40.

Gluck, Frederick. "The Dilemmas of Resource Allocation." *Journal of Business Strategy* (Fall 1981): 67–71.

Gluck, Frederick, Stephen Kaufman, and A. Steven Walleck. "The Four Phases of Strategic Management." *Journal of Business Strategy* 2 (Winter 1982): 11–12.

Harrigan, Kathryn Rudie. "A Framework for Looking at Vertical Integration." *Journal of Business Strategy* 3 (Winter 1983): 30–37.

Haspeslagh, Philippe. "Portfolio Planning: Uses and Limits." *Harvard Business Review* 60 (January–February 1982): 58–73.

Hax, Arnoldo C., and Nicolas S. Mailuf. "The Concept of Strategy and the Strategy Formation Process." *Interfaces* 18 (May–June 1988): 99–109.

Isenberg, Daniel J. "The Tactics of Strategic Opportunism." *Harvard Business Review* 65 (March–April 1987): 92–97.

Kenny, Graham K., Richard J. Butler, David J. Hickson, David Gray, Geoffrey R. Mallory, and David D. Wilson. "Strategic Decision Making: Influence Patterns in Public and Private Sector Organizations." *Human Relations* 10 (September 1987): 613–622.

MacMillan, Ian C., Donald C. Hambrick, and Diana L. Day. "The Product Portfolio and Profitability: A PIMS-Based Analysis of Industrial-Product Businesses." *Academy of Management Journal* 25 (December 1982): 733–755.

Marcus, Alfred A. "Responses to Externally Induced Innovation: Their Effects on Organizational Performance." *Strategic Management Journal* 9 (July–August 1988): 387–402.

Morrisey, George L. "Who Needs a Mission Statement? You Do." *Training and Development Journal* 42 (March 1988): 50–52.

Paquette, Laurence, and Thomas Kida. "The Effect of Decision Strategy and Task Complexity on Decision Performance." *Organizational Behavior & Human Decision Processes* 41 (February 1988): 128–142.

Peters, Thomas J., and Robert H. Waterman, Jr. *In Search of Excellence.* New York: Harper & Row, 1982.

Polyczynski, James J., and Jason Leniski. "Inviting Front-Line Managers into the Strategic Planning and Decision Making Process." *Appalachian Business Review* 9 (1982): 2–5.

Pryor, Austin K., and William K. Foster. "The Strategic Management of Innovation." *Journal of Business Strategy* 7 (Summer 1986): 38–42.

Robinson, Richard B., Jr. "The Importance of 'Outsiders' in Small Firm Strategic Planning." *Academy of Management Journal* 25 (March 1982): 80–93.

Ross, Joel E., and Ronnie Silverblatt. "Developing the Strategic Plan." *Industrial Marketing Management* 16 (May 1987): 103–110.

Sass, C. Joseph, and Teresa A. Keefe. "MIS for Strategic Planning and a Competitive Edge." *Journal of Systems Management* 39 (June 1988): 14–17.

Schilit, Warren Keith. "Upward Influence Activity in Strategic Decision Making." *Group & Organization Studies* 12 (September 1987): 343–368.

Shaffer, James C. "Mission Statements: Why Have Them? (Corporate Mission Statements)." *Communication World* 4 (June 1987): 14–16.

Tang, Ming-Je. "An Economic Perspective on Escalating Commitment." *Strategic Management Journal* 9 (Summer 1988): 79–92.

Thackray, John. "The Fall of Corporate Planning." *Management Today* (July 1986): 17.

Uttal, Bro. "The Corporate Culture Vultures." *Fortune* (17 October 1983): 66–72.

Weigelt, Keith, and Ian MacMillan. "An Interactive Strategic Analysis Framework." *Strategic Management Journal* 9 (Summer 1988): 27–40.

Wilson, Ian. "The Strategic Management Technology: Corporate Fad of Strategic Necessity." *Long-Range Planning* 19, no. 2 (April 1986): 21–22.

CHAPTER

7

Chapter Outline

Managerial Decision Making

Learning Objectives

After completing this chapter students should be able to

1. Define decision making, identify the steps in the decision-making process, and identify major factors that can have an impact on managerial decision making.
2. Explain the scientific method of decision making and describe the group methods used in decision making.
3. Explain the requirements that must be present before a decision problem can exist and relate how models are used in decision making.
4. Describe barriers to effective decision making, participation and the decision-making process, and advantages and disadvantages of group decision making.

FRED AND TERRY RANDALL were puzzled about what to do. This married couple had operated The Craft Cottage for four years and were thinking of expanding. Two similar businesses were available for purchase in Jefferson City, where The Craft Cottage was located. Not only would buying one of them eliminate a competitor, it would also be a way of growing quickly.

The inventory at The Craft Cottage included handmade craft items, artists' supplies, and prints of original paintings and etchings. The prints were supposedly purchased for their investment value, although Fred and Terry believed most customers bought the prints mainly for their decorative appeal. The Craft Cottage also offered picture-framing services and painting lessons.

The Randalls had started the business in their garage, converting it to a store and later adding a woodworking shop to the back. The Craft Cottage was in one of the better residential areas of town, one block off a state highway and less than a mile from Chancellor State University. The Randalls identified their primary customers as wives of educators and other professionals, mostly in the twenty-five to thirty-five age range. They felt that the noncommercial location and atmosphere of The Craft Cottage had positive appeal to these customers.

Fred commented, "It is difficult to get good help." Except for the Randalls, all the employees worked part-time. The bookkeeper was a doctoral candidate in history, who had no formal training in accounting and who worked mainly at her convenience. Two or three college students were employed to help in woodworking and framing as well as janitorial and yard work.

The Randalls viewed word-of-mouth and direct mail as their most effective forms of advertising. They distributed a newsletter every two months or so, mainly to people who had been in the store. The Craft Cottage also placed ads in local newspapers, including the high school and university papers. The Randalls had resolved to drop their yellow pages listings because they considered them ineffective and thought they invited calls for "stupid things."

The Craft Cottage had reported losses totaling $18,000 in its first four years of operation. The Randalls had hoped to break even within five years, but that seemed unlikely, because fourth-year losses were the highest ever. Fred Randall received a military pension, but most of the family savings were tied up in the business. In fact, inventory alone had recently exceeded $40,000, most of it in original works on paper. The true value of these prints was uncertain.

The Randalls knew they would have to borrow to buy either of the businesses they were considering, and this was of concern to them. One owner, the leading seller of prints in town, wanted $125,000 for his frame shop and sales operation. The other firm sold art supplies and did framing. The Randalls thought they could buy that store for $35,000. Neither price included the building, which would have to be purchased or leased separately.[1] ■

T HE CRAFT COTTAGE story suggests the extensive need for decision making in business. **Decision making** is the process of generating and evaluating alternatives and making choices among them. The need for decision making is so pervasive that decision making may be considered synonymous with managing. It is a large portion of the manager's job. Every employed person is required to engage in decision-making activities as part of the work performed. College professors make decisions about the nature of the information they will present to their students. Physicians diagnose problems and prescribe treatments. Scientists formulate hypotheses and select experiments for testing them.

Decisions made by professional managers may be no more or less crucial than those of the physicians or scientists. However, a managerial decision typically affects a great number of people—customers, stockholders, employees, and the general public. Professional managers see the results of their decisions reflected in the firm's earnings report, the welfare of employees, and the economic health of the community and the country. As Levitt contends, unlike lawyers, scientists, or physicians, "the manager is judged not for what he knows about the work that is done in his field, but by how well he actually does the work."[2] To survive and prosper, the manager must be able to make professional decisions.

In this chapter, the decision-making process and several important factors that affect decision making are discussed first. Next, the scientific method and group methods of decision making are described. Then, the requirements for decision making are presented, followed by a discussion of the use of models in decision making and a review of the barriers to effective decision making. The final sections are devoted to helping readers understand how worker participation is involved in the decision-making process and the advantages and disadvantages of group decision making.

THE DECISION-MAKING PROCESS

Companies do not want dynamic failures; they want individuals who are properly equipped to make decisions. This does not mean that the managers must be right 100 percent of the time; no one is perfect. It does suggest that successful managers have a higher batting average than less successful managers.

Chrysler Chairman Lee A. Iacocca usually distinguishes himself as an effective decision maker. After all, Iacocca is the savior of the Chrysler Corporation. He is the same guy who decided to purchase the hot-selling Jeep. But in 1984 Iacocca struck a deal with his buddy Alejando de Tomaso, the boss of Maserati. This was an effort to upgrade Chrysler's image and get a toehold in Europe in the luxury two-passenger coupe market. The Chrysler TC turned out to be an inelegantly styled Chrysler with a Maserati emblem. Car magazines complained that the new car is under-powered, noisy, and marred by cheap plastic finishes. "Such inattention to detail in a car that cost almost as much as the Porsche 944," raged *Automobile Magazine* in June 1988, "is grotesque—like finding a lava lamp in William F. Buckley's reading room."[3] Obviously, the car that Iacocca envisioned is not the one that was produced by the joint effort of Chrysler-Maserati. In 1988, Chrysler dropped an option to increase their Maserati stake to 51 percent, modified TC production plans, and killed other projects. This

FIGURE 7.1 ■
The Decision-Making
Process

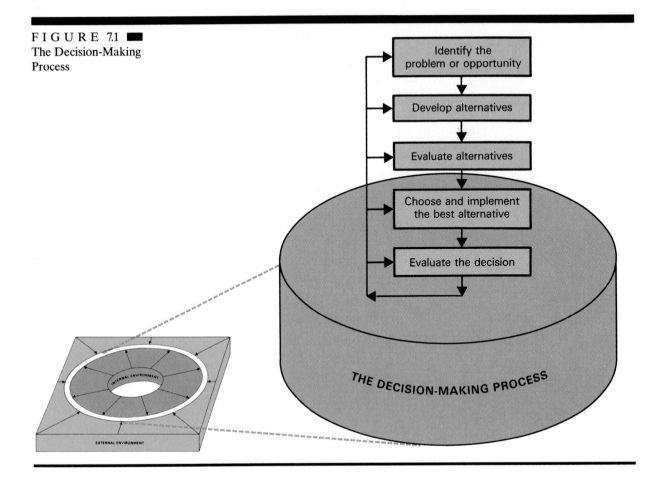

action indicates that Iacocca realizes that his original decision was obviously flawed and is a probable attempt to cut his losses. However, Iacocca is still a successful manager, because, among other attributes, he normally makes quality decisions.

Managers are evaluated primarily on the results of their decisions. Some apparently successful executives follow an intuitive approach to decision making, basing their decisions on hunches and gut feelings. However, a more formalized approach to decision making, such as that illustrated in Figure 7.1, can usually increase a manager's batting average.

The implementation of a decision does not complete the decision-making process. The arrows in the decision-making process model indicate that there is constant reevaluation and feedback to every phase of decision making. The outcome—whether good or bad—provides information that can contribute to future decisions. The environment of decision making and the steps in the process are discussed below.

Environmental Factors

Decision making does not occur in a vacuum. Notice in Figure 7.1 that the elements of the organization's external environment are the same as those identified in Chapter 3. Variations in any of these factors can affect decision making. In a similar manner, the internal environment helps determine what decisions are made and who makes them. For instance, the Randalls have problems with their competitors, and also with their approach to inventory control.

Identify the Problem or Opportunity

Some people view decision making only as problem solving; however, problems are usually better treated as opportunities. The first step in the decision-making process should be to look more for decision-making opportunities than for problems. Eventually problems will make themselves evident. Often the distinction between a problem and an opportunity is not clear.

In defining a problem (or opportunity), it is important to consider not just the problem itself but the underlying causes. For instance, the problem may be an increased number of defects coming off a production line. Untrained workers may have been assigned to the department. Maintenance people may have been doing a poor job of servicing the equipment. Or materials may have been defective, due to sloppy purchasing practices. The causes of a problem must be understood before the problem can be corrected.

Often, solving a problem or taking advantage of an opportunity requires working with other departments. Defining the problem in terms of what caused it, or seeing the problem as an opportunity, will help identify the persons and groups who need to be involved. If a problem is due to poor maintenance, for instance, it may be necessary to involve the maintenance supervisor in deciding how to correct it.

Develop Alternatives

A problem can usually be "solved" in any of a number of ways. The only alternative that really counts, of course, is the one judged best among those considered. At this point in the decision-making process, however, it is important to consider all feasible ways by which a problem can be solved. Naturally, the number of alternatives generated is limited by the amount of time available for the decision, as well as by the importance of the decision itself. Obviously, however, the best alternative cannot be chosen if no one thinks of it. Until all alternatives have been evaluated, it is best not to eliminate any one from consideration.

Evaluate Alternatives

Usually advantages and disadvantages can be found in every possible solution. One alternative may be clearly superior, but it may also have some weak points. It is essential that managers realistically appraise arguments for or against a particular alternative. Sometimes an idea sounds good initially, but taking time to weigh the pros and cons of alternatives usually pays off; it prevents the manager from having to say, "I wish I had put more effort into making that decision."

There are a number of ways of evaluating alternatives. One way is to list the pros and cons of each. This often results in one alternative being identified as clearly superior to the others. Care should be taken, however, not to place too much emphasis on the number of pros and cons, but rather to consider the overall importance of those relating to each alternative.

Another way to evaluate alternatives is to determine the expected payoff associated with each alternative. This "payoff relationship," as discussed later on in this chapter, requires consideration of both costs and benefits. It is also necessary to consider the probability of occurrence of the expected payoff. For example, an alternative that offers a 50-percent probability of a $1 million payoff generally will be chosen over one with a 10-percent probability of a $2 million payoff. There are mathematical techniques available to calculate expected payoffs, but these are beyond the scope of this chapter.

Choose and Implement the Best Alternative

The ability to select the best course of action from several possible alternatives often separates successful managers from less successful ones. The alternative offering the highest promise of attaining the objective, taking into consideration the overall situation, should be selected. This step may sound easy, but for managers it is the toughest part of their job. However sophisticated the selection technique followed, a manager can never be sure that the results of a decision will be favorable. Fear of making a wrong decision sometimes causes a manager to make no decision at all. It is no wonder that relatively high salaries are paid to managers who have a reputation for having the fortitude to make decisions and for making correct ones most of the time. It is easy to be a Monday morning quarterback and criticize the coach's decisions. The coach, however, has to make decisions on the football field under pressure of time; no coach has the luxury of knowing how those decisions will turn out. Many thought it wrong when Chrysler managers received large bonuses after having seen their company through its recent crisis, but the bonuses may have been justified by the difficulty of the decisions these managers had to make. If those decisions had been wrong, the

The ability to select the best course of action often separates successful managers from unsuccessful ones.
(© Lawrence Migdale/Photo Researchers, Inc.)

YOU ARE THE personnel director for a manufacturing firm that is involved in a major change in direction. This will mean hiring young energetic workers, and you have some difficult decisions to make. The firm is building two new technologically advanced plants in Tennessee and will close four of the five old-line plants in Michigan and Ohio. John Morrow, a fifty-six-year-old production worker, who has been with your firm ten years, is, in your opinion, not capable of being retrained, but he is not old enough to receive any retirement benefits. You can place John in the only existing old-line plant the company has left, or you can release him.
What would you do?

company might have failed, and Lee Iacocca, along with his faithful lieutenants, would have been out on the street.

It is easy to see how the managers of Chrysler felt a responsibility not only to make correct decisions, but also to ensure that those decisions were implemented properly. Even if decision making is not done in a crisis situation, like that which faced Chrysler, the responsibility for implementation cannot be avoided. No matter how technically correct the decision, and no matter how faithfully a manager follows the recommended process, a decision has no value except through its implementation.

Evaluate the Decision

No decision-making process is complete until the decision has been exposed to the realities of the business environment. Evaluation requires an objective assessment of how the decision has solved the problem or taken advantage of the problem-turned-opportunity. This is particularly important for firms that stress decentralized management. In these companies, lower-level managers are allowed to become more involved in decision making. This provides junior managers with decision-making experience, improving their intuition and judgment.

■ FACTORS AFFECTING DECISION MAKING

Many factors can have an impact on the manager's decision making. Some of the more important ones may be seen in Figure 7.2 and are described below. All of these factors influence managers as they make decisions, though some are more important at higher levels than at lower levels and vice versa.

Routine versus Nonroutine Decision Making

Management decisions may range from such major ones as whether to build a new plant or to enter a new business all the way down to rather routine decisions

F I G U R E 7.2 ■
Factors Affecting
Decision Making

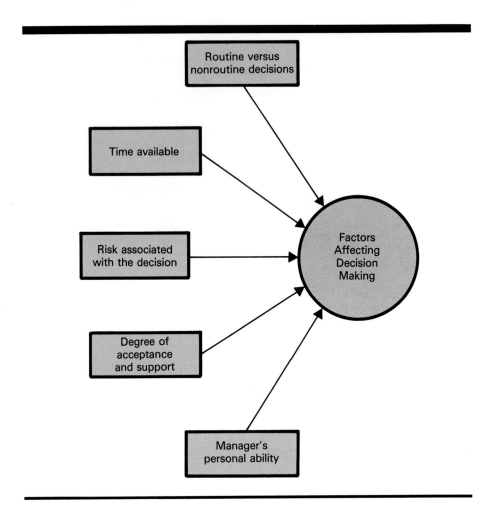

such as deciding on a supplier of bathroom tissue. Decisions may be viewed as routine or nonroutine.

ROUTINE DECISIONS

Most managers make numerous routine decisions in the performance of their jobs. Routine decisions made by managers are governed by the policies, procedures, and rules of the organization, as well as by the personal habits and preferences of managers. Managers certainly should not devote as much time to making routine decisions as they would to making nonroutine or more serious ones. It would be silly, for example, to follow a formal procedure in deciding whom to assign to a certain machine on a given day. Managers should be flexible in their decision making, just as in any other aspect of their job.

Policies, procedures, and rules provide a framework for routine decision making, thus freeing managers for more challenging and difficult problem solving. Managers are little more than clerks, however, if they simply adhere to the rule book and do not exercise some personal judgment for the betterment of all concerned.

NONROUTINE DECISIONS

Even though routine decisions may take up a considerable portion of a manager's time, individuals succeed or fail as managers on the basis of their nonroutine decisions. **Nonroutine decisions** are designed to deal with unusual problems or situations. Whether to expand to foreign markets, build a new production plant, or buy a more advanced computer system are examples of nonroutine decision situations. Nonroutine decisions are made by managers at all levels in the organization. Ones made by a first-line supervisor might involve firing an employee or changing the layout or procedures in the department. But the nonroutine decisions that will result in the success or the failure of the organization must be made by the upper-level managers, including individuals such as the CEO, the president, and the owner.

When real estate mogul Donald Trump agreed to buy the venerable Eastern Shuttle in October 1988 for $365 million, he aimed to slice into rival Pan American World Airways' share of the $400 million market. The nonroutine decisions he made soon after taking over included revamping both aircraft and terminals, redecorating each plane's interior, sending all planes back to Boeing to fix any defects, and a $50 discount shopping coupon. Trump may outfit each seat with a phone, TV, and radio; may provide valet airport parking; and is toying with the idea of handing out gambling chits redeemable at his Atlantic City casinos.[4] Such nonroutine decisions are probably essential if Trump is to take over a reasonable share of Pan Am's market. Obviously, such nonroutine decisions could only be made by Trump, because of their sheer magnitude.

Figure 7.3 illustrates the relationship among three levels of management and the amounts of routine and nonroutine decisions. As a manager progresses to higher levels, the number of nonroutine decisions increases. Nonroutine decisions require that managers exercise creativeness, good judgment, and intuition.

Nonroutine decisions Decisions that are designed to deal with unusual problems or situations.

FIGURE 7.3 ■
Managerial Levels and the Relative Amounts of Routine and Nonroutine Decisions

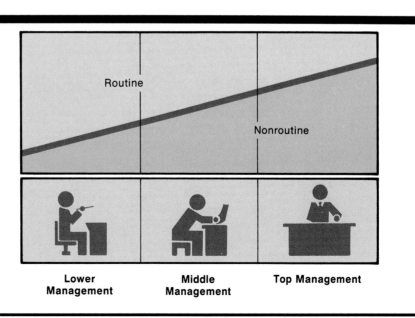

Time Available

The amount of time that can be devoted to decision making is often a critical factor. Managers would prefer to have sufficient time to evaluate and analyze thoroughly all alternatives prior to making a decision, but few have this luxury. Decisions frequently must be made in time-pressure situations. Assume that a customer makes the Randalls an offer to make a large purchase at a low, though profitable, price. Assume further that the order must be accepted today or the buyer will go to another supplier. Even if the Randalls have a good reason for taking time with such decisions, the Randalls dare not do so.

Risk Associated with the Decision

Decision risk
Exposure to the probability that an incorrect decision will have an adverse effect on the organization.

Decision risk is exposure to the probability that an incorrect decision will have an adverse effect on the organization. It is a factor that all managers consider, consciously or unconsciously, in decision making. For instance, Betty Harris, president of a small book publishing company, is considering paying $100,000 to a well-known author to write a book. If the book sells well, the firm could make $500,000, but if the book does not, Harris's company will lose the $100,000 plus an additional $75,000 in developmental and promotional costs. She may decide not to take the risk if the loss of $175,000 could seriously harm the company.

On the other hand, the purchasing manager for General Motors often signs contracts for automobile parts that greatly exceed $1 million. The risk in such decisions is low because of the size of the organization. Even the loss of $1 million for General Motors would not have a disastrous effect on the firm. As the decision risk increases, more time and effort are often devoted to individual decisions.

Degree of Acceptance and Support by Equals and Superiors

At times new managers are not immediately accepted. Reasons for lack of acceptance vary. Perhaps the manager is in a division where most of the other managers are much older, or perhaps the work group does not like outsiders. A similar concern exists for a female manager in a male-dominated organization. If the acceptance and support by other managers is lacking, decision making will be affected, and it is up to the individual manager to overcome the problem.

A lack of acceptance on the part of subordinates can limit a manager's ability to make decisions and get them implemented. Solutions requiring close cooperation may not even be feasible if subordinate acceptance is lacking. Perhaps the best way for a manager to gain acceptance is to earn subordinates' respect. Making an effort to improve communication and involve workers in the decision-making process helps develop a feeling of mutual respect. The extremely successful Wal-Mart stores are distinguished by a top management that keeps employees closely informed about company plans and practices and includes them in corporate decision making.[5] When Lee Iacocca came to Chrysler, he kept his reputation for working harder than anyone else, coming to work early and staying late. It was also clear that he knew his job and was willing to put out extra effort to get the job done. Any manager who wishes to gain subordinate acceptance may have to work hard to get it.

There is another side to the matter of gaining the support of subordinates. Lee Iacocca had to make drastic changes at Chrysler, and he knew that many managers would resist his efforts. His decision was to simply replace a number of them with faithful subordinates he had known in his previous position at Ford Motor Company. This decision, coupled with his charismatic leadership qualities, undoubtedly improved the cooperativeness of other managers.

The Manager's Personal Ability as a Decision Maker

Perhaps the most important factor affecting decision making is a manager's own ability and attitude. As owners of The Craft Cottage, Fred and Terry Randall are responsible for making the decisions within their organization; although one would have to wonder about their personal ability as decision makers—The Craft Cottage lost $18,000 during the first four years of operation. No matter how willing a manager is to make decisions and be responsible for them, that individual needs the ability to make correct decisions if he or she is to be successful. To some degree, this ability depends on following an appropriate decision-making process.

A manager's own experiences and level of understanding also help determine the quality of that manager's decisions. Experience tends to be a good teacher. For example, many college recruiters place major emphasis on the experience a student has gained from business and extracurricular activities. They believe the learning process for a particular job may be shortened if a student has been active in other endeavors while in college. But decision makers who rely only on their own experience may base their judgments mainly on their feel for the situation, and, if they are confronted with unfamiliar situations, faulty decisions may result. Basing decisions only on experience has several obvious shortcomings, among them:

1. Learning from experience is usually random.
2. Although we may have experience, there is no guarantee that we learned from it.
3. What we learn from experience is necessarily circumscribed by the limits of our experience.
4. Conditions change, and the past may not be a good indicator of current or future conditions.[6]

The question might be asked, "Do you have twenty years of experience, or do you have one year of experience twenty times?" Ralph C. Davis's classic statement summarizes the need for a bond between experience and intellect for a professional decision maker:

A man who has nothing but background is a theorist. A man who has nothing but practical experience is a business mechanic. A professionally trained executive is one in whom there is an effective integration of these two general types of experiences, combined with adequate intelligence regarding the types of problems with which he must deal.[7]

▮ THE SCIENTIFIC METHOD

Many corporations use a scientific approach to carry out the individual phases of the decision-making process. As may be seen in Figure 7.4, the **scientific method** is a formal way of doing research, which comprises observation of events, hypothesis formulation, experimentation, and acceptance or rejection of the hypothesis.

Observation of Events

The scientific method requires that people explore fully the relationships among the elements of a system and have a curiosity to know how and why they produce a particular outcome. The process usually begins with the discovery that something is not as it should be. For example, several years ago Ram, Inc., an Omaha, Nebraska, parts distributor, was experiencing a high level of employee turnover. This problem was forcibly brought to the attention of Geri Hodges, Ram's personnel manager, when she had to recruit seven new workers in a single week.

Hypothesis Formulation

The second step in the scientific method is the creation of one or more possible explanations of the causes of the problem. A **hypothesis** is a tentative statement of the nature of the relationship that exists between a cause and an effect, which

Scientific method
A formal way of doing research, which comprises observation of events, hypothesis formulation, experimentation, and acceptance or rejection of the hypothesis.

not responsible for

Hypothesis
A tentative statement of the nature of the relationship that exists between a cause and an effect, which provides an explanation of the cause that brought about the observed effect.

F I G U R E 7.4 ▮
The Scientific Method

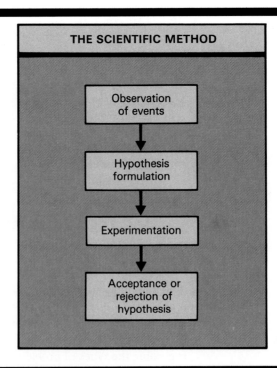

provides an explanation of the cause that brought about the observed effect. For instance, after some study, Geri Hodges decided that a possible cause of the high turnover was the perception of low pay by employees.

Experimentation

After the hypothesis has been clearly stated, it should be subjected to one or a series of tests to determine whether the tentatively stated relationship does in fact exist. Tests confirm or support the hypothesis or prove it to be unsound. Geri Hodges decided to do a simple survey to determine if her initial hypothesis was correct. In the survey, she asked employees to offer suggestions for improvements at Ram.

Acceptance or Rejection of the Hypothesis

The final step in the scientific method is the acceptance or rejection of the hypothesis. Upon studying the results of her survey, Geri Hodges noted that seven out of ten of the employees surveyed listed higher pay first or second among the ways suggested to improve conditions. This convinced her that her initial hypothesis was correct.

▉ GROUP METHODS INVOLVED IN DECISION MAKING

Up to this point, decision making has been discussed as if it were a process carried out by the individual manager. In most organizations, individuals are responsible for the outcomes of decisions under their control. Effective decisions generally combine high quality with acceptance by the decision makers.[8] Group decision making brings different resources to the task situation than does individual decision making. For example, studies indicate that work-team systems allow autoworkers real participation in decision making, and produce better quality cars more efficiently than do plants with traditional work organizations.[9]

There are several techniques through which groups can be involved in any stage of the decision-making process. Four of these are brainstorming, nominal grouping, the Delphi technique, and consensus mapping.

Brainstorming

Brainstorming
An idea-generating technique wherein a number of persons present alternatives without regard to questions of feasibility or practicality.

Brainstorming is an idea-generating technique wherein a number of persons present alternatives without regard to questions of feasibility or practicality. Through brainstorming, individuals are encouraged to identify a wide range of ideas. Usually one individual is assigned to record the ideas on a chalkboard or writing pad. Brainstorming may be used at any stage of the decision-making process, but it is most effectively used at the beginning, once a problem has been stated. Sometimes the alternatives produced through brainstorming may be rather bizarre. No criticism is allowed, because the purpose of brainstorming is to come up with innovative possibilities. Evaluation can wait until later and is not part of brainstorming.

Brainstorming can be an effective technique for generating alternatives once a problem has been stated.
(© Joseph Nettis/Photo Researchers, Inc.)

Although brainstorming is useful for all types of decisions, it is most effective for simple, well-defined problems.[10] It encourages enthusiasm and a competitive spirit among group members in generating ideas; it also prevents group members from feeling hopeless in regard to the range of possibilities in a given situation.[11] Brainstorming can result in many shallow and useless ideas, but it can spur members to offer new ideas as well.

Nominal Grouping

Nominal grouping represents an attempt to move toward a structured approach, which encourages individual creativity.[12] *Nominal* refers to the fact that members, acting independently, form a group in name only. An important feature of this technique is that it allows the members to meet face to face but does not restrict individual creativity as traditional group discussions do. **Nominal grouping,** then, is an approach to decision making that involves idea generation by group members, group interaction only to clarify ideas, member rankings of ideas presented, and alternative selection by summing ranks. The steps are shown in Figure 7.5 and discussed below:

Nominal grouping
An approach to decision making that involves idea generation by group members, group interaction only to clarify ideas, member rankings of ideas presented, and alternative selection by summing ranks.

1. *Statement of the problem.* After the nominal group is assembled, the group leader states the decision problem clearly and succinctly. No discussion is allowed, although group members may ask questions to clarify the problem.
2. *Idea generation.* Group members silently record and number their ideas for solving the problem.
3. *Round-robin recording.* The group members alternate in presenting their ideas while the group leader lists the ideas on a flip chart or chalkboard. This process continues without discussion until all of the ideas have been recorded.
4. *Clarification of ideas.* Under the leader's guidance, group members question one another to clear up any confusion about what each idea means. No evaluation is allowed yet.

F I G U R E 7.5 ■
Steps in Nominal Grouping

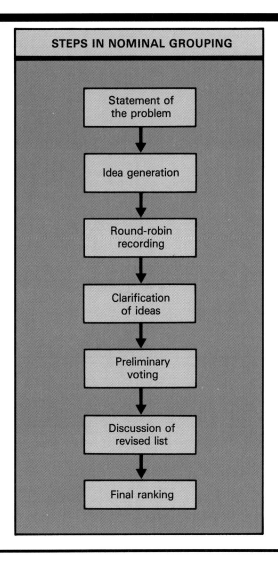

STEPS IN NOMINAL GROUPING

Statement of
the problem

Idea generation

Round-robin
recording

Clarification
of ideas

Preliminary
voting

Discussion of
revised list

Final ranking

5. *Preliminary voting.* Each group member independently ranks what are considered the best several of the decisions presented. The ideas that receive the lowest average ranks are eliminated from further consideration.
6. *Discussion of revised list.* Individual group members question one another to clarify the ideas that remain. The purpose is not to persuade but to understand.
7. *Final ranking.* Group members rank all of the ideas. The one with the highest total ranking is adopted.

Delphi technique
A formal procedure for obtaining consensus among a number of experts through the use of a series of questionnaires.

The Delphi Technique

The **Delphi technique** is a formal procedure for obtaining consensus among a number of experts through the use of a series of questionnaires. The procedure is similar to nominal grouping, but participants do not meet. In fact, ideally, the

everybody verbalizes ideas

FIGURE 7.6 ■
Steps in the Delphi
Technique

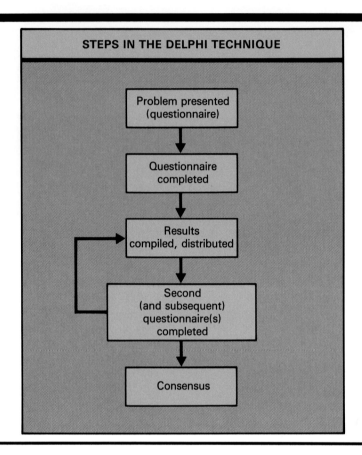

experts do not know who else is involved. The steps in the Delphi technique are shown in Figure 7.6 and discussed below:

1. The problem is presented to group members through means of a questionnaire that asks them to provide potential solutions.
2. Each expert completes and returns the questionnaire.
3. Results are compiled and provided to the experts, along with a revised and more specific questionnaire.
4. The experts complete the second questionnaire. The process continues until a consensus emerges.

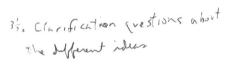

The Delphi technique prevents the respondents from being influenced by the personalities of the other participants and at the same time allows for the sharing of ideas. Unlike nominal grouping, the end result is a consensus decision. This method was conceived by the Rand Corporation to forecast how seriously a nuclear attack would affect the United States. It is expensive and time-consuming and generally has been limited to important and futuristic ideas.

Delphi is very useful in instances where

• The problem does not lend itself to precise analytical techniques but can benefit from subjective judgments on a collective basis;

- The individuals needed to contribute to the examination of a broad or complex problem have no history of adequate communication and may represent diverse backgrounds with respect to experience or expertise;
- More individuals are needed than can effectively interact in a face-to-face exchange;
- Time and cost make frequent group meetings infeasible;
- The efficiency of face-to-face meetings can be increased by a supplemental group-communication process;
- Disagreements among individuals are so severe or politically unpalatable that the communication process must be refereed and/or anonymity assured; and/or
- The heterogeneity of the participants must be preserved to assure validity of the results; that is, avoidance of domination by quantity or by strength of personality ("bandwagon effect").[13]

Consensus Mapping

The technique begins after a task group—task force or project team—has developed, clarified, and evaluated a list of ideas. It includes the following steps:[14] First, the facilitator encourages participants to search for clusters and categories of listed ideas. This search for structure includes the listing and discussion of alternative clusters and categories by the entire group or subgroups, and then production of a single classification scheme by group members working as a group or in pairs or trios. Then the facilitator consolidates the different schemes developed by the subgroups into a single representative scheme that acts as a map for the entire group. Group members next work to revise the map into a mutually acceptable solution. When there is more than one task group, a representative from each group presents its revised map to other task groups' members. Finally, representatives from each of the task groups work to produce a single, consolidated map. In general, this technique works best with complex problems that are multidimensional, have interconnected elements, and many sequential steps.[15]

■■ DECISION-MAKING REQUIREMENTS

As previously stated, there is perhaps no other attribute that so frequently distinguishes the excellent manager from mediocre ones as does the ability to make wise and innovative decisions. However, as may be seen in Figure 7.7, there are certain requirements that must be met in effectively carrying out the decision-making process.

Decision Maker

When Harry Truman was president of the United States, he always kept a plaque on his desk that stated, "the buck stops here." He was the person responsible, and he made the final decision. At The Craft Cottage, Fred and Terry Randall

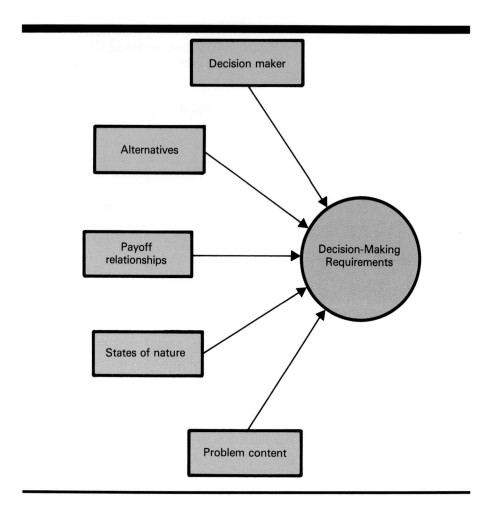

are jointly responsible for decision making. The decision maker is not always so easy to identify. The role of decision maker may be assumed by an individual or by a group of individuals, depending on how the organization is managed. Whoever the decision maker may be, he or she must choose from among a group of alternatives, a task many individuals do not like. Contrary to some thinking, not everyone enjoys making decisions, even though charged with the responsibility to do so.

Alternatives

Alternatives
Choices that the decision maker has to decide on.

Choices that the decision maker has to decide on are referred to as **alternatives.** To have a decision problem, the decision maker must have more than one alternative to choose from. Alternatives may be many or few in number. They may merely represent the option of "doing something" or "doing nothing." A good decision maker, however, attempts to identify and evaluate as many alternatives as possible, given time and resource restrictions. The Randalls are thinking about expanding and are considering two alternative locations in Jefferson City.

Payoff Relationships

be as specific as you can

Payoff relationship
Evaluating alternatives in terms of their potential benefits or costs.

pros & cons tend to be very vague

Evaluating alternatives in terms of their potential benefits or costs is the **payoff relationship.** Ultimately the decision maker should be attempting to choose the decision that will either maximize benefits or minimize costs. When the profits and costs associated with a particular alternative cannot be expressed mathematically, the decision maker suffers severely. For example, decision making is made much easier if one can state that a particular decision will result in a savings of $50,000, as compared with one's merely expressing the option that "costs will be lowered." Fred and Terry Randall have apparently forgotten about this decision-making requirement, because they have not estimated the costs or benefits associated with either of the two alternatives.

States of Nature

States of nature
Refers to the various situations that could occur and the probability of each of these situations happening.

States of nature refers to the various situations that could occur and the probability of each of these situations happening. For example, you have all heard a weather reporter say, "There is a 20-percent chance of rain." The 20-percent chance of rain would be one state of nature and the 80-percent chance of *no* rain would be the other. The Randalls have also been deficient in this decision-making requirement, because they have not estimated the probability of success of purchasing either of the two alternative businesses.

Choice may be required in either of two situations: when the precise relationships among alternatives are known, and the problem is merely to define what the relationships mean in terms of an objective; or when there is uncertainty about the future environment, or precise relationships between alternatives are not known. Good decision makers study situations thoroughly in the hope that their decisions will be correct more often than not. Because of the nature of doubt, it is most likely that decision makers will never be 100 percent correct.

Problem Content

Problem content
The environment in which the problem exists, along with the decision maker's knowledge of that environment, and the environment that will exist after a choice is made.

The **problem content** is the environment in which the problem exists, along with the decision maker's knowledge of that environment, and the environment that will exist after a choice is made. The Randalls realize that the purchase of one of the alternatives will eliminate one competitor.

Because the environment is taken into consideration in decision making, a decision that may be considered proper in one organization may be improper in another. For example, managers in two different firms producing similar products and presented with the same problem may make different decisions because of the internal environment each faces. One firm may stress maximum risk-taking for their managers, thereby permitting even lower-level managers to make important decisions. Another firm may want to have this same decision approved by upper-level management. Even though a lower-level manager in the second firm might be perfectly capable of making the decision, the situation does not permit it.

A Decision-Making Problem

To understand how the components of decision making interact, imagine how a student (the decision maker) might choose a part-time job. Suppose the student needs to take a job to supplement her student aid funds. She needs to analyze each element of decision making with regard to the decision-making requirements. The only job openings are at a recently opened local pizza restaurant. Two alternatives are present—one alternative is the job of assistant manager and the other is to be a pizza baker.

The payoff for each position is different. The baker receives an hourly wage of $4, no matter what the level of sales. However, as assistant manager, the estimated payoff for high sales will be $8 an hour, the payoff for average sales will be $6 an hour, and the payoff for low sales will be $1 an hour.

Because the restaurant is relatively new, the sales potential of the business has not been established. However, based on her experience within the community, she estimates that there is a 20-percent chance of high sales, a 50-percent chance of average sales, and a 30-percent probability of low sales. These states of nature will have a major impact on the amount of money received in the assistant manager's position.

Now the student is in a position to evaluate the two alternatives. One technique to accomplishing this task is known as "determining expected value," and the computation is as follows:

Expected earnings (pizza cook) = .2(4.00) + .5(4.00) + .3(4.00)
= $4.00

Expected earnings (assistant manager) = .2(8.00) + .5(6.00) + .3(1.00)
= $4.90

Thus, if the student is willing to accept the alternative that has the higher expected value, the assistant manager position that offers commission (expected value of $4.90 versus $4.00 per hour guaranteed) is the best decision.

But one factor remains to be examined—the problem content. There may be other facts that must be considered before an actual decision is made. The student's financial situation may prevent her from taking the chance of receiving only $1 per hour if sales are poor. On the other hand, this individual may desire the status of being an assistant manager. Other alternatives also could be evaluated. For instance, there may be other jobs available. Although there may be numerous other considerations, this example should provide some insight into the factors involved in decision making.

■■■ THE USE OF MODELS IN DECISION MAKING

Model
An abstraction of a real-world situation.

A technique that has proven quite beneficial to managers in the decision-making process is model building. A **model** is defined as an abstraction of a real-world situation. A model attempts to portray reality through various means without having to work directly with the real world. In business, models can be expressed in many ways and can have many meanings. This is true because managers often must deal with highly complex business systems that must be simplified to be understood. Model building provides the means for simplifying a complex situation.

Model builders first determine the purpose of the model, as it relates to depicting a real-world situation. Next, one must decide which parts should be included. This factor alone is a major advantage of model building. Certain components, which would be included in the real world but have no effect on the problem under consideration, can be omitted. Finally, the model builder must define the relationships that exist among the parts. Understanding these interrelationships is vital in model building. In a true sense, the model is merely a tool for assisting managers in decision making. Models are more widely employed than is commonly realized. Many times a manager may not even realize a model is being used when actually it is. In this section, two well-known models of the decision-making process, the rational-economic model and the administrative model, are discussed.

Rational-Economic Model

Rational-economic model
A model that outlines how decisions should be made rather than describing how decisions actually are made.

The **rational-economic model** outlines how decisions should be made rather than describing how decisions actually are made. The model proposes that people are economically rational and that decision makers seek to maximize outcomes by searching out and evaluating all possible alternatives before selecting the one best alternative. In addition, people are assumed to have exacting information about all available alternatives and the repercussions of each alternative. Individuals also are believed to process information in a logical, impartial, and systematic manner.

The rational-economic model depicts decision making as a straightforward process, but this is seldom the case. In practice, decision making is never quite that simple. First, the reason why decision making is rarely as simple as it is portrayed is that people rarely have access to absolute and perfect information. Second, even if the information received concerning all possible alternatives were available, an individual's cognitive limitations would make it difficult to accurately process such a vast amount of information. Third, decision makers seldom have adequate knowledge about the future consequences of every alternative.

This model portrays the ideal decision-making process and has provided the foundation for much of the empirical research and current knowledge relating to the decision-making process. Unfortunately, however, this model is seriously limited as a practical tool for understanding many common decision-making situations.

The Administrative Model

Administrative model
A model that is descriptive and provides a framework for comprehending the nature of the process that decision makers actually use when selecting among various alternatives.

The **administrative model**[16] is descriptive and provides a framework for comprehending the nature of the process that decision makers actually use when selecting among various alternatives. This model also assumes that people generally attempt to find the best possible alternative among the possible options. The administrative model acknowledges the human limitations that make rational decisions difficult to achieve.

This model suggests that a person's cognitive ability to process information is limited. In other words, a human being can handle only so much information before information overload occurs. Even if complete information were available to the decision maker, these cognitive limitations would impede making a completely rational decision; subsequently, decision makers have what is referred to as *bounded rationality*.

Bounded rationality affects several key aspects of the decision-making process. First, the decision maker does not search out all possible alternatives before selecting the best one. Instead, once the various alternatives are isolated and evaluated, a solution that is acceptable is selected. Once a satisfactory alternative is selected, the search for additional solutions stops. Other potentially better alternatives may exist, but they will not be identified or considered because a workable solution has been found.

Second, the search for alternatives is guided primarily by past experiences or rules of thumb, which provides a method for promptly identifying solutions with the greatest likelihood of success. The search for alternatives is usually conducted within the familiar aspects of the decision situation.

Finally, bounded rationality implies that decision makers satisfice instead of maximize. **Satisficing** occurs when an alternative is selected that meets minimum rather than optimum standards of acceptance. In other words, a decision maker, because of various constraints such as time and cost, selects an alternative that is satisfactory rather than ideal. The administrative model presents a much more realistic description of how decisions are often made. Some situations require a rational-economic approach, but most people probably satisfice more than they maximize.

Satisficing
Occurs when an alternative is selected that meets minimum rather than optimum standards of acceptance.

■ BARRIERS TO EFFECTIVE DECISION MAKING

Decision making can be a complex and perplexing process. As may be seen in Figure 7.8, there are several barriers to making informed and effective decisions. An awareness of such barriers can help improve the decision-making process.

Tunnel Vision

Tunnel vision
Occurs when people have mental blinders, such as individual biases, that can restrict the search for an adequate solution to a relatively narrow range of alternatives.

Tunnel vision occurs when people have mental blinders, such as individual biases, that restrict the search for an adequate solution to a relatively narrow range of alternatives. To the extent that it inhibits identifying additional and worthwhile alternatives, tunnel vision has a detrimental effect on the decision-making process.[17]

Previous Commitments

Previous commitments is another barrier to effective decision making. Decisions usually occur in an interrelated sequence and therefore impact other decisions. Possibly the most difficult decision a person makes relates to choices about the fate of an entire sequence of decisions. Research by Staw[18] indicates that people who feel personally responsible for a previously selected bad decision often tend to commit additional resources to that alternative. The most significant implication is that the escalating commitment to a particular decision makes it increasingly

F I G U R E 7.8 ■
Barriers to Effective
Decision Making

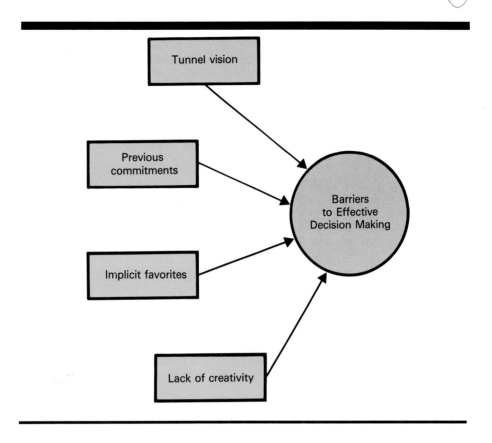

difficult to objectively evaluate other alternatives and to change the already initiated course of action.

Implicit Favorites

Research by Soelberg[19] indicates that many people select a favorite alternative early in the decision-making process but continue to evaluate additional solutions. Subsequent alternatives are therefore distorted perceptually, evaluated using decision criteria that emphasize the superiority of the preferred solution. Such decision makers will process information in such a way that final selection of the implicit favorite is virtually guaranteed.

Lack of Creativity

Most people possess creative ability, which can be developed through training and application.[20] **Creativity** is the ability to generate ideas that are both innovative and functional. This ability is an obvious requirement for managerial effectiveness, and it is especially important in making nonroutine decisions.

Unfortunately, creativity rarely receives adequate attention within organizations. The first reason for this neglect is that organizational policies and procedures are usually designed to promote order, consistency, and uniformity, thereby

Creativity
The ability to generate ideas that are both innovative and functional.

limiting creativity. Second, managerial work is fast paced and action oriented, whereas creativity requires time for preparation, incubation, inspiration, and validation.[21] Finally, most individuals do not understand creativity and therefore overlook rather than advocate or reinforce it.

All of the barriers that can impact decision making have not been discussed, but hopefully the reader now recognizes that barriers such as the ones described here do exist, and do affect the decision-making process.

■■■ WORKER PARTICIPATION AND THE DECISION-MAKING PROCESS

Worker participation
The process of involving workers in the decision-making process.

Although participation as a factor in corporate culture will be discussed in Chapter 20, participation as involved in the decision-making process is discussed here. **Worker participation** is the process of involving workers in the decision-making process. Most managers assume that they must be either participative or nonparticipative when involving workers in decision making. Also, some managers

FIGURE 7.9 ■
Degrees of Worker
Participation

Skip

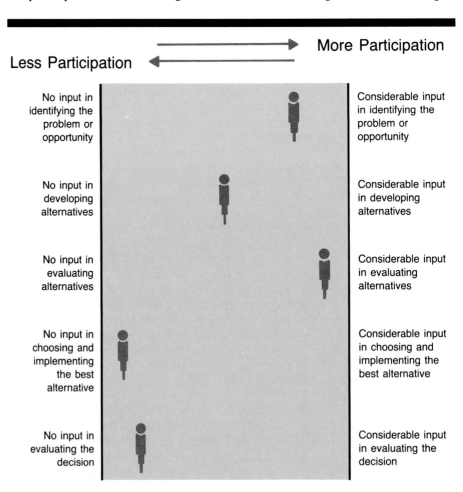

believe that if they involve workers in decision making they will lose control over the work unit.[22] Certainly that is not necessarily the case, since the degree of worker participation differs in each step of the decision-making process.

As can be seen in Figure 7.9, a worker's participation may be high in some steps and low in others. Note that the worker shown participates extensively in identifying the decision-making opportunity and developing alternatives, but takes almost no part in making and evaluating the decision. For other workers (or other managers), the pattern of participation might be entirely different.

Virtually every manager receives some input from employees before making important decisions. From a motivational standpoint, encouraging input is probably useful only when the employees feel they play a meaningful part. The manager should be completely honest about this. If a decision has already been made, the manager should not ask employees for advice about it. Employees should be consulted only when they have information or insight that will help managers make better decisions.

▪▪ ADVANTAGES AND DISADVANTAGES OF GROUP DECISION MAKING

When a group makes a decision, the involvement of more than one individual brings additional knowledge and skills to the decision, which tends to result in higher quality decisions. In the same way that individuals involved in making a decision generally become committed to it, group consensus expedites acceptance of the decision by the group. Therefore, both individual and group commitment to the decision is increased.

Of course, group decision making generally takes more time than decision making by individuals. The exchange of information among many individuals, as well as effort spent on obtaining consensus, is time-consuming. Sometimes, to reach a decision more quickly, or to reach a decision all group members will accept, groups satisfice rather than optimize; that is, they select a satisfactory but not the best solution.

Groups tend to make riskier decisions. Because no single person shoulders the consequences of a decision made by a group, individuals may feel less accountable and will accept riskier, more-marginal solutions. In addition, groups may ignore individual expertise, opting instead for group consensus. Strong personality types and high-status group members may dominate the discussion, causing less assertive and lower-status members to go along with them.[23] Cohesive groups may develop **groupthink**—a mode of thinking with a norm of concurrence-seeking behavior.[24] The symptoms of groupthink arise when members of decision-making groups are critical of ideas outside the groups, prefer to entertain ideas within the groups, and focus too heavily on developing concurrence within the group. It occurs most frequently in highly cohesive groups, particularly in stressful situations.

Table 7.1 presents a summary of the advantages and disadvantages of group decision making. By making a decision as a group, the partnership task force brings diverse knowledge and skills to the decision-making process and therefore should reach a decision that is of a higher quality, as well as one that is accepted by everyone. However, because the group seems to have problems with its

Groupthink
A mode of thinking with a norm of concurrence-seeking behavior.

TABLE 7.1 ■ Advantages and Disadvantages of Group Decision Making	
Advantages	Disadvantages
Brings multiple knowledge and skills to the decision	Requires more time Ignores individual expertise, at times
Expedites acceptance by the group	Satisfices often
Generally results in higher quality decisions	Encourages riskier decisions
Increases commitment to decision	Creates the possibility of groupthink

interpersonal and rational processes, the decision-making process requires extensive time and does not use individual expertise well.

Groups frequently produce better decisions if problems have multiple parts that can be addressed by a division of labor. Group performance also tends to be better than the average performance of individual members, which requires estimates to be made. In contrast, however, individual decision making tends to lead to more effective decisions on problems that require completion of a series of complex stages, as long as the individual receives input from many sources.[25] When group members choose a colleague whose solution they are willing to accept as the group's, the resulting decision equals the quality and is no riskier than those obtained by group decision making.[26] But the effectiveness of such a "best-member" strategy depends on the probability of the group's selecting the *real* best member and on the potential for subjectivity in the solution.[27] Table 7.2 provides a comparison of individual and group decision making.

Vroom and Yetton[28] and Maier[29] suggest that decision makers should consider the following six factors in managing decision making:

1. *The type of problem or task to be solved.* Individual decision making results in greater creativity, as well as more efficiency; group decision

TABLE 7.2 ■ Comparison of Individual and Group Decision Making		
Factor	Individual	Group
Type of problem or task	when creativity or efficiency is desired	when diverse knowledge and skills are required
Acceptance of decision	when acceptance is not important	when acceptance by group members is valued
Quality of the solution	when "best member" can be identified	when several group members can improve the solution
Characteristics of individuals	when individuals cannot collaborate	when group members have experience working together
Climate surrounding decision making	when the climate is competitive	when the climate is supportive of group problem solving
Amount of time available	when relatively little time is available	when relatively more time is available

making is superior when a task or problem requires a variety of expertise.

2. *The necessity of acceptance of the decision for its implementation.* Group decision making more often leads to acceptance than does decision making by individuals.

3. *The importance of the quality of the solution.* Group decision making generally leads to higher quality solutions, unless an individual has expertise in the decision area and this is identified in advance of the process.

4. *The personalities and capabilities of the people involved in the decision.* Some individuals have difficulty collaborating in a group setting; also, groups can ignore individual expertise.

5. *The climate surrounding decision making.* Supportive climates encourage group problem solving; competitive climates stimulate individual responses.

6. *The amount of time available.* Group decision making takes much more time than individual decision making.

Research supports the fact that group decision making often results in the most effective decision.[30] Participation may also reduce any role conflict and role ambiguity experienced by the task force members.[31]

SUMMARY

Decision making is the process of generating and evaluating alternatives and making choices among them. Some people view decision making only as problem solving; however, problems are usually better treated as opportunities. Often the distinction between a problem and an opportunity is not clear. In any event, no decision-making process is complete until the decision has been exposed to the realities of the business environment.

Decisions may be routine or nonroutine. Many other factors may impact a manager's decision making: the amount of time, decision risk, acceptance of new managers, and a manager's own ability and attitude. The scientific method—observation of events, hypothesis formulation, experimentation, and acceptance or rejection of the hypothesis—is one approach to decision making. It requires that people want to explore fully the relationships among the elements of a system and have a curiosity to know how and why they produce a particular outcome. Groups can be involved in any stage of the decision-making process. Four ways are brainstorming, nominal grouping, the Delphi technique, and consensus mapping.

There are certain decision-making requirements in addition to a decision maker. Choices that the decision maker has to decide on are referred to as alternatives. Evaluating alternatives is the payoff relationship. States of nature are the various situations that could occur and the probability of each. The problem content is the environment in which the problem exists.

The rational-economic model outlines how decisions should be made, while the administrative model describes and provides a framework for comprehending the nature of the actual decision-making process. The decision-making process can be complex and perplexing. An awareness of barriers such as tunnel vision, previous commitments, implicit favorites, and lack of creativity can help improve the decision-making process.

Most managers assume that they must be either participative or nonparticipative when involving workers in decision making. Also, some managers believe they will lose control if they involve workers in decision making. Certainly that is not necessarily the case, since the degree of worker participation differs in each step of the decision-making process. When a group makes a decision, additional knowledge and skills are brought into play, which tends to result in higher quality decisions. In addition, since individuals involved in making a decision generally become committed to it, group consensus expedites acceptance of the decision by the group. Therefore, both individual and group commitment to the decision is increased.

REVIEW QUESTIONS

1. Define decision making and identify the steps in the decision-making process. How important do you think it is to a manager?
2. What is meant by the following statement: "The ability to select the best course of action from several possible alternatives often separates successful managers from less successful ones"?
3. This text identifies several factors that can have an impact on the manager's decision making. Identify and briefly discuss each.
4. What are the steps involved in the scientific method?
5. Define each of the following terms:
   a. Brainstorming
   b. Nominal grouping
   c. Delphi technique
   d. Consensus mapping
6. List and briefly define each of the requirements that must be present before a decision problem can exist.
7. Define a model. How can a model be used to assist in the decision-making process?
8. What are the barriers to effective decision making?
9. Describe how worker participation may differ in each step of the decision-making process.
10. What are the advantages and disadvantages of group decision making?

KEY TERMS

decision making	Delphi technique	administrative model
nonroutine decisions	alternatives	satisficing
decision risk	payoff relationship	tunnel vision
scientific method	states of nature	creativity
hypothesis	problem content	worker participation
brainstorming	model	groupthink
nominal grouping	rational-economic model	

CASE
STUDY

A REQUEST FOR SPECIAL FAVORS

"**M**Y HUSBAND has made plans for us to go, and he says we are going," said Barbara Kener. Barbara was a payroll clerk at Wellingham Corporation, a Brockton, Massachusetts, shoe manufacturer. Barbara had just asked Jerry Wall, the payroll department manager, if she could take a week of vacation the first week of January to visit her husband's family. Jerry had tried to talk her out of it because of the heavy work load during that period, but Barbara clearly felt strongly about taking the time off.

It had been customary for payroll department clerical personnel to schedule their vacations at times other than during January, because it was then that the payroll department had the most to do. All of the individual payroll records had to be finished, and a wide range of reports, including the employee W-2 forms for 2,000 employees, had to be completed. Jerry was not even sure he would be able to meet the deadlines for preparation of the reports without Barbara's help. Barbara was an

especially efficient worker, and, although she had been employed only since March, Jerry had come to depend on her.

Jerry recalled that when Barbara was hired, he had failed to discuss the need for avoiding January vacations, telling her only that she would be eligible for one week of vacation for each six months of employment. Jerry felt somewhat responsible for the misunderstanding. But he knew that letting Barbara take her vacation as requested might hurt morale in the department, even if the work load could be handled. Not only would the others have to work harder, but Jerry remembered having turned down two special requests for January vacations in the past.

QUESTIONS
1. What should Jerry do about Barbara's request? In answering this question, use the decision-making process developed in the chapter.
2. What situational factors should Jerry consider in making the decision? Why?

CASE
STUDY

A DECISION TO PURCHASE A COMPUTER

IN AUGUST 1989, Leon and Roy Sivils were hotly debating whether their small company ought to buy a computer. For the fourth time in as many years, Roy had brought up the subject. "I think we have a pretty good system now," said Leon. "Look, Leon," replied Roy, "I don't know of any other company the size of ours that doesn't have a computer. Besides, the cost has gotten so low, an Apple or a Radio Shack costs only a little more than a typewriter. We might even want to consider buying a clone. Anyway, I don't think we can afford not to computerize."

Roy and Leon are the owners of the TAC Agency, Inc., which owns and operates a number of residential sewer and water systems around Fort Wayne, Indiana. The TAC Agency had about 3,000 customers in 1989. Each customer was billed every month for sewer or water service or both. Presently, the bills are prepared by hand. Cash receipts are manually recorded on individual ledger cards. The work is done by part-time employees hired at minimum wage.

Going back over the records for the previous year, Roy had found eighty posting errors in customer-account records. Some payments had been credited to the wrong accounts, and other customers had been credited with payments that had not been made. Most of the mistakes made in the company's favor had been pointed out by customers and corrected. The ones that Roy found in the customer's favor had generally remained undiscovered.

After Roy explained this to Leon, Leon still wasn't totally convinced. "Let's study it a little more before we rush into a decision. I just want to make sure that the right one is made."

QUESTIONS
1. What additional information might Leon use to help him in the decision-making process?
2. From the little you know about the TAC Agency, what uses might be found for a microcomputer if the company buys one?

EXPERIENTIAL EXERCISE

In this exercise, each group of five persons will be working on the same thing at the same time. Members of each group will be asked to participate in solving a job-related problem. Often when a group of employees work on a joint task, there are problems. When the job problem affects the employees involved in resolving it, group problem solving becomes even more difficult.

Assume you are a store manager for a supermarket chain. Your store is typical of the stores in the chain, with all of the problems such an operation involves. You naturally take pride in your store. You want others to feel that your store is tops. An important company decision affecting all store managers is about to be made. Specifically, your district manager Harry Hines has been called on to make the decision regarding who will be the manager for the new store in his district. You are anxious about the outcome. Here are some facts about the store managers and their stores:

Alice:	seventeen years with the company; her store is ten years old.
Claude:	five years with the company; his store is four years old.
Butch:	ten years with the company; his store is one year old.
Lawanda:	one year with the company; her store is seventeen years old.

Two of the stores are in older, well-developed areas of the city, but Alice and Butch's stores are in relatively undeveloped areas. Alice's store is an older store, but the area never did develop as it was expected to. Each of the store managers is eager to get a store in a location where business potential is greater and where their performance will look better.

In the past it seemed that no matter who was chosen, most of the managers were unhappy, and felt the decision was wrong. The new store is in a newly developing residential area, which is growing very rapidly. It is the first supermarket in the area. Harry has decided to let his store managers make the decision this time. As far as Harry is concerned, they are all capable of handling the job. He just wants them to be satisfied with the decision.

Select five individuals; one to serve as Harry Hines, the district manager, and four individuals to serve as Alice, Claude, Butch, and Lawanda. Your instructor will provide the additional information you need to participate in this exercise.

NOTES

1. An adaptation of a case by Wayne H. Decker and Thomas R. Miller of Memphis State University.
2. Theodore Levitt, "The Managerial Merry-Go-Round," *Harvard Business Review* 52 (July–August 1974): 120.
3. John Rossant and Wendy Zellner, "How Chrysler's $30,000 Sports Car Got Side-swiped," *Business Week,* 23 January 1989, 68.
4. Seth Payne, "War of the Shuttles," *Business Week,* 20 February 1989, 38.
5. Thomas J. Murry, "Wal-Mart Stores Penny Wise," *Business Month,* December 1988, 42.
6. Adapted from Alvar O. Elbing, *Behavioral Decision in Organizations* (Glenview, Ill.: Scott, Foresman, 1970), 14.
7. Ralph C. Davis, *The Fundamentals of Top Management* (New York: Harper, 1951), 55.
8. N. R. F. Maier, "Assets and Liabilities in Group Problem Solving: The Need for an Integrative Function," *Psychological Review* 74 (1967): 239–249.
9. John Hoerr, "Is Teamwork a Management Plot? Mostly Not," *Business Week,* 20 February 1989, 70.
10. J. L. Adams, *Conceptual Blockbusting: A Guide to Better Ideas,* 2d ed. (New York: W.W. Norton, 1979).
11. Adams, *Conceptual Blockbusting.*
12. A. L. Delbecq and A. H. Van de Ven, "A Group Process Model for Problem Identification and Program Planning," *Journal of Applied Behavioral Science* 7 (1971): 466–492.
13. Delbecq and Van de Ven, "Group Process Model," 466–492.
14. S. Hart, M. Boroush, G. Enk, and W. Hornick, "Managing Complexity Through Consensus Mapping: Technology for the Structuring of Group Decisions," *Academy of Management Review* 10 (1985): 587–600.
15. Hart et al., "Consensus Mapping," 587–600.
16. H. Simon, *Models of Man* (New York: John Wiley & Sons, 1957).
17. Donald D. White and David A. Bednar, *Organizational Behavior: Understanding and Managing People at Work* (Newton, Mass.: Allyn and Bacon, 1986), 285.
18. B. M. Staw, "The Escalation of Commitment to a Course of Action," *Academy of Management Review* 6 (October 1981): 577–587.
19. P. O. Soelberg, "Unprogrammed Decision Making," *Industrial Management Review* 8 (1967): 19–29.
20. D. J. Treffinger and J. D. Gowan, "An Updated Representative List of Methods and Educational Programs for Stimulating Creativity," *Journal of Creative Behavior* 5 (1971): 127–139.
21. C. Patrick, *What Is Creative Thinking?* (New York: Philosophical Library, 1955).
22. Larry Hatcher and Timothy L. Ross, "Gainsharing Plans—How Managers Evaluate Them," *Business* 36 (October–December 1986): 30.
23. A. H. Van de Ven and A. L. Delbecq, "Nominal versus Interacting Group Processes for Committee Decision Making Effectiveness," *Academy of Management Journal* 14 (1971): 203–212.
24. I. Janis, "Groupthink," *Psychology Today* (June 1971).
25. L. N. Jewell and H. J. Reitz, *Group Effectiveness in Organizations* (Glenview, Ill.: Scott, Foresman, 1981).
26. P. W. Yetton and P. C. Bottger, "Individual versus Group Problem Solving: An Empirical Test of a Best-member Strategy," *Organizational Behavior and Human Performance* 29 (1982): 307–321.
27. H. J. Einhorn, R. M. Hogarth, and E. Klempner, "Quality of Group Judgment," *Psychological Bulletin* 84 (1977): 158–172.

28. V. H. Vroom and P. Yetton, *Leadership and Decision-Making* (Pittsburgh, Pa.: University of Pittsburgh Press, 1973).
29. Maier, "Assets and Liabilities," 239–249.
30. M. Sashkin, "Participative Management Is an Ethical Imperative," *Organizational Dynamics* 12 (Spring 1984): 4–22.
31. S. E. Jackson, "Participation in Decision Making as a Strategy for Reducing Job-Related Stress," *Journal of Applied Psychology* 68 (1983): 3–19.

REFERENCES

Archer, Ernest R. "How to Make a Business Decision: An Analysis of Theory and Practice." *Management Review* 69 (February 1980): 54–61.

Baron, Jonathan, and John C. Hershey. "Outcome Bias in Decision Evaluation." *Journal of Personality and Social Psychology* 51 (April 1988): 569–579.

Bommer, Michael, Clarence Gratto, Jerry Gravender, and Mark Tuttle. "A Behavioral Model of Ethical and Unethical Decision Making." *Journal of Business Ethics* 6 (May 1987): 265–280.

Daniel, D. W. "What Influences a Decision? Some Results from a Highly Controlled Defense Game." *Omega* 8 (November 1980): 409–419.

Dodd-McCue, Diane, J. Matejka Kenneth, and D. Neil Ashworth. "Deep Waders in Muddy Waters: Rescuing Organizational Decision Makers." *Business Horizons* 30 (September–October 1987): 54–57.

Dutton, J. E., L. Fayey, and V. K. Naraynan. "Toward Understanding Strategic Issue Diagnosis." *Strategic Management Journal* 4 (October–December 1983): 307–324.

Etzioni, Amitai. "Normative-Affective Factors: Toward a New Decision-Making Model." *Journal of Economic Psychology* 9 (June 1988): 125–150.

Fombrun, Charles J. "Structural Dynamics Within and Between Organizations." *Administrative Science Quarterly* 31 (September 1986): 103–121.

Frederickson, James W. "The Strategic-Decision Process and Organizational Structures." *Academy of Management Review* 11 (April 1986): 280–297.

Heiner, Ronald A. "Imperfect Decisions in Organizations: Toward a Theory of Internal Structure." *Journal of Economic Behavior & Organization* 9 (January 1988): 25–44.

Henderson, John C. "Influence of Decision Style on Decision-Making Behavior." *Management Science* 26 (April 1980): 371–386.

Hogarth, Robin M., and Spyors Mankridaks. "Value of Decision Making in a Complex Environment—An Experimental Approach." *Management Science* 27 (January 1981): 93–107.

Holloway, Clark, and Herbert H. Hand. "Who's Running the Store? Artificial Intelligence!!!" *Business Horizons* 31 (March–April 1988): 70–76.

Hornstein, Harvey A. "Managerial Courage: Individual Initiative and Organizational Innovation." *Personnel* 63 (July 1986): 16–22.

Iselin, Errol R. "The Effects of Information Load and Information Diversity on Decision Quality in a Structured Decision Task." *Accounting, Organizations and Society* 13 (April 1988): 147–164.

Isenberg, Daniel J. "Thinking and Managing: A Verbal Protocol Analysis of Managerial Problem Solving." *Academy of Management Journal* 29 (December 1986): 775–788.

Malik, S. D., and Kenneth N. Wexley. "Improving the Owner/Manager's Handling of Subordinate Resistance to Unpopular Decisions." *Journal of Small Business Management* 24, no. 3 (July 1986): 22–28.

Mangrum, Claude T. "Determining the Right Regimen of Managerial Exercises." *Supervisory Management* 26, no. 2 (February 1981): 26–30.

Meyer, Alan D. "Mingling Decision-Making Metaphors." *Academy of Management Review* 9 (January 1984): 6–17.

Nitzan, Shmuel, and Jacob Paroush. "Small Panels of Experts in Dichotomous Choice Situations." *Decision Sciences* 14 (July 1983): 314–325.

O'Reilly, C. A., III. "Variations in Decision Makers' Use of Information Sources: The Impact of Quality and Accessibility of Information." *Academy of Management Journal* 25 (1982): 756–771.

Paquette, Laurence, and Thomas Kida. "The Effect of Decision Strategy and Task Complexity on Decision Performance." *Organizational Behavior & Human Decision Processes* 41 (February 1988): 128–142.

Pitz, Gordon F., Natalie J. Sachs, and Joel Heerboth. "Procedures for Eliciting Choices in the Analysis of Individual Decisions." *Organizational Behavior and Human Performance* 26, no. 3 (December 1980): 396–408.

Roy, Delwin A., and Claude A. Simpson. "Expert Attitudes of Business Executives in a Smaller Manufacturing Firm." *Journal of Small Business Management* 19 (April 1981): 16–22.

Schilit, Warren Keith. "Upward Influence Activity in Strategic Decision Making." *Group & Organization Studies* 12 (September 1987): 343–368.

Schweiger, David M., William R. Sandberg, and James W. Ragan. "Group Approaches for Improving Strategic Decision Making: A Comparative Analysis of Dialectical Inquiry, Devil's Advocacy, and Consensus." *Academy of Management Journal* 29 (March 1986): 51–71.

Simon, H. "On the Concept of Organizational Goal." *Administrative Science Quarterly* 9 (1964): 1–22.

Singh, Jitendra V. "Performance, Slack, and Risk Taking in Organizational Decision Making." *Academy of Management Journal* 29 (September 1986): 562–585.

Sova, Dawn. "No Margin, No Mission; Without Training in Financial Decision Making, Managers May Not Be Able to Help Fulfill the Corporate Mission." *Computer Decisions* 19 (23 February 1987): 68.

Suedfeld, Peter. "Are Simple Decisions Always Worse?" *Society* 25 (July–August 1988): 25–27.

Tjosvold, Dean. "Effects of Crisis Orientation on Managers' Approach to Controversy in Decision Making." *Academy of Management Journal* 27 (March 1984): 130–138.

Tylecote, Andrew. "Time Horizons of Management Decisions: Causes and Effects." *Journal of Economic Studies* 14 (November 1987): 51–64.

CHAPTER

8

Chapter Outline

The Organizing Process

Learning Objectives

After completing this chapter students should be able to

1. Define organization and describe the organizing process.
2. Define specialization of labor and identify its benefits and limits.
3. Identify and describe the primary means of departmentation and describe organizational differentiation.
4. Describe the informal organization and explain the benefits and costs of the informal organization.

FREEPORT, MAINE, IS well known as the home of L.L. Bean Company, a catalog merchandiser of sporting goods and clothing. L.L. Bean also operates a 50,000-square-foot retail store in Freeport. The store is open day and night and attracts celebrities and others from all over the world.

Woodrow Shepherd, who now owns Freeport Firestone, started out as an L.L. Bean employee in 1969. The owner of the only Gulf Oil station in Freeport died in 1974, and the service station came up for sale. Woodrow quit his job with L.L. Bean and invested his life savings plus $20,000 in borrowed funds in the service station. At first, Woodrow worked from daylight to dark six days a week. He employed only one helper, Joe Gross, who pumped gas, fixed flats, and did whatever else Woodrow needed him to do. As Freeport grew over the next ten years, Woodrow's business did also. It was not long before the bookkeeping was too much for him, so he asked his wife to start coming in half-days to take care of that.

Woodrow added on to his service station and in 1976 got the Firestone tire franchise. The tire business was especially profitable, so Woodrow spent most of his time in the tire department, selling, installing, and repairing tires. By that time, Joe Gross had become a seasoned and dependable attendant. So Woodrow hired another man to help Joe take care of the service island. He also hired a helper in the tire department.

By 1980, Woodrow found it necessary to replace his wife with a full-time bookkeeper. He also employed an additional worker and a supervisor in the tire department. This freed Woodrow to keep a watch on the work Joe was doing at the service island and to spend a little more time keeping track of bookkeeping and financial matters.

Until 1981, Woodrow called the place simply "Shepherd's Gulf Station." That year, he had a nice sign painted and changed the name to Freeport Firestone. Business continued to expand, and by 1984 Woodrow had installed another service island and added a tire and battery showroom next to the tire-service bays. Because the L.L. Bean store was open all night and generated significant traffic, Woodrow hired a night manager to keep the service island open until midnight. By then Freeport Firestone employed fourteen persons full-time and two part-time.

The town of Freeport had grown to about 25,000 in population, and Woodrow thought about opening a smaller service station and tire center at the opposite end of Main Street. He missed waiting on customers himself and realized that if he opened another outlet, he would have to hire managers for both stores and would probably have to spend all his time solving problems and coordinating the activities of his subordinates. He decided to do it anyway, and by 1987 ground had been broken for the new branch of Freeport Firestone. The organization function as it evolved at Freeport Firestone is similar to that at many other firms, whether small or large, domestic or international, service or manufacturing. ∎

I N THIS CHAPTER, organization and the components of the organizing process are described. Next, organizational differentiation, which becomes necessary as an organization grows, will be discussed. Finally, the informal organization and its benefits and costs will be addressed.

WHAT IS AN ORGANIZATION?

The word "organization" is used widely; most of us are reminded of it each day when we read newspapers, walk about the university campus, watch television programs, or listen to the radio. Some of us, when we hear the word, envision large companies such as Sears and General Motors. Certainly Freeport Firestone would be considered an organization. But few of us think of the local grocery store, service station, fast-food restaurant, or nursery school. Each of these, however, is an organization, too.

Organizations, large or small, have at least these three common characteristics:

1. They are composed of people.
2. They exist to achieve goals.
3. They require some degree of limitation on member behavior.

Organization
Two or more people working together in a coordinated manner to achieve group results.

Thus, an **organization** is defined as two or more people working together in a coordinated manner to achieve group results. Because most people spend a considerable part of their lives working in organizations, it is important to understand fully how organizations function and how organizations can be managed effectively. To be effective, a manager must be capable of organizing *human resources, physical factors,* and *functions*—production, marketing, finance, personnel—in a manner designed to ensure the achievement of the goals of the firm. This process is crucial to the success of every organization where people work together as a group. Rubbermaid Inc. is a corporation that appears to epitomize what a corporation should be. According to Stanley C. Gault, chairman and chief executive officer, their success is built on being well positioned to compete in all areas, "people, product, production, and promotion." In 1988, Rubbermaid Inc. was named by *Business Month* magazine as one of the five best-managed companies, largely because of their emphasis on effectively organizing human resources, physical factors, and functions.

Organizing
The process of prescribing formal relationships among people and resources to accomplish goals.

Organizing is the process of prescribing formal relationships among people and resources to accomplish goals. The organizing process, as illustrated in Figure 8.1, takes place within the constraints of the organization's external and internal environments.

Management has authority & responsibility over who makes decision & gets responsibilities

External Environment

In Chapter 3 we saw how the external environment affects the management of corporations. The external environment also affects the organizing process. For instance, laws and public concern about clean water and air may create a need for a manufacturer to add personnel, to monitor any possibly toxic substances that may be discharged. The necessity to deal with a wide range of suppliers, and

FIGURE 8.1 ■■
The Organizing Process

Consider organizational
objectives

↓

Determine types
of work activities

↓

Departmentation

THE ORGANIZING PROCESS

INTERNAL ENVIRONMENT

EXTERNAL ENVIRONMENT

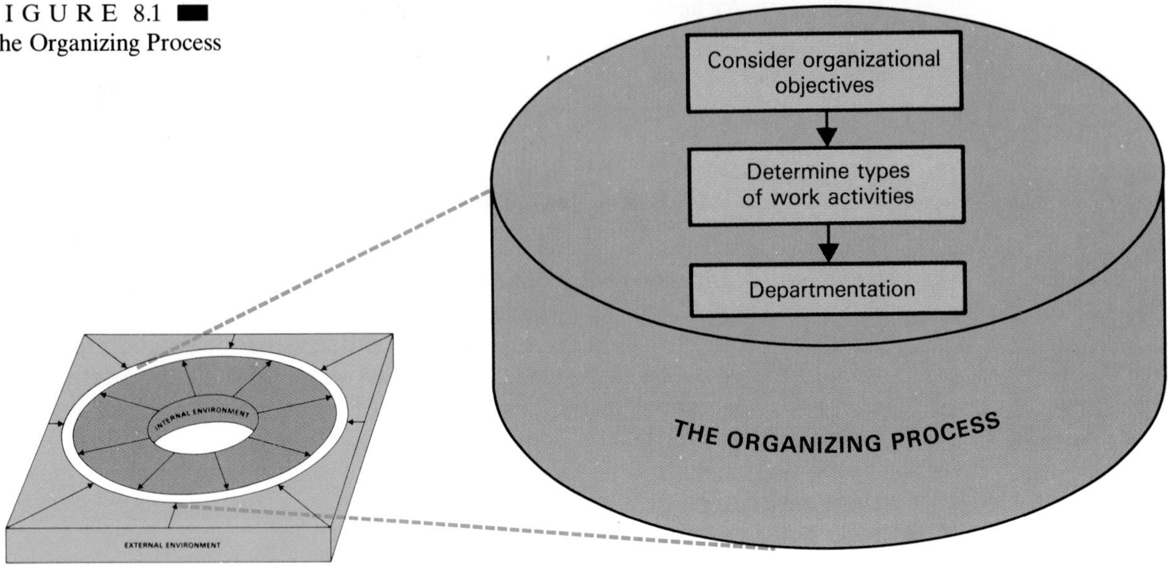

to buy in large volumes, requires a sophisticated purchasing department at company headquarters. Differences in legislation from state to state require that someone be responsible for helping individual store managers stay within the law.

More than in the past, rapidly changing technological factors influence the organizing process. For example, new automotive technology requires U.S. automobile manufacturers to make major changes in assembly lines, which had changed little from those developed by Henry Ford before 1920. Robots now do repetitive tasks previously done by humans. In some plants, cars are assembled at work stations rather than on mile-long assembly lines. Similar rapid technological change is occurring in virtually every industry segment. As changes in the manufacturing process occur, organizations must be able to respond with new and more flexible ways of assigning persons and machines to jobs.

Surprisingly, even the once-hidebound British labor unions have allowed changes in organization. Japan-based British industries now have work rules, and British companies have adopted the Japanese management style, just-in-time inventory and quality assurance systems. Flexible ways of assigning persons and machines to jobs apparently work for Japanese companies operating in Britain, so the British are adapting their methods. According to Roy Sanderson, national secretary of Britain's electricians' union, the Japanese have "set the pace for British manufacturing productivity and technology."[1] No longer can business leaders ignore the obvious advantages of new and more flexible ways of assigning persons and machines to jobs.

Internal Environment

The organizing process is also influenced by the internal environment that individual managers face. The approach to organizing that an individual manager uses must be compatible with the internal environment. For example, a company's procedures manual may specify the manner in which machinery can be rearranged, and personnel regulations may restrict reassignment of workers.

The boss's view of the company's strategic and operating plans will limit the way a manager can organize resources to carry out those plans. At Chrysler Corporation, for example, it is well known that Lee Iacocca places emphasis on product quality as well as on low cost. Therefore, managers at Chrysler must create organizational units that tightly control quality *and* contain no "fat" in the form of additional management levels or positions.

The discussion will now focus on the steps in the organizing process, as Figure 8.1 illustrates. First, it is necessary to consider the organizational objectives and then attempt to determine the kind of organization needed to accomplish those objectives. Next, management must determine the types of functions, or work activities, that will be required to meet company goals. Finally, activities that are similar are grouped together. A number of departments or otherwise separate organizational units are set up, each designed to carry out a different function or group of functions.

■■■ CONSIDER ORGANIZATIONAL OBJECTIVES

Everything the manager does should be directed toward goal accomplishment, and organizing is no exception. Organizing should have as its purpose arranging people and resources in the best way possible to support the organization's objectives. It is vitally important that every phase of the organizing sequence be directed at goal accomplishment. Wal-Mart's goal is to expand their basic business—offering name-brand merchandise to a vast low- to middle-income population. Organizing for Wal-Mart therefore involves arranging people and resources in the best way possible to support that goal. One principle that

The purpose of organizing is to arrange people and resources in the best way possible to support the objectives of the organization.
(© Lawrence Migdale/Stock, Boston, Inc.)

distinguishes Wal-Mart from its competitors is the unusual depth of employee involvement in company affairs. Wal-Mart's highly motivated personnel are the envy of its competitors. For example, employee suggestions resulted in the successful practice of installing official greeters in all Wal-Mart stores to offer advice, give directions, or just be friendly to customers. Wal-Mart has an inventory control system that is recognized as one of the most sophisticated in retailing.[2] Simply by having arranged their people and resources effectively, Wal-Mart may become the nation's largest retailer within the next five years; or at least that is what many on Wall Street predict.

■■■ DETERMINE TYPES OF WORK ACTIVITIES

Once objectives, and the kind of organization needed to accomplish them, are established, it is possible to determine the kinds of work activities that should be involved. On a typical baseball team, players perform the tasks of fielding, hitting, and pitching. A good team must develop competent specialists in each of these activities. Pitching can be further broken down into starting, long relieving, and short relieving. Fielding involves playing the infield and the outfield. And playing second base requires talents that are different from those needed to do the other infield jobs.

Similarly, the work activities required to accomplish the objectives of business firms can be identified. In a manufacturing concern, raw materials must be procured and the product must be made and sold. Each of these major phases involves hiring and supervising people, processing paperwork, and numerous other activities. At Freeport Firestone, as at any other business, there are many tasks that require special skills. For example, tires must be sold and tires must be repaired. So all these types of activities must be distinguished from one another before the organizing process can proceed. An important concept in specifying different kinds of tasks is specialization of labor.

■■■ SPECIALIZATION OF LABOR

Specialization of labor
The division of a complex job into simpler tasks so that one person or group may carry out only identical or related activities.

In his 1776 book, *The Wealth of Nations,* Adam Smith explained how he was able to increase the productivity of a group of pin makers by more than a thousandfold through specialization (division) of labor. **Specialization of labor** means the division of a complex job into simpler tasks so that one person or group may carry out only identical or related activities. A purpose of organizing, like everything else a manager does, is to improve productivity. Through specialization of labor, it is possible for members of the organization to concentrate in a single area, resulting in increased output. To achieve efficiency, specialization is especially essential in mass-production industries. But in fact, in nearly all organizations, most work activities are of a specialized nature.

Organizations have endless options as to the degree of specialization associated with each job. For instance, if a company produces small transistor radios, several different approaches, shown in Figure 8.2, might be available.

FIGURE 8.2 ■
Degrees of Specialization
Associated with the Job of
Producing Small Transistor
Radios

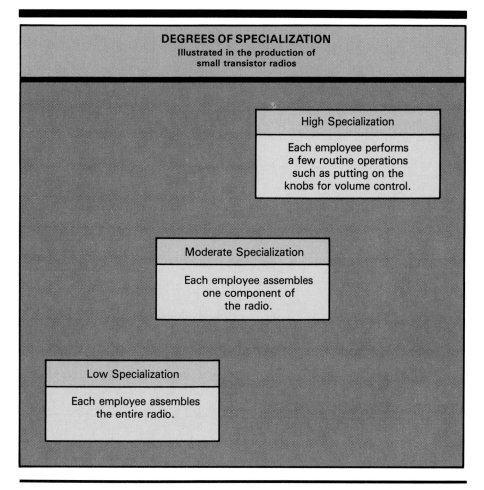

DEGREES OF SPECIALIZATION
Illustrated in the production of
small transistor radios

High Specialization

Each employee performs
a few routine operations
such as putting on the
knobs for volume control.

Moderate Specialization

Each employee assembles
one component of
the radio.

Low Specialization

Each employee assembles
the entire radio.

Advantages of Specialization

As seen in Figure 8.3, there are five specific advantages of specialization. First, specialization often increases productivity. A worker who is allowed to concentrate skill and effort on just a small number of tasks can usually achieve a high level of output. In manufacturing electronic components, output per worker tends to be much higher in situations where employees perform highly specialized work activities. Similarly, high performance results are apparent in many fast-food restaurants. At McDonald's, employees perform specialized functions, for example, cooking hamburgers or french fries.[3] This is in contrast to more traditional restaurants, where employees may perform a wide variety of jobs.

Second, specialization permits managers to more efficiently supervise a larger number of employees, thereby increasing the span of management. A manager may be able to supervise thirty workers who are performing the same specialized tasks. If workers are performing a number of diverse tasks, the employees that a manager can effectively supervise are much less.

Third, it decreases training time. A more specialized job can be learned more quickly than a job that entails numerous different work activities. When

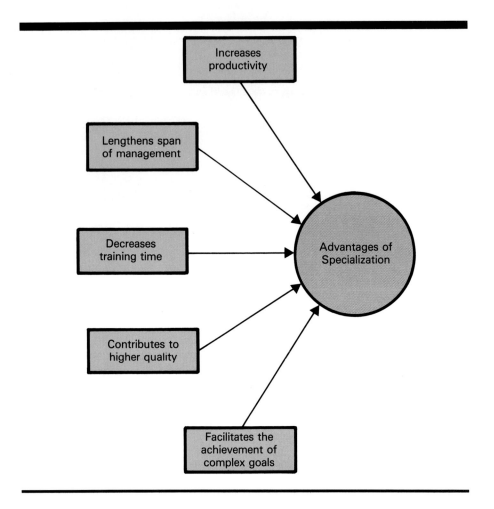

training time is reduced, the workers become productive at a faster rate. For instance, the time required to train a worker to cook french fries or prepare milk shakes is minimal compared with the time required to learn all the jobs performed in a fast-food restaurant.

Fourth, specialization contributes to consistently higher quality products and services. It has been said that we live in an age of specialization, one in which most people are employed as specialists. Many students who choose to pursue a degree in business administration specialize in accounting, management information systems, finance, management, or marketing. Few professions better demonstrate the move to specialization than does medicine. As more is learned about each phase of medicine, entire careers emerge, concentrating on specific parts of the body or specific symptoms. Forty or fifty years ago, most doctors treated all of the ailments of all members of the family. Now most physicians specialize, becoming gynecologists, pediatricians, cardiologists, ophthalmologists, proctologists, and so forth. By specializing in a narrow range of the medical profession, a physician is able to offer the best diagnosis and treatment medical research and technology has available.

Finally, specialization can facilitate the achievement of highly complex goals. Complex projects usually require large numbers of specialists. The U.S. space program would not have been possible without the contributions of the thousands of specialists assembled by the National Aeronautics and Space Administration. Teams of specialists, each knowledgeable in a particular phase of the project, contributed to its success. Similarly, the design and construction of airplanes, or the construction of large buildings, requires the contributions of many different specialists.

Disadvantages of Specialization

Despite its advantages, specialization of labor is not always a desirable alternative. In some organizations, due to too much specialization, certain jobs have become oversimplified, causing boredom and fatigue among employees. For example, some people find it very difficult to tighten bolts 1,000 times a day. Typically, the highest degree of specialization is found in this kind of assembly-line work, and the result is employee turnover, absenteeism, and a deteriorating quality of output. These negative consequences may offset the advantages and increase the costs of specialization.

A number of companies have established programs to overcome the disadvantages of specialization. Others have actually reduced the degree of specialization. General Motors is experimenting with using work teams, with team monitors assigned on a rotating basis. This gives each worker a feeling of involvement in company efforts to increase the quality and quantity of output. Shaklee Corporation has a unique management philosophy for its new plant in Norman, Oklahoma. There, small groups of employees make, inspect, and package a diverse array of products. The teams establish their own production schedules and working hours. They select new workers from a pool approved by the personnel department and can even initiate discharges.[4]

Efforts to overcome the detrimental effects of specialization were intensified in the 1980s. Books such as *Theory Z* and *In Search of Excellence* touted what has come to be called "Japanese management." The result was the institution of quality circles and other such participative devices, especially in industries that compete directly with the Japanese.

■■ DEPARTMENTATION

Departmentation
The process of grouping related work activities into manageable units.

The process of grouping related work activities into manageable units is known as **departmentation.** The purpose of departmentation is to contribute to more effective and efficient use of organizational resources. In this section we discuss first the ways functions should be grouped in an organization. Then, common types of departments are described.

Functional Similarity

Ideally, each department or division in the organization should be made up of people performing similar tasks. This is the concept of *functional similarity,* a guiding principle in the creation of sections, departments, and divisions. Jobs with similar objectives and requirements are grouped to form a section, and the

FIGURE 8.4 ■
Factors Affecting
Functional Similarity

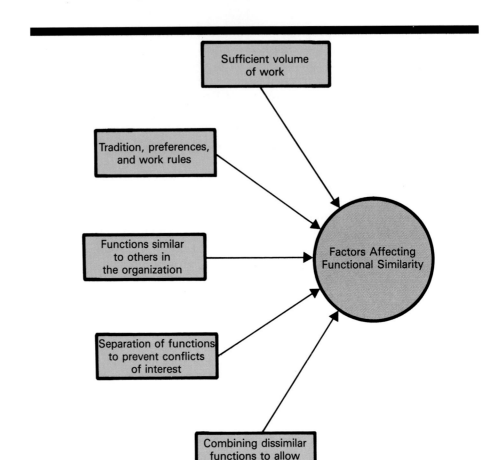

person with the background necessary to supervise these functions effectively is assigned as the manager. For example, a construction company might employ a plumbing crew, an electrical crew, and so forth. Each different crew performs a group of related functions.

The achievement of functional similarity, important as it is, nevertheless depends on a number of factors. Several of these are shown in Figure 8.4 and are discussed below.

VOLUME OF WORK

Sometimes the volume of the work does not allow for specialization. In small firms, personnel have to cope with a wide assortment of jobs. At Freeport Firestone, for example, workers have to do a variety of tasks ranging from pumping gas to fixing flats. But with increases in volume, the concept of functional similarity can be applied more rigorously. For example, compare the operations of a small grocery store with those of a large supermarket. In the small store, one person might perform such functions as stocking shelves, working in the produce section, checking, and bagging groceries. In the large supermarket, personnel will tend to specialize in one or only a few of the basic functions. It is common for individual managers to oversee the produce section and the stocking, checking, and bagging functions.

TRADITIONS, PREFERENCES, AND WORK RULES

Although two tasks may be similar, traditions, work rules, and personal preferences may prevent their assignment to one individual. For example, the function of installing electrical conduit (the steel pipe that protects electrical wire) is quite similar to the function of running water piping; however, few plumbers would be willing to run conduit, and electricians would usually object to installing water pipes. This is because individuals associate a set of behavioral expectations, duties, and responsibilities with a given position.[5]

SIMILAR FUNCTIONS IN DIFFERENT DEPARTMENTS

A third complicating factor is that a particular function often occurs in different departments. For example, inventory control would appear to fit logically in the purchasing department, which buys materials and thus has need for records of inventory levels. However, the production department uses the same materials and, in scheduling, must work with these same inventory records. Inventory control could be placed in either department.

SEPARATION OF FUNCTIONS
TO PREVENT CONFLICTS OF INTEREST

Sometimes similar functions are not combined because doing so might create conflicts of interest. Quality control is intimately involved in production; inspectors frequently work side by side with production employees. The inspector, however, should not be unduly influenced by the production manager's interest in quality and costs. Thus, inspection, although similar to production, should be separate from production, to protect its independence.

COMBINING DISSIMILAR FUNCTIONS TO ALLOW COORDINATION

Finally, there are occasions when two dissimilar functions must be combined for purposes of effective action and control. In a factory organization, purchasing is clearly differentiated from selling. But in department stores, buying and selling are so interdependent that one person is often made responsible for both. The theory is that a well-bought dress or hat is half-sold.

Kinds of Departments

There is no standard way to divide an organization. Even companies in the same industry often have vastly different kinds of departments; however, it is possible to identify five bases on which departmentation normally occurs: (1) function, (2) product, (3) customer, (4) geographic territory, and (5) project. Additionally, a combination approach may be utilized.

DEPARTMENTATION BY FUNCTION

Departmentation by function is perhaps the most common means of dividing an organization. By grouping related functions, organizations form their departments on the basis of specialized activities such as finance, marketing, production, engineering, and personnel (Figure 8.5). Grouped together, specialists become more efficient. Departmentation by function is especially useful in stable

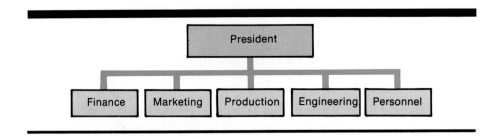

environments where technical efficiency and quality are important.[6] Undoubtedly, functional specialists also feel more comfortable working with others of similar background and experience. At an LTV Steel Co. plant in Cleveland, Ohio, teams of highly trained technicians manage a huge electrogalvanizing line practically by themselves and participate in decisions on hiring, scheduling of work and hours, and operations planning.[7] Departmentation by function may create certain problems for management, however. Employees in specialized departments may become more concerned with their own department than with the overall company. Because of the sometimes conflicting purposes of various departments, upper management must ensure that an effective means of coordination exists. An example of interdepartmental conflict occurred at Tennco Products Company's Tubular Products facility near Memphis, Tennessee. The personnel director asked the production manager to hire more women machine operators, thinking that this would be a simple task. The production manager argued that qualified women were not available and that top management demands for increased efficiency made taking time to train women impractical. In the end, more women were hired, but only after the president became involved and encouraged production and personnel to settle their differences.

DEPARTMENTATION BY PRODUCT

Product departmentation is concerned with organizing according to the type of product being produced and/or sold by the firm. This method, through which efficiency is enhanced by the application of specialized knowledge of particular products or services, is often used by rather large, diversified companies. Figure 8.6 shows the organization of a large electronics firm divided into three product divisions. Firms manufacturing and selling technologically complex products are often set up in this way.[8]

Until 1983, General Motors was divided into five product divisions: Chevrolet, Pontiac, Oldsmobile, Buick, and Cadillac. Because of what GM executives call

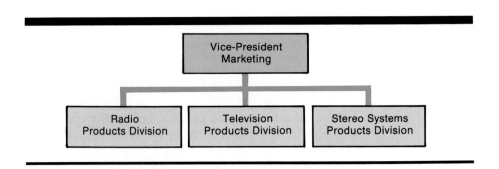

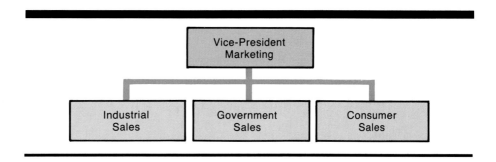

F I G U R E 8.7 ■
Departmentation by
Customer

"creeping complexity," the company has recently been reorganized, resulting in only two product divisions: the Chevrolet, Pontiac, and GM Canada division and the Buick, Cadillac, and Oldsmobile division. Small cars are designed and manufactured by the first group and intermediate and large cars by the latter.[9]

DEPARTMENTATION BY CUSTOMER

Departmentation by type of customer is used by organizations that have a special need to provide better service to different types of customers. As illustrated in Figure 8.7, a diversified manufacturing company may have industrial, government, and consumer sales divisions. A USX salesperson who deals with obtaining government contracts simply maintains good relations with purchasing agencies and makes sure that USX has opportunities to bid. Selling to industrial customers, in contrast, requires greater emphasis on personal persuasion and long-standing relationships. A person who does well in one area may be a failure in the other. Banks also use departmentation along customer lines. For example, commercial loan officers deal only with business customers, while consumer-lending specialists make personal loans. When client satisfaction is the main competitive issue, especially in an uncertain environment, customer departmentation is often appropriate.[10]

DEPARTMENTATION BY GEOGRAPHIC TERRITORY

Grouping activities according to geographic territory is used by organizations that have physically dispersed and/or noninterdependent operations or markets to serve. The marketing function of the company shown in Figure 8.8 is organized into the southern, western, and eastern regional divisions. Geographic departmentation offers the advantages of better services with local or regional personnel, often at less cost. Division by geography is the single most common scheme for international companies. For example, when Wendy's decided to expand into Europe, the company faced a competitive and legal environment very different

F I G U R E 8.8 ■
Departmentation by
Geographic Territory

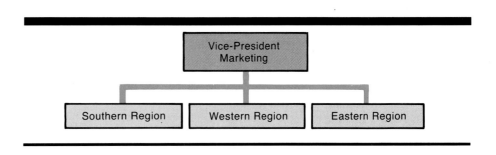

FIGURE 8.9 ■
Departmentation by
Project

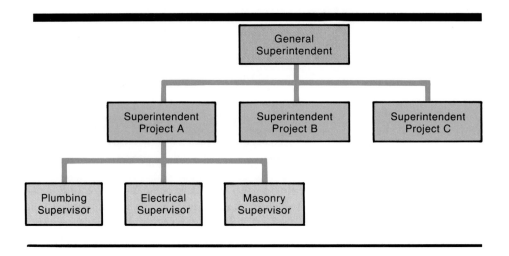

from that in the United States and therefore established a separate division for
the European operations. Geographic departmentation is most effective when
the corporation's activities are widespread and there are few product lines.[11]

DEPARTMENTATION BY PROJECT

When the work of an organization consists of a continuing series of major
projects, departmentation by project normally occurs. This is especially common
in the construction industry. Figure 8.9 shows how a typical construction operation
might be departmentalized. In this example, each project superintendent, under

FIGURE 8.10 ■■■ Organization Chart: A Combination Approach to Departmentation

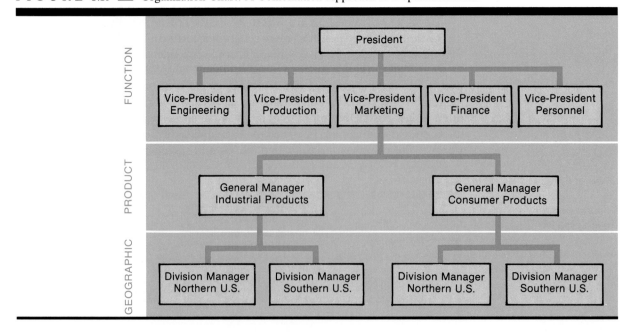

the direction of the general superintendent, is responsible for a separate contract. Such an organization changes frequently as projects are completed and new ones started. The superintendent in charge of Project A may transfer to a new project or back to headquarters or be laid off when Project A is finished. In addition, the plumbing supervisor currently working on Project A may move to Project C when the plumbing on Project A is complete.

DEPARTMENTATION: A COMBINATION APPROACH

Unless the organization is quite small, it is likely that several different bases for departmentation will be used in combination. No one form of departmentation can meet the needs of most firms, particularly in such large companies as General Motors, General Electric, and Exxon. In the product-type organization at GM, portions of the design function continue to be performed by the corporate staff rather than by the product divisions. Also, GM still uses district managers in its marketing organization. An organization chart illustrating various forms of departmentation is shown in Figure 8.10. In this case, the manufacturing company is departmentalized on three levels, by type of functions performed (engineering, production, marketing, and so on), by type of products produced (industrial and consumer), and by geographic territory. The precise form of departmentation a firm chooses must be based on its own needs.

■ ORGANIZATIONAL DIFFERENTIATION

In a newly formed small organization, a single owner-manager performs all of the major functions of the business, such as financing, procuring materials, designing the product, and making and selling the product. This was the case with Woodrow Shepherd of Freeport Firestone when he first opened his service station. As the volume of business grows, the work required increases beyond the capacities of one person. The employment of additional personnel requires vertical and horizontal differentiation. When Woodrow Shepherd decided to hire Joe Gross, he had to describe those tasks that Joe would perform, that is, he had to differentiate them from the other tasks of the organization. Joe was to pump gas and fix flats, among other duties. A new level in the organization had been created, even though Freeport Firestone was only a two-person firm (Section A of Figure 8.11).

Vertical differentiation
The process of creating additional levels in the organization.

The process of creating additional levels in the organization is defined as **vertical differentiation.** Initially, there are just two levels, managerial and operative, but managers like Woodrow Shepherd usually do not assign all the operative work to a subordinate. Woodrow continued to wait on customers and often worked alongside Joe Gross, in addition to supervising him. In the early stages of organizational growth, functions considered vital to success and that require special expertise, like sales and finance, often continue to be done by the manager.

Horizontal differentiation
The process of forming additional units at the same level in the organization.

As the volume of business continues to grow, additional personnel will be added and more operative functions differentiated and allocated. The process of forming additional units at the same level in the organization is called **horizontal differentiation.** The result is shown in Section B of Figure 8.11. For Freeport

FIGURE 8.11 ■
Functional Differentiation
Downward and Outward

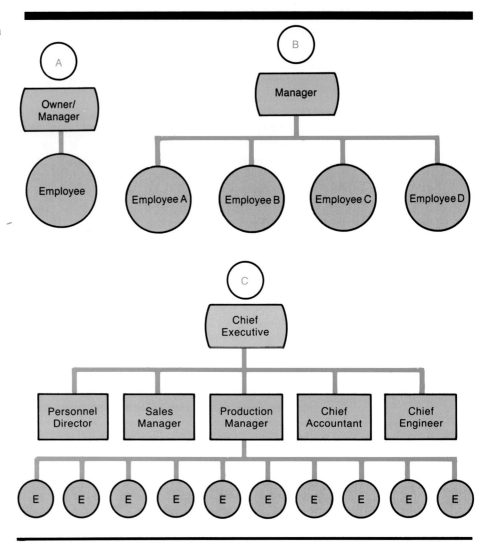

Firestone, this occurred when Woodrow hired a person to help Joe on the service
island and a helper for the tire department. Although Woodrow continued to do
operative work for a time, he knew that the management job would soon become
too demanding for him to continue. Woodrow Shepherd employed horizontal
differentiation because the work load became too great. There is another reason
for adding additional workers or departments at a given level. The original
manager may find that certain functions can be more effectively and economically
performed by a specialist. For example, a manager may find sales a weak area,
because of ineffective or inadequate training programs. Therefore, a sales trainer
would be employed to take over that phase of the business, so that the manager
could devote more time to other areas. As in the case of Freeport Firestone,
horizontal growth usually occurs at lower levels as additional workers are required.
When the number of workers exceeds that which one manager can supervise,
additional supervisors must be added. As the organization grows, horizontal

differentiation usually results in the splitting off of those functions that are most complex and least similar to other functions of the firm.

As shown in Section C of Figure 8.11, horizontal differentiation usually results in the creation of several functional departments. If the organization continues to grow, further differentiation will be needed, both horizontal and vertical. Figure 8.12 shows how personnel, production, and engineering might be further subdivided, resulting in an additional level of managers.

Coordination
The process of ensuring that persons who perform interdependent activities work together in a way that contributes to overall goal attainment.

When differentiation occurs, coordination is required. **Coordination** is the process of ensuring that persons who perform interdependent activities work together in a way that contributes to overall goal attainment. Coordination assumes a greater importance as the organization becomes more complex. For example, the manager of the company illustrated in Figure 8.12 would have to be much more concerned with coordination than was Woodrow Shepherd when his only employee was Joe Gross. For large, multibusiness companies, separate business units are often set up. Usually, the more diverse the products such a company makes, the more authority will be decentralized.[12]

F I G U R E 8.12 ▮▮ Horizontal Differentiation of Functional Departments

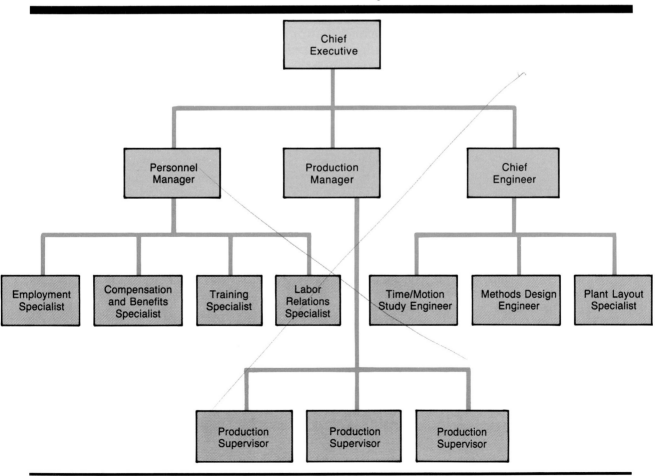

■ THE INFORMAL ORGANIZATION

Informal organization
The set of evolving
relationships and patterns
of human interaction within
an organization that are
not officially prescribed.

It is possible to identify many groups, of varying size, within a typical firm. Naturally, many of these groups have a place in the formal organization. These groups also have a place in the informal organization. In fact, all of these groups blend together to form the **informal organization,** which is the set of evolving relationships and patterns of human interaction within an organization that are not officially prescribed.

In the formal organization, managers establish what employees should do through formal organizational charts and job descriptions. Traditional managers tend to emphasize the values of organizational and personal loyalty. Many will tolerate incompetence more readily than disloyalty. The formal organization represents management's attempt to specify the way things should be done in the various sections, departments, and divisions of the firm. But the official organizational structure is only part of the story. There emerges another structure, existing alongside the formal one, which consists of informal relationships created not by officially designated managers but by organizational members at every level.

Because of the impact of the informal organization, an increasing number of firms are training their managers to cope with it. The director of corporate personnel for a large insurance company says, "We teach our managers/supervisors to be alert to the formation of 'informal work groups' and that such groups can be either a positive or a negative influence on a department or company objective." Corning Glass Works has an extensive management development program devoted to understanding how the informal group functions and to designing ways to have the informal group work in a positive manner.

The informal organization has definable characteristics. First, its members are joined together to satisfy needs. However, these needs may be completely different; one worker may want to make friends, another may be seeking advancement. Second, the informal organization is continuously changing. Relationships that exist one day may be gone the next. Third, members of various organizational levels may be involved. The informal organization does not adhere to the boundaries established by the formal one. A manager in one area may have close ties to a worker in another. Fourth, the informal organization is affected by

The manager should always be aware of the informal organization that exists within the department or company. (© Allen Green/Photo Researchers, Inc.)

relationships outside the firm. A top-level manager and a supervisor may associate with each other because they are members of the same golf club. Finally, the informal organization has a pecking order: certain people are assigned greater importance than others. Workers who adhere more closely to the norms of the informal group tend to gain greater respect.

Although not capable of being placed into a formal organizational chart, an informal organization does have its own structure. Like the formally structured organization, the informal organization may have a chain of command, which is sometimes charted after the fact by management. Managers should recognize that informal work groups exist at all levels of the organization. A formal organization chart can be very misleading in terms of who has "real" authority and influence.

The nature of the informal structure is dynamic and constantly changing. As different members enter and exit the group, the structure is modified. The structure is based heavily on the communication patterns that develop among group members. If many people attempt to gain the advice of one individual, this individual is often the informal leader, and the structure develops around this individual. Just as formal organizations have vice-presidents, the informal group may have an equivalent counterpart. The informal structure evolves rather than being formally laid out, yet it is often as rigid as the formal stucture.

Contact chart

A diagram showing various individuals in the organization and the numbers of interactions they have with others.

The organizational structure of the informal work group may be studied by means of a contact chart. A **contact chart** is a diagram showing various individuals in the organization and the numbers of interactions they have with others. These charts are developed to identify the connections that an individual has with other members of the organization. As may be seen from the contact chart in Figure 8.13, all contacts do not follow the formal organizational chart. In various instances, certain levels of management are bypassed; others show cross-contact from one chain of command to another. In Figure 8.13, individual 19 appears to be very popular, based on the number of contacts.

F I G U R E 8.13 ■■■ A Contact Chart

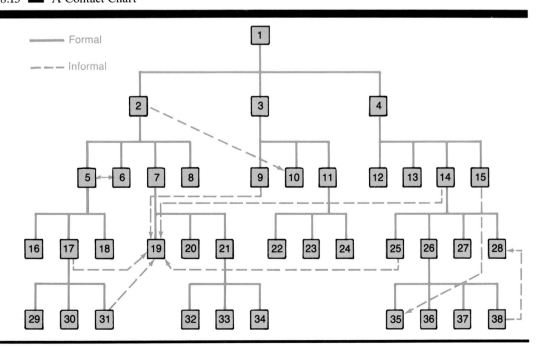

One difficulty with a contact chart is that it does not show the reasons for relationships. Also, it is never clear whether contacts shown will work for, or against, the organization. Individual 19 could be helping other employees accomplish their tasks. On the other hand, this individual could be talking down the organization and promoting disharmony among company employees. Once managers have identified the major contact points, they are in a position to either encourage or discourage the individual within the work group.

■■ BENEFITS AND COSTS OF THE INFORMAL ORGANIZATION

Managers often have mixed emotions about the informal organization. Although it is capable of contributing to greater organizational effectiveness, it is not without its drawbacks. There are certain costs. But if management is properly trained to understand and work with the informal organization, the benefits should exceed the costs, as Figure 8.14 suggests. If management is not careful, the reverse may be true.

F I G U R E 8.14 ■■ Benefits and Costs of the Informal Work Group

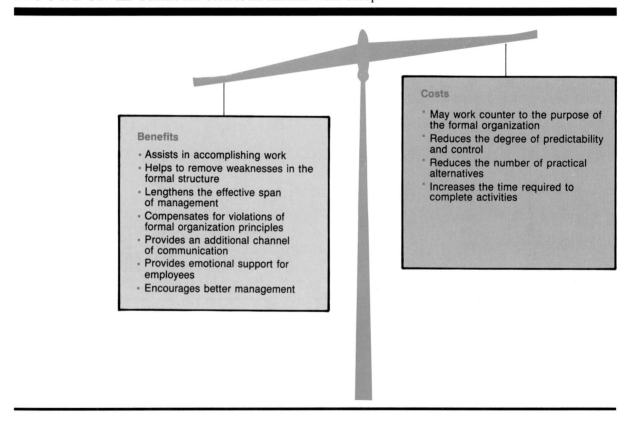

Benefits
- Assists in accomplishing work
- Helps to remove weaknesses in the formal structure
- Lengthens the effective span of management
- Compensates for violations of formal organization principles
- Provides an additional channel of communication
- Provides emotional support for employees
- Encourages better management

Costs
- May work counter to the purpose of the formal organization
- Reduces the degree of predictability and control
- Reduces the number of practical alternatives
- Increases the time required to complete activities

Benefits of the Informal Organization

It is fortunate that management cannot destroy the informal organization, because it is capable of contributing in significant ways to an organization's effectiveness. Several of the means by which the informal organization can benefit the work group are discussed below.

ASSISTS IN ACCOMPLISHING WORK

For managers to be effective, their subordinates must be permitted a certain degree of flexibility in accomplishing assigned tasks. Monitoring subordinates' every move is detrimental to their achieving success. If in business, employees act only when they are told to act, following standard instructions to the letter at all times and contacting others only when duly authorized, the business would have to cease operations. Still, there are the traditionalists, who tend to rely more heavily on formal decisions based on scientific study of business problems.

There are also decision-making situations for which the formal command is inadequate, even wrong. If the atmosphere is heavily traditional, subordinates may exhibit malicious obedience by executing a command faithfully despite personal knowledge that their action will ultimately result in failure. Many managers have discovered that a subordinate can agree with them all day, follow every directive to the letter, and yet fail miserably. When managers place more faith in informal relationships, subordinates may voluntarily adapt the formal order to the requirements of the actual situation. Loosely structured groups are often more effective in achieving organizational objectives.

HELPS TO REMOVE WEAKNESSES
IN THE FORMAL STRUCTURE

The formal organization often has a number of gaps that the informal group can fill. Consider a person who is promoted to a position that exceeds that individual's current capabilities. This is not an unusual occurrence in the armed services, for instance, where a young officer is appointed unit commander. Without the advice and assistance of an experienced sergeant, young officers might not survive their first assignments. In fact, most likely there are many officers who are unsuccessful in the military because they fail to recognize the power of the informal organization. Formal orders and regulations may state that someone is the commander, with certain responsibilities and authorities. But in reality that person may be deficient. By admitting temporary weaknesses, the commander might be able to obtain help from other officers and enlisted personnel. In such a case, deficiencies in the formal structure are overcome by decision making with others. In time, the informal organization may conform to the formal one more closely.

WIDENS THE EFFECTIVE SPAN OF MANAGEMENT

Span of management
The number of people a manager can effectively supervise.

The number of people a manager can effectively supervise is referred to as the **span of management.** As individuals and small groups learn to interact more effectively and are permitted to do so by their supervisors, the manager should be able to devote less time to each individual worker. This may allow widening of a manager's effective span of management.

COMPENSATES FOR VIOLATIONS
OF FORMAL ORGANIZATION PRINCIPLES

Informal relationships can compensate for the ineffectiveness of certain traditional principles of formal organizations. For example, even though authority should equal responsibility, the principle is often violated. As a result, managers often try to develop informal contacts with personnel over whom they have no formal authority. As favors are traded and friendships formed, one quickly learns that the formal prescription of authority often is not sufficient. This does not negate the desirability of having responsibility equal to authority. We discuss these organizing principles further in Chapter 9.

PROVIDES AN ADDITIONAL CHANNEL OF COMMUNICATION

Grapevine
The informal means by which information is transmitted in an organization.

The informal means by which information is transmitted in an organization is referred to as the **grapevine.** To some traditional managers, the grapevine constitutes an obstacle, to be destroyed. They seek to channel and control most, if not all, communications through the official chain of command. However, the grapevine can add to organizational effectiveness if the manager will use it. The grapevine is fast and usually accurate in the information it transmits.

Use of the grapevine does not decrease the importance of maintaining an official channel of communication and command. Although the grapevine can spread much information in a short period, it cannot provide the authority necessary to ensure that action will take place.

PROVIDES EMOTIONAL SUPPORT FOR EMPLOYEES

Over half of all voluntary resignations in many organizations occur within the first six months of employment. This is often due to poor induction procedures, when little help is provided the new employee in joining and being accepted within the group. Friendships, or at least speaking acquaintances, are highly essential to a satisfactory working environment for most people. In one hospital where the termination rate among janitorial personnel was high, the formation of clean-up teams reduced turnover considerably. Such personnel felt isolated and uncomfortable when working alone among physicians, nurses, and patients.

ENCOURAGES BETTER MANAGEMENT

Awareness of the nature and impact of the informal organization often leads to better management decisions. The acceptance of the fact that formal relationships will not enable full accomplishment of organizational tasks should stimulate management to seek other means of increasing motivation. Managers should seek to improve their knowledge of the nature of the people in general and subordinates in particular. They should realize that organizational performance can be affected by the workers' willingness to grant cooperation and enthusiasm. Means other than formal authority must be sought to develop attitudes that support effective performance.

Costs of the Informal Organization

The informal organization is not without its drawbacks. Here are some of the possible detrimental effects of the informal organization.

ETHICAL DILEMMA

Y‌OU ARE A supervisor with a medium-sized manufacturing firm. Your company is in financial difficulty; however, it recently bid on, and has a good chance of obtaining, a major federal government contract. The contract, if obtained, would permit the firm to open up a second shift and even hire some new workers. Since the contract bid was for an amount in excess of $1,000,000 annually, your firm is required to analyze the composition of its labor force in relation to minority employees and correct discrepancies if they exist. When the analysis was conducted, it was determined that few minorities were employed by the company. Top management has stated that it intends to work toward increasing the number of minorities in the firm. However, there is considerable resistance to this policy throughout the firm, especially in your department, which has no minorities. You have a minority applicant and a Caucasian applicant for one job opening on the line. In your opinion, the minority worker is slightly better qualified than the Caucasian applicant. You are aware of the firm's policy toward hiring minority workers, but you believe that a minority worker on the line would cause you a lot of problems with the other workers. You can hire the better qualified minority applicant, or you can hire the less qualified Caucasian applicant.

What would you do?

MAY WORK COUNTER TO THE PURPOSES OF THE FORMAL ORGANIZATION

It is apparent to most managers that individuals in informal groups can and sometimes do work contrary to the formal goals of an enterprise. Few would object to the existence of the informal organization if its goals could always be the same as those of the formal organization. However, informal groups sometimes pressure workers to exhibit disinterest in company requirements, disloyalty, and insubordination, or to engage in unauthorized actions that work at cross-purposes with the organization.

REDUCES THE DEGREE OF PREDICTABILITY AND CONTROL

A goal of most organizations is to ensure predictability and control of behavior so that individuals will work effectively toward organizational goals. This depends, however, on people interpreting and following the formal guidelines. If managers recognize and accept the possibility of a good outcome from permitted flexibility, they must also accept the risks that accompany this lesser degree of control. Informal relationships can and do add much to an organization's effectiveness; they also can and do add much to the degree of uncertainty.

The effect of reassignments on relationships

REDUCES THE NUMBER OF PRACTICAL ALTERNATIVES

A study of the U.S. Army during World War II concluded that the natural unit of personal commitment is the informal group, not the formal organization.[13] For example, the soldiers reported that one of the major reasons for moving forward in combat was to avoid letting the other fellows down. In all organizations, business or military, the solidarity of the informal group can be a major constraint on management actions.

This solidarity may create problems in the reassigning of personnel. If informal groups are broken up by moving individual members in and out, members may feel insecure and show decreased motivation and cooperation. This may suggest that management should think in terms of moving whole groups, rather than individuals. If management wishes to capitalize on the considerable values issuing from the development of informal relationships in work groups, it must be willing to accept some loss of flexibility in decision making.

INCREASES THE TIME REQUIRED TO COMPLETE ACTIVITIES

If the cooperative efforts of the informal work groups can be aligned with the objectives of the firm, management has the best of both worlds. The collective power generated can be phenomenal. But informal work group activities such as gossiping, betting pools, long coffee breaks, and general horseplay are time-consuming and may be detrimental to efficient operations. These are acts that often tax the patience of managers; however, if effective work groups are to be established, some of these activities will have to be permitted, possibly even encouraged. Managers must realize that, despite concern for goal accomplishment, they must allow the group time and opportunity to maintain itself in good working order. People can usually sustain action for a longer period of time under an informal atmosphere than they can when the situation is highly rigid, controlled, and formal.

SUMMARY

An organization is defined as two or more people working together in a coordinated manner to achieve group results. Organizing is the process of prescribing formal relationships among people and resources to accomplish goals. It is affected by both the external environment of the firm and by the firm's internal environment, which individual managers must face. Organizing should be directed toward goal accomplishment; once objectives are established, work activities can be determined. Complex goals are often achieved through specialization of labor, which offers a number of specific benefits, including increased productivity. There are also negative consequences of specialization, such as boredom and fatigue.

The process of grouping related work activities into manageable units is known as departmentation. Ideally, each department should be made up of people performing similar tasks. This is the concept of functional similarity. In addition to function, there are four other ways to divide an organization: by product, by customer, by geographic territory, and by project. Perhaps the most common way is by grouping related functions, such as production, marketing, engineering, finance, and personnel. Unless the organization is quite small, it is likely that several different bases for departmentation will be used.

Additional levels in the organization are created through vertical differentiation; additional units at the same level through horizontal differentiation. Coordination ensures that persons who perform interdependent activities work together in a way that contributes to overall goal attainment.

The informal organization is the set of evolving relationships and patterns of human interaction within an organization that are not officially prescribed. It has a number of definable characteristics and may be studied by means of a contact chart, a diagram showing various individuals in the organization and the numbers of interactions they have with others. Managers often have mixed emotions about the informal organization. Although it is capable of contributing to greater organizational effectiveness, it is not without its drawbacks. But if management is properly trained to understand and work with it, the benefits of the informal organization should exceed the costs. However, if management is not careful, the reverse may be true.

REVIEW QUESTIONS

1. Define organization. What are the three common characteristics of an organization?
2. Describe the process of organizing. What tasks must managers perform in the organizing process?
3. In terms of the organizing process, what types of work activities are needed on a baseball team? a football team? a fast-food restaurant? a small appliance assembly plant?
4. Define specialization of labor. What are its advantages and disadvantages?
5. What guidelines should be used in grouping work activities?
6. Define departmentation. What are the primary means of departmentation?
7. Distinguish, by example and definition, between horizontal and vertical differentiation.
8. Describe the benefits and losses that may be attributed to the informal work group. What is the purpose of a contact chart?

KEY TERMS

organization	vertical differentiation	contact chart
organizing	horizontal differentiation	span of management
specialization of labor	coordination	grapevine
departmentation	informal organization	

CASE STUDY

THE ORGANIZATION OF QUALITY CONTROL

SHELTON LEWIS IS production manager for Memorand, Inc., a company that manufactures small component parts for the hydraulics industry. Shel, as his employees call him, came to Memorand fifteen years ago as a production foreman. He believes the company has been good to him and has chosen not to leave, even though he has had a number of offers of better paying jobs with competing firms.

Gloria Honeycutt is in charge of the quality control section at Memorand and reports directly to Shelton. Gloria started out as Shelton's secretary five years ago. With his encouragement she attended college and recently obtained a degree in industrial management with a concentration in quality control. She then was reassigned to the quality control job, but she continued to report directly to Shelton. Like Shelton, Gloria is intensely loyal to Memorand.

Yesterday, a delicate situation arose, creating a strain on the usually excellent relationship between Shelton and Gloria. The problem began with the following conversation:

Gloria: "Shel, I'm finding a large number of imperfections in the cylinders we're making for Ingersol Rand. I know you're facing a deadline, but I believe we should slow down and inspect all the cylinder parts before they are assembled."

Shelton: "Have you found more than the standard number of defectives?"

Gloria: "No, but a number of cylinders barely passed the leakage tests, and many of the mounting holes are just within specs. If you don't slow down, we may miss a chance at future orders from Ingersol Rand. You know how quality conscious they are."

Shelton: "If we do slow down, we won't make the scheduled delivery date. If we don't do that, Memorand may not even be considered for future contracts. I don't expect you, of all people, to stand in the way of getting the order out on time."

Gloria didn't know what to do, so she just left the office. She still felt she was right. The contract with Ingersol Rand was a lucrative one, and it had been given to Memorand only because Shelton had guaranteed quick delivery. Pleasing Ingersol Rand could easily result in a 10-percent sales increase for the company as a whole. Ingersol Rand has a reputation for selecting suppliers carefully and sticking with them as long as delivery and quality are up to par.

QUESTIONS

1. Is there anything amiss with the organizational relationship between Gloria and Shelton? If so, what? How would you change it? Defend your answer.
2. What do you believe Gloria should do at this point? Explain.

CASE STUDY

MATERIALS ORGANIZATION AT NEWCO MANUFACTURING

TOM JOHNSON, the new materials manager for the Newco Manufacturing Company, was concerned about the lack of organization in his department. Newco had 250 employees and manufactured small electrical motors. Tom reported to the vice-president of manufacturing, Charles McDowell. Tom's fifteen subordinates performed such functions as stocking, receiving, inventory control, purchasing, and outside sales.

Partly because the work flow was unpredictable, the previous materials manager had allowed the department's personnel to do whatever job they thought necessary at the time. They often shifted from job to job—working the parts-issue window while mechanics ordered parts, stocking the parts bin when time permitted, receiving parts when deliveries were made, and shipping orders to customers. The same employees answered the phone and handled outside sales as required. Employee complaints over matters such as inadequate pay, unclear work assignments, and lack of competent leadership had been frequent.

Tom's boss gave him a rather detailed account of the past performance of the materials operation. McDowell had described the materials department as performing very poorly, and he attributed this to a lack of overall direction, ineffective organization, and incompetent personnel. McDowell described several of the department's personnel as "dope heads," who did as little work as possible. The turnover rate had been in excess of 200 percent per year for the past three years. McDowell suggested that Tom "clean house" by firing most of the employees in the department and starting with a fresh crew.

Tom was obviously shaken by the comments made by McDowell and by the complaints of the personnel, and he considered finding a new position; however, he chose not to leave the company before giving the assignment his best efforts for at least a few months.

QUESTIONS

1. Using concepts and principles discussed in this chapter, how would you recommend that Tom Johnson improve the materials department?
2. What type of organization chart would you recommend Tom develop?

EXPERIENTIAL EXERCISE

This exercise will involve you in organizing people. You will have to consider the personalities of both supervisors and subordinates. The situation described here exists in many companies. You either will be assigned a role by your instructor or will serve as an observer. See if you can help these people out.

There are three shifts. An increasing number of grievances have been coming from Shift 3, and the general foreman, Bob Jones, is concerned. They are usually petty complaints, but they are time-consuming and interfere with overall operations. The general foreman wonders if the makeup of the crews might be the problem. Bob has just called a meeting of his three shift supervisors.

If you are not assigned a role, then you are to serve as an observer. As an observer, you should note the following things:

1. Behavior of each supervisor
2. Personalities of individual crewmembers and the combination of personalities on each shift
3. Who has influence
4. Who creates conflict
5. Alternatives considered
6. Issues stressed
7. Who exerts the *most* influence
8. Changes, if any, made in the organization of the crews
9. Degree of acceptance of the decision by the supervisory personnel
10. Degree of acceptance of the decision by the crewmembers

The instructor will provide more information to participants.

Shift 1

J. R. McNasty: J. R. is not well liked by the others on the crew. Nobody wants to work with him. He is a hard worker, but he is also a "Don Juan." All he talks about are his "exotic exploits."

Sam Spade: Sam is the youngest crewman on his shift. His father is a supervisor in another division. He really does not care much for the work or the people. But it has served as a good base of operations for his bookmaking activities, since most of the people here like to gamble.

Bill Dart: Bill is the senior crewmember on his shift. He knows his job and takes pride in being the fastest in the entire plant on his particular operation. He is not liked by the others on the crew, but he figures they are jealous. Besides, as he would put it, he can live without them. He enjoys a good argument and often engages in shouting matches with other crewmembers, or even supervisors.

Shift 2

Jim Hardy: Jim is a quiet, easy going, but hard-working crewman. He never causes trouble and can always be counted on to do a good job on every assignment. He has no complaints about his job. He just wants to be given work to do and to be left alone.

Maggie Spellman: Maggie is the union steward. However, she is sensitive to both sides of issues regarding production and comes to the defense of the company when she believes it is right. She is respected by co-workers and by company management. She has a reputation as a good worker and intends to keep it.

Buddy Goode: Buddy is considered to be the best all-around crewmember in his department. He has mastered every operation and consistently turns out high-quality work. Other crewmembers often go to him with their problems, both work-related and personal. He has good rapport with the shift supervisors—in fact, Tommy Starr, supervisor on the first shift, is his brother-in-law.

Shift 3

Charlie Striker: Most people consider Charlie to be very belligerent. He is having marital problems, which keeps him in a bad mood most of the time. He is on the union committee and plans to become president of the local.

Al Loner: Al looks out for himself. He worked overtime every day for three weeks prior to the last pre-strike inventory buildup. He has been having some back problems lately, which have slowed him down. He does not seem to fit in with the other workers.

C. C. Krier: C. C. really loves a good argument or fight. He prides himself on being a professional agitator. His previous supervisor labeled him an incompetent, but the company hasn't found any way to get rid of him.

NOTES

1. Richard A. Melcher, Mark Maremont, Amy Borrus, and Thane Peterson, "The Japanese Are Coming—And Thatcher Is All Smiles," *Business Week,* 20 February 1989, 46.
2. Thomas J. Murry, "Wal-Mart Stores Penny Wise," *Business Month,* December 1988, 42.
3. "The Fast-Food War: Big Mac Under Attack," *Business Week,* 30 January 1984, 45.
4. "The New Industrial Relations," *Business Week,* 11 May 1981, 85–98.
5. W. G. Astley and A. H. Van de Ven, "Central Perspectives and Debates in Organization Theory," *Administrative Science Quarterly* (June 1983): 248.
6. R. L. Daft, *Organization Theory and Design* (St. Paul, Minn.: West, 1983), 227.
7. John Hoerr, "Is Teamwork a Management Plot? Mostly Not," *Business Week,* 20 February 1989, 70.
8. Theodore T. Herbert, "Strategy and Multinational Organization Structure: An International Relationships Perspective," *Academy of Management Review* (April 1984): 263.
9. "Can GM Solve Its Identity Crisis?" *Business Week,* 23 January 1984, 32–33.
10. Daft, *Organization Theory,* 23.
11. Herbert, "Strategy," 263.
12. Vijay Govindaragan, "Decentralization, Strategy, and Effectiveness of Strategic Business Units in Multibusiness Organizations," *Academy of Management Review* 11, no. 4 (October 1986): 844–856.
13. Samuel A. Stouffer and Arthur A. Lumsdain, *The American Soldier: Combat and Its Aftermath,* Vol. 2 (Princeton: Princeton University Press, 1949): 1974.

REFERENCES

Astley, W. G., and A. H. Van de Ven. "Central Perspectives and Debates in Organization Theory." *Administrative Science Quarterly* (June 1983): 248.

Bobbitt, H. R., Jr., and J. D. Ford. "Decision-Maker Choice as a Determinant of Organizational Structure." *Academy of Management Review* 5 (January 1980): 13–23.

"Can GM Solve Its Identity Crisis?" *Business Week* (23 January 1984): 32–33.

Daft, R. L. *Organization Theory and Design.* St. Paul, Minn.: West, 1983.

Dalton, D. R., W. D. Todor, J. Spendelini, J. Fielding, and L. W. Porter. "Organization Structure and Performance: A Critical Review." *Academy of Management Review* 5 (January 1980): 61–64.

Fleming, Mary M. K. "Keys to Successful Project Management." *CMA—The Management Accounting Magazine* 60 (November–December 1986): 58–61.

Fombrun, Charles J. "Structural Dynamics Within and Between Organizations." *Administrative Science Quarterly* 31 (September 1986): 103–121.

Govindaragan, Vijay. "Decentralization, Strategy, and Effectiveness of Strategic Business Units in Multibusiness Organizations." *Academy of Management Review* 11, no. 4 (October 1986): 844–856.

Handy, C. "Through the Organizational Looking Glass." *Harvard Business Review* 58, no. 1 (January–February 1980): 115–121.

Herbert, Theodore T. "Strategy and Multinational Organization Structure: An International Relationships Perspective." *Academy of Management Review* (April 1984).

"The New Industrial Relations." *Business Week* (11 May 1981): 85–98.

Peters, Thomas J. "The Destruction of Hierarchy: The Information Revolution Is Killing Traditional Corporate Hierarchy." *Industry Week* 237 (15 August 1988): 33–35.

Quinlivan-Hall, Dave. "Involving Your People in Organizational Problem Solving." *Training & Development Journal* 41 (July 1987): 73–74.

Scanlan, K. "Maintaining Organizational Effectiveness—A Prescription for Good Health." *Personnel Journal* 58, no. 5 (May 1980): 381–386.

Sussman, Susan. "Corporations Urged to Improve How They Organize Information." *PC Week* 1 (17 March 1987): 1–2.

CHAPTER

9

Chapter Outline

Organizing

Structure

Learning Objectives

After completing this chapter students should be able to

1. Describe the concepts of responsibility, authority, delegation, and accountability.
2. List several important organizing principles.
3. Contrast the advantages of centralization and decentralization.
4. Identify the basic types of organizational structures and the advantages and disadvantages of each.

"ONE SMALL STEP for man, one giant leap for mankind." The words of Neil Armstrong in July 1969 as he stepped onto the surface of the moon have become part of the American legend. They represent the realization of the dream to explore space and walk on the moon. More than that, though, landing on the moon was the culmination of a determined ten-year effort initiated by President John F. Kennedy. It was one of the most highly organized and technically complex endeavors ever undertaken.

The "Vision of Apollo," which resulted in Neil Armstrong's moonwalk, was hardly characteristic of the support that has been given the U.S. space program since then. In 1986, for example, funding for NASA as a percentage of the federal budget, was less than one half the yearly funding for Apollo during the 1960s.

Still, NASA moved forward with some challenging goals. The space shuttles Columbia, Challenger, and Discovery were immensely complex to build and launch. Just to process the shuttle orbiter, external tank, and boosters required 6,027 contractor employees. NASA clearly had to be well organized to coordinate such complex activities. In addition, participant corporations like Lockheed, Rockwell International, and Martin Marietta had to align their own organizations to accomplish the tasks at hand. For example, Lockheed established competing teams, each including a former astronaut; each team formed an alliance with a major airline to take advantage of the airline's operational experience.

Just the proposals on the shuttle processing contracts ran over 500 pages. Organizing and coordinating the extremely complex technology, the diverse and highly trained personnel, and the contributions of hundreds of subcontractors was a monumental task. The future presented even greater challenges. President Reagan charged NASA with developing "more visionary, long-term space program goals." Among the ideas being seriously promoted were a lunar base and a systematic exploration of the solar system.

But all that was interrupted by the Challenger accident in 1986. A leaking rocket booster caused a mighty explosion and loss of mission, vehicle, and crew just over a minute after liftoff. A presidential panel investigated and found numerous organizational failings within NASA. NASA examined itself closely and by late in 1988 was back on line, as successful as ever. During the period between 1986 and late 1988, two more space shuttle missions were completed without a hitch. ■

IN CHAPTER 8 the organizing process and the ways departmentation occurs as organizations grow were presented. In this chapter we first discuss four important management concepts, responsibility, authority, delegation, and accountability. Then, several principles or guidelines of the organizing function, important to a manager's performance, are reviewed. Next, the trade-off between the needs of centralization and those of decentralization is discussed. In the final section of the chapter, the common types of organizational structures are described.

RESPONSIBILITY

Responsibility
An obligation to perform work activities.

In accepting a certain job, a person takes responsibility for performing the tasks involved. **Responsibility** is an obligation to perform work activities. For example, Joan Lewis, a manager with NASA, is responsible for the data-processing center. As such, she must plan, organize, influence, and control the work of computer operators and analysts. And that is not all. She must also provide for the maintenance of the computer equipment and programs and engage in numerous other activities essential to the success of the data-processing department.

In this regard, responsibility is a felt obligation. The degree to which a manager feels the obligation to perform is enhanced if responsibilities are clearly defined. Nothing is more frustrating to a manager or a worker than being confused about the nature, scope, and details of specific job responsibilities. For instance, suppose Susan James, a first-line supervisor for a large insurance company, has the following conversation with her boss, Phil Williams:

Susan: Am I responsible for processing the new commercial fire insurance policies, or should Joe Davis's unit handle them?

Phil: I don't think it really matters too much which unit handles these policies so long as it's done correctly and thoroughly.

Susan: But what do you expect me to do?

Phil: I'll get back to you later on this—I'm busy at the moment.

Obviously, Phil's comments leave Susan unsure of her responsibility. In fact, in cases such as this, managers often assume that someone else will do what needs to be done. Therefore, Phil should not be surprised if the new policies do not get processed at all. When this occurs, he may be upset with Susan, but the real fault is his own.

Ambiguous instructions can be dangerous. In 1979 Metropolitan Edison's nuclear plant at Three Mile Island in Pennsylvania overheated. Public safety in the area was seriously endangered. The fear was that clouds of radioactive gas would expose citizens to high levels of radioactivity and that radiation would show up later in cows' milk and other food products. A study of the Three Mile Island nuclear incident showed that job-related tension, brought on by confusion over what was expected of employees, contributed to the accident.[1] It seems that some important steps were omitted from various safety measures. Apparently the reactor operators were not sure who was responsible.

■ AUTHORITY

Authority
The right to decide, to direct others to take action, or to perform certain duties in achieving organizational goals.

A common complaint of managers is that, although they have unlimited responsibility, their authority is often inadequate. **Authority** is the right to decide, to direct others to take action, or to perform certain duties in achieving organizational goals. The definition suggests that authority has at least three key characteristics:

1. Authority is a right.
2. Exercising authority involves making decisions, taking actions, or performing duties.
3. Authority is granted for the purpose of achieving organizational goals.

Every manager must have some authority in order to organize and direct the use of resources to attain the goals of the organization. At every level in the organization there are various degrees of authority that may be given to a manager. For example, a supervisor made responsible for staffing a department may have the authority to do so at any of the degrees of authority shown in Figure 9.1. At the lowest level, the supervisor will feel that he or she lacks the authority to staff the department adequately.

F I G U R E 9.1 ■
Degrees of Authority in Staffing a Department

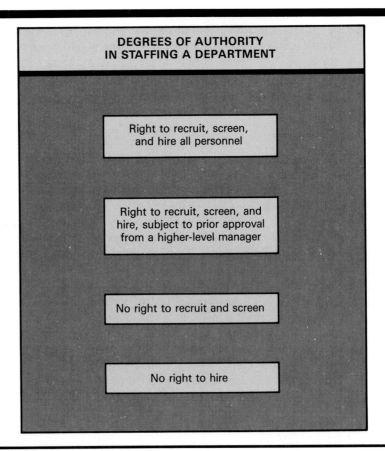

**DEGREES OF AUTHORITY
IN STAFFING A DEPARTMENT**

Right to recruit, screen, and hire all personnel

Right to recruit, screen, and hire, subject to prior approval from a higher-level manager

No right to recruit and screen

No right to hire

■■ DELEGATION

Delegation
The process of assigning responsibility along with the needed authority.

The process of assigning responsibility along with the needed authority is referred to as **delegation.** Delegation is one of the most significant concepts or practices affecting a manager's ability to get the job done. It creates a risk for managers, however, because the success or failure of an operation is ultimately their responsibility. When a manager delegates a responsibility to a subordinate, the relationship between the two is based on an obligation. Managers should remember an important point: one cannot relieve oneself of any portion of the original responsibility; delegation only allows for someone else doing the work. Some managers attempt to reduce risk by avoiding delegation and doing everything themselves. Delegation of responsibility and authority is essential, though, if managers are to provide opportunities for the development of people. Also, few managers have the capability to personally perform all of the duties for which they are responsible. A frequent cause of operational failure is the unwillingness or inability of some managers to delegate responsibility and authority.

Some of the more important reasons for delegation are illustrated in Figure 9.2. First, delegation of authority often leads to quicker action and faster, better decisions. Action can be taken much faster if we can avoid going to a higher level in the organization for a decision. For example, at Sears, Roebuck, store managers

FIGURE 9.2 ■
Reasons for Delegation

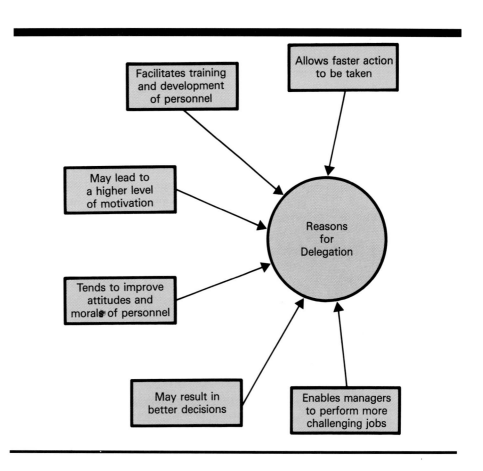

subordinate

supervisor

> #### TABLE 9.1 ■ Limitations or Potential Problems with Delegation
>
> 1. • If improper feedback is provided, the manager may lose control and may not have the time to correct the situation should a problem occur.
> 2. • Delegation can fail if the level of responsibility and authority is not clearly defined and understood.
> 3. • If the delegatee does not possess the ability, skills, and experience to accomplish the job or to make decisions, delegation can prove disastrous.
> 4. • Problems can result if an employee is given responsibility but insufficient authority to perform the task.

can decide within very broad limits what items to stock. In general, however, when routine matters are handled at a level that is higher than necessary, work output will likely be less than optimum.

Second, delegation tends to be an important factor in training and developing personnel in the organization. Managers cannot learn to perform a certain function or make decisions unless they are given the opportunity to do so. Delegation of responsibility and authority is essential if the firm is concerned about developing personnel to assume more challenging and demanding jobs in the future.

Third, delegation may lead to a higher level of motivation. Persons who are given authority and responsibility by their superiors often see this as a reflection of trust in their abilities. This may become a self-fulfilling prophecy as subordinates try to live up to that trust.

Fourth, closely related to improved motivation are the attitudes and the morale of employees. Persons who are given responsibility and authority tend to have a better attitude toward their superiors. They are often easier to manage and more cooperative, and their morale is higher.

Fifth, delegation may result in better decisions. The person who is closest to the job being done is often the one who knows how to do it best.

Finally, it is through delegation that managers are able to perform especially challenging jobs, such as putting a man on the moon. Delegation can be thought of as a way of extending the manager's capabilities. Evidence suggests that managers recognize this. A recent study of graduating MBAs and practicing managers revealed that the ability to perform a wide variety of tasks tends to be associated with increasing delegation.[2]

Despite these and other advantages of delegation, certain limitations, or potential problems managers should be considering, may be seen in Table 9.1.

■ ACCOUNTABILITY

Accountability
Any means of ensuring that the person who is supposed to do a task actually performs it and does so correctly.

No organization can function effectively without a system of accountability. **Accountability** is any means of ensuring that the person who is supposed to do a task actually performs it and does so correctly. Situations can rapidly get out of control when people are not held accountable.

FIGURE 9.3 ■
Conditions for Holding a
Manager Accountable

*Things managers should
do to be accountable*

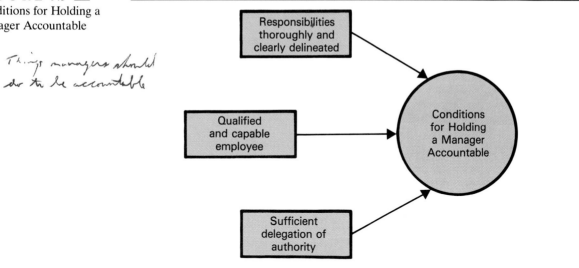

Before a manager can be held accountable for results, certain conditions, seen in Figure 9.3, should be present. First, responsibilities must be thoroughly and clearly understood. An individual who is unaware of what is expected cannot be properly held accountable. Second, the person must be qualified and capable of fulfilling the obligation. It would be inconceivable to assign the responsibility and authority for performing engineering or accounting functions to individuals having no previous educational background or experience in these areas. Finally, sufficient authority to accomplish the task must be delegated. Assigning a manager the total profit responsibility for a department but no authority to hire or fire employees might mean that insufficient authority has been delegated. This manager probably would object to being held accountable for results.

Because it is so closely related to responsibility, a manager's accountability cannot be delegated to someone else. Managers are usually accountable not only for their own actions and decisions, but also for the actions of their subordinates. In navy tradition, the captain should go down with the ship, but this is an extreme case.

Accountability can be established in several ways. The first method is through *monitored* personal inspection by the manager. After assigning a person to do the task, the manager observes to see that it is done properly. The second method is to have the subordinate complete reports and give them to the manager. However, because it is human nature to want to be seen in the best possible light, such reports might be biased in favor of the subordinate. A third method is through reporting done by others. A quality control inspector might report the number of defective units for each worker to the manager. Customers may report poor service or faulty products. This method of accountability is out of the hands of the person held accountable and is therefore reasonably free of bias. Finally, accountability may be obtained through a machine with a counter or other measuring device. In a grocery store, a cash register tape of all sales does this. Most modern retailers use point-of-sale accounting systems, where most mistakes are immediately logged for correction.

■ ORGANIZING PRINCIPLES

To accomplish organizational goals, organizations may follow any or all of a number of important organizing principles. These principles, briefly discussed below, are summarized in Table 9.2.

Unity of Command

Fayol

Unity of command principle
The belief that each person should answer to only one immediate superior; each employee has only one boss.

The **unity of command principle** is the belief that each person should answer to only one immediate superior; each employee has only one boss. Unity of command enables better coordination and understanding of what is required and improves discipline. An employee with two or more bosses can receive contradictory orders. Although unity of command is a sound concept, it does have certain limitations. In large organizations especially, a person may be accountable to more than one boss.

Equal Authority and Responsibility

An important principle of management is that degree of authority should equal degree of responsibility. Following this principle ensures that work will be performed more efficiently and with a minimum amount of frustration on the part of personnel. By not delegating an adequate amount of authority, energies

TABLE 9.2 ■ Organizing Principles

Principle	Definition of	Reason for	Possible Causes of Violation	Possible Results of Violation
Unity of command	A person should report to only *one* boss	Clarity and understanding, to ensure unity of effort and direction and to avoid conflicts	Unclear definition of authority	Dissatisfaction or frustration of employees and perhaps lower efficiency
Equal authority and responsibility	The amount of authority and responsibility should be equal	Allows work to be accomplished more efficiently, develops people, and reduces frustration	Fear on the part of some managers that subordinates might "take over"	Waste of energies and dissatisfaction of employees, thereby reducing effectiveness
Scalar principle	There should be a clear definition of authority in the organization ("to go through channels")	Clarity of relationship avoids confusion and improves decision making and performance	Uncertainty on the part of the employee or a direct effort by the employee to avoid chain of command	Poor performance, confusion, and/or dissatisfaction
Span of management	There is a limit to the number of employees a manager can effectively supervise	Increased effectiveness in direction and control of a manager	Overloading a manager due to growth in number of personnel	Lack of efficiency and control, resulting in poor performance

and resources are wasted, and employee dissatisfaction often results. Unfortunately, many managers continue to give their subordinates more responsibility than authority.

The Scalar Principle and the Chain of Command

Scalar principle
The philosophy that authority and responsibility should flow from top management downward in a clear, unbroken line.
Chain of command
The line along which authority flows from the top of the organization to any individual.

The **scalar principle** is the philosophy that authority and responsibility should flow from top management downward in a clear, unbroken line. If the scalar principle is followed, there is a clear chain of command for every person in the organization. The **chain of command** is the line along which authority flows from the top of the organization to any individual. A clear chain of command clarifies relationships, avoids confusion, and tends to improve decision making, thus often leading to more effective performance. When the scalar principle is followed, superiors and subordinates communicate by going through channels.

Span of Management

Span of management (control)
The number of direct subordinates reporting to any manager.

The number of direct subordinates reporting to any manager is referred to as the **span of management (control).** Although the span of management may vary greatly, there is a maximum number of employees a manager can effectively supervise in a given circumstance. Efficient use of managerial talent also dictates that there also be a minimum number of subordinates assigned to each manager. Organizations that value a flat structure, with few levels of management, can achieve this only by having large spans of management.

Although it is not appropriate to attempt to specify what the correct span of management should be in every situation, it is useful to think about how relationships increase when a manager has more than about eight direct subordinates. This was the subject of research done by V. A. Graicunas, a management consultant of the 1930s. Graicunas derived a formula to determine the potential interactions or relationships possible when managers have a given number of employees.[3] Graicunas's formula is as follows:

$$R = n + n(n - 1) + n(2^{n-1} - 1)$$

where R represents the number of relationships or interactions and n is the number of subordinates reporting to the manager.

According to the Graicunas formula, a manager with two employees would have six potential relationships. For example, if Ed Bishop has two subordinates, John and Susan, there would be six possible interactions, as Table 9.3 illustrates. As Table 9.4 shows, each additional employee creates a substantial increase in the number of potential relationships.

Accepted spans of management have historically been relatively narrow, usually ranging from six to fifteen. Narrow spans of management permit closer supervision of personnel but tend to create tall organizational structures with a large number of levels. This may cause difficulties in communications and result in managers and workers at lower levels feeling isolated. Wide spans result in relatively fewer levels, or flat organizations, and greater freedom for the individual employee.

Relationships	Number of Relationships	Example
TABLE 9.3 ■ Possible Relationships with Two Employees		
Direct relationships	2	• Ed may meet and talk with John • Ed may meet and talk with Susan
Group relationships	2	• Ed may meet and talk with John with Susan present, or Ed may meet and talk with Susan with John present
Cross relationships	2	• John may interact with Susan without Ed being present, or Susan may meet with John without Ed being present
TOTAL	6	

A number of factors affect the span of management:

1. In general, the more complex the work, the shorter the optimum span of management.
2. The span can be longer if the manager is supervising employees performing similar jobs.
3. If jobs are closely interlocked and interdependent, the manager may have greater problems with coordination, creating the need for a rather limited span of management.
4. If the organization is operating in an unstable environment, a narrow span may prove to be more effective.
5. The establishment of numerous standards increases predictability and provides the basis for effective control, thereby resulting in a wider effective span.
6. Managers and employees who are highly skilled, experienced, and motivated generally can operate with wider spans of management and with less supervision.
7. Where high commitment to the organization is as important as technical efficiency, such commitment can be enhanced through wider spans of management.[4]

Number of Employees	Potential Number of Relationships
TABLE 9.4 ■ Possible Relationships with Different Numbers of Employees	
1	1
2	6
3	18
4	44
5	100
6	222

The span of management can be significantly longer for an assembly line type of organization than for unit or small-batch processing. (COMSTOCK, Inc./Ed Pieratt)

In addition, technology can have a significant impact on the span of management. Joan Woodward, a British researcher, conducted studies in 100 English manufacturing firms. She discovered that the type of production technology actually used in business organizations affected the span of management. Woodward classified production technology on the basis of the following categories:

- Unit or small-batch processing (for example, made-to-order goods such as custom-tailored clothing)
- Mass production (assembly-line operations)
- Process production with continuous long runs of a standardized product such as oil, chemicals, or pharmaceuticals

She discovered that spans of management were widest in firms using mass-production technology. The jobs in a mass-production situation tend to be more routine and similar to one another, thereby leading to wider appropriate spans of management.[5] On the other hand, unit and process production were marked by narrower spans of management.

CENTRALIZATION VERSUS DECENTRALIZATION

Centralization
The degree to which authority is retained by higher-level managers within an organization rather than being delegated.

It is important that management determine the appropriate levels of responsibility and authority to be delegated. **Centralization** is the degree to which authority is retained by higher-level managers within an organization rather than being delegated. If a limited amount of authority is delegated, the organization is usually characterized as being centralized. If a significant amount of authority is delegated to lower levels, the enterprise is described as being decentralized. There are many degrees of centralization. The real question is not whether a company should decentralize, but what degree of decentralization is appropriate.

In a highly centralized structure, individual managers and workers at lower levels in the organization have a rather narrow range of decisions or actions they can initiate. By contrast, the scope of authority to make decisions and take actions is rather broad for lower-level managers and employees in decentralized organizations. In a highly centralized organizational structure, upper management makes all decisions regarding the hiring or firing of personnel, approval of purchasing of equipment and supplies, and similar activities. In a decentralized structure, lower-level management may make these decisions.

Decentralization is advocated by many who believe that a greater share in management decision making should be given to lower organizational levels. Decentralization tends to create a climate for more rapid growth and development of personnel. If virtually all decisions and orders come from one central source, organization members tend to act as robots and unthinking executors of someone else's commands. On the other hand, there are exceptionally competent managers in high positions, like Lee Iacocca at Chrysler, who are better able to make valid decisions than are their subordinates. When this is the case, a reasonable tendency is to lean toward centralization. In addition, many employees and lower-level managers do not wish to be involved at high levels in the organization.

In addition to the human behavior implications of decentralization and centralization, several other factors affect a manager's decision in this regard. Centralization

1. produces uniformity of policy and action.
2. results in few risks of errors by subordinates who lack either information or skill.
3. utilizes the skills of central and specialized experts.
4. enables closer control of operations. by top managers

On the other hand, decentralization

1. tends to make for speedier decisions and actions on the spot without consulting higher levels.
2. results in decisions that are more likely to be adapted to local conditions.
3. results in greater interest and enthusiasm on the part of the subordinate to whom the authority has been entrusted (these expanded jobs provide excellent training experiences for possible promotion to higher levels).
4. allows top management to utilize time for more study and consideration of the basic objectives, plans, and policies of the enterprise.

Additional factors to be taken into account concerning the degree of centralization are discussed below.

Size and Complexity of the Organization

The larger the enterprise, the more authority the central manager is forced to delegate. If the firm is engaged in many separate businesses, the limitations of expertise will usually lead to decentralization. Authority will be delegated to the heads of these units. Each major product group is likely to have different product problems, various kinds of customers, and different marketing channels. If speed and adaptability to change are necessary for success, decentralization is a must.

Dispersion of the Organization

When the difficulties of size are compounded by geographic dispersion, it is evident that a greater degree of decentralization must occur. General Motors Company is a prime example of decentralization because of size and geographic dispersion. Not every decision or every function must be decentralized, however. Control of operations may have to be pushed down to lower levels in the organization, even though control of financing may still be centralized. Because of the increasing complexity of federal and state legislation affecting employment practices and unionization, centralization of labor relations is often established for purposes of uniformity throughout the company.

Competence of Personnel Available

A major limiting factor in centralization is the degree of competence of present personnel. If an enterprise has grown up under centralized decision making and control, subordinate personnel are often poorly equipped to start making major decisions. They were hired and trained to be followers, not leaders and decision makers. In some convenience store chains, this has developed into a major problem. Store managers are promoted to supervisor, not because of their decision-making ability, but because they are experienced in basic store functions and can ensure that store managers follow standard operating procedures. In

ETHICAL DILEMMA

You RUN THE Medallion Construction Company, and your company is bidding on a $2.5 million public housing project. A local electrical subcontractor submitted a bid that you know is 20 percent too low and could put him out of business. In fact, the bid was $30,000 below the other four contractors' bids. But accepting it will improve your chance of winning the contract. You are asking yourself the same question over and over again, "Is it right to allow someone to drive themselves into possible bankruptcy when they don't know it, but you do?" You can accept the low subcontractor bid and almost assure that your company can get the $2.5 million contract, or you can throw out the too-low subcontractor bid and submit a realistic overall bid on the contract.
What would you do?

Source: Adapted by permission, *Nation's Business,* August 1987. Copyright © 1987, U.S. Chamber of Commerce.

such situations, people who eventually make it to the top may not be equipped to cope with all the decisions that must be made that are not based on established practices and procedures. Those inclined toward more independent thought and action may be driven away from the centralized firm.

Adequacy of the Communication System

Greater size, complexity, and geographic dispersion lead to the delegation of larger amounts of authority for decision making to lower levels in the organization. Unwanted decentralization can be avoided through the development of a communication system that will provide for the speed, accuracy, and capacity of information top management needs to exercise centralized control. In effect, although large size and geographic dispersion may preclude being on the spot, one can control subordinates by detailing standards of performance and by ensuring that information flows quickly and accurately to the central authoritative position.

The lack of an effective communication channel has caused problems for the joint venture between Chrysler and Maserati. Size, complexity, and geographic dispersion led to communication problems in the building of the Chrysler TC automobile. Making 780 trips to Italy—to resolve the problem of whether the car's top should be made of composite materials, steel, or aluminum—caused the final cost to be 14 percent over budget. There were also inventory problems; at one point, $23 million worth of Chrysler components were discovered piled up in a Milan warehouse. Because of financial loss, due to these communication problems, Chrysler dropped an option to increase their stake in Maserati to 51 percent, modified TC production plans, and killed other joint projects.[6]

Computer Technology

The widespread use of computers in business gives managers more flexibility in deciding whether to decentralize. Today, computers or terminals are available at virtually all site locations and information can be supplied to headquarters virtually instantaneously. In the past, an organization might have decided to decentralize because of the time delay involved in getting decision-making information to top-level managers. Today this is less of a problem.

Even when it is not feasible to centralize all aspects of management, certain functions can be handled at headquarters. For example, the functions of accounting and finance have been centralized to some degree in most major companies. Other firms have formed data communications networks, which link computers and terminals throughout the organization. It appears likely that widespread use of such "networking" may be the next major wave in the evolution of information technology.[7]

Organizational structure
The formal relationships among groups and individuals in the organization.

TYPES OF ORGANIZATIONAL STRUCTURES

The formal relationships among groups and individuals in the organization are called **organizational structure.** The organizational structure provides guidelines essential for effective employee performance and overall organizational success. The structure clarifies and communicates the lines of responsibility and authority within the firm and assists management in coordinating the overall operation.

Although it is common to think only of large companies when discussing organizational structures, every firm, large or small, has a structure of some kind. It may or may not have an organizational chart. Small businesses may have structures that are simple and easy to understand. In fact, the organizational structure may be informal and highly changeable in small, uncomplicated businesses. By contrast, large, diverse, and complex organizations usually have a highly formalized structure, but that does not mean that the structure is so rigid that it does not change, perhaps even frequently. Determining the most appropriate organizational design or structure is not a simple matter if one must consider frequency of reorganization as a factor. Newly formed high-technology companies are the most likely companies to restructure or reorganize frequently, but even some of the largest Fortune 500 industrial firms often experience major reorganization.

Many variations of organizational structures are used today, but line, line and staff, functional authority, project, and matrix structures are discussed separately to instill in the reader an understanding of the most common types of structures from which variations are developed. Mechanistic and organic structures were discussed in Chapter 2. They are also discussed here because of their impact on organizational structure.

Line organizations
Those organizations that have only direct, vertical relationships between different levels within the firm. They include only line departments.

Line departments
Departments directly involved in accomplishing the primary purpose of the organization.

Line Organization

Line organizations are those organizations that have only direct, vertical relationships between different levels within the firm. They include only line departments. **Line departments** are those departments directly involved in accomplishing the primary purpose of the organization. In a typical company, line departments include production and marketing. In a line organization, authority follows the chain of command. Figure 9.4 is an illustration of a simple line organization structure.

FIGURE 9.4 ■
A Line Organization
Structure

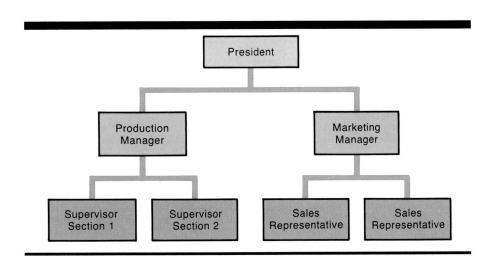

Several advantages are quite often associated with the pure line organization structure.

1. A line structure tends to simplify and clarify responsibility, authority, and accountability relationships within the organization. The levels of responsibility and authority of personnel operating within a line organization are likely to be precise and understandable.
2. A line structure promotes fast decision making and allows the organization to change direction rapidly, because there are few people to consult when problems arise.
3. Because pure line organizations are small, there are greater feelings of closeness between management and employees, and all personnel usually have an opportunity to know what is going on in the firm.

There are also certain disadvantages to the line structure. The major disadvantage is that as the firm grows larger, there is an increasing lack of effectiveness. At some point, improved speed and flexibility does not offset the lack of specialized knowledge and skills. This point occurs long before a company reaches the size of Sears, for example. In other words, a line structure may reduce the effectiveness of managers by forcing them to be experts in too many fields. In a line organization, firms tend to become overly dependent on the one or few key people who can perform numerous jobs. If the organization is to remain purely line, management can create additional levels to share the managerial load. This, however, will result in a longer chain of command and consequent loss of some of the values of speed, flexibility, and centralized control. Therefore, there are few pure line organizations of any substantial size.

Line and Staff Organization

Most large organizations are of the line and staff type. **Line and staff organizations** are those organizations that have direct, vertical relationships between different levels and also specialists responsible for advising and assisting other managers. Such organizations have both line and staff departments. **Staff departments** provide line people with advice and assistance in specialized areas.

As shown in the line and staff organization chart in Figure 9.5, staff functions under the president typically include personnel, research, accounting, and quality control. The line functions are marketing and production. Each staff manager has responsibilities to persons at every level within the organization. For simplicity, only the staff relationships between the personnel director and persons in the production department are shown. Notice the dotted lines from personnel to superintendents, supervisors, and workers. The personnel director, however, also has staff responsibilities to the other department heads. Personnel, research, accounting, and quality control are separate, specialized staff functions, but the managers of these functions have a direct-line reporting relationship to the president.

Three separate types of specialized staffs can be identified: (1) advisory, (2) service, and (3) control. It is possible for one unit to perform all three functions. For example, a personnel manager advises line managers on labor relations topics. The department simultaneously provides a service by procuring

Line and staff organizations Organizations that have direct, vertical relationships between different levels and also specialists responsible for advising and assisting other managers.
Staff departments Provide line people with advice and assistance in specialized areas.

FIGURE 9.5 ■■ Line and Staff Structure of a Typical Manufacturing Company

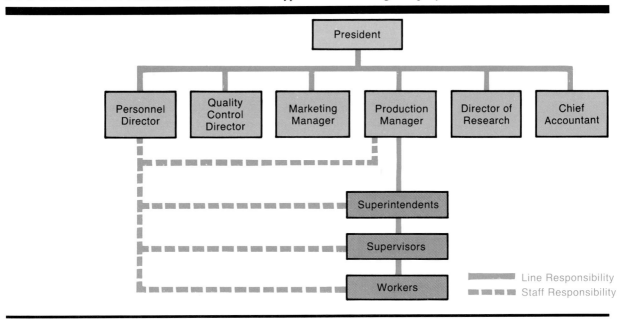

and training needed production and sales personnel. A control orientation enters when the personnel manager audits salaries actually paid, to ensure conformity to line-approved pay ranges. Some staffs are predominantly one or the other in character. For example, a staff economist advises the establishment of long-range plans, and a quality control staff unit enforces authorized product standards. It is apparent that the potential for conflicts in coordination between line and staff tends to grow as one moves from advice to service to control. One can possibly ignore advice, but service is needed, and control is often unavoidable.

There are both advantages and disadvantages. The primary advantage of a line and staff organization structure is that it uses the expertise of staff specialists. Their concentrated and skillful analysis of business problems allows a manager to be more scientific. In addition, a manager's effective span of management can be lengthened—that is, once relieved of technical details, the manager can supervise more people. Some staff personnel even operate as an extension of the manager and assist in coordination and control.

Despite the fact that a line and staff structure allows for increased flexibility and specialization, it may create conflicts. When various specialists are introduced into the organization, line managers may feel that they have lost authority over certain specialized functions. These managers do not want staff specialists telling them what to do or how to do it, even though they recognize specialists' knowledge and expertise. It is important to use staff personnel without destroying unity of command. The authority of line managers should be preserved while their ability to produce is enhanced. Some staff personnel have difficulty adjusting to the role, especially if line managers are reluctant to accept advice. Staff personnel may resent not having authority, and this may cause line and staff conflict.

There is a tendency for specialists to seek to enlarge personal influence by assuming line authority in their specialty. This tendency is compounded by the realization that the fundamental purpose of all staff is to produce greater economy and effectiveness of operation. This means that staff must attempt to introduce changes that result in more efficiency. These changes will not always be welcomed with open arms by line personnel. Thus, the introduction of specialized, noncommand personnel into what was once a fairly simple organization structure often complicates relationships. At an LTV Steel Co. plant in Cleveland, Ohio, teams of highly trained technicians manage a huge electrogalvanizing line practically by themselves, and participate in decisions on hiring, scheduling of work and hours, and operations planning.[8] These specialists probably have enlarged personal influence because they have assumed some line authority in their specialty; nevertheless, this approach appears to produce greater economy and effectiveness of operation.

Functional Authority Organization

Functional authority organization
A modification of the line and staff organization whereby staff departments are given authority over line personnel in narrow areas of specialization.

Functional authority
This is the right of staff specialists to issue orders in their own names in designated areas.

The **functional authority organization** is a modification of the line and staff organization whereby staff departments are given authority over line personnel in narrow areas of specialization. In a pure line organization, there is limited use of specialists by management. In the line and staff organization, specialization of particular functions characterizes the structure, but the specialists only advise and assist. In the functional organizational structure, however, specialists are given **functional authority.** This is the right of staff specialists to issue orders in their own names in designated areas.

The principle of unity of command (having one boss) is violated when functional authority exists. Even though few if any organizations give all of their staff managers functional authority, it is quite common to do so for one or two specialists. If a function is considered to be of crucial importance, it may be necessary for the specialist to exercise direct rather than advisory authority. The violation of unity of command is intentional. The possible losses resulting from confusion and conflicting orders from multiple sources may be more than offset by increased effectiveness.

Examples of specialists often given functional authority are the managers of quality control, safety, and labor relations. Figure 9.6 shows a functional authority organizational structure. Notice that this is quite similar to the line and staff organization shown in Figure 9.5, except for the nature of the relationship between the staff specialist and other managers. Quality control is a very important function in most manufacturing firms, and its level of authority and status within the organization has increased over the years. A traditional staff department would merely advise. Because of the critical nature of its work, however, a quality control department often directs as well as advises.

Safety and labor relations specialists may exercise functional authority over personnel in other areas throughout the organization, but only in relation to their specific specialties. A safety manager may issue compliance guidelines and give direct interpretations of the Occupational Safety and Health Act (OSHA) throughout the organization. The labor relations specialist often will have complete authority in contract negotiations with the union. In each of the above illustrations—quality control, safety, and labor relations—the traditional chain of command has been split. As long as this splitting process is restricted,

F I G U R E 9.6 ■ Functional Authority Organizational Structure

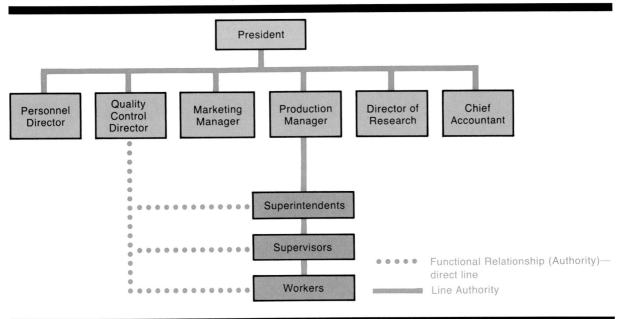

coordination and unity of action are not in excessive danger. Many organizations that utilize functional relationships attempt to confine the impact to managerial rather than operative levels. Thus, a department supervisor may have to account to more than one boss, but the employees are protected from this possible confusion.

The major disadvantages of a functional authority organizational structure are: (1) the potential conflicts resulting from the violation of the principle of unity of command, and (2) the tendency to keep authority centralized at higher levels in the organization. If the functionalized structure is used extensively, there may be a tendency for the line department supervisor to become little more than a figurehead. The structure can become very complicated when there are functional specialists on various levels in the organization.

Project and Matrix Organization Structures

The line, line and staff, and functional authority organizational structures have been the traditional approaches to organization. The primary goal of these forms of organizations has been the establishment and distribution of authority to coordinate and control the firm by emphasizing vertical, rather than horizontal, relationships. In major aerospace projects like Apollo, however, work processes may flow horizontally, diagonally, up, or down. The direction of work flow depends on the distribution of talents and abilities in the organization and the need to apply them to the problem that exists. The organizations that have emerged to cope with this challenge have been referred to as project and matrix organizations.

TABLE 9.5 ■■ When Project Organization Structures Are Most Valuable
• Work is definable in terms of a specific goal and target date for completion.
• Work is somewhat unique and unfamiliar to the existing organization.
• Work is complex with respect to interdependence of activities and specialized skills necessary for accomplishment.
• Work is critical in terms of possible gain or loss.
• Work is temporary with respect to duration of need.

PROJECT ORGANIZATION

Project organization
A temporary organization designed to achieve specific results by using teams of specialists from different functional areas within the organization.

A **project organization** is a temporary organization designed to achieve specific results by using teams of specialists from different functional areas within the organization. The team focuses all of its energies and skills on the assigned project. Once the specific project has been completed, the project team is broken up, and personnel are reassigned to their regular positions in the organization or to other projects. Many business organizations and government agencies make use of project teams or task forces to concentrate efforts on specific project assignments, like the development of a new product or technology or the construction of a new plant.

NASA provides the most widely known example of the use of the project organization. Until the Challenger accident in 1986, NASA had seen success after success. Terms like Gemini and Apollo are remembered with pride by millions of U.S. citizens. Each mission was a distinct project at NASA. Although the disaster reflects poorly on NASA's recent application of organizing principles, the previous successes probably would not have been possible without project organizations. NASA, and most of the rest of the aerospace industry, remain committed to this form of organization, and two recent successful missions attest to its continued success. As may be seen in Table 9.5, there are times when project organization structures are probably most valuable.

Figure 9.7 illustrates a highly simplified project structure attached to an existing organization. Personnel are assigned to the project from the existing permanent organization and are under the direction and control of the project manager. The project manager specifies what effort is needed and when work will be performed, whereas the concerned department managers may decide who in their unit is to do the work and how it is to be accomplished. Home base for most personnel is the existing department—engineering, production, purchasing, personnel, or research and development.

The authority over each of the four project members is shared by the project manager and the respective function managers in the permanent organization. The four specialists are temporarily on loan and spend only a portion of their time on the project assignment. It is apparent that authority is one of the crucial questions of the project structure. A deliberate conflict has been established between the project manager and managers within the permanent organization. The authority relationships are overlapping, presumably in the interest of ensuring that all problems will be covered.

Project managers and department heads are often forced into using means other than formal authority to accomplish results. Informal relationships become

F I G U R E 9.7 ■ Project Structure

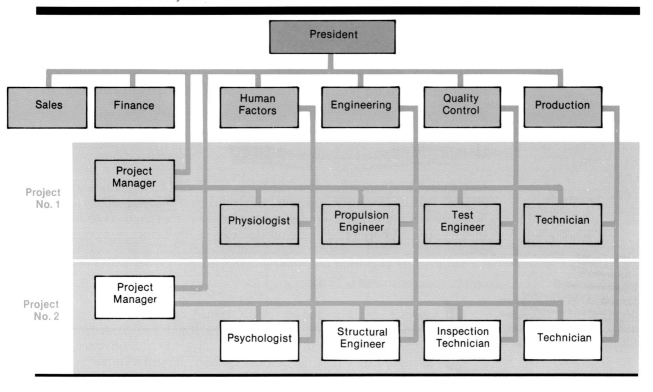

more important than formal prescriptions of authority. In the event of conflict and dispute, discussion and consensus are required, rather than the forcing of compliance by threat or punishment. Full and free communication, regardless of formal rank, is required among those working on the project. More attention is allocated to roles and competencies in relation to the project than to formal levels of authority.

MATRIX ORGANIZATION

Matrix organization
A permanent organization designed to achieve specific results by using teams of specialists from different functional areas within the organization.

A **matrix organization** is a permanent organization designed to achieve specific results by using teams of specialists from different functional areas within the organization. They are often used when it is essential for the firm to be highly responsive to a rapidly changing external environment. For example, an electronics firm might find that the matrix structure facilitates quick response by the company to its environment. Matrix organization structures have been used successfully in such industries as banking, chemicals, computers, and electronics. However, matrix organizations require the use of an effective coordinating mechanism to offset the negative effect of dual authority.[9]

In matrix organizations, there are functional managers and product (or project) managers. Functional managers are in charge of specialized resources such as production, quality control, inventories, scheduling, and selling. Product managers are in charge of one or more products and are authorized to prepare product strategies and call on the various functional managers for the necessary resources. When a firm moves to a matrix structure, functional managers must realize that they will lose some of their authority and will have to take some direction from the product managers, who have the budgets to purchase internal resources. In fact, true matrix organizations imply that project and line managers will have roughly equivalent power.[10]

Despite limitations, the effectiveness of the project and matrix management concepts demonstrates that people can work for two or more managers and that managers can effectively influence those over whom they have only partial authority. There is the possibility of conflict and frustration, but the opportunity for prompt, efficient accomplishment is great.

Mechanistic versus Organic Structures

As discussed in Chapter 2, Burns and Stalker originally identified two types of organizations, mechanistic and organic, while studying Scottish electronics firms.[11] As the technology became less stable and more dynamic, they found, organizations tended to evolve from mechanistic to organic. How do these types of organizations differ?

Mechanistic organizations emphasize relatively less flexible and more stable organizational structures.[12] That is,

Mechanistic organization
An organization that emphasizes relatively less flexible and more stable organizational structures.

1. Activities are specialized into clearly defined jobs and tasks. A manufacturing organization with a single assembly line divided into innumerable specialized activities is typically a mechanistic structure.
2. Persons of higher rank typically have greater knowledge of the problems facing the organization than those at lower levels. Unresolved problems are thus passed up the hierarchy. In these structures, the president has greater knowledge of problems than the vice-presidents, who in turn have greater knowledge than managers, who in turn have greater knowledge than nonmanagerial employees. When a clerk or technician faces a problem that he or she cannot solve, he or she brings it to the supervisor for resolution. If the supervisor cannot solve it, the problem is referred up the hierarchy until resolution occurs.
3. Standardized policies, procedures, and rules guide much of the decision making in the organization. Mechanistic organizations often have detailed manuals of organizational policies, and supervisors frequently answer questions or problems by referring employees to the correct section of the procedures manual. When such organizations are unionized, the extent of standardization and formalization typically increases; the union contract may list a majority of the organization's employment policies.
4. Rewards are chiefly obtained through obedience to instructions from supervisors. Mechanistic organizations encourage conformity and discourage innovation, since innovation often means disobedience of company regulations.

Organic organizations
Organizations that have flexible organizational designs and can adjust rapidly to change.

Organic organizations, on the other hand, have flexible organizational designs and can adjust rapidly to change.[13]

1. There is de-emphasis on job descriptions and specialization. People become involved in problem solving when they have the knowledge or

skill that will help solve the problem. A marketing analyst, rather than the vice-president of marketing, may be asked to contribute to the organization's strategic plan if that person has the required knowledge.

2. People holding higher positions are not necessarily assumed to be better informed than employees at lower levels. Such organizations emphasize decentralization of decision making, where responsibility and accountability are pushed as low in the organization as is possible and effective. Organic organizations frequently include large numbers of professional employees, for whom involvement in decision making is natural.

3. Horizontal and lateral organization relationships are given as much or more attention than vertical relationships. Project teams, matrix structures, integrating or liaison roles, and task forces, which bring together individuals with diverse functional expertise, are frequently introduced.

4. Status and rank differences are de-emphasized. Individuals are valued for their expertise rather than for their position in the hierarchy. Thus, computer operators are viewed as equal but different in function from their managers, when it comes to accomplishing the organization's goals.

5. The formal structure of the organization is less permanent, more changeable. Integrating (such as a matrix organization) and adhocratic structures (which use a variety of liaison devices, such as project teams) are organic.

■ COMMITTEES

Committee
A group of people assigned to work together to do something not included in their regular jobs.

Committees have been the brunt of many harsh jokes. For example, it has been said that a camel is a horse designed by a committee. A **committee** is a group of people assigned to work together to do something not included in their regular jobs. Other names used to designate committees include board, council, and task force. A permanent committee is referred to as a standing committee. Committees are necessary for several reasons. They can bring together experts from various areas to handle difficult problems. At least in theory, two heads are better than one. Even if the decisions that committees make are technically no better than those made by individuals, such decisions are often more readily accepted. In fact, it is common practice to make sure that persons likely to oppose an expected decision be placed on the committee responsible for making it.

Committees also have weaknesses. Often the decision process is slow. One person can make decisions faster than a group can. Committees are also costly. If five people are on a committee and the average cost of each is $25 an hour, it costs $250 to have a two-hour meeting. Another weakness of committees is that they often encourage compromise, even though the best decision may be at one extreme or the other.

The shortcomings of committees can be minimized if a few simple rules are followed:

A committee can be used to bring together workers or managers from different areas of the organization for a specific purpose. (© Jeffry W. Myers/Stock, Boston, Inc.)

1. The purpose of the committee should be clearly stated in writing.
2. The size of the committee should be just adequate to obtain the representation and intellectual input required.
3. There should be an odd number of members so that the committee will not deadlock on important issues.
4. Every committee meeting should have a specific written agenda.
5. The committee should be immediately disbanded when it has accomplished its purpose.

SUMMARY

In this chapter we have first discussed four concepts essential in the management of a successful organization. Responsibility is a felt obligation to perform work activities; authority is the right to decide, to direct others, and to perform certain duties; and delegation is the process of assigning responsibility along with the needed authority. Finally, no organization can function effectively without a system of accountability—the means of ensuring that the person who is supposed to do a task actually performs it and does so correctly. Situations can rapidly get out of control when people are not held accountable.

These concepts are basic to the organizing process. In addition, managers follow certain guidelines in performing the organizing function. The unity of command principle is the belief that each person should answer to only one immediate superior. Another important principle is that degree of authority should equal degree of responsibility. The scalar principle is the philosophy that authority and responsibility should flow from top management downward in a clear, unbroken line, called the chain of command. A clear chain of command clarifies relationships, avoids confusion, and tends to improve decision making. The number of subordinates reporting directly to any manager is referred to as the span of management (control). Although the span of management may vary greatly, there is a maximum number of employees a manager can effectively supervise in a given circumstance.

Management must determine appropriate levels of responsibility and authority to be delegated. Centralization is the degree to which authority is retained by higher-level managers. If a significant amount of authority is delegated to lower levels, the enterprise is described as being decentralized. The larger the enterprise, the more authority is delegated. Size, complexity, and geographic dispersion lead to greater decentralization.

The organizational structure is the formal relationships among groups and individuals in the organization. Line organizations have direct, vertical relationships between different levels within the firm. They include only line departments, those directly involved in accomplishing organizational objectives. Line and staff organizations also have direct, vertical relationships, but also specialists responsible for advising and assisting other managers. The functional authority organization is a modification of the line and staff organization. Staff departments are given authority over line personnel in narrow areas of specialization. A project organization is a temporary organization designed to achieve specific results, using teams of specialists from different functional areas within the organization. A matrix organization is the same as a project organization, except that it is permanent rather than temporary. Mechanistic organizations emphasize relatively less flexible and more stable organizational structures. Organic organizations, on the other hand, have flexible organizational designs and can adjust rapidly to change.

In the final section we considered committees, groups of people working together to do something not included in their regular jobs. Committees bring together experts from various areas to handle difficult problems. The theory is, two heads are better than one.

REVIEW QUESTIONS

1. Distinguish by definition among the following terms:
   a. Responsibility
   b. Authority
   c. Delegation
   d. Accountability
2. Describe each of the following organizing principles:
   a. Unity of command
   b. Equal authority and responsibility
   c. Scalar principle
3. Distinguish between centralization and decentralization. Briefly describe the primary factors to be considered in determining the degree of centralization that is appropriate for an organization.
4. What are the basic forms of organizational structure? Briefly describe each form.
5. Under what circumstances are project and matrix structures the most appropriate?
6. Discuss the merits of this statement: "A camel is a horse designed by a committee."

KEY TERMS

responsibility
authority
delegation
accountability
unity of command
   principle
scalar principle
chain of command
span of management
   (control)

centralization
organizational structure
line organizations
line departments
line and staff
   organizations
staff departments
functional authority
   organization

functional authority
project organization
matrix organization
mechanistic organization
organic organizations
committee

AN OPPORTUNITY IN DISGUISE

IT WAS ONLY seven months after Glen Frost took over as postmaster in Norman, Oklahoma, that he received notice of a 20-percent RIF (reduction in force) to take effect at the end of the next pay period. Glen was really worried. He was not sure he could do the job with eight people, which would be the number remaining after the RIF.

Glen finally decided that this might really be an opportunity in disguise. He had tried to rearrange the work area several times in the past, but to no avail. Even though he had suggested a number of layouts, any of which would have improved efficiency, one worker or another—or several—always objected. The postal workers were comfortable with the arrangement of the stamp machine, the sorting boxes, and the counters just where they were, and where they had been for years.

Glen seized on the opportunity created by the reduction in force. He asked the remaining workers to help him select the best work space arrangement. Within a few days, there was a consensus about how the work stations, machines, and counters should be arranged for maximum efficiency. Glen was also able to reassign some of the work and to eliminate several operations that did not need to be performed at all. As soon as the postal workers became accustomed to the new organization, the post office provided better service than it ever had, and the workers actually had an easier time. Although Glen had already lost two people, he decided not to hire a replacement when the next one quit or retired.

QUESTIONS
1. Explain why you believe the postal workers cooperated with Glen after the RIF.
2. Do you approve of Glen's failure to impose a new arrangement of the work flow prior to the RIF? How would you have handled the situation? Defend your answer.
3. Do you believe that Glen's authority was equal to his responsibility? Explain.

MISCO PAPER CONVERTERS

WHEN DICK VALLADAO and George Smeltzer, owners of Misco Paper Converters, began their business, it was only a part-time operation. The operation involved buying rolls of brown kraft paper, such as that used for grocery bags, cutting the paper into various shapes and sizes, bundling the sheets together, and shipping the bundles to industrial customers. The pieces of paper were used for various purposes: as vapor barriers in electronic equipment, to place between glass or china plates and bowls prior to shipping, and as a protective wrapping for many small manufactured items.

As the business grew and became more profitable, Dick and George decided to leave their jobs and work at Misco full-time. They had been doing the work in a small metal building behind George's house, but when they went into the business full-time they rented a 6,000-square-foot warehouse. They also purchased a shear press and a stripper in addition to the press and stripper they already owned, as well as a truck to pick up the raw paper at the paper mill and to make some deliveries. Usually the bundles of paper were shipped by common carrier to customers, some of which were as much as 600 miles distant.

Dick and George found it necessary to hire six operators. The operation was simple. The paper was fed off the large rolls through a stripper, which cut it to the appropriate widths. The stripping machine was set to clip the paper off every fifty feet or so. Then the strips were stacked on top of one another on a set of rollers that allowed the paper to be fed back into one of the shear presses. When a stack of strips was fifty layers thick, it was fed into the shear press, which clipped it to the appropriate length. The resulting rectangular stacks of brown paper were tied with twine and stacked onto shipping pallets. When a pallet was full, it was set aside to wait for shipment.

At first, George and Dick worked with the operators as a team, with each worker doing whatever needed to be done. Each person soon learned to operate the forklift, the strippers, and the shear presses and tie bundles as well. Dick and George felt themselves to be relative equals, so neither attempted to exercise authority over the other. As time went on, however, Dick began to think that the whole operation could be accomplished more efficiently if some kind of structure were imposed.

QUESTIONS

1. Do you believe that anything is to be gained at Misco by establishing an organizational structure, including specialization and lines of authority and responsibility? Explain your answer.
2. Assuming that George and Dick decided to set up a typical kind of organization, how should they decide who is to be chief executive? Should they have to decide that at all? Explain.

EXPERIENTIAL EXERCISE

Ampex Tool & Die has recently been acquired by Hugh Tool Company. The former owner of Ampex Tool & Die, Milton Bradley, was kept on to manage the division he founded. The management of Hugh Tool Company often resolves problems of integrating a newly acquired company into the main operation by means of committee. Since Milton had no substantial experience with committees, Trezzie Pressley, the Training and Development Manager, was sent from the main office to show Milton how committees should be used.

Milton is somewhat uncomfortable with the changes ordered by Hugh Tool Company. However, he will meet with Trezzie, who is considered an "expert" on organizing people and resources by committee. Trezzie insists on putting George Jones, a long-term supervisor, in charge of the committee instead of Milton. Milton believes that this decision will be a disaster because, although very competent, George is also very critical. Milton thinks, "I've got to convince Trezzie to let me handle the transition alone. I have always heard that committees are slow, costly, and only result in compromises, not real solutions. As I have always said, 'A camel is a horse designed by a committee!' "

Trezzie Pressley has come to Ampex Tool & Die to explain the necessity of committees, and to get a transition committee organized. Trezzie expects to have trouble with Milton, because Milton normally just does what comes naturally. Milton always runs the show by instinct, often with little input from others.

Obviously, Milton Bradley and Trezzie Pressley will have different views on the subject of management by committee. These different viewpoints should make for an interesting discussion. This is a committee problem, and if you feel you cannot handle the pressures of committee work, you should not volunteer. Otherwise, volunteer as one of the two participants chosen. The rest of you observe carefully. The instructor will provide more information to participants.

NOTES

1. R. F. Chisholm and S. V. Kasl, "The Nature and Predictors of Job-Related Tension in a Crisis Situation: Reactions of Nuclear Workers to the Three Mile Island Accident," *Academy of Management Journal* (September 1983): 401.
2. J. D. Ford and W. H. Hegarty, "Decision Makers' Beliefs about the Causes and Effects of Structure: An Exploratory Study," *Academy of Management Journal* (June 1984): 281.
3. V. A. Graicunas, "Relationships of Organizations," in *Papers on the Science of Administration,* ed. L. Gulick and L. Urwick (New York: Columbia University Press, 1947).
4. L. W. Fry and J. W. Slocum, Jr., "Technology, Structure, and Workgroup Effectiveness: A Test of a Contingency Model," *Academy of Management Journal* (June 1984): 236.
5. Joan Woodward, *Industrial Organization: Theory and Practice* (London: Oxford University Press, 1965), 52–62.

6. John Rossant and Wendy Zellner, "How Chrysler's $30,000 Sports Car Got Side-swiped," *Business Week,* 23 January 1989, 68.

7. Ronald M. Locklin, "Choosing a Data Communications Network," *The Journal of Business Strategy* 6, no. 3 (Winter 1986): 14.

8. John Hoerr. "Is Teamwork a Management Plot? Mostly Not," *Business Week,* 20 February 1989, 70.

9. J. L. C. Cheng, "Interdependence and Coordination in Organizations: A Role-System Analysis," *Academy of Management Journal* (March 1983): 160–161.

10. William F. Joyce, "Matrix Organization: A Social Experiment," *The Academy of Management Journal* 29, no. 3 (September 1986): 537.

11. T. Burns and G. M. Stalker, *The Management of Innovation* (London: Tavistock, 1966).

12. C. R. Gullett, "Mechanistic vs. Organic Organization: What Does the Future Hold?" *The Personnel Administrator* 20 (November 1975): 17.

13. Gullett, "Mechanistic vs. Organic Organization," 17.

REFERENCES

Arnold, John D. "The Why, When, and How of Changing Organizational Structures." *Management Review* (March 1981): 17–20.

Bellman, Geoffrey M. "The Quest for Staff Leadership." *Training & Development Journal* 10 (January 1986): 36–41.

Briscoe, Dennis R. "Organizational Design: Dealing with the Human Constraint." *California Management Review* 23 (Fall 1980): 71–80.

Brown, J. L., and N. M. Agnew. "The Balance of Power in a Matrix Structure." *Business Horizons* 25 (November–December 1982): 51–54.

Cheng, J. L. C. "Interdependence and Coordination in Organizations: A Role-System Analysis." *Academy of Management Journal* (March 1983): 156–162.

Chisholm, R. F., and S. V. Kasl. "The Nature and Predictors of Job-Related Tension in a Crisis Situation: Reactions of Nuclear Workers to the Three Mile Island Accident." *Academy of Management Journal* (September 1983): 385–405.

Daft, R. L. *Organization Theory and Design.* St. Paul, Minn.: West, 1983.

Fleming, Mary M. K. "Keys to Successful Project Management." *CMA—The Management Accounting Magazine* 60 (November–December 1986): 58–61.

Ford, J. D., and W. H. Hegarty. "Decision Makers' Beliefs about the Causes and Effects of Structure: An Exploratory Study." *Academy of Management Journal* (June 1984): 271–291.

Fry, L. W., and J. W. Slocum, Jr. "Technology, Structure, and Workgroup Effectiveness: A Test of a Contingency Model." *Academy of Management Journal* (June 1984): 221–246.

Gibson, James L., John M. Ivancevich, and James H. Donnelley, Jr. *Organizations: Behavior Structure and Processes.* Dallas: Business Publications, 1981.

Haynes, M. E. "Delegation: There's More to It Than Letting Someone Else Do It." *Supervisory Management* 25 (January 1980): 9–15.

Isenberg, Daniel J. "The Tactics of Strategic Opportunism." *Harvard Business Review* 65 (March–April 1987): 92–97.

Joyce, William F. "Matrix Organization: A Social Experiment." *The Academy of Management Journal* 29, no. 3 (September 1986): 537.

Lawrence, P. R., and J. W. Lorsch. "Differentiation and Integration in Complex Organizations." *Administrative Science Quarterly* 12 (June 1967): 1–47.

Lawrence, P. R., and J. W. Lorsch. *Organization and Environment.* Boston: Harvard University Graduate School of Business, Division of Research, 1967.

Lider, R. C., and T. R. Mitchell. "Reactions to Feedback: The Role of Attributions." *Academy of Management Journal* 28 (1985): 291–308.

Lucas, Rob. "Political-Cultural Analysis of Organizations." *Academy of Management Journal* 12, no. 1 (January 1987): 144–156.

Miller, Danny. "Configurations of Strategy and Structure: Towards a Synthesis." *Strategic Management Journal* 7, no. 3 (May–June 1986): 233–249.

Nicholson, P. J., Jr., and S. C. Goh. "The Relationship of Organization Structure and Interpersonal Attitudes to Role Conflict and Ambiguity in Different Work Environments." *Academy of Management Journal* (March 1983): 148–155.

Pate, Larry E., and Warren R. Nielsen. "Integrating Management Development into a Large-Scale System-Wide Change Programme." *Journal of Management Development* 6 (Winter 1987): 16–30.

Phillips, Jack J. "Authority: It Doesn't Just Come with Your Job." *Management Solutions* 31 (August 1986): 35–37.

Quinlivan-Hall, Dave. "Involving Your People in Organizational Problem Solving." *Training & Development Journal* 41 (July 1987): 73–74.

Roos, L. L., Jr., and R. I. Hall. "Influence Diagrams and Organizational Power." *Administrative Science Quarterly* 25 (March 1980): 57–71.

Sherman, J. D., and H. L. Smith. "The Influence of Organization Structure on Intrinsic versus Extrinsic Motivation." *Academy of Management Journal* 27 (December 1984): 877–884.

Sinclair, J. M. "Is the Matrix Really Necessary?" *Project Management Journal* 15 (March 1984): 49–55.

Walker, A., and J. Lorsch. "Organizational Choice: Product versus Function." *Harvard Business Review* 46 (November–December 1968): 129–138.

Waterman, H., Jr., J. Peters, and R. Phillips. "Structure Is Not Organization." *Business Horizons* 23, no. 3 (June 1980): 14–26.

CHAPTER

10

Chapter Outline

Human Resource Management (HRM) Functions

Laws and Executive Orders Affecting Equal Employment Opportunity

The Staffing Process

The Selection Process

Internal Staffing Administration

Special Considerations in Selecting Managerial Personnel

Summary

Staffing the Organization

Learning Objectives

After completing this chapter students should be able to

1. Identify and briefly describe the basic human resource functions that must be accomplished if the firm's employment needs are to be met.
2. List the predominant laws and Executive Orders that affect equal employment opportunity.
3. Describe what is involved in human resource planning and recruitment.
4. Explain each phase of the selection process.
5. Describe the factors involved in internal staffing administration.
6. State some special considerations involved in selecting managerial personnel and identify some techniques for identifying managerial talent.

THE ECONOMIC RECESSION of 1979–1984 hit Cleveland, Ohio's Lincoln Electric Company especially hard. In 1982 alone, the firm's revenue dropped 30 percent. For most companies, this would have spelled disaster; in fact, for many it did, as business bankruptcies climbed to record highs. But Lincoln was ready. The company remained profitable, not a single worker was laid off, and Lincoln was prepared to meet the demand for its products that the inevitable recovery would bring. By 1987 sales and profits had recovered, and now the company appears stronger than ever.

How did Lincoln do it? In the opinion of many, credit should be given to the ability, loyalty, and enthusiasm of the Lincoln work force. In large measure, this in turn springs from a number of unusual personnel policies. Workers at Lincoln are guaranteed lifetime employment. In exchange, they have to be willing to accept transfer to different jobs when changes in product demand occur. Also, the company promotes managers only from within. Every job opening is advertised internally, and any employee can apply. If workers are needed from outside, they are hired only at the entry level.

Almost every worker is paid on a piece-rate basis, so much per item produced. Part of the company profits, usually about half, is paid out as employee bonuses just before Christmas each year. These bonuses have averaged about the same as annual wages, and wages without the bonuses are on a par with those of other Cleveland workers.

New workers are placed on one year's probation. Normally, those who are not attuned to the rapid pace at Lincoln leave on their own accord within the year. Outsiders who apply for Lincoln jobs are carefully screened—first by the personnel department, then by a committee of vice-presidents and supervisors—before being placed in the qualified-applicant pool. Supervisors can hire whomever they please from this pool to fill vacancies at the entry level. There are no employment tests and no educational requirements, except for salespeople, who must be graduate engineers.

Significant credit must be given to Lincoln managers, who eschew executive pursuits. There are no reserved parking places. The executive offices are austere, purely functional, and carpetless. Even the company president eats in the cafeteria and pays for his own meals. More important than self-effacement, however, is the management discipline practiced at Lincoln. The work force is expanded only reluctantly, and employees normally work several hours of overtime each week. That way, a significant sales decline can be absorbed without cutting anyone back below forty hours.

Managers at Lincoln responded quickly to the recession, immediately making the difficult decision to cut workers back to the guaranteed minimum thirty hours per week before that action actually had to be taken. Because the cutback occurred in a timely manner, it was possible to return to a normal work week sooner than otherwise might have been possible if an early, definitive decision had not been made.

Some of the employees complained, however, when their hours were cut back and their bonuses reduced; they had become accustomed to a total compensation level that was double that of other Cleveland firms. But no one was fired. And Lincoln Electric remains economically sound and optimistic about its ability to take the good and the bad in stride.[1] ∎

INCOLN ELECTRIC IS KNOWN the world over as a leader in human resource management. The Lincoln example illustrates that the personnel policies and practices a company follows must be integrated into a sound, overall management system.

A major focus of the organizing function discussed in the preceding chapters is the people who work together in pursuit of organizational goals. Making sure that the organization has the right people in the right jobs at the right time is vital. In this chapter, we will first define the basic functions related to human resource management. Then, the major legislation affecting equal employment opportunity will be identified. The major portion of the chapter is devoted to the elements of the staffing process. The final section discusses some special considerations involved in selecting managerial personnel and some techniques for identifying managerial talent.

■ HUMAN RESOURCE MANAGEMENT (HRM) FUNCTIONS

Managers must work with the firm's human resources if organizational goals are to be accomplished. The firm must attract, select, train, and retain qualified people. If the human resource functions do not assure a pool of qualified employees, the organization could have problems attaining organizational goals. This fact became all too real at the Boeing Company's main location. In 1989, for the first time in twenty years, Boeing missed a delivery deadline. According to Dean D. Thornton, president of Boeing's commercial airplane subsidiary, "we overcommitted." Even though employment at Boeing jumped 83 percent to 155,000 workers, from 1983 to 1989, the increase did not relieve the pressure of contract backlogs.[2] Occurrences such as this interfere with goal attainment. To prevent them, management must assure that HRM functions are carried out successfully. To meet the firm's human resource needs, there are six basic HRM functions that must be accomplished. As may be seen in Figure 10.1, these are staffing, human resource development, compensation, health and safety, employee and labor relations, and human resource research.[3] Let us discuss each of these in turn.

Staffing

Staffing
The formal process of ensuring that the organization has qualified workers available at all levels to meet its short- and long-term business objectives.

Staffing is the formal process of ensuring that the organization has qualified workers available at all levels to meet its short- and long-term business objectives.[4] Frank Lorenzo, the embattled president of Eastern's parent company, Texas Air, would have been thrilled to have had pilots waiting in the wings to take over for the striking pilots at Eastern Air Lines. According to a recent article in *Business Week*, it will take Eastern about a month to recruit and certify enough new pilots to resume many more of its flights.[5] Meanwhile, Texas Air continues to lose money, and Eastern has filed for bankruptcy protection. Proper staffing could have assisted Lorenzo in accomplishing his short- and long-term goals. The staffing process involves job analysis, human resource planning, recruitment, selection, and internal staffing administration. These topics are the focus of this chapter and will be covered in greater detail later.

FIGURE 10.1 ■
The Human Resource
Management System

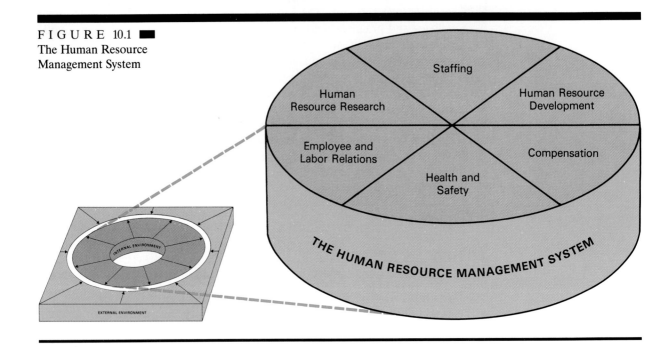

F I G U R E 10.1 ■
The Human Resource
Management System

Human Resource Development

Human resource development (HRD) programs are designed to assist individuals, groups, and the entire organization in becoming more effective. HRD is needed because people, jobs, and organizations are always changing. HRD should begin when individuals join the firm, and it should continue throughout their careers. Large-scale HRD programs are referred to as organization development (OD). The purpose of OD is to alter the environment within the firm to assist employees in performing more productively.

Other aspects of HRD include career planning and performance appraisal. Career planning is a process whereby human resource goals are set and the means to achieve them are established. Individual careers are not separate and distinct from organizational careers. The goals of both can be met if organizations assist employees in career planning. Through performance appraisal, employees are evaluated to determine how well they are performing their assigned tasks. Performance appraisal affords employees the opportunity to capitalize on their strengths and overcome identified deficiencies, thereby becoming more satisfied and productive employees.

Compensation

Compensation
Includes all rewards
individuals receive as a
result of their employment.

The question of what constitutes a fair day's pay has been a major concern for centuries. Employees must be provided with adequate and equitable rewards for their contributions to organizational goals. **Compensation** includes all rewards individuals receive as a result of their employment. As such, it is more than monetary income. The rewards may include one or any combination of the following:

- **Pay:** The money that a person receives for performing a job.
- **Benefits:** Additional financial rewards other than pay such as paid holidays, medical insurance, and retirement programs.
- **Nonfinancial:** Nonmonetary rewards that an employee may experience, such as enjoyment of the work performed and a pleasant working environment.

Health and Safety

Health
Refers to the employees' freedom from illness and their general physical and mental well-being.

Safety
The protection of employees from injuries due to work-related accidents.

Health refers to the employees' freedom from illness and their general physical and mental well-being. **Safety** is the protection of employees from injuries due to work-related accidents. These topics are important to management because employees who enjoy good health and who work in a safe environment are more likely to be efficient. For this reason, forward-thinking managers have long advanced safety and health programs. Today, because of federal legislation, all organizations have become concerned with their employees' safety and health.

Employee and Labor Relations

In 1989, unions represented 17 percent of all nonfarm workers. Estimations are that by the year 2000, unions will represent only 13 percent of all nonfarm workers.[6] Even with the projected decline in union membership, a business firm is required by law to recognize a union, and bargain with it in good faith, if the firm's employees want the union to represent them. In the past, this relationship was an accepted way of life for many employers. Today, however, according to a recent Conference Board survey on labor-management relations, preventing the spread of unionism and developing instead effective employee relations systems is more important to *some* managers than achieving sound collective bargaining results.[7]

Additional changes could be on the horizon in the area of union-management relations, due to a recent revolt of sorts at the huge General Motors engine and

BUSINESS BRIEFS

INSIDE BUSINESS

The Fate of Unionism

IN 1989, UNIONS represented approximately 17 percent of all nonfarm workers. Estimations are that by the year 2000, unions will represent only 13 percent of all nonfarm workers. Mr. Jay Mazur, the president of the International Ladies Garment Workers Union (ILGWU), discusses the state of unionism in the apparel industry, the threat of foreign domination of the industry, and possible remedies to address union woes. According to Mazur, reports of the death of the apparel union and of unionism in general are premature. Judge for yourself if Mazur's views on unionism are realistic, or simply naive. Mazur's opinions are analyzed by the CNN business news team of Kandel, Perry, and Schuch.

Y OU RUN THE Sunbelt Construction Company, and you are currently having problems with certain individuals who want to unionize your company. Three of your employees have extreme influence over the other members of the work force. Clearly these three are the impetus for the organizing effort. The source of the discontent is the current wage and benefits package offered by your company. This is the maximum wage and benefits package that you can provide and still remain competitive. You have just received word from your boss that you are to stop the unionizing effort or you will have to answer to him. A supervisor has just told you that he believes that if raises are given to the three primary organizers, they will turn the tide of unionization and accept the current wage and benefits package. "All we need to do is keep the raises quiet." You can either give the three employees raises, or you can stand firm and try and make your employees understand why you can't give a larger wage and benefits package.
What would you do?

assembly complex in the Pontiac, Michigan, plant. In 1989, management and union executives, intent on saving jobs by driving down costs, nurtured team production systems, relaxed work rules, and backed union-management cooperation. Union executives expected that union members would approve the contract. Instead, union members dealt them a stunning defeat. The discontent has spread far beyond the Pontiac plant. Throughout the UAW an increasingly vocal group of dissentients is challenging the move toward union-management cooperation led by the union's leadership.[8] This state of flux in the area of union-management relations may further complicate dealing with unionized employees and make the staffing function more difficult.

Human resource managers in union-free organizations are often quite knowledgeable about union goals and activities. Union-free firms typically strive to satisfy their employees' needs in every reasonable manner, to make it clear to them that unions are not necessary for individuals to achieve personal goals. Remaining union free requires, in addition to a totally communicative and open environment, a strong commitment to do so by *all* managers in a company; but in many ways, it requires even more effort on the part of those in the human resource department. Some companies fail to maintain commitment and therefore become vulnerable to organizing efforts. The old maxim is still true: "Unions don't organize employees, managers do"—through mistakes, neglect, and, unfortunately, just plain greed.[9] The human resource manager, therefore, must ensure that an employee relations system is created whereby employees are treated in a positive manner, so that individual workers can maintain their self-esteem and grow individually as the organization advances.

Human Resource Research

The human resource manager's research laboratory is the entire work environment. Research needs permeate every human resource management function.

For instance, research may be conducted to determine the type of workers who will prove to be most successful in the firm. Or it may be directed toward determining the causes of certain work-related accidents. Human resource research is expected to be increasingly important to all forms of organizations in the future.

■■ LAWS AND EXECUTIVE ORDERS AFFECTING EQUAL EMPLOYMENT OPPORTUNITY

There have been numerous national laws passed and Executive Orders signed that impact equal employment opportunity. Their passage signified an attitude in the general population that changes should be made in employment practices. The most significant laws are briefly described in the following sections.

Civil Rights Acts of 1866 and 1871

The 1866 Civil Rights Act is based on the Thirteenth Amendment to the Constitution and prohibits race discrimination in hiring, placement, and continuation of employment. Private employers, unions, and employment agencies are all included in this act. The 1871 act is based on the Fourteenth Amendment and prohibits deprivation of equal employment rights under state employment laws. State and local government employers are included. Thus, in the case of *Brown* v. *Gaston County Dyeing Machine Company* (1972), the court ruled that a black was entitled to back pay for the period during which discrimination occurred. The time period involved was between 1960 and 1961, three years prior to the 1964 Civil Rights Act. There is virtually no effective statute of limitation in filing charges under these acts.[10]

In 1987, the Supreme Court ruled that Jews, Arabs, and other similar groups may file civil charges if they have convincing evidence of discrimination "because of . . . ancestry or ethnic characteristics." The decision was based on the above-mentioned 1866 statute, which guarantees all "races" the "full and equal benefit of all laws . . . as is enjoyed by white citizens." Jews, Arabs, and other groups such as Swedes, Norwegians, Germans, and Greeks constitute races covered under this ruling.[11]

Title VII of the Civil Rights Act of 1964—Amended 1972

One law that has had an extensive influence on human resource management is Title VII of the 1964 Civil Rights Act, as amended by the Equal Employment Opportunity Act of 1972. This legislation prohibits discrimination based on race, color, sex, religion, or national origin. Title VII covers employers engaged in industries affecting interstate commerce with fifteen or more employees for at least twenty calendar weeks in the year in which a charge is filed, or the year preceding the filing of a charge. Included in the definition of employers are state and local governments, schools, colleges, unions, and employment agencies. The act created the Equal Employment Opportunity Commission (EEOC), which is responsible for its enforcement.

Age Discrimination in Employment Act of 1967— Amended in 1978 and 1986

As originally enacted, the Age Discrimination in Employment Act (ADEA) prohibited employers from discriminating against individuals who were from forty years of age to sixty-five. The 1978 amendment provided protection for individuals who were at least forty, but less than seventy years old. On October 31, 1986, President Reagan signed into law an amendment to the ADEA making it illegal for employers to discriminate against anyone because of age. The latest amendment gives older employees the option to continue working past seventy; and the health care provision of the amendment provides them with an additional incentive to continue to do so.[12] The act pertains to employers with twenty or more employees for twenty or more calendar weeks (in either the current or the preceding calendar year), unions of twenty-five or more members, employment agencies, and federal, state, and local government subunits. Administration of the act was transferred from the U.S. Department of Labor to the EEOC in 1979.

Enforcement may begin once a charge is filed, or the EEOC can review compliance even if no charge is filed. The Age Discrimination Act differs from Title VII of the Civil Rights Act in that it provides for trial by jury and there is a possible criminal aspect to a charge. The trial by jury is important in that the jury may have greater sympathy for older people who may have been discriminated against. The criminal aspect means that an employee may receive more than lost wages if discrimination is proven. In addition, because of the 1978 amendment, class action suits are now possible.

Rehabilitation Act of 1973

The Rehabilitation Act covers certain government contractors and subcontractors and organizations that receive federal grants in excess of $2,500. Individuals are considered handicapped if they have a physical or mental impairment that substantially limits one or more major life activities, or have a record of such impairment. The Office of Federal Contract Compliance Programs (OFCCP) administers the act. If a contract or subcontract exceeds $50,000, or if the contractor has fifty or more employees, an affirmative action program must be prepared. In it, the contractor must specify the reasonable accommodations that are being made in hiring and promoting handicapped persons.

This act is expected to have even more impact in the future, because the definition of "handicapped" has not been thoroughly tested by the courts. As more and more cases go to court, additional ailments will probably be labeled as handicapping conditions. For example, in the recent *Vickers* v. *Veterans Administration* case, it was determined that a person who is hypersensitive to tobacco smoke is handicapped.[13]

Pregnancy Discrimination Act of 1978

Passed as an amendment to Title VII of the Civil Rights Act, the Pregnancy Discrimination Act prohibits discrimination in employment based on pregnancy, childbirth, or related medical conditions. The basic principle of the 1978 act is that women affected by pregnancy, and related conditions, must be treated the same as other applicants and employees on the basis of their ability or inability to work. A woman is therefore protected against such practices as being fired, or being refused a job or promotion, merely because she is pregnant or has had an abortion. She usually cannot be forced to take a leave of absence so long as she can work. If other employees on disability leave are entitled to return to their jobs when they are able to work again, so too are women who have been unable to work because of pregnancy.

The same principle applies in the benefits area, including disability benefits, sick leave, and health insurance. A woman unable to work for pregnancy-related reasons is entitled to disability benefits or sick leave on the same basis as employees unable to work for medical reasons. Also, any health insurance provided must cover expenses for pregnancy-related conditions on the same basis as expenses for other medical conditions. However, health insurance for expenses arising from an abortion is not required, except where the life of the mother would be endangered if the fetus were carried to term, or where medical complications have arisen from an abortion.

Immigration Reform and Control Act (IRCA) of 1986

This law establishes criminal and civil sanctions against employers who hire an individual knowing he or she is an unauthorized alien and makes it unlawful to hire anyone without verifying employment authorization and identity. Employers who unlawfully hire an illegal alien will be subject to fines of $250 to $2,000 per worker for the first offense; $2,000 to $5,000 for the second offense; and $3,000 to $10,000 for the third offense. In addition, employers who fail to comply with the record-keeping provisions of the law will be subject to a penalty of $100 to $1,000 for each individual they have failed to document, even if the individual is legally entitled to be employed. Further, when dealing with the national origin provision of the Civil Rights Act, the new IRCA reduces the threshold coverage from fifteen to four employees. The effect of this extension of the 1964 law will be to curtail the actions of employers who may choose a policy to hire only U.S. citizens and thereby avoid any potential violation of the IRCA. Many aliens are in the United States legally, and refusal to hire would violate their civil rights.[14]

Executive Order 11246, as Amended by EO 11375

Executive Orders (EOs)
Directives issued by the president that have the force and effect of laws enacted by Congress.

Executive Orders (EOs) are directives issued by the president that have the force and effect of laws enacted by Congress. On September 24, 1965, President Lyndon B. Johnson signed EO 11246. This EO made it the policy of the government of the United States to provide equal opportunity in federal employment for all qualified persons. It prohibits discrimination in employment because of race, creed, color, or national origin. The EO also requires promoting the full realization of equal employment opportunity through a positive, continuing program in each executive department and agency. The policy of equal opportunity applies to every aspect of federal employment policy and practice.

A major provision of EO 11246 is that every executive department and agency that administers a program involving federal financial assistance will require adherence to a policy of nondiscrimination in employment as a condition for the approval of a grant, contract, loan, insurance, or guarantee. During the performance of a contract, contractors agree not to discriminate in employment because of race, creed, color, or national origin. **Affirmative action** is performance required to ensure that applicants are employed, and that employees are treated appropriately during employment, without regard to race, creed, color, or national origin. Human resource practices covered relate to employment, upgrading, demotion, transfer, recruitment or recruitment advertising, layoffs or termination, rates of pay or other forms of compensation, and selection for training including apprenticeships. Employers are required to post notices to this effect in conspicuous places in the workplace. In the event of the contractor's noncompliance, contracts can be canceled, terminated, or suspended, in whole or in part, and the contractor may be declared ineligible for future government contracts. In 1968, EO 11246 was amended by EO 11375, which changed the word "creed" to "religion" and added sex discrimination to the other prohibited items. These EOs are enforced by the Department of Labor through the Office of Federal Contract Compliance Programs (OFCCP).

Affirmative action
Performance required to ensure that applicants are employed, and that employees are treated appropriately during employment, without regard to race, creed, color, or national origin.

Skip

■ THE STAFFING PROCESS

Staffing, defined earlier in the chapter, is an integral part of human resource management. There are several components of the staffing process, each closely linked to the others. Figure 10.2 illustrates these basic components, which are discussed separately below.

 Fredrick Taylor

Job Analysis

Job analysis
The systematic process of determining the skills and knowledge required for performing jobs in the organization.

Job analysis is the systematic process of determining the skills and knowledge required for performing jobs in the organization.[15] As may be seen in Figure 10.2, it impacts every aspect of staffing. Job analysis involves a careful investigation of job duties and responsibilities, as well as of relationships to other jobs and working conditions. Job facts are gathered, analyzed, and recorded as the job is performed. This information is necessary when preparing job descriptions and specifications. Without properly conducted job analyses, it would be difficult to perform the other human resource management functions. In order to help assure quality, the Boeing Company has conducted a job analysis for employees who will build their planes. Boeing has stepped up training, and new workers take blueprint-reading classes and practice riveting and drilling before starting assembly-line jobs. Boeing also conducts "pre-employment" training for serious job candidates at local vocational-technical schools.[16] Several techniques may be used in conducting a job analysis, including the following:

- Observations of, and interviews with, present employees performing the jobs
- Questionnaires completed by present employees or supervisors of the work
- Analysis by experts
- A diary of activities performed by present employees

FIGURE 10.2 ■
The Staffing Function

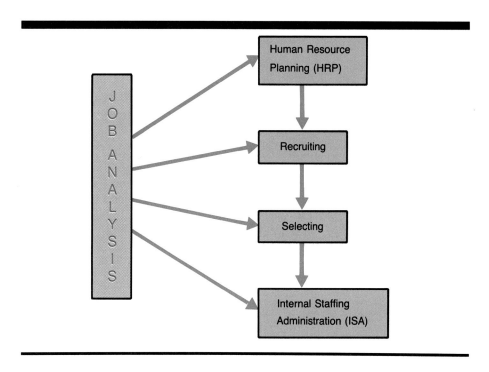

Information obtained through job analysis is crucial to the development of job descriptions. The **job description** is a document that provides information regarding the tasks, duties, and responsibilities of the job. Job descriptions are accurate, concise statements of what employees are expected to do on their jobs. They should indicate what employees do, how they do it, and the conditions under which the duties are performed. Among the items often included in a job description are

Job description
A document that provides information regarding the tasks, duties, and responsibilities of the job.

- Major duties performed
- Percentage of time devoted to each duty
- Performance standards to be achieved
- Working conditions and possible hazards
- Number of persons working on each job and their reporting relationships
- The machines and equipment used on the job

Job descriptions are useful in virtually every HRM function. They facilitate the recruitment process by clarifying the specific nature of objectives and responsibilities of jobs. They are also a helpful tool in the orientation and training of new employees. Even though job descriptions exist in many large firms, managers sometimes do not understand or use them properly. For instance, some managers believe that having job descriptions restricts management's flexibility and creativity in staffing the organization.

Job specification
A statement of the minimum acceptable qualifications that a person should possess to perform a particular job.

A statement of the minimum acceptable qualifications that a person should possess to perform a particular job is the **job specification.** Items typically included in the job specification are education requirements, experience, personality, and physical abilities. In practice, job specifications are often included as a major section of a job description.

Human Resource Planning

Human resource planning
The process of systematically reviewing personnel requirements to ensure that the required number of employees with the required skills are available when they are needed.

Human resource planning (HRP) is the process of systematically reviewing personnel requirements to ensure that the required number of employees with the required skills are available when they are needed. There are two aspects to HRP: requirements and availability. Forecasting human resource requirements involves determining the number and type of employees needed by skill level and location. When the analysis indicates a personnel shortage, the firm must initiate recruitment efforts. When the analysis projects a personnel surplus, restricted hiring, reduced hours, early retirement, or layoffs may be required. Referring to the story at the start of the chapter, when Lincoln's sales dropped in the early 1980s, that company chose to reduce working hours and reassign workers rather than lay anyone off.

In order to forecast human resource availability, the organization looks to both internal sources (current employees) and external sources (the labor market). With a long waiting list of prospective workers, Lincoln Electric has less concern than most other companies about whether or not workers are available.

Human resource planning, when performed properly, can do the following:

- Enable management to anticipate shortages and surpluses of labor, allowing the development of plans for avoiding or correcting problems before they become serious
- Permit forecasts of recruitment needs in terms of both the numbers and the types of skills sought
- Help in the analysis of sources of supply of labor in order to focus recruitment efforts on the most likely supply sources
- Provide for identification of replacements or backup for present key managers from either inside or outside the organization
- Integrate personnel plans with financial plans and forecasts.[17]

As stated in the beginning of the chapter, employment at Boeing jumped 83 percent to 155,000 workers during the years from 1983 to 1989. Boeing was able to forecast their human resource requirements, but lack of ability of qualified personnel continues to plague them.

Recruitment

Recruitment
The process of attracting individuals—in sufficient numbers and with appropriate qualifications—and encouraging them to apply for jobs with the organization.
Employment requisition
A form issued to activate the recruitment process; it typically includes such information as the job title, starting date, pay scale, and a brief summary of principal duties.

Recruitment is the process of attracting individuals—in sufficient numbers and with appropriate qualifications—and encouraging them to apply for jobs with the organization.[18] In most large organizations, this begins with an employment requisition. An **employment requisition** is a form issued to activate the recruitment process; it typically includes such information as the job title, starting date, pay scale, and a brief summary of principal duties. Recruitment can range from locating individuals within the firm who are qualified to a sophisticated and extensive search for a new president.

This affirmative action recruiter helps his company to attract qualified minority applicants for employment. (© Ellis Herwig/Stock, Boston, Inc.)

The usual means of internal recruiting is through the use of a job bidding and posting system. The purpose of job posting is to communicate the fact that job openings exist. Job bidding permits individuals in the organization, who believe that they possess the required qualifications, to apply (bid) for the job. At Lincoln, every job above the entry level is filled from within. Internal recruitment or promotion from within is an important source of personnel for positions above the entry level. Promotion from within has several advantages; it

1. increases morale of employees;
2. improves the quality of selection, since an organization usually has a more complete evaluation of the strengths and weaknesses of internal applicants as compared to that of applicants from outside the firm;
3. motivates present employees to prepare for more responsible positions;
4. attracts a better quality of external applicants if chances for promotion from within are good; and
5. assists the organization to utilize personnel more fully.

Despite the advantages of internal recruiting, there are several disadvantages to be considered. Two of these are:

1. there may be an inadequate supply of qualified applicants.
2. internal sources may lead to inbreeding of ideas—current employees may lack new ideas on how to do a job more effectively.

Some well-known companies in addition to Lincoln that practice promotion from within are Delta Airlines, IBM, and Hewlett-Packard.

Even if a company is committed to promotion from within, external recruitment is required just to maintain a stable work force. It is particularly necessary in light of the change and growth most organizations experience. Some companies use outside recruitment to bring new skills into the firm and to prevent inbreeding. Possible external sources of recruitment include high schools and vocational schools, community colleges, colleges and universities, the competition and other firms, and unsolicited applicants. Some recruiting methods are advertising, employment agencies, recruiters, and employee referrals. Essentially, the firm must first determine where potential employees may be found and then use appropriate methods to encourage them to make application. Only when a firm has applicants for a job can the selection process begin.

Selection
The process of identifying those recruited individuals who will best be able to assist the firm in achieving organizational goals.

■ THE SELECTION PROCESS

The ultimate objective of recruitment is to select individuals who are most capable of meeting the requirements of the job. **Selection** is the process of identifying

FIGURE 10.3 ■■
The Selection Process

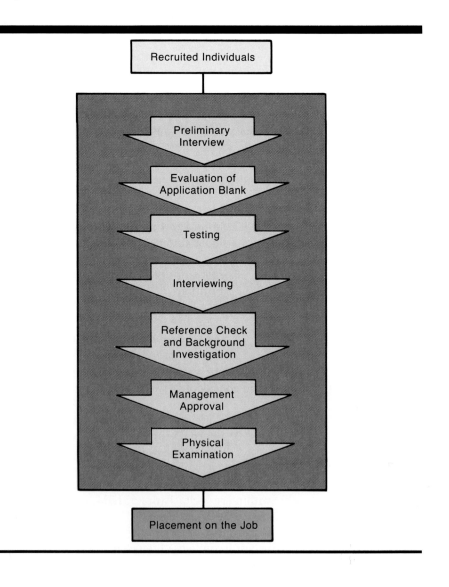

those recruited individuals who will best be able to assist the firm in achieving organizational goals. The selection process is shown in Figure 10.3.

Preliminary Interview

Preliminary interviews
Interviews used to
eliminate the obviously
unqualified applicants.

Preliminary interviews are those interviews used to eliminate the obviously unqualified applicants. Reasons for elimination may include excessive salary requirements, inadequate training or education, or lack of job-related experience. An applicant who appears to qualify for a position is asked to complete the application blank.

Evaluation of Application Blank

The next step in the selection process is to have the prospective employee complete an application blank. The employer should evaluate the application with regard to whether there appears to be a match between the individual and the position. The specific type of information requested in an application blank may vary from firm to firm and by positions within the organization. Separate sections of an application typically relate to education, work experience, and other specific job-related data.

An application blank must fill the firm's informational needs while meeting legal requirements. Only questions that have job relevance should be included. Questions related to sex, age, national origin, religion, color, or race should not be asked. Answers to questions regarding criminal convictions should be considered only if job related. For jobs such as pilot positions, the application blank may ask for licensing information.

Testing

Traditionally, testing has been an integral component in the selection process. Tests have been used to screen applicants in terms of skills, abilities, aptitudes,

A successful candidate for employment has completed a multi-step process of testing and evaluation. (© Barbara Burnes/Photo Researchers, Inc.)

interest, personality, and attitudes. The Civil Rights Act and interpretations by the federal courts have had the effect of reducing the use of selection tests. For instance, in the 1973 *Griggs* v. *Duke Power Company* decision, the U.S. Supreme Court ruled that pre-employment requirements, including tests, must be job related. It has proved to be very difficult to design tests consisting totally of job-related items.

Certain conditions should be met if tests are to be used for employee selection. First, a test should be reliable; that is, it should provide consistent results. If a person takes the same test a number of times, scores should be similar. Second, tests should be valid; they should measure what they are designed to measure. If a test is designed to predict job performance, prospective employees who score high on the test should prove to be high performers. Third, a selection test should be objective. When different scorers interpreting the results of the same test arrive at similar interpretations, the test is said to be objective. Finally, a test should be standardized. This requires that it be administered under standard conditions to a large group of persons who are representative of the individuals for whom it is intended. The purpose of standardization is to obtain norms, so that specific test scores are meaningful when compared to other scores in the group.

Interviewing

The interview is the most widely used and probably the most important method of assessing the qualifications of job applicants. At Lincoln Electric, it is almost the only method used. The subjective judgments that are often made during employment interviews sometimes reduce their reliability. However, interviews do accomplish the following purposes:

1. Obtain additional information about the applicant
2. Provide information regarding the firm
3. Sell the applicant on the company

Interviews may be distinguished by the amount of structure they possess. Probing, open-ended questions are asked in nondirective interviews. Usually only highly trained interviewers use the nondirective technique because it requires a highly subjective appraisal of the job candidate. On the other hand, the patterned interview consists of standardized questions that are asked of all applicants for a specific group of jobs. This standardization permits the candidates to be compared easily and greatly aids the validation process.

Interviews can be conducted in several ways. A majority of employment interviews consist of the applicant's meeting with an interviewer in a one-on-one situation. This form of interviewing is the least threatening type. Another form of interviewing is the group interview. Here, several applicants interact in the presence of one or more company representatives. Or one candidate may be quizzed by several interviewers. The latter type is called a board interview.

Sometimes the stress interview is used in the selection of managers and sales personnel. The stress interview puts the applicant on the defensive. The interviewer attempts to put pressure on the person in order to observe his or her reactions to stress and tension.

Regardless of the type of method used, the interview is the most relied upon element in the selection of new personnel. When selecting new employees and evaluating candidates for promotion, most managers rely on the interview, so following sound practices is essential. The following guidelines have been found to be helpful in conducting effective interviews:

1. *Plan for the interview*—review job specification and description as well as the applications of candidates.
2. *Create a good climate for the interview*—try to establish a friendly, open rapport with the applicant.
3. *Allow sufficient time for an uninterrupted interview.*
4. *Conduct a goal-oriented interview*—seek the information needed to assist in the employment decision.
5. *Avoid certain types of questions*—try not to ask leading questions or questions that may imply discrimination.
6. *Seek answers to all questions and check for inconsistencies.*
7. *Record the results of the interview immediately on completion.*[19]

Over the years, the interview, much like testing, has received considerable criticism concerning its ability to predict success on the job. Many factors influence the decision of the interviewer in interviewing an applicant for employment. Interviews can be instruments of discrimination, and for this reason, they have received close scrutiny by the EEOC in recent years. Charges of possible discrimination have led to an increase in the use of the patterned interview, since it has significantly higher reliability and validity than other methods of interviewing.

An effective means of assessing the success of an organization's interviewing process is to compare the later performance of employees with their earlier evaluations during the interview. Obviously, the goal is to determine how effective or valid the interview is in predicting job success.

Reference Check and Background Investigation

Once an applicant has successfully cleared the interview hurdle, the practice of many organizations is to conduct reference checks and background investigations. The purpose of reference checks is to provide additional insight regarding applicants. Reference checks have their weaknesses, too. For example, job applicants normally provide their own list of references, most of which are obviously biased in the applicant's favor. Also, since the passage of the Federal Privacy Act of 1974, persons who have been employed by the federal government have the legal right to review reference checks, unless they waive this right.

Although a reference check often provides enough information to verify the information on the application blank, there are many times when it does not. Often it is important to perform a background investigation into the applicant's past employment history. Background investigations help determine if past work experience is related to the qualifications needed for the new position. Another reason for the background investigation is credential fraud, which has increased in recent years.[20] It has been found that between 7 and 10 percent of job applicants are not what they present themselves to be.[21]

Management Approval

In most large organizations, many of these selection functions are performed by the personnel department. However, the personnel department does not usually make the final decision as to which person is selected for a particular position. Under most circumstances, the final hiring decision is made by the manager or supervisor who will be the immediate superior of the new employee. The selection decision is usually made after interviewing the applicants and reviewing the recommendations of the personnel department. The immediate supervisor knows the needs of his or her unit or department and is in the best position to evaluate the qualifications and characteristics of prospective employees. The supervisor or manager should be able to identify the factors in the applicant's background or work experience that will help the new employee in fitting into the work unit.

Physical Examination

Once a decision to make a job offer has been reached, a physical examination is often conducted. Typically, job offers are contingent on the applicant's passing the physical. Physicals screen out individuals who have contagious diseases and help determine if applicants are physically capable of performing the work. An often-ignored purpose of physical examinations is to provide records, which protect the company against claims for previously existing medical conditions.

■■ INTERNAL STAFFING ADMINISTRATION

Staffing encompasses much more than planning, recruiting, and selecting employees. It is also vitally concerned with these employees after they have become organizational members. Internal staffing administration (ISA) (Figure 10.4) includes these activities: career management, performance appraisals, employee assistance programs, orientation, and employee status changes such as promotions, transfers, demotions, resignations, discharges, outplacements, layoffs, and retirements.

Career management is a formalized approach to ensure that employees have opportunities to maximize their potential. When individual career needs are not consonant with organizational needs, the employee will probably choose to leave the firm.

Performance appraisal is an integral part of the staffing function. It provides the periodic feedback needed to evaluate the effectiveness of recruitment and selection. It also identifies individuals who are trainable and who possess the essential skills to meet current and future job requirements. However, the major contribution of the performance appraisal process may be the development of work environments in which employees and their managers set objectives, monitor results, and formally evaluate success against predetermined performance goals. Properly administered, the performance appraisal process ensures improved communication throughout the organization.

Employee assistance programs (EAPs) are systematic efforts to help employees cope with problems that interfere with their productive ability on the job

Career management
A formalized approach to ensure that employees have opportunities to maximize their potential.

Employee assistance programs
Systematic efforts to help employees cope with problems that interfere with their productive ability on the job and their personal happiness.

F I G U R E 10.4 ▮
Internal Staffing
Administration

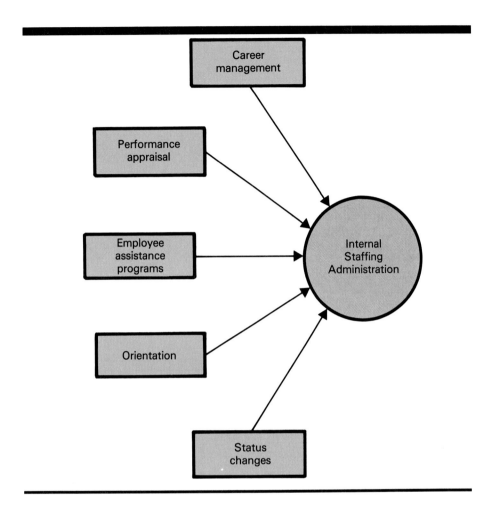

and their personal happiness. Personal problems often go unresolved, either because management is reluctant to bring up personal issues or because workers simply do not know where to go for help. Firms that understand this use EAPs as a comprehensive, problem-solving approach to a multitude of difficulties, such as burnout, alcoholism, drug abuse, and family conflict. A firm may choose to provide confidential, in-house professional counselors, or it may refer employees to an external agency.

Orientation
The process of introducing new employees to the job, the company, and other employees.

Orientation is the process of introducing new employees to the job, the company, and other employees. When employees are brought into a new work group, they often confront many confusing situations. An understanding of the formal and informal work environment can help new employees adjust more quickly to the job and its requirements.

The purposes of orientation are the following:

1. to create in the new employee a favorable impression of the organization and its work,
2. to help ease the new employee's adjustment to the organization, and
3. to provide specific information concerning the task and performance expectations of the job.[22]

TABLE 10.1 ■ Orientation Outline

1. History and nature of the business
2. Goals of the company
3. Basic products/services provided by the firm
4. Organizational structure
5. Policies, procedures, and rules covering such areas as:
   a. Work schedules
   b. Salaries and payment periods
   c. Physical facilities
   d. Attendance and absenteeism
   e. Working conditions and safety standards
   f. Lunch and coffee breaks
   g. Discipline and grievance
   h. Parking
6. Company benefits
   a. Insurance programs
   b. Pension and/or profit sharing plans
   c. Recreational programs—bowling, tennis, golf, etc.
   d. Vacations and holidays
7. Opportunities
   a. Advancement, promotion
   b. Suggestion systems
8. Specific departmental responsibilities
   a. Department functions
   b. Job duties/responsibilities/authority
   c. Introduction to other employees in work group

[handwritten margin note: mission of organization]

Every new employee goes through an orientation period, regardless of whether the firm has a formal orientation program or not. New recruits must "learn the ropes" or the "rules of the game" if they are to succeed. Much of the new employee orientation takes place on an informal basis—during coffee breaks, at lunch, or during work—through interactions with those employees who are often referred to as "old-timers." However, most organizations have formal orientation programs. These are designed to acquaint new personnel with areas such as those outlined in Table 10.1.

Employees typically do not remain in the same job, with the same company, throughout a career. In fact, there are several kinds of job or status changes, which must be managed effectively. These include:

[handwritten margin note: skip]

- **Promotion**—advancement to a more responsible job in the organization
- **Lateral move**—transfer to another job at the same level of responsibility
- **Demotion**—assignment within the organization to a job with less responsibility
- **Resignation**—a voluntary termination of employment initiated by the employee
- **Discharge**—an involuntary termination of employment initiated by the employer
- **Outplacement**—an involuntary separation, but with help from the employer in finding other work for the employee

- **Layoff**—an involuntary separation with the expectation of returning when business conditions improve
- **Retirement**—separation from the company, typically with some form of income and medical protection
- **Reduction in force**—a systematic process intended to reduce staff

To ensure the highest level of productivity, better-managed firms strive to achieve a proper match between individuals and jobs. Careless or random selection of employees can seriously impair the ultimate ability of the company to survive. It is not surprising, then, that the staffing function consistently ranks high with top executives as a business activity requiring their attention.

SPECIAL CONSIDERATIONS IN SELECTING MANAGERIAL PERSONNEL

In recruiting and selecting nonmanagerial personnel, it is usually possible to use objective factors in identifying potentially successful employees; however, more subjective judgment is often involved in selecting managerial personnel. Here, proper selection is even more important. The actions of a senior manager at Lincoln, for example, might affect the lives of many Lincoln employees and others outside the firm. In selecting managers, concern is typically focused on an evaluation of skills, abilities, attitudes, and characteristics, many of which are intangible. Some of these include:

- Planning skills *technical*
- Communication ability
- Decision-making skills *technical*
- Organizing ability *tech*
- Motivation and leadership skills *human*
- Conceptual skills
- Adaptability to change
- Qualities such as self-confidence, aggressiveness, and empathy *human*

The recruitment and development of high-quality managerial personnel is essential to the continuing success of every organization. Because of this, organizations must be concerned with determining needs for managerial personnel and identifying persons with managerial potential.

Techniques for Identifying Managerial Talent

Identifying individuals with potential executive talent has become an increasingly important activity in large organizations. In general, the activity has taken these two directions:

1. determining the significant personal characteristics or behaviors that seem to predict managerial success, and
2. establishing managerial talent assessment centers.

PERSONAL CHARACTERISTICS

Over the years, there has been considerable interest in determining the personal characteristics related to managerial success. Major companies such as AT&T, Sears, General Electric, and many others have engaged in research within their firms to identify a series of traits or characteristics necessary for success. In the studies, measures of job performance—such as productivity, salary level, and quality of work of successful managers—were related to the personal characteristics and attitudes of these managers, including grades in college, level of self-confidence, organized and orderly thought, personal values of a practical and economic nature, intelligence, nonverbal reasoning, and general attitudes. Research at AT&T found a significant relationship between grades in college and salary level achieved. In a study of 10,000 managers in the Bell System, it was found that 51 percent of those in the top 10 percent of their college class were located in the top third of the salary levels in the company. For the most part, however, studies of personal characteristics of managers have not yielded accurate predictions of managerial success.

ASSESSMENT CENTER

The assessment center, used to improve managerial selection, has become popular in recent years. It is designed to provide for the systematic evaluation of the potential of individuals for future management positions. The assessment center requires individuals to participate in a series of activities similar to what they might be expected to do in an actual job. Such activities typically include in-basket exercises, management games, leaderless group discussions, mock interviews, and tests. Assessors observe the employees over a period of time. Table 10.2 illustrates a three-day assessment center schedule, which uses a number of different techniques as bases on which to evaluate executive candidates. The American Telephone and Telegraph Company introduced the assessment center approach to American business in the mid-1950s, and since then it has grown in popularity. More than 200 large companies now utilize assessment centers.

A survey of thirty-three companies revealed that the three most widely used assessment techniques are in-basket exercises (thirty-one firms), business games (thirty firms), and leaderless group discussion (thirty-one firms).[23] An in-basket consists of a set of notes, messages, telephone calls, letters, and reports that the candidate is expected to handle within a period of one or two hours. The candidate's decisions can be rated by assessors with respect to such abilities as willingness to take action and organizing of interrelated events.

A business game is a competitive simulation, in which teams, in competition with each other, are required to make decisions concerning production, marketing, purchasing, and finance. The leaderless group discussion assesses participant activities such as taking the lead in discussion, influencing others, mediating arguments, speaking effectively, and summarizing and classifying issues. In addition, various other exercises are often designed to fit the firm's particular situation. For example, J. C. Penney utilizes the "Irate Customer Phone Call," made by an assessor, in order to rate the candidate's ability to control emotions, demonstrate tact, and satisfy the complaint.[24] Psychological tests and in-depth interviewing are frequently used, but these techniques generally show lower levels of accuracy in predicting future success. Personality tests appear to be the weakest predictor.

TABLE 10.2 ■ Typical Assessment Center Schedule

Day 1	Orientation of a dozen candidates
	Break up into groups of four to play a *Management Game* (observe and assess organizing ability, financial acumen, quickness of thinking, efficiency under stress, adaptability, leadership)
	Psychological Testing (measure and assess verbal and numerical abilities, reasoning, interests, and attitudes) and/or *Depth Interviews* (assess motivation)
	Leaderless Group Discussion (observe and assess aggressiveness, persuasiveness, expository skill, energy, flexibility, self-confidence)
Day 2	*In-Basket Exercise* (observe and assess decision making under stress, organizing ability, memory and ability to interrelate events, preparation for decision making, ability to delegate, concern for others)
	Role-playing of Employment or Performance Appraisal Interview (observe and assess sensitivity to others, ability to probe for information, insight, empathy)
	Group Roles in preparation of a budget (observe and assess collaboration abilities, financial knowledge, expository skill, leadership, drive)
Day 3	*Individual Case Analyses* (observe expository skill, awareness of problems, background information possessed for problems, typically involving marketing, personnel, accounting, operations, and financial elements)
	Obtain *Peer Ratings* from all candidates
	Staff assessors meet to discuss and rate all candidates
Weeks later	Manager with assessor experience meets with each candidate to discuss assessment with counseling concerning career guides and areas to develop

The initial study at AT&T in the mid-1950s was most impressive in determining the predictive accuracy of the assessment center approach. Assessor ratings were not communicated to company management for a period of eight years, in order to not contaminate the results. In a sample of fifty-five candidates who achieved the middle-management ranks during that period, the center had correctly predicted 78 percent of them.[25] Of seventy-three persons who did not progress beyond the first level of management, 95 percent had been correctly predicted by the assessment staff. As a result, AT&T has maintained its assessment centers, processing an average of 10,000 candidates a year. Review of rates and of actual progress of 5,943 individuals over a ten-year period has demonstrated a high validity of assessment center predictions.

SUMMARY

If organizational goals are to be accomplished, firms must attract, select, train, and retain qualified people. To meet the firm's human resource needs, six basic

HRM functions must be accomplished: staffing, human resource development, compensation, health and safety, employee and labor relations, and human resource research.

Numerous national laws have been passed and amended and Executive Orders signed that impact equal employment opportunity, thus signifying an attitude in the general population that changes should be made in employment practices. The most significant include Title VII of the 1964 Civil Rights Act and Executive Order 11246. Affirmative action was a major provision of EO 11246.

Staffing is an integral part of human resource management. The basic elements of the staffing process, job analysis, human resource planning, recruitment, selection, and internal staffing administration are closely linked. The ultimate objective of recruitment is to attract individuals who are most capable of meeting the requirements of the job. Selection is the process of identifying those recruited individuals who will best assist the firm in achieving organizational goals. Traditionally, testing is an integral component in the selection process. The interview is the most widely used, probably the most important method of assessing the qualifications of job applicants. In most large organizations, many selection functions are performed by the personnel department. However, the personnel department does not usually make the final decision as to which person is selected for a particular position.

Staffing encompasses much more than planning, recruiting, and selecting employees. It is also vitally concerned with these employees after they have become organizational members. Internal staffing administration (ISA) includes career management, performance appraisals, and employee assistance programs, among other activities.

In recruiting and selecting managerial personnel, more subjective than objective judgment is often required, focusing on evaluation of skills, abilities, attitudes, and characteristics, many of which are intangible. In general, the activity involves determining the significant personal characteristics or behaviors that seem to predict managerial success and establishing managerial talent assessment centers.

REVIEW QUESTIONS

1. What are the basic components of human resource management? Briefly define each.
2. What are the major federal laws that affect the staffing process?
3. Distinguish between a job description and a job specification.
4. Describe the advantages and disadvantages of promotion from within.
5. List and discuss the two basic types of employment interviews.
6. What steps are involved in the personnel selection process?
7. What is the purpose of an assessment center? Discuss.
8. List the various types of employee status changes.

KEY TERMS

staffing	job description	selection
compensation	job specification	preliminary interviews
health	human resource	career management
safety	planning	employee assistance
Executive Orders (EOs)	recruitment	programs
affirmative action	employment requisition	orientation
job analysis		

CASE STUDY

BUSY?

AS PRODUCTION MANAGER for Thompson Manufacturing, Jack Stephens has the final authority to approve the hiring of any new supervisors who work for him. The personnel manager performs the initial screening of all prospective supervisors and then sends the most likely candidates to Jack for interviews.

One day recently Jack received a call from Pete, the personnel manager. "Jack, I've just spoken to a young man who may be just who you're looking for to fill that final line supervisor position. He has some good work experience and it appears as if his head is screwed on straight. He's here right now and available if you could possibly see him." Jack hesitated a moment before answering. "Gee, Pete," he said, "I'm certainly busy today but I'll try to squeeze him in. Send him on down."

A moment later Allen Guthrie, the new applicant, arrived at Jack's office and introduced himself. "Come on in, Allen," said Jack. "I'll be right with you after I make a few phone calls."

Fifteen minutes later Jack finished the calls and began talking with Allen. Jack was quite impressed. After a few minutes Jack's door opened and a supervisor yelled, "We have a small problem on line number one and need your help."

"Sure," Jack replied. "Excuse me a minute, Allen." Ten minutes later Jack returned and the conversation continued for at least ten more minutes before a series of phone calls again interrupted them.

The same pattern of interruptions continued for the next hour. Finally, Allen looked at his watch and said, "I'm sorry, Mr. Stephens, but I have to pick up my wife."

"Sure thing, Allen," Jack said as the phone rang again. "Call me later this week."

QUESTIONS

1. What specific policies might a company follow to avoid interviews like this one?
2. Explain why Jack and not Pete should make the selection decision.

CASE STUDY

SOMETHING'S MISSING

JOHN CASE, accounting supervisor, was clearly annoyed as he approached his boss, Gerald Jones. He began, "Gerald, this note you sent me says I have to update descriptions for all ten of the jobs in my department within the next two weeks."

"Well," asked Gerald, "what's the problem with that?"

John explained, "This is a waste of time, especially since I have other deadlines. It will take at least thirty hours. We still have two weeks of work left on the internal audit reviews. You want me to push that back and work on *job descriptions*? No way.

"We have not looked at these job descriptions in years. They will need a great deal of revision. And

as soon as they get into the hands of the employees, I will get all kinds of flak."

"Why would you get flak for getting the job descriptions in order?" asked Gerald. John answered, "This whole thing is a can of worms. Just calling attention to the existence of job descriptions will give some people the idea they don't have to do things that are not on the description. And if we write what the people in my division really do, some jobs will have to be upgraded, and others will be downgraded I'll bet. I just can't afford the morale problem and the confusion right now."

Gerald replied, "What do you suggest, John? I have been told just to get it done, and within two weeks." "I don't want to do it at all," said John, "and certainly not during the audit period. Can't you just go back up the line and get it put off until next month?"

QUESTIONS

1. What have John and Gerald forgotten to perform prior to the creation of job descriptions? Why is this step important?

2. Evaluate John's statement, "Just calling attention to the existence of job descriptions will give some people the idea they don't have to do things that are not on the description."

EXPERIENTIAL EXERCISE

Selecting the best persons to fill vacant positions is a most important task of human resource management. As all managers recognize, there are many factors that must be considered in order to ensure proper selection. The selection decision you will be dealing with in this exercise is a necessary one, because George Hendricks has just been promoted, and before he starts his new job, his replacement must be determined. George's firm is an affirmative action employer, and presently there are few women in management. George has some excellent subordinates to choose from, but there are many factors to consider before a decision can be made. The people upstairs made it perfectly clear that they expect George to select an individual who can perform as well as he did over the last six years. The individuals he worked with on the line have made it clear that they want Sam Philips. The women on the line have indicated, to everyone who will listen, that it is time for a female supervisor, in at least one division. But it is George's decision, and he must select the best person, regardless of the heat.

Sam Philips, an employee of the company for the past eleven years, is one possible candidate. He wants this promotion, needs the higher pay, the respect and influence to be gained, and the nice office that George has now. Sam is recognized as one of the most technically capable individuals in the division. He is from the old school: "We get things done through discipline. We don't put up with people allowing their personal problems to interfere with work."

Fredda Lott, an employee for seven years, is another candidate. She wants the promotion primarily because she can do a good job and can represent the women on the line. She was an excellent student in college, and she believes she can deal effectively with the personal problems of others. She is recognized as technically capable and has an undergraduate degree in management.

Fred Rubble, an employee of the company for six years, is the final candidate for the promotion. He believes he should get the promotion primarily because he can do the best job. Fred is very capable, but not quite as familiar with all the technical aspects of the job as is Fredda or Sam. He has an associate's degree in liberal arts, and is taking business classes at night. Fred is also actively involved in the community, having held various civic offices.

Four individuals will participate in this exercise; one as George Hendricks, the current supervisor, and three as the candidates for the promotion. Your instructor will provide the participants with the additional information necessary to participate.

NOTES

1. Arthur Sharplin, "The Lincoln Electric Company," *Case Research Journal* (1982): 59–84; Arthur Sharplin, "Lincoln Electric's Unique Policies," *Personnel Administrator* (June 1983): 8–10; Arthur Sharplin, "Lincoln Electric Company, 1984," in *Strategic Management* (New York: McGraw-Hill, 1985).
2. Maria Shao, Seth Payne, John Templeman, and Mark Maremont, "Trying Times at Boeing," *Business Week*, 13 March 1989, 35.

3. Based on the discussion in R. Wayne Mondy and Robert M. Noe III, *Personnel: The Management of Human Resources,* 3d ed. (Newton, Mass.: Allyn and Bacon, 1987): 6–11.

4. R. Wayne Mondy, Robert M. Noe, and Robert E. Edwards, "What the Staffing Function Entails," *Personnel* 63 (April 1986): 55.

5. Todd Vogel, Gail De George, Pete Engardio, and Aaron Bernstein, "Texas Air: Empire in Jeopardy," *Business Week,* 27 March 1989, 30.

6. "Beyond Unions: A Revolution in Employee Relations Is in the Making," *Business Week,* 8 July 1985, 72.

7. Alexander B. Trowbridge, "A Management Look at Labor Relations," *Unions In Transition* (San Francisco: ICS Press, 1988), 414.

8. Wendy Zellner, "The UAW Rebels Teaming Up Against Teamwork," *Business Week,* 27 March 1989, 110.

9. Trowbridge, "Labor Relations," 417.

10. Howard C. Lockwood, "Equal Employment Opportunities," in *Staffing Policies and Strategies,* ed. Dale Yoder and Herbert G. Heneman (Washington, D.C.: Bureau of National Affairs, 1979), 4–252.

11. Ted Gest, "An Old Anti-bias Law's Widened Bite," *U.S. News & World Report,* 1 June 1987, 10.

12. Michael R. Carrell and Frank E. Kuzmits, "Amended ADEA's Effects on HR Strategies Remain Dubious," *Personnel Journal* 66 (May 1987): 112.

13. George E. Stevens, "Exploding the Myths about Hiring the Handicapped," *Personnel* 63 (December 1986): 57.

14. Art L. Bethke, "The IRCA: What's an Employer to Do?" *Wisconsin Small Business Forum* 6 (Fall 1987): 26.

15. Mondy and Noe III, *Personnel,* 101.

16. Shao et al., "Trying Times," 35.

17. "A Bleak New Year for Airline Profits," *Business Week,* 10 January 1983, 38; James Ott, "Delta Expanding Route System with 737-200s," *Aviation Week and Space Technology,* 2 April 1984, 32–33; "Delta: The World's Most Profitable Airline," *Business Week,* 31 August 1981, 68–71; James Ott, "Delta Anticipates Savings in Flight-Planning System," *Aviation Week and Space Technology,* 30 April 1984, 34–39; and numerous articles from *The Wall Street Journal.*

18. Mondy, Noe, and Edwards, "Staffing Function," 55–56.

19. C. Harold Stone and Floyd L. Ruch, "Selection, Interviewing, and Testing," in *ASPA Handbook of Personnel and Industrial Relations,* ed. Dale Yoder and Herbert G. Heneman (Washington, D.C.: Bureau of National Affairs, 1974), 152–154.

20. Kenneth C. Cooper, "Those 'Qualified' Applicants and Their Phony Credentials," *Administrative Management* 38 (August 1977): 44.

21. Scott T. Rickard, "Effective Staff Selection," *Personnel Journal* (June 1981): 477.

22. Diana Reed-Mendenhall and C. W. Millard, "Orientation: A Training and Development Tool," *Personnel Administrator* 25 (August 1980): 40.

23. Joseph M. Bender, "What Is 'Typical' of Assessment Centers?" *Personnel* 50 (July–August 1973): 51.

24. William C. Byham, "Assessment Centers for Spotting Future Managers," *Harvard Business Review* 48 (July–August 1970): 158.

25. Douglas W. Bray and Donald L. Grant, "The Assessment Center in the Measurement of Potential for Business Management," *Psychological Monographs* 80, no. 17 (1966): 24.

REFERENCES

Baier, L. L. "Job Searching and the Advertising Dilemma." *Personnel Administrator* 29 (April 1984): 22–24.

Berger, Raymond M., and Donna H. Tucker. "How to Evaluate a Selection Test." *Personnel Journal* 66 (February 1987): 88–90.

Briscoe, Dennis R., and Susan Harwood. "Improving the Interview Process." *Personnel* 61 (September 1987): 18–20.

Buonocore, Anthony J., and Dallas R. Crable. "Equal Opportunity: An Imcomplete Evolution." *Personnel Journal* 65 (August 1986): 32–35.

Carrell, Michael R., and Frank E. Kuzmits. "Amended ADEA's Effects on HR Strategies Remain Dubious." *Personnel Journal* 66 (May 1987): 111–119.

Davidson, Jeffrey P. "Checking References." *Supervisory Management* 31 (January 1986): 29–31.

Dennis, Donn L. "Evaluating Corporate Recruitment Efforts." *Personnel Administrator* 30 (January 1985): 21–26.

Feild, Hubert S., and Robert D. Gatewood. "Matching Talent with the Task: To Find the Right People, First Define the Jobs You Want Them to Do." *Personnel Administrator* 32 (April 1987): 113–123.

Grider, Doug, and Mike Shurden. "The Gathering Storm of Comparable Worth." *Business Horizons* 30 (July–August 1987): 81–86.

Halcrow, Allan. "Anatomy of a Recruitment Ad." *Personnel Journal* 64 (August 1985): 64–65.

Hixon, Allen L. "Why Corporations Make Haphazard Overseas Staffing Decisions." *Personnel Administrator* 31 (March 1986): 91–94.

Huber, Vandra L., Margaret A. Neale, and Gregory B. Northcraft. "Decision Bias and Personnel Selection." *Organizational Behavior and Human Decision Processes* 40 (August 1987): 136.

Hunt, Gary T., and William F. Eadie. *Interviewing: A Communication Approach.* New York: Holt, Rinehart, and Winston, 1987.

Kleinman, Dan. "What to Look for in Tomorrow's Employee." *Personnel Journal* 66 (October 1987): 192–206.

Kohl, John P., and David B. Stephens. "Expanding the Legal Rights of Working Women." *Personnel* 64 (May 1987): 46–51.

LoPresto, Robert. "Ethical Recruiting." *Personnel Administrator* 31 (November 1986): 90–92.

Magnus, Margaret. "Is Your Recruitment All It Can Be?" *Personnel Journal* 66 (February 1987): 54–63.

Markowitz, Jarroid. "Managing the Job Analysis Process." *Training & Development Journal* 41 (August 1987): 64–67.

Martin, Bob, and Stephanie Lawrence. "Personnel Executives Respond to Reaffirmation of Affirmative Action." *Personnel Journal* 66 (May 1987): 9–15.

Mercer, Michael W., and John J. Seres. "Using Scorable Interview 'Tests' in Hiring." *Personnel* 61 (June 1987): 57.

Mondy, R. Wayne, Robert M. Noe, and Robert E. Edwards. "What the Staffing Function Entails." *Personnel* 63 (April 1986): 55–58.

Nkomo, Stella M. "The Theory and Practice of HR Planning: The Gap Still Remains." *Personnel Administrator* 31 (August 1986): 71–81.

Paunonen, Sampo V., Douglas N. Jackson, and Steven M. Oberman. "Personnel Selection Decisions: Effects of Applicant Personality and the Letter of Reference." *Organizational Behavior and Human Decision Processes* 40 (August 1987): 97.

Powell, Gary N. "The Effects of Sex and Gender on Recruitment." *Academy of Management Review* 12 (October 1987): 731–743.

Premeaux, Shane R., R. Wayne Mondy, and Art Bethke. "Decertification: Fulfilling Unions' Destiny?" *Personnel Journal* 66 (June 1987): 144–148.

Schenkel-Savitt, Susan, and Steven P. Seltzer. "Recruitment as a Successful Means of Affirmative Action." *Employee Relations Law Journal* 13 (Winter 1987): 165–179.

Schneider-Jenkins, C., and N. Carr-Ruffino. "Smart Selection: Three Steps to Choosing New Employees." *Management World* 14 (March 1985): 38–39.

Smart, Bradford D. "Progressive Approaches for Hiring the Best People." *Training and Development Journal* 41 (September 1987): 46–53.

Voluck, Philip R. "Recruiting, Interviewing and Hiring: Staying within the Boundaries." *Personnel Administrator* 32 (May 1987): 15–19.

CHAPTER

11

Chapter Outline

The Controlling Process

Learning Objectives

After completing this chapter students should be able to

1. Define controlling and describe the control process.
2. Describe the most frequent types of standards used and explain control tolerances.
3. Relate controlling to the business system and describe and identify the characteristics of strategic control points.
4. Relate the reasons for negative reactions to controls, and describe ways of overcoming negative reactions to controls.
5. Explain the importance of disciplinary action and describe what is meant by the concepts of progressive discipline and discipline without punishment.

THROUGH ITS 7-ELEVEN STORES division, the Southland Corporation operates more than 10,000 convenience stores throughout the world, most of them in the United States. For more than twenty years the company's revenues and earnings have grown, recently exceeding $8 billion and $131 million, respectively, per year. Yearly gains of 15 and 20 percent have not been unusual for Southland.

The 7-Eleven organization is well known for its system of tight control and disciplined management. The efficiency of the company's control system may be a reflection of the personality of the founder, Joe C. Thompson. His sister wrote, "The biggest influence on Joe's life, I believe, was discipline." Even competitors give the company good marks. The president of a rival convenience store chain said, "I think it has to be said that Southland is one of the great retailing stories of our time."

To make sure its small, 2,400-square-foot stores are successful, Southland studies potential sites extensively and uses computer programs to forecast a proposed store's sales for the first five years. A store that does not measure up to standards is often closed. John Thompson, son of the founder and now chairman, says that when stores look like losers, "we would rather close them and take our licks."

7-Eleven has been a leader in the computerization of store operations. Five automated distribution centers supply 7-Eleven stores in the United States. Specially designed trucks deliver pre-priced items, along computer-designed routes, to individual stores. Careful analysis is made of which items sell best in which stores. Even shelf location is the subject of careful computerized evaluation. When trends change, items that no longer sell well are replaced by others, which are being continually tested in a few strategically located stores. A product that appears to be a rapid seller is tried nationwide.

The range of products and services offered at 7-Eleven stores continues to evolve. In 1984, Southland began installing automatic teller machines (ATMs) in some high-traffic stores. In 1986, an agreement was reached with Hardee's to feature that company's fast-food products in 7-Elevens.

Because of the limited floor space and wide array of merchandise, inventories must be tightly controlled. Using central computers in Dallas, Southland is able to determine which items to stock and what prices to charge. In addition, it is possible to analyze the operations of each store in the system in terms of profitability, inventory turnover, and so forth.

The ability of the Southland Corporation to respond to changing conditions is illustrated by the company's experience with gasoline marketing. In 1972, only 200 7-Eleven stores sold gasoline; but by the mid-1970s, when gasoline prices skyrocketed due to the Arab oil embargo, the self-service pumps at 7-Eleven stores had become very popular. The company began to relocate a few stores from the traditional mid-block location to corners, a proven marketing technique for gasoline stations but not for convenience stores. The corner locations produced 50 percent extra sales. Of several thousand stores added since the mid-1970s, almost all sell gasoline and almost all are on corners. Although gasoline produces a very small profit margin for 7-Eleven, gasoline customers must come inside to pay, and many make purchases other than gasoline.[1] ■

S THE 7-ELEVEN STORY illustrates, the control function is a vital part of the management process. A properly designed control system alerts managers to the existence of potential problems and helps them to take corrective actions. At first, one might think that properly performing the functions of planning, organizing, and influencing would eliminate the need for controlling. Nothing could be further from the truth. First, it is impossible to anticipate every situation; consequently the organization must be ready to respond to unexpected changes. Consider what might happen if 7-Eleven were not ready to change product selection in response to customer preferences. Even when likely events can be identified, no one is certain what the future holds, so some adjustment is always necessary. An effective control system provides for these adjustments.

This chapter first describes the controlling process. Next, three types of controls are discussed. Then, procedures for establishing strategic control points are described, followed by a discussion of the reasons why controls often produce negative reactions and a description of how these negative reactions may be overcome. Finally, disciplinary action as a means of controlling employee behavior is described.

▓ THE CONTROLLING PROCESS

Controlling

The process of comparing actual performance with standards and taking any necessary corrective action.

Controlling is the process of comparing actual performance with standards and taking any necessary corrective action. The control process has three steps: (1) establish standards, (2) evaluate performance, and (3) take corrective action. Figure 11.1 illustrates these steps. Notice that like the other management functions, the controlling function is subject to environmental influences. For example, in 1984, 7-Eleven stores were picketed by fundamentalist Christian groups opposed

FIGURE 11.1 ▆
The Controlling Process

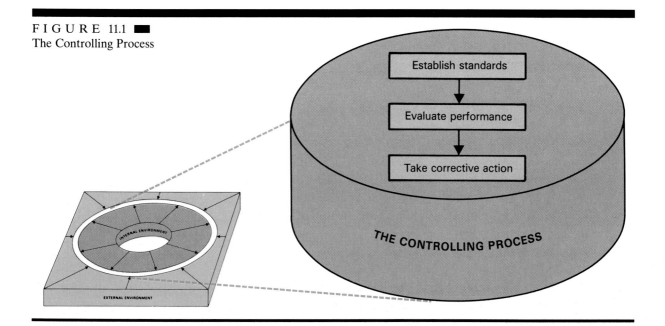

303

to the distribution of *Penthouse* and *Playboy* magazines. This effort by members of the public undoubtedly caused some 7-Eleven customers to start shopping elsewhere. It was also of concern to the stockholders because of the probable impact on sales and profits. Southland ultimately stopped selling magazines of this type, most likely because of the pressure from the external environment. Southland's controlling process has to be carried out in the context of these and other external forces and must produce the proper responses. The phases of the controlling process are the same at Southland as in any other organization.

Establish Standards

Standards
Established levels of quality or quantity used to guide performance.

pg 111 – 115

Workers must know what is expected before the control process can be implemented. **Standards** are established levels of quality or quantity used to guide performance. For example, a shaft might have a standard diameter, and the machinist must try to cut the shaft to that size. Standards are sometimes viewed as goals. American standards, often rigidly stated, are frequently ignored to get the products out the door. Foreign manufacturers keep setting new, far tougher standards of performance, reliability, and durability, which American manufacturers, for the most part, cannot meet.[2] Wherever possible, standards should be expressed numerically, to reduce subjectivity. This tends to depersonalize the control process.[3] The most frequently used types of standards are listed and described below.

1. *Time standards.* Time standards state the length of time it should take to make a certain product or perform a certain service. An airline pilot has a standard time span in which to make a certain trip. Most organizations have a standard lunch time.
2. *Productivity standards.* These standards are based on the ~~amount~~ of *per unit of input* product or service produced during a set time period. For instance, a

or per employee

Controls are established by setting appropriate standards and then evaluating performance as measured against those standards. (© 1987 Lawrence Migdale/Photo Researchers, Inc.)

productivity standard might be to produce 10 units per hour or to serve 150 customers per hour in a Wendy's restaurant.

3. *Cost standards.* These standards are based on the cost associated with producing the goods or service. For example, the material cost might be $10 per unit. Cost standards are usually set in the expense budget for the supervisor's unit. At 7-Eleven, strict quality standards are observed in selecting which brands of products to stock. Because of limited shelf space, 7-Eleven carries only the best selling one or two brands of any particular item.

4. *Quality standards.* These are based on the level of perfection desired. For instance, no more than a certain percentage of impurities may be allowed in a chemical, or a valve may have to hold pressure for ten minutes in order to pass inspection. American quality is improving to a point just below the Japanese at best. For example, as many as one quarter of American factory workers do not produce anything; they simply fix other workers' mistakes.[4]

5. *Behavioral standards.* These are based on the type of behavior desired of workers in the organization. Expressing these standards precisely is difficult. The convenience store industry, in particular, imposes strict standards of behavior on store managers and clerks. Workers in 7-Eleven stores are required to wear standard clothing, be neat, and treat customers courteously. Employees who violate behavioral standards are often subject to disciplinary action, the topic of a later section of this chapter.

Control tolerances
Specifications of how much deviation will be permitted before corrective action is taken.

Although standards may be clear, control tolerances also need to be established. **Control tolerances** are specifications of how much deviation will be permitted before corrective action is taken. For instance, a standard size for a particular part may be 3.1 inches (see Table 11.1), but a tolerance of ± 0.05 inch may be permitted. If a part is produced within the range of 3.05 to 3.15 inches, it is accepted. If it falls outside this range, it is rejected. As another example, a company might allow only two unexcused absences per month. A standard workday might be eight hours, but most managers have a certain control tolerance of lateness, perhaps five minutes. Whether the standard relates to a product, a service, or behavior, it is important to communicate both the standard and the control tolerances to workers. If this is done, many workers will control themselves.

TABLE 11.1 ■ Standards and Control Tolerances

Standards	Tolerances
3.1″ shaft diameter	$\pm 0.05''$
Perfect attendance	Two absences per month
8:00 A.M. starting time	Five minutes late
One minute waiting time	Fifteen seconds more
Clear polished surface	Two visible defects

TABLE 11.2 ■ QC Tread Checklist

	Standard	Minimum	Maximum	Actual
Width	22.15″	22.0″	22.3″	22.1″
Length	72.25″	72.0″	72.5″	72.1″
Thickness	.845″	.82″	.87″	.85″
Weight	8.7#	8.6#	8.8#	8.7#
Number of visible defects	0	0	2	0

Evaluate Performance

Evaluating performance consists of checking for deviation from standard and determining if those deviations exceed control tolerances. Evaluation requires accurate measurement of what is taking place and an effective means of comparison with standards.

When the process being controlled is a mechanical one, measurement and comparison may be quite simple. For example, a quality control inspector may use a micrometer or other instrument to measure a part. Table 11.2 illustrates a QC checklist that a tire inspector for a major tire manufacturer uses. The inspector need only glance at the checklist after measuring a tire to see if a deviation from standard exceeds control tolerances.

The latest technique for meeting manufacturing standards is called statistical process control, or SPC. Basically, **statistical process control** gauges the performance of the manufacturing process by carefully monitoring changes in whatever is being produced. The goal is to detect potential defects before they result in off-quality products, then pinpoint the reasons for the deviations and adjust the process to make it more stable. The Japanese, who have been honing statistical quality methods for over thirty years, picked up on SPC quickly. Few U.S. companies have a tradition of quality consciousness, but the majority of those that do have applied SPC as vigorously as have the Japanese. AT&T, Corning Glass, Du Pont, Ford, Hewlett-Packard, IBM, Kodak, and Westinghouse are frequently cited as leaders in management by quality.[5] American companies that really key on quality are considered to be among the most successful.

Other processes, especially behavioral ones, are more difficult to measure. The courtesy with which a 7-Eleven employee serves customers is an example. When one of the authors was a young navy personnel officer, he reprimanded a clerk for working too slowly. The leading chief petty officer showed the young officer that, although the clerk appeared to be working slowly, he was actually doing more than his share. Managers should be careful to measure accurately before taking corrective action.

Statistical process control
A procedure that gauges the performance of the manufacturing process by carefully monitoring changes in whatever is being produced.

see pg 338

Take Corrective Action

The manager must consider what action to take to correct performance when deviations occur. Often the real cause of the deviation must be found before corrective action can be taken. Assume that the number of allowable defects produced by a certain machine exceeds standard. The cause may be a faulty machine or it may be a careless operator. Clearly, proper corrective action depends on which one is the case.

Not all deviations from standard justify corrective action. In some cases, personal judgment is necessary. Suppose that a worker is fifteen minutes late for work (a deviation from the standard), but you realize the lateness was unavoidable. As manager you may decide to take no action, even though a deviation occurred. In this case, the standard is to be on time.

Corrective action may be either immediate or permanent. Immediate corrective action is often aimed at correcting *symptoms*. Permanent corrective action corrects the *cause* of the symptoms or problem. Most frequently, corrective action is of the immediate type; it is done right away to correct the situation. For example, a particular project is a week behind schedule. If the delay is not corrected, other projects will be seriously affected. The first thing to do is to not worry about who caused the difficulty but to get the project back on schedule. Depending on the authority of the manager, the following corrective actions may be ordered: (1) overtime hours may be authorized; (2) additional workers and equipment may be assigned; (3) a full-time director may be assigned to push the project through; (4) an extra effort may be asked from all employees; or (5) if all these fail, the schedule may have to be readjusted, requiring changes all along the line.

After the degree of urgency has been diminished, attention can be devoted to more permanent corrective action. Just how and why did events stray from their planned course? What can be done to prevent a recurrence of this type of difficulty? It is at this phase that many managers fail. Too often they find themselves "putting out fires"; and they never discover the actual cause of the problem. For instance, managers may find themselves constantly having to interview and hire new people to replace those who quit. A manager may be working twelve hours a day locating new employees. But the high turnover problem is not solved merely by this type of immediate corrective action. Some type of permanent corrective action must be taken, once managers determine what is causing the high turnover. A supervisor may be extremely difficult to work with, or the pay scale may not be competitive for the area. Whatever the problem, it must be identified and corrected, or high turnover will likely continue. Permanent corrective action must be taken for the sake of future economical and effective operations.

Managers may discover that there are a number of fundamental causes for a deviation from standard. In this particular project, the schedule may not have been met because of an ongoing problem in one department. Or it may be discovered that not only was this particular project in trouble, but most of the other projects in this company are also behind schedule. In the first instance, investigation may reveal that poor equipment in the one department is the major source of difficulty. Thus, a basic corrective action would be to provide new or improved equipment or new or improved management. It is not likely that this particular project will be helped by this action, but future projects should be improved. If, on the other hand, most of the projects in the firm are also usually behind schedule, an even more serious type of basic corrective action may be demanded; perhaps a drastic overhaul of general control procedures, or even reorganization of the entire company.

■ CONTROLLING AND THE BUSINESS SYSTEM

Recall from Chapter 3 that in the business system, inputs are converted to outputs through a transformation process. As is fairly obvious from Figure 11.2, the controlling efforts by management may concentrate on inputs, on the process itself, or on outputs.

Controlling Inputs

With input controls, managers attempt to monitor the resources—material and personnel—that come into the organization, to ensure that they can be used effectively to achieve organizational objectives.

MATERIAL CONTROLS

The material resources an organization requires must meet specified quality standards and be available when needed by the firm. If Ethan Allen, a major furniture manufacturer, purchased low-quality wood with which to manufacture furniture, the company would not maintain its reputation for producing excellent furniture. Statistical sampling (discussed in greater detail in Chapter 12) is often used to assist in material control. With statistical sampling, a portion of the items

FIGURE 11.2 ■
The Business System

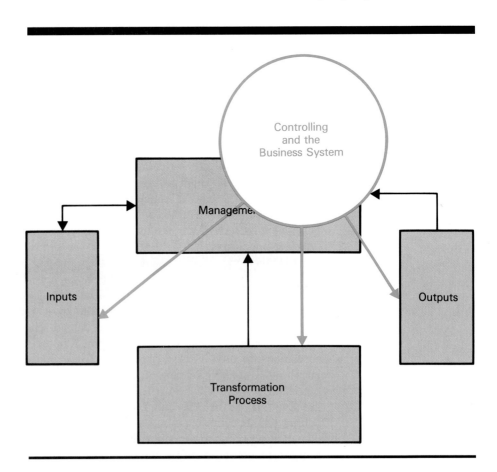

received into the firm are checked to estimate the quality of the entire lot. For instance, 5 percent of the lumber Ethan Allen receives might be examined. In many cases, failure of even a small percentage of the incoming items could create difficulty. Components for commercial aircraft engines are an example. Statistical sampling is not typically used in such situations. Rather, each item is inspected individually.

PERSONNEL SELECTION CONTROLS

If a firm is to maintain stability or growth, it continually needs new workers, due to factors such as death, retirement, loss of employees to other organizations, and growth, in and of itself. In order to obtain new workers capable of sustaining the organization, certain controls must be established regarding their selection. The skill requirements of each job must be determined, and new employees should meet or exceed these requirements before they are employed.

As discussed in Chapter 10, the basic document that delineates the qualifications needed to perform a job is the job specification. Requirements such as education, work experience, and physical abilities are stated in the job specification. Knowing these requirements permits the firm to seek out those individuals who are best qualified to perform jobs in the organization. Without job specifications serving as standards, recruiters would be unprepared and unable to staff the organization.

Controlling the Process

Overseeing the actual process of producing goods and services offers an opportunity to correct problems before outputs have been affected. Most of a typical supervisor's time is spent overseeing the process. Effective supervisors usually become familiar with the sights and sounds of the workplace and can often tell when something unusual is occurring. A wide range of possible signals is available to the supervisor. A noisy bearing on a bolt machine might warn the supervisor that the machine will begin to make defective bolts. Before a single faulty bolt has been produced, the bearing can be replaced.

Perhaps the most important aspect of this kind of control is observation and correction of employee behavior. A 7-Eleven store supervisor might observe an individual store manager failing to put excess cash into the "drop safe" (to keep the amount of cash exposed to potential theft at a minimum). Before this causes a problem, the supervisor can correct the store manager's behavior. In fact, this is such a serious violation in the convenience store business that it often prompts disciplinary action. An observant supervisor will often notice a worker looking around or behaving carelessly and will take action before output has been affected.

Observing workers, managers, and machines in the process of doing the organization's work is a tool of management at every level. A senior manager might observe a junior one cursing or otherwise behaving inappropriately and stop the misbehavior before it affects morale or productivity.

Controlling Outputs

The ultimate purpose of controlling focuses on the quality and quantity of outputs produced. In fact, most people think of controlling as simply checking what has

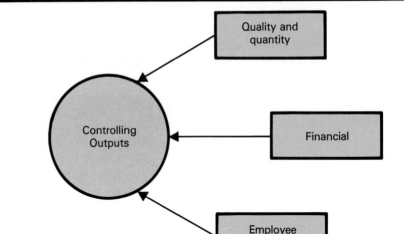

occurred and taking corrective action. In the business system, this consists of quality and quantity controls, financial controls, and evaluation of employee performance based on output (see Figure 11.3).

QUALITY AND QUANTITY CONTROLS

The purpose of quality control is to ensure that a certain level of excellence is attained. There has been more emphasis on quality ever since Americans became convinced that foreign manufacturers typically produce better automobiles, stereos, bicycles, and other products. Quality control must also be concerned with the costs of increasing quality. Therefore, it is important that the quality necessary to meet company objectives be determined in the planning stage. The

ETHICAL DILEMMA

Y OU ARE THE president of Lincoln Laser Company, a $5 million-a-year manufacturer in Phoenix, and you thought you had an airtight deal with a Japanese distributor. You spent months negotiating a deal to sell your equipment in Japan. In order to offer the best product possible, you dissected the innards of the $300,000 machine at Lincoln that scans printed circuit-board wiring for minute cracks and breaks and totally refined the product. Finally, the Japanese ordered eight. You deliver the product, and the Japanese distributor tells you it is not what the customer expected. They want you to re-engineer the equipment, even though it clearly meets the written specifications. You can either re-engineer the equipment even though it clearly meets the written specifications, or you can refuse to re-engineer the product.
    What would you do?

Source: Adapted by permission, *Nation's Business*, August 1987. Copyright © 1987, U.S. Chamber of Commerce.

F I G U R E 11.4 ■
Monthly Quality
Comparison Report, by
Shifts

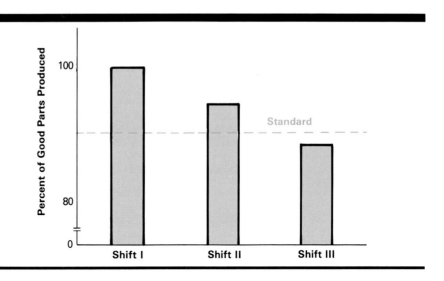

Southland Corporation makes many of the items sold at 7-Eleven stores. The octane of the gasoline Southland makes at its Louisiana refinery is an indicator of quality; however, producing only 100-octane fuel would be prohibitively expensive, so the company ensures that its gasoline is only (but at least) of standard quality in terms of octane. A similar situation exists in the manufacture of ice cream and yogurt by Southland's dairy products division. Trade-offs are necessary between the quality level one might prefer and the cost of achieving that level.

A common approach to evaluating quality is to seek comparison with other organizations or subunits. Figure 11.4 shows how three shift crews compare in terms of the acceptable parts they produce. The supervisor for shift 3 probably feels the third shift is deficient in comparison to the other two and should take corrective action.

Productivity is normally thought of in terms of the quantity of output. Most companies also expect a certain amount of production from each individual or organizational unit, often expressed in terms of a quota. Sales quotas specify the amount of sales an individual, district, or region is expected to meet. Production quotas specify the amount or number of an item that needs to be produced. Control of quotas at every level is important if the organization is to achieve its objectives. When a 7-Eleven store does not live up to sales expectations, it is closed. This is only done, of course, after a good deal of effort has been expended to bring the store up to standard.

FINANCIAL CONTROLS

The ultimate output that most companies desire is net profit. The quality and quantity of goods and services is often seen as a means to this end. Financial statements provide valuable information with regard to whether a company, department, or unit is effectively using its financial resources. Intelligent interpretation of financial data provides an excellent means by which management can control its financial welfare.

Budgetary controls (discussed in the next chapter) also offer a way of ensuring that the company is performing well financially. Plans are made for certain levels

TABLE 11.3 ■ Summary of Financial Ratio Analysis

Category of Ratio	Name of Ratio	Formula for Calculation	Purpose of Ratio
Liquidity	Current ratio	$\dfrac{\text{current assets}}{\text{current liabilities}}$	Measures ability to meet debts when due—short-term liquidity
	Quick ratio	$\dfrac{\text{current assets-inventory}}{\text{current liabilities}}$	Measures ability to meet debts when due—very short-term liquidity
Leverage	Debt to total assets	$\dfrac{\text{debt}}{\text{total assets}}$	Measures percentage of total funds that have been provided by creditors (debt = total assets − equity)
	Times interest earned	$\dfrac{\text{profit before tax + interest charges}}{\text{interest charges}}$	Measures the extent to which interest charges are covered by gross income
Profitability	Return on sales (net profit margin)	$\dfrac{\text{net income}}{\text{sales revenue}}$	Measures percent of profit earned on each dollar of sales
	Return on total assets	$\dfrac{\text{net income}}{\text{total assets}}$	Measures the return on total investment of a firm
	Return on equity	$\dfrac{\text{net income}}{\text{stockholder equity}}$	Measures rate of return on stockholders' investment
	Earnings per share	$\dfrac{\text{net income}}{\text{number of common shares outstanding}}$	Measures profit earned for each share of common stock
Activity	Total asset turnover	$\dfrac{\text{revenues}}{\text{total assets}}$	Measures effectiveness of assets in generating revenues
	Collection period	$\dfrac{\text{accounts receivable}}{\text{revenues per day}}$	Measures time required to collect for an average sale
	Inventory turnover	$\dfrac{\text{sales}}{\text{inventory}}$	Measures number of times inventory is sold each accounting period

of revenues and expenses. If at any time the company is not on track toward achieving those levels, a good budgeting system will initiate corrective action.

In order to analyze financial position, a firm would likely begin with ratio analysis. Financial ratio analysis provides management with a basis for comparing current to past performance. In addition, financial ratios can be compared not only to past trends within the company, but also to other divisions within the company and to other firms in the industry. If the ratios are not in line with acceptable standards, the manager is in a position to make corrections. There are four basic types of ratios:

Liquidity ratios
Ratios that measure a firm's ability to meet its current obligations.

Leverage ratios
Ratios that measure whether a firm has effectively used outside financing.

- **Liquidity ratios** measure a firm's ability to meet its current obligations.
- **Leverage ratios** measure whether a firm has effectively used outside financing.

- **Activity ratios** measure how efficiently the firm is utilizing its resources.
- **Profitability ratios** measure the overall operating efficiency and profitability of the firm.

Names of ratios, the formula for their calculation, and the purpose of the ratio may be seen in Table 11.3.

Activity ratios
Ratios that measure how efficiently the firm is utilizing its resources.

Profitability ratios
Ratios that measure the overall operating efficiency and profitability of the firm.

Performance Appraisal (PA)
A formal system that provides a periodic review and evaluation of an individual's job performance.

EVALUATION OF EMPLOYEE PERFORMANCE *discussed under control, not staffing*

For a top producer in a work group, nothing is more discouraging than getting the same pay increase a marginal employee gets. In such a situation, the incentive to do superior work will certainly decline. While employees at all levels, management and nonmanagement alike, are continuously appraised informally, it is desirable to formally summarize these evaluations periodically. **Performance Appraisal (PA)** is a formal system that provides a periodic review and evaluation of an individual's job performance.[6] An effective employee performance system is a means of control, whereby individuals learn of their strengths and weaknesses and are told what they should do to overcome deficiencies. Collaborative approaches to performance appraisal done in a realistic, objective manner help subordinates grow and become more effective employees.[7] Employee performance evaluation systems that give each worker the same rating are not fair to the individual who is a superior performer, nor do they assist the substandard worker who desires to improve.

The overall goal of performance appraisal systems is to improve the organization's effectiveness by developing and communicating vital information about the firm's human resources. This requires providing feedback to employees on their performance. When the manager evaluates employees against pre-established standards on the appraisal form, the manager is involved in controlling.

■■ ESTABLISHING STRATEGIC CONTROL POINTS

Management is centrally concerned with controlling the business system, consisting of inputs, processes, and outputs. A frequent problem is determining what part of the system to monitor. Ideally, every resource, processing activity, and output should be measured, reported, and compared to a predetermined standard. This can be extremely costly and time-consuming. A manager must determine what activity to measure and when to measure it. Critical points selected for monitoring in the process of producing goods or services are called **strategic control points.**

Strategic control points
Critical points selected for monitoring in the process of producing goods or services.

Strategic control points should have a number of basic characteristics (see Figure 11.5). First, they should relate to key operations or events. If a difficulty occurs at a vital strategic control point, the entire operation may grind to a halt. For instance, if the word processing manager in a bank does not have control of the type and quality of equipment purchased, inaccurate and untimely information may be sent to depositors. The problem created by poor-quality equipment may have a detrimental impact on the sales of a company, even though the word processing personnel and sales force are of exceptional quality.

A second important characteristic of strategic control points is that they must be set up so that problems can be identified before serious damage occurs. If the

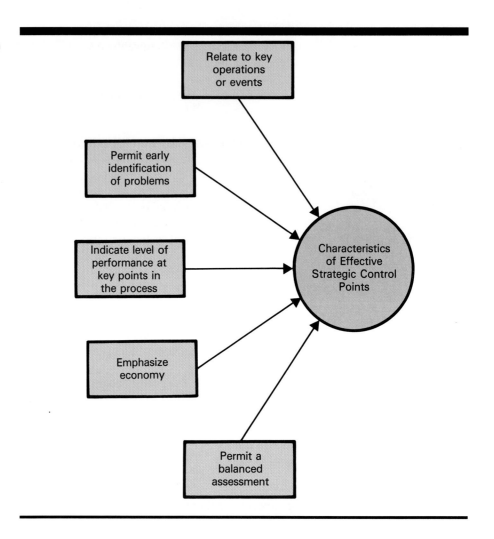

control point is properly located, action can be taken to stop or alter a defective process before major harm is done. Testing for defects early in the process typically cuts costs and improves both production and quality.[8] It does little good to discover that a million defective parts have been produced. The control point should be located so as to quickly identify and correct deviations.

In the early days of one of the authors' careers, he had the opportunity to observe how the improper selection of strategic control points almost caused a major tire manufacturer to be forced to cease operation. In the manufacture of a tire, four basic phases are required (see Figure 11.6). The mixing department must obtain the proper blend of rubber for the type of tire that is being produced. The tread is then shaped, with attention being given to length, width, and thickness. The next phase, building, entails placing the various components such as the tread, steel belting, and white walls together. In the molding department, the tires are heated and shaped into final form.

A major problem forced the tire company to reevaluate their entire control procedure. In the old system of control, a tire was inspected only after it had

F I G U R E 11.6 ■■ Example of Placement of Strategic Control Points

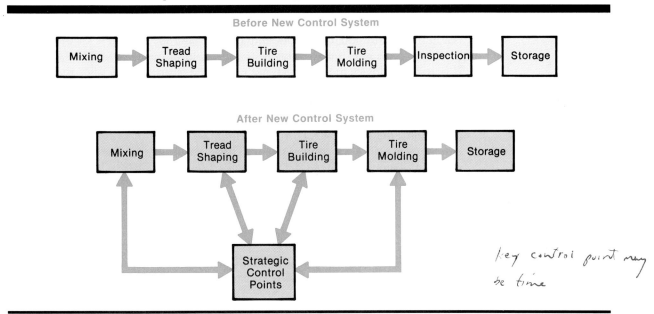

key control point may be time

been molded. At that stage, there was already a large investment in the tire, and it would have to have a major defect before it would be rejected. The deficiency in the control process was recognized when the tire manufacturing firm delivered a several-million-dollar order to a company that purchased tires and sold them at retail outlets under its own brand name. The retail chain, after careful inspection of the tires, rejected the order and demanded that the entire batch be redone. The tire manufacturing firm nearly went out of business because of the large investment tied up in rejected inventory. The firm had to go heavily into debt to remake the order.

After this experience, major changes were made in the control process. A separate quality control department, reporting directly to the president, was established. Quality control inspectors were hired and given authority to stop operations, even over the advice of the production superintendent. Strategic control points were located in the four major departments (see Figure 11.6). If a problem occurred in the mixing department, it would be discovered before the tire progressed to the other stages. Because of this intensive effort to improve quality, the firm was able to survive and prosper.

A third consideration in selecting strategic control points is that together they should indicate the level of performance for a broad spectrum of key events. At times, comprehensiveness conflicts with the need for proper timing. Net profit, for example, is a comprehensive strategic control point, indicating the progress of the entire enterprise. Yet if one waits until the regular accounting period to obtain this figure, one loses control of the immediate future. It does little good to recognize that the firm is now bankrupt; managers need to have accounting figures ahead of time so that corrective action may be taken.

Economy is the fourth consideration in the choice of proper control points. With computer and management information systems so readily available, there is a strong temptation to demand every conceivable bit of information. But there is only a limited amount of information that an executive can effectively use. With so much information available to the executive, critical information may be lost in the masses of data. Simply stated, "You can't see the forest for the trees."

Finally, the selection of various strategic control points should be balanced. If only credit losses are watched and controlled, for example, sales may suffer because of an overly stringent policy in accepting credit risks. If sales are emphasized too strongly, credit losses will mount. There is a tendency to place tight control over tangible functions, such as production and sales, while maintaining limited control over the intangible functions such as employee development and other staff services. This often leads to a state of imbalance where production executives are held to exact standards, and staff executives are seemingly given blank checks.

■■■ REASONS FOR NEGATIVE REACTIONS TO CONTROLS

Controls are important to effective management, yet employees often view them in a negative way. When the term *controls* is mentioned, it reminds some individuals that other people have the power to regulate their activities. There is a natural resistance to controls, because controls take away a certain amount of individual freedom. Employees may not like being controlled, but they will usually accept the fact that some controls are necessary. As may be seen in Figure 11.7, it is when controls are inappropriate, unattainable, unpredictable, related to uncontrollable variables, or contradictory that major resistance is encountered.[9]

Inappropriate Controls

Often controls are not related to the goals of the organization. If the wrong thing is being controlled, this will not contribute to doing the right thing efficiently.

Unattainable Standards

Employees usually realize when a standard is unrealistic. When unattainable controls are established, it may actually cause some employees to work below their capabilities. For instance, suppose that a machine operator has been producing effectively at a standard of twenty units an hour. If management arbitrarily increases the standard to forty units, the worker may feel that the standard is unattainable. The worker's output may actually be lowered below the original twenty units.

Unpredictable Standards

When the control system is unpredictable and constantly changed, much frustration and resentment of the control process can result. For instance, if a 7-Eleven store manager is told to increase sales and, once sales have increased, is told that

FIGURE 11.7 ■ Negative Reactions to Controls: Causes and Cures

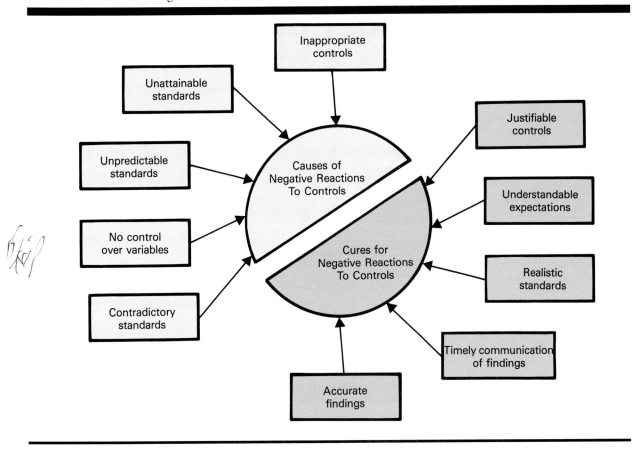

store maintenance is more important, frustration will likely result. The store manager could not predict what standard he or she was to be evaluated on.

No Control Over the Situation

It is frustrating to anyone to be reprimanded for something they cannot control. Suppose, for instance, that a manager is told that she will be evaluated regarding the profit and loss of her department, but she does not have the authority to hire and fire employees. Situations such as this can cripple the entire control system.

Contradictory Standards

At times, various controls may be established that contradict each other. It may appear to the manager that if one standard is achieved, it would be impossible to accomplish the other. For instance, it might appear to some managers that high quality and maximum output are contradictory in nature. To a marketing manager, a control system that stresses both increased sales and reduced advertising costs may appear contradictory.

■ OVERCOMING NEGATIVE REACTIONS TO CONTROLS

Although people may be inclined to resist controls, there are means that managers can use to assist in reducing negative reactions. Some of the solutions seen in Figure 11.7 and discussed below may appear obvious, but the ineffectiveness of some control systems makes it clear that they are not always employed.

Justifiable

If employees believe that there is a need for a particular control, compliance is much easier to obtain. For instance, the firm may have to increase the quality of its product in order to obtain future contracts. These contracts may mean not only profit for the firm, but job stability for the employees. A control system will have higher acceptability if the reason for the control appears justifiable to those who must comply.

Understandable

Employees who know exactly what is expected of them with regard to a control system tend to exhibit less resistance. For instance, a statement by a manager that quality should increase does not clearly convey what is expected. A requirement that the percentage of defective parts should decrease by 10 percent is precise and understandable. When workers do not understand what is expected of them, frustration and resentment can occur.

Realistic

A realistic control system involves standards that are obtainable by the employees who work within the control system. At times it may appear that controls are established merely to harass the worker. Standards that are higher than needed to accomplish the purpose of the organization are not only expensive, but may well be resisted by company employees.

Timely

For a control system to be effective, information regarding deviations needs to be communicated to employees as quickly as is practical. For instance, it does little good to tell workers that their performance was below standard three weeks ago. If a problem is to be corrected, it must receive timely attention.

Accurate

Nothing could be worse than to have a control system that provides inaccurate information. If information feedback has proved incorrect in the past, employees may not trust the control system. If workers consistently find errors made by supervisors, all management input may be questioned. In such a case, for example, an employee who receives a low performance evaluation may have reason to suspect the evaluation is inaccurate even if it is not.

At times, a manager must take disciplinary action to correct unacceptable behavior by an employee. (© Stacy Pick/Stock, Boston, Inc.)

■ DISCIPLINARY ACTION

A necessary but often trying aspect of control is taking disciplinary action.[10] A firm needs a program to administer disciplinary action when violations of company policies or rules occur. Firms not only need such programs, they also need procedures for assisting employees in appealing disciplinary actions. Unjustified disciplinary action has contributed to the loss of union-free status in many firms. It has also resulted in unauthorized wildcat strikes, walkouts, and slowdowns in unionized firms. The effects of these actions can include unnecessary expense and loss of production time.

Discipline
The state of employee self-control and orderly conduct present within an organization.

Disciplinary action
Action taken to correct unacceptable behavior.

Discipline is the state of employee self-control and orderly conduct present within an organization. Remember what the sister of Joe C. Thompson, founder of 7-Eleven, said: "The biggest influence on Joe's life, I believe, was discipline." In disciplined management can be found the potential for genuine teamwork. **Disciplinary action** is action taken to correct unacceptable behavior. Many of the problems a manager deals with require disciplinary actions. Approximately half of all grievance cases appealed to an impartial arbitrator by labor unions involve disciplinary action, and in approximately half of these, management's decisions are overturned. It is evident from the statistics that managers are not applying disciplinary action in a generally accepted manner.

In spite of a firm's desire to solve its employee problems in a positive way, at times this is not possible. A major purpose of disciplinary action is to ensure that employee behavior is consistent with the firm's goals. Rules are established to assist the organization in accomplishing its objectives. When a rule is violated, the effectiveness of the organization is diminished to some degree, depending on the severity of the infraction. For instance, if a worker reports late to work, the loss to the firm may be minimal. However, if a worker fails to use the safety guard on a machine and is severely injured, the loss may be substantial. Managers must realize that disciplinary action can be a positive force for the company. The firm benefits from developing and implementing effective disciplinary action policies.

Without a healthy state of discipline, or the threat of disciplinary action, the firm's effectiveness may be severely limited.

The Disciplinary Action Process

The disciplinary action process is dynamic and ongoing. One person's actions can affect others in the group. For instance, if a worker receives disciplinary action, it is likely that this action will influence other workers when they learn that such mistakes will not be tolerated.

The disciplinary action process is shown in Figure 11.8. Note that the external environment affects the process, as it does with all management activities. Laws that affect company policies are constantly changing. For instance, OSHA has caused many firms to establish new safety rules. Unions are another external factor. Specific punishments for rule violations are subject to negotiation. For instance, a union may negotiate three written warnings for tardiness instead of the two warnings a present contract might require.

Changes in the internal environment of the firm can also alter the disciplinary action process. Through organizational development, the firm may alter its

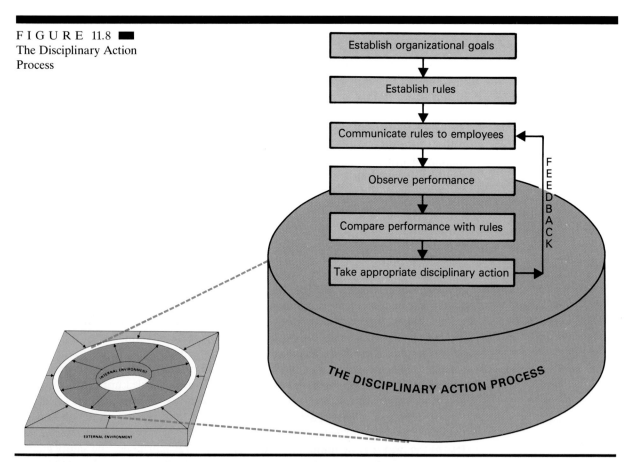

F I G U R E 11.8 ■
The Disciplinary Action Process

Source: Adapted from R. Wayne Mondy and Robert M. Noe, III, *Personnel: The Management of Human Resources,* 3d ed. (Newton, Mass.: Allyn and Bacon, 1987), p. 628.

culture. This change may result in first-line supervisors handling disciplinary action in a more positive manner. Organization policies can also have an impact on the disciplinary action process. Seeing employees as mature adults rather than as irresponsible children could significantly affect the process.

The disciplinary action process deals largely with infractions of rules. Rules—specific guides to action—are created to facilitate the accomplishment of organizational objectives. The do's and don't's associated with accomplishing tasks are highly inflexible. A company rule may prohibit smoking in a given area or require wearing hard hats in hazardous areas. And, of course, after rules have been established, they must be communicated to the affected employees. Individuals cannot obey a rule if they do not know it exists. As long as employee behavior does not vary from acceptable practices, there will be no need for disciplinary action. But when an employee's behavior violates a rule, corrective action may be taken. The purpose of this action is to alter the types of behavior that can have a negative impact on achievement of organizational objectives.

Note that Figure 11.8 shows a feedback loop from "take appropriate disciplinary action" to "communicate rules to employees." Some employees find out that a rule is being enforced only when a peer receives disciplinary action. Employees will then conform to the rule to avoid similar disciplinary action.

Approaches to Disciplinary Action

Several concepts regarding the administration of disciplinary action have been developed. Two of these—progressive discipline, and discipline without punishment—are discussed below.

Progressive discipline is a disciplinary-action approach designed to ensure that the minimum penalty appropriate to the offense is imposed. It involves answering a series of questions about the severity of the offense (see Figure 11.9). If the improper behavior is minor and has not previously occurred, perhaps an oral warning will be sufficient. Or, an individual may receive several written warnings before a violation warrants more than another written warning. The manager does not consider termination until each lower-level question has been answered "yes." However, major violations, such as hitting a supervisor, may justify the immediate termination of the employee.

Discipline without punishment is a process whereby a worker is given time off with pay when disciplinary action is suggested to determine if he or she really wants to follow the rules and continue working for the company.[11] When a rule is violated, there are three steps that are taken. The first is an "oral reminder," the next a "written reminder," and then the worker is given one, two, or three days off (with pay) to be allowed time to think. During the first two steps the manager tries to gain the employee's agreement to solve the problem.[12] If the third step must be taken, when the employee returns to work there is a meeting with the supervisor to affirm the employee's agreement that the rule violation will not occur again. When discipline without punishment is used, it is especially important that all rules be explicitly stated in writing. At the time of orientation, workers are told that repeated violations of different rules will be viewed in the same way as a number of violations of one rule. This helps to prevent workers from taking undue advantage of the program.

Progressive discipline
A disciplinary-action approach designed to ensure that the minimum penalty appropriate to the offense is imposed.

Discipline without punishment
A process whereby a worker is given time off with pay when disciplinary action is suggested to determine if he or she really wants to follow the rules and continue working for the company.

FIGURE 11.9 ■
The Progressive Discipline
Approach

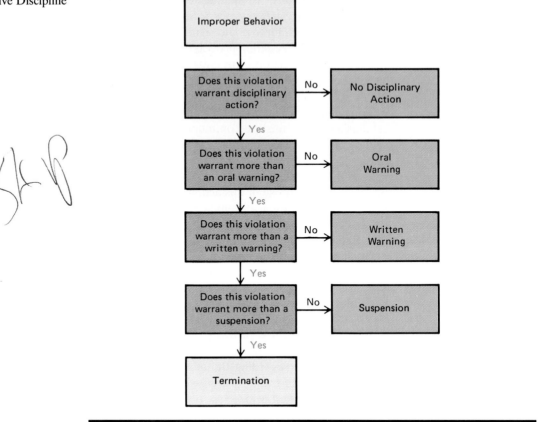

Source: R. Wayne Mondy and Robert M. Noe, III, *Personnel: The Management of Human Resources,* 3d ed. (Newton, Mass.: Allyn and Bacon, 1987), p. 630.

TABLE 11.4 ■■■ Guidelines for Disciplinary Action

- The manager should assume that all employees desire to conform to reasonable organizational requirements.
- The act, rather than the person, should be condemned.
- Future desired behavior should be described.
- Reasonable promptness is important, so that the employee can connect the penalty to the violation.
- A managerial listening role is highly essential (1) to effect greater understanding of the reasons for the act and (2) to prevent hasty decisions that may lead to unjustified penalties.
- Negative disciplinary action should be administered in private.
- Definite, but tactful, follow-up should occur, to determine the degree of success of the disciplinary action.
- Consistency and flexibility, though apparently contradictory, are both desirable elements of a good program of disciplinary action.

Managers should keep in mind that the main purpose of disciplinary action is not to punish or eliminate employees, but to improve their contribution to the organization. Rehabilitation achieves this goal more often than termination. Table 11.4 lists guidelines that assist managers in handling disciplinary action cases, whether or not managers explicitly practice the progressive disciplinary action approach discussed in the paragraph above.

SUMMARY

Controlling is the process of comparing actual performance with standards and taking any necessary corrective action. The control process has three steps: (1) establish standards, (2) evaluate performance, and (3) take corrective action. Standards are established levels of quality or quantity used to guide performance. Although standards may be clear, control tolerances may also need to be established. Control tolerances are specifications of how much deviation will be permitted before corrective action is taken. Evaluating performance consists of checking for deviation from standard and determining if those deviations exceed control tolerances. The manager must consider what action to take to correct performance when deviations occur. Immediate corrective action corrects symptoms. Permanent corrective action corrects the cause of the symptoms or problem.

With input controls, attempts are made to monitor the resources—material and personnel—that come into the organization to ensure that they can be used effectively to achieve organizational objectives. Overseeing the actual process of producing goods and services offers an opportunity to correct problems before outputs have been affected. The ultimate purpose of controlling focuses on the quality and quantity of outputs produced. In monitoring the process of producing goods or services, critical points, called strategic control points, are selected. Despite the importance of controls to effective management, employees often view them in a negative way because controls take away a certain amount of individual freedom. However, there are means that managers can use to assist in reducing negative reactions.

Discipline is the state of employee self-control and orderly conduct present within an organization. It indicates the potential for genuine teamwork. Disciplinary action is action taken to correct unacceptable behavior.

Progressive discipline ensures that the minimum penalty appropriate to the offense is imposed. In discipline without punishment, workers are given time off with pay to determine if they really want to follow the rules and continue working for the company.

REVIEW QUESTIONS

1. Define *controlling*. What are the steps in the control process?
2. What are the most frequently used types of standards? Briefly discuss each.
3. What are specific means of controlling inputs and outputs? Briefly describe each.
4. What factors should a manager consider in establishing strategic control points?

5. List and describe the reasons for negative reactions to controls. What are the ways of overcoming negative reactions to controls?
6. Define *disciplinary action* and *progressive discipline*. What guidelines should a manager follow when disciplinary action must be taken?

KEY TERMS

controlling	leverage ratios	discipline
standards	activity ratios	disciplinary action
control tolerances	profitability ratios	progressive discipline
statistical process control	Performance Appraisal (PA)	discipline without punishment
liquidity ratios	strategic control points	

CASE STUDY — FLEXTIME

KATHY COLLIER IS a supervisor of a government office in Washington, D.C. Morale in her office has been quite low recently. The workers have gone back to an 8:00 A.M. to 4:30 P.M. work schedule after being on flextime for nearly two years.

When the directive came down allowing Kathy to place her office on flextime, she spelled out the rules carefully to her people. Each person was to work an eight-hour day, during the core period from 10:00 A.M. to 2:30 P.M. and at any other time between 6:00 A.M. and 6:00 P.M. Kathy felt her workers were honest and well motivated, so she did not bother to set up any system of control.

Everything went along well for a long time. Morale improved, and all the work seemed to get done. In November 1988, however, an auditor from the General Accounting Office investigated and found that Kathy's workers were averaging seven hours a day. Two employees had been working only during the core period for more than two months. When Kathy's department manager reviewed the auditor's report, Kathy was told to return the office to regular working hours. Kathy was upset and disappointed with her people. She had trusted them and felt they had let her down.

QUESTIONS
1. What type of controls should Kathy have used to prevent the problem? Explain your answer.
2. Should Kathy be disappointed with her people? Why or why not?

CASE STUDY — DIFFERENT PHILOSOPHIES

COLLINS AND BRADFORD is a manufacturing company near Denver with sales of approximately $250 million. C&B employs twelve college-trained accountants at its headquarters. These positions are divided among financial accounting, cost accounting, accounts payable, and auditing. Tom Brown came to work at C&B in the financial accounting department. He had a B.B.A. from Penn State and two years of previous work experience in accounting. He caught on quickly, did a good job, and was well liked by his supervisor and fellow employees. After eleven months, a position became available in the cost accounting department that offered Tom a higher salary and an opportunity to develop professionally in another area.

Tom took the job in the cost accounting department. Ed Blake is the supervisor in the department. Ed is basically a self-taught, hard-working individual, who rose through the ranks by out-working everyone and taking on difficult jobs. After three months in the cost accounting department it became apparent to Tom that he and Ed could not work together. Tom disagreed with Ed's training techniques and Ed's philosophy on how certain problems should be handled. It also became evident that they had a severe personality conflict. After a full month of deliberation on what to do, Tom decided to go to John Collins, Ed's supervisor, and ask for a transfer. He explained that he wanted to remain at C&B, but that neither he nor the cost accounting department was benefiting from his being in his present position.

Ed and John had been friends and working associates for years, and John's initial reaction was to blame Tom for the bad situation. He surveyed the other accounting positions and did not see any openings coming up in the near future. John felt that he had three alternatives: to create an additional accounting position in another department and transfer Tom, to work with Ed and Tom to reconcile the problems, or to terminate Tom.

QUESTIONS
1. What might have caused the conflict between Tom and Ed? How can this type of conflict be controlled so as not to affect adversely a firm's operations?
2. What action should John take? Is he limited to the three alternatives mentioned at the end of the case?
3. If you were Tom Brown, what would you do?

EXPERIENTIAL EXERCISE

Phyllis Long, the production manager, has just finished talking to the efficiency expert from the main office. The news is not good. According to the efficiency expert, there are productivity problems in Unit 2, which must be rectified as quickly as possible. It will be necessary to meet with Larry Kurth, the supervisor of that unit, and get this situation straightened out quickly. Problems in that unit have been suspected for some time, but now proof exists. Phyllis believes that the problem with Larry is that he insisted on staying friends with everybody when he was promoted. Larry really believes that a supervisor can be a friend and a boss. He tells everybody what to do and expects the work to be accomplished. When it does not get done, he makes excuses. This dual role worked out for about six months, but now the workers believe they can get away with anything. Being a friend and a boss has not been successful for this supervisor. This has to stop, now!

Larry believes that productivity problems are not anyone's fault, the employees of Unit 2 are hard workers, and everybody has known everybody for quite a long time. According to Larry, "These individuals would never let down their other friends on the line." Larry believes that any logical person can readily see that these problems are due to circumstances. They are not the fault of improper supervision or personnel problems!

This is an interesting situation that you might enjoy straightening out. It is unlikely that Phyllis and Larry will readily see eye-to-eye on this matter. Phyllis has the difficult job of describing the situation to Larry. Larry has the unenviable task of attempting to convince the production manager to see his side of the situation. This exercise will require only two of you to actively participate, so get in the game quickly. The rest of you pay attention. For the participants, more information is on the way.

NOTES

1. This story is a composite taken from a number of published sources, including: Shawn Tully, "Look Who's a Champ of Gasoline Marketing," *Fortune,* 1 November 1982, 149–154; Mitchell Gordon, "A Matter of Convenience: Southland's Sprawling 7-Eleven Chain Rings Up Fresh Gains," *Barrons,* 6 December 1982, 43–47; Tom Bayer, "7-Eleven Takes Steps to Move Beyond Image," *Advertising Age,* 7 December 1981, 77–78; "From Super to Merely Excellent," *Financial World,* 1 October 1980, 22–23; "Southland's Risky Plunge into Refining," *Business Week,* 11 April 1983, 33.
2. Karen Pennar, "America's Quest Can't Be Half-Hearted," *Business Week,* 8 June 1989, 136.
3. S. M. Klein and R. R. Ritti, *Understanding Organizational Behavior* (Boston: Kent, 1984), 509.
4. Pennar, "America's Quest," 136.
5. Port, "The Push for Quality," 132.
6. R. Wayne Mondy, Robert M. Noe, and Robert E. Edwards, "What the Staffing Function Entails," *Personnel* 63 (April 1986), 55.

7. R. L. Taylor and R. A. Zawachi, "Trends in Performance Appraisal: Guidelines for Managers," *Personnel Administrator* 29, no. 3 (March 1984): 71.

8. Jon Turino, "Test Strategies That Cut Manufacturing Costs," *SAM Advanced Management Journal* 49, no. 1 (Winter 1984): 53.

9. Robert N. Anthony and Regina E. Herzlinger, *Management Control in Nonprofit Organizations* (Homewood, Ill.: Irwin, 1975), 222–226.

10. Portions of the discussion regarding disciplinary action were adapted from R. Wayne Mondy and Robert M. Noe III, *Personnel: The Management of Human Resources,* 3d ed. (Newton, Mass.: Allyn and Bacon, 1987), 626–630.

11. Laurie Baum, "Punishing Workers with a Day Off," *Business Week,* 16 June 1986, 80.

12. David N. Campbell, R. L. Fleming, and Richard C. Grote, "Discipline Without Punishment—at Last," *Harvard Business Review* 63 (July–August 1985), 168.

REFERENCES

Baum, Laurie. "Punishing Workers with a Day Off." *Business Week* (16 June 1986): 80.

Buffa, Elwood S. *Modern Production-Operations Management.* 8th ed. New York: John Wiley & Sons, 1987.

Camillus, John C. "Six Approaches to Preventive Management Control." *Financial Executive* 48 (December 1980): 28–31.

Chase, Richard B., and Nicholas J. Aquilano. *Production and Operations Management: A Life Cycle Approach.* Homewood, Ill.: Irwin, 1981.

Dalton, Dan R., and William D. Todor. "Win, Lose, Draw: The Grievance Process in Practice." *Personnel Administrator* 26 (March 1981): 25–29.

Lippert, F. G. "Quality Indicators." *Supervision* (March 1984): 16–17.

Mondy, R. Wayne, and Robert M. Noe III. *Personnel: The Management of Human Resources.* 3d ed. (Newton, Mass.: Allyn and Bacon, 1987).

Morris, Richard M., III. "Management Control and Decision Support Systems—an Overview." *Industrial Management* 28 (January–February 1986): 8–15.

Olson, D., and R. Bangs. "No-Fault Attendance Control: A Real World Application." *Personnel Administrator* 29, no. 6 (June 1984): 53–56.

Ouchi, W. G. "Relationship Between Organizational Structure and Organizational Control." *Administrative Science Quarterly* 22, no. 1 (March 1981): 95–113.

Pingpank, Jeffery C., and Thomas B. Mooney. "Wrongful Discharge: A New Danger for Employers." *Personnel Administrator* 26 (March 1981): 31–35.

Schroeder, Roger G. *Operations Management: Decision Making in the Operations Function.* New York: McGraw-Hill, 1981.

Swann, James P., Jr. "Formal Grievance Procedures in Nonunion Plants." *Personnel Administrator* 26 (August 1981): 66–70.

Taylor, R. L., and R. A. Zawachi. "Trends in Performance Appraisal: Guidelines for Managers." *Personnel Administrator* 29, no. 3 (March 1984): 71–80.

Turino, Jon. "Test Strategies That Cut Manufacturing Costs." *SAM Advanced Management Journal* 49, no. 1 (Winter 1984): 42–53.

Wueste, Richard A. "A Matter of Inconsequence: Mastering the Art of Executive Triviality." *Management World* 17 (March–April 1988): 40–41.

CHAPTER

12

Chapter Outline

Placing Quantitative Controlling Tools in Perspective

Budgetary Control

Quality Control

Inventory Control

Network Models

Summary

Controlling Techniques

Learning Objectives

After completing this chapter students should be able to

1. Define various types of budgets and identify the benefits and limitations of budgets.
2. Explain quality control and state the usefulness of control charts.
3. Describe the importance of inventory control and explain various methods of inventory control.
4. Explain network models and describe how PERT can assist in both planning and control.

A THIRTY-FIVE-YEAR veteran autoworker at General Motors's Pontiac engine plant number 18 in Detroit describes how it was in the old days when he found out a tool was going bad. "I'd tell the supervisor, and he'd say, 'Leave it for the second shift.' The second shift would leave it for the third shift, and the third shift would leave it for me in the morning. Then my supervisor would say, 'Leave it for the weekend.' Well, now we've got only the day shift left, and if we didn't do better, there just wouldn't be a day shift."

Today worker participation and training are the rule rather than the exception at plant 18. Workers and union officials even helped design a new production line recently, which years earlier would have been left to the process engineers. Every worker takes a four-week course and leaves with a magnifying glass (to help see defects in the tools), a pocket calculator, and a good understanding of statistical controls. With many new quantitative controls in effect, workers find frequent uses for what they have learned.

The output of the plant shows the changes that have occurred. Pontiac struggled for years to improve the quality of its engines. Now improvements happen every day. Plant 18 had trouble with threads on the connecting-rod bolts it bought from four suppliers. As it turned out, practically all the defective bolts came from one supplier. When that supplier was dropped, the failures stopped. A certain camshaft gear has to be accurate within a few ten-thousandths of an inch. If the gear does not meet the standard, the engine has to be pulled and the gear replaced, at a cost of over $1,000. One year thirty-eight engines required the costly repair job. After it was discovered that checking three successive gears once an hour kept the boring from going out of kilter, failures dropped next year to six, and to none last year.

What accounts for the change? The main factor is Dr. W. Edwards Deming, the eighty-three-year-old statistician who is given credit for much of Japan's manufacturing preeminence and for whom two of that country's national productivity prizes are named. Deming was invited to the Pontiac plant after General Manager William Hogland saw an NBC documentary, "If Japan Can, . . . Why Can't We?" Deming was then already back in the United States at Nashua Corporation. Hogland invited him to come to plant 18.

Hogland had no idea what a difference Deming would make. "His message shook the foundations of our approach to quality," says Hogland. Workers and managers alike at plant 18 view Deming—who looks more like Charles de Gaulle than Albert Einstein—with awe. Many have memorized his "14 points to improve quality." A few of his points follow:

- Don't rely on mass inspection.
- Drive out fear by encouraging open, two-way communication.
- Teach statistical techniques. The rudiments can be learned in five-day crash courses.
- Make maximum use of the statistical knowledge and talent in your company.

The new concern for qualitative controls applies not only to product quality but to costs as well. Thus, budgeting has taken on a new importance at plant 18.

Deming claims that a company can improve quality best by controlling its purchasing system. "Work with fewer vendors," he says. "First, find one good supplier; then you can look for more." Deming continues, "Insist on evidence of quality through control charts from every vendor. Without the charts, neither vendor nor buyer can prove that the quality levels are constant—day after day, lot after lot—or what his costs are."

Just as the system worked in Japan, so it is working at plant 18. James Harbour, an auto industry consultant, writes, "The Pontiac engine plants are superb examples of what can be accomplished when you decide that quality and productivity go hand in hand."[1] ▪

I N THE LAST CHAPTER the controlling process was discussed. Today, this process uses many quantitative techniques to derive the greatest level of quality productivity possible. The Deming system provides an excellent example of a properly implemented quantitative control system. In fact, statistical control systems are credited with causing the turnaround of plant 18. The control systems that are imposed must support and encourage employees, not constrain them.

In this chapter, the quantitative controlling tools available to management are first placed in proper perspective. Applications of quantitative techniques in industry are then described, beginning with budgetary control. The latter sections of the chapter are devoted to quality control, inventory control, and networking techniques.

▬ PLACING QUANTITATIVE CONTROLLING TOOLS IN PERSPECTIVE

Numerous quantitative techniques are available to managers. The techniques have application in every area of management, especially planning and controlling. The emphasis on quantitative tools should not be taken to mean that a manager is always expected to know the detailed mathematics of each. Managers should become as familiar as possible with all techniques, but maintain enough detachment from them to allow clear thinking to take place. A manager should at least have an appreciation of the following: the quantitative tools available, the situations for which they are designed, and how they are used in business.

Among students of management, there is an apparent misconception: that quantitative tools cannot be used without a complete knowledge of, and skill in, the techniques themselves. *This need not be the case.* To solve control problems, prudent managers want to utilize their resources to the maximum extent reasonable. But to do so, a manager need only recognize what control tools are applicable, know when they should be used, and identify the factors that should be considered in solving the problem. Once the manager has made this determination, a mathematician, statistician, or computer specialist can perform the actual calculation. These individuals are trained to implement quantitative techniques. In many cases, specialists like W. Edwards Deming are available to help in deciding which tools to use. The Japanese respect Deming so much that they named an award for excellence in manufacturing after him, the coveted Deming Prize.[2]

Once a mathematical answer has been obtained, managers must still use personal judgment in evaluating mathematical models, since no mathematical model can satisfactorily emulate all aspects of most decision problems. It is sound judgment that is required, not unquestioning reliance on simple quantitative results. Once all factors are considered, managers must decide whether to use the solutions that have been derived through the use of quantitative techniques.

■ BUDGETARY CONTROL

Budget
A statement of planned allocation of resources expressed in financial or numerical terms.

The most basic and widely used quantitative controlling technique is the budget. A **budget** is a statement of planned allocation of resources expressed in financial or numerical terms. Budgetary control is concerned with the comparison of actual to planned expenditures. Most areas of operations in a business enterprise—marketing, production, materials, labor, manufacturing expense, capital expenditures, and cash—have budgets. The operating budget for Pontiac's plant 18 includes specific allowances for every major activity involved in making engines.

Types of Budgets

Capital budget
A statement of planned expenditures of funds for facilities and equipment.

Often the budget is the most important document a manager uses in planning and controlling operations. There are basically two broad categories of budgets: capital budgets and operating budgets. A **capital budget** is a statement of planned expenditures of funds for facilities and equipment. The machines that will be required to make engines at plant 18 must be designed and even ordered years in advance. The capital budget therefore typically extends over several years. When it is first known that a new or replacement machine will be needed, the capital budget is modified to include the expected expenditure.

Operating budget
A statement of the planned income and expenses of a business or subunit.

An **operating budget** is a statement of the planned income and expenses of a business or subunit. The expenditures for material and labor expected to be made at plant 18 during a given year are included in the plant's operating budget. There are also allowances for utilities, maintenance, and all other recurring expense items. For a subunit of a large organization, like plant 18, the "income" the subunit can expect is just an allocation of funds from headquarters.

An Illustration of Budgetary Control

The use of a budget as a control device is relatively simple. Assume that Table 12.1 shows the monthly budget for the cylinder block boring department at plant 18. The major expense items include direct labor (such as wages for the unit's boring machine operators), indirect labor (the department manager's salary), operating supplies (grinding disks), maintenance expenses (repair of machines), and miscellaneous expenses. In the table, actual expenditures are compared with budgeted or planned expenditures. In this department, actual exceeded budgeted expenditures for direct labor and operating supplies by $800 and $250, respectively. Actual spending for maintenance and miscellaneous was under the budgeted amount by $440. Budgetary control enables the manager to identify significant

TABLE 12.1 ■ Department Operating Budget: Cylinder Block Boring Department, January 13

Item	Budget	Actual	Over	Under
Direct labor	$10,000	$10,800	$800	
Indirect labor	1,800	1,800		
Operating supplies	1,250	1,500	250	
Maintenance	1,800	1,400		$400
Miscellaneous expense	190	150		40
TOTAL	$15,040	$15,650	Over $610	

deviations in actual versus budgeted or planned expenses and to take corrective actions when necessary. For example, the $800 over budgeted expenses for the wages of boring machine operators may have been caused by the necessity to pay overtime wages. The need for overtime may have resulted from ineffective work scheduling or the sudden appearance of a rush job. This situation, if it occurs in several successive periods, may cause the manager to take corrective actions, such as requesting additional personnel or improving the scheduling of work. Clearly, budgeting control is useful for managers at virtually every level of an organization.

Benefits of the Budgeting Process

The fact that virtually every type of organization—profit or nonprofit—operates within the framework of budgets attests to the benefits of budgeting. Budgeting is a significant part of both the planning and the controlling processes. Budgets are widely used by managers to plan, monitor, and control various activities and operations at every level of an organization. There are several important advantages for preparing and using budgets. Some of the benefits of the budgeting process are as follows:

1. *Provides standards against which actual performance can be measured.* Budgets are quantified plans that allow management to measure and control performance objectively. If, for instance, a departmental manager knows that the budgeted expenditure for supplies is $1,000 per month, the manager is in a position to monitor and control the expenses for supplies.
2. *Provides managers with additional insight into actual organizational goals.* Monetary allocation of funds, as opposed to mere lip service, more often than not is the true test of a firm's dedication to a particular goal. For instance, suppose that two firms of relatively equal size have a stated policy of hiring minority personnel, but Firm A allocates $100,000 to minority programs and Firm B budgets $10,000. A manager from Firm A may conclude that a much stronger commitment to minority hiring exists at Firm A.

Budgets are one means of monitoring control of the activities and operations of an organization. (© Catherine Ursillo/Photo Researchers, Inc.)

3. *Tends to be a positive influence on the motivation of workers.* People typically like to know what is expected of them, and budgets clarify specific performance standards.

4. *Causes managers to divert some of their attention from current to future operations.* To some extent, a budget forces managers to anticipate and forecast changes in the external environment. For example, an increase in transportation costs created by higher-priced petroleum might force the firm to seek an alternative transportation or distribution system.

5. *Improves top management's ability to coordinate the overall operation of the organization.* Budgets are blueprints of the company's plans for the coming year. They greatly aid top management in coordinating the operations/activities of each division or department.

6. *Enables management to recognize and/or anticipate problems in time to take the necessary corrective action.* For example, production costs substantially ahead of the budgeted amount will alert management to make changes that may realign actual costs with the budget. At Pontiac plant 18, this use of budgeting is enhanced by the existence of supporting controls. Not only are overall departmental costs monitored, but the costs of individual activities are isolated and controlled. Long before departmental expenditures are out of control, corrective action can begin.

7. *Facilitates communication throughout the organization.* The budget significantly improves management's ability to communicate the objectives, plans, and standards of performance important to the organization. Budgets are especially helpful to lower-level managers. They let them know how their operations relate to other units or departments within the organization. Also, budgets tend to pinpoint managers' responsibility and improve their understanding of the objectives of the

organization. This usually results in increased morale and commitment on the part of managers.

8. *Helps managers recognize when change is needed.* The budgeting process requires managers to review carefully and critically the company's operations to determine if the firm's resources are being allocated to the *right* activities and programs. The budgeting process causes management to focus on such questions as: Which products appear to have the greatest demand? Which markets appear to offer the best potential? What business are we in? Which businesses should the firm be in?[3]

Limitations of the Budgeting Process

Although numerous benefits can be attributed to the use of budgets, problems may arise. If the budgetary process is to achieve maximum effectiveness, these difficulties must be recognized, and attempts made to reduce the potentially damaging side effects associated with the use of budgets. Some of the major problems are as follows:

- Some managers believe that all funds allocated in a budget must be spent. This attitude may actually work against the intent of the budgetary process. These managers learned from experience that if they do not spend the funds that have been budgeted, their budget will be reduced the following year. Managers have found that such a conscientious cost-effectiveness approach can actually hurt their departments. A manager who operates in this type of environment may make an extraordinary effort to spend extra funds for reasons that may be marginal at best. Undoubtedly this kind of attitude existed at plant 18 in the "old days," as described by the thirty-five-year veteran autoworker.
- A budget may be so restrictive that supervisors are permitted little discretion in managing their resources. Actual amounts that can be spent for items may be specified, and funds may not be transferable from one account to another. This sometimes results in seemingly ludicrous situations. For example, there may be funds to purchase personal computers but no money for printer ribbons.
- In evaluating a manager, the main criterion may be conformity to the budget, rather than what the manager has actually accomplished. If this philosophy is prevalent within the firm, poor managers will be recognized as superior because they met the budget and good managers will, in all likelihood, be reprimanded for failure to follow the exact budgetary guidelines. This state of affairs can severely reduce the amount of risk a manager will be willing to take. Managers may spend a majority of their time ensuring that they are in compliance with the budget, when their time might be better spent developing new or innovative ideas.

Zero Base Budgeting

Zero base budgeting (ZBB), originally developed by Texas Instruments, is a system of budgeting that requires management to take a fresh look at all programs

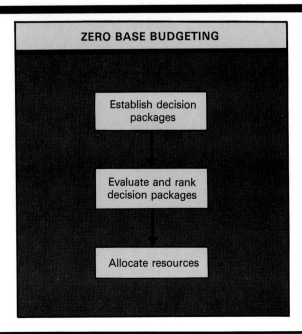

and activities each year, rather than merely build on last year's budget. In other words, last year's budget allocations are not considered as a basis for this year's budget. Each program, or "decision package," must be justified on the basis of cost-benefit analysis. There are three main features of zero base budgeting, shown in Figure 12.1 and discussed below.

1. The activities of individual departments are divided into *decision packages,* which provide information to management so that management can compare the costs and benefits of each program or activity.
2. Each decision package is first evaluated and then ranked in order of decreasing importance to the organization. Thus, priorities are established for each program and activity. Each of these is evaluated by top management to arrive at a final ranking.
3. Resources are allocated according to top management's final rankings of the programs. As a rule, decisions to allocate resources for high-priority items will be made rather quickly, whereas closer scrutiny will be given lower-priority programs or activities.[4]

ZBB is not a panacea for solving all problems associated with the budgeting process. Organizations may experience problems in implementing the ZBB system. Most managers are reluctant to admit that all of their activities are not of the highest priority, or to submit their programs to close scrutiny. However, with ZBB, a system is established whereby an organization's resources can be allocated to the higher-priority programs. Under this system, programs of lower priority can be reduced or eliminated. Thus, the benefits of zero base budgeting appear to outweigh the costs.

■■ QUALITY CONTROL

Quality
The degree of excellence of a product or service.

Quality is a concern of most Americans. But what exactly is meant by the term? **Quality** is the degree of excellence of a product or service. Quality control is the means by which a firm makes sure that its product or service will serve the purpose for which it is intended. Quality standards are determined by the company's objectives. If the company wishes to gain a reputation for high-quality products, standards will have to be high, and the company must have a very rigid quality control program to meet these high standards. Increased quality, although it generally results in higher costs, allows for higher prices. On the other hand, some firms may sell to market segments that desire lower prices and will accept lower quality. Certain standards remain, but they are not as high as those of quality-oriented firms. American quality is at best improving to a point just below the Japanese. As many as one quarter of American factory workers do not produce anything; they simply fix other workers' mistakes.[5]

There are numerous ways to maintain product quality. A company could decide on 100 percent inspection of all items manufactured. Even so, some defects may not be discovered. When the human element is made part of the quality control environment, it is inevitable that mistakes will occasionally be made. Some good items may be rejected, and some bad items may be accepted.

In most instances it is not feasible to have 100 percent inspection. For instance, if the standard for the life of a light bulb were 200 hours, the bulb would have to be burned for that many hours to determine if it met the standard. Naturally, there would be no product to sell after the inspection. Tire manufacturing provides a similar example. Companies set standards for their tires that specify the number of miles they can be safely driven. If each tire were placed on a machine to run the assigned number of miles, there would be no product to market. In still other instances, the costs involved in 100 percent inspection would be prohibitive. If each nail in a keg were inspected separately, for example, the cost to inspect might be higher than the price of the nails.

The technique that is available to overcome the above deficiencies is known as *statistical quality control*. In statistical quality control, a portion of the total number of items is checked. For instance, inspectors might select five out of one hundred items and estimate the characteristics of the other ninety-five. Some degree of error exists. For instance, if only five out of one hundred items are defective (this amount of error may be perfectly acceptable), it is conceivable that all five defective samples might be selected for testing and the entire lot subsequently rejected. On the other hand, there might be only five good parts. These five good parts might be the ones drawn. Then the entire batch would be accepted. Statistical quality control involves risk, but in many instances the benefits justify the risks. Recall that it was possible to essentially eliminate gear failures at General Motors plant 18 by inspecting just three gears each hour.

Acceptance Sampling

Acceptance sampling
The inspection of a portion of the output or input of a process to determine acceptability.

Acceptance sampling is the inspection of a portion of the output or input of a process to determine acceptability. Assume that it has been statistically determined that taking a sample of fifteen items from each batch of one hundred and limiting allowable defective units to one will result in the desired quality. In this case, if two or more items are defective, the entire lot will be rejected. When an entire lot is rejected, every item in it may have to be inspected. Or the lot may have to be returned to the supplier, who must evaluate the problem. Through this kind of sampling, plant 18 was able to identify the supplier of defective connecting-rod bolts.

There are two basic approaches to sampling: sampling by variables and sampling by attributes. Both methods are used, but under different circumstances.

SAMPLING BY VARIABLES

A plan developed for variable sampling consists of determining how closely an item conforms to an established standard. In essence, degrees of goodness and degrees of badness are permitted. For instance, a stereo speaker is designed to project a certain tone quality. But all speakers will not behave the same. Some speakers will perform above the standard, and some will have tone quality that is below standard. The variance does not necessarily mean that the speaker will be rejected. It will only be rejected when the measure of quality is outside a certain range.

SAMPLING BY ATTRIBUTES

With sampling by variables, degrees of conformity are considered; with attribute sampling, the item is either acceptable or unacceptable. The product is either good or bad; there are no degrees of conformity to consider. For example, at plant 18 an engine block that has a hole in the side of any cylinder is rejected.

either good or bad product

Control Charts

Control chart
A graphic record of how closely samples of a product or service conform to standards over time.

A **control chart** is a graphic record of how closely samples of a product or service conform to standards over time. The chart is used with both variable and attribute sampling, although the statistical procedures for developing the chart are different. In both instances, the standard is first determined (Figure 12.2). A variable sampling plan in the manufacture of tire treads might have standards that test thickness, weight, length, and width. If the average thickness of a certain tire tread is expected to be 0.87 inch, this becomes the standard.

F I G U R E 12.2 ■
An Example of a Control Chart

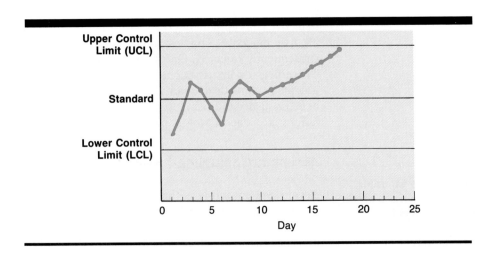

Once the standard has been established, the manager must determine the amount of deviation that will be acceptable. The maximum level that will be allowed is referred to as the *upper control limit* (UCL), and the minimum level is called the *lower control limit* (LCL). In the tire tread example, the UCL might be 0.89 inch and the LCL might be 0.84 inch. If a thickness of a tread being evaluated falls within the two extremes, it will be accepted. If it falls outside the limits, it will be rejected.

Another benefit of control charts is that potential problems may be recognized prior to their actual occurrence. Figure 12.2 shows that from day 10 until day 17, the quality of the product progressively worsened. The item is still within the limits of acceptability, but if the problem is not corrected, the process may soon go above the upper control limit. When managers see this pattern developing, they are in a position to take corrective action.

How Much Quality?

Managers cannot simply have an objective to maximize quality. Through their understanding of the objectives of the firm, managers establish standards and levels of quality that are in line with organizational objectives. They realize that as quality increases, costs go up; in other words, quality costs. In terms of maximizing profits, there is an optimum level of quality for each product. The quality level that is appropriate is determined primarily by top management. Supervisors usually monitor the quality on a day-to-day basis, to ensure that the stated level of quality is being maintained.

U.S. industry has been criticized for not matching the competition, especially the Japanese, in the quality of its output. For example, a *Harvard Business Review* article revealed that room air-conditioning assembly lines in the United States produced eighty times (not 80 percent more, but *eighty times*) as many defects as those in Japan.[6] Today consumers, who now have the alternative of buying quality

ETHICAL DILEMMA

Y OUR FIRM RECEIVED a large contract last summer to manufacture transaxles to be used in a new line of front-wheel-drive cars, which a major auto manufacturer plans to introduce in the near future. The contract is very important to your firm. As you began examining test reports, you discovered that the transaxle tended to fail when loaded at more than 20 percent over rated capacity and subjected to strong torsion forces. Such a condition could occur with a heavily loaded car braking hard for a curve down a mountain road. The results would be disastrous. The manufacturer's specifications call for the transaxle to carry 130 percent of its rated capacity without a failing. However, since the likelihood of a disastrous occurrence is fairly low, and since there is no time or money to redesign the assembly, your options seem limited. You can refuse to deliver the transaxles that are rated at 120 percent over capacity, and possibly financially ruin the company, or you can deliver the transaxles, which will probably never fail.

What would you do?

Quality control is of increasing importance, as American firms find themselves competing in the new global marketplace. (©David Woo/ Stock, Boston, Inc.)

products from abroad, are demanding a higher level of quality. The result has been that U.S. manufacturers are now more and more willing to pay the costs that quality entails, in order to remain competitive with foreign producers. For example, the trucks made at Ford Motor Company's Louisville, Kentucky, assembly plant once had the lowest quality rating of all U.S.-made Ford vehicles. Because Ford was willing to invest in statistical controls, a tougher inspection system, and tighter standards for vendors, the Ranger trucks made in Louisville today get Ford's highest quality rating.[7] However, American quality still lags behind that of foreign competitors. Regardless of the product, foreign competitors keep setting new, far tougher standards for performance, reliability, and durability.[8]

▰▰ INVENTORY CONTROL

Inventory
Refers to the goods or materials available for use by a business.

Inventory refers to the goods or materials available for use by a business. Concern with inventory is almost continuous. A car dealer has excessive inventory and will offer a special deal to sell a car. A furniture dealer provides a similar offer. Although there may be a bit of sales promotion in these offerings, inventory does represent a cost that must be controlled. A product in inventory constitutes a valuable, although idle, resource. The Purchasing Management's Association says that total inventory carrying costs exceed 25 percent of the inventory value each year, and one expert estimates that they run between 30 and 36 percent.[9] Much of the resources of many major companies are inventories, so failure to control inventories can mean the difference between profit and loss.

Purposes of Inventory

One is that it permits relative independence of operations between two activities. For instance, if Machine A makes a product that will be used by Machine B and

Machine A breaks down, Machine B will have to cease operation unless inventory of the product has been previously built up.

Inventories also provide for continuous operations when demand for the product is not consistent. Electric razors are sold primarily during the Christmas holiday season, but a manufacturer of electric razors typically keeps production going through the entire year. That way, a skilled work force can be maintained and equipment usage can be kept at an optimal level.

Another purpose of inventory is to allow filling orders quickly, thereby maintaining customer satisfaction. If orders arrive at a constant rate, there may be no need to maintain inventory. But if five orders come in this month and a hundred next month, a company without product inventory might be hard-pressed to fill the hundred requests.

Economic Order Quantity (EOQ) Method of Inventory Control

The **economic order quantity (EOQ)** method is a procedure for balancing ordering costs and carrying costs so as to minimize total inventory costs (see Figure 12.3). **Ordering costs** are administrative, clerical, and other expenses incurred in initially obtaining inventory items and placing them in storage. **Carrying costs** are the expenses associated with maintaining and storing the products before they are sold or used. Taxes, insurance, interest on capital invested, storage, electricity, and spoilage are some of the items associated with carrying costs. The total inventory cost associated with a particular order is represented by the following general formula:

Total inventory cost = ordering cost + carrying cost

Economic order quantity (EOQ)
A procedure for balancing ordering costs and carrying costs so as to minimize total inventory costs.

Ordering costs
Administrative, clerical, and other expenses incurred in initially obtaining inventory items and placing them in storage.

Carrying costs
Expenses associated with maintaining and storing the products before they are sold or used.

FIGURE 12.3 ■
Economic Order Quantity
Illustration

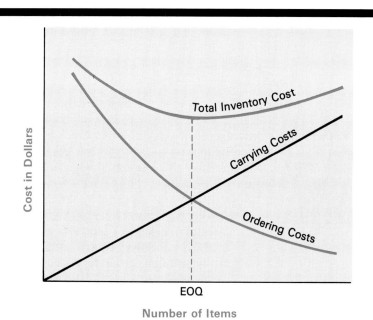

F I G U R E 12.4 ■
Basic Equation for EOQ

Skip

$$\text{EOQ} = \sqrt{\frac{2\binom{\text{ordering}}{\text{cost}}\binom{\text{annual}}{\text{demand}}}{\text{unit carrying costs}}} = \sqrt{\frac{2(O) \times (D)}{C}}$$

Economic order quantity is the amount of an inventory item that should be purchased to minimize total inventory cost. If orders are made less frequently ordering costs go down, but carrying costs go up. If frequent orders are submitted, ordering costs go up but carrying costs are reduced. This is graphically illustrated in Figure 12.3. The optimum number of items to order at any one time is represented by the lowest point on the total cost curve. This is where the carrying costs and ordering costs lines intersect.

Calculus was used in the development of the EOQ model. Managers do not have to be quantitative wizards to determine EOQ. Any manager, however, should be able to identify two primary costs: carrying cost (C) and ordering cost (O). Using calculus, the EOQ formula is determined from the total cost equation. The basic equation for EOQ is presented in Figure 12.4.

If the assumption is made that annual demand is 1,000 units, carrying cost is $2 per unit, and ordering cost is $4, the economic order quantity is 63.25, or 63 when rounded to the nearest unit. No other order quantity would lower the total cost.

The model described is one of the simplest to develop. The sophistication level of the model a manager will prescribe depends on the actual needs of the company. The manager must be capable of realizing when inventory control procedures may be useful and must identify what costs may be associated with the problem. Then specialists such as accountants and mathematicians are called on to assist in the development of the model. The manager establishes guidelines and ensures that appropriate results are obtained.

ABC Inventory Method

Sometimes it is impractical to monitor every item in inventory with the same degree of intensity. In such cases it is useful to categorize the items of inventory according to the degree of control needed. The **ABC inventory method** is the classification of inventory items for control purposes into three categories according to unit costs and number of items kept on hand. The usual categories are

ABC inventory method
The classification of inventory items for control purposes into three categories according to unit costs and number of items kept on hand.

- A—Items in this group account for 70 percent of the dollar value of the inventory used. They represent a small number of items but high unit cost. They receive frequent, even daily, attention.
- B—Items in this group represent the next 20 percent of the dollar value of the inventory usage. These items are not as important as Group A items, but they do represent a substantial investment and should receive moderate attention.
- C—Items in this group are less expensive and may be used less often, and therefore, require less-frequent attention.

10 percent

In order to calculate an item's classification, multiply the cost of the item by how often the item is used in a specific period. Then, list all items in order of total dollar amounts. Items representing 70 percent of the total dollars constitute the A group, the items constituting the next 20 percent would be the B group, and the remainder would be in C.[10]

A manager using the ABC method should carefully monitor A items. This category might include automobiles, machinery, and tractors. B items require less vigorous control. C items might not even be formally controlled, especially if the cost associated with monitoring the items is prohibitive, as may be the case for pencils and paper.

Just-In-Time Inventory Method

Just-In-Time inventory method (JIT)
The practice of having inputs to the production process delivered precisely when they are needed, thereby assigning the responsibility for keeping inventories to a minimum to suppliers.

The Japanese success in cutting manufacturing costs is partly attributed to their use of the **Just-In-Time inventory method (JIT).** This is the practice of having inputs to the production process delivered precisely when they are needed, thereby assigning the responsibility for keeping inventories to a minimum to suppliers. Traditionally, U.S. factories attempted to manage inventories internally. More and more, however, they are using the just-in-time method. One expert suggests that use of this method can even result in "zero" inventory.[11] Zero inventory may seem unrealistic; nevertheless JIT can reduce inventory considerably.

U.S. automobile manufacturers have led the way in adopting JIT. At GM's Buick City plant in Flint, Michigan, a number of suppliers have been encouraged to place their facilities within walking distance of the assembly line. Buick has given them complete responsibility for quality, inventory, and delivery of the items they supply.[12] Attempting to spring back from its near collapse in 1980, Chrysler too has adopted JIT. "In the past," says Chrysler's production control chief, "suppliers paid very little attention to inventory. Now they have to because inventory costs so much. Automakers may not be able to afford suppliers who do not control inventory."[13]

Automobile makers are not alone in efforts to improve inventory control. Woolworth's department stores have adopted a computerized system of inventory control called *visual electronic ordering (VEO)*. Under VEO, the variety chain is able to order just what it needs and program delivery just as old stock is likely to sell out.[14] Paragon Industries, a six-store home center chain headquartered in Fresno, California, has a similar system in effect.[15] To win back customers in the apparel market, America's textile companies are mounting a just-in-time delivery campaign. Swift Textiles Inc. each morning ships just enough denim for a day's production at the nearby Levi Strauss & Co. plant in Valdosta, Georgia. With Swift certifying the quality of the denim, Levi closed its warehouse and quality testing lab and gained a competitive advantage.[16]

Evidence suggests that just-in-time purchasing has produced substantial benefits for U.S. companies.[17] In a survey conducted in 1986, inventory turnover increased by an average of 97 percent, delivery promises kept increased from 67 percent to 83 percent, and scrap cost declined 40 percent. However, some problems remain in moving toward a just-in-time system. For example, some managers are concerned about how dependent they should be on their suppliers.[18] The level of trust between firms and suppliers may be higher in Japan than it is in the United States.

■ NETWORK MODELS

The many complex tasks involved in building a skyscraper or a dam are almost impossible for the average person to comprehend. When a project is nonrecurrent, large, complex, and involves multiple organizations, a tool is needed to assist in coordinating this complicated network of interdependencies.

The primary tools available to coordinate such projects are the program evaluation and review technique (PERT) and the critical path method (CPM). PERT was developed under the Navy Special Projects Office to assist in the rapid development of the Polaris submarine program. During approximately the same time period (1957–1958), researchers for E.I. Du Pont de Nemours and Company and computer specialists from what was the Remington Rand's Univac division combined their talents to develop CPM. The initial purpose of CPM was to schedule and control all activities involved in constructing chemical plants.

Both PERT and CPM have received widespread acceptance. One major advantage of these techniques is the ease with which they can be computerized. PERT and CPM are used primarily for construction projects. But some firms, such as 3M Corporation, use the techniques to assist in the development of new products. Firms that do major construction work for the government are often required by their contracts to use PERT. Because of the similarity of PERT and CPM, only PERT will be discussed in detail. The primary difference between the two is that, in CPM, time and cost are known factors. In PERT, time must be estimated and costs determined.

PERT

PERT (Program Evaluation and Review Technique) A planning and control technique that involves the display of a complex project as a network of events and activities with three time estimates used to calculate the expected time for each activity.

PERT (Program Evaluation and Review Technique) is a planning and control technique that involves the display of a complex project as a network of events and activities with three time estimates used to calculate the expected time for each activity. An event is the beginning or completion of a step. It does not consume time or resources. An event is represented by a circle or node in the network. An activity is a time-consuming element of the program. It is represented by an arrow.

In order to assist in the understanding of PERT, in this section the technique will be applied to a specific project. The project entails obtaining a production contract award for an aircraft. The principal steps in doing this are described below.

1. Define the objective of the project and specify the factors (time, cost) that must be controlled—for example, how quickly must the project be completed and how much money will be allocated for completion.
2. List the activities involved in the project. In this example, these are as follows:
   - Preparing specifications
   - Establishing quantity requirements
   - Negotiating contract
   - Preparing test facilities
   - Developing airframe

FIGURE 12.5 ■■ PERT Network with Activities and Events

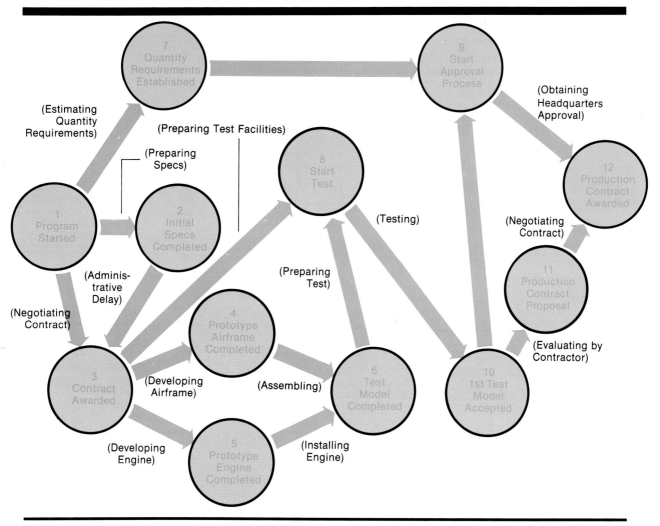

- Developing engine
- Assembling airframe
- Installing engine
- Preparing test
- Testing
- Obtaining headquarters' approval
- Evaluating by contractor
- Negotiating contract

3. Develop a statement of the relationship among project activities. The order in which each task is to be accomplished must be specified. A PERT network is then drawn (see Figure 12.5). As may be seen, the prototype airframe and the prototype engine must be completed before the test model is completed.

4. Determine the expected times that will be required to complete each activity. PERT requires three time estimates:

F I G U R E 12.6 ■ Expected Times to Complete Each Activity

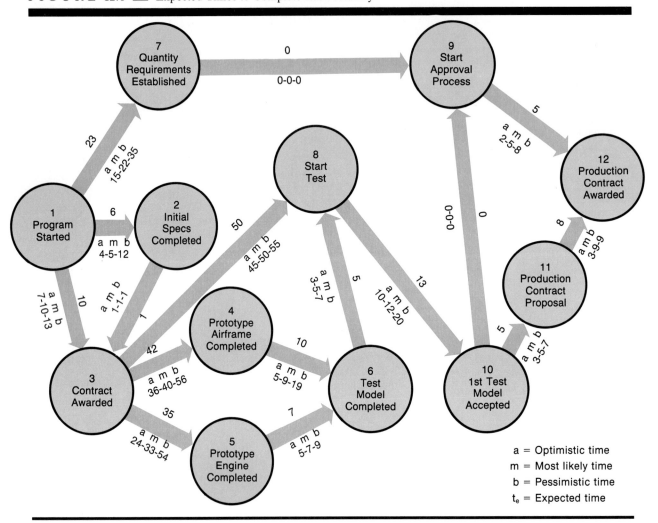

- *Optimistic time*—If everything goes right and nothing goes wrong, the project can be completed in this amount of time.
- *Most likely time*—The most realistic completion time for the activity.
- *Pessimistic time*—If everything goes wrong and nothing goes right, the project will be completed in this amount of time. The expected time for the completion of each activity may be seen in Figure 12.6. For instance, the optimistic time for "developing airframe" is thirty-six weeks, the pessimistic time is fifty-six weeks, and the most likely time is forty weeks. Expected time is then computed by inserting the three time estimates in the following formula:

Expected time (te)

$$= \frac{\text{optimistic time} + 4(\text{most likely time}) + \text{pessimistic time}}{6}$$

$$= \frac{36 \text{ weeks} + 4(40 \text{ weeks}) + 56 \text{ weeks}}{6} = 42 \text{ weeks}$$

5. Determine the *critical path,* that is, the longest path from start to finish of the project. Computer programs are available to perform the mechanics of this task. The critical path for this project is represented by the broken line seen in Figure 12.7. If any activity along the critical path is a week late, the entire project will be delayed an additional week.

F I G U R E 12.7 ■■■ Critical Path for the Project

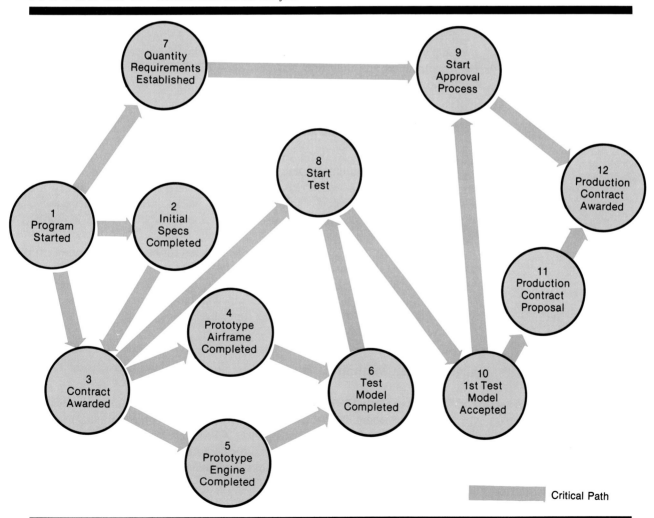

6. Determine the probability of completing the entire project or a particular activity on time. The capability of doing this is an important feature of PERT. Again, computer programs are available to calculate the probabilities. The optimistic and pessimistic times are necessary to assist in this operation. If there were but one time estimate—the most likely time—probabilities could not be computed.

A manager usually finds it beneficial to compare the optimistic and pessimistic times to the most likely time. For instance, the activity "developing engine" would likely cause greater concern to the manager than the activity "developing airframe." The difference between the optimistic time and pessimistic time is thirty weeks (54 − 24), while the difference for the activity "developing airframe" is but twenty weeks (56 − 36). A manager will likely monitor the activities that have the greatest difference between optimistic and pessimistic times, because they have the greatest potential for delaying the project.

Once the critical path is identified, the manager can quickly determine what activities to monitor closely. If an activity along the critical path slips one day, the entire project will be delayed one day. Activities that are not on the critical path may be of less immediate concern.

PERT may serve as both a planning and a control tool. In planning, it *forces* a manager to think thoroughly through a project and identify the tasks that must be accomplished and how they interrelate. PERT facilitates control mainly by highlighting the critical path.

PERT/Cost

Typically it is possible to use additional resources to reduce required time for most activities. Additional workers might be hired or more equipment brought in. Although expenses would rise, the shortened time frame might justify the added costs. For example, if spending $1,000 on additional electricians will advance the completion date of an urgently needed factory by even a few days, the expenditure will likely be justified.

Improvements in information processing capabilities have expanded the inclusion of cost consideration in PERT analysis. The purpose of PERT/Cost is to reduce the entire project completion time by a certain amount at the least cost. Reducing completion time might be especially important to a company that faces costly penalties for being late with a project. Also, there may be very high fixed costs for every day of the project.

Critical Path Method

CPM (Critical Path Method) A planning and control technique that involves the display of a complex project as a network, with one time estimate used for each step in the project.

CPM (Critical Path Method) is a planning and control technique that involves the display of a complex project as a network, with one time estimate used for each step in the project. The developers of CPM were dealing with projects in which the times and costs of tasks (activities) required to complete the project are known. In CPM, the points or nodes of the CPM network represent activities rather than events, as in PERT. In PERT three time estimates are used. There is but one time estimate in CPM, because CPM was designed to accommodate situations in which sets of standardized activities are required for the completion of a complex project. Time for completion of a task is relatively easy to determine accurately. Because there is but one time estimate, probabilities for completing the project on time cannot be computed. With these minor exceptions, PERT and CPM are similar.

SUMMARY

There are numerous quantitative techniques in every area of management, especially planning and controlling. Managers should become familiar with all techniques. They need not know the detailed mathematics of each, but should at least have an appreciation of the quantitative tools available, the situations for which they are designed, and how they are used in business.

Budgetary control is concerned with the comparison of actual to planned expenditures. A budget is a statement of planned allocation of resources expressed in financial or numerical terms. There are basically two broad categories: capital budgets and operating budgets. A capital budget is a statement of planned expenditures of funds for facilities and equipment. An operating budget is a statement of the planned income and expenses of a business or subunit. Although there are numerous benefits in the use of budgets, problems may arise. These must be recognized and attempts made to reduce potentially damaging side effects. Zero base budgeting is a system of budgeting that requires management to take a fresh look at all programs and activities each year, rather than merely build on last year's budget. Each program, or "decision package," must be justified on the basis of cost-benefit analysis.

Quality control, through which firms make sure their product or service serves the purpose for which it is intended, involves quality standards derived from company objectives. Inspection may be by acceptance sampling, either sampling by variables or sampling by attributes. Control charts show how closely samples conform to standards over time.

Inventories, the goods or materials available for use by a business, permit independence of operations between activities, provide for continuous operations when demand is not consistent, and allow orders to be filled quickly. One method of inventory control is the economic order quantity method (EOQ), which balances ordering costs and carrying costs to minimize total inventory costs. The ABC inventory control method classifies items into three categories according to unit costs and number of items kept on hand. The Japanese success in cutting manufacturing costs is partly attributed to their use of the just-in-time method of inventory control. Inputs to the production process are delivered precisely when they are needed, thereby assigning the responsibility for keeping inventories to a minimum to suppliers.

Network models are used in planning and controlling large complex projects, usually construction projects. PERT (program evaluation and review technique) involves the display of a complex project as a network of events and activities with three time estimates used to calculate the expected time for each activity. The purpose of PERT/Cost is to reduce the entire project completion time by a certain amount at the least cost. CPM (critical path method) also involves the display of a complex project as a network, but with one time estimate used for each step in the project. In the model, circles designate activities rather than events, as in PERT. The developers of CPM were dealing with projects in which the times and costs of activities (tasks required to complete the project) are known. PERT is used when these factors are not known.

REVIEW QUESTIONS

1. What information should a manager have an appreciation of with regard to quantitative tools?
2. Define a budget. What are the two broad categories of budgets?
3. What are the benefits and limitations of budgets?
4. What is zero base budgeting?
5. Define quality control. What is the purpose of quality control?
6. What are the two basic types of acceptance sampling plans? How are control charts used?
7. Explain the purposes of inventory. What is the economic order quantity (EOQ) method of inventory control?
8. Distinguish between PERT and CPM.

KEY TERMS

budget	Economic Order	PERT (Program
capital budget	Quantity (EOQ)	Evaluation and
operating budget	ordering costs	Review Techniques)
quality	carrying costs	CPM (Critical Path
acceptance sampling	ABC inventory method	Method)
control chart	Just-In-Time inventory	
inventory	method (JIT)	

CASE STUDY

POOLING OUR KNOWLEDGE

"THIS IS THE third batch of sticks we've gotten back from Brunswick this quarter," said Jerry Hodges, "and it's been different problems each time." Along with the returned pool sticks, Brunswick had provided a checklist of defects, and Jerry and his shop manager, John Kenner, were looking it over. The sticks had been made by Jerry's company, Hodges Woodworks. Brunswick is a major distributor of recreation equipment of all kinds, and Hodges had contracted to provide the company with 5,000 pool sticks per month during 1988.

There were 200 defective sticks in the returned batch. Defects ranged from misaligned leather tips on two of the sticks, to thread defects on four sticks where the sticks screwed together in the middle, to an incomplete covering of varnish on the wood sections of four other sticks. Altogether, sixteen types of defects were noted in the batch.

"The costs are just too high to inspect every piece of every stick," said Jerry. "Yeah, I know," replied John, "but it's not as expensive as having to rework an entire batch. Anyway, Brunswick uses 100 percent inspection. Why shouldn't we?" Jerry replied, "We may have to do that. But if the number of defectives is below 2 percent, Brunswick will accept the batch. Let's see if we can figure out a cheaper way to accomplish that."

The manufacturing process for pool sticks is complex. The wood parts are cut from solid maple and machined to shape on numerically controlled lathes. Then they are drilled and shaped on other machines to fit plastic, metal, and rubber parts purchased from other parts manufacturers. After being assembled, the pool cues are varnished in batches of twenty with a spray gun. Because of the small volume, most of the assembly work is done by hand.

After some discussion, John and Jerry determined that, except for the varnish problem, all of the defects in the present batch resulted from parts purchased from others. "Obviously," said Jerry, "we should do the same thing to our suppliers that Brunswick is doing to us: check the parts when we get them, and return them if they are defective."

QUESTIONS
1. What techniques are available to help Hodges Woodworks get the defective rate down below 2 percent?
2. Should the company attempt to prevent any defective cue sticks at all from leaving the factory? Explain.

CASE STUDY

A PROBLEM OF INVENTORY CONTROL

MARTHA YOUNG is the supervisor of ten stores in a convenience store chain. Each of these small stores has a day manager and two assistant managers who work the evening and midnight shifts. These "managers" are mistitled; they have no subordinates reporting directly to them. The day manager is typically the senior person, who has chosen the day shift.

Mark McCall is the day manager of one of the stores. Mark has worked at the store for three months, and sales have been increasing steadily. Mark maintains his store in good order, and the first two monthly inventory checks have been satisfactory. But as Martha reads the inventory report for this month, she becomes quite disturbed. Inventory is $1,000 short over the previous month (anything over $200 is considered out of the ordinary).

Martha realizes that this report is extremely serious. Other managers have been terminated for

inventory shortages of this amount. She likes
Mark, but something must be done to keep this
situation from occurring in the future. Martha sits
down and reviews the situation regarding the store.
The following points come to mind:

- The store is located close to a school. When Mark took
  control of the store, school was not in session. There
  might be some shoplifting occurring.
- One of the assistant managers has been with the store
  only one month. There is a possibility that there could
  be internal theft.

- The other assistant manager broke up with his
  girlfriend last month. There is a possibility that he has
  not been paying close attention to his job.

QUESTIONS
1. What type of controls, if any, should Martha
   instigate?
2. If the inventory is short next month, what do you
   think Martha should do?

EXPERIENTIAL EXERCISE

The "fix-it crew" is in a fix. You and the other participants in this exercise will have the opportunity to help solve a tough, important problem. The fix-it people are managers, mechanics, and quality control inspectors in an engine overhaul facility owned by a major U.S. airline. The jet engines the facility overhauls are returned to other facilities for reinstallation in commercial airliners. The requirement for quality is extremely high, since the aircraft are put right back into service afterward. An engine failure could be disastrous.

Ninety people are employed in the facility. The shop superintendent is responsible for the entire shop operation, which includes an administrative office, disassembly, reassembly, shipping/receiving, and the test cell. The test cell is where the completed engines are operated to test them before they are shipped off for reinstallation. The engine overhaul process is like a traditional assembly-line operation, except that engines are both taken apart and put back together. The engines enter at one end of the facility and leave at the other.

Although Quality Control is located in the engine repair facility building, the chief of Quality Control, Bill Wright, reports directly to the maintenance director, who is responsible for the entire airline maintenance effort. The quality control inspectors can inspect at any station along the assembly line. Also, about 20 percent of the finished engines are randomly selected for a thorough inspection by teams of two inspectors.

The overhaul facility has an outstanding record. However, within the past two months inspection failures have increased. Production is down due to additional hours spent correcting defects. Normally an engine is overhauled, tested, and shipped in two to four working days, depending on the number of parts requiring replacement. Within the past two months, this average has increased to between four and five days. This has occurred in spite of extensive overtime.

Upper management has noticed the problems. The shop superintendent, Kim Green, has decided that he must get things back under control quickly. He has scheduled a meeting to identify the problem, and to seek solutions. If you are selected for one of the major roles in this exercise, you will sit in on that meeting. In any case, you will be able to watch the drama unfold. Select five individuals to serve as other supervisors—Kim Green, Bill Wright, Houston Morris, J. D. Greco, and Bob Williams. The instructor will provide more information to participants.

NOTES

1. This story is a composite from a number of sources, including: "Dr. Deming Shows Pontiac the Way," *Fortune,* 18 April 1983, 19–36; and Daniel W. Gottlieb, "Purchasing's Part in the Push for Quality," *Purchasing,* 10 September 1981, 75–78.
2. Otis Port, "The Push for Quality," *Business Week,* 8 June 1989, 132.
3. Robert N. Anthony and Regina E. Herzlinger, *Management Control in Nonprofit Organizations* (Homewood, Ill.: Irwin, 1975), 222–226.

4. Gordon Shillinglaw, *Managerial Cost Accounting: Analysis and Control,* 4th ed. (Homewood, Ill.: Irwin, 1977), 142–143.
5. Karen Pennar, "America's Quest Can't Be Half-Hearted," *Business Week,* 8 June 1989, 136.
6. David A. Garvin, "Quality on the Line," *Harvard Business Review* (September–October 1983): 67.
7. Jerry Main, "Ford's Drive for Quality," *Fortune,* 18 April 1983, 62.
8. Pennar, "America's Quest," 136.
9. William E. Dollar, "The Zero Inventory Concept," *Purchasing,* 29 September 1983, 43.
10. Peter E. Alcide, "The ABCs of Inventory Management," *Practical Accountant* 19 (August 1986): 36.
11. Dollar, "Zero Inventory Concept," 43.
12. "Buick City Places Suppliers in Backyard," *Purchasing,* 10 November 1983, 15.
13. "U.S. Auto-Makers Adopt Just-in-Time Methods." *Iron Age,* 5 July 1982, 15.
14. "Woolworth's Wanding Is Made to Order," *Chain Store Age Executive* (April 1984): 52.
15. "Paragon Tracks Inventory with Customized System," *Chain Store Age Executive* (April 1984): 59.
16. Port, "Push for Quality," 134.
17. A. Ansari and Batoul Modarress, "Just-in-Time Purchasing: Problems and Solutions," *Journal of Purchasing and Materials Management* 22 (Summer 1986): 11–12.
18. Milt Ellenbogen, "Face of Purchasing," *Industrial Distribution* 75 (September 1986): 40.

REFERENCES

Ansari, A., and Batoul Modarress. "Just-in-Time Purchasing: Problems and Solutions." *Journal of Purchasing and Materials Management* 22 (Summer 1986): 12–15.

Backes, Robert W. "Cycle Counting—A Better Way for Achieving Accurate Inventory Records." *Production and Inventory Management* 21 (Second Quarter 1980): 36–44.

"Buick City Places Suppliers in Backyard." *Purchasing* (10 November 1983): 15.

Dollar, William E. "The Zero Inventory Concept." *Purchasing* (29 September 1983): 43.

Ellenbogen, Milt. "Face of Purchasing." *Industrial Distribution* 75 (September 1986): 40.

Garvin, David A. "Quality on the Line." *Harvard Business Review* (September–October 1983): 67.

———. "Quality Problems, Policies, and Attitudes in the United States and Japan: An Exploratory Study." *Academy of Management Journal* 29 (December 1986): 653–674.

Hutchins, Dave. "Quality Is Everybody's Business." *Management Decision* 24 (Winter 1986): 4.

Main, Jeremy. "Ford's Drive for Quality." *Fortune* (18 April 1983): 62.

Nelson, Andre. "Who Really Controls Quality?" *Supervisory Management* 31 (April 1986): 8–11.

"Paragon Tracks Inventory with Customized System." *Chain Store Age Executive* (April 1984): 59.

Ross, Joel E., and Y. K. Shetty. "Quality and Its Management in Service Businesses." *Industrial Management* 27 (December 1985): 7–13.

Solomon, S. L. "Building Modelers: Teaching the Art of Simulation." *Interfaces* 10 (April 1980): 65–72.

"U.S. Auto-Makers Adopt Just-in-Time Methods." *Iron Age* (5 July 1982): 15–17.
"Woolworth's Wanding Is Made to Order." *Chain Store Age Executive* (April 1984): 52.
Wueste, Richard A. "A Matter of Inconsequence: Mastering the Art of Executive Triviality." *Management World* 17 (March–April 1988): 40–41.

CHAPTER
13

Chapter Outline

Communication
and
the
Influencing
Process

Learning Objectives

After completing this chapter students should be able to

1. Describe the basic components of the communication process and state what should be communicated to workers.
2. Explain the basic forms of organizational channels of communication and describe intergroup communication.
3. Identify the barriers to individual and group communication.
4. Explain ways available to improve communication and describe the influencing process.

DELTA, THE FREE world's sixth largest airline, has earned the respect of the airline industry and financial markets as well. Except for one year, the company has been continuously profitable since before World War II. Delta also claims the smallest number of passenger complaints to the Federal Aviation Administration of any major airline.

Delta began in Monroe, Louisiana, in 1924 as a crop-dusting operation. C. E. Woolman, an entomologist (specialist in insects) by profession and an aviation enthusiast, is credited with causing what was then Huff Daland Dusters to become the world's largest privately owned aircraft fleet. In addition to its internal growth, the company merged with Chicago and Southern Airlines in 1953 and with Northeast Airlines in 1972. Today, Delta serves nearly 100 cities in the United States and six foreign countries, operating a fleet of more than 300 planes and employing nearly 40,000 people.

The airline industry was in a state of turmoil in the mid-1980s. A major recession had begun in 1979 that was to last for several years. The air traffic controllers' strike, which occurred in 1981, was never really settled, placing a great strain on the air traffic system. At the same time, the airline industry, like several other major industries, was deregulated, resulting in an intensification of competition. While other airlines were failing, throwing thousands out of work, Delta's employees were optimistically buying the company its first Boeing 767 aircraft. They named the plane the *Spirit of Delta.* Delta's workers are nonunionized, but pay scales and employee benefits surpass averages for the industry.

An open-door policy enables employees to air any grievances, hopefully before they become major problems. Flexibility in work assignments—a ticket agent willingly shifts to baggage handling, for example—has helped to increase productivity. Guaranteed employment and a promotion-from-within policy are credited with giving employees a feeling of security. All of the company's top managers have been with the company for over two decades, and no one at Delta expects to be kept from a promotion by someone's being hired from outside.

When some major airlines were selling off planes in order to survive during the early 1980s, Delta was modernizing its fleet with new Boeing 737s, 757s, and 767s. In 1986 the company ordered more new planes and began selling some of its older DC-8s to United Parcel Service. That same year Delta bought Western Air Lines, to become the nation's third largest airline, behind United and American. Delta has also improved its competitive edge in the unregulated market by developing its DATAS II computerized reservation system, expanding its hubs at Dallas and Cincinnati, and carefully managing its long-term debt. The company put into effect a new flight-planning system, which is expected to save the company several million dollars a year, reduce fuel costs, and give a smoother ride.

Looking into the future, President David C. Garrett, Jr., said, "In the longer term, we have great confidence in the future of the company. Our aircraft and ground facilities are superior. Our family of Delta professionals is unexcelled in the industry. Our financial position is strong. We have virtually everything we need to maintain and extend our position as the leader in the airline industry."[1] ∎

Having an open-door policy, a promotion-from-within policy, and a commitment to remaining union free probably directly impacts Delta's continuing success. Perhaps the worst criticism managers receive from peers, superiors, and subordinates is that they cannot communicate effectively. A concern regarding communication was expressed quite accurately by one executive vice-president: "Unless individuals are capable of clear and timely communication with deputies, peers, and principals, they are nearly totally ineffective."

In Chapter 1, management was defined as the accomplishment of objectives through the efforts of other people. In order for employees to achieve the objectives identified by the manager, they must have a clear understanding of those objectives. A statement by a frustrated manager such as, "You did what you thought I meant very effectively. Unfortunately, that was not what I wanted you to do" reveals that effective communication did not take place. Effective communication should not be considered an end in itself, but a means of achieving company goals. The most encouraging feature of communication is that it is learned. Individuals who truly desire to improve their ability to communicate can do so by giving proper attention to the task.

This chapter begins with a discussion of the communication process. Next, the various channels of communication will be presented, followed by a discussion of intergroup communication. Then, the items that can cause a breakdown in communication are reviewed. Next, factors that can assist or facilitate the communication process will be presented. A brief presentation of influencing comprises the final portion of the chapter.

THE COMMUNICATION PROCESS

Communication
The transfer of information, ideas, understanding, or feelings between people.

Communication is the transfer of information, ideas, understanding, or feelings between people. In an organization, communication provides the means by which the objectives of the firm may be accomplished. The manner in which plans are to be implemented and actions coordinated to achieve a particular objective must be communicated to the individuals who must accomplish the task. In fact, it has been estimated that managers spend a large portion of their time—approximately 75 percent—communicating. Communication provides the means by which members of the firm may be stimulated to accomplish organizational plans willingly and enthusiastically.

Source
The person who has an idea or message to communicate to another person or persons.

Communication must always take place between two or more people. Shouting for help on a desert island is not communication; similarly, if the professor lectures and no one listens or understands, there is no communication. The basic elements of the communication process are shown in Figure 13.1. Each step in the sequence is critical to success. The **source** (sender) is the person who has an idea or message to communicate to another person or persons. A problem that often affects the communication process is that each person has different backgrounds, experiences, and goals. As the first step in the communication process, a sender must encode the message or idea into a set of symbols that the receiver will understand. Words on this page are symbols to the reader. The sound of a car's horn on a busy freeway may mean that an accident appears likely. Thus, the blast of the horn becomes a symbol of danger.

When communication is attempted, messages are transmitted through such means as speaking, writing, acting, and drawing. A number of channels may be

FIGURE 13.1 ■
The Communication
Process

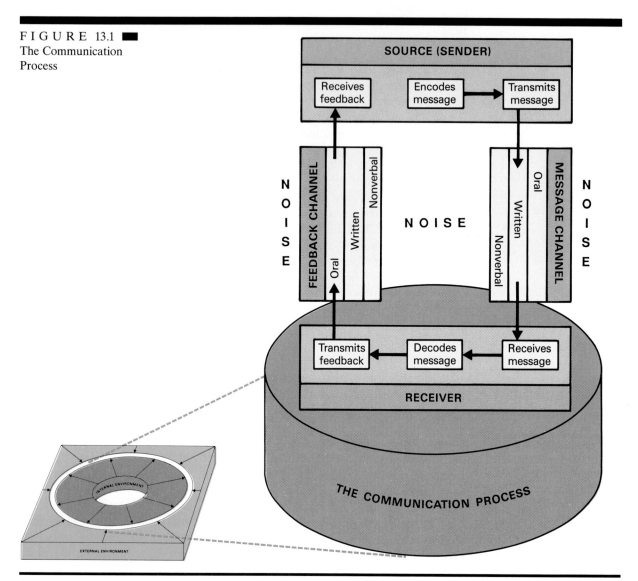

Source: Adapted from H. Joseph Reitz, *Behavior in Organizations* (Homewood, Ill.: Irwin, 1981), 310. Copyright © 1981 by Richard D. Irwin, Inc. Used with permission.

used to transmit any message. Words can be communicated orally through such methods as face-to-face conversations, telephone conversations, radio, and television. Books, articles, and letters can serve as written channels. The senses of touch, smell, and taste are nonverbal channels (although for a blind person reading braille, touch is a verbal channel). Much meaningful communication takes place without a word being spoken.

Continuing to the lower part of Figure 13.1, the receiver must decode the message by converting the symbols into meaning. Like senders, receivers have diverse backgrounds, experiences, and aspirations. *Communication is effective to the extent that the receiver's decoding matches the sender's encoding.* Based on the meaning transmitted, the receiver will act in response to the communication. This action can be to ignore the message, perform some task, store the information for future use, or something else. Feedback is provided so that the sender will know if the message was accurately received and the proper action taken.

In business, communication is vital to success. If communication breakdowns occur, costly mistakes frequently result. As was mentioned in a previous chapter, Chrysler Corporation and Maserati created a joint venture to build the Chrysler TC. From October 1986 to August 1988 Chrysler executives took 780 trips to Italy. Evidently such trips did not help communication. Months were wasted trying to determine whether the top on the Chrysler TC would be made of composite materials, steel, or aluminum. After months of ineffective communication, Chrysler got its way, but the cost for tooling to produce the new composite top was $7 million, about triple the original cost estimate. Maserati managers claim that Iacocca exploded in August 1988 when $23 million of Chrysler components were discovered piled up in a Milan warehouse. It took Chrysler four weeks to determine who had the responsibility for ordering them.[2] As is evident from this example, effective communication is essential for successful business ventures, because ineffective communication can severely reduce profit potential.

■■■ WHAT SHOULD BE COMMUNICATED?

Some managers limit their communication with subordinates to the issuance of orders. But communication should take on a much larger scope. Every day it becomes dramatically apparent that communication with employees is a critical requirement of good management. Behavioral scientists have demonstrated that worker motivation is impossible without effective communication.

Research has also underscored the need for subordinates to be heard and understood by their supervisors. The 1980s have seen continued organizational budget tightening. Heightened competition over already-scarce resources at all levels has been experienced. The need for an effective communication system that advances the goals of the organization is quite obvious. The responsibility to maintain a good communication climate clearly falls to management.[3]

Determining the specific topics to be communicated is often difficult. The manager who believes that everything is suitable for transmission will not only clog the channels with insignificant trivia but may harm operations by releasing wrong information. To sustain employee cooperation in the pursuit of organizational objectives, the needs of the employee must be considered, and how those needs will be addressed must be communicated. As may be seen in Table 13.1, employees want to know certain things.

TABLE 13.1 ■ Information Employees Want to Know

- Their standing in relation to the official, formal authority structure
- Their standing in relation to the informal organization, with respect to individual status, power, acceptance, and so forth
- Events that have a bearing on their own and the company's future economic security
- Operational information that will enable them to develop pride in their job

■■ CHANNELS OF COMMUNICATION

Communication channels `
Means by which information is transmitted.

Formal communication channels
Communication channels that are officially recognized by the organization.

Informal communication channels
Ways of transmitting information within an organization that bypass formal channels.

As may be seen in Figure 13.2, organizations provide many channels for communication. **Communication channels** are the means by which information is transmitted. Communication channels may be classified as formal and informal. **Formal communication channels** are those communication channels that are officially recognized by the organization. Instructions and information are passed downward along these channels, and information flows upward. Information also travels through informal channels. **Informal communication channels** are ways of transmitting information within an organization that bypass formal channels.

Formal Downward Channels

Many managers emphasize the importance of the downward channels of communication. They are aware of the necessity for conveying upper management's orders and viewpoints to subordinates, although perhaps unaware of how subordinates will perceive the communicated information. It is believed that the logic of these orders will stimulate desired action. Some of the various channels available to carry the information downward are examined next.

CHAIN OF COMMAND
Orders and information can be given personally or in written fashion and transmitted from one level to another. This is the most frequently used formal channel and is appropriate on either an individual or a group basis. The most common way in which communication flows downward is face-to-face interaction. Therefore, the subordinate, whether manager or worker, should become a good listener. The junior person can usually ask questions to clarify the message.

F I G U R E 13.2 ■■ Communication Channels in an Organization

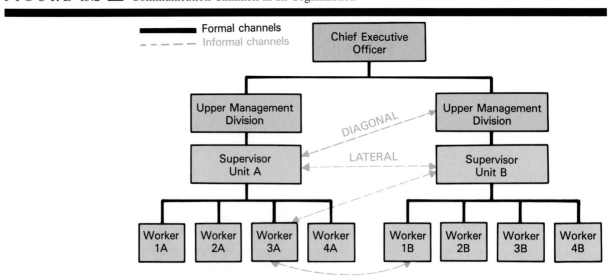

Communication between a supervisor and a subordinate is usually verbal and face to face.
(© Larry Mulvehill/Photo Researchers, Inc.)

BUSINESS BRIEFS

PINNACLE

Changes at Xerox, including Communication Changes

MANY MANAGERS EMPHASIZE the importance of the downward channels of communication. They are aware of the necessity for conveying upper management's orders and viewpoints to subordinates. Clear communication frequently will stimulate desired action. Mr. David Kearns, Chairman of the Xerox Corporation, has been sparking radical change inside Xerox since May of 1982 when he stepped in as the company's third chief executive officer in a year. Kearns is credited by Wall Street analysts with putting the company back on the revolutionary road it embarked on in 1959 with its first copier machine, and that was no easy task. Mr. David Kearns proposes that the way to simplify things is to take out layers of management so that the communication process from the people who actually do the work up through the top of the business is a much thinner thing. According to Kearns, the key to simplifying the bureaucracy is an efficient communication system. Through enhanced communication the management process at Xerox is much more effective and efficient. CNN correspondent Tom Cassidy discusses these and other issues with Mr. David Kearns.

Written documents also provide a major means of downward communication through the chain of command. Letters and memoranda should be written with consideration for how they will be understood. Incorrect interpretations are frequent, however. Lower and middle managers may not have originated the confusing communication, but they can help subordinates understand any from upper management. The directive may require some translation into the language of subordinates.

Written communications should be used for matters that are extremely important to either the manager personally or the company. Relatively permanent information such as policies, procedures, and rules usually should also be written. Additionally, managers should write communications that they suspect might otherwise be misunderstood.

POSTERS AND BULLETIN BOARDS

Information of concern to company employees is often communicated on posters and bulletin boards. Some workers may not read them, however. This is especially true when the posters or bulletins are not kept current. Information often remains on the board long after its usefulness has passed. Thus, this channel may be useful only as a supplementary device.

THE HOUSE ORGAN

Many firms have company newsletters or newspapers, often referred to as house organs. A great deal of information regarding the organization can be communicated in this way. Information about new products, how well the company is doing, and even policies is often contained in the newsletter. Readership is increased if some space is allocated to personal items of interest to employees. For instance, scores of the company bowling team or an award to a long-term employee might be mentioned.

LETTERS AND PAY INSERTS

Direct mail may be used when top management wants to communicate matters of importance. Since the letter is sent directly to the employee from the company, there is a reasonable chance that it will be read. Inserting a letter with the paycheck may also encourage readership. It at least ensures that each worker receives a copy. Also, the worker may be in a better mood because it is payday. Such letters also help to stimulate interest in company matters by employee spouses.

EMPLOYEE HANDBOOKS AND PAMPHLETS

Handbooks frequently are used during the hiring and orientation process as an introduction to the organization. Too often, however, they are unread, even when the firm demands a signed statement that the employee is acquainted with their contents. When special systems are being introduced, such as a pension plan or a job evaluation system, concise, well-illustrated pamphlets are often prepared to facilitate understanding and stimulate acceptance.

ANNUAL REPORTS

Annual reports are increasingly written not only for stockholders but also for the employees. A worker may be able to obtain information about the firm in this way. Information about new plants, new products, and company finances is often included.

LOUDSPEAKER SYSTEMS

The loudspeaker system is used not only for paging purposes but also to make announcements while they are "hot." Such systems can also be misused, as in the case of a certain company president on vacation, who thoughtlessly sent greetings from his cool mountain retreat to the hot, sweaty workers on the production floor.

Formal Upward Channels

Advocates of participative management emphasize the establishment of upward channels of communication. This is necessary not only to determine if subordinates have understood the information that was sent downward, but also to satisfy the need of subordinates to be involved. A communication effectiveness survey of thousands of employees showed that only half believed that significant upward communication was present. The others saw little chance of discussion or dialogue with upper management.[4] An upward flow of information is also necessary if management is to coordinate the various activities of the organization. There are many channels from which to choose for the upward flow of information.

OPEN-DOOR POLICY

Open-door policy
An established guideline that allows workers to bypass immediate supervisors concerning substantive matters without fear of reprisal.

An **open-door policy** is an established guideline that allows workers to bypass immediate supervisors concerning substantive matters without fear of reprisal. Delta Airlines encourages an open-door policy, which has no doubt contributed to Delta's success. Managers are encouraged to create an environment in which subordinates will feel free to come to them with problems and recommendations. An open-door policy can go a long way toward reducing tension among subordinates and improving trust. It is important that employees know of the open-door policy and believe management is sincere about it. At Rubbermaid Inc., the chairman and chief executive officer, Stanley C. Gault, takes an open-door policy one step further, by strolling through the factories and talking directly with workers.[5]

The advantages of an open-door policy are well known, but the disadvantages should also be recognized. Managers often feel insecure when they know that subordinates can take complaints directly to upper managers. At times, a supervisor only knows a problem exists when an upset upper manager calls. Also, an open-door policy may cost management time. Feeling obligated to stop work any time a worker shows up at the door may make it hard to complete administrative tasks.

SUGGESTION SYSTEMS

Many companies have formal suggestion systems. Some have suggestion boxes. Others have "beneficial suggestion" forms that workers are encouraged to complete. When a suggestion system is used, every suggestion should receive careful consideration. Workers should be promptly informed of the results of the decision on each suggestion.

Wal-Mart is one company that distinguishes itself in their dedication to employee involvement in company affairs. Management keeps employees closely informed about company plans and practices, and includes them in corporate decision making. Employee suggestions for improvements or changes are made on a weekly basis, and these recommendations are taken seriously at headquarters.[6]

QUESTIONNAIRES

Anonymous questionnaires sometimes are given to workers in an attempt to identify problem areas within the organization. When a large number of workers rate the firm low in a given area, management should search for solutions. For instance, if a significant number of workers indicate dissatisfaction with pay, an investigation is certainly warranted. Pay may actually be too low, or the workers may just be unaware of what other firms are paying. Whatever the case, the company should take some action, or workers' faith in the use of the questionnaires may be lost.

THE GRIEVANCE PROCEDURE

Grievance procedure
A systematic process that permits employees to complain about matters affecting them.

A systematic process that permits employees to complain about matters affecting them is referred to as a **grievance procedure.** The grievance procedure is a mechanism that gives subordinates the opportunity of settling disputes within the organization. Most unions have negotiated formal grievance procedures. When employees do not have avenues to voice their complaints, even small gripes may grow into major problems. Some managers believe that formal grievance procedures weaken their authority. Others see the grievance procedure as a way of keeping minor problems from becoming serious.

OMBUDSPERSON

Ombudsperson
A complaint officer with access to top management who hears employee complaints, investigates, and sometimes recommends appropriate action.

The ombudsperson provides a means of resolving grievances in nonunion organizations. Ombudspersons have been used for some time in Europe, and the practice is becoming more popular in the United States. Ombudspersons act as top management's eyes and ears. An **ombudsperson** is a complaint officer with access to top management who hears employee complaints, investigates, and sometimes recommends appropriate action. Because of their access to top management, ombudspersons can often resolve problems swiftly. In many cases, the ombudsperson simply helps employees find people who can solve their problems. Sometimes ombudspersons recommend specific action to managers.

In recent years the ombudsperson has assumed the additional duties of assisting to uncover scandals within organizations. Large defense contractors, such as McDonnell Douglas and General Electric, have used ombudspersons to respond to questions raised regarding safety of product design or the billings on a defense contract. Workers who believe that a problem exists can now bypass the supervisor and gain an audience with the ombudsperson.[7]

SPECIAL MEETINGS

Special employee meetings to discuss particular company policies or procedures are sometimes scheduled by management to obtain employee feedback. The keystone of teamwork in the Pitney Bowes Company, for example, is monthly departmental meetings of all employees. In addition, a central employee council of thirteen employee representatives meets with top executives on a monthly basis. Employees on this main council are elected for two-year terms and devote time to investigating company problems and improving communication processes.

Informal Communication Channels

As may be seen in Figure 13.2, informal communication channels are not included in the formal organization structure. If a manager has a problem that is affected by another department, the two managers involved may get together informally over coffee. Informal communication may be either lateral or diagonal (see Figure 13.2). When managers communicate at the same organizational level, it is known as lateral communication. This form of communication benefits from established personal relationships. Mutual trust must first develop. This often takes time, but if effective, lateral communication can improve the productivity of both departments. Some companies provide for lateral communication as part of the formal organizational structure.

Another type of informal channel is diagonal communication. This also bypasses the formal chain of command. Information is exchanged with those higher or lower in the organization, but not directly in the formal chain of command. Again, this is not an automatic process. Trust must first develop. Care must be taken in using diagonal communication because immediate superiors might take offense. Used effectively, diagonal communication can be an important information source for managers.

The grapevine is the organization's informal communication system. It exists within the organization, but it may also extend beyond it. The grapevine does not respect formal lines of authority. Its tentacles reach into every unit and level throughout an organization. However, most of the information it transmits derives from the formal organization. The grapevine usually transmits information more rapidly than the formal system does, although sometimes not as accurately. Employees generally rate the grapevine as one of the primary sources of current information.[8]

The grapevine has four basic characteristics. First, it transmits information throughout the organization in every direction. Information on the grapevine can go down, up, laterally, and diagonally, all at the same time. It can connect organizational units that have very indirect formal relationships. Second, the grapevine transmits information rapidly. It is not restricted by any formal policies and procedures. The chain of command does not have to be followed. Once a message gets into the grapevine, it can move almost instantaneously to any point in the organization. Third, the grapevine is selective in who receives the information. Some people are tuned in to it and others are not. There are certain persons to whom even gossips do not talk. Consequently, some managers are not even aware of the grapevine. Finally, the grapevine extends beyond the formal organization. Considerable communication about the firm occurs off the job. Workers may be at a party and pass on or receive information about the company. There are usually hundreds or even thousands of such connections.

Managers should not ignore the grapevine, because it cannot be eliminated. Wise managers attempt to remain tuned in to the grapevine. Not only will they obtain useful information, but they will be able to replace incorrect messages with accurate information. The grapevine is a very important part of the communication process, even for enlightened companies that try to make the formal communication system as effective as possible.

▬ INTERGROUP COMMUNICATION

Many of the concepts regarding interpersonal communication apply equally to intergroup communication. The extent and quality of two-way communication among groups can be diagnosed in the following manner: First, analyze the quality of encoding, transmission, and decoding of information; second, assess the extent to which groups create either a supportive or a defensive climate during interactions; and third, determine the network that best describes the communication between the groups. This analysis parallels that for communication within groups.

Special Roles

Organizational structure influences intergroup as well as interpersonal communication. Two positions, or special roles—gatekeeper and boundary spanner—facilitate effective communication between groups.

GATEKEEPERS

Gatekeepers
Individuals in positions that allow them to screen information and control access to it.

Gatekeepers are individuals in positions that allow them to screen information and control access to it.[9] Situated at the crossroads of communication channels, these roles, or positions, are like nerve centers, where information is "switched" among people and groups.[10] Gatekeepers communicate extensively internally, as well as externally, with professionals outside the parent organization.[11] Staff specialists, such as human resource professionals, who interact with line management groups, fill such roles.[12] In a research laboratory, technical gatekeepers bring supplier information to their own group and to other groups in the organization.[13] Managers also act as gatekeepers, sharing information with subordinates, superiors, and peers. Research has shown that gatekeeping supervisors can affect the turnover of members of research and development projects. These supervisors reduce turnover by teaching R&D professionals, as part of their early socialization, of the value of professional and organizational orientation.[14]

BOUNDARY SPANNERS

Boundary spanners
Individuals who serve the roles of information processor and representative for an organization or its subunits to others outside the unit's boundary.

Boundary spanners are individuals who serve the roles of information processor and representative for an organization or its subunits to others outside the unit's boundary.[15] These roles exist where two groups or units, such as the R&D and marketing departments, interact. Product managers, department representatives to a task force, or individuals holding other liaison positions act as boundary spanners. A purchasing agent, sales representative, or public relations director, for example, can act as a liaison between a department's or organization's internal and external environments.

Individuals in boundary-spanning roles perform significant communication activities in R&D laboratories.[16] These individuals gather information from other groups and external sources as a way of remaining technologically current and coordinating with other organizational work groups.[17] In these R&D units, project supervisors generally act as boundary spanners.[18] One study of an engineering laboratory demonstrated that such roles stem from the perceived competence of the individual and the extent of colleague consultation in which that person engages.[19] In the study, researchers found that the role of internal spanner or liaison between the laboratory and the rest of the organization was frequently a prerequisite for the role of external liaison—between the laboratory or the larger organization and an outside organization.

Communication Networks and Their Characteristics

Communication networks
The flow of messages between and among people in organizations.

Organizations are made up of individuals occupying certain positions or roles. Relatively permanent role arrangements in groups describe in part the group's structural configuration, or group structure. Group structure may also be described by the enduring patterns of communication that may be seen among the role holders. The flow of messages between and among people in organizations occurs through pathways called **communication networks.** Figure 13.3 illustrates five such communication patterns or networks. The wheel network has a single person who alone communicates with all others in the work group. The Y (particularly if inverted) and the chain networks resemble the chain of command in a formal communication channel. Communication flows up and down a hierarchy, with little skipping of levels or communication outside the hierarchy. The circle resembles the chain, except the communication loop is closed. For example, the lowest-level member of a group may have a top manager as a mentor and communicate with him or her. In the completely connected network, all group members regularly communicate with all other members.

Of course, a single network does not precisely describe the communication in any one group. Rather, a group's communication may be typified by one

FIGURE 13.3 ■
Communication Networks and Their Characteristics

Network:

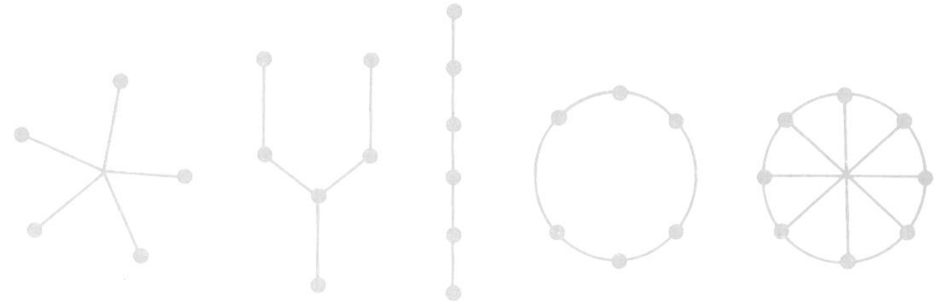

	Wheel	Y	Chain	Circle	Completely connected
Characteristics of Information Exchange:					
Speed	Fast	Slow	Slow	Slow	Fast-Slow
Accuracy*	Good	Fair	Fair	Poor	Good
Saturation	Low	Low	Moderate	High	High
Characteristics of Members:					
Overall satisfaction	Low	Low	Low	High	High
Leadership emergence	Yes	Yes	Yes	No	No
Centralization	Yes	Yes	Moderate	No	No

*These accuracy estimates may change according to the nature and complexity of the task.

Source: Based on A. Bavelas, "Communication Patterns in Task-Oriented Groups." *Journal of Accoustical Society of America* 22 (1950): 725–730.

network, or the group may use variants of one or more networks. Identifying the predominant structural configuration, however, helps explain or predict the performance and satisfaction of the group and its members. These networks differ along two sets of dimensions:

1. The characteristics of an exchange of information
   a. The *speed* of problem solving by the group
   b. The *accuracy* of problem solving by the group; that is, the extent, frequency, and type of mistakes made
   c. The *saturation* of the network; that is, the amount of information being passed along the network's segments
2. The characteristics of network members
   a. Their *satisfaction*
   b. The emergence and existence of *leadership*; that is, whether a single position typically demonstrates leadership or whether several positions share leadership
   c. The *centralization* of decision making in the group; that is, whether a single person has primary responsibility for decision making or whether it is decentralized to many members of the group

In the wheel configuration, information exchange occurs relatively quickly between the center position and peripheral ones. Information flows somewhat slower between two spoke positions because it must pass through a third position, the center, which acts as an intermediary. Compare this speed of information exchange with the speed between two positions in the chain. Obviously, passing information through two positions requires less time than moving it through three. In the wheel, accuracy of information remains high, because little filtering occurs; only one person, the central person, can pass information on to others. Contrast this to the chain or Y network, where distortions increase as information passes through several positions. The links of the wheel, chain, and Y receive less information than the links in the circle and the completely connected network. In the circle and completely connected network, the greater opportunity for feedback seems to be associated with greater member satisfaction. This satisfaction may also be due to the sharing of leadership responsibility and the decentralized decision making.

The effectiveness of the structural configuration selected will vary among groups and at different times within the same group. For example, when a group is newly formed, a wheel configuration may be best, so that a large quantity of information can be conveyed as rapidly as possible to the new members. But in an established group, whose members must identify and evaluate alternatives, discussion is more essential than conveying information, and a completely connected network would be more appropriate. Effectiveness occurs when a *fit* exists between the network, group members, and task characteristics.

■■■ BARRIERS TO COMMUNICATION

Effective communication means that the receiver correctly interprets the message of the sender. Often this is not the case, due to various communication breakdowns

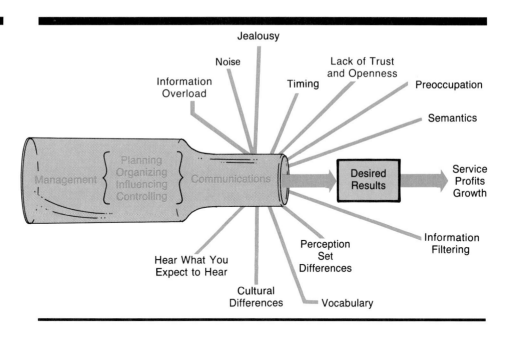

that can occur. A survey of 32,000 employees in twenty-six organizations showed that only half of the employees thought that the organization's communications were accurate and candid, and two thirds felt them to be incomplete.[20] If a manager tells an employee to "produce a few more parts," and the employee makes two but the manager wants 200, a breakdown in communication certainly took place. If managers are to develop their communication ability, the ways in which communication breakdowns can occur must be fully understood.

As seen in Figure 13.4, successful management decisions must pass through the bottleneck, or barriers to communication, if organizational objectives are to be achieved. If the barriers are excessive, communication may be reduced to the point where the firm's objectives simply cannot be met. Barriers may be classified as technical, language, or psychological. Each of these is discussed below.

Technical Barriers

Environmental barriers to communication are referred to as "technical breakdowns." Timing, information overload, and cultural differences are three such technical barriers.

TIMING

Timing
The determination of when a message should be communicated.

The determination of when a message should be communicated is referred to as **timing.** It is often quite important for a manager to determine the most appropriate time to transmit a message. For instance, a manager who must reprimand a worker for excessive tardiness will want to speak to the worker as soon as possible after the event. If, say, six months passes before the reprimand is made, the worker will likely have forgotton the event.

INFORMATION OVERLOAD

Information overload
A condition that exists
when an individual is
presented with too much
information in too short a
time.

Information overload is a condition that exists when an individual is presented with too much information in too short a time. With the many channels and media available, as well as the changed philosophy toward a greater sharing of information, it is little wonder that information overload occurs. A person can absorb only so many facts and figures at any one time. When excessive information is provided, a major breakdown in communication can occur.

As a professor, one of the authors experienced information overload in a classroom. The course was a statistics class, which met one day a week for four hours. In the first hour, students were eager to take notes. By the fourth hour, few students could repeat what the instructor had said. Information overload had occurred. Some students have discovered that their grades suffer when they attempt to take all of their classes in the morning on Monday, Wednesday, and Friday. By the end of the last class, many of the students have no idea what the instructor said, and their grades suffer.

CULTURAL DIFFERENCES

Cultural differences can also cause a breakdown in communication. In the United States, time is a highly valuable commodity, and a deadline suggests urgency. But in the Middle East, giving another person a deadline is considered rude, and the deadline is likely to be ignored. If a client is kept waiting in the outer office for thirty minutes in the United States, the delay may mean that the client is perceived to have low status. In Latin America, a thirty-minute wait is common. If a contract offer in this country has not been acted on over a period of several months or a year, an American might conclude that the other party has lost interest. In Japan, long delays mean no slackening of interest; delay is often a negotiation tactic, known to be effective in dealing with impatient Americans.

Americans conduct most business at an interpersonal distance of from five to eight feet; a distance of one to three feet suggests more personal or intimate undertakings. The normal business distance in Latin America is closer to the personal distance in the United States. This results in some highly interesting communication difficulties. Consider the back-pedaling North American as his or her Latin American counterpart presses ever closer. Regarding status symbols, consider a manager's office in the United States. Spacious, well furnished, and located on the top floor, it conveys meanings of high prestige. In the Middle East, size and decor of office mean little or nothing; and in France, managers are likely to be located in the midst of their subordinates, in order to control them.

Language Barriers

Language problems can result from the vocabulary used and from different meanings applied to the same word (semantics).

VOCABULARY

A manager must understand the type of audience being addressed. Statisticians, skilled mechanics, and unskilled laborers likely have different vocabulary sets. Words that the statistician might fully understand have little meaning to the

FIGURE 13.5 ■■
Common Vocabulary Base

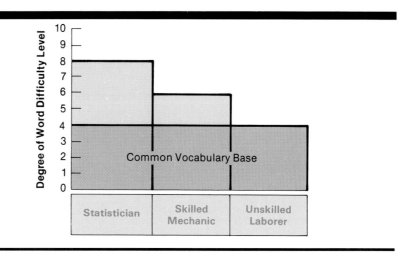

unskilled laborer, and vice versa. Breakdowns in communication often occur when the sender does not tailor the message to match the knowledge base of the receiver. This problem is most severe when someone deliberately uses fancy words just to seem more knowledgeable.

Certain words are part of practically every person's vocabulary. Figure 13.5 illustrates these as the common vocabulary base. Arbitrarily selected difficulty levels from zero to 4 on a scale of 10 are used. If a person speaks using words of level 4 or less, both the statistician and the unskilled laborer will understand. As an individual progresses above this base level, more and more people will be unable to comprehend the message. If the statistician uses words above the level of 6, communication with the skilled mechanic is lost. Naturally, there will be times when higher-level words must be used to communicate a technical concept, but if managers can concentrate their messages in the common vocabulary base, they have a much better chance of being understood.

SEMANTICS

When a sender sends words to which a receiver attaches meanings different from those intended by the sender, a semantic—or meaning of words—communication breakdown will likely occur. A major difficulty with the English language is that multiple meanings may be attached to a single word, for instance, the word *charge*. A manager may place an employee *in charge* of a section. The company *charges* for its services. A person gets a *charge* out of a humorous story. When two individuals attach different meanings to a word, a breakdown in communication can occur.

Jargon also creates barriers to communication. Virtually every industry develops a certain jargon, which is used in everyday business. The statistician, computer programmer, word processor, or unskilled laborer likely develops expressions peculiar to his or her specific jobs. When speaking to an individual not associated with the trade—and therefore unfamiliar with the jargon—a breakdown in communication may occur. For this reason many firms provide new employees with a list of definitions of terms associated with the particular industry.

Psychological Barriers

Technical factors and semantic differences cause considerable breakdown in communication, but it is the psychological barriers that tend to be the major cause for miscommunication. These include various forms of distortion and problems involving interpersonal relationships.

INFORMATION FILTERING

Information filtering refers to the process by which a message is altered through the elimination of certain data as the communication moves up from person to person in the organization. As subordinates contribute information to superiors, they know the information will be used for at least two purposes: (1) to aid management in controlling and directing the firm (and therefore the worker), and (2) to evaluate the worth of their performance. Managers often discover that information that has been provided to them by subordinates has been filtered. Managers at all levels are also tempted to filter information as it progresses up the chain of command. Even the president may filter information before it goes to the board of directors.

Filtered information may result in an incorrect impression of the true situation. There have been many managerial attempts to reduce both the number and thickness of the authority filters that clog organization communication channels. Decentralization reduces the number of levels of authority within the organization. One organization reduced the number of managerial levels from eight to four, with a consequent speeding up of the communication process. Such reorganizations are drastic and require considerable efforts in the areas of retraining and establishing realistic control standards.

A consultant can serve as a means of reducing communication filters. In one company, there was a steady decrease in productivity for no reason that could be identified by management. The consultant systematically interviewed all employees over a six-month period. The results of these many interviews indicated strong feelings on the part of many employees that work standards were too high. Older employees resented the high wage scales of the new employees, and temporary transfers to new jobs to avoid layoff were widely resented. In each case, management had felt that it had effectively communicated its intent to the employees.

LACK OF TRUST AND OPENNESS

Openness and trust on the part of both managers and employees must exist if orderly changes in the organization are to occur. When employees feel that openness and trust do not exist, barriers to communication are present. The open-door policy at Delta can be effective only if workers believe the company's promises of confidentiality and no reprisals when workers bypass the chain of command.

Feedback is encouraged when employees perceive the manager to be open and receptive to ideas. Managers need this feedback to do their job, as was illustrated in Figure 13.1. On the other hand, if managers give the impression that their orders should never be questioned, communication tends to be stifled.

A major factor in the success of Japanese business is that Japanese managers trust their peers and superiors as well as their workers. This attitude results in a simpler organizational structure. In the United States the many layers of

Information filtering
The process by which a message is altered through the elimination of certain data as the communication moves up from person to person in the organization.

organizational structure cause high overhead and much red tape. Japanese firms assume that personnel at all levels are trustworthy, and they do not have to employ highly paid executives to review the work of other highly paid executives.[21]

JEALOUSY

It is perhaps a difficult lesson for a manager to learn, but everyone may not be pleased by his or her successful performance. A manager's competency may actually be viewed by peers and superiors as a threat to their security. They may even try to minimize the manager's accomplishments in the eyes of upper management. Because of the jealousy of peers, the effectiveness of communication between the manager and upper management may be severely reduced.

PREOCCUPATION

Some people are so preoccupied with themselves that they listen but do not hear the message. Preoccupation causes people to respond in certain, rather predictable, though inappropriate ways. A New York columnist tells the story of attending a party at a well-known socialite's home. The socialite was famous for being so preoccupied with making a favorable impression on her guests that she did not listen to what the guests said. The columnist decided to play a trick on the socialite, so he deliberately arrived late. As he entered, he gave this explanation of being late: "I'm sorry to be late, but I killed my wife this evening and had a difficult time stuffing her body into the trunk of my car." The charming hostess beamed and said, "Well, darling, the important thing is that you have arrived; now the party can really begin."

WE HEAR WHAT WE EXPECT TO HEAR

Most of us are often conditioned to hear what we expect to hear, not what is actually said. Because of past experiences, we develop preconceptions of what is being said. Sometimes we hear what we want to hear. An employee who has been reprimanded quite a few times by a certain supervisor may even interpret a compliment by that supervisor as a negative statement.

PERCEPTION SET DIFFERENCES

Perception set
A fixed tendency to interpret information in a certain way.

A **perception set** is a fixed tendency to interpret information in a certain way. Differences in past experiences, educational background, emotions, values, beliefs, and many other factors affect each person's perception of a message or of words. The word *management,* for example, may provoke an entirely different image in the minds of two persons. The parents of one may have been business managers, while the parents of the other may have been labor union organizers. Perception set differences even affect the meanings of words like *chair, pencil,* and *hat,* which represent tangible objects. The impact is clearly much greater for such terms as *liberal* and *conservative.*

NOISE

Noise
Anything that interferes with or disrupts the accurate transmission and/or reception of messages.

Noise is anything that interferes with or disrupts the accurate transmission and/or reception of messages. Noise can occur at several or all points within the communication process. Noise is the principal source of error in communication. In reality, it cannot be eliminated from the communication process. However, through careful application of the communication process, the negative impact of noise can be controlled.

ETHICAL
DILEMMA

YOU ARE THE public relations manager for the J. L. Shiely Company, the St. Paul mining concern. Your company and the small community in which it is located have always co-existed harmoniously. Suddenly, the town turns against your mining company. A new town board views digging for profit immoral, and in order to punish your company, passes an ordinance laying title to fifteen acres of your property. In 1955 Shiely deeded the 15-acre park to the town, with a provision that the firm could eventually reclaim it for mining. You could probably win a lawsuit against the town, but that would sour the relationship even further. You can either take the town to court, and show them who is boss, or you can lobby residents to intervene and start treating your company fairly.
What would you do?

Source: Adapted by permission, *Nation's Business,* August 1987. Copyright © 1987, U.S. Chamber of Commerce.

■■ BARRIERS TO EFFECTIVE GROUP COMMUNICATION

Barriers to communication also affect groups. Additionally, group attitudes toward collaboration and competition can also create barriers. Parties with a competitive attitude

- define conflict as win-lose;
- pursue only their own goals;
- understand their own needs but publicly disguise them;
- aggrandize their power;
- use threats to get submission;
- overemphasize their own needs, goals, and position;
- adopt an attitude of exploiting the other party whenever possible;
- emphasize only differences in positions and the superiority of their own position; and
- isolate the other person or group.[22]

The win-lose perspective is a major barrier to intergroup communication. This kind of "we-they" attitude polarizes the interacting groups, and communications take on an aura of bargaining, rather than transmission of facts or problem solving. Union and management are especially prone to this type of interaction.

■■ IMPROVING COMMUNICATION

When breakdowns in communication occur, often the result is lowered productivity. Sometimes, when managers believe they have told a worker to do one thing, the employee perceives it as a directive to do something else. In this case, the manager not only may lose the worker's time, but also may discover that harm was done when the worker performed the wrong task. Thus, learning how to communicate effectively can significantly improve productivity. As mentioned earlier, the main thing to remember is that communication skills can be learned. If we truly want to improve our communication ability, there are means available to do so. Empathy, listening, reading skills, observation, word choice, body language, actions, and transactional analysis are discussed as ways to improve communication.

Empathy

Empathy
The ability to identify with the various feelings and thoughts of another person.

You have likely heard the expression, "I not only have sympathy for you. I have empathy." **Empathy** is the ability to identify with the various feelings and thoughts of another person. It does not mean you necessarily agree with the other person, but you understand why that person speaks and acts in a certain way. If someone is bitter, an empathetic person is able to "feel" the bitterness. Managers should take the time to understand as much as possible about the people they work with daily. By being empathetic, managers can more easily get to the heart of many workers' problems.

Listening

To facilitate communication, one of the most effective tools managers have at their disposal is the ability to listen. Constant talking interferes with listening and learning. Listening skills help managers discover problems and determine solutions.

Communication cannot take place unless messages are received and understood. It has been observed that the average speaking speed is about 120 words

A manager who listens to employees can identify problems and determine solutions. (Courtesy of International Business Machines Corporation)

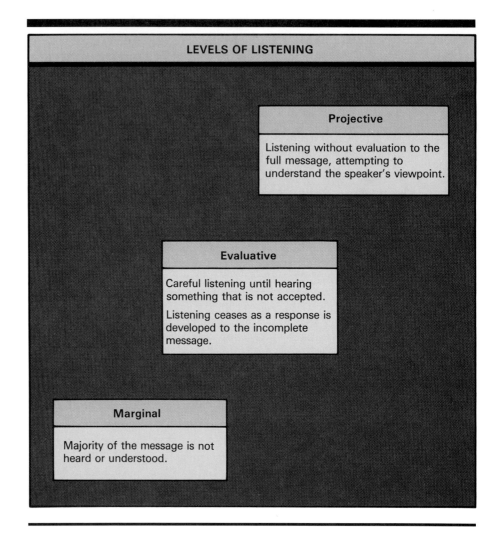

per minute. The speed at which most people are able to comprehend words is more than four times the speed at which the words are spoken. The question therefore arises, what does the listener do with the free time that results from this difference in speeds?

As may be seen in Figure 13.6, at least three types of listening have been identified: marginal, evaluative, and projective. The slower speed of the speaker provides the listener with an opportunity for marginal listening, that is, letting the mind stray while someone is talking. This can lead to misunderstanding and even insult. Most of us have experienced the situation in which, when speaking to someone, we realize that their mind is "a million miles away." The person may have heard a few words, but most of the message was not understood.

Evaluative listening requires the listener to pay reasonably close attention to the speaker. Any free time is devoted to evaluating the speaker's remarks. Forming rebuttal while the speaker is still speaking may lead to marginal listening. As soon as the sender says something that is not accepted, communication ceases, as the receiver begins to develop a response. Instead of one idea being transmitted and held by two people, two ideas develop, neither of which is really communicated. If the listener allocates too much time to disapproving or approving of what is heard, there may not be time to understand fully. This is particularly true when the remarks are loaded with emotion or threats to the security or status of the receiver.

Projective listening holds the greatest potential for effective communication. To fully utilize their time, listeners attempt to project themselves into the position of the speaker and understand what is being said from the speaker's viewpoint. Effective listening should precede evaluation. After understanding what has been said, individuals are better able to evaluate it. Carl Rogers has suggested a rule to follow to ensure some degree of projective listening: "Each person can speak for himself only *after* he has related the ideas and feelings of the previous speaker accurately and to that speaker's satisfaction."[23] There is no necessity to agree with the statements, but there is a need to understand them as the speaker intended. Only in this way is it possible to frame a reply that will actually respond to the speaker's remarks. Effective listening is empathetic listening. It requires an ability to listen for feeling as well as for words. The listener attempts to "stand in the shoes" of the other person.

Reading Skills

Reading skills receive much attention in our society. The amount of written material managers must cover has increased significantly, and some attempt should first be made to consolidate and reduce it. Particularly in larger organizations, the ability to read rapidly and with understanding is an essential communication skill. It has been found that reading speeds can be doubled and tripled with little or no loss in comprehension.

Observation

As in the case of listening, there are too few attempts to increase skill in observation, outside of training for law enforcement. Most individuals have heard of police reports of traffic accidents where there were many witnesses. When the police question the different witnesses, there are many different versions of what actually occurred. "The blue car went through the stop light," says one witness. "No, that is not correct," says another. "The light was green." Most people miss a great deal by failing to carefully observe important elements in the environment. We mentioned earlier how some managers are very adept at assessing the general atmosphere of an organization merely by strolling through its workplaces. Observation of furnishings, housekeeping, dress of personnel, and activities can convey much information. Using our powers of observation to supplement listening and reading adds immeasurably to our understanding of what is actually going on.

Word Choice

There is a certain threshold of words that virtually everyone can understand (refer back to Figure 13.5). Managers who want to communicate effectively must choose their words carefully. The words transmitted by the sender must be in the vocabulary set of the receiver. Generally, for effective communication, simple or common words are best.

Body Language

Research has shown that 90 percent of first impressions are based on nonverbal communication and only 10 percent on verbal communications.[24] Because it is the manager's job to get things done through the efforts of other people, it is important for managers to be aware of how they are communicating nonverbally. **Body language** is defined as a nonverbal method of communication in which physical actions such as motion, gestures, and facial expressions convey thoughts and emotions.

An infinite variety of body positions are available to the receiver at any one moment. The manager will find it useful to know the language of body position and to use it correctly. Although each person's body language is highly individualized, some generalizations, used cautiously, may be helpful. Crossed legs or ankles and folded arms may indicate a defensive posture or a dislike of the situation. A more open position may indicate the opposite, as may leaning forward or backward in a relaxed manner. A worker facing away from the manager, or putting hands in pockets, may be adopting a negative posture.

Many people almost literally talk with their hands. Usually, the meaning of hand gestures is readily understandable; and, as part of the total message, their importance should not be ignored by the manager. Free use of hand gesturing is likely to indicate one of two contrasting psychic states—highly emotional and animated, or relaxed and relatively carefree. If the emotional zeal of the first state develops into stress, gesturing becomes more restricted. The really tense individual is likely to be rigid of body, with limited hand movement.

While free use of hand gestures generally reflects a positive attitude toward the other person, it sometimes can indicate other states. Nervousness, discomfort, or an unfavorable attitude may be reflected by such things as clenching the fists, drumming the fingers, twiddling the thumbs, and tugging at the nose, ear, or chin. The more neutral stance of thinking or evaluating may be indicated by stroking or rubbing the chin or forehead.

Facial expressions are readily understood. By observing a person's face, we can usually distinguish among such emotions as anger, interest, happiness, disgust, contempt, surprise, fear, and love. As messages, facial expressions may indicate true feelings more reliably than verbal messages. In fact, when these two types of messages are contradictory, the receiver is more likely to believe the facial expression. For most people, it is more difficult to communicate false information through facial expression than through any speaking or writing.

Effective managers appreciate the importance of body language in the communication process. All people—managers, superiors, and subordinates—give off physical signals in attempting to communicate. These provide significant insight into the exact meaning of the message. Managers particularly must be aware of the signals they are presenting. Employees grasp at these small symbols to determine what "the boss" means. A frown may cause words, even though the words are positive in nature, to be taken wrong. A sarcastic smile, along with "you did a good job," will likely be interpreted to mean that the worker actually

Body language
A nonverbal method of communication in which physical actions such as motion, gestures, and facial expressions convey thoughts and emotions.

did not do a good job. A blank stare may mean to the employee that the manager is not interested.

A manager must also be aware of the signals that a subordinate may be giving off. Sweaty hands or nail biting may mean that the worker feels ill at ease. Managers need to recognize these signs and be prepared to adjust their actions.

Most nonverbal signals are given subconsciously; hence, it takes more effort to change the traditional nonverbal signals, particularly perhaps for women. In today's corporate environment, women as a group have risen far above the level of secretary. Nevertheless, studies show that the unconscious communications of female managers to their male counterparts still tend to convey the message that they perceive their status to be lower than that of men.[25]

Actions

The manager must also recognize that one communicates by what one does or does not do. If a man comes to work one day and finds his desk moved from a location in a private office to one in an open area, communication of a sort has taken place. If no verbal explanation accompanies the action, people will interpret it their own way; the missing symbol or signal will be supplied by the observer. And despite any verbal statement to the contrary, such a move will likely be interpreted as a demotion.

In one company, management had introduced a change in procedure for a small crew of employees. The new method was timed, and standards were established. The workers all produced less than half the standard. They all filed grievances protesting the unfairness of the standard. Management tried everything it could think of to correct the problem, from all-day time studies to providing each employee with a private instructor in the new method. A check on similar jobs in other companies revealed that the standard was in line. Thus, management concluded that a concerted work restriction was involved.

The next move was one of communication by *action*. An engineer was sent to the production department, and he proceeded to measure various angles and spaces on the floor. He volunteered no information to the group. Finally, one man's curiosity got the best of him, and he asked the engineer what he was doing. The engineer indicated that management wanted to see if there was sufficient room to locate certain machinery that could do the work of this crew. He continued about his business of measuring. The next day, all work crew members were producing amounts well above the established standard.

Transactional Analysis

Transactional analysis (TA)
A training and development method that considers the three ego states of Parent, Adult, and Child in helping people understand interpersonal relations.

Transactional analysis has been used for a number of years as a technique for teaching behavioral principles to individuals and small groups in training and development programs. **Transactional analysis (TA)** is a training and development method that considers the three ego states of Parent, Adult, and Child in helping people understand interpersonal relations.[26] As such, TA serves as a facilitator in communication.

PARENT
The Parent ego state may take on the characteristics of either the Nurturing or the Negative Parent. When the Nurturing Parent dominates, the person gives

praise and recognition, comfort in time of distress, and reassurance in time of need. Statements such as "you have done a good job" or "I am certain the problem will work out all right" might be associated with the Nurturing Parent. The Negative Parent is overcontrolling, suffocating, critical, and oppressive. Comments such as "women should be seen and not heard" or "be careful, you can hurt yourself with the knife" might be associated with the Negative Parent. When the Negative Parent dominates, the person tends to lecture, believes that his or her moral standard is best for everyone, and often will not accept other ideas.

CHILD

The Child may take on the characteristics of the Natural Child, the Little Professor, or the Adaptive Child. The Natural Child is spontaneous, impulsive, untrained, expressive, self-centered, affectionate, and curious. The Little Professor tends to be intuitive, manipulative, and creative. The Adaptive Child tends to react in a way determined by parental figures.

ADULT

A person who tends to evaluate the situation and who attempts to make decisions based on information and facts is in the Adult ego state. No emotions are involved, and the individual tends to function like a computer, with all decisions based on logic.

The interaction of ego states can have a significant impact on behavior in organizations. The manager must recognize that an employee will not always be in the Adult state and will not always make decisions based entirely on logic. In fact, the greatest amount of creativity is associated with the Child. Also, the

FIGURE 13.7 ■
A Crossed Transaction
Involving All Three Ego
States

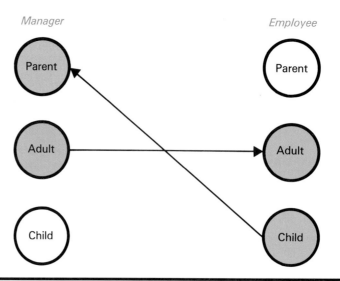

Manager: This task needs to be completed today.
Employee: Why are you always pushing me to work harder?

manager will be able to recognize when communication is impossible. For instance, the manager who is in the Adult state may attempt to speak to the Adult of the employee. But the Child state of the employee returns the conversation to the Parent of the manager. The conversation shown in Figure 13.7 illustrates such a communication problem. Communication has broken down, because the employee is not addressing the problem that the manager was attempting to communicate.

Crossed transactions also occur when the message sent gets an unexpected response. Note that in Figure 13.8 the manager delivers a message from the Parent ego state intended for the employee's Child state, "I never want you to interrupt me again like you did in that meeting yesterday." Instead, the employee replies from the Parent state, "Who are you to dominate the whole conversation?" The manager expected an apologetic response but instead received one that was unexpected. Here, the transaction was crossed. These types of transactions are generally unproductive and represent a breakdown in communication.

Managers should also be aware of the ego state that they themselves are speaking from. If the ego state is properly interpreted, employees will recognize and possibly change their actions. Should managers recognize that they are in one state and an employee is in a state that precludes effective communication, it may be best to postpone discussion. For instance, if the manager is in the Child state and the employee is in the Adult state, communication may be postponed. The employee who is in the Adult state is serious about work at this time and may misinterpret joking remarks.

Applying TA concepts on a broad basis may prove valuable in producing desired organizational change. As individuals in a firm learn to analyze their own social interactions, better communication and greater organizational effectiveness can occur.

FIGURE 13.8 ■■
An Unexpected Response
Results in a Crossed
Transaction

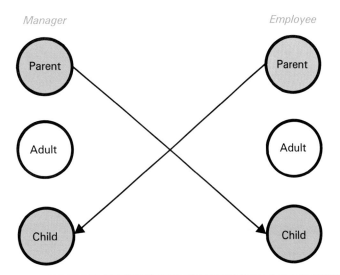

Manager: "I never want you to interrupt me again like you did in that meeting yesterday."
Employee: "Who are you to dominate the whole conversation?"

▆ THE INFLUENCING PROCESS

Effective communication has a significant impact on the manager's efforts to influence the employees' activities. *Influencing* is the process of determining or affecting the behavior of others. In earlier years, directing was the term commonly used.

When using the functional approach to the study of management, the four functions—planning, organizing, influencing, and controlling—are typically discussed. Students study each of these functions basically in the order described above. The organization of a book was neat and effective.

When dealing with a book entitled *Management and Organizational Behavior,* however, the manner in which to organize it becomes a bit fuzzy. From a functional standpoint, the natural placement of influencing would be as in the sequence above. But from an organizational behavior viewpoint, influencing topics are a major part of organizational behavior and should be included in those sections. For example, the topics of leadership, motivation, and communication are major components of influencing, but they are also important organizational behavior topics.

In the time-honored tradition of management, a compromise was reached. Influencing is presented briefly in the management process section to maintain continuity of management thought. However, the topic is placed at the end of this section, because of the relationship between communication and influencing, and as a means of introducing the next three organizational behavior sections (see Figure 13.9). Influencing—the process of determining or affecting the behavior of others—is important in the study of both management and organizational behavior and is, in fact, a composite of various organizational behavior topics.

FIGURE 13.9 ▆
Management and
Organizational Behavior

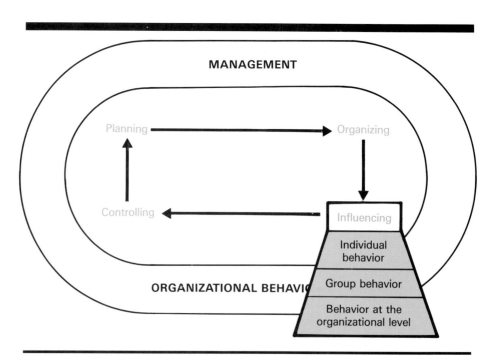

SUMMARY

Communication is the transfer of information, ideas, understanding, or feelings between people. Through communication, organizational objectives may be accomplished. The manner in which plans are to be implemented and actions coordinated is communicated to those who must accomplish the task. Each step in the sequence is critical to success.

In the communication process, a sender encodes a message into a set of symbols that the receiver will understand. Messages are transmitted through speaking, writing, acting, and drawing. The receiver decodes the message by converting the symbols into meaning. Communication is effective to the extent that the receiver's decoding matches the sender's encoding. Based on the meaning transmitted, the receiver can ignore the message, perform some task, or store the information. Through feedback, the sender knows if the message was accurately received and the proper action taken.

Communication channels, the means by which information is transmitted in organizations, may be formal or informal. Formal channels are those that are officially recognized by the organization. Instructions and information are passed downward, and information flows upward. Information also travels through informal channels, which bypass formal channels. The grapevine is an informal communication system that extends in every direction throughout an organization and even beyond it. Although it does not respect lines of authority, it does get much of its information from the formal organization. Information moves rapidly, although not as accurately. Employees generally rate the grapevine as one of the primary sources of current information.

Organizational structure influences intergroup as well as interpersonal communication. To facilitate communication, gatekeepers screen information and control access to it. Boundary spanners are information processors and representatives for organizations or its subunits to others outside the unit's boundary.

Messages flow along communication networks, such as the wheel or chain configuration. In a group, communication may be through one type of network, or the group may use variants of one or more networks. Identifying the predominant structural configuration, however, helps explain or predict the performance and satisfaction of the group and its members.

Communication breakdowns often occur when messages are not interpreted correctly. Barriers to communication may be technical, language, or psychological. Environmental barriers such as timing, information overload, and cultural differences are referred to as technical breakdowns. Language problems can result from vocabulary and semantics. A manager must understand the type of audience being addressed. When a sender sends words to which a receiver attaches different meanings than those intended by the sender, a semantic—or meaning of words—communication breakdown has occurred.

Psychological barriers tend to be the major causes of miscommunication and communication breakdown. These include various forms of distortion and problems involving interpersonal relationships. Through information filtering, for example, messages are altered through the elimination of certain data as the communication moves from person to person in the organization. Openness and trust must exist if orderly changes are to occur. Jealousy is often a barrier to communication, as is self-preoccupation and the tendency to interpret information in a certain way. Differences in past experiences, emotions, and beliefs affect each person's perception of a message.

When groups take a competitive stance, a "we-they" attitude is projected, which polarizes the interacting groups and thus establishes a communication barrier between them. Communications take on an aura of bargaining, rather than transmission of facts or problem solving. Union and management are particularly prone to this type of interaction.

Empathy, listening, reading, observation, word choice, body language, actions, and transactional analysis are all facilitators of communication. These are skills that can be learned. Body language is a nonverbal method of communication. Physical actions such as motion, gestures, and facial expressions convey thoughts and emotions. An infinite variety of body positions is available to the receiver at any one moment. The manager will find it useful to know the language of body position and to use it correctly. Transactional analysis (TA) has been used for a number of years as a technique for teaching behavioral principles to individuals and small groups in training and development programs. TA considers the three ego states of Parent, Adult, and Child in helping people understand interpersonal relations. As such, TA serves as a facilitator in communication.

REVIEW QUESTIONS

1. Define communication. Describe the basic communication process.
2. Distinguish by definition between formal and informal channels of communication. Provide examples of both types of channels of communication.
3. Distinguish among technical, language, and psychological barriers to communication.
4. Describe barriers to effective *group* communication.
5. List the factors that have the ability to improve communication.
6. Explain how empathy may be used to assist a person in becoming a better listener.
7. What is transactional analysis? How can it be used as a facilitator?

KEY TERMS

communication	grievance procedure	information filtering
source	ombudsperson	perception set
communication channels	gatekeepers	noise
formal communication channels	boundary spanners	empathy
informal communication channels	communication networks	body language
open-door policy	timing	Transactional Analysis (TA)
	information overload	

CASE STUDY

A FAILURE TO COMMUNICATE

"COULD YOU COME to my office for a minute, Bob?" asked Terry Geech, the plant manager. "Sure, be right there," said Bob Glemson. Bob was the plant's quality control director. He had been with the company for four years. After completing his degree in mechanical engineering, he worked as a production supervisor and then as maintenance manager, prior to promotion to his present job. Bob thought he knew what the call was about.

"Your letter of resignation catches me by surprise," began Terry. "I know that Wilson Products will be getting a good man, but we sure need you here, too." "I thought about it a lot," said Bob, "but there just doesn't seem to be a future for me here." "Why do you say that?" asked Terry. "Well," replied Bob, "the next position above mine is yours. With you only thirty-nine, I don't think it's likely that you'll be leaving soon."

"The fact is that I am leaving soon," said Terry. "That's why it's even more of a shock to know that you are resigning. I think I'll be moving to the corporate offices in June of next year. Besides, the company has several plants that are larger than this one. We need good people in those plants from time to time, both in quality control and in general management."

"Well, I heard about an opening in the Cincinnati plant last year," said Bob, "but by the time I checked, the job had already been filled. We never know about job opportunities in the other plants until we read about them in the company paper."

"All this is beside the point now. What would it take to get you to change your mind?" asked Terry. "I don't think I can change my mind now," replied Bob. "I've already signed a contract with Wilson."

QUESTIONS
1. Evaluate the communication system at this company.
2. What actions might have prevented Bob's resignation?

CASE STUDY

OPEN THE DOOR!

BARNEY CLINE, THE NEW human resource manager for Ampex Utilities, was just getting settled in his new office. He had recently moved from another firm to take over his new job. Barney had been selected over several in-house candidates and numerous other applicants because of his record for getting things done. He had a good reputation for working through people to get the job accomplished.

Just then his phone rang. The person on the other end of the line said, "Mr. Cline, could I set up an appointment to talk with you?" "Certainly," Barney said, "when do you want to get together?" "How about after work? It might be bad if certain people saw me speaking to anyone in management."

Barney was a bit puzzled, but he set up an appointment for 5:30 P.M., when nearly everyone would be gone. At the designated time there was a knock on his door; it was Mark Johnson, a senior maintenance worker who had been with the firm for more than ten years.

After the initial welcome, Mark began by saying, "Mr. Cline, several of the workers asked me to talk to you. The grapevine has it that you're a fair person. The company says it has an open-door policy. We're afraid to use it. Roy Edwards, one of the best maintenance men in our section, tried it several months ago. They hassled him so much that he quit only last week. We just don't know what to do to get any problems settled. There have been talks of organizing a union. We really don't want that, but something has to give."

Barney thanked Mark for his honesty and promised not to reveal the conversation. In the weeks following the conversation with Mark, Barney was able to verify that the situation existed as Mark had described it. There was considerable mistrust between managers and the operative employees.

QUESTIONS

1. What types of communication breakdowns had occurred in the case?
2. Discuss the impact of the grapevine on resolution of this case.

EXPERIENTIAL EXERCISE

Chuck Rader is the new supervisor of the Accounting/Finance department and wants to make some major changes. He thinks, "I am fed up with the grapevine, and it must be eliminated. I am tired of the leaks of information, because they are very damaging to the company. The former supervisor could not handle his people and put a stop to all these rumors, but I can. The primary cause of the problem is the accounting coordinator. She has been with the company for eighteen years, knows everybody, and she is always giving out information without authorization. If I want someone to know something, I'll let them know when the time is appropriate and not before. That goes for all my people, if they can't keep quiet they don't belong here. This is going to stop and it will stop today, whether she likes it or not."

Lorie Blalock, the accounting coordinator, is totally convinced that everything said to others will help them get their jobs done, or assist them in understanding the nature of changes. The department has always been fairly effective even with these leaks of information. Lorie has been with the company longer than the newly appointed supervisor, and has always performed well. In fact, she has served to facilitate the accomplishment of some projects in the past. She has connections and a good performance record.

When the supervisor and the accounting coordinator get together the result will be, at the very least, interesting, and at the very worst, volatile. Either way, it should be a learning experience. If you want to stop it, or spread it, there is a place for you here. This exercise requires only two to actively participate. One of you will play the forceful supervisor and the other will play the aggressive accounting coordinator. Volunteer for your preference now. The rest of the class observe carefully. Additional information necessary to perform your roles will be provided by the instructor.

NOTES

1. Lewis E. Albright, "Staffing Policies and Strategies," in *ASPA Handbook of Personnel and Industrial Relations*, ed. Dale Yoder and Herbert G. Heneman (Washington, D.C.: Bureau of National Affairs, 1974): 4–21.
2. John Rossant and Wendy Zeller, "How Chrysler's $30,000 Sports Car Got Sideswiped," *Business Week*, 23 January 1989, 68, 73.
3. M. L. Fahs, "Communication Strategies for Anticipating and Managing Conflict," *Personnel Administrator* (October 1982): 28–34.
4. R. Foltz and R. D'Aprix, "Survey Shows Communication Problems," *Personnel Administrator* (February 1983): 8.
5. Christy Marshall, "Rubbermaid, Yes Plastic," *Business Week*, December 1988, 37.
6. Thomas J. Murry, "Wal-Mart Stores Penny Wise," *Business Month*, December 1988, 42.
7. Michael Brody, "Listen to Your Whistleblower," *Fortune*, 24 November 1986, 77–78.
8. Foltz and D'Aprix, "Survey," 8.
9. J. P. Barnard, "The Principal Players in Your Organization's Information System," *Supervisory Management* 28 (June 1983): 21–24.

10. H. Mintzberg, *The Structuring of Organizations* (Englewood Cliffs, N.J.: Prentice-Hall, 1978).

11. R. Katz and M. L. Tushman, "A Longitudinal Study of the Effects of Boundary Spanning Supervision on Turnover and Promotion in Research and Development," *Academy of Management Journal* 26 (1983): 437–456.

12. G. Strauss, "Tactics of Lateral Relationship: The Purchasing Agent," *Administrative Science Quarterly* 8 (1962–1963): 161–186.

13. T. J. Allen and S. I. Cohen, "Information Flow in Research and Development Laboratories," *Administrative Science Quarterly* 14 (1969): 12–19; Strauss, "Tactics of Lateral Relationships," 161–186.

14. Katz and Tushman, "Boundary Spanning Supervision," 437–456.

15. H. Aldrich and D. Herker, "Boundary Spanning Roles and Organization Structure," *Academy of Management Review* 2 (1977): 217–230.

16. M. Tushman and D. Nadler, "Communication and Technical Roles in R&D Laboratories," in *Management of Research and Innovation,* ed. B. Dean and J. Goldhar (North Holland, N.Y.: TIMS, 1980), 91–111.

17. E. B. Roberts and A. R. Fusfeld, "Critical Functions: Needed Roles in the Innovation Process," in *Career Issues in Human Resource Management,* ed. R. Katz (Englewood Cliffs, N.J.: Prentice-Hall, 1982), 182–207.

18. Katz and Tushman, "Boundary Spanning Supervision," 437–456.

19. M. L. Tushman and T. J. Scanlan, "Characteristics and External Orientations of Boundary Spanning Individuals," *Academy of Management Journal* 24 (1981): 83–98.

20. Tushman and Scanlan, "Boundary Spanning Individuals," 83–98.

21. "Trust: The New Ingredient in Management," *Business Week,* 6 July 1981, 104.

22. D. W. Johnson and F. P. Johnson, *Joining Together: Group Theory and Group Skills* (Englewood Cliffs, N.J.: Prentice-Hall, 1975).

23. Carl R. Rogers and F. J. Roethlisberger, "Barriers and Gateways to Communication," *Harvard Business Review* 30 (July–August 1952): 48.

24. Murray Mizock, "What You Aren't Saying May Be Everything," *Data Management* (September 1986): 33.

25. L. R. Cohen, "Minimizing Communication Breakdown Between Male and Female Managers," *Personnel Administrator* (October 1982): 57–58.

26. For an expanded coverage of transactional analysis, see Thomas A. Harris, *I'm O.K.—You're O.K.* (New York: Harper & Row, 1969).

REFERENCES

Atchison, Sandra D. "These Top Executives Work Where They Play." *Business Week* (27 October 1986): 132, 134.

Brody, Michael. "Listen to Your Whistleblower." *Fortune* (24 November 1986): 77–78.

Brush, J. M., and D. P. Brush. "Companies Tune In to Video." *Management World* (January 1984): 25.

Calise, P. F., and M. Locke. "Office Automation: Who's in Control?" *Management World* (March 1984): 17.

Caruth, Don. "Words: A Supervisor's Guide to Communications." *Management Solutions* 31 (June 1986): 34–35.

Donath, Bob. "Corporate Communications." *Industrial Marketing* 65 (July 1980): 52–53.

Earley, P. Christopher. "Trust, Perceived Importance of Praise and Criticism and Work Performance: An Examination of Feedback in the United States and England." *Journal of Management* 12 (Winter 1986): 457–473.

Ewing, David W., and Pamela M. Banks. "Listening and Responding to Employees' Concerns." *Harvard Business Review* 58 (January–February 1980): 101–114.

Foltz, Roy G. "Internal Communications, Give Them Facts." *Public Relations Journal* 36 (October 1980): 25.

Gildea, Joyce A., and Myron Emanuel. "Internal Communications: The Impact on Productivity." *Public Relations Journal* 36 (February 1980): 8–12.

Graham, L. G. A. "Audiographics for Sound Teleconferencing." *Computer World* (28 September 1983): 63.

Isenberg, Daniel J. "Thinking and Managing: A Verbal Protocol Analysis of Managerial Problem Solving." *Academy of Management Journal* 29 (December 1986): 775–788.

Keller, John J. "The Rewiring of America." *Business Week* (15 September 1986): 188–196.

Kikoski, John F. "Communication: Understanding It, Improving It." *Personnel Journal* 59 (February 1980): 126.

Laing, G. J. "Communication and Its Constraints on the Structure of Organizations." *Omega* 8 (1980): 287–301.

McKenzie, C. L., and C. J. Qazi. "Communication Barriers in the Workplace." *Business Horizons* 26 (March–April 1983): 70–72.

March, James G., and Martha S. Feldman. "Information in Organizations as Signal and Symbol." *Administrative Science Quarterly* 26 (June 1981): 171–186.

Mizock, Murray. "What You Aren't Saying May Be Everything." *Data Management* (September 1986): 33.

Moorhead, Gregory, and John R. Montanari. "An Empirical Investigation of the Groupthink Phenomenon." *Human Relations* 30 (May 1988): 300–311.

Morley, Donald Dean, and Pamela Schockley-Zalabak. "Conflict Avoiders and Compromisers: Toward an Understanding of Their Organizational Communication Style." *Group & Organization Studies* 11 (December 1986): 387–402.

Nelton, Sharon. "Beyond Body Language." *Nation's Business* 74 (June 1986): 73–74.

Targowski, Andrew S. "The Management Wheels: A Technique of Applying Management Philosophies." *Data Management* 25 (October 1987): 12–14.

Tavernier, Gerard. "Improving Managerial Productivity: The Key Ingredient Is One-on-One Communication." *Management Review* 70 (February 1981): 13–16.

CHAPTER

14

Chapter Outline

Understanding Perception, Attribution, and Learning

Learning Objectives

After completing this chapter students should be able to

1. Describe the perception process and explain perceptual distortions.
2. Explain the attribution process and describe attributional biases.
3. Describe the learning process.

THE LAST BATTLE was almost over between the union official, known as Little Napoleon, and the company chairman, called the Colonel. The pre-dawn standoff between these two individuals was the final attempt to save Eastern Airlines. Although the struggle involved billions of dollars, huge debts, and labor strife, it was to a large degree because of intensely personal alliances that the dramatic corporate conflict reached its climax.

Basically, Eastern decided to stick with Colonel Frank Borman and not give in to machinist union head Charles Bryan, who was called "Little Napoleon." The conflict between the Colonel and Little Napoleon came down to the union official wanting Borman's head and the Colonel standing firm in his demand for union concessions. When the lines for the last battle were drawn, Bryan would not negotiate while Borman was in charge, and Borman's friends and associates on the Eastern board would not let Borman take the fall.

Eventually, the fifty-eight-year-old company, the nation's third largest airline, was sold to Texas Air Corporation, not so much as a result of Eastern management being foiled by labor, but in many ways because of the conflict between these two men. Once these two men had been allies in rebuilding Eastern, but now they were enemies, defending their respective institutions until the sale papers were finalized and Texas Air had won.

Bryan at one time had great respect for Borman and once called him the "Christopher Columbus of our time in history." Although the two battled fiercely over the years, in 1983 they struck an historic agreement, cited as one of corporate America's greatest success stories. The union, in exchange for a 20-percent wage giveback, won a 25-percent stake in the company and four seats on the board. Bryan's negotiation strategy was that for every union concession there had to be a gain.

According to Professor John Simmons of the University of Massachusetts at Amherst, "For a time, there was an amazing sense among employees that 'we are the airline, we are building a better company.' But the problem was, after labor came on the board, Borman never worked with them like they were part of the company. It was like having four new vice-presidents in your office, but you never take them out for beer."

Borman viewed the situation quite differently, however. According to Borman, "In retrospect, maybe I was a little naive in thinking that labor could accept the role of working in a competitive marketplace."

Having Bryan and Borman in the boardroom sets the stage for what would end with the purchase of Eastern by Texas Air. The board wanted to cut labor costs to cope with deregulation and the arrival of discount airlines. Union leaders on the board argued against labor cuts and decried autocratic management.

It soon became evident that Eastern could not compete with the discounters. Where People Express paid 20 percent for labor costs, Eastern paid 37 percent. Where People Express had gas-guzzling planes during an oil price plunge, Eastern had fuel-efficient planes that cost 10 times as much. Eastern's 60 lenders precipitated the crisis by demanding that Eastern get wage concessions by week's end or they would call in the airline's $2.5 billion debt.

Bryan said Borman made many mistakes in enacting fare wars at the wrong time and in not flying as many flights as possible. Borman said the most recent problems began when United cut fares last summer. Board member

Julian Scheer, a close personal friend of Borman, summed up his assessment of the situation as follows: "We knew that, absent the ability to get wage concessions, the losses in 1986 would have been so horrendous the airlines would not survive."

Borman told the board he had an offer from Texas Air. He said the airline would have to be sold unless Bryan agreed to a 20-percent wage concession. Borman told Bryan that management and labor could work together. But Bryan believed that thus far Borman's deeds had not matched his words.

When Borman shoved the microphone in Bryan's face and asked him if he was going to cooperate, the stunned Bryan just sat there and didn't say anything. According to board member John T. Fallon, "this was a very impressionable move, and after Bryan said nothing, Frank said to him, 'Well, you just destroyed this airline.'" According to Bryan, he then responded, "And I'll say you did it, so where does that get us?"

Outside the boardroom, some of Bryan's aides approached Borman's aides. Bryan's group offered a 15-percent wage giveback on the condition that Borman quit. It was classic Bryan: If you must give something away, get something from management they don't want to give. Fallon said the offer was never officially given to the board, although board members said they were aware of it. Borman said in the interview, "I heard that was going around the boardroom halls."

Borman left the boardroom and went to his office. The board was set to decide his fate. Borman said the board knew he had a standing offer to resign and, "I didn't want to influence their decision." With Borman gone, there were some last angry words. Said Scheer, "I turned to Charlie Bryan and said, 'Do you realize what you are doing? I just want to hear it from your own lips.' He said, 'I have not changed my position.'"

Fallon, chairman of R.M. Bradley and Company, a Boston-based real estate firm, took over the meeting. He made a last appeal to Bryan, then asked for a silent prayer. There was no turning back on either side. The board voted to sell Eastern to Texas Air.

Borman's extraordinarily close ties with his board made the difference. Borman had recommended longtime friends and associates for many of the board memberships, with the notable exception of the four union representatives. It was no coincidence that the vote to back Borman was 15–4, with the union affiliates in opposition.

Frank Borman and Charles Bryan disagreed about their respective roles as well as the causes of Eastern's situation and the necessity of selling the company. Why did their perceptions differ? Why did they perceive different causes for the airline's financial situation? What happened when the two men tried to talk about the situation and determine who was to blame for it? How did their previous experiences—their learned behaviors and attitudes—influence the events described here? ■

Q UESTIONS SUCH AS THESE are fundamental, because they deal with the description of events and the reasons given for the events. As the Eastern example suggests, different observers of an incident may describe and diagnose it very differently.

In this chapter, areas of organizational behavior are explored that deal with the way individuals perceive—and thus describe—events and other people. An attempt will also be made to show how individuals understand, and thus diagnose and analyze, events and people. The chapter also focuses on the way past experiences influence description and understanding. Because they deal with people, perception, attribution, and learning will be explained with a greater utilization of the Eastern story.

▪▪ THE PERCEPTION PROCESS

This discussion begins with the situation at Eastern Airlines. First, a review of the final board meeting seems appropriate, along with the decision to sell, as seen from several different perspectives. Think of yourself as Frank Borman. What do you notice? From his position, which features of the situation stand out? What thoughts come to mind? Now think of yourself as Charles Bryan. What do the events feel like? What features of the events do you notice? What thoughts come to mind? Finally, think of yourself as a member of the board. What is the setting in which you are hearing about the situation? Which features of the situation stand out? What thoughts come to mind?

When individuals put themselves in these different positions, they probably notice different features of the situation. They will think about the meeting of the board and the decision to sell in different ways. Objectively, this situation is a single event. However, when playing the role of different observers of the event, a single individual's perception of the event will vary.

Perception is the understanding or view people have of things in the world around them.[1] Different individuals may have totally different views of a group, such as organized labor, which influence their business decisions differently. For example, Frank Lorenzo, chairman of Texas Air Corporation, views labor as the enemy and therefore handles labor with an *iron hand*. According to one company veteran, Lorenzo uses "subtle intimidation" when dealing with labor. According to others, demanding pay cuts from Eastern's three unions and threatening to transfer Eastern's jobs to Continental's non-union work force are acts of extreme intimidation.[2] On the other hand, AT&T views labor as more of a business partner. Currently, AT&T management prefers common interest forums between local union officials and division managers, instead of traditional adversarial relationships. AT&T has tried both confrontation and cooperation and found that cooperation is better.[3] Lorenzo's perception of organized labor is quite different from that of AT&T management, and therefore the actions of Lorenzo and AT&T management, in regard to organized labor, will also likely differ. Perception can significantly influence business actions.

As the introductory case illustrates, different people are likely to have somewhat different, and sometimes contradictory, views or understandings of even the same event or person. Rarely do different observers describe events or persons in exactly the same way. For this reason, presenting a clear, well-documented description of a situation is the first step in understanding behavior. Because a person's perceptions have a strong impact on that individual's descriptions, analysis of events, and subsequent behavior, it is important to examine the perceptual process and some of the factors that affect it. Basically, the perceptual process takes place in two stages, as seen in Figure 14.1. The first is *selection;* the second is *organization.*[4]

Perception
The understanding or view people have of things in the world around them.

FIGURE 14.1 ■
The Perceptual Process

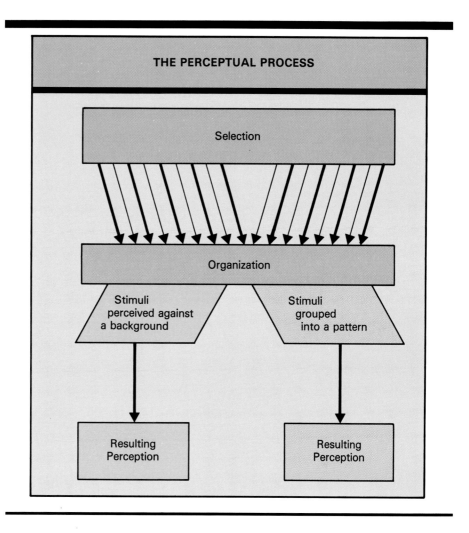

Selection

Selection
Identifying certain features
of an event to notice.

Identifying certain features of an event to notice is referred to as **selection.** In the situation at Eastern Airlines, the workers, managers, top executives, union officials, and board members of the company *select* certain features of the event to notice. Quite possibly because of their different concerns, perspectives, and vantage points, the features they select to notice would be quite different. For example, Bryan focused on the poor timing of fare cuts, while Borman focused on wage concessions.

Individuals are continually faced by a mélange of sounds and sights. In a situation, so many stimuli bombard the individuals concerned that they find it difficult to take full account of all of them. Consider the board meeting at Eastern. There, one might observe several members preoccupied with the written documentation of the situation. Others might be seen talking loudly among themselves.

Borman's confrontation with Bryan might also be noticed, or Bryan's silent response to Borman's question.

Individuals tend to select and attend to only some of the features that are present in any situation. Attention is paid to the actions and conversations of only certain workers. Or attention is paid to only some of the characteristics of a worker. A manager might be alert to a worker's experience with a particular piece of machinery or the worker's age or sex. This selection process helps people avoid dealing with information that seems to them to be irrelevant. Further, by focusing on the most relevant information, it helps them avoid information overload. Unfortunately, in some cases, selection also causes individuals to overlook important stimuli.

CHARACTERISTICS OF THE STIMULI

Certain characteristics of the stimuli themselves influence what stimuli individuals select. Stimuli tend to be selected that are larger, more intense, in motion, repetitive, either novel or very familiar, or in contrast to their background.[5] Stimuli are often overlooked that are small, less intense, stationary, or that blend in with the background.

Consider, for example, an error in bookkeeping. A manager is more likely to see a large error than a small one. An accountant will probably notice the small errors. Consider next a salesperson's response to a ringing telephone, a relatively intense stimulus. A salesperson frequently answers a phone before helping a customer waiting in person, because that customer—unless very vocal or demanding—offers a less intense stimulus. Now consider two workers who come to work late. One worker has been late three times already during the week, while the second has not been late for two months. Whose tardiness will the manager likely notice? It might be suggested that the manager would notice the first worker's tardiness because of the repetitiveness of the stimulus (tardy behavior). Alternatively, the manager might notice the second worker's tardiness because it is a novel stimulus. Think about the student who constantly asks the professor for extensions on assignments. Now compare that student to one who has asked for an extension only once. Which student will the professor most likely question? The novelty of the second student's request causes the professor to focus on it. In another work situation, employees may not hear (or select) the voice of a supervisor who continually complains about the quality of their work, because the voice may lack sufficient intensity, novelty, or contrast. Finally, consider the bank teller who wears flamboyant clothes, rather than the more conservative dress usually worn by bank employees. A manager may be more likely to focus on this worker's behavior than on other workers' actions, because the teller contrasts with the background of the bank.

In the case of the decision to sell Eastern, which characteristics of the stimuli attracted the attention of the various board members? John Fallon may have noted Borman's putting the mike up to Charlie Bryan's face, because the action was intense and in motion. He may have noted Bryan's lack of response, possibly because it contrasted with the background and was new and novel.

CHARACTERISTICS OF SELECTORS

Stimuli are also selected according to the internal state of the selector. Such states evolve from the individual's experiences,[6] motivation, and personality.[7] Figure 14.2 illustrates the role learning plays in our perceptions. Parts (a) and (b) are optical illusions. In parts (c), (d), (e), and (f), lengths that look different are in fact, identical. In (g), all three men are the same height.

In organizations, an employee's tardiness might be seen, for example, in terms of the manager's own education or experience in viewing key events—as a function of the manager's social class, educational background, or job history.

FIGURE 14.2 ■
Influence of Learning
on Perception

Source: (c) E. P. Johnson, *Student's Manual to Accompany Psychology,* 2d ed. Boston: Houghton Mifflin, 1951; (g) F. Luthans, *Organizational Behavior,* 4th ed. New York: McGraw-Hill, 1985, 166. Reproduced by permission.

PINNACLE

**The Perceptions of Dr. Armand Hammer,
One of the World's Preeminent Capitalists**

PERCEPTION IS THE UNDERSTANDING or view people have of things in the world around them. Different individuals may have totally different views of the same group, such as leaders of major countries throughout the world, which influence their business decisions. Dr. Armand Hammer, Chairman of Occidental Petroleum, wakes up every day with an unusual perception of reality. He really views each day as a real challenge. His perceptions of the world has made Dr. Hammer one of the world's preeminent capitalists. Dr. Hammer has had a front-row seat on history during most of the twentieth century, at times taking an active, sometimes controversial role in shaping history itself. Since 1921, when he went to Russia to fight the spread of Tifus and reportedly collected money owed his family, Hammer maintained an extraordinary relationship with Soviet leaders from Lenin to Gorbachev. Dr. Hammer's two goals are to find a cure for cancer and bring peace to this troubled world. CNN correspondent Tom Cassidy discusses these and other issues with Dr. Armand Hammer.

The situation might also be seen in terms of the person's own physiological requirements for sleep. Or it might be seen in terms of the individual's personality, aggressiveness, enthusiasm, or introversion. Similarly, an advertisement for a new restaurant may be seen one way if a person has experience with that type of restaurant. It might be seen differently if a need for food is the motivation, rather than a need for security or a need for self-esteem. Or, a person with an extroverted personality might shake the hand of a person who extends a hand, whereas a person with an introverted personality might not "see" the proffered hand. A person with an extroverted personality might not "hear" a supervisor's raised voice, whereas a person with an introverted personality might focus immediately on that stimulus.

Think of Eastern's situation. Which stimuli did Borman select? Why did he select them? Why, for example, did he focus on labor's refusal to give wage concessions? Why did he choose to hear the rumors of Bryan's deal if he resigned? Which stimuli did Bryan select? Why did he select them? Both men were likely influenced by their learning processes, motivation, and personality in selecting the stimuli to see and hear. Their different experiences, needs, and personalities might have resulted in their different perceptions of the situation.

Organization

Once stimuli have been selected, individuals categorize and organize them so that the new material makes sense. If possible, the new stimuli are made to fit in with how people already understand and know the world. For example, if a manager sees current employees as being lazy, this individual will likely see new employees as lazy, too. Disconfirming evidence will rarely be noticed.

Stimuli are organized in two basic ways. First, stimuli are perceived as figures standing against a background. A plant supervisor sees, for example, assembly-line workers against a background of the plant's equipment, or the actions of one worker against that of the entire group of workers. The distinctions made between figure and background will influence which attitudes and behaviors the supervisor ultimately chooses to focus on.

Such distinctions influence performance evaluations in particular. The uniqueness of the subject being rated is significant. If someone is being interviewed for a job, the people whose interviews immediately precede will affect the way the interviewer will perceive that person. The previous interviews act as a background against which the current interviewee is assessed. In one study, interviewees who had average qualifications were judged differently, depending on whether the preceding person had very high or very low qualifications.[8] As might be expected, the average interviewees were rated much more highly when they followed a person with low qualifications, because their "better" features stood out against the background of the lower-qualified person. When the average interviewees followed people with high qualifications, their "worse" features were noted, so they were rated poorly.

Another study determined the effects of the proportion of noncompliant clerical workers on supervisors' ratings of compliant clerical workers.[9] As in the study above, contrasts made a difference. The greater the proportion of noncompliant workers, the more favorably the supervisors judged the compliant workers, and the more they gave them pay raises and recommended them for promotion.

Closure

The tendency to form a complete mental image out of incomplete data among related stimuli.

In addition to perceiving figures against a background, individuals group discrete stimuli into a pattern.[10] For example, individuals try to create **closure,** which is the tendency to form a complete mental image out of incomplete data among related stimuli.[11] Figure 14.3 illustrates closure for physical stimuli. Notice that you tend to complete the square and ignore the duplication of words in the three sayings. How does this principle apply to behavior in organizations? The supervisor who has thirty subordinates has a complete mental picture of each worker, generally based on just a few details.

Grouping of stimuli occurs when they are similar, are near other stimuli, form a continuous pattern, or create a completed pattern. For example, a vice-president in an insurance firm may have difficulty distinguishing between the performance of two actuaries who have adjacent offices. A headmaster in a high school may mentally group all tardy students and have difficulty differentiating

FIGURE 14.3 ■
Closure for Physical
Stimuli

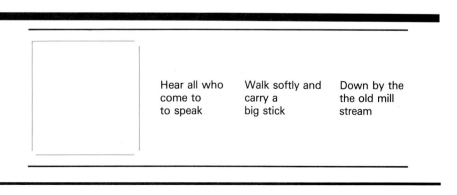

| Hear all who come to to speak | Walk softly and carry a big stick | Down by the the old mill stream |

among them, regardless of the legitimacy of their tardiness. Grouping of stimuli underlies their interpretation and contributes to the distortions of perceptions described in the next section.

■ PERCEPTUAL DISTORTIONS

In reality, both selection and organization generally suffer from inaccuracies or distortions. These distortions include (1) stereotyping, (2) halo effect, (3) projection, and (4) expectancy.

Stereotyping

Stereotyping
The situation when an individual attributes behaviors or attitudes to a person on the basis of the group or category to which that person belongs.

Stereotyping is the situation when an individual attributes behaviors or attitudes to a person on the basis of the group or category to which that person belongs. "Blondes have more fun" and "All managers are smart" illustrate stereotyping.

Stereotyping often occurs with ethnic groups, women, managers, white-collar workers, and blue-collar workers. A common stereotype is that the average Japanese factory worker is dedicated to quality, whereas the average American worker is sloppy, and unconcerned with quality.[12] What stereotypes do you think existed at Eastern Airlines? Borman says, "In retrospect maybe I was a little naive in thinking that labor could accept the role of working in a competitive workplace," stereotyping labor as uncooperative and inflexible. Bryan earlier called Borman "the Christopher Columbus of our time"—a more positive stereotype.

Stereotyping often occurs because individuals do not gather sufficient data about others to describe their behaviors or attitudes accurately. They may look for shortcut ways of describing certain phenomena without spending the time to completely analyze them. Alternatively, some individuals have personal biases

Women and minorities in the work place can be stereotyped by having certain behaviors or attitudes attributed to them. (COMSTOCK, Inc.)

against certain groups of individuals. Using stereotypes reduces the accuracy of our perceptions about these groups. Even when overwhelming disconfirming evidence should cause the perceiver to admit that a person or thing does not conform to the stereotype, the perceiver often maintains the stereotype and views the exception as an anomaly.[13]

There are ways that can be used to reduce stereotyping in organizations. First, individuals must gather sufficient information about other people's behavior and attitudes to encourage objective perceptions. Second, they must check the conclusions they draw to ensure their validity. Third, they must differentiate between facts and assumptions in determining the basis of their perceptions.

Halo Effect

Halo effect
Refers to an individual's using a general impression of a person to evaluate that individual's specific behaviors or attitudes.

The **halo effect** refers to an individual's using a general impression of a person to evaluate that individual's specific behaviors or attitudes. Working overtime, for example, can lead to a person being evaluated as highly cooperative. A neat personal appearance can cause a person to be judged as precise in his or her work. A talkative person may be judged less responsible than a quieter, seemingly pensive individual.

The halo effect frequently affects assessments of employee performance. Research suggests, for example, that such assessments are highly influenced by the quality of recent behavior—either good or bad—rather than by the behavior throughout the rating period.[14] A particularly outstanding report completed just prior to a performance evaluation may result in a highly positive appraisal for the entire preceding period. For this reason, supervisors must seek accurate and complete descriptions of employee behavior. Other research suggests that a supervisor who has information suggesting identical performance by two female subordinates will give them different evaluations according to their attractiveness.[15] Attractiveness increased the performance evaluations, pay raises, and promotions of women in nonmanagerial positions, but decreased these same outcomes for women in managerial positions. No differences occurred in the evaluations or compensation of men. In addition, some raters tend to be consistently lenient, consistently strict, or consistently in the middle, in evaluating workers. These raters do not make *individual* evaluations.

There are means by which the halo effect can be reduced. Those who gather complete data about an individual generally reduce their reliance on the halo effect for assessing behavior. In addition, distinguishing among various aspects of an individual's behavior, rather than grouping even superficially related aspects, should reduce the impact of the halo effect. Managers must separate appearance from performance, productivity from attendance, and personality from creativity. Finally, recognizing the proven correlates of performance should decrease an individual's use of the halo effect, rather than assuming unsupported correlates, such as the relationship between personal appearance and precision or speaking ability and responsibility.

Projection

Projection
An emotional biasing of perceptions.

Projection involves an emotional biasing of perceptions. Fear, hatred, love, or distrust can influence an individual's perceptions. Older workers who fear that

ETHICAL DILEMMA

Y̶OU ARE ONE of the managers for the Orlando, Florida-based company which operates 11 upscale mobile-home parks owned by Clayton, Williams & Sherwood, Inc. These parks maintain high quality by strictly enforcing rules. You hike rents to support the parks' facilities and services. A group of residents on fixed incomes say they cannot pay and will be made homeless if rents rise. You can either make exceptions to the rent increase for those who cannot pay, or you can enforce the rules and make everyone pay.
What would you do?

Source: Adapted by permission, *Nation's Business,* August 1987. Copyright © 1987, U.S. Chamber of Commerce.

their skills are becoming obsolete may translate this fear into a dislike or distrust of younger workers. This in turn may be reflected in their perceptions of the attitudes and behaviors of the younger workers. They may state that the new recruits do not like the experienced employees, for example. Thus, projection has decreased perceptual accuracy.

Have you ever heard someone say, "My boss is prejudiced." "The boss doesn't like women." "The boss doesn't like black workers." "The boss doesn't trust people over forty"? These observations about the boss may be accurate, or they may instead reflect the worker's prejudices. The speaker, rather than the boss, may not like women, black workers, or workers over forty. Projection refers to individuals attributing their own attitudes to another person. Individuals use projection as a defense mechanism, to transfer blame to another person, or as protection from their own unacceptable feelings. In business, individuals frequently attribute their own prejudices against minorities, managers, and employees to the other party.

Projection frequently occurs in union-management relations. Each side attributes feelings of mistrust (its own) to the other side. Management might state that the union mistrusts them, when, in fact, it is management that mistrusts the union. They project their own feelings onto the other group, representing them to others as the feelings of the other group. This projection was obvious in Bryan and Borman.

Examples of projection are numerous. In order to reduce or eliminate projection, a person must first identify his or her true feelings. Once true feelings are recognized, the person must repeatedly assess whether and how they are influencing the person's perceptions of others. Further, in situations where projection is common, such as in union-management relations, managers must carefully evaluate the accuracy of their perceptions.

Expectancy

Expectancy
When participants anticipate certain behaviors from other participants.

When participants anticipate certain behaviors from other participants it is referred to as **expectancy.** They may expect workers to be lazy, bossy, or tardy. These expectations may be associated with the participants' anticipating certain types of behavior from different groups of workers (stereotyping), from workers who demonstrate specific or bad behavior (halo effect), or from workers onto whom they project their own attitudes (projection). Thus, expectancy is also a type of perceptual distortion and underlies the other three types.

Assume that a market research supervisor has two subordinates. The first subordinate has demonstrated great creativity and productivity in the advertising campaigns she has developed. The second subordinate follows the directions given by the manager to the letter, but she has demonstrated neither initiative nor enthusiasm for special projects. The supervisor just found an innovative marketing plan on his desk. Which subordinate will likely be congratulated for the excellent work? If expectancy is operating, the supervisor would likely approach the first subordinate, who had demonstrated creativity in the past. This evaluation could be incorrect. Of course, either subordinate could have developed the plan. Expectations influence and bias perceptions of others, reducing the accuracy of the perceptions. Expectations of managers have been shown to influence even the performance of subordinates.

How did Frank Borman expect Charles Bryan to behave? How did Bryan expect the board to behave? To reduce the distortions that result from expectancy, individuals must carefully test the assumptions they make about behavior in organizational situations.

■■■ THE ATTRIBUTION PROCESS

Attribution
Determining the cause of a situation.

But is it sufficient to merely describe different events or people? For example, would the stockholders or employees of Eastern Airlines be content with a simple description of the decision to sell? Most likely they would move to the next step, determining the cause of the situation. Determining the cause of a situation is referred to as **attribution.** In reading the case, most would likely try to determine the cause (or causes) for the decision to sell.

The need to determine why events occur is a common one. Many people, whether consciously or not, ponder the reasons for many events and then decide *why* the events occurred. In this way, individuals *attribute causes* to the events. Individuals move from *description to diagnosis*. As might be expected, different people often attribute different causes to the same event. In this book, a wide range of explanations are presented for various phenomena so that individuals can attribute causes as accurately and *completely* as possible.

Think again of the sale of Eastern Airlines. How do Borman and Bryan explain the sale? Borman attributes it to excessive union demands. Bryan cites larger equipment purchases, and Borman's unwillingness to resign. Why do these men differ?

Theoretical Antecedents

Kurt Lewin defined behavior as being a function of both an individual's personality and the environment.[16] He suggested that any time a person acts, the action probably results from both the person's personal characteristics and situational influences. It is inaccurate to assume that behavior results from just one of the two causes. Frank Lorenzo, chairman of Texas Air Corporation, appears to be an individual who personally believes that business managers should have the ability to do whatever they want with the company they oversee. This belief, combined with the extremely competitive nature of the airline industry, probably resulted in Lorenzo's firm actions with labor.[17] When individuals try to understand reasons for behavior, however, they often ignore one of these types of causes—personal or situational. There is a tendency to overestimate the influence of either a person's personality characteristics or environmental influences and to typically discount the other factor. Thus, in the Eastern example, people who blame Bryan likely discount the fare structure and Borman's management decisions as possible causes. People who blame Borman likely discount labor's refusal to offer concessions. Study of the behavioral theories in this text should in part increase the accuracy of the attributions we make, and improve the understanding of organizational phenomena.

The Steps in Attribution

Attribution theorists and researchers study the process of determining the causes of specific events, the responsibility for particular outcomes, or the personal qualities of individuals participating in a situation.[18] They also study the process by which individuals come to attribute people's behavior primarily to either their personality or situational causes.[19] One researcher has suggested that this process occurs in three stages: A person (1) observes another person's behavior; (2) determines whether the behavior was intended; and (3) assigns a reason for the behavior.[20] More specifically, the process takes place as follows (see Figure 14.4):

Stage 1. First, individuals observe or are told about some action. Consider the sale of Eastern Airlines, for example. People are told that Borman and the board voted to sell the company to Texas Air.

Stage 2. Second, a determination is made on whether the observed behavior was intended or accidental. Did the sale occur on purpose, or did it just happen by accident? By answering this question, a first-level determination is made of the cause of the behavior.

If it is assumed that the sale occurred accidentally, no attempt is made to determine its causes. It is attributed to fate, luck, accident, or a similar uncontrollable phenomenon. If, however, it is assumed that the sale was intended, that the board chose to sell Eastern to Texas Air, progression moves to stage 3.

Stage 3. Third, questions arise as to whether situational causes or personal characteristics explain the person's behavior. For example, was competition in the industry the main impetus for the sale? If price wars were believed to be the key, Borman's and the board's vote to sell would be attributed to situational factors. Or, it might be suspected that the banks insisted on the sale. In this case Borman's and the board's behavior would also be attributed to situational factors. On the other hand, if people believed that Borman's personality influenced his decision to sell, that his past management actions and refusal to resign were factors, or that his conflict with Bryan was a major cause, then they would more likely conclude that personal dispositions motivated the sale. A similar analysis can be made for Charles Bryan's refusal to give wage concessions.

Although *both* situational *and* personal factors may influence an event, most of us generally try to simplify our understanding of the event and so attend

FIGURE 14.4 ■■
The Attribution Process

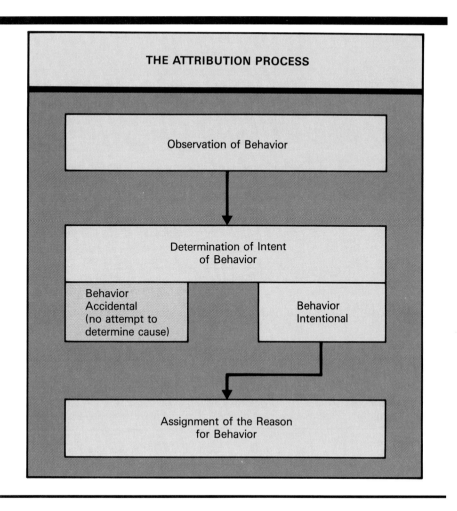

THE ATTRIBUTION PROCESS

Observation of Behavior

Determination of Intent
of Behavior

Behavior
Accidental
(no attempt to
determine cause)

Behavior
Intentional

Assignment of the Reason
for Behavior

primarily to only one type of cause or the other, rather than to both. Recognizing this tendency to simplify our understanding, and the resulting inaccurate attributions, this book encourages students to systematically apply a series of behavior perspectives to understanding a situation and attributing causes to it.

■■ ATTRIBUTIONAL BIASES

The reasons for behavior may be attributed to either situational or personal factors. But, these attributions are made in predictable ways, based on an individual's point of view and the effectiveness of the behavior.

Point of View

An individual can participate in a situation as an *actor* or an *observer*. In looking at the Eastern situation, Borman can be viewed as the actor and Bryan as the observer. Who is the actor and who is the observer depends on the behavior to which the cause will be attributed. If Bryan's behavior is viewed with regard to wage concessions, then he becomes the actor and Borman becomes the observer.

Research on attributions indicates that actors emphasize situational causes of a behavior and de-emphasize personal factors, to protect their self-image and ego.[21] For example, Borman, as the actor, would emphasize economic conditions, including labor's position, and de-emphasize his personal attitudes as contributory aspects. The observer would emphasize the personal factors of the actor and de-emphasize situational factors as explanations for the situation.[22] Thus, Bryan would emphasize Borman's autocratic management and de-emphasize the possibility that the banks were primarily responsible for the decision to sell.

Consider the employee who arrives at work late. Does the worker attribute the cause of the tardiness to personal characteristics, or to situational factors such as traffic, a malfunctioning alarm clock, or changed work rules? To what does the worker's boss attribute the cause of the tardiness? According to the attributional biases just discussed, the worker attributes behavior to the situation—a delayed subway, perhaps; the boss attributes the worker's behavior to personal characteristics—laziness, for example. Recognizing this tendency toward bias should alert individuals to possible inaccuracies in their attributions and diagnoses.

Effectiveness of the Behavior

The perceived success or failure of a behavior complicates the attribution of its cause, as shown in Table 14.1. Actors attribute successes to personal factors, and failures to situational factors.[23] For observers the reverse is true. They attribute successes to situational factors and failures to personal factors.[24] Consider the case of Eastern again. If Borman views the sale as a successful behavior, he would attribute it to his personal skill or ability. If he views it as a mistake or a failure, he likely attributes it to the situation, such as economic circumstances, the bank's actions, or labor intransigence. One study of 181 annual reports indicates that unfavorable corporate outcomes were attributed to external and uncontrollable causes more often than were favorable ones.[25]

Now consider the case of a student who has just completed a final examination. If the student obtains an A on the exam, how will the excellent performance likely be explained? If that student obtains an F on the exam, how will the poor performance be explained? To what will the professor attribute the student's performance? The student—as an actor—will attribute an A (success) to personal factors, such as knowledge or effort, but an F to situational factors, such as poor teaching or noise in the examination room. The professor will make the reverse

TABLE 14.1 ■ Summary of Attributions				
	Actor's Actions		Observer's Actions	
	Success	Failure	Success	Failure
Actor	Personal	Situational	Situational	Personal
Observer	Situational	Personal	Personal	Situational

attributions. The teacher will attribute an A to excellent teaching (aspects of the situation) and an F to the student's laziness or low IQ. Which of these attributions is correct? Of course, any of these attributions probably represents an oversimplification of the causes.

Rectifying Attributional Factors

Testing the nature of attributions in a problem situation should be an early and recurring step of diagnosis. As much as possible, individuals should be *actively* involved in processing information about the situation, rather than remain passive.[26] Individuals can learn reasonable causes for various behaviors as well as methods for testing their assumptions. By knowing the typical attributional biases, individuals can be alert to these biases in their own attributions and verify the accuracy of the causes they identify.

■■■ THE LEARNING PROCESS

Learning
The acquisition of skills, knowledge, abilities, and attitudes through patterned actions and practice.

In addition to perception and attribution, learning influences both the description and diagnosis of organizational behavior. **Learning** refers to the acquisition of skills, knowledge, abilities, and attitudes through patterned actions and practice. Individuals can learn in a variety of ways. Behaviorists emphasize the reinforcement between various behaviors through trial-and-error experiences. Social learning theorists integrate both behaviorist and cognitive approaches.

Behaviorist Approach

Beginning with research on animal responses, behaviorist theorists emphasized the link between a given stimulus and response. Recall Pavlov's work with dogs.[27] He noted that, upon presentation of a piece of meat (unconditioned stimulus) to a dog, the dog salivated (unconditioned response). The ringing of a bell (neutral stimulus) initially yielded no salivation response. After pairing the ringing bell with the piece of meat several times, Pavlov then rang the bell without presenting the meat—and the dog salivated (conditioned response). In classical conditioning, after repeated pairing of neutral and unconditioned stimuli, solitary presentation of the neutral stimulus leads to a conditioned response, as illustrated in Figure 14.5.

Operant conditioning extends classical conditioning to focus on the consequences of a behavior.[28] A stimulus still cues a response, but what happens after the response—a desired or undesired consequence—determines whether the response will recur (see Figure 14.5). For example, an individual who receives a bonus (a positive consequence) after creative performance response on a work assignment (stimulus) is more likely to repeat the creative response than if his or her performance is ignored (a negative consequence). Thus, repetition of Bryan's refusal to concede to management's requests may depend on the consequences associated with it. If he receives a reprimand, he will be less likely to repeat the behavior than if his peers or bosses praise his action.

F I G U R E 14.5 ■■ Behavioral Learning Models

Classical Conditioning Model

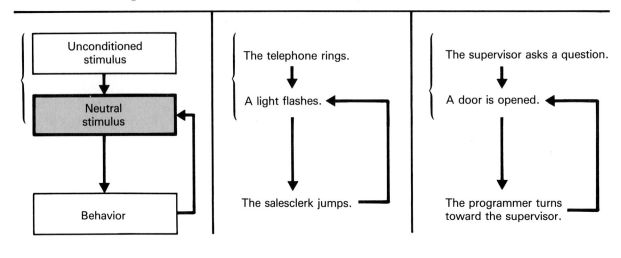

Operant Conditioning Model

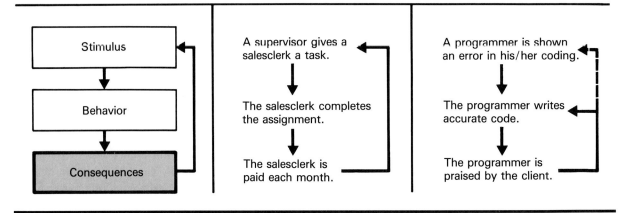

Cognitive Approach

In contrast to the stimulus-response links that are key to behaviorist theories, cognitive theorists look at the significance of cognitive environmental cues and expectations.[29] In Edward Tolman's early experiments, rats learned to run through a maze to a goal of food. Repeated trials allowed the rat to develop cognitive connections that identified the correct path to the goal. Each time the rat reached its goal, the connections between the cognitive cues and the expectancies of reaching the goal were strengthened. According to Tolman, the rat developed a cognitive map of the path to the goal, so that one cue or stimulus led to the next cue or stimulus, rather than to a response. Figure 14.6 depicts these links. Thus, Bryan's attribution of Borman's personal responsibility for the sale could have resulted from the sequence of cues he perceived to be associated with that behavior.

FIGURE 14.6 ■
Cognitive Learning Model

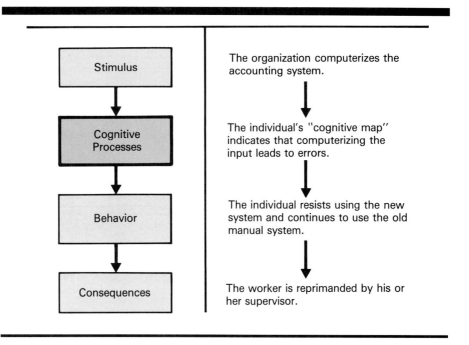

Cognitive learning theories have also been integrated into expectancy and goal-setting theories. For example, programs that link job and organizational rules, regulations, and activities with worker expectations about goals emphasize the cognitive connections between environmental cues, worker expectancies, and goals.[30]

Social Learning Approach

Extending beyond both behavioral and cognitive learning theories, social learning theory suggests that learning results from modeling behaviors. Using observations to gather information, learners imitate the behavior of others.[31] According to Albert Bandura, a learner first watches others and develops a mental picture of the behavior and its consequences.[32] The observer then tries out the behavior. If positive consequences result, the behavior is repeated, but if negative consequences occur, no repetition takes place. The learner's assessment of response consequences parallels behaviorist theories. The learner's development of a cognitive image of the situation incorporates ideas of cognitive learning.

Applications of modeling theory to understanding and improving behavior in organizations are increasing.[33] Luthans and Kreitner suggest the following modeling strategy:

1. Precisely identify the goal or target behavior(s) that will lead to performance improvement.
2. Select the appropriate model(s) and modeling media, e.g., live demonstration, training film, videotape, or the like.
3. Make sure the employee is capable of meeting the technical skill requirements of the target behavior(s).

Managers can encourage learning in the work place by providing learning opportunities and rewarding desired results. (© Lincoln Russell/Stock, Boston, Inc.)

4. Structure a favorable and positive learning environment to increase the probability of attention and reproduction and to enhance motivation to learn and improve.

5. Model the target behavior(s) and carry out supporting activities such as role playing. Clearly demonstrate the positive consequences of engaging in the model target behavior(s).

6. Positively reinforce reproduction of the target behavior(s) both in training and back on the job.

7. Maintain and strengthen the target behavior(s), first with a continuous schedule of reinforcement, and later with an intermittent schedule.[34]

Enhancing Effective Learning

How can managers encourage learning in the workplace? First, they can ensure that appropriate conditions for learning exist. This can be done by providing appropriate stimuli (e.g., complete and understandable information or material) to facilitate acquisition of skills, knowledge, or attitudes. Second, managers should reinforce desired learned behaviors. They should also provide environmental cues that encourage learning—by structuring a context (a physical and emotional climate) that supports learning. Finally, managers should select individuals who can model desired behaviors.

SUMMARY

Perception is the understanding or view people have of things in the world around them. Perceptions have a strong impact on an individual's descriptions, analysis of events, and subsequent behavior. Basically, perception is a two-stage process of selection and organization.

So many stimuli bombard us daily it is difficult to attend to all of them. So we select and attend to only some of the features present in a situation. Certain characteristics of stimuli, such as size, intensity, and novelty, influence what individuals attend to. An important characteristic is how stimuli contrast to their background. Stimuli are also selected according to our internal state. Once stimuli have been selected, individuals categorize and organize them so that the new material makes sense. In reality, though, both selection and organization generally suffer from perceptual distortions, including stereotyping, halo effect, projection, and expectancy.

Because of perceptual distortion, rarely will the description we give of any particular event or person be totally objective or accurate. Rather, many factors will color our descriptions and cause them to differ from another person's descriptions. Incorporating many people's perceptions into an account of a person or event should improve the accuracy of a situation's description.

Most people, whether consciously or not, ponder the reasons for events and then decide why the events occurred. In this way, they attribute causes to events. Individuals thus move from description to diagnosis. One researcher has suggested that diagnosis occurs in three stages: A person (1) observes another person's action; (2) determines whether the behavior was intended; and (3) assigns a reason for the behavior. Behavior, according to Kurt Lewin, results from two causes, a person's personal characteristics and situational influences, not just one or the other. But often the behavior may be attributed to one or the other cause. These attributions, however, are made in predictable ways, based on an individual's point of view and the effectiveness of the behavior. Individuals participate in situations as actors or observers. Actors emphasize situational causes and de-emphasize personal factors, to protect their self-image. The perceived success or failure of a behavior complicates the attribution of its cause. Actors attribute successes to personal factors, and failures to situational factors. For observers the reverse is true.

Learning refers to the acquisition of skills, knowledge, abilities, and attitudes through patterned actions and practice. Individuals can learn in a variety of ways. Behaviorists emphasize the reinforcement between various behaviors through trial-and-error experiences. Social learning theorists integrate both behaviorist and cognitive approaches. Managers can enhance learning in the workplace by providing an appropriate and supportive environment.

REVIEW QUESTIONS

1. Define perception and describe the stages of the perception process.
2. List and define the types of perceptual distortions described in the text.
3. What are the steps in the attribution process? Briefly describe each.
4. What is meant by the statement, "An individual can participate in a situation as an actor or an observer"?
5. Define learning. Describe the different ways that individuals learn.

KEY TERMS

perception	stereotyping	expectancy
selection	halo effect	attribution
closure	projection	learning

A MANAGEMENT TRAINEE IN TROUBLE

MIRIAM SIMPSON WENT to work with Centurion Electric Company two weeks after she graduated from Michigan State University. Centurion, though relatively unknown to the general public, is one of the nation's largest manufacturers of electric transformers and generators. The company is headquartered in Detroit, with branch offices in a number of cities. Miriam was one of 200 management trainees Centurion hired that year and one of fifteen trainees who were to be prepared for branch office management.

During the preliminary two weeks of training at corporate headquarters in Detroit, Miriam learned that she was to develop competence in the following areas: shipping and receiving, inventory control, purchasing, personnel, production, order service, and outside sales. In addition to on-the-job experience in these areas, the branch manager trainees were to return to Detroit four times a year for a week of classroom instruction. During that time, they were also expected to compare notes and review individual progress with members of upper management.

Miriam was assigned to the Indianapolis branch and was placed under the direct supervision of Jerry Mundy, the branch manager. Mr. Mundy, fifty-eight, had been with Centurion for thirty-seven years, having joined the company at the end of World War II. He had not attended college but instead had worked his way up. He believed this way of making it into management provided better training than the company's one-year rotation program. After Miriam's arrival she was assigned to perform a number of jobs in the branch, but not according to the planned program. Asked to fill in as needed, she found herself doing mostly clerical work. In the first three months, she never got out of shipping and receiving.

When Miriam returned to headquarters for the first one-week training session, she discussed her problem with the coordinator of training and development, James Simpson. Mr. Simpson assured Miriam that he would check into the matter and attempt to make sure that she was properly prepared for her future management job.

When Miriam returned to the branch, Mr. Mundy reprimanded her for "putting him on report." The conversation proceeded as follows:

Mr. Mundy	"Miriam, you work for me. At least as long as you are at this branch. If you have anything negative to say, you should say it to me, not to Simpson. Why did you do that?"
Miriam	"I don't know. I guess I was just frustrated with the training I've received."
Mr. Mundy	"You're just like a lot of young college graduates. You think your degree should entitle you to special treatment. Well, I'm sorry. But in my book it doesn't mean a thing."
Miriam	"I understand. What do you want me to do now?"
Mr. Mundy	"Go back to work and don't cause any more trouble."

QUESTIONS

1. Is there a problem of perception in this case? Discuss.
2. Was Mr. Mundy attempting learning in this case? Discuss.

CLOSE TO THE VEST

FOR THE PAST few years, sales at Glenco Manufacturing had been falling. The decline was industrywide. Still, Glenco had been able to increase its share of the market slightly.

Although forecasts indicated that demand for the products would improve in the future, Joe Goddard, the company president, believed that something needed to be done immediately to help

the firm survive this temporary slump. As a first step he employed a consulting firm to determine whether a reorganization might be helpful.

A team of five consultants arrived at the firm. They told Mr. Goddard that they first had to gain a thorough understanding of the current situation before they could make any recommendations. Mr. Goddard assured them that the company was open to them. They could ask any questions that they thought were necessary.

The grapevine was full of rumors virtually from the day the consulting group arrived. One employee was heard to say, "If they shut down the company, I don't know if I could take care of my family." Another worker said, "If they move me away from my friends I'm going to quit."

When workers questioned their supervisors, they received no explanations. No one had told the supervisors what was going on either. The climate began to change to one of fear. Rather than being concerned about their daily work, employees worried about what was going to happen to the company and their jobs. Productivity dropped drastically as a result.

A month after the consultants departed, an informational memorandum was circulated throughout the company. It stated that the consultants had recommended a slight modification in the top levels of the organization to achieve greater efficiency. No one would be terminated. Any reductions would be the result of normal attrition. By this time, however, some of the best workers had already found other jobs, and company operations were severely disrupted for several months.

QUESTIONS

1. What difference might it make if the workers were participating in the situation as actors or observers? Answer with regard to the discussion in the text.
2. What effect did attributional biases have in this situation? Discuss.

EXPERIENTIAL EXERCISE

Career planning and development is extremely important to many individuals. They want to know how they fit into the future of the organization. Employees who believe they have a future with their company are often more productive than those who do not. This exercise is designed to assist in understanding what it takes for one individual to climb the organizational ladder to success. The climb depends partly on the individual's self-perceptions and perceptions of past experiences with the company. This exercise provides a method of individual career planning for the manager described in the scenario below.

The individual being evaluated is thirty-five years old and is at a crossroads in his career. Upon self-reflection and appraisal at his birthday party, he realizes that while he has achieved only moderate successes in his ten years with the organization, few others in the organization of comparable age and experience have any more "book or common-sense intelligence." In fact, the company is inundated with middle- and upper-level managers much older, and often less intelligent, who seem to spend an inordinate amount of time at the country club.

Assume that you are this person and have set your sights on an important middle management position in the next five to seven years, and a top management position with your organization in the next ten to fifteen years. You have determined that there are twenty factors that determine upward movement in your organization. You are now trying to determine which are most important for survival and success, and which are least important. This decision will determine whether you take the road to organizational survival and success, or the road to career failure and stagnation.

You will each be given a list of twenty factors that have been determined as essential for an individual's survival and success in an organization. You will rank the importance of each factor for your survival and success in the organization. Write the number "1" beside the most important factor, the number "2" beside the second most important factor, and so on through the number "20," the least important factor.

Everyone in the class can participate in this exercise. Each student will complete Exhibit 1, the "Business Survival and Success Factors," as he or she believes the individual described in the scenario would. Your instructor will provide the participants with the additional information necessary to participate.

NOTES

1. J. A. Litterer, *The Analysis of Organizations,* 2d ed. (New York: John Wiley & Sons, 1973), 106.
2. Jo Ellen Davis and Pete Engardio, "What It's Like to Work for Frank Lorenzo," *Business Week,* 18 May 1987, 76.
3. Aaron Berstein, "Labor Relations: Reconnecting the Lines," *Business Week,* 18 January 1988, 59.

4. T. R. Mitchell, *People in Organizations: Understanding Their Behavior* (New York: McGraw-Hill, 1978); and H. C. Triandis, *Interpersonal Behavior* (Monterey, Cal.: Brooks/Cole, 1977).

5. D. Coon, *Introduction to Psychology: Exploration and Application* (St. Paul, Minn.: West, 1977).

6. W. V. Haney, *Communication and Interpersonal Relations: Text and Cases* (Homewood, Ill.: Irwin, 1979).

7. D. Hellriegel and J. W. Slocum, Jr., *Organizational Behavior,* 3d ed. (St. Paul, Minn.: West, 1983).

8. K. N. Wexley, G. A. Yukl, S. Z. Kovacs, and R. E. Sanders, "Importance of Contrast Effects in Employment Interviews," *Journal of Applied Psychology* 63 (1978): 579-- 588.

9. R. J. Grey and D. Kipnis, "Untangling the Performance Appraisal Dilemma: The Influence of Perceived Organizational Context on Evaluative Processes," *Journal of Applied Psychology* 61 (1976): 329–335.

10. E. Gibson, *Principles of Perceptual Learning and Development* (New York: Appleton-Century-Crofts, 1969).

11. D. Fisher, *Communication in Organizations* (St. Paul, Minn.: West, 1981).

12. Karen Pennar, "America's Quest Can't Be Half-Hearted," *Business Week,* 8 June 1987, 136.

13. Gordon Allport, *The Nature of Prejudice* (Reading, Mass.: Addison-Wesley, 1954).

14. F. J. Landy and J. L. Farr, "Performance Rating," *Psychological Bulletin* 87, no. 1 (1980): 72–107.

15. M. E. Hellman and M. H. Stopeck, "Being Attractive, Advantage or Disadvantage? Performance Evaluations and Recommended Personnel Actions as a Function of Appearance, Sex, and Job Type," *Organizational Behavior and Human Decision Processes* 35 (1985): 202–215.

16. K. Lewin, *Field Theory in Social Science* (New York: Harper, 1951).

17. Jo Ellen Davis and Pete Engardio, "What It's Like to Work for Frank Lorenzo," *Business Week,* 18 May 1987, 76.

18. H. H. Kelley, "The Process of Causal Attribution," *American Psychologist* 28 (1973): 107–128; V. L. Hamilton, "Intuitive Psychologist or Intuitive Lawyer: Alternative Models of the Attribution Process," *Journal of Personality and Social Psychology* 39 (1980): 767–772; E. E. Jones and K. E. Davis, "From Acts to Dispositions: The Attribution Process in Person Perception," in *Advances in Experimental Social Psychology* 2, ed. L. Berkowitz (New York: Academic Press, 1965), 219–266.

19. S. G. Green and T. R. Mitchell, "Attributional Processes of Leaders in Leader-Member Interactions," *Organizational Behavior and Human Performance* 23 (1979): 429–458; D. R. Ilgen and W. A. Knowlton, Jr., "Performance Attributional Effects on Feedback from Superiors," *Organizational Behavior and Human Performance* 25 (1980): 441–456; W. A. Knowlton, Jr., and T. R. Mitchell, "Effects of Causal Attributions on a Supervisor's Evaluation of Subordinate Performance," *Journal of Applied Psychology* 65 (1980): 459–466.

20. E. K. Shaver, *An Introduction to Attribution Processes* (Cambridge, Mass.: Winthrop, 1975).

21. E. E. Jones and R. E. Nisbett, *The Actor and the Observer, Divergent Perceptions of the Causes of Behavior* (Morristown, N.J.: General Learning Press, 1971).

22. Jones and Nisbett, *Actor and Observer.*

23. J. Bartunek, "Why Did You Do That? Attribution Theory in Organizations," *Business Horizons* 24, no. 5 (1981): 66–71.

24. H. H. Kelley and J. L. Michela, "Attribution Theory and Research," *Annual Review of Psychology* (1980): 457–501.

25. J. R. Bettman and B. A. Weitz, "Attributions in the Board Room: Causal Reasoning in Corporate Annual Reports," *Administrative Science Quarterly* 28 (1983): 165–183.

26. R. G. Lord and J. E. Smith, "Theoretical, Information Processing, and Situational Factors Affecting Attribution Theory Models of Organizational Behavior," *Academy of Management Review* 8 (1983): 50–60.

27. I. P. Pavlov, *Conditioned Reflexes: An Investigation of the Physiological Activity of the Cerebral Cortex,* ed. and trans. G. V. Anrep (London: Oxford University Press, 1927).

28. B. F. Skinner, *About Behaviorism* (New York: Alfred A. Knopf, 1974); B. F. Skinner, *The Behavior of Organisms: An Experimental Approach* (New York: Appleton-Century-Crofts, 1932).

29. E. C. Tolman, *Purposive Behavior in Animals and Men* (New York: Appleton-Century-Crofts, 1932).

30. F. Luthans, *Organizational Behavior,* 4th ed. (New York: McGraw-Hill, 1985).

31. Luthans, *Organizational Behavior.*

32. A. Bandura, *Social Learning Theory* (Englewood Cliffs, N.J.: Prentice-Hall, 1978).

33. C. C. Manz and H. P. Sims, "Vicarious Learning: The Influence of Modeling on Organizational Behavior." *Academy of Management Review* 6 (1981): 105–113.

34. F. Luthans and R. Kreitner, *Organizational Behavior Modification and Beyond* (Glenview, Ill.: Scott, Foresman, 1985), 157.

REFERENCES

Allen, Judith L., Lydia D. Walker, David A. Schroeder, and David E. Johnson. "Attributions and Attribution-Behavior Relations: The Effect of Level of Cognitive Development." *Journal of Personality and Social Psychology* 52 (June 1987): 1099–1109.

Allport, Gordon. *The Nature of Prejudice.* Reading, Mass.: Addison-Wesley, 1954.

Bartunek, J. "Why Did You Do That? Attribution Theory in Organizations." *Business Horizons* 24, no. 5 (1981): 66–71.

Bettman, J. R., and B. A. Weitz. "Attributions in the Board Room: Causal Reasoning in Corporate Annual Reports." *Administrative Science Quarterly* 28 (1983): 165–183.

Forsterling, Friedrich, and Udo Rudolph. "Situations, Attributions, and the Evaluation of Reactions." *Journal of Personality and Social Psychology* 54 (February 1988): 225–232.

Holloman, Russ, and Barbara Coleman. "The Individual and the Organization: Their Search for Accommodation." *Arkansas Business and Economic Review* 20 (Summer 1987): 19–26.

Jones, E. E., and R. E. Nisbett. *The Actor and the Observer, Divergent Perceptions of the Causes of Behavior.* Morristown, N.J.: General Learning Press, 1971.

Kaplan, Steven E. "Improving Performance Evaluation." *CMA—The Management Accounting Magazine* 61 (May–June 1987): 56–59.

Kelley, H. H., and J. L. Michela. "Attribution Theory and Research." *Annual Review of Psychology* (1980): 457–501.

"Learning by Teaching." *Training: The Magazine of Human Resources Development* 25 (July 1988): 12–13.

Lewin, K. *Field Theory in Social Science.* New York: Harper, 1951.

Lider, R. C., and T. R. Mitchell. "Reactions to Feedback: The Role of Attributions." *Academy of Management Journal* 28 (1985): 291–308.

Lord, R. G., and J. E. Smith. "Theoretical, Information Processing, and Situational Factors Affecting Attribution Theory Models of Organizational Behavior." *Academy of Management Review* 8 (1983): 50–60.

Luthans, F. *Organizational Behavior.* 4th ed. New York: McGraw-Hill, 1985.

Luthans, F., and R. Kreitner. *Organizational Behavior Modification and Beyond.* Glenview, Ill.: Scott, Foresman, 1985.

McElroy, James C., and Charles B. Shrader. "Attribution Theories of Leadership and Network Analysis." *Journal of Management* 12 (Fall 1986): 351–361.

Manz, C. C., and H. P. Sims. "Vicarious Learning: The Influence of Modeling on Organizational Behavior." *Academy of Management Review* 6 (1981): 105–113.

March, James G., and Martha S. Feldman. "Information in Organizations as Signal and Symbol." *Administrative Science Quarterly* 26 (June 1981): 171–186.

Pavlov, I. P. *Conditioned Reflexes: An Investigation of the Physiological Activity of the Cerebral Cortex.* Edited and translated by G. V. Anrep. London: Oxford University Press, 1927.

Roskies, Ethel, Jeffrey K. Liker, and David B. Roitman. "Winners and Losers: Employee Perceptions of Their Company's Technological Transformation." *Journal of Organizational Behavior Management* 9 (April 1988): 123–137.

Skinner, B. F. *About Behaviorism.* New York: Alfred A. Knopf, 1974.

───── . *The Behavior of Organisms: An Experimental Approach.* New York: Appleton-Century-Crofts, 1938.

Tolman, E. C. *Purposive Behavior in Animals and Men.* New York: Appleton-Century-Crofts, 1932.

Wexley, K. N., G. A. Yukl, S. Z. Kovacs, and R. E. Sanders. "Importance of Contrast Effects in Employment Interviews." *Journal of Applied Psychology* 63 (1978): 579–588.

CHAPTER

15

Motivation

Learning Objectives

After completing this chapter students should be able to

1. Describe management influences that impact motivation theories and explain needs theory.
2. Describe equity and reinforcement theory.
3. Explain expectancy theory, goal setting and motivation, and the reward system.

CAROL HARRINGTON JOINED Market Research Associates (MRA) as a senior analyst after receiving her MBA from a prestigious business school. She entered graduate school directly after graduation from college with a major in psychology, so MRA was her first full-time work experience. MRA was a small consulting firm that provided market research assistance for a wide range of clients. With the exception of the secretary, Carol was the first full-time employee hired by the firm's four partners.

For the first few months at MRA, Carol assisted the four partners in completing their projects. It became clear to her bosses right away that Carol was a quick learner and a strong performer, so they immediately gave her additional responsibility and autonomy in performing her job. Within six months Carol was completing projects with little assistance from the firm's partners. She relished the independence they gave her and felt challenged to become an outstanding performer.

During this time, the business community increasingly recognized the quality work performed by MRA. The number of requests for services began to exceed what Carol and the four partners could reasonably provide themselves. During the next six months, the partners hired two additional professional staff members. Within the following six months they hired six more analysts, bringing the total number of professionals, including the four partners, to thirteen. The firm also added six additional employees, who provided clerical, secretarial, and limited technical assistance to the professional staff.

Carol's outstanding performance continued. Although the other new hires required significant amounts of training and supervision, Carol functioned independently. She dealt directly with clients, designing, negotiating, and implementing market research projects. She completed her work on schedule and within the allocated budget. Although her bosses never praised her work, her clients expressed their satisfaction with it. When questioned about her attitude toward her job, Carol responded with enthusiasm and satisfaction. She frequently worked extra hours beyond the required thirty-five, even though her salary was relatively low in comparison to that of her friends who held similar positions in other firms.

In the middle of the second year of Carol's employment at MRA, the firm's partners decided to reorganize the professional staff. Carol was made an assistant vice-president and given supervisory responsibility for three other professionals. She was also told to report directly to one of the partners, who had the title of vice-president. Rather than perform all aspects of the market research studies herself, she was told to oversee her three subordinates' performance of them. The studies had been designed for the clients either by Carol or by the vice-president to whom Carol reported.

Although Carol was enthusiastic about her new supervisory responsibilities, she was concerned about her new relationship to the partner. She felt that this particular partner did not do his share of the work. She knew that his projects were frequently completed behind schedule and over budget. When she worked with him before, he had delayed the submission of her reports and failed to make substantive changes in them. During the next few months, however, he began to exert great control over the team's projects and Carol's activities, as she expected he would. He frequently changed Carol's plans, or he would give new directions to her subordinates without informing her or discussing with her his reasons for doing so. Although some of her co-workers had commented about the high quality of her work, her boss offered neither praise nor constructive criticism. Carol complained that she was bored. Her boss did not allow her to be creative. He only wanted her to follow his directions precisely.

Other difficulties developed. Her subordinates expressed dissatisfaction in working with such a young supervisor. Some of the men expressed dissatisfaction in working with a woman. Carol expressed her own dissatisfaction to the bosses concerning the performance of her subordinates. She felt they were not committed to their jobs or to MRA and that she was doing much more work than they were. Carol became even less enthusiastic about her job. Before long she began to perform her work in a relatively perfunctory manner, completing the tasks she could within the regular work day, eliminating any overtime, and meeting her boss's requests to the letter.

When Carol learned that one subordinate, who had a large family but less experience and less education than she had, was receiving the same salary as she, she was incensed. She complained to her bosses and they agreed to raise her salary by $200. Carol continued her job to the letter, but six months later she resigned and took a supervisory position with another market research firm at a considerably higher salary. ■

Motivation
The willingness to put forth effort in the pursuit of organizational goals.

WHAT CAUSED THE DECLINE in Carol Harrington's productivity, creativity, involvement, and satisfaction? At least in part, it can be attributed to a decline in her motivation. **Motivation** is defined as the willingness to put forth effort in the pursuit of organizational goals. The goal of motivation in organizations is to keep high performers challenged and productive and to cause less effective performers to intensify their contributions to the organization.

Management traditionally has relied on the use of rewards—such as increased pay, job security, and good working conditions—or punishments—such as dismissal, demotions, or withholding rewards—to motivate employees to achieve high performance. Management in today's environment, however, cannot rely solely on the manipulation of pay, benefits, or working conditions to encourage personnel to perform effectively. Motivation is a much more complicated process.

The manager must seek to understand the forces that energize workers' behavior. He or she has the responsibility to develop a work environment that makes use of the enormous energy that is within every person. In essence, then, a manager's major task is to create and develop an effective environment in which employees will be motivated to become productive, contributing members of the organization.

In this chapter, three philosophies of human nature will be discussed first. Then, four major motivation theories—needs theories, equity theory, reinforcement theory, and expectancy theory—are described. Goal setting as a technique for increasing motivation is also reviewed. The chapter concludes with a consideration of the nature of reward systems in organizations.

▨ PHILOSOPHIES OF HUMAN NATURE

In order to create an environment conducive to a high level of employee motivation, managers must understand some basic philosophies of human nature. The assumptions that managers have regarding other people is a major factor in establishing a motivated work force. These assumptions of management can be directly and positively influenced by an understanding of the following philosophies of human nature.

McGregor's Theory X and Theory Y

Douglas McGregor stressed the importance of understanding the relationships between motivation and philosophies of human nature.[1] In observing the practices and approaches of traditional managers, McGregor believed that managers usually attempt to motivate employees by one of two basic approaches. He referred to these approaches as Theory X and Theory Y. **Theory X** is the traditional view of management that suggests that managers are required to coerce, control, or threaten employees in order to motivate them. The vice-president, in the opening case, seems to have a Theory X philosophy, because he exercised too much control over Carol's work and discouraged her creativity, thereby decreasing her level of motivation. McGregor proposed an alternative philosophy of human nature, which he referred to as Theory Y. In contrast to Theory X, **Theory Y** is a view of management by which a manager believes people are capable of being responsible and mature. Thus, employees do not require coercion or excessive control by the manager in order to perform effectively. McGregor's belief was that Theory Y is a more realistic assessment of people.

Theory X
The traditional view of management that suggests that managers are required to coerce, control, or threaten employees in order to motivate them.

Theory Y
A view of management by which a manager believes people are capable of being responsible and mature.

PINNACLE

People, the Key to Corporate Success!

IN ORDER TO learn how to create an environment conducive to a high level of employee motivation, managers must develop an understanding of the philosophies of human nature. The assumptions that managers have regarding other people are a major factor in establishing a motivated work force. George Gillett, Chairman of the Gillett Group, has what appears to be a true understanding of what is necessary to establish and maintain a motivated work force. The Gillett Group operates, among other ventures, the largest ski resort and non-network affiliate TV operation in the United States. He has built an empire on the old-fashioned virtues of honesty and integrity. His strategy for managing his empire is to key on people, utilize consensus decision making, and give good people total freedom to grow. He hires the best people possible and aggressively promotes the hiring of women and blacks. He views a corporation as a chain of people. According to Gillett, the corporation is no stronger than its weakest people link. CNN correspondent Tom Cassidy discusses with Mr. Gillett his philosophies of management and other issues relevant to his business success.

TABLE 15.1 ■ A Comparison of McGregor's Theory X and Theory Y Assumptions	
Theory X	Theory Y
The average person inherently dislikes work and will avoid it if possible.	The expenditure of physical and mental effort in work is as natural as play or rest.
Because of the dislike of work, most people must be coerced, controlled, directed, and threatened with punishment to get them to perform effectively.	People will exercise self-direction and self-control in the service of objectives to which they are committed.
The average person lacks ambition, avoids responsibility, and seeks security and economic rewards above all else.	Commitment to objectives is a function of the rewards associated with achievement.
Most people lack creative ability and are resistant to change.	The average person learns, under proper conditions, not only to accept but to seek responsibility.
Since most people are self-centered, they are not concerned with the goals of the organization.	The capacity to exercise a relatively high degree of imagination, ingenuity, and creativity in the solution of organizational problems is widely, not narrowly, distributed in the population.

Source: Based on material in Douglas McGregor, *The Human Side of Enterprise* (New York: McGraw-Hill, 1960).

Table 15.1 illustrates the different assumptions of these two philosophies of human nature. The Theory Y assumptions represent the manager's high degree of faith in the capacity and potential of people. If one accepts the Theory Y philosophy, managerial practices such as the following will be seriously considered: (1) abandonment of time clocks, (2) flexible work hours on an individual basis, (3) job enrichment, (4) management by objectives, and (5) participative decision making. All are based on the beliefs that abilities are widespread in the population and that each person can be trusted to behave in a responsible manner. Thus, management would create an environment that permits workers to be motivated to fully utilize their potential.

One should not conclude that McGregor advocated Theory Y as a panacea for all managerial problems. The Theory Y philosophy is not utopia, but, as McGregor argued, it does provide a basis for improved management and organizational performance.

Argyris's Maturity Theory

The research of Chris Argyris has also aided managers in developing a more complete understanding of human behavior as it relates to motivation. Argyris emphasized the importance of the process of maturity. He suggests that there is a basic difference between the demands of the mature personality and the demands of the typical organization. Argyris concluded that if plans, policies, and methods/procedures are described in detail, an employee will need to be submissive and passive, which suggests a Theory X type of organization. The demand is for the subordinate to concentrate on the orders as given and not question or attempt to understand these orders in a broader perspective. In brief, such a detailed prescription may ask individuals to work in an environment where

1. They have little control over their workaday world.
2. They are expected to be passive, dependent, and subordinate.
3. They are expected to have a short time perspective.
4. They are induced to be perfect and to value the frequent use of a few shallow abilities.
5. They are expected to produce under conditions leading to psychological failure.[2]

When the mature employee encounters the conditions described above, three reactions are possible:

1. *Escape.* An employee may escape by quitting the job, being absent from work, or attempting to climb to higher levels in the firm where the structure is less rigid.
2. *Fight.* A person can fight the system by exerting pressure on the organization by means of informal groups or through formally organized labor unions.
3. *Adapt.* The most typical reaction of employees is to adapt, by developing an attitude of apathy or indifference. The employee "plays the game," and pay becomes the compensation for the penalty of working. According to Argyris, adaptation least represents good mental health.

Argyris argues that a highly structured environment will cause employees to act immaturely. One could argue as well, that maturity involves the ability to adapt to any kind of environment, structured or not. Many people can and do adjust to tightly regimented work situations; one need only observe workers on an assembly line to recognize this. In U.S. business, only a fraction of jobs are of the highly structured, totally controlled type. Workers who prefer challenges can find them. To the degree that an open job market operates effectively, there will be a matching of various human needs and organizational demands. The ideas of Argyris do, of course, have some relevance to the practice of management and the application of motivational techniques, but the suggestion that this philosophy is an adequate guide for managers in *all* situations is erroneous. Nevertheless, managers who understand maturity theory, as purported by Chris Argyris, are in a better position to apply the theories of motivation to best advantage.

The Self-Fulfilling Prophecy

Self-fulfilling prophecy
The idea that the manager's positive or negative expectations will have significant influence on employee motivation and performance.

The idea that the manager's positive or negative expectations will have significant influence on employee motivation and performance is the **self-fulfilling prophecy.** According to J. Sterling Livingston:

- A manager's expectations of employees and the way that the manager treats them largely determines their performance and career progress.
- A unique characteristic of superior managers is their ability to create high performance expectations that subordinates fulfill.
- Less effective managers fail to develop high performance expectations, and, as a consequence, the productivity of their subordinates suffers.
- Subordinates, more often than not, appear to do what they believe they are expected to do.[3]

High performance expectations tend to be self-fulfilling prophecies. A manager communicates expectations through both verbal and nonverbal means. The manager's facial expressions, eye contact, body posture, or tone of voice can indicate high approval and high expectations, or the reverse.

Numerous studies support the notion of the self-fulfilling prophecy. In one, eighteen elementary school teachers were informed that about 20 percent of their students were "intellectual bloomers" and as such would achieve remarkable progress during the school year. The 20-percent sample had been chosen at random and so did not differ in intelligence or abilities from the rest of the students in the teachers' classes. The only variable was the expectations of the teachers. During the school year, these students actually did achieve significantly greater progress. Thus, the teachers' expectations of them became a self-fulfilling prophecy.

Similar results have been achieved by managers in relation to motivation in business. More often than not, if managers have high expectations of their employees, the employees' performance will meet those expectations. For example, the manager of a large computer center at a major university was able to substantially change the life and work of a janitor. The manager had high expectations and believed that George Johnson, who had only limited formal education, had the potential to become a computer operator. After several months of training, George Johnson not only fulfilled the expectations of the manager but ultimately progressed to the point of providing training to others. This illustrates how the expectations of one person (in this case, the manager of the computer center) can have significant impact on the actions of another.

Managers in every organization interested in high productivity must meet the challenge of encouraging the development of subordinates in ways that contribute to their high performance, career development, and personal satisfaction. Effective managers who have high expectations of subordinates tend to build the employees' self-confidence and to develop their performance capabilities. By contrast, ineffective managers, who have low expectations of subordinates, tend to create a negative organizational culture. As a result, levels of motivation and performance are lower, and the employees' self-esteem or self-image, as well as their careers, may be severely damaged.[4] In their attempts to motivate workers, managers should assess their own preconceived notions and eliminate any assumptions that might interfere with the proper application of the theories of motivation.

■■ NEEDS THEORIES

As may be seen in Figure 15.1, there are four major theories of motivation. The first of these is needs theories. Human beings have various needs and behave

F I G U R E 15.1 ■
Major Theories of
Motivation

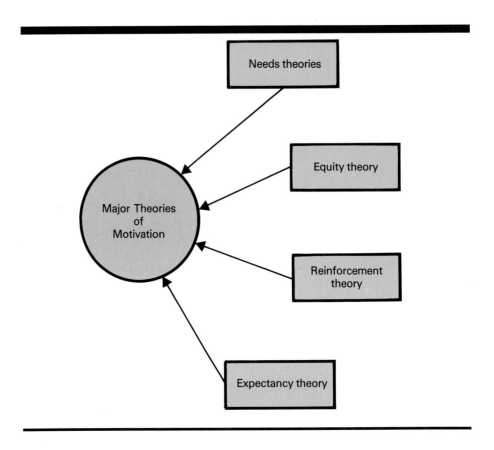

accordingly. Therefore, many researchers in the area of human behavior, in their attempt to explain motivation, have developed theories based on the concept of needs. In this section, four of the most popular needs theories, as they relate to motivation, are presented: (1) Maslow's hierarchy of needs theory; (2) Alderfer's ERG theory; (3) McClelland's needs theory; and (4) Herzberg's two-factor theory. Each theory proposes and describes a specific set of needs that individuals have. As Table 15.2 shows, the needs associated with each differ somewhat. The

TABLE 15.2 ■ Comparison of Needs in Four Theories of Motivation

Maslow	Alderfer	McClelland	Herzberg
Physiological	Existence		Hygiene
Safety and Security			
Belongingness and Love	Relatedness	Need for affiliation	
Self-esteem	Growth	Need for achievement Need for power	Motivators
Self-actualization			

theories also differ as to the ways through which unfulfilled needs influence motivation.

Maslow's Hierarchy of Needs

In 1935 Abraham Maslow began to develop the first and one of the most popular and well-known motivation theories.[5] Maslow stated that individuals have five needs (as shown in Figure 15.2), which he arranged in a hierarchy from the most basic level to the highest: physiological, safety, belongingness and love, esteem, and self-actualization.[6]

Physiological needs refer to the most basic needs an individual has. These include, at a minimum, a person's requirements for food, water, and shelter. Today in organizations such needs must be viewed more broadly. For example, for some workers, the ability to care for their children might be included among these basic physiological needs. The wages individuals receive for working, as well as supplementary benefits, often address these most basic needs. Some companies provide subsidized lunch programs, or company housing. An increasing number of organizations are now providing workers with child-care facilities, or subsidized child care at home. Physiological needs, then, motivate individuals to

FIGURE 15.2 ■■
Maslow's Hierarchy of Needs

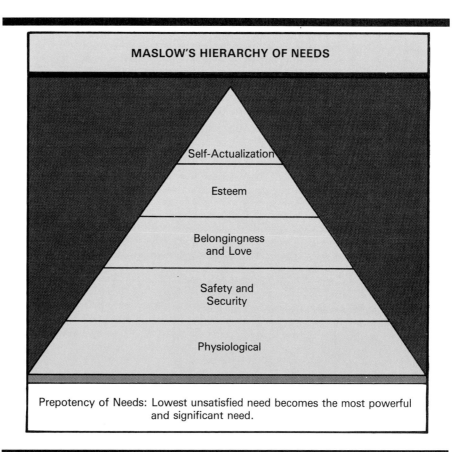

perform so that they will continue to be employed and will thus continue to have their needs satisfied.

Safety needs refer to a person's desire for security or protection. This type of need translates most directly into a concern for both short- and long-term job security. In the automobile industry, for example, recent contracts signed between labor and management meet workers' needs for security by guaranteeing employment to workers.[7] Other employers offer pension benefits to motivate workers to produce and to remain with the organization. More recently, some organizations have attempted to protect the physical safety of those workers who park their cars in distant or dark parking lots by offering an escort service at the end of the work day.

Belongingness and love needs focus on the social aspects of work as well as nonwork situations. Some individuals desire affectionate relationships or regular interaction with others. Organizations meet these social needs by providing opportunities for social interactions, such as regular coffee breaks, organized sports, or other recreational opportunities. Increasingly, organizations encourage workers to perform their jobs as members of work teams, which provides work-related opportunities for meeting social needs. At an LTV Steel Company plant in Cleveland, teams of highly trained technicians manage a huge electrogalvanizing line practically by themselves and participate in decisions on hiring, scheduling of work, and operations planning.[8] Such work-related closeness could easily satisfy social needs.

Esteem needs refer to a person's desire to (1) master his or her work; (2) demonstrate competence and accomplishments; (3) build a reputation as an outstanding performer; and (4) hold a position of prestige. Some employers might attempt to motivate their employees by offering them increasingly larger and more plush offices as their performance increases. Employers may also offer titles that reflect prestige. Or employers may give public recognition for good performance, through "Employee of the Month" awards, for example.

Self-actualization needs reflect individuals' desires to grow and develop to their fullest potential. Individuals often want the opportunity to be creative on the job. Or they may want autonomy and responsibility. Organizations try to motivate these individuals by offering them challenging positions as well as opportunities to advance in the organization.

PREPOTENCY OF NEEDS

Maslow ordered the five basic needs in a hierarchy, from the basic physiological needs up through safety, belonging and love, esteem, and self-actualization. In his scheme, the lowest unsatisfied need becomes the *prepotent,* or most powerful and significant, need. The individual acts to fulfill the prepotent need first. Once satisfied, that need no longer motivates. For example, a person who lacks sufficient food and clothing will act to satisfy those basic physiological needs. This person would most likely work in order to receive pay or other benefits to satisfy those needs. On the other hand, a person whose physiological, safety, and belongingness needs are already satisfied would be motivated to satisfy needs at the next level—the esteem needs. For this person, pay will not motivate performance, unless it increases esteem; but a promotion, or other changes in job titles or status, which satisfy esteem needs, are likely to motivate.

Maslow recognized that the hierarchy of needs could, under certain circumstances, vary in order. He noted, for example, that some people may value self-esteem over love, autonomy over other needs, or physiological needs over all others. Some may value higher-order needs (esteem or self-actualization) over lower-order ones (physiological, safety, or security).[9] In addition, higher needs can be distinguished from lower ones in that, as Maslow suggests, higher needs develop later, require less immediate gratification, cause less stress, depend more on the environment for their existence, and are less tangible and observable.[10]

Carol Harrington of MRA, like everybody, has all five types of needs. It is fairly safe to assume that Carol has already satisfied her physiological, security, belongingness, and esteem needs and that, for her, self-actualization needs are, according to Maslow, prepotent. During her first year at MRA, it was the increasing opportunity to express creativity and to work independently that motivated her, because these working conditions satisfied her prepotent need for self-actualization. However, the vice-president exercised too much control over Carol's work and discouraged her creativity. By not allowing her to continually meet her self-actualization needs, he thereby decreased her level of motivation, and ultimately caused her to resign from the company.

RESEARCH SUPPORT

The popularity of Maslow's theory of motivation stems primarily from its simplicity and logic. One study, for example, found that the autonomy, esteem, and security needs of lower management were less satisfied than those of middle management; higher-order needs were the least satisfied in both groups.[11] Ironically, the research that has been conducted to test the theory does not provide consistent support for it. Rather, in general, it indicates that there are two or three categories of needs, not five.[12] In particular, the lower-order needs, such as the needs for security and safety, and the higher-order needs, such as the needs for love, esteem, and self-actualization, cluster independently. Thus, individuals are motivated to satisfy either lower-order needs or higher-order needs. This observation would separate employees into two groups: (1) those for whom **extrinsic motivation**—motivation by factors outside the job itself, such as pay, job title, or tenure—is most appropriate; and (2) those for whom **intrinsic motivation**—motivation by factors within the job, such as creativity, autonomy, and responsibility—is most appropriate. These two types of motivation will be contrasted in the final section of the chapter on motivation and the reward system. Finally, the research suggests that prepotent needs do not necessarily occur one at a time.[13] Rather, several needs are most often present simultaneously, to varying extents.

Extrinsic motivation
Motivation by factors outside the job itself, such as pay, job title, or tenure.

Intrinsic motivation
Motivation by factors within the job, such as creativity, autonomy, and responsibility.

Alderfer's ERG Theory

As may be seen in Figure 15.3, Clayton Alderfer reorganized Maslow's needs hierarchy into three levels of needs: (1) existence, (2) relatedness, and (3) growth.[14] *Existence* includes both physiological and safety needs; it corresponds to the lower-order needs described in the research related to Maslow's theory. *Relatedness* comprises love and belongingness needs. *Growth* incorporates both self-esteem and self-actualization needs. Together with relatedness needs, growth needs comprise the higher-order needs.

THE MECHANISM OF NEEDS SATISFACTION

Alderfer agreed with Maslow that unsatisfied needs motivate individuals. For example, workers with unsatisfied relatedness needs (love and belongingness) are motivated to produce if their performance results in their satisfying these needs.

FIGURE 15.3 ▅
Alderfer's Hierarchy of
Needs

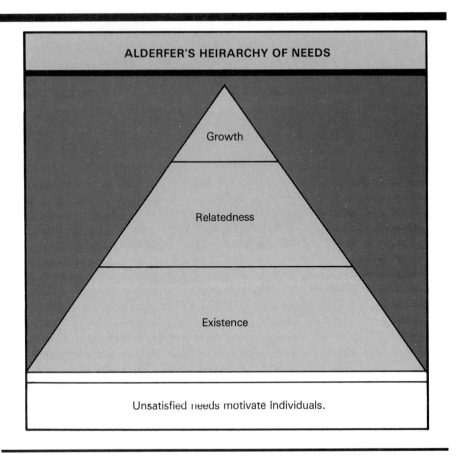

Alderfer also agreed that individuals, in satisfying their needs, generally move up the hierarchy; that is, they satisfy lower-order before higher-order needs. Like Maslow, he believed that as lower-order needs are satisfied they become less important; but he also believed that as higher-order needs are satisfied they become more important. Under some circumstances, however, individuals might return to a lower need. An employee frustrated in efforts to satisfy growth needs, for example, might be motivated to satisfy the lower-level relatedness needs.

Consider the employee who earns a good salary, has a reasonably high standard of living, and has made many friends at work. According to Maslow and Alderfer, this person is probably motivated to satisfy growth needs. What if the individual finds that he or she is continually frustrated in attempts to get more autonomy and responsibility, features of a job that generally encourage individual growth? When asked, the employee reports that having friends at work and getting together with them outside of work is most important. Frustration in satisfying a higher (growth) need has resulted in regression to a lower level of (relatedness) needs.

Alderfer's theory for diagnosing motivational problems asks six questions: (1) What needs do the individuals involved in the situation have? (2) What needs have been satisfied? How? (3) Which unsatisfied need is the lowest in the hierarchy? (4) Have some higher-order needs been frustrated? How? (5) Has the person refocused on a lower-level need? (6) How can the unsatisfied needs be satisfied? The opening case suggests that the new structure is frustrating Carol's attempts to meet her growth needs. Carol left the company. But what might have happened if she had not? Over time, if her frustration continued, satisfying either existence or relatedness needs might have become more important for Carol.

OTHER INFLUENCES ON NEEDS
Different individuals have different needs. Alderfer attributes these differences in part to the individual's developmental level, as well as to the different needs a person experiences as a group member. For example, after receiving her MBA, Carol's existence needs might predominate; as she attains financial security, her needs might shift to primarily growth ones. Later, as she adds financial responsibilities such as a family or aged parents, satisfying her existence needs may again become important.

McClelland's Needs Theory

David McClelland and his associates, beginning in the 1950s, focused on needs similar to the higher-order needs identified by Maslow.[15] Whereas Maslow's theory stresses a universal hierarchy of needs, the research of David McClelland emphasizes that there are certain needs that are learned and socially acquired as the individual interacts with the environment. McClelland's needs theory is concerned with how individual needs and environmental factors combine to form three basic human motives: the need for achievement (*n Ach*), the need for power (*n Pow*), and the need for affiliation (*n Aff*). McClelland conducted numerous studies attempting to define and measure basic human needs.

NEED FOR ACHIEVEMENT
A person with a high need for achievement tends to be characterized as a person who

- Wants to take personal responsibility for finding solutions to problems
- Is goal oriented
- Seeks a challenge—and establishes moderate, realistic, and attainable goals that involve risk but are not impossible to attain
- Desires concrete feedback on performance
- Has a high level of energy, and is willing to work hard

People exhibiting a high *n Ach* find this pattern of behavior personally rewarding. For these people, the value of goal accomplishment is enhanced if the goals are at least moderately difficult to achieve and if there is a significant degree of risk involved.[16] McClelland's research has shown that a high *n Ach* is probably a strong or dominant need in only 10 percent of the U.S. population. Persons high in the need for achievement tend to gravitate toward entrepreneurial and sales positions. In these occupations, individuals are better able to "manage" themselves and satisfy the basic drive for achievement. In the opening case, Carol Harrington has a high need to achieve. The vice-president's interference obviously caused motivational problems for Carol.

NEED FOR POWER

A high need for power means that an individual seeks to influence or control others. Such an individual tends to be characterized as a person who

- Is concerned with acquiring, exercising, or retaining power or influence over others
- Likes to compete with others in situations that allow him or her to be dominant
- Enjoys confrontations with others

Often top-level managers and politicians have a high need for power. Frank Lorenzo and Donald Trump appear to fit into this power mold. These individuals seem to have a burning desire to control their respective environments. McClelland says that there are two basic aspects of power: positive and negative. Positive use of power is essential if a manager is to accomplish results through the efforts of others. The negative side of power is seen in an individual who seeks power for personal benefit, which may prove detrimental to the organization.[17]

NEED FOR AFFILIATION

The need for affiliation is related to the desire for affection and establishing friendly relationships. A person with a high need for affiliation tends to be characterized as one who

- Seeks to establish and maintain friendships and close emotional relationships with others
- Wants to be liked by others
- Enjoys parties, social activities, and bull sessions
- Seeks a sense of belonging by joining groups or organizations

To varying degrees, each person possesses all three motives; however, one of the needs will tend to be more characteristic of the individual than the other

An individual with a high need for affiliation values friendships and social interaction in the work place.
(© James Foote/Photo Researchers, Inc.)

two.[18] People in a given culture may have the same needs, but the relative strength of those needs differs. For example, the strength of Japanese workers' need for affiliation may be stronger than that of U.S. workers. Therefore, the family feeling that Nissan promotes may have less appeal in the United States than in Japan.

Each of McClelland's three motives evokes a different type of feeling of satisfaction. For example, the achievement motive tends to evoke a sense of accomplishment, whereas a manager may have a feeling of being in control or influencing others when the power motive is prevalent. According to this theory, the probability that an individual will perform a job effectively and efficiently depends on a combination of

- The strength of the motive or need relative to other needs
- The possibility of success in performing the task
- The strength value of the incentive or reward for performance

The most effective mixture of these three motives depends on the situation. In studies of over 500 managers, it was concluded that the most effective managers have a high need for power, a moderate need for achievement, and a low need for affiliation. These managers tend to use their power in a participative manner for the good of the organization. The best managers have a moderate need for achievement not strong enough to interfere with the management process. Persons with high needs for both power and achievement have high managerial motivation but they may not make the best managers.[19] After all, management is getting work done through the efforts of others, not overpowering them.

Outstanding sales personnel tend to be high in the need for achievement and moderately high in the need for power. Entrepreneurs who develop ideas and promote specific enterprises tend to be high in achievement motivation. They delight in personally solving problems and getting immediate feedback on the degree of success. Entrepreneurs sometimes are unable to make the transition to top-level management positions. Their need for personal achievement gets in the way of the requirements for effectively influencing the organization's employees.

MEASURING NEEDS FOR ACHIEVEMENT, AFFILIATION, AND POWER

Determining the level of effort and performance possible in an organization involves determining its members' *n Ach*. A variety of instruments are used to measure all three needs. McClelland used the projective Thematic Apperception Test (TAT). The TAT comprises a series of pictures of one or more people in various settings similar to that shown in Figure 15.4. The respondent describes what he or she thinks is occurring in the picture. What do you see in Figure 15.4? Are these individuals holding a sales meeting to discuss problems related to the introduction of a new product? Are they chatting during a coffee break? Or is the man in the back of the picture assigning projects to members of the group?

McClelland proposed that respondents project their own needs into their description of the picture. For example, if an individual views the picture as a problem-solving meeting, then that individual would receive positive scores on the need for achievement. If this picture is perceived as a social gathering, then positive scores on the need for affiliation are recorded. If the picture is viewed as

F I G U R E 15.4 ■
Picture Representative of
Those Used in Projective
Tests Such as the TAT

a situation being controlled by a single person, then positive scores on the need for power are recorded. Professional administrators have detailed protocols for scoring the pictures included in the TAT and similar tests. Because of the time and skill required in the administration and scoring of the test, its cost is relatively high and only trained professionals can administer and score it. For this reason, others prefer the use of nonprojective tests, such as the questionnaire shown in Table 15.3.

IDENTIFYING NEEDS ACCORDING TO McCLELLAND

Table 15.3 is a list of questions to help identify a person's predominant need at any given time. Scoring responses provides a rough estimate of an individual's predominant need at this particular time. Carol obviously has the need to achieve. Note that occasionally individuals may experience more than one of these needs equally strongly.

McClelland and his colleagues devoted their initial attention and energy to studying the need for achievement, which they linked to effective managerial performance in the United States and abroad. These researchers proposed that those higher in the need for achievement performed better than those with a low need for achievement. McClelland also stated that he could teach an individual the need for achievement and thereby improve his or her performance. Some of McClelland's earliest work involved measuring the extent of achievement

---

TABLE 15.3 ■ Identification of Needs According to McClelland

1. Do you like situations where you personally must find solutions to problems?
2. Do you tend to set moderate goals and take moderate, thought-out risks?
3. Do you want specific feedback about how well you are doing?
4. Do you spend time considering how to advance in your career, how to do your job better, or how to accomplish something important?

If you responded yes to questions 1–4, then you probably have a high need for achievement.

5. Do you look for jobs or seek situations that provide an opportunity for social relationships?
6. Do you often think about the personal relationships you have?
7. Do you consider the feelings of others to be very important?
8. Do you try to restore disrupted relationships when they occur?

If you responded yes to questions 5–8, then you probably have a high need for affiliation.

9. Do you try to influence and control others?
10. Do you seek leadership positions in groups?
11. Do you enjoy persuading others?
12. Are you perceived by others as outspoken, forceful, and demanding?

If you responded yes to questions 9–12, then you probably have a high need for power.

Source: Based on R. M. Steers and L. W. Porter, *Motivation and Work Behavior* (New York: McGraw-Hill, 1979), pp. 57–64.

---

motivation in different countries by analyzing and comparing their folk tales.[20] He found a high positive correlation between an achievement theme in a folk tale and the level of industrial development in that country. Once again, the results suggested the value of a need for achievement for performance.

More recently, McClelland, with David Burnham, has studied the need for power in individuals. Contrasting male managers in a sales organization with a high need for power to those with a high need for affiliation, for example, they found that managers with a high need for power tended to run more productive departments than did managers with a high need for affiliation.[21] These results suggest the importance of power to organizational performance.

ACQUISITION OF MOTIVES

McClelland, unlike other theorists, emphasizes the means through which one might acquire various motives. He says, in particular, that training can increase an individual's need for achievement. In this way, he offers a prescription for individuals deficient in needs that might influence their work efforts and subsequent performance. He directs them to focus on developing certain desirable needs; for example, he teaches them how to develop a higher need for achievement. For this reason, some have argued that *n Ach* is not a need but a value.

McClelland's theory differs from Maslow's and Alderfer's, which focus on satisfying existing needs rather than on creating or developing needs. Like these other needs theories, however, McClelland's approach suggests that increasing the environment's compatibility with individual needs should improve motivation and, consequently, performance.

F I G U R E 15.5 ■ Herzberg's Two-Factor Theory

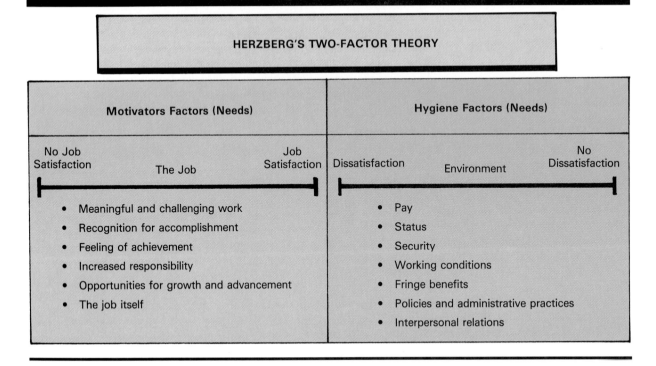

Herzberg's Two-Factor Theory

Frederick Herzberg and his associates' view of motivation complements that of the other needs theorists.[22] They suggest that *motivators*—features of a job's content including responsibility, autonomy, self-esteem, and self-actualization opportunities—are factors that satisfy higher-order needs, motivate a person to exert more effort, and hence encourage the person to perform better. *Hygiene factors*—factors that can meet physiological, security, or social needs, including physical working conditions, salary, company policies and practices, benefits, and other features of a job's context—satisfy lower-order needs and prevent dissatisfaction. Thus, for Herzberg, two independent outcome continuums exist: (1) no satisfaction–satisfaction, and (2) dissatisfaction–no dissatisfaction, rather than a single dissatisfaction–satisfaction continuum (see Figure 15.5). Unlike the other needs theories, the two-factor theory focuses on increasing overall satisfaction, rather than relying simply on meeting individual needs. "It is primarily the 'motivators' that serve to bring about the kind of job satisfaction and . . . the kind of improvement in performance that industry is seeking from its work force."[23]

Hygiene factors do not motivate because they do not encourage individuals to exert more effort. But hygiene factors must first be satisfied to bring the individual to a point of neutrality so that the motivators will have an effect. For example, offering autonomy and responsibility when working conditions and other context factors are not resolved will still result in worker dissatisfaction. Making provision for hygiene factors will cause workers to be neutral in the job situation (not be dissatisfied); then motivators can be introduced and will be expected to cause satisfaction and ultimately improve performance.

RESEARCH SUPPORT

Herzberg's theory has been subjected to significant criticism. This criticism focuses on the research method used to collect data, as well as on the classification of some factors (e.g., pay) as both a motivator and a hygiene factor.[24] The theory also ignores individual differences, and it may overemphasize the importance of pleasure as a desired outcome. Still, this theory can offer significant insights into, if not definitive answers for, motivational problems.

For example, according to Herzberg, a manager's giving an individual a new job title without additional job responsibilities would not change his or her performance, because the manager has increased the hygiene factors (which affect dissatisfaction) but not the motivators (which affect satisfaction, effort, and performance). Similarly, if pay is considered a hygiene factor, merely giving pay increases without changing a job's content will not increase performance.

Organizational Responses to Needs

Organizations can attempt to meet individuals' needs through the introduction of special programs such as food or housing plans, the organization of individuals into work teams, the design of the reward system, and the design of jobs. Table 15.4 gives an overview of the ways in which organizations can satisfy different kinds of needs.

TABLE 15.4 ■ Ways of Satisfying Individual Needs in the Workplace

Need	Organizational Conditions
Physiological Existence Hygiene	pay mandatory breakfast or lunch programs company housing
Safety Security Existence Hygiene	company benefits plans pensions seniority pay
Love Belongingness Relatedness Affiliation Hygiene	coffee breaks sports teams company picnics and social events work teams pay
Self-esteem Growth Achievement Motivators	autonomy responsibility pay (as symbol of status) prestige office location and furnishings job challenge
Self-actualization Growth Power Motivators	challenge autonomy leadership positions authority

Changing a job's content by increasing challenge, autonomy, and responsibility addresses the higher-order needs of esteem, achievement, and growth. Changes in a reward system, such as introducing pensions and new benefits, influence the lower-level physiological and security needs. The introduction of work teams focuses on social needs. Note that pay is a particularly powerful organizational change: it can meet both lower-order and higher-order needs.

Evaluation of Needs Theories

The extent to which any of the current needs theories explains motivation in organizations has been questioned by some researchers. They maintain that the concept of needs is popular in psychology but is difficult to prove or disprove, for several reasons.[25] First, needs are difficult to specify and measure. Often, for example, managers must assume what the needs of their subordinates are; few instruments exist that can reliably or validly measure them.[26] When possible, managers should talk to subordinates about their needs, asking for suggestions as to how the organization could better meet those needs.

Second, relating needs to various job characteristics can be problematic. It cannot be completely certain that a new company-benefits plan will better meet an individual's security needs, or that increasing autonomy will respond to self-actualization needs. The complexity of human behavior and organizational life makes it difficult to determine direct cause-and-effect relationships.

Third, need-satisfaction models fail to account for variances in behaviors and attitudes. For example, decreasing job performance can be a function of ineffective leadership or of dysfunctional organizational design.

Fourth, attributing needs to individuals fails to take into account the external forces that influence behavior. For example, declining performance may result from changes in the technology required to do the job or changes the company faces with its competition, rather than from a failure of the firm to meet an employee's needs.

Finally, care must be taken to avoid stereotyping individuals by applying a single, one-time categorization of their needs. Individual needs may change over time, as a function of the situation in which the person is involved. Assessment of individual needs that affect motivation must be an ongoing process in order to be truly effective.

Equity theory
A theory which assumes that people assess their performance and attitudes by comparing both their contribution to work and the benefits they derive from it to the contributions and benefits of a "comparison other" whom the person selects—who in reality may be like or unlike the person.

■ EQUITY THEORY

The second major type of motivation theory is generally credited to J. Stacy Adams.[27] It has evolved from social comparison theory, which suggests that individuals must assess and know their degree of performance and the "correctness" of their attitudes in a situation. Lacking objective measures of performance or correct attitudes, they compare their performance and attitudes to those of others. **Equity theory** assumes that people assess their performance and attitudes by comparing both their contribution to work and the benefits they derive from it to the contributions and benefits of a "comparison other" whom the person selects—who in reality may be like or unlike the person. For example, workers

YOU ARE IN charge of a think tank that supports the research and development department for your company. Your company manufactures microchips and is a leader in advanced chip technology. The main reason the company is so successful in staying on the cutting edge of chip technology is the think tank. The think tank has been so successful that another has been organized to support the company's newest manufacturing operation on the Gulf Coast. The individuals to be included in the new think tank have already been selected, and your boss has just assigned you the task of deciding who from your group of thinkers will be its head. The best-qualified person for the job is Tim Matherson. Tim is an MIT graduate, the informal team leader, and the individual who personally spearheaded three of the team's five most successful product advancements. However, if Tim were given the promotion, the void created by his leaving would be difficult to fill. On the other hand, there is the boss's niece, Marthanne, who was forced on the group by the boss. She is sharp, a graduate of Tech, but she is not a team player, and she is always trying to push you around. You can either recommend Tim and illustrate how those who produce the most benefit the most, or you can recommend Marthanne, make the boss happy, and get rid of her.

What would you do?

might compare their effort and rewards to the effort and rewards of other professionals in the firm, as Carol Harrington did, or to friends or associates in other firms, or even to the CEO of the organization.

Determination of Equity

Equity theory further states that a person is motivated in proportion to the perceived fairness of the rewards received for a certain amount of effort as compared to others.[28] A colleague may have been heard to say, "I'm going to stop working so hard—I work harder than Susan and she gets all the bonuses." This individual has compared his effort and the rewards he received to the effort exerted and rewards received by Susan. In fact, no actual inequity may exist, but the *perception* of inequity influences subsequent actions.

Specifically, one compares two ratios: (1) the ratio of their outcomes to their inputs to (2) the ratio of another's outcomes to inputs (see Figure 15.6). Outcomes may include pay, status, and job complexity; inputs include effort, productivity, age, sex, and experience. For example, one worker may feel that he receives $20 for each hour of effort he contributes to the job; in contrast, he may assess that another worker receives $40 for each hour of effort she contributes to the job. The first (A) worker perceives that his ratio of outcomes to inputs (20 to 1) is less than the second (B) worker's (40 to 1). In fact, the second individual may only receive $10 for each hour of effort she contributes to the job. But, according to equity theory, the facts do not influence motivation; perceptions of the situation

FIGURE 15.6 ■■
Equity Theory

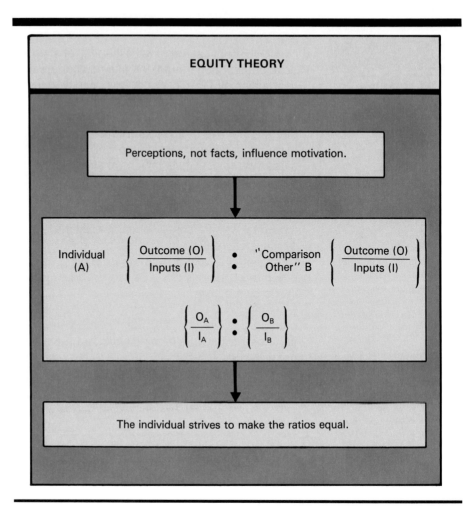

do. Some workers may feel that they have more experience than a "comparison other"—a worker to whom they compare themselves—but receive less complex jobs to perform; here, again, perceived inequity exists.

Reduction of Inequity

According to equity theory, individuals are motivated to reduce any perceived inequity. They strive to make the ratios of outcomes to inputs (O/I) equal.[29] When inequity exists, the person making the comparison strives to make the ratios equal by changing either the outcomes or the inputs.

The Overjustification Effect

Theoretically, the same adjustment process occurs when a person perceives that he or she receives too great a reward for the input or has too complex a job in comparison to others.[30] For example, individuals who feel that they received undeserved time off would increase their inputs, perhaps by working longer hours, so that the perceived ratios are equal. Research has questioned whether this *overjustification effect* really occurs.[31] Many researchers believe, however, that overpaying some people will improve their performance.[32]

Determining Equity in the Workplace

When inequity exists in an organization, individuals react in a variety of ways, some of which have been described earlier.[33] Some people adjust their inputs; for example, they exert less effort or spend more time at work. Others change the outcomes; they request pay increases or more vacation time. Still others adjust their perception of their own or others' inputs and outcomes; they might revalue their own or others' effort, experience, or education. Some workers leave the situation entirely. The remaining people choose a different comparison person. Table 15.5 illustrates the conditions under which these alternatives occur. This table can be used to diagnose potentially inequitable situations and the likely consequences.

Thus, when high absenteeism, low productivity, high turnover, or other such symptoms exist, the following questions can be asked to determine whether or not inequity exists:

1. What contributions or inputs does the person make to the situation? What is the person's level of education, effort, or experience?
2. What benefits or outcomes does the person receive? What is the level of job complexity, pay, or status of that person?
3. What is the ratio of inputs to outcomes? (Some quantification of both inputs and outcomes should occur. These can then be compared in ratio form. If the inputs or outcomes cannot be quantified, qualitative determination of the ratio must occur.)
4. Is the ratio the same, greater than, or less than the ratio of comparison others?

Answers to the first three questions must also be obtained for relevant others. The resulting ratios can then be compared.

TABLE 15.5 ■ Conditions of Perceived Inequity

Condition	Responses of Perceiver (A)
$\frac{O_A}{I_A} > \frac{O_B}{I_B}$	A increases inputs A asks for reduced outcomes A changes comparison person A leaves the situation
$\frac{O_A}{I_A} < \frac{O_B}{I_B}$	A reduces inputs A asks for increased outcomes A changes comparison person A leaves the situation

Equity theory does not negate needs theory. Rather, it provides another perspective for analyzing motivational problems and predicting individuals' behaviors and attitudes. Both needs theories and equity theory can be used together in diagnosis.

Empirical Evidence

Equity theory basically makes strong intuitive sense, but the empirical evidence for it has been mixed. One study showed that individuals will exert an amount of effort that will lead to the greatest payoff for the lowest expenditure of effort.[34] Another showed that employees' perceptions of the fairness of their pay relative to their co-workers' and others' outside the organization, as well as the fairness and administration of rules for pay increases and promotion, were related most significantly to absenteeism; only their perceptions of the fairness of their pay to that of others' outside the organization were significantly related to turnover.[35] Recent research suggests that a time lag may exist in some individuals reacting to inequity.[36] Further, individual characteristics such as sex, IQ, and social values may affect an individual's perception of inequity.[37]

In a sense, equity theory may oversimplify motivational issues by not explicitly considering individual needs, values, and personalities. Thus, equity theory should be supplemented with other theoretical approaches to motivation. To understand complex organizational behavior completely, diverse perspectives must be applied. Nevertheless, ensuring equity in organizational policies, specifically in the reward system, is essential to effective motivation.

■ REINFORCEMENT THEORY

Reinforcement theory
The idea that human behavior can be explained in terms of the previous positive or negative outcomes of that behavior.

Reinforcement theory applies the behaviorist learning theories to motivation. Prompted most directly by B. F. Skinner's research, it emphasizes the importance of feedback and rewards in motivating behavior through diverse reinforcement techniques.[38] **Reinforcement theory** is the idea that human behavior can be explained in terms of the previous positive or negative outcomes of that behavior. People tend to repeat behaviors that they have learned will produce pleasant outcomes. Behavior that is reinforced will be repeated; behavior that is not reinforced will not be repeated.

Skinner contends that people's behavior can be controlled and shaped by rewarding (reinforcing) desired behavior while ignoring undesirable actions. Over time, the reinforced behavior will tend to be repeated, whereas the unrewarded behavior will tend to be extinguished and disappear. Punishment of undesired behavior is to be avoided, since it may contribute to feelings of restraint and actions of rebellion. Thus, over a period of years, one can control the behavior of another without that person being aware of it. In his book, *Beyond Freedom and Dignity,* Skinner says that people can be controlled and shaped while at the same time feeling free.[39] Skinner's theory of shaping behavior is useful to managers, although one should not assume that human behavior is simple to understand and/or modify.

Positive Reinforcement

Positive reinforcement
Also known as *operant conditioning* or *behavior modification,* involves repeatedly pairing desired behaviors or outcomes with positive reinforcement, rewards, or feedback.

Positive reinforcement, also known as *operant conditioning* or *behavior modification,* involves repeatedly pairing desired behaviors or outcomes with positive reinforcement, rewards, or feedback. For example, if a person who packs tea sets receives ten cents for each one packed, the desired behavior—packing the tea sets—is directly paired with the financial rewards. If a person who completes a project in a way desired by the supervisor receives praise for the project, this verbal feedback, which accompanies good performance, encourages the performance of the behavior to recur. According to reinforcement theory, this praise, or reinforcement, of the behavior should stimulate its repetition.

Feedback shapes behavior by encouraging the reinforced or rewarded behavior to recur. If the behavior is not precisely what is desired by a superior or client, repeated reinforcements in the desired direction can move the actual behavior closer to the desired behavior. For example, if an individual often comes to work late, that person's superior might comment positively when that person comes to work less late; additional praise might follow if that person comes to work more and more promptly; and praise would continue until the desired behavior occurred. This behavior would then be reinforced with praise, or even financial incentives, until it became more or less permanent, but praise would be discontinued if any reversion to previous behaviors occurred.

Other Reinforcement Techniques

While positive reinforcement motivates behavior by attaching desired reinforcements to desired behavior, other techniques attach undesired reinforcements, as shown in Table 15.6. In *negative reinforcement,* an individual acts to stop an undesired behavior that has already occurred by applying a desired reinforcer when the behavior stops. The term *negative* stems from either (1) the removal of the individual from a negative situation when the desired behavior occurs, or (2) the application of the reinforcer when an undesired or negative behavior ceases. A word processing operator who is chronically late is assigned the department's least desirable work; but when the operator arrives on time for a month of work days, that individual is given interesting and desired work. The undesirable behavior is reinforced with an undesirable reinforcer; but when the behavior changes, a desirable reinforcer replaces the undesirable one.

TABLE 15.6 ■ Reinforcement Options

	Application Serves As:	Withdrawal Serves As:
Desirable reinforcement (Reward)	Positive reinforcement	Withholding reinforcement (leading to discontinuance of desired/productive behavior)
Undesirable reinforcement (Adverse stimulus)	Punishment	Negative reinforcement (leading to extinction of undesirable behavior)

Withholding reinforcement also causes the discontinuation of certain behaviors. Extinction of behavior results when a specific reinforcer causing a particular desired or undesired behavior is withheld. In other words, failure to apply reinforcements causes a behavior to cease. Removing positive reinforcements contributes to a decline in performance. The withholding of reinforcement causes people to discontinue the productive behavior. A person who repeatedly works overtime but receives neither compensation, status, nor praise for this added effort will likely stop the overtime. By withholding reinforcement, a supervisor will often cause desired behaviors—productivity, creativity, attendance—to stop or be extinguished.

Punishment also eliminates undesirable behaviors, but often creates the secondary consequences of tension and stress. Thus, punishment should be used only as a last resort. In addition, the results of punishment tend to be less predictable and less permanent than those of other operant conditioning techniques.

The word *punishment* here refers to the application of an undesirable reinforcer to an undesirable behavior. In this way it differs from negative reinforcement, which refers to reinforcing the cessation of an undesirable behavior. Using punishment, a superior officer would assign kitchen patrol (KP—an undesirable reinforcer) to a newly recruited army private who questions a directive (an undesirable behavior) about using computers on the job. Using negative reinforcement, the superior officer would take the private off KP when the soldier adheres to directives without question for a month. How would the private react to punishment? Most likely the recruit would feel bitterness or anger toward the superior. This attitude, which often results from the use of punishment, may result in a long-term negative attitude toward the activity—the use of computers—that the superior was conducting. Negative attitudes toward the administrator of the punishment often accompany negative attitudes toward the activity that inspired the punishment.

Punishment may also suppress behavior, but not permanently eliminate it. This results because punishment does not offer an alternative to the undesirable behavior. If a worker repeatedly misuses a piece of equipment and receives punishment each time, the behavior may not change because no correct way of using the equipment (an alternative behavior) is presented.

Punishment may also be offset by positive reinforcement for the same undesirable behavior from another source, such as peers.[40] The newly recruited private's "speaking back" to a superior may be applauded by other recruits. Or the worker's co-workers may encourage the misuse of equipment, particularly if the worker is otherwise perceived to violate the group's standards for expected and acceptable behavior. Table 15.7 summarizes the types of reinforcement and their consequences.

Reinforcement Schedules

The timing and frequency of reinforcement significantly influence its impact. Reinforcement schedules differ along two dimensions:

1. *Fixed/variable*—the extent to which reinforcement is regular and known in advance. A weekly paycheck is administered according to a fixed schedule. Often this type of reinforcer loses power quickly

TABLE 15.7 ■ Types of Reinforcement and Their Consequences

Type	Effect on Behavior When Applied to the Individual	Effect on Behavior When Withdrawn from the Individual
Positive	Increased frequency over preconditioning level	Return to preconditioning level
Negative	Decreased frequency over preconditioning level	Return to preconditioning level
Punishment	Decreased frequency over preconditioning level	Return to preconditioning level
Withholding	Decreased frequency over preconditioning level	Return to preconditioning level

Source: Based on O. Behling, C. Schriesheim, and J. Tolliver, Present trends and new directions in theories of work effort, *Journal Supplement, Abstract Service of the American Psychological Association* 385 (1974): 57.

because it is received regardless of the individual's behavior. Praise, however, is typically given according to a variable schedule—the praiser does not determine in advance precisely when to comment about an employee's behavior.

2. *Interval/ratio*—the extent to which reinforcement corresponds to the passing of specific time intervals or with the occurrence of a given number of responses. Christmas bonuses illustrate reinforcements given according to an interval schedule: they are given once a year at a predetermined time. Piecework rates illustrate reinforcement according to a ratio schedule: piecework pay is given after a specific number of items (or responses) are produced.

Table 15.8 illustrates the four schedules resulting from the combination of these two dimensions and suggests some applications for them. The four schedules differ in their ability to encourage desired behavior in the short term and the long run. In general, fixed and interval schedules more effectively encourage desired

TABLE 15.8 ■ Schedules of Reinforcement (Examples in Parentheses)

	Fixed	Variable
Interval	Reinforcement or reward given after a specified period of time (Weekly or monthly paycheck)	Reinforcement or reward given after a certain amount of time with that amount changing before the next reinforcement (Supervisor who visits shop floor on different unannounced days each week)
Ratio	Reinforcement or reward given after a specified number of responses (Pay for piecework)	Reinforcement or reward given after a number of responses with that number changing before the next reinforcement (Praise)

behaviors in the short term; variable and ratio schedules more effectively sustain desired behaviors over the long run. Managers must select the reinforcement schedule that best fits with their goals.

Most frequently a diversity of rewards should be applied, each according to different schedules. For example, a manager might use the weekly paycheck to encourage attendance, a merit bonus to motivate exceptional behavior, and periodic praise to stimulate day-to-day and longer-term productivity. In trying to motivate an employee to show initiative, for example, a manager should begin praising the worker each time the employee demonstrates initiative, then gradually decrease the use of praise until only exceptional behavior receives comments. This movement from a fixed-ratio schedule to a variable-ratio schedule sustains behavior over the long term. Or a manager might rely on weekly paychecks to reward a mechanic's productivity, and ultimately add yearly bonuses, with the timing of the award unannounced. This shift from a fixed-interval to a variable-interval schedule also sustains productivity.

Operant Conditioning Programs

Operant conditioning is widespread in work settings to increase performance levels. The distribution of the weekly paycheck, the delivery of merit raises, and the promotion of an employee who does a good job are typical examples. Some firms, however, use more extensive behavior modification programs.[41] Emery Air Freight applied a combination of positive incentives, goal setting, and praise to increase container utilization in freight packing. In one program, the freight packers set capacity goals for the shipping crates, which they then compared to their actual packing record. Meeting their goals provided feedback about the quality of their performance and reinforced the behavior that led to goal accomplishment. Praise from supervisors often accompanied the goal accomplishment and helped to shape the desired behaviors. This program increased container utilization from approximately 40 percent to over 85 percent and saved $600,000 in 1970 and over $2 million in 1975.

Similarly, at Michigan Bell, a program combining goal setting and positive reinforcement for telephone operators increased performance in such areas as service promptness and average time per call from 50 percent to 90 percent. Garbage collectors in Detroit received a bonus when financial savings accrued from their higher productivity. The city saved over $1 1/2 million in 1974 and each worker received a $350 bonus.

Other applications of reinforcement theory have also received public attention.[42] Programmed instruction, for example, combines motivation theory and learning theory. Students have learned algebra, accounting, and typing, among other subjects, in this way. Typically, programmed instruction has been used for teaching relatively simple subject matter. The learner responds to a series of questions about a given subject in a written text or on a computer terminal. After each correct answer, the learner moves to the next question, which helps to refine his or her knowledge of the subject by asking about a slightly different aspect of it. Thus, correct answers are reinforced by the learner's having the opportunity to move forward in the instructional program. After an incorrect answer, the learner moves to a separate series of questions, which provide additional information about the current, unmastered subject. Thus, many questions are available to reinforce the learning of a particular subject. In this approach the learner gets immediate feedback about the accuracy of a response. Zenith Corporation has used programmed instruction to teach the features of their color televisions to wholesale sales representatives. IBM has also used it to train computer programmers.

Fitting Reinforcers to Behavior

Although the popularity of positive reinforcement has increased, researchers now believe that the assignment of reinforcers is more complicated than they once thought. What, for example, does the weekly paycheck or the annual Christmas bonus reinforce? Do supervisors praise their subordinates enough or at the best times? In universities, society hopes that teachers will not neglect their teaching responsibilities, yet in some disciplines rewards them, almost entirely, only for research and publications.[43] In business, organizations are often in a position where they hope for employee efforts in the areas of team building, interpersonal relations, and creativity, among others, but formally reward none of these.[44]

Misguided reward systems, where undesired behaviors are reinforced or perceived to be reinforced, occur for three reasons.[45] First, organizational members may substitute measurable outcomes for true organizational goals. For example, organizations may reward the quantity of work produced by computer programmers and overlook the quality or efficiency of the programs written. They may rely on measuring tardiness or absenteeism of schoolteachers, which are easily observable and quantifiable, rather than evaluating teacher performance, which is more difficult to assess.

Second, managers may overemphasize the visible parts of a task. They may reward machine operators who have few breakdowns, rather than those who look for more efficient ways of producing. Likewise, a manager may reward a secretary's word processing speed, rather than the individual's initiative or interpersonal skills.

Third, organizational leaders may show simple hypocrisy about the outcomes they desire. Supervisors, for example, might tell workers that they value creativity, when in fact they seek employees who quietly implement their requests. Or they might state that employee service is their foremost goal, whereas in fact profit is the sole driving force. In this last situation, employees' perceptions of the reward system differ significantly from the actual reinforcement program.

Rules for Effective Operant Conditioning

What principles guide the effective use of reinforcement theory? How can "the folly of rewarding A, while hoping for B" be avoided? And how can an individual's perception of the use of reinforcement theory match its actual implementation? Clay Hamner offers six rules for using operant conditioning techniques.[46]

1. *Do not give all people the same rewards.* As in equity theory, pay and other reinforcements should be distributed fairly to all employees according to relevant performance criteria.
2. *Realize that failure to respond has reinforcing consequences: withdrawing reinforcement causes a behavior to cease.*
3. *Be sure to tell individuals what they can do to get reinforcement.* This type of communication increases the similarity between perceptions and reality.

4. *Be sure to tell individuals what they are doing wrong.* In universities, good teachers often do not receive tenure because they have not done sufficient research or published enough. Department chairpersons, senior faculty, or other personnel with knowledge of tenure standards must regularly evaluate their performance on all dimensions and communicate the results to the nontenured faculty member.

5. *Do not punish in front of others.* In using punishment, attempt to reduce the dysfunctional, secondary consequences associated with it. Keeping punishment private reduces a worker's need to "save face" with co-workers or subordinates, which often causes workers to act in ways detrimental to the organization's goals.

6. *Make the consequences equal to the behavior.* Reinforcements such as praise, bonuses, promotions, and demotions should fit the type of behavior being reinforced. Giving a 20 percent pay increase to an employee to reinforce prompt attendance will confuse the employee about the importance of other work behaviors.

Reinforcement theory should only be applied in conjunction with the principles of social learning. Rewards or reinforcement must meet an employee's specific needs and must be applied equitably. Managers must be clear about the behaviors they want to encourage and consistent in reinforcing them. They must also apply appropriate rewards according to effective schedules.

■ EXPECTANCY THEORY

Expectancy theory
An approach to motivation that attempts to explain behavior in terms of an individual's goals and choices and the expectations of achieving these goals.

In recent years, one of the more popular theories of motivation has been expectancy theory.[47] The approaches to motivation developed by Maslow, Herzberg, and McClelland do not adequately account for differences in individual employees or explain why people behave in certain ways. Victor Vroom developed an approach to motivation, known as **expectancy theory,** that attempts to explain behavior in terms of an individual's goals and choices and the expectations of achieving these goals.[48] It assumes that people can determine which outcomes they prefer and can make realistic estimates of their chances of obtaining them. Expectancy theory, perhaps more than the preceding ones, offers a comprehensive view of motivation and integrates many of the elements of the needs, equity, and reinforcement theories.

Victor Vroom popularized expectancy theory in the 1960s. His model states that motivation is a function of expectancy, valence, and instrumentality.[49] In other words,

$$\text{Motivation} = \text{E} \times \text{V} \times \text{I (Expectancy} \times \text{Valence} \times \text{Instrumentality)}$$

This simple formulation identifies the three basic components of expectancy theory.

E, or expectancy, refers to a person's perception of the probability that effort will lead to performance. For example, a person who perceives that if he or she works harder then he or she will produce more, has a high expectancy that hard work leads to productivity. A person who perceives that if he or she works harder then he or she will be ostracized by other workers, has a high expectancy that effort leads to exclusion. A person who sees no link between effort and performance will have zero expectancy about this relationship. If expectancy is zero, then motivation will be lower than if expectancy is positive.

V, or valence, refers to a person's perception of the value of the projected outcomes; that is, how much the person likes or dislikes receiving those outcomes. An individual with high esteem needs generally will attach a high valence to a new job title or a promotion. An individual with strong security needs will value pension and retirement programs or the awarding of tenure. An individual with growth or self-actualization needs will view challenging jobs or increased responsibility as motivating because of their high valence. When valence is high, motivation is likely to be higher than when valence is less positive, or negative.

I, or instrumentality, refers to a person's perception of the probability that certain outcomes, positive or negative, will be attached to performance. For example, a person who perceives that he or she will receive greater pay or benefits if he or she produces, has high instrumentality. A person who sees no link between performance and pay will have zero instrumentality. Motivation is a function of the value of instrumentality.

The Intrinsic-Extrinsic Motivation Formulation

Barry Staw, among others, introduced a revised expectancy theory in the late 1970s.[50] Rather than limiting his model to extrinsic motivation, which links action to a desirable outcome such as increased pay or promotion,[51] Staw also considers intrinsic motivation, which links action to the satisfaction obtained from performing an action, such as exploration or competence.[52] In short, performing a task has intrinsic and extrinsic valence, both of which enter into the calculation of motivation.

In this model, motivation is reduced if an individual does not value either the intrinsic outcomes or the extrinsic outcomes, or if the person perceives that the intrinsic, or the extrinsic, performance-to-outcome expectancies (rewards) are low. For example, a worker's motivation will be reduced if (1) he or she does not like doing certain tasks, or if (2) he or she does not receive the rewards desired for performing them. A manager can increase extrinsic motivation either by depriving a worker of a valued outcome or by giving the worker the extrinsic rewards valued most; the manager can also ensure that rewards accompany task performance.[53] Managers can increase intrinsic motivation by changing the characteristics of work activities, such as by redesigning jobs.[54]

Empirical Support

Evidence for the validity of the expectancy model is mixed.[55] Conceptual and methodological problems have been emphasized, with critics stating that (1) the model is too complex to measure; (2) the key variables of performance, effort, and valence lack consistent definition and operationalization; and (3) repeated measures of the model's validity over time (reliability) do not exist.[56] Still, expectancy theory has dominated research on motivation since the early 1970s, principally because it has provided three factors useful to managers in their efforts to increase employee motivation. Its emphasis on the individual and its ability to highlight individual differences can also be useful to the practicing manager.

The expectancy perspective implies both the value of equity in the work situation and the importance of consistent rewards; in fact, both equity theory and reinforcement theory have been viewed as special cases of expectancy theory.[57] Although it does not explicitly address individual needs, valences and instrumentalities might be considered as functions of such needs, as noted earlier. Thus, it addresses the issue of individual differences to a much greater extent than needs theories. In addition, it offers the opportunity for quantification of the various facets of motivational problems. Hence, expectancy theory, more than any other presented so far, offers a comprehensive guide for understanding motivation.

▪▪ GOAL SETTING AND MOTIVATION

Just as expectancy theory can serve as an integrative model of motivation, goal setting can act as a common technique in the application of the motivation theories presented so far. Setting goals can help individuals identify ways of meeting their needs. Accomplishing goals can be reinforcing in itself. In these ways, goal setting encourages individuals to exert effort, and goal accomplishment motivates individuals to perform.

Goals, which any member of an organization can set, describe desired future states. Once established, goals can focus behavior and motivate individuals to achieve the desired end state. Examples in organizations are cutting costs, reducing absenteeism, increasing employee satisfaction, and changing the work climate. In 90 percent of the reported studies, goal setting has shown a positive effect on performance.[58]

Goals can vary in three ways: (1) specificity, (2) difficulty, and (3) acceptance. The specificity or clarity of goals refers to the extent to which their accomplishment is observable and measurable. "Reducing absenteeism by 20 percent" is a highly specific goal for a manager; "developing subordinates" is a much less specific one. Goal difficulty, or the level of performance desired, can also vary significantly. A salesperson's setting a goal to open ten new accounts per month might be easy, but a goal to open 100 new accounts is extremely difficult. Third, individuals' acceptance of stated goals, or their commitment to accomplishing the goals, may vary. A subordinate is much less likely to accept a goal and try as hard as possible to accomplish it if a manager assigns the goal rather than setting it jointly with the subordinate.

Research suggests that goals that are specific, moderately difficult, and yet accepted by a worker are more likely to be motivating than those that are not. A study of goal setting by truck drivers in a logging operation illustrates the motivational value of this technique.[59] The drivers loaded logs and drove them to the mill for processing. When their supervisors first instructed them to "do their best," they underloaded their trucks, filling them to only 58–63 percent of truck capacity. The researchers then assigned the drivers a goal of 94 percent of capacity and promised that no disciplinary action would take place if they did not meet the goal. In the first three months, they loaded 80 percent, 70 percent, and 90 percent of truck capacity, respectively. (In the second month the loggers tested the promise of no discipline, causing the drop in loading, but evidently fully accepted the goal thereafter.) Further research recognized the role of feedback as a key component in the success of goal setting.[60]

Even when employees are given the opportunity to jointly set goals with managers, the characteristics of the participants, such as authoritarianism and education, can have an impact on the effectiveness of goal setting.[61] One study of 140 technicians and engineers indicated that the level of acceptance of goals affects the relationship of goal difficulty to task performance: goal difficulty is positively and linearly related to task performance for accepted goals; it is negatively and linearly related for rejected goals.[62] In a second study, subjects were assigned goals on the first trial and chose their own goals on the second. They chose harder goals if the assigned goals were easy, and easier goals if the assigned goals were hard.[63] In addition, performance was a function of ability, acceptance of the goals, level of the goals, and the interaction of the goals with ability.

Research has indicated that goal-setting programs improve performance at both managerial and nonmanagerial levels over an extended period of time in a variety of organizations.[64] In very complex jobs, however, goal setting may not be feasible; in fact, it may lead to bureaucratic behavior, where setting goals becomes an end in itself. Feedback through performance reviews and pay can also enhance performance, but only when these incentives lead individuals to set higher goals.[65] Thus, goal setting provides a link between motivational perspectives and issues of interpersonal communication, since a clear statement and sharing of goals is a prerequisite to resolving motivational dilemmas.

■■■ MOTIVATION AND THE REWARD SYSTEM

Rewards that an individual receives are very much a part of the understanding of motivation. Research has suggested that rewards now cause performance later, and rewards now cause satisfaction later.[66] Edward Lawler concluded that five factors influence satisfaction with a reward.[67] First, satisfaction depends on the amount received and the amount the individual feels he or she should receive. Typically, the larger the reward, whether extrinsic such as pay or intrinsic such as job challenge, the more satisfied people feel. However, this feeling is moderated somewhat by the individuals' perception of whether the reward is justified. Some people feel uneasy if they receive a disproportionately large reward, particularly for the amount of effort they exert or in comparison to co-workers whom they perceive as similar. Second, comparison to what happens to others influences people's feelings of satisfaction. If an employee feels that he is being over- or under-rewarded in comparison to other employees whom he views as similar to himself, he probably feels less satisfied than if he feels he is being treated equitably. Third, an employee's satisfaction with both the intrinsic and extrinsic rewards received affects overall job satisfaction. Fourth, people differ widely in the rewards they desire and in the value they attach to each. For instance, some individuals are willing to trade off flexible working hours for increased compensation; others choose benefits (sick leave, medical insurance, pension contributions) over salary increases. And fifth, many extrinsic rewards satisfy only because

---

TABLE 15.9 ■ Requirements of an Effective Reward System

Quality of Work Life

Reward level	A reward level high enough to satisfy the basic needs of individuals
External equity	Rewards equal to or greater than those in other organizations
Internal equity	A distribution of rewards that is seen as fair by members
Individuality	Provision of rewards that fit the needs of individuals
Membership	High overall satisfaction, external equity, and higher reward level for better performers
Absenteeism	Important rewards related to actually coming to work (high job satisfaction)
Performance motivation	Important rewards perceived to be related to performance
Organization structure	Reward distribution pattern that fits the management style and organization structure

Source: Reprinted by permission of E. E. Lawler III, Reward systems. In *Improving Life at Work,* ed. J. R. Hackman and J. L. Suttle (Santa Monica, Cal.: Goodyear, 1977), p. 172.

they lead to other rewards. For example, increased pay may satisfy because it results in more recreational opportunities or increased status for an employee.

These observations suggest the need for a diverse reward system. They also suggest that a comprehensive reward system demands a complete analysis of the organizational members and their work situation before rewards are chosen and allocated. They emphasize the nature and consistency of rewards, while not ignoring the individual members and their specific needs.

Table 15.9 summarizes the requirements of an effective reward system. Such a system must create a high quality of work life by offering sufficiently high and equitable rewards to meet individuals' needs. It must also encourage organizational effectiveness by rewarding better performance and attendance at work, and by offering rewards that are congruent with management's style and the organization's structure.

Characteristics of the Reward System

The design of a reward system includes the two major types of rewards mentioned earlier: intrinsic and extrinsic. People who work because they find the work itself rewarding are intrinsically motivated. Those who work because they receive such rewards as pay, promotions, or benefits are extrinsically motivated. Most researchers and practitioners agree that motivation in a work setting can occur because of the availability of both intrinsic and extrinsic rewards, the value attached to them, and the quality of their distribution in the organization (see Figure 15.7).

FIGURE 15.7 ■■
The Reward System

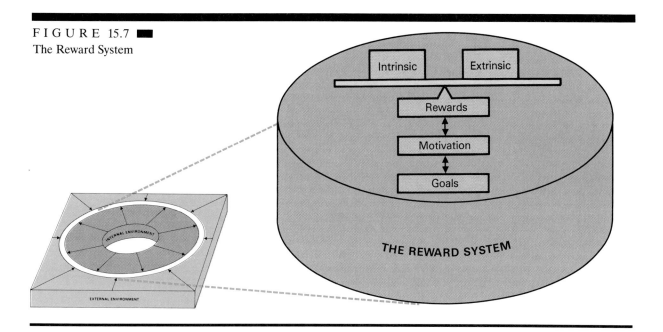

Various characteristics of the reward system respond to the organization's environment, help accomplish its goals, and contribute to its culture (the pattern of basic assumptions about the way employees adapt externally and integrate internally). Top management must determine, for example, whether it will assign pay on the basis of the jobs held by the workers or the skills or competencies that workers have. Job-based pay rewards people for performing specific jobs and moving up the hierarchy, whereas skill-based programs reward people for building more competencies and developing their skills. Job-based pay reinforces the link between organizational design and the accomplishment of organizational goals. It emphasizes the relationship between an individual's job performance and organizational outcomes. It supports a culture that emphasizes bottom-line performance. Skill-based programs can be used either independently or in conjunction with a job-based system. They support a culture that reflects a concern for individual development and learning, and an environment that requires relative flexibility from a relatively permanent work force.[68]

Reward systems must also consider the market position of the pay levels offered. If a firm pays, on average, higher wages than its competitors, and learns that another firm—a major competitor—pays lower wages, would management continue to offer high pay levels? How would employee motivation be affected if management lowered pay across the firm? Some companies prefer to take a leadership position in pay; management of these organizations assumes that paying well will result in attracting the best employees. Others are willing to risk attracting somewhat less qualified workers by offering lower compensation. The market position chosen certainly influences the organization's ability to cope with its environment; when a tight labor market exists, organizations with an aggressive, "leader" strategy typically fare best in securing the workers they need. When, on the other hand, labor is very available, these pay leaders may unnecessarily spend a premium for compensation.

Top management must also determine which organizational members will make pay decisions. Responsibility can be decentralized throughout the organization to supervisors, who should know their employees' needs and the value they attach to various rewards. Or it can be centralized and systematized in a corporate compensation system, which emphasizes equity and pay for performance. The decision-making process chosen frequently complements the organization's structure and reinforces its culture.

Criteria of an Effective Reward System

An effective reward system ties rewards to performance. Individuals who work harder, produce more, or produce better quality outputs should receive greater rewards than poorer performers. Reward systems should also offer a sufficient number and diversity of rewards. Some organizations lack the resources to offer enough extrinsic rewards to motivate employees to perform or to encourage their satisfaction. These organizations should instead consider job-enrichment or quality-of-work-life programs as ways of increasing intrinsic rewards.

The criteria for the allocation of rewards must be clear and complete. Individual organizational members should know whether they receive rewards for level or quality of performance, attendance, innovativeness, or effort, for example. The criteria for receipt of specific wages, benefits, and incentives must be clearly defined. But different individuals should be treated differently when appropriate.

An effective reward system links the reward to the individual's performance. (© Dave Schaefer/The Picture Cube)

Workers who perform at different levels or who have different needs often should not receive the same rewards. At the same time, management must ensure that workers perceive that the distribution of rewards is equitable. Finally, organizational rewards should compare favorably with rewards in similar organizations. For organizations to attract, motivate, and retain qualified and competent employees, they must offer rewards comparable to their competitors.

SUMMARY

Motivation is the willingness to put forth effort in the pursuit of organizational goals. To create an environment conducive to a high level of motivation, managers must understand some philosophies of human nature, such as McGregor's Theory X and Theory Y, Argyris's maturity theory, and the self-fulfilling prophecy.

Four popular needs theories have been discussed: (1) Maslow's hierarchy of needs theory; (2) Alderfer's ERG theory; (3) McClelland's needs theory; and (4) Herzberg's two-factor theory. Maslow states that individuals have a hierarchy of five needs, from the most basic physiological level to the highest level of self-actualization. Alderfer reorganized Maslow's needs hierarchy into three needs levels: (1) existence, (2) relatedness, and (3) growth. McClelland and his associates focused on needs similar to the higher-order needs identified by Maslow; specifically, needs for (1) achievement *(n Ach)*, (2) affiliation *(n Aff)*, and (3) power *(n Pow)*, the need to control one's own work or the work of others. Herzberg and his associates' view of motivation complements those of the other needs theorists. They suggest that motivators—features of a job's content, such as responsibility—satisfy higher-order needs, motivate a person to exert more effort, and encourage better performance. Hygiene factors, which meet physiological, security, or social needs, satisfy lower-order needs and prevent dissatisfaction.

Equity theory assumes that people assess their performance and attitudes by comparing their contribution to work and the benefits they derive from it to those of a "comparison other." In reinforcement theory, human behavior is explained in terms of the previous positive or negative outcomes of that behavior. Vroom's expectancy theory states that motivation is a function of expectancy, valence, and instrumentality.

Just as expectancy theory can serve as an integrative model of motivation, goal setting can act as a common technique in the application of the motivation theories presented so far. Setting goals helps individuals identify ways of meeting their needs, and accomplishing goals can be reinforcing in itself. Goal setting thus encourages individuals to exert effort, and goal accomplishment tends to motivate individuals.

Research suggests that rewards now cause performance later, and rewards now cause satisfaction later. A complete analysis of organizational members and their work situation is prerequisite to choosing and allocating rewards.

REVIEW QUESTIONS

1. Define motivation.
2. Compare and contrast McGregor's Theory X and Theory Y. What are some

      examples of managerial practices that are consistent with a Theory Y philosophy of human nature?

3. What is Argyris's maturity theory? How does it apply to motivation?
4. Relate Herzberg's theory of motivation to the theory developed by Maslow.
5. Describe McClelland's theory of human motives. How does it relate to motivation, and what are the basic characteristics of individuals described by the theory?
6. What is expectancy theory?
7. Briefly describe reinforcement theory.
8. Define equity and describe it as it relates to motivation.
9. How can goal setting act as a common technique in the application of motivation theories?
10. What are the factors that Edward Lawler concluded influence satisfaction with a reward?

KEY TERMS

motivation	extrinsic motivation	reinforcement theory
Theory X	intrinsic motivation	positive reinforcement
Theory Y	equity theory	expectancy theory
self-fulfilling prophecy		

A BIRTHDAY PRESENT FOR KATHY

BOB ROSEN COULD hardly wait to get back to work Monday morning. He was excited about his chance of getting a large bonus. Bob is a machine operator with Ram Manufacturing Company, a Wichita, Kansas, maker of electric motors. He operates an armature winding machine. The machine winds copper wire onto metal cores to make the rotating elements for electric motors.

Ram pays machine operators on a graduated piece-rate basis. Operators are paid a certain amount for each part made, plus a bonus. A worker who produces 10 percent above standard for a certain month receives a 10-percent additional bonus. For 20 percent above standard, the bonus is 20 percent. Bob realized that he had a good chance of earning a 20-percent bonus that month. That would be $287.

Bob had a special use for the extra money. His wife's birthday was just three weeks away. He was hoping to get her a new Chevrolet Citation. He had already saved $450, but the down payment on the Citation was $700. The bonus would enable him to buy the car.

Bob arrived at work at seven o'clock that morning, although his shift did not begin until eight. He went to his work station and checked the supply of blank cores and copper wire. Finding that only one spool of wire was on hand, he asked the fork truck driver to bring another. Then he asked the operator who was working the graveyard shift, "Sam, do you mind if I grease the machine while you work?"

'No," Sam said, "that won't bother me a bit."

After greasing the machine, Bob stood and watched Sam work. He thought of ways to simplify the motions involved in loading, winding, and unloading the armatures. As Bob took over the machine after the eight o'clock whistle, he thought, "I hope I can pull this off. I know the car will make Kathy happy. She won't be stuck at home while I'm at work."

QUESTIONS

1. Explain the advantages and disadvantages of a graduated piece-rate pay system such as that at Ram.
2. Explain Bob's high level of motivation in terms of needs theory, reinforcement theory, and expectancy theory.

THE NEW ANALYST

HARRY NEAL HAS BEEN employed with Trimark Data Systems (TDS) for five years and during that time has progressed to his current position of senior programmer analyst. He is generally pleased with the company and thoroughly enjoys the creative demands of his job.

One Saturday afternoon during a golf game with his friend and co-worker Randy Dean, Harry discovered that his department had hired a recent state university graduate as a programmer analyst. Harry, although a good-natured fellow, got upset when he learned that the new man's starting salary was only $30 a month lower than his own. Harry was bewildered. He felt that he was being treated unfairly.

The following Monday morning, Harry confronted Dave Edwards, the personnel director, and asked if what he had heard was true. Dave apologetically admitted that it was and attempted to explain the company's situation: "Harry, the market for programmer analysts is very tight, and in order for the company to attract qualified prospects, we have to offer a premium starting salary. We desperately needed another analyst, and this was the only way we could get one."

Harry asked Dave if his salary would be adjusted accordingly. Dave answered, "Your salary will be reevaluated at the regular performance appraisal time. You're doing a great job, though, and I'm sure the boss will recommend a raise." Harry thanked Dave for his time but left the office shaking his head and wondering about his future with TDS.

QUESTIONS

1. Do you feel that Dave's explanation was satisfactory? Discuss.
2. What is likely to be the impact of this incident on Harry's motivation to work?
3. What action do you think the company should have taken with regard to Harry? Explain.

EXPERIENTIAL EXERCISE

Marty Allen, the production manager, is anxious to get his well-deserved promotion, but a recent occurrence has interfered with his clearing out the last orders of business prior to moving up. The deadline on the Borring Aircraft contract has been moved up three weeks, and he will have to deal with the problems associated with meeting the new deadline. If the previous deadline had remained in force, the new production manager would be the one responsible for meeting it. Marty does not really have the time to bring the Borring contract in by deadline, but if the assistant manager and the production foreman will help, the deadline can be met. Marty will meet with these two key individuals today to enlist their support.

Mary Paris, the assistant manager, is aware that the boss is getting a promotion and that he does not want to mess with the Borring Aircraft project. She believes that extra performance in meeting the new deadline could help her secure a promotion to the production manager's position. A recommendation by Marty Allen is essential. She realizes that the extra push needed to get the promotion must be made immediately, so now is the time to volunteer to take over the Borring project.

The production foreman's unit is responsible for completion of the Borring Aircraft project, and the production foreman, Alex Fontneau, is aware that the production manager is getting a promotion and would like to go upstairs in a blaze of glory. Alex also realizes that only he can get that kind of work out of the work group because they all owe him. Alex's wife's birthday is next week, and he needs the production bonus early for a down payment on the new car he wants to get her as a present. The only problem is that bonuses are paid only when quotas are actually exceeded. However, Alex knows that the deadline can be met, and the resulting bonus will be substantially above the $600 needed for the down payment. So now is the time to offer to do whatever it takes to meet the deadline, and ask for the advance bonus.

Only with the help of very special people can this deadline be met. If you want to be one of these special individuals you can participate just by volunteering. Determine whether you want to be the production manager or a key employee and let the instructor know. All others observe carefully. Participants will be given additional information necessary to participate.

NOTES

1. Douglas McGregor, *The Human Side of Enterprise* (New York: McGraw-Hill, 1960).
2. Chris Argyris, *Personality and Organization* (New York: Harper & Row, 1957).
3. J. Sterling Livingston, "Pygmalion in Management," *Harvard Business Review* (July–August 1969).
4. John L. Single, "The Power of Expectations: Productivity and the Self-Fulfilling Prophecy," *Management World* (November 1980): 19, 37–38.
5. A. H. Maslow, *Motivation and Personality* (New York: Harper & Row, 1954), ix.
6. Maslow, *Motivation*, 30–92.

7. See "Agreements Between Ford Motor Company and the UAW," dated February 1982, for an example of such an agreement.

8. John Hoerr, "Is Teamwork a Management Plot? Probably Not," *Business Week,* 20 February 1989, 70.

9. Maslow, *Motivation,* 98–99.

10. Maslow, *Motivation,* 147–150.

11. L. W. Porter, "A Study of Perceived Need Satisfactions in Bottom and Middle Management Jobs," *Journal of Applied Psychology* 45 (1961): 1–10.

12. See M. A. Wahba and L. G. Bridwell, "Maslow Reconsidered: A Review of Research on the Need Hierarchy Theory," *Organizational Behavior and Human Performance* 15 (1976): 212–240; V. F. Mitchell and P. Moudgill, "Measurement of Maslow's Need Hierarchy," *Organizational Behavior and Human Performance* 16 (1976): 334–349; E. E. Lawler III, *Motivation in Work Organizations* (Monterey, Cal.: Brooks/Cole, 1973).

13. Wahba and Bridwell, "Maslow Reconsidered," 212–240; Mitchell and Moudgill, "Maslow's Need Hierarchy," 334–349; Lawler III, *Motivation.*

14. C. P. Alderfer, *Existence, Relatedness, and Growth: Human Needs in Organizational Settings* (New York: Free Press, 1972).

15. D. McClelland, *The Achieving Society* (Princeton, N.J.: D. Van Nostrand, 1961).

16. S. M. Klein and R. R. Ritti, *Understanding Organizational Behavior* (Boston: Kent, 1984), 257.

17. D. C. McClelland and David H. Burnham, "Power Is the Great Motivator," *Harvard Business Review* 54 (March–April 1976): 103.

18. David R. Hampton, Charles E. Summer, and Ross A. Webber, *Organizational Behavior and the Practice of Management* (Glenview, Ill.: Scott, Foresman, 1978), 11–15.

19. M. J. Stahl, "Achievement Power and Managerial Motivation: Selecting Managerial Talent with the Job Choice Exercise," *Personnel Psychology* (Winter 1983), 786.

20. Stahl, "Achievement Power," 786.

21. D. McClelland and D. H. Burnham, "Power Driven Managers: Good Guys Make Bum Bosses," *Psychology Today,* December 1975.

22. F. Herzberg, B. Mausner, and B. B. Snyderman, *The Motivation to Work* (New York: John Wiley & Sons, 1959).

23. Herzberg, Mausner, and Snyderman, *Motivation.*

24. See B. L. Hinton, "An Empirical Investigation of the Herzberg Methodology and Two-factor Theory," *Organizational Behavior and Human Performance* 3 (1968): 286–309, for a discussion of methodological problems; M. D. Dunnette, D. Campbell, and M. Hakel, "Factors Contributing to Job Satisfaction and Dissatisfaction in Six Occupational Groups," *Organizational Behavior and Human Performance* 2 (1967): 143–174; R. House and L. Wigdor, "Herzberg's Dual Factor Theory of Job Satisfaction and Motivation: A Review of the Evidence and Criticism," *Personnel Psychology* 20 (1968): 369–389; J. Schneider and E. Locke, "A Critique of Herzberg's Classification System and a Suggested Revision," *Organizational Behavior and Human Performance* 14 (1971): 441–458; and P. Smith, L. Kendall, and C. Hulin, *The Measurement of Satisfaction in Work and Retirement* (Chicago: Rand McNally, 1969), for discussion of evidence that shows a factor causing satisfaction for one person may cause dissatisfaction for another.

25. G. R. Salancik and J. Pfeffer, "An Examination of Need-Satisfaction Models of Job Attitudes," *Administrative Science Quarterly* 22 (1977): 427–456.

26. J. R. Gordon, *A Diagnostic Approach to Organizational Behavior,* Second Edition (Boston: Allyn and Bacon, 1987). Activity 3–1 shows one instrument for measuring needs.

27. J. S. Adams, "Toward an Understanding of Inequity," *Journal of Abnormal and Social Psychology* 67 (November 1963): 422–436.

28. J. S. Adams, "Inequity in Social Exchange," in *Advances in Experimental and Social Psychology,* vol. 2, ed. L. Berkowitz (1965): 267–300; see also E. Walster, W. Walster, and E. Berscheid, *Equity: Theory and Research* (Boston: Allyn and Bacon, 1978).

29. R. P. Vecchio, "Predicting Worker Performance in Inequitable Settings," *Academy of Management Review* 7 (1982): 103–110, presents four mathematical models of equity theory.

30. G. R. Oldham and H. E. Miller, "The Effect of Significant Others' Job Complexity on Employee Reactions to Work," *Human Relations* 32 (1979): 247–260.

31. D. Schwab, "Construct Validity in Organizational Behavior," in *Research in Organizational Behavior,* vol. 2, ed. B. Staw (Greenwich, Conn.: JAI Press, 1980); M. R. Carrell and J. E. Dittrich, "Equity Theory: The Recent Literature, Methodological Considerations, and New Directions," *Academy of Management Review* 3 (1978): 202–210; Walster, Walster, Berscheid, *Equity,* 128.

32. J. Greenbert and G. S. Leventhal, "Equity and the Use of Overreward to Motivate Performance," *Journal of Personality and Social Psychology* 34 (1976): 179–190.

33. Adams, "Toward an Understanding"; Walster, Walster, Berscheid, *Equity,* 131–141.

34. R. E. Kopelman, "Psychological Stages of Careers in Engineering: An Expectancy Theory Taxonomy," *Journal of Vocational Behavior* 10 (1977): 270–286.

35. M. R. Carrell and J. E. Dittrich, "Employee Perceptions of Fair Treatment," *Personnel Journal* 55 (1976): 523–524.

36. R. A. Cosier and D. R. Dalton, "Equity Theory and Time: A Reformulation," *Academy of Management Review* 8 (1983): 311–319.

37. M. R. Carrell and J. E. Dittrich, "Equity Theory: The Recent Literature, *Personnel Journal* 55 (1976).

38. B. F. Skinner, *The Behavior of Organisms: An Experimental Approach* (New York: Appleton-Century-Crofts, 1938).

39. B. F. Skinner, *Beyond Freedom and Dignity* (New York: Alfred A. Knopf, 1971).

40. S. F. Jablonsky and D. L. DeVries, "Operant Conditioning Principles Extrapolated to the Theory of Management," *Organizational Behavior and Human Performance* 7 (1972): 340–358.

41. H. W. Babb and D. G. Kopp, "Applications of Behavior Modification in Organizations: A Review and Critique," *Academy of Management Review* 3 (1978): 281–292; and W. C. Hamner and E. P. Hamner, "Behavior Modification on the Bottom Line," *Organizational Dynamics* 4 (1976): 8–21.

42. Note that the radical behaviorists do not support goal setting and accomplishment as legitimate reinforcers.

43. S. Kerr, "On the Folly of Rewarding A, While Hoping for B," *Academy of Management Journal* 18 (1975): 773.

44. Kerr, "On the Folly," 773.

45. Kerr, "On the Folly," 773.

46. W. C. Hamner, "Reinforcement Theory and Contingency Management in Organizational Settings," in *Organizational Behavior and Management,* ed. H. L. Tosi and W. C. Hamner (Chicago: St. Clair, 1974).

47. Adrian Harrell and Michael Stahl, "Additive Information Processing and the Relationship Between Expectancy of Success and Motivational Force," *Academy of Management Journal* 29 (June 1986): 424–425.

48. Victor Vroom, *Work and Motivation* (New York: John Wiley & Sons, 1964).

49. Vroom, *Work.*

50. B. M. Staw, *Intrinsic and Extrinsic Motivation* (Morristown, N.J.: General Learning Press, 1976).

51. See S. Koch, "Behavior as 'Intrinsically' Regulated: Work Notes Towards a Pretheory of Phenomena Called Motivation," in *Nebraska Symposium on Motivation,* ed. M. R. Jones (Lincoln: University of Nebraska, 1956); Lawler III, *Motivation.*

52. K. C. Montgomery, "The Role of the Exploratory Drive in Learning," *Journal of Comparative Physiological Psychology* 47 (1954): 60–64.

53. Staw, *Motivation*.

54. Staw, *Motivation*.

55. R. J. House, H. J. Shapiro, and M. A. Wahba, "Expectancy Theory as a Predictor of Work Behavior and Attitudes: A Reevaluation of Empirical Evidence," *Decision Sciences* 5 (1974): 481–506.

56. See T. Connolly, "Some Conceptual and Methodological Issues in Expectancy Models of Work Performance," *Academy of Management Review* 1 (1976): 37–47; H. G. Heneman and D. P. Schwab, "Evaluation of Research on Expectancy Theory and Predictions of Employee Performance," *Psychological Bulletin* 78 (1972): 1–9; and M. A. Wahba and R. J. House, "Expectancy Theory in Work and Motivation: Some Logical and Methodological Issues," *Human Relations* 27 (1974): 121–147.

57. See J. P. Campbell and R. D. Pritchard, "Motivation Theory in Industrial and Organizational Psychology," in *Handbook of Industrial and Organizational Psychology,* ed. M. D. Dunnette (Chicago: Rand McNally, 1976); and E. E. Lawler III, *Motivation in Work Organizations* (Belmont, Cal.: Brooks/Cole, 1973).

58. E. A. Locke, K. N. Shaw, L. M. Saari, and G. P. Latham, "Goal Setting and Task Performance," *Psychological Bulletin* 90 (1981): 125–152.

59. G. Latham and J. J. Baldes, "The Practical Significance of Locke's Theory of Goal Setting," *Journal of Applied Psychology* 59 (1975): 122–124.

60. M. Erez, "Feedback, a Necessary Condition for the Goal Setting-Performance Relation," *Journal of Applied Psychology* 62 (1977): 624–627.

61. M. Erez, P. C. Earley, and C. L. Hulin, "The Impact of Participation on Goal Acceptance and Performance: A Two-Step Model," *Academy of Management Journal* 28 (1985): 50–66.

62. M. Erez and I. Zidon, "Effect of Goal Acceptance on the Relationship of Goal Difficulty to Performance," *Journal of Applied Psychology* 69 (1984): 69–78.

63. E. A. Locke, E. Frederick, E. Buckner, and P. Bobko, "Effect of Previously Assigned Goals on Self-set Goals and Performance," *Journal of Applied Psychology* 69 (1984): 694–699.

64. G. P. Latham and G. A. Yukl, "A Review of Research on the Application of Goal Setting in Organizations," *Academy of Management Journal* 18 (1975): 824–845.

65. G. P. Latham and E. A. Locke, "Goal-setting—A Motivational Technique That Works," *Organizational Dynamics* 7 (1979): 68–80.

66. C. N. Greene and R. E. Craft, Jr., "The Satisfaction-performance Controversy," *Business Horizons* 15 (1972): 31–41.

67. E. E. Lawler III, "Reward Systems," in *Improving Life at Work,* ed. J. R. Hackman and J. L. Suttle (Santa Monica, Cal.: Goodyear, 1977).

68. See E. E. Lawler III, "Reward Systems in Organizations," in *Handbook of Organizational Behavior,* ed. J. Lorsch (Englewood Cliffs, N.J.: Prentice-Hall, 1983).

REFERENCES

Alderfer, C. P. *Existence, Relatedness, and Growth: Human Needs in Organizational Settings.* New York: Free Press, 1972.

Bahrami, Bahman. "Productivity Improvement Through Cooperation of Employees and Employers." *Labor Law Journal* 39 (March 1988): 167–168.

Bailey, James E. "Personnel Scheduling with Flexshift: A Win/Win Scenario." *Personnel* 63 (September 1986): 62–67.

Ciancutti, Arthur R. "There's No Need for Excuses." *Management World* 17 (July–August 1988): 23–24.

Cook, C. W. "Guidelines for Managing Motivation." *Business Horizons* 23 (April 1980): 61–69.

Cosier, R. A., and D. R. Dalton. "Equity Theory and Time: A Reformulation. *Academy of Management Review* 8 (1983): 311–319.

Cummings, L. L. "Compensation, Culture, and Motivation: A Systems Perspective." *Organizational Dynamics* (Winter 1984): 33–44.

Erez, M., and I. Zidon. "Effect of Goal Acceptance on the Relationship of Goal Difficulty to Performance. *Journal of Applied Psychology* 69 (1985): 69–78.

Ernz, M., P. C. Earley, and C. L. Hulin. "The Impact of Participation on Goal Acceptance and Performance: A Two-Step Model." *Academy of Management Journal* 28 (1985): 50–66.

Gregory, Gene. "The Japanese Enterprise: Sources of Competitive Strength." *Business and Society* 24 (Spring 1985): 13–21.

Handy, Charles. "Management Training: Perk or Prerequisite?" *Personnel Management* (May 1987): 28–31.

Harrell, Adrian, and Michael Stahl. "Additive Information Processing and the Relationship Between Expectancy of Success and Motivational Force." *Academy of Management Journal* 29 (June 1986): 424–433.

Hatcher, Larry, and Timothy L. Ross. "Gainsharing Plans—How Managers Evaluate Them. *Business* 36 (October–December 1986): 30–37.

Hennecke, Matt. "How Do You Know It Works?" *Training: The Magazine of Human Resources Development* 25 (April 1988): 49–51.

Herzberg, Frederick. "One More Time: How Do You Motivate Employees?" *Harvard Business Review* 65 (September–October 1987): 109–120.

Howard, A., et al. "Motivation and Values among Japanese and American Managers." *Personnel Psychology* (Winter 1983): 883–898.

Jordan, Paul C. "Effects of an Extrinsic Reward on Intrinsic Motivation: A Field Experiment." *Academy of Management Journal* 29 (June 1986): 405–412.

Kennedy, C. W., J. A. Fossum, and B. J. White. "An Empirical Comparison of Within-Subjects and Between-Subjects Expectancy Theory Models." *Organizational Behavior and Human Performance* (August 1983): 124–143.

Klein, S. M., and R. R. Ritti. *Understanding Organizational Behavior.* Boston: Kent, 1984.

Klimoski, R. J., and N. J. Hayes. "Leader Behavior and Subordinate Motivation." *Personnel Psychology* 33 (Autumn 1980): 543–555.

McCullers, John C., Richard A. Fabes, and James D. Moran III. "Does Intrinsic Motivation Theory Explain the Adverse Effects of Rewards on Immediate Task Performance?" *Journal of Personality and Social Psychology* 52 (May 1987): 1027–1033.

"Management Incentives: Motivating Managers to Achieve Goals." *Small Business Report* 13 (May 1988): 48–52.

Maslow, A. H. *Motivation and Personality.* New York: Harper, 1954. ix.

Mateika, J. Kenneth, and Richard J. Dunsing. "Managing Employee Rewards." *Administrative Management* 47 (June 1986): 22–24.

Miller, William B. "Motivation Techniques: Does One Work Best?" *Management Review* (February 1981): 47–52.

Mitchell, T. R. "Motivation: New Directions for Theory, Research, and Practice." *Academy of Management Review* 7 (1982): 80–88.

Mondy, R. Wayne, Shane R. Premeaux, and Arthur Sharplin. "Motivation In Practice." *Manage* 39, 2d Qtr (1986): 13, 22–23.

"Motivating the Plateaued Employee: The Art of Awakening the Dormant Performer." *Manage* 38 (Annual 1988): 11–16.

Neider, L. L. "Experimental Field Investigation Utilizing an Expectancy Theory View of Participation." *Organizational Behavior and Human Performance* 26 (December 1980): 425–442.

Ordiorne, G. S. "Uneasy Look at Motivation Theory." *Training and Development Journal* 34 (June 1980): 106–112.

Ouchi, William G. "Organizational Paragrams: A Commentary on Japanese Management and Theory Z Organizations." *Organizational Dynamics* 9 (Spring 1981): 36–42.

———. "Theory Z Corporations." *Industry Week* (4 May 1981): 49–51.

Porter, L. W. "A Study of Perceived Need Satisfactions in Bottom and Middle Management Jobs." *Journal of Applied Psychology* 45 (1961): 1–10.

Rehder, R. R. "What American and Japanese Managers Are Learning about Each Other." *Business Horizons* 24 (March–April 1981): 63–70.

Runcie, John F. "By Days I Make the Cars." *Harvard Business Review* (May–June 1980): 106–115.

Schmitt, N., and L. Son. "Evaluation of Valence Models of Motivation to Pursue Various Post-High School Alternatives." *Organizational Behavior and Human Performance* 27 (February 1981): 135–150.

Sievers, Burkard. "Beyond the Surrogate of Motivation." *Organization Studies* 7 (Fall 1986): 335–351.

Skinner, B. F. *The Behavior of Organisms: An Experimental Approach.* New York: Appleton-Century-Crofts, 1938.

Snyder, Neil H., Bernard A. Morin, and Marilyn A. Morgan. "Motivating People to Build Excellent Enterprises." *Business* 38 (April–June 1988): 14–19.

Stahl, M. J. "Achievement Power and Managerial Motivation: Selecting Managerial Talent with the Job Choice Exercise." *Personnel Psychology* (Winter 1983): 775–790.

Vecchio, R. P. "Predicting Worker Performance in Inequitable Settings." *Academy of Management Review* 7 (1982): 103–110.

Vroom, V. H. *Work and Motivation.* New York: John Wiley & Sons, 1964.

Wagel, William H. "Opening the Door to Employee Participation." *Personnel* 63 (April 1986): 4–6.

CHAPTER
16

Chapter Outline

Individual Differences in Personality

Individual Development

Stress in Organizations

Burnout

Summary

Individual Differences, Development, and Stress

Learning Objectives

After completing this chapter students should be able to

1. Describe individual differences in personality.
2. Explain biosocial, family, and career development.
3. Describe the causes of stress and burnout in organizations.

STEVEN BUCHANAN IS the manager of the data-processing department of Fresh-Foods Industries. Fresh-Foods imports and distributes quality specialty foods throughout the eastern half of the United States. The data-processing department maintains the in-house computerized systems for such functions as purchasing, accounting, and personnel.

The department currently employs a variety of technical and managerial personnel. Steve has been particularly concerned lately about the performance of the five programmers in his department. (Table 16.1 describes these programmers along a variety of dimensions.) He has complained that although the programmers are writing more lines of code than previously, the quality of their work has decreased. No one seems willing to work overtime or put in enough extra effort to be both productive and accurate.

The five programmers have also been absent a great deal during the past six months. When Steve has inquired about these absences, some programmers have cited personal reasons. Others noted that they have been sick a great deal; one complained of severe migraine headaches; another had "stomach problems." Steve's boss has also told him that one of the programmers has complained about a personality clash between himself and his boss.

We might attribute the problems in this situation to the workers' lack of motivation. Perhaps their needs are not being met, the situation lacks equity, desired behaviors are not being reinforced, or their expectancies are low. Or we might hypothesize that the programmers have not learned the behaviors expected for their jobs. We have already identified some individual differences in perception, attribution, learning, and motivation. But can other differences between individuals explain performance problems and dysfunctional attitudes? In managing the programmers, Steve may be overlooking differences among them due to personality, personal development, role pressures, or the ability to manage stress constructively. ∎

I N THIS CHAPTER, individual differences in personality are examined, followed by discussions of biosocial, family, and career development. Specific consideration is given to the impact these have on individual behavior and job performance. To illustrate the many unique concepts involved, we examine the lives of five members of a data-processing department who have fairly extreme personality differences and who are in various stages of individual development. In the final sections of the chapter we discuss stress, role conflict and ambiguity as causes of stress, and burnout.

Personality
Consists of a wide range of motives, emotions, values, interests, attitudes, and competencies regarding an individual.

Differences in personality can significantly affect individual behavior, and subsequently individual and group performance, in organizations. **Personality** consists of a wide range of motives, emotions, values, interests, attitudes, and competencies regarding an individual. These characteristics are frequently organized into patterns that reflect an individual's heredity and social, cultural, and family environments. A true appreciation of the nature of differences in personality allows managers to more effectively manage, thereby enhancing both individual and group performance.

Personality Types

Internalizers
Individuals who feel that they control their own lives and actions.

Externalizers
Individuals who believe that others control their lives and actions.

Machiavellianism
The extent to which an individual has a tendency to manipulate others.

Psychological research has identified a wide range of psychological characteristics that comprise an individual's personality. Rotter described the extent to which individuals believe that their behaviors influence what happens to them, referred to as locus of control.[1] **Internalizers** feel that they control their own lives and actions; **externalizers** believe others control their lives and actions. Internalizers would agree, for example, that "promotions are earned through hard work and persistence," and "when I am right, I can convince others."[2] Externalizers would agree that "making a lot of money is largely a matter of getting the right breaks" and "it is silly to think that one can really change another person's basic attitudes."[3]

Other researchers have described **Machiavellianism,** or the extent to which an individual has a tendency to manipulate others.[4] Those who score high on this

BUSINESS BRIEFS

PINNACLE

Sculley versus Jobs—Individual Differences in Personality Bring about Fundamental Changes at Apple

DIFFERENCES IN PERSONALITY can significantly affect individual behavior in organizations and subsequently individual and group performance. John Sculley, Chairman of Apple Computers, replaced a much different personality, Steven Jobs. The small, informal organization that Jobs and Wozniak favored has become significantly more structured under John Sculley, the former PepsiCo executive. John Sculley has plotted the course for the future by assuring that Apple's top management team develop a comprehensive product-line strategy designed to keep Apple positioned as the technology-marketing leader in the fast-growing personal computer industry. The progression of Sculley as the youngest president of PepsiCo, up until the point where he took over the leadership role at Apple Computers, is addressed. Sculley, working in the revolutionary technological atmosphere of the computer business, has streamlined management, shared his marketing expertise, and restored discipline to the Apple Computer Corporation. Senior CNN correspondent Tom Cassidy discusses these, and other issues, with John Sculley.

FIGURE 16.1 ■
Problem-Solving
Orientations

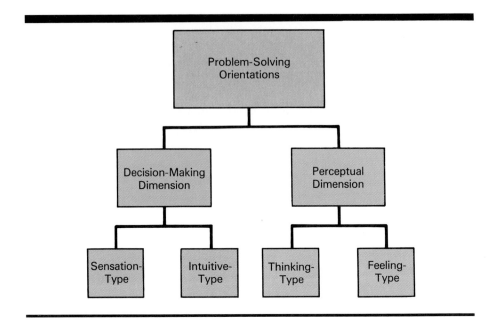

Type A individuals
Individuals who tend to
feel very competitive, be
prompt for appointments,
do things quickly, and
always feel rushed.

Type B individuals
Individuals who tend to be
more relaxed, take one
thing at a time, and
express their feelings.

Introverted person
An individual who is shy
and withdrawn.

Extroverted person
An individual who is
outgoing, often aggressive,
and dominant.

**Sensation-type
individuals**
Individuals who dislike new
problems unless there are
standard ways to solve
them, like an established
routine, must usually work
all the way through to
reach a conclusion, show
patience with routine
details, and tend to be
good at precise work.

personality trait agree that "anyone who completely trusts anyone else is asking for trouble" and "the best way to handle people is to tell them what they want to hear."[5]

A third personality dimension, which relates to stress (discussed later in this chapter), is Type A or Type B characteristics. Individuals with these two types of personalities differ in the ability to relax and their desire for achievement, perfectionism, and competitiveness.[6] **Type A individuals** tend to feel very competitive, be prompt for appointments, do things quickly, and always feel rushed. **Type B individuals** tend to be more relaxed, take one thing at a time, and express their feelings.[7]

Jungian psychology, on the other hand, identifies two basic personalities: introversion and extroversion.[8] The **introverted person** is shy and withdrawn, whereas the **extroverted person** is outgoing, often aggressive, and dominant. As may be seen in Figure 16.1, the problem-solving orientation of these personality patterns can be classified along two dimensions: (1) the decision-making dimension—how individuals make decisions; and (2) the perceptual dimension—how individuals perceive (or select and organize stimuli) in a situation. The decision-making dimension involves two problem-solving orientations—sensation-type and intuitive-type. Further, the perceptual dimension also involves two problem-solving orientations—feeling-type and thinking-type.

Sensation-type individuals dislike new problems unless there are standard ways to solve them, like an established routine, must usually work all the way through to reach a conclusion, show patience with routine details, and tend to be good at precise work. For instance, GM Chairman Roger B. Smith appears to be this type of individual. GM is the archetypical conservative, mature bureaucracy, with layer upon layer of managers following well-defined procedures. In an attempt to change, Smith supported GM's acquisition of EDS. But when H. Ross Perot became a GM director and recommended changing their current approach to business, he was bought out for $700 million.

Intuitive-type individuals
Individuals who like solving new problems, dislike doing the same thing over and over again, jump to conclusions, are impatient with routine details, and dislike taking time for precision.

Feeling-type individuals
Individuals who are aware of other people and their feelings, like harmony, need occasional praise, dislike telling people unpleasant things, tend to be sympathetic, and relate well to most people.

Thinking-type individuals
Individuals who are unemotional and uninterested in people's feelings, like analysis and putting things into logical order, are able to reprimand people and fire them when necessary, may seem hard-hearted, and tend to relate well only to other thinking types.

Intuitive-type individuals like solving new problems, dislike doing the same thing over and over again, jump to conclusions, are impatient with routine details, and dislike taking time for precision. **Feeling-type individuals** are aware of other people and their feelings, like harmony, need occasional praise, dislike telling people unpleasant things, tend to be sympathetic, and relate well to most people. **Thinking-type individuals** are unemotional and uninterested in people's feelings, like analysis and putting things into logical order, are able to reprimand people and fire them when necessary, may seem hard-hearted, and tend to relate well only to other thinking types.[9] The Myers-Briggs Scale provides a more valid assessment of these dimensions.[10]

Measuring Personality

Personality is assessed primarily in three ways. First, individuals can complete inventories—lists of questions that describe the respondent's personality—such as the California Psychological Inventory or the Minnesota Multiphasic Personality Inventory (known as the MMPI). On the MMPI, for example, respondents are asked to indicate the truth of over 400 statements about their health, social attitudes, and phobias.[11]

Second, trained psychologists can administer projective tests, such as the Thematic Apperception Test and the Rorschach Inkblot Test. In these tests, the respondent tells the administrator what he or she sees in a picture (the TAT) or in relatively ambiguous inkblots (the Rorschach). This description is then scored using a detailed protocol. The scores describe the individual along a variety of personality dimensions.

The third assessment approach involves individuals in simulations, role-playing exercises, and stress interviews. The participants' behavior is observed and scored along a series of dimensions. These instruments describe personality by helping to define consistent patterns of psychological functioning.

Significance for Performance

Based on the description of an individual's personality or personal style, one can predict the way he or she is likely to behave in organizations. For example, individuals who are internalizers perceive that they determine, and are responsible for, their own level of performance. People who are externalizers believe that

ETHICAL
DILEMMA

YOU ARE A LAND SYNDICATOR with Hilby Wilson, Inc., a San Diego investment firm. You buy a hotel and later discover that it will never turn a profit. Investors have already sent you checks to get in on the deal. You can either bury your beliefs that the project will certainly fail and keep the investment money to cover a portion of your losses, or you can absorb the losses invested in renovations and return the checks.

What would you do?

Source: Adapted by permission, *Nation's Business,* August 1987. Copyright 1987, U.S. Chamber of Commerce.

others control their life and actions and therefore determine their level of performance. How might an internalizer and an externalizer differ in their view of the best way to advance in an organization? Internalizers would likely view advancement as within their control. Externalizers would view it as being out of their control. Similarly, internalizers might attribute success to themselves rather than to the situation; but externalizers might conclude the reverse. Or internalizers might view landing a new client as within their control, whereas externalizers might consider such an occurrence as a matter of luck.

Now consider a manager with a thinking-type personal style. How would this manager deal with a poor-performing employee? This individual would likely analyze the situation, paying little attention to the subordinate's feelings. Compare this behavior to that of a feeling-type manager in the same situation. The feeling-type individual would be more concerned with the employee's feelings. Consider how these two managers might deal with a worker experiencing personal problems. It can be hypothesized that the first manager would focus on the organizational implications of the dilemma, whereas the second would be most concerned with its consequences for the employee.

In considering the implications of personality for individual and organizational performance, managers must be careful not to stereotype individuals on the basis of their traits. Rather, it is better to use knowledge about an individual's personality to help predict, but not guarantee, future behavior. Although personality and personal style are relatively stable dimensions, their manifestation may differ over an individual's life, as described in the next section.

■■■ INDIVIDUAL DEVELOPMENT

Research suggests that adults, like children, have clearly defined stages of biological, social, and family development, as well as stages of career growth and

An organization is composed of individuals who may have different backgrounds, personality traits, and be at different stages of personal development. (© Charles Gupton/Stock, Boston, Inc.)

TABLE 16.1 ■ Profiles of Five Programmers

Dimensions	Leslie Slater	Jasper Phipps	Patricia Robertson	John Sales	Jeffrey Sachs
Age	22	28	34	41	57
Marital status	single	married	married	divorced	widower, remarried
Number of children	0	0	2 preschoolers	3 teenagers	7 grown children or stepchildren
Education	B.A. 1 year ago	M.B.A. 4 years ago	M.S. in computer science 3 years ago	B.S. in engineering 20 years ago	high school diploma 40 years ago
Number of jobs held previously	0	2	3	10	8
Number of years at Fresh-Foods	1	4	15	20	15
Number of years in current job	1	4	7	1	5
Locus of control	Internalizer	Internalizer	Externalizer	Internalizer	Externalizer
Type A or B	A	B	B	A	A
Decision-making orientation	Sensation	Sensation	Intuitive	Intuitive	Intuitive
Perceptual orientation	Feeling	Thinking	Feeling	Thinking	Thinking

development.[12] Most individuals at a particular stage will likely have common needs and similar ways of coping with situations. Of course, these ways of coping are modified by an individual's personality and personal style, so there can be variations within stages. Still, developmental stages do help explain individuals' responses to organizational situations. Employees at different stages of biosocial development may respond differently, for example, to overtime work or supervisory responsibility. Or certain features of the work situation may create dilemmas for people who are at different family stages.

Consider the information in Table 16.1. These members of the data-processing department at Fresh-Foods Industries likely do not respond to their work in the same way. They may have different values regarding their jobs. Their involvement in their work may be different. Extra work issues may influence their work behavior. Because these individuals are in different stages of biosocial, family, and career development, they probably do not react to their work in the same way.

Biosocial development
Involves the different developmental stages that influence an individual's behavior and attitudes at work.

Biosocial Development

Biosocial development involves the different developmental stages that influence an individual's behavior and attitudes at work. We explain how biosocial development influences individual behavior and performance by examining the information in Table 16.1 regarding Leslie Slater, Jasper Phipps, Patricia Robertson, John Sales, and Jeffrey Sachs. Leslie Slater, at 22, is primarily concerned with getting into the adult world, developing her sense of identity, and building a life that reflects her personality and personal style. She can experiment with various combinations of work and nonwork in her life. At times she may spend seventy or eighty hours at work; at other times she may work only the minimum time required. Leslie likely devotes energy to establishing her independence and looking for individuals, at work and elsewhere, to replace her parents as models of behavior.

Whether individuals in this stage find a mentor or sponsor seems to be particularly important.[13] Mentors can influence an employee's movement through the organization and exert a significant influence over that person's life-style.[14] Thus, individuals should select a mentor who can help and who has the confidence of the young worker; whom the protégé can help and make look good in the eyes of others; and who has a successful track record.[15] Recent research suggests that in some situations a worker's peers can act as effective mentors.[16] One study indicates that two thirds of the executives surveyed had mentors and that they received greater compensation than executives without mentors.[17] Thus, mentorship seems to be a critical tool for career success.[18]

At this stage some women may consciously emphasize their work life more than their nonwork life so that they can establish the flexibility they need later. In other words, they try to make themselves indispensable to their organizations so that later they may have the option of part-time work or more flexible hours.

Jasper Phipps's focus is probably less single-minded than Leslie's. Because of his responsibilities outside of work, he may be both more economical with his time at work and more committed to achieving. He most likely has spent the past several years establishing his own identity and life-style; for example, he may be part of a dual-career family, or he may be a workaholic. At this point Jasper must review all past commitments and reappraise his personal and career progress to date. The precise approach Jasper would take depends on his personality. For example, as a thinking person he likely takes a more analytical approach to his developmental tasks than if he were a feeling person, in which case he would be more likely to focus on his own and others' emotions.

Patricia Robertson has entered her thirties. During this decade individuals face different challenges and dilemmas from those they faced in their twenties. At this time, individuals such as Patricia come to terms with both their careers and their marriages. They may feel pressure to have children if they do not have them already. If they have children, they might have conflict over how much time and energy to devote to family versus career. Robertson would react differently than other people to these family and career demands, depending on her perceptual and decision-making styles. As an intuitive type, how might she respond? How would she react if she were a sensation type? Although women have traditionally withdrawn from the work force for a period of five to ten years to raise young children, increasing numbers with preschoolers are remaining in the work force and juggling work and nonwork responsibilities. In the last decade, men, too, have become more involved in family responsibilities: an increasing number share child-rearing and housekeeping responsibilities with their wives.

John Sales faces the difficulties encountered at mid-life. He may face a mid-career crisis, where he is questioning the fundamental value, appropriateness, and real accomplishment in both the career and family domains so far. John must reassess his own accomplishments, locate his own life goals and values, and make final decisions about his career. These mid-career requirements may temporarily distract him from his job responsibilities while he reassesses his commitment to them. Ultimately he may reaffirm his commitment to his work, or choose to switch to another career.

Men and women such as Jeffrey Sachs have basically two options at their life stage. Sachs can enjoy the relative stability he is experiencing in his life and career. Alternatively, he can focus his energies on retirement, since this becomes a viable option when he reaches the early sixties. Coping with occupational retirement, however, may create uncertainty during this transition time. Thus, adjusting to reduced status or work role may create performance problems for Sachs.

Clearly, then, individuals confront different issues at each stage of their biological and social development. Their ability to deal with these issues, as well as the organization's success in responding to their different needs, will influence both their individual and job performance. Managers should not overlook the fact that their subordinates' behavior and attitudes may be explained by their biosocial developmental stage. They should also remember that their own behavior and attitudes might be explained in the same way.

Family Development

Consider again Leslie Slater, Jasper Phipps, Patricia Robertson, John Sales, and Jeffrey Sachs, profiled in Table 16.1. Do you think that the interaction between work and family is identical or even similar for these five programmers? What issues must each face? Are the issues the same for male and female employees with the same family configurations?

FAMILY STAGES

Table 16.2 shows some representative stages and tasks of family development. While Leslie Slater is getting into the adult world and developing her sense of self, she is also managing the balance between partial and complete independence from her family. She must decide where to live and how much time to spend with her parents. Managing her relations with men may also require some time and attention. She must decide whether to date, whether to marry, and how much time to devote to her social life. Professional people are increasingly focusing more on their career than on nonwork issues at this time, delaying close involvements until their late twenties or early thirties.

In contrast, Jasper Phipps is learning to live with a spouse. Balancing his own needs with the needs of another may create performance dilemmas for him at work. For example, his wife's work demands may require a geographical relocation that would affect his own career. Or conflicting work schedules could limit the amount of time he and his wife spend together. Clearly, Jasper's choice of a family style, such as whether he is part of a dual-career family, influences the nature of his work involvement and commitment.

Patricia Robertson may face very real conflicts between her work and home responsibilities. In addition to adjusting to parenthood emotionally, she must resolve the more practical issues of establishing a workable division of responsi-

TABLE 16.2 ■ Sample Stages, Issues, and Tasks of the Family Cycle

State or Stage	Issues	Specific Tasks
Dependent child	Learning to adapt to the environment	Getting own needs met
Transition to adulthood	Managing the delicate balance between total and partial independence to allow for some trial and error in an environment of safety and support	
Single adult	Managing relations with those of the opposite sex	
Married adult	Learning to live with a mate	Balancing one's own needs and styles with those of another
	Making a long-term commitment to a family style and financial requirements	
Parent of a young child	Adjusting to parenthood emotionally	Setting up a workable schedule of child care
Parent of adolescents	Dealing with the independence needs and rebellion of their children	Setting reasonable standards and limits
		Enforcing limits
	Coming to terms with changing values	
Parent of grown children	Adjusting to the departure of children	Developing new work role, hobbies, etc.
	Building new relationship with spouse	
Grandparent	Establishing a relationship with a small child	
	Dealing with own children in parent role	
	Assessing own role as a mentor	

Source: Edgar Schein, *Career Dynamics,* © 1978, Addison-Wesley Publishing Co., Inc., Reading, Massachusetts. Chart adapted from pages 50–52. Reprinted with permission.

bility in her marriage. Work demands may limit the amount of time she can devote to home responsibilities. Women at this stage often face the dilemma of whether to continue working at all. For those with young children who continue to work, their comfort with this decision influences their behavior at work. The quality of child care they arrange, the flexibility of their employer in allowing them to respond to family problems, and the cooperation of their spouse in sharing home responsibilities all influence individual performance.

John Sales's mid-career crisis may be compounded by the difficulty in his family arrangements. Dealing with the independence needs and rebellion of his own children may reinforce his feelings of inadequacy or dissatisfaction, which in turn may restrict his ability to perform effectively at work. The financial demands of supporting his own and his former spouse's households may further intensify the stress he feels.

At the same time that Jeffrey Sachs's work requirements are declining, his family requirements are also decreasing. He must adjust to the departure of children and build a new relationship with a new spouse. And both men and women at this stage may face the decision of whether to withdraw from the work world to accompany spouses into retirement.

DUAL-CAREER FAMILY

Organizations are increasingly employing individuals who are members of families in which both partners have professional careers.[19] Such workers often experience conflicts between their work and family responsibilities. For example, which spouse will stay home with a sick child? What will happen if one person's career advancement depends on geographical relocation? Who will perform the social responsibilities that a wife has traditionally performed for a fast-track husband?

Individuals in dual-career families often use one or more of the following five strategies for dealing with role pressures.[20] First, family members develop commitment to both careers. Each person agrees to his or her spouse's need and right to pursue a career.

Second, they build in flexibility in home and on the job. Each person must be willing to adjust and revise his or her plans as required. For example, in dual-career families, one or both members may forego a particular advancement opportunity if it requires moving. In addition, where possible, they hold jobs that give them autonomy or other means of adaptability. A university professor, for instance, often has greater flexibility in his or her career than would the branch manager of a bank.

Third, two-career families use several different coping mechanisms that help members negotiate responsibilities such as child care. They may change their own attitudes about the priorities they attach to certain activities, such as eating certain types of meals at regular times. Or they may find better ways to fulfill all their responsibilities, through increased attention to the scheduling of activities. An example would be shopping for food only once a week instead of twice or three times.

Fourth, members of two-career families must be skilled at time management. They generally employ their energy carefully and pare their lives down to high priority activities. Thus, they often limit the number of social activities in which they participate and carefully choose volunteer responsibilities.

Fifth and finally, they develop career competencies, such as self-assessment, collection of vocational information, goal setting, planning, and problem solving, to facilitate their mutual career advancement. Organizations that wish to retain a valued worker who is a member of a dual-career family often assist by securing a job for the spouse of the employee.

Organizations must recognize that transitions in personal life often accompany career transitions.[21] Therefore, they must be concerned with the consequences of major career moves within the organization and help individuals to develop strategies for managing the accompanying changes in their personal lives.

Career Development

Career

Individually perceived sequence of attitudes and behaviors associated with work-related experiences and activities over the span of a person's life.

A **career** is the individually perceived sequence of attitudes and behaviors associated with work-related experiences and activities over the span of a person's life.[22] In the following sections we discuss career stages, professional careers in particular, and organizational socialization important to career development.

CAREER STAGES

A variety of schemes have been used to represent career development, or the changes in attitudes and behaviors over time. Table 16.3 presents four groups of

TABLE 16.3 ■ Career Stages According to Edgar Schein	
Age	Schein
0	
5	Growth, fantasy
10	Exploration
15	
20	Entry into work
25	world/training
30	Full membership in early career
35	Full membership in mid-career
40	Mid-career crisis
45	
50	Late career in nonleadership and leadership roles
55	decline and
60	disengagement
65	
70	Retirement

Source: Edgar Schein, *Career Dynamics,* © 1978, Addison-Wesley Publishing Co., Inc., Reading, Massachusetts. Chart adapted from pages 40–46. Reprinted with permission.

stages, including approximate age correlates, as developed by Edgar Schein. In Schein's scheme, the first stage is that of establishing identity. This stage is typically reached between the ages of ten and twenty. In this stage, career alternatives are explored and an attempt is made to move into the adult world. The next group of stages involves growing and getting established in a career. These stages typically last from after age twenty to forty, when a person chooses an occupation and establishes a career path. In the next group, self-maintenance and self-adjustment generally last to age fifty and beyond. At this point, a person either accepts life as it is or makes adjustments. Career change and divorce often occur at this time, because people are seriously questioning the quality of their lives. It is a period of decline and disengagement when diminishing physical and mental capabilities may accelerate. Aspirations and motivations may be lowered, resulting in additional career adjustments. The final stage, according to Schein, is retirement.

Most career development activities are directed at an organization's new, younger workers. However, for most individuals, different career development needs occur at different stages in their lives. For example, because of the Age Discrimination in Employment Act, as amended in 1986, there is no longer a mandatory retirement age; therefore, for many individuals, the maintenance-and-adjustment period of career development is likely to be extended.[23] Consequently, it is likely that in the future, career development activities will not be limited to

---

TABLE 16.4 ■ Sample Stages, Issues, and Tasks of the Career Cycle

Stages	Issues	Specific Tasks
Growth, fantasy, exploration	Developing a basis for making realistic vocational choices	Developing and discovering one's own needs and interests
	Obtaining education or training	Getting maximum career information
Entry into world of work	Becoming a member of an organization or occupation	Learning how to look for and secure a job
Training	Becoming an effective member quickly	Overcoming the insecurity of inexperience
		Learning to get along with boss and co-workers
Full membership in early career	Accepting the responsibility and discharging duties	Performing effectively
		Accepting subordinate status
	Developing and displaying special skills	Developing initiative and realistic expectations
Full membership in mid-career	Choosing a specialty	Gaining a measure of independence
	Remaining technically competent	
	Establishing a clear identity	Assessing own motives, talents
		Assessing organizational and occupational opportunities
Mid-career crisis	Reassessing own progress relative to ambitions	Becoming aware of career anchor
	Deciding relative importance of work and family	Making specific choices about the present and future
Late career in nonleadership role	Becoming a mentor	Remaining technically competent
	Broadening interests	Developing interpersonal skills
	Deepening skills	Dealing with younger persons
Late career in leadership role	Using skills and talents for organization's welfare	Becoming more responsible for organization
	Selecting and developing subordinates	Handling power
		Balancing career and family
Decline and disengagement	Learning to accept reduced power and responsibility	Finding new sources of satisfaction
Retirement	Adjusting to more drastic life-style changes	Maintaining a sense of identity and self-worth without job

Source: Edgar Schein, *Career Dynamics,* © 1978, Addison-Wesley Publishing Co., Inc., Reading, Massachusetts. Chart adapted from pages 40–46. Reprinted with permission.

the initial years of an employee's life. Table 16.4 presents the career stages according to Edgar Schein and a sample of issues and tasks associated with each.

Recall the five members of the data-processing department shown in Table 16.1. Are these five department members at the same stage in their career cycle? What do they expect from their jobs in relation to their career development? Are they likely to react in the same way to the requirements of their jobs and the organization?

Leslie Slater is most likely trying to become an effective and accepted member of Fresh-Foods Industries while she learns the ropes and routines of her first job. She must spend time learning to get along with her boss and co-workers while trying to become an effective member quickly.

Jasper Phipps strives for a high level of recognition early in a career. His primary emphasis must be on performing effectively, accepting responsibility, discharging duties, and developing special skills. Young professionals like Jasper often experience difficulties in accomplishing these tasks.[24] The expectations of superiors, peers, and subordinates (if any) may conflict: subordinates may expect compassion; superiors, obedience to orders. Their first supervisors may be incompetent and limit their acquisition of knowledge and advancement. In addition, young professionals, particularly young managers, may be insensitive to the internal political environment of the organization. Personal passivity and ignorance of real evaluative criteria may prevent them from actively improving their status or performance. These young professionals may not recognize that they must relinquish technical involvement or train successors if they are to advance. Tensions between older and younger managers, dilemmas about the person to whom the young professional owes loyalty, as well as ethical dilemmas and anxiety about integrity, commitment, and dependence, may all contribute to the problems experienced by employees like Jasper Phipps.

Patricia Robertson performs career tasks similar to those of Jasper Phipps. She has become increasingly autonomous in her job while assuming additional responsibilities. Yet she is concerned with remaining technically competent. She must assess whether she wishes to remain a technical employee or advance into a managerial position. Regular reassessment of her own motives and talents, as well as of organizational and occupational opportunities, must occur. She must also be concerned with **obsolescence,** or the failure to maintain up-to-date knowledge in a career field.[25] She must ensure that she does not become a plateaued performer. "Plateaued individuals are by and large 'solid citizens,' people who are doing their present jobs well but who are seen as having little likelihood of achieving positions at the highest level; they constitute the bulk of the managerial work force in most organizations—those who 'get the work done.'"[26]

John Sales may face a mid-life crisis in his career as well as his personal life. The mid-life transition or "mid-life decade," which typically occurs between ages thirty-five and forty-five, causes individuals to appraise their life's accomplishments to date. They pose questions such as "What have I done with my life?" "What do I really get from and give to my (spouse), children, friends, work, community, and self?" "What are my real values and how are they reflected in my life?"[27] In one study of men at mid-career, 80 percent experienced significant struggles over career or family. These frequently resulted in moderate or severe crises, where individuals questioned every facet of their lives.[28] To resolve these crises, individuals frequently make new choices about career and family or finally accept their old choices as appropriate. Eventually they come to terms with time, accept that life is finite, and view themselves as stable and accomplished.[29]

Jeffrey Sachs must find a way to continue contributing to the organization. He might be involved with shaping its direction by acting as a sponsor for younger workers.[30] Professionals older than forty are considered above-average performers

Obsolescence
The failure to maintain up-to-date knowledge in a career field.

only if they have moved into this stage or one where they train, assume responsibility for, and act as mentors for others.[31]

For employers, "the basic challenge is not to weed out deadwood but to maintain the motivation and performance of managers (and other workers) who no longer see the prospect of vertical mobility."[32] Although employees must assume some responsibility for preventing their own stagnation, unless organizations can respond with continuous challenges and additional responsibilities, the plateaued employee will probably experience performance problems. To identify causes of performance problems, managers should diagnose the career development of key employees:

1. At what career stage are the relevant organizational members?
2. What developmental issues and tasks are they confronting?
3. How might these interface with their current organizational roles?
4. Are employees in appropriate roles for their career stages?
5. Are employees' skills obsolete?
6. Have any employees plateaued in their careers?

PROFESSIONAL CAREERS

Professional employees are those who bring specialized expertise to organizations, frequently as a result of advanced education or special training. These individuals (scientists, engineers, teachers, and accountants) often face career and organizational issues different from those experienced by managers and other employees. Managers who do not share their professional background may have difficulty motivating or supervising them. Recognition for the technical quality of their work may be limited by management's lack of technical knowledge: professionals often disagree with managers over the technical sophistication required to complete their tasks. Professionals also frequently demand extensive autonomy in their work. They may be more committed to their specialty and profession than to the organization. And professionals may insist on professional standards of conduct, which can sometimes be dysfunctional for the organization.[33]

In most organizations, professional employees cannot advance in the organization without assuming some managerial responsibility.[34] Unfortunately, "dual ladders," where individuals can assume increasingly higher positions (with greater pay, status, and responsibility) *without* assuming managerial or supervisory responsibility, are uncommon in most organizations (see Figure 16.2). Without them, professionals may experience career dissatisfaction, which in turn leads to either deviant or adaptive behaviors.[35] Figure 16.3 shows the range of deviant or adaptive behaviors that might occur, vis-à-vis management, the job, oneself, or one's career. For example, a professional may show adaptive behavior vis-à-vis management: this individual may seek and obtain freedom from professional constraints, utilize privileges such as flexible work hours, demonstrate more autonomy, or rely on technology such as the computerization of interactions with management. In contrast, the dissatisfied professional may demonstrate deviant behaviors, such as divulging company secrets or resorting to unethical practices. Behaviors that have both adaptive and deviant elements include refusal to implement management's requests, work-to-rule (that is, working by the letter of the professional's contract), and interpersonal sabotage.

To ensure the productivity of professionals, managers must use accommodative mechanisms, including job redesign, "dual ladders," professional reward

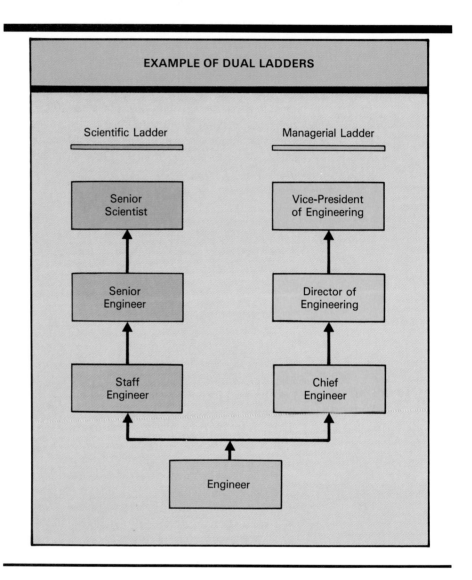

systems, and mentorship for managers. Professionals, for their part, must learn about the organization they are about to enter and check its "fit" with their own personal and professional goals.

Career effectiveness and the individual job effectiveness that accompanies it are often a result of organizational socialization, the organization's ability to integrate the employee into the organization and help that person make career transitions effectively.

ORGANIZATIONAL SOCIALIZATION

"The process of 'learning the ropes,' the process of being indoctrinated and trained, the process of being taught what is important in an organization or subunit thereof" is an inherent part of career development.[36] Organizational socialization is "the process by which a new member learns:

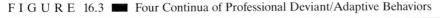

FIGURE 16.3 ■■ Four Continua of Professional Deviant/Adaptive Behaviors

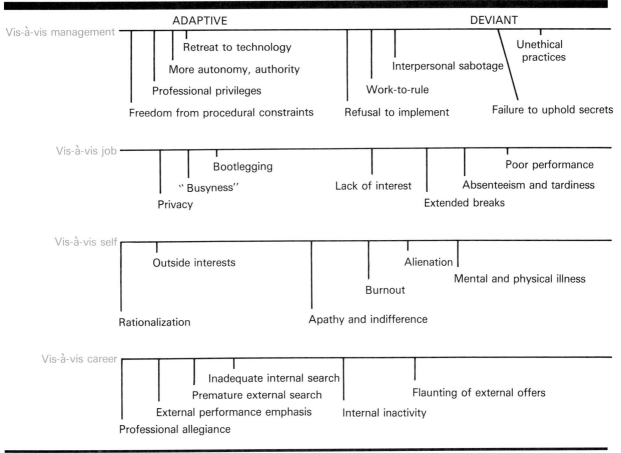

Source: J. Raelin, Examination of deviant/adaptive behaviors in the organizational careers of professionals, *Academy of Management Review* 9 (1984): 413–427. Reprinted with permission.

1. the basic *goals* of the organization;
2. the preferred *means* by which those goals should be attained;
3. the basic *responsibilities* of the member in the role which is being granted him by the organization;
4. the *behavior patterns* which are required for effective performance in the role;
5. a set of rules or principles which pertain to the *maintenance of the identity and integrity* or the organization."[37]

Orientation programs frequently provide the initial socialization of organization members. In some organizations, top managers meet with new recruits to discuss their philosophy and vision of the organization. In others, the human resource management department meets with newly hired employees and presents them with the organization's rules and standard operating procedures. In still other organizations, small groups of new employees meet with managers to discuss their concerns. Or individual recruits may receive orientation from their own supervisor. Do you think the participants in these various types of orientation sessions will perceive the same things as being important in their organizations? Certainly the formality or informality of orientation provides cues about the operation of the organization; so, too, does the choice to orient newly hired employees individually or in a large group.

Socialization occurs continually, but it is most intense when an individual makes a career transition in an organization by entering a new, often higher,

TABLE 16.5 ■ Names, Definitions, Examples, and Hypothesized Consequences of Socialization Strategies

Strategy	Definition	Example	Hypothesized Consequences
Collective	Puts newcomer through a common set of experiences as part of a group	Freshman orientation	Conformity, less stress
Individual	Processes recruits singly and in isolation from each other	On-the-job training	Innovation, more stress
Formal	Segregates newcomers from regular organizational members	Basic military training	Conformity, more stress
Informal	Treats newcomers as undifferentiated from other members	Transferred employees	Innovation, less stress
Sequential steps	Requires entrant to move through a series of discrete and identifiable steps to achieve a defined role	Specialized medical training	Conformity, less stress
Nonsequential steps	Accomplishes achievement of a defined role in one transitional stage	Promotion	Innovation, more stress
Tournament	Separates clusters of recruits into different programs on the basis of presumed differences	Academic tracked programs	Innovation, more stress
Contest	Avoids sharp distinctions between clusters of recruits	Law school	Conformity, less stress
Fixed	Gives the recruit complete knowledge of time required to complete passage	Six-week managerial training program	Conformity, less stress
Variable	Offers a timetable that does not fix the length of socialization	Doctoral program	Innovation, more stress
Serial	Provides experienced members as role models for newcomers about to assume similar positions to follow	Apprenticeship program	Conformity, less stress
Disjunctive	Has no role models available for newcomers about to assume similar positions to follow	First holder of newly defined job	Innovation, more stress
Investitive	Ratifies and documents the usefulness of personal characteristics of new recruits	New faculty orientation	Innovation, less stress
Divestiture	Seeks to deny and strip away recruits' personal characteristics	Training for the priesthood	Conformity, more stress

Source: Reprinted by permission of publisher, from *Organizational Dynamics,* 7/1978 © 1978. American Management Association, New York. All rights reserved.

position or a different department. A newly promoted manager must "learn the ropes" of the new position. Workers whose supervisor has just been replaced must learn how the new boss operates.

Organizational socialization often occurs unconsciously, with no analysis of the strategies employed or of their likely consequences. John Van Maanen describes seven dimensions of socialization strategies that are associated with career transitions.[38] Table 16.5 lists and defines these strategies and provides a brief example and some hypothesized consequences of each. Consider a one-day orientation program for bank tellers in which a group of new recruits sees a film about the company, receives a lecture about the benefits they are to receive, tours the organization, and undergoes classroom training about bank procedures. What types of socialization strategies are incorporated into this orientation? The orientation program uses collective and formal strategies, where newcomers go through a common set of experiences as part of a group that does not include regular organizational members. The program also avoids distinctions between recruits (contest strategy), requires them to move through a series of identifiable steps (sequential steps) in a prespecified time period (fixed), and encourages newcomers to model their behavior on that of previously successful tellers (serial strategy). In addition, newcomers are not encouraged to retain their personal characteristics (divestiture strategy). Assuming that the socialization of the new tellers continues to use similar strategies, such as providing training for all tellers as a group in a formal classroom setting, Van Maanen and Schein would hypothesize that most of these strategies would result in conforming behavior.[39] It would be expected that the tellers would demonstrate limited innovation in performing their jobs. Of course, this type of outcome seems appropriate for bank tellers. Would orientation that uses these strategies be appropriate for salespeople or middle managers?

It can be hypothesized that a different set of strategies would result in innovative behavior. Training that uses individual, informal, tournament, nonsequential steps, variable, disjunctive, and investitive strategies encourages this outcome. The strategies used may result in either less stress or more stress for the individuals involved.

■ STRESS IN ORGANIZATIONS

Problems related to individual differences in personality and development may lead to dysfunctional behaviors and attitudes in organizations. Together with role conflict, the inability of organizations to respond to worker needs at various stages of biosocial, family, and career development may result in significant stress for the worker. Such stress can have positive or negative consequences for both the workers and the organization.

Stress
The body's reaction to any demand made on it.

Hans Selye first used the term stress in the 1930s.[40] **Stress** is the body's reaction to any demand made on it. It is a psychological and physiological state that results when certain features of an individual's environment, including noise, pressures, job promotions, monotony, or the general climate, impinge on that person. Both positive and negative occurrences can give rise to stress. As may be seen in Figure 16.4, in stress situations individuals generally go through three stages: (1) alarm, (2) resistance, and (3) exhaustion.[41] In the alarm stage a

FIGURE 16.4 ■
Stages of Stress

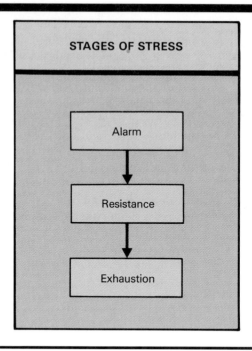

stressor causes a rise in adrenaline, or anxiety. If the stressor persists, individuals respond to it during the resistance stage. They may attack the stressor directly, adopt a previously but no longer successful coping behavior, deny the stressor, withdraw physically or psychologically from the situation, or persist in responding whether or not the response is effective.[42] When a stressor is allowed to persist to the point of physiological or psychological damage, exhaustion occurs.

Some respond to stress by becoming more productive and creative. Have you ever heard a friend or co-worker say, "I work best when I have a deadline in sight; I can't do anything productive unless I feel some pressure"? This person likely uses the stress resulting from the time pressure constructively—to increase individual productivity. Others experience gastrointestinal, glandular, and cardio-vascular disorders or respond to stress by overeating, drinking excessively, or taking tranquilizers.[43] Others become impatient, detached, or filled with despair. Such physiological and psychological reactions can decrease a person's creativity and productivity, which in turn often increases a person's level of stress, in turn causing a further decrease in effectiveness.

Causes of Stress

Stress has become increasingly common in organizations, largely because of increased job complexity and increased economic pressures on individuals. Individuals at the beginning of their career, who are trying to establish themselves, often experience stress; the mid-career crisis is virtually synonymous with stress; and facing the changes retirement brings creates significant stress for many individuals. Table 16.6 lists the major life-stress events and provides a way of calculating the probability of experiencing stress-related illness.

TABLE 16.6 ■ Life-Stress Events

Complete the scale by circling the mean value figure to the right of each item if it has occurred to you during the past year. To figure your total score, add all the mean values circled (if an event occurred more than once, increase the value by the number of times). Life-stress event totals of 150 or less indicate generally good health, scores of 150 to 300 indicate a 35–50 percent probability of stress-related illness, and scores of 300+ indicate an 80 percent probability.

Life Event	Mean Value	Life Event	Mean Value
1. Death of spouse	100	24. In-law troubles	29
2. Divorce	73	25. Outstanding personal achievement	28
3. Marital separation from mate	65	26. Wife beginning or ceasing work outside the home	26
4. Detention in jail or other institution	63	27. Beginning or ceasing formal schooling	26
5. Death of a close family member	63	28. Major change in living conditions	25
6. Major personal injury or illness	53	29. Revision of personal habits	24
7. Marriage	50	30. Troubles with the boss	23
8. Being fired at work	47	31. Major change in working hours or conditions	20
9. Marital reconciliation with mate	45	32. Change in residence	20
10. Retirement from work	45	33. Changing to a new school	20
11. Major change in the health or behavior of a family member	44	34. Major change in usual type and/or amount of recreation	19
12. Pregnancy	40	35. Major change in church activities	19
13. Sexual difficulties	39	36. Major change in social activities	18
14. Gaining a new family member	39	37. Taking out a mortgage or loan for a lesser purchase	17
15. Major business readjustment	39	38. Major change in sleeping habits	16
16. Major change in financial state	38	39. Major change in number of family get-togethers	15
17. Death of a close friend	37	40. Major change in eating habits	15
18. Changing to a different line of work	36	41. Vacation	13
19. Major change in the number of arguments with spouse	35	42. Christmas	12
20. Taking out a mortgage or loan for a major purchase	31	43. Minor violations of the law	11
21. Foreclosure on a mortgage or loan	30		
22. Major change in responsibilities at work	29		
23. Son or daughter leaving home	29		

Source: Thomas H. Holmes, Social Readjustment Rating Scale, *Journal of Psychosomatic Research* 11(2) (1967): 213–218. Reprinted with permission from Pergamon Press, Ltd.

Interpersonal variables, such as leadership style and extent of group cohesion and participation, also contribute to stress both in and out of the workplace. Where the personalities of leaders and followers conflict, such as when an extroverted employee is supervised by an introverted manager, or when an individual with a thinking decision-making orientation clashes with an individual with a feeling decision-making orientation, stress often occurs. Thus, the relationship between stressors and stress may be affected by an individual's personality, culture, or nonwork environment. Professional women experience

Stress is becoming more common in organizations because of increasing job complexity and economic pressures on the individual.
(COMSTOCK, Inc./Michael Stuckey)

unique stressors: discrimination, stereotyping, conflicting demands of work and family, and feelings of isolation, which can dramatically impact performance and health.[44]

The National Institute for Occupational Safety and Health (NIOSH) is one organization that has studied stress as it relates to work. This organization's research indicates that some jobs are more stressful than others. The twelve most stressful jobs are listed in Table 16.7.

Role Conflict and Role Ambiguity

Each of the data-processing professionals profiled in Table 16.1 has a prescribed set of activities, or potential behavior, that constitutes the roles that individuals perform.[45] For example, the role of programmer might include reviewing the specifications for programs, writing the code for a program, reviewing it with the client, or keeping it current.

Typically, an individual in a particular work role relates to, or interacts with, others in comparable or related roles, known as the *role set*. In the case of the data-processing department at Fresh-Foods Industries, each programmer may interact with the other programmers in the department, with the department manager, and with clients. These other persons generally have expectations of how the role holder will operate. For example, Steve Buchanan may expect Leslie to follow his specifications precisely and complete the program as quickly as

TABLE 16.7 ■ Stressful Jobs

12 Jobs with the most stress

1. Laborer	5. Office manager	9. Machine operator
2. Secretary	6. Foreman	10. Farm owner
3. Inspector	7. Manager/administrator	11. Miner
4. Clinical lab technician	8. Waitress/waiter	12. Painter

Other high-stress jobs (in alphabetical order)

■ Bank teller	■ Machinist	■ Railroad switchman
■ Clergy	■ Meatcutter	■ Registered nurse
■ Computer programmer	■ Mechanic	■ Sales manager
■ Dental assistant	■ Musician	■ Sales representative
■ Electrician	■ Nurses' aide	■ Social worker
■ Fireman	■ Plumber	■ Structural-metal worker
■ Guard/watchman	■ Policeman	■ Teachers' aide
■ Hairdresser	■ Practical nurse	■ Telephone operator
■ Health aide	■ Public relations person	■ Warehouse worker
■ Health technician		

Source: From a ranking of 130 occupations by the federal government's National Institute for Occupational Safety and Health.

possible. Others in the department may expect her to act as a resource for questions they have, even if this delays completion of a required program. Subordinates may expect Steve to provide training. Clients may ask the programmer to revise existing code. The programmers may or may not conform to these expectations. They may conform to the clients' expectations of "user-friendly" programs; or they may act contrary to these expectations by writing programs that allow them to use a complex programming language that is not as user-friendly. They may meet their boss's requirements for many lines of code but ignore the request for highly accurate code.

Generally, an individual will operate *in role;* that is, the person will behave according to the expectations associated with the role. For example, the factory worker will assemble engines, or the professor will counsel students. On occasion, role holders operate *out of role;* that is, they perform activities typically not associated with their roles. The factory worker or the professor may indulge in heated political oratories or write personal letters at work.

THE DEFINITION OF ROLE CONFLICT

It might be said, however, that behaviors such as those cited above are not really out of role, according to the role holder. Different people often have different expectations about the activities that are appropriate for a role holder. These different expectations result in conflicting pressures on the role holder to perform in one way rather than another. This in turn results in role conflict, where compliance with one set of pressures prevents (or makes more difficult) compliance with a different set of pressures. Role conflict and role ambiguity (described below) at work lead to such dysfunctional work-related behaviors as tension, job dissatisfaction, propensity to leave the organization, and lowered commitment.[46] For example, top management expects an accountant to perform as a detail person, processing as many accounts as possible. But the supervisor expects the accountant to sacrifice quantity in favor of quality and creativity. To which set of pressures does the accountant respond? Let's look at another situation. An individual with strong religious beliefs is asked to work on a religious holiday. Or consider a programmer who is asked to write programs for a project to which he or she has ethical objections. Such situations offer a high possibility of role conflict.

As these examples suggest, role conflict is inherent within a single role; but persons play multiple roles to meet diverse, and potentially conflicting, expectations. For example, a manager who is also a wife and mother, or a manager who is also a husband and father, plays different roles inside and outside the organization. She or he might experience role conflict when attending a PTA meeting conflicts with attending a business meeting. A lawyer, who also serves as a local school committee member, may find that work responsibilities infringe on time required to deal with school business, or vice versa.

TYPES OF ROLE CONFLICT

Role conflict can come from different sources. There are five types of role conflict: (1) intrasender, (2) intersender, (3) inter-role, (4) person-role, and (5) role overload.

Intrasender conflict
Conflict that occurs when one person sends a role holder conflicting or inconsistent expectations.

Intrasender conflict occurs when one person sends a role holder conflicting or inconsistent expectations. In the case of the five programmers, Steven may tell them, on the one hand, to write as many lines of code as possible and, on the other hand, to write programs that are error-free.

Intersender conflict
Conflict that occurs when different people with whom the role holder interacts have different expectations of him or her.

Intersender conflict occurs when different people with whom the role holder interacts have different expectations of him or her. The programmers may "hear" different expectations about their role from their clients and from their supervisor. A client may want a program as quickly as possible, regardless of the overtime and cost required, but the supervisor wants to maintain a ceiling on salaries and overtime.

Inter-role conflict
Conflict that occurs when the expectations associated with different roles come into conflict.

Inter-role conflict occurs when the expectations associated with different roles come into conflict. The working mother who has a sick child is expected to be at work performing her job and to be at home caring for her sick child simultaneously. Both partners in a dual-career marriage are expected to be fully committed to both work and family.

Person-role conflict
Conflict that occurs when the activities expected of a role holder violate the individual's values and morals.

Person-role conflict occurs when the activities expected of a role holder violate the individual's values and morals. The employee who is asked to work on a religious holiday or to participate in activities that contradict personal values may experience this type of conflict. The employee who is asked to distort data to represent the company favorably in an affirmative action report may also experience such conflict.

Role overload
A more complex form of conflict, that occurs when the expectations sent to a role holder are compatible, but their performance exceeds the amount of time available to the person for performing the expected activities.

Role overload, a more complex form of conflict, occurs when the expectations sent to a role holder are compatible, but their performance exceeds the amount of time available to the person for performing the expected activities. A person who holds a full-time job, attends graduate school part-time, has family and child-care responsibilities, and is actively involved in volunteer activities will likely experience role overload. So, too, will a person who is asked to perform tasks that exceed that person's knowledge, skills, or abilities. Overload also typifies top management jobs, where the role holder often has more responsibilities than a single individual can handle.

Each type of role conflict involves pressure on the role holder to conform to expectations. For example, a supervisor will create intrasender conflict by pressuring a subordinate to act each way the supervisor demands, even if the ways contradict or conflict. This is particularly common where trade-offs between quality and quantity, or between quality and expense, must occur. Generally, the more extreme the pressure, the more extensive the conflict, and the greater the stress that often results. Further, the ability of different individuals to deal with conflict may be linked to their personality and personal style. For example, sensation-oriented individuals, who are more focused on details, may be better able to deal with role overload than those individuals who cannot organize details or diverse activities.

ROLE AMBIGUITY

Role ambiguity
A role holder who lacks sufficient information to perform the activities associated with that individual's role.

A role holder who lacks sufficient information to perform the activities associated with that individual's role experiences **role ambiguity.** New employees who receive no orientation often experience role ambiguity, because they lack complete information about both the activities and responsibilities of the job and about the organization. Also, employees who do not know what activities the organization rewards often experience role ambiguity. Does the company promote individuals who conform to company policies completely, or does it reward those who take some risks and who demonstrate creativity? Does the company value a perfect attendance record, or is high production quotas the criterion? New employees need to know what will be expected of them.

Kahn and his associates suggest that role holders must know six basic types of information.[47] First, role holders must know what the expectations of others are. For example, what attitudes and behaviors does a supervisor require of subordinates? What types of interactions do peers and subordinates expect?

Second, role holders must know the activities they should perform and the interpersonal interactions they should demonstrate to fulfill these expectations of others. For example, how should the five programmers complete their work? Must they work at the office, or can they work at home? How extensively should they consult peers or supervisors? They must also determine the best ways to perform the required activities. They can gather this information from discussions with supervisors and co-workers.

Third, role holders must know the consequences of performing or not performing the activities or of interacting with others in certain ways. For example, if a program is not written on time, will the programmer be given an extension, reprimand—or be fired? If an employee never eats lunch with co-workers, will this result in isolation on the job? Knowing the precise consequences of actions reduces role ambiguity and often the stress and tension that accompany it.

Fourth, role holders must know the kinds of behaviors or attitudes that will be rewarded or punished. In the data-processing department, is tardiness a punishable offense? What happens if other departments complain (justifiably or not) about a programmer's performance? On the other hand, what might result if top management is extremely satisfied with the data-processing department's performance? What happens if a programmer disregards the advice of the other programmers, or assumes a competitive attitude toward them?

Fifth, role holders must find out what types of rewards and punishments will be given and assess the likelihood of their receiving them. They can get this information by asking supervisors or by observing the past organizational behavior of others.

Finally, role holders must determine the kinds of behaviors and attitudes that will satisfy or frustrate personal needs. Do the rewards offered meet employees' needs? Do the required behaviors help the individuals accomplish their tasks?

DIAGNOSING ROLE PRESSURES

To determine whether role conflict or role ambiguity exists in a situation, questions such as the following can be asked:

- Do any symptoms of role conflict or role ambiguity, such as stress, confusion, or low productivity, exist?
- How is each person's role defined by the role holder and by relevant others?
- Are the expectations for the role holder clear?
- Do any of the identified role expectations conflict?
- What socialization processes does the organization use?
- What are the outcomes of the socialization processes? Are they appropriate to the individuals involved and the situation?

Individuals respond to both role conflict and role ambiguity in a variety of ways. Think about an experience you may have had that involved role conflict or role ambiguity. How did you handle it? Some cope by adjusting to the situation, by setting priorities, or by ignoring certain expectations. For example, members of dual-career families may, at different stages, give priority to one or the other spouse's career. Early in their careers, a husband's need to relocate may be given priority. Working parents may decide that family responsibilities (e.g., a sick child or a conference with a child's teacher) have a higher priority than work responsibilities (e.g., staff meetings), or vice versa. A computer programmer who is a perfectionist may ignore the boss's demands to program quickly, even if errors result. Or a project manager who observes certain religious holidays may on those days leave work, even though a lot remains to be done. Any of these people might experience anxiety and stress.

The Stress Audit

In many organizations today, managers find that they must be more sensitive to potential stressors in order to maintain productive, involved employees. At the same time, employees today often opt for minimizing stress, sometimes at the expense of promotions or significant pay increases. But managers and employees alike must recognize that a certain amount of stress may be necessary for creative and productive work. A total absence of stress in the work place can result in complacency.

Predicting the level of stress in a situation can be difficult, largely because stress is often person-specific, meaning that what is highly stressful for one person may effect another very little. Oftentimes, features of jobs intuitively rated as stressful—such as the mental demands on and responsibilities of air-traffic controllers, or the life-and-death situations police officers face—are neither disliked nor experienced as stressful by the actual job holders.[48] Alternatively, simple requests for overtime or revisions of completed work may cause stress.

Stress audit
An audit that helps identify the symptoms and causes of stress.

Let us consider again the five programmers in the data-processing department described in Table 16.1. The extent of dysfunctional stress in that situation could be evaluated by performing a **stress audit,** which helps identify the symptoms and causes of stress.[49] To perform an audit, ask questions such as the following:

1. Do any individuals demonstrate cardiovascular, gastrointestinal, allergy-respiratory, or emotional distress irregularities?
2. Is job satisfaction low, or job tension, turnover, absenteeism, strikes, or accident proneness high?
3. Does the organization's design contribute to the symptoms?
4. Do interpersonal relations contribute to the symptoms?
5. Do career-development variables contribute to the symptoms?
6. What effects do personality, sociocultural influences, and the nonwork environment have on the relationship between stressors—individual careers, interpersonal relations, and organizational design—and stress?

To answer questions 1 and 2 completely and accurately for the five programmers would require a more thorough description of the situation than that provided by Table 16.1. Yet even a brief scenario can offer evidence of gastrointestinal irregularities, high job tension, and high absenteeism—all indicators of stress. To answer questions 3 through 6 requires understanding of the various issues discussed throughout the chapters of this book.

Managing Stress

To be effective, organizational members must recognize when to increase and when to decrease stress. The key to constructively managing stress is to first recognize its energizing or destructive effects.[50] Managers can encourage productive stress. They can help employees build challenge into their work and assume incremental responsibility and autonomy over time.[51]

Managers can also help individuals cope with dysfunctional stress in three basic ways.[52] First, individuals can secure treatment at work for the symptoms of stress. Many organizations now provide free employee health and counseling services, as well as stress-reduction workshops, to help individuals deal with symptoms. Second, stress-reduction activities can be directed to changing the person—by improving resistance to stress through yoga, exercise, diet, or psychological support. Third, individuals and organizations can change or remove the stressors: they can redesign jobs to reduce role overload, role ambiguity, or conversely, boredom. They can also change organizational policies to give individuals more control over their work activities.

Alternatively, individuals can attempt to prevent stress altogether.[53] Thus, managers should be trained in stress symptom identification, and to ask questions such as the following:[54]

- What are the stress symptoms that I observe? Have these symptoms been observed before? When? For how long?
- What has happened around work that could trigger a severe stress reaction? Is this what the employee is stressed about?
- Have I been a stress carrier, contributing to the employee's problems? How sure am I?
- Is there a possible medical (or physical) problem? How sure am I?
- Does this employee have a long-standing personality problem that was noted long before these symptoms occurred?
- Has the employee effectively coped with stress in the past? How?
- Are there resources available (work counseling, co-worker support, managerial support) to help reduce the symptoms?

Managers can help individuals cope with stress by encouraging adaptive behaviors. They can reduce the work load of overworked employees, encourage an employee who has a poor working relationship with a colleague to confront him or her, and clarify ambiguous roles.[55] Managers can simultaneously discourage maladaptive behaviors. They can discourage overworked employees from accepting additional work, discourage employees with poor co-worker relationships from avoiding or attacking the co-workers, and prevent workers from withdrawing from ambiguous roles.

The costs of stress are high. In one study of a hypothetical organization, which had 2,000 employees and gross sales of $60 million per year, it was estimated that stress-related factors cost the organization $1,780 per employee per year.[56] Another study estimated the cost of executive stress at almost $10 billion annually.[57] Clearly, the diagnosis and reduction of stress can contribute significantly to increased individual and organizational effectiveness.

■■ BURNOUT

Burnout
A state of fatigue or frustration, which stems from devotion to a cause, way of life, or relationship that did not provide the expected reward.

Burnout has been described as a state of fatigue or frustration, which stems from devotion to a cause, way of life, or relationship that did not provide the expected reward.[58] Burnout is often associated with a mid-life or mid-career crisis, but it can happen at different times to different people.[59] Individuals in the helping professions, such as teachers and counselors, seem to be susceptible to burnout because of their jobs, whereas others may be vulnerable because of their upbringing, expectations, or personalities.[60] Burnout is frequently associated with people whose jobs require close relationships with others under stressful and tension-filled conditions.[61] While any employee may experience this condition, perhaps 10 percent of managers and executives are so affected.[62] The dangerous part of burnout is that it is contagious. A highly cynical and pessimistic burnout victim can quickly transform an entire group into burnouts. Therefore, it is important that the problem be dealt with quickly. Once it has begun, it is difficult to stop.[63] Some of the symptoms of burnout include: (1) chronic fatigue, (2) anger at those making demands, (3) self-criticism for putting up with demands, (4) cynicism, negativism, and irritability, (5) a sense of being besieged, and (6) hair-trigger display of emotions.[64] Other symptoms might include recurring health problems, such as ulcers, back pain, or frequent headaches. The burnout victim is often unable to maintain an even keel emotionally. Unwarranted hostility may occur in totally inappropriate situations. Subsequently, burnout is harmful to the individual's mental and physical health, resulting in performance problems both individually and organizationally.

SUMMARY

Personality consists of a wide range of motives, emotions, values, interests, attitudes, and competencies. Differences in personality can significantly affect behavior and job performance in organizations. The characteristics that comprise an individual's personality can be differentiated or organized along a number of different dimensions. For example, internalizers feel that they control their own lives; externalizers believe others do. Type A individuals are competitive, prompt for appointments, and always feel rushed. Type B individuals tend to be more relaxed and to express their feelings. Introverted persons are shy and withdrawn; extroverted persons are outgoing, often aggressive, and dominant. Sensation-type individuals dislike new problems unless there are standard ways to solve them, like an established routine, must usually work all the way through to reach a conclusion, show patience with routine details, and tend to be good at precise work. Intuitive-type individuals, unlike sensation-type individuals, like solving new problems, jump to conclusions, and are impatient with details. Feeling-type individuals are aware of other people and their feelings, like harmony, and need occasional praise. Thinking type individuals are unemotional and uninterested in people's feelings, like putting things into logical order, and can reprimand people when necessary. Effective managers understand these personality types.

Research suggests that adults, like children, have clearly defined stages of biological, social, and family development. Most individuals at a particular stage are likely to have common needs and similar ways of coping with their situations. Career development also occurs in stages. A career is the individually perceived sequence of attitudes and behaviors associated with work-related experiences and activities over the span of that person's life. A variety of schemes have been used to represent career development, and managers should diagnose the career development of key employees to identify causes of performance problems. Orientation programs are particularly important in the socialization and development of organization members. Socialization occurs continually but is most intense at career transition points. Socialization strategies may result in either conforming or innovative behavior.

Stress is a psychological and physiological state that results when features of an individual's environment impinge on that person. Individual personality and development differences that lead to dysfunctional behaviors and attitudes can, along with role conflict and ambiguity, give rise to stress in organizations. Stress has become increasingly common in organizations today, due largely to increased job complexity and economic pressures. Stress often leads to burnout, or a state of fatigue or frustration. Burnout is often associated with a mid-life or mid-career crisis. Managers today must be more sensitive than ever to potential stressors in order to maintain a productive, involved work force.

REVIEW QUESTIONS

1. Define personality. What are the various personality types?
2. What are the strategies dual-career families use for dealing with role pressures?
3. What is a career? Describe the various career stage schemes.
4. Define stress. What are the basic causes of stress?
5. What are the various types of role conflict? Briefly describe each.
6. What is burnout? Why is it important for a manager to understand burnout?

KEY TERMS

personality	sensation-type	intrasender conflict
internalizers	individuals	intersender conflict
externalizers	intuitive-type individuals	inter-role conflict
Machiavellianism	feeling-type individuals	person-role conflict
Type A individuals	thinking-type individuals	role overload
Type B individuals	biosocial development	role ambiguity
introverted person	career	stress audit
extroverted person	obsolescence	burnout
	stress	

CASE STUDY   A STAR IS FALLING

"JUST LEAVE ME alone and let me do my job," said Manuel Gomez. Dumbfounded, Bill Brown, Manuel's supervisor, decided to "count to ten" before responding to Manuel's fury. As he walked back to his office, Bill thought about how Manuel had changed over the past few months. He had been a hard worker and extremely cooperative when he went to work for Bill two years earlier. The company had sent Manuel to two training schools and had received glowing reports about his performance in each of them.

Until about a year ago, Manuel had a perfect attendance record and was virtually an ideal employee. At about that time, however, he began to have personal problems, which resulted in a divorce six months later. Manuel had requested a day off several times to take care of personal business, and Bill had attempted to help in every way he could. He tried not to get involved in Manuel's personal affairs. But he was aware of the strain Manuel must have experienced as his marriage broke up and as he and his wife engaged in the inevitable disputes over child custody, alimony payments, and property.

During the same time period, top management initiated a push for improving productivity. Bill found it necessary to put additional pressure on all of his workers, including Manuel. He tried to be considerate, but he had to become much more performance oriented, insisting on increased output from every worker. As time went on, Manuel began to show up late for work and actually missed two days without calling Bill in advance. Bill attributed Manuel's behavior to extreme stress, and because Manuel had been such a good worker for so long, he excused the tardiness and absences, only gently suggesting that Manuel should try to do better.

Sitting at his desk, Bill thought about what might have caused Manuel's outburst of a few minutes earlier. Bill had simply suggested to Manuel that he shut down the machine he was operating and clean up the surrounding area. This was a normal part of Manuel's job and something he had been careful to do in the past. Bill thought that the disorderliness around Manuel's machine might account for the increasing number of defects in the parts he was making. "This is a tough one— I think I'll talk to the boss about it," thought Bill.

QUESTIONS

1. What do you think is likely to be Manuel's problem? Discuss.
2. If you were Bill's boss, what would you recommend that he do?

CASE STUDY   A CASE OF PERCEPTION

THE LAW FIRM of Maconi, Smith, and Solomon employs seventy-five employees: twenty partners, thirty junior law associates, ten paralegals, and fifteen secretaries. Founded in 1955, Maconi, Smith, and Solomon had become a major force in corporate law. For the first twenty-five years, the firm experienced slow but steady growth. They recruited law students from top law schools who were interested in becoming corporate lawyers and in receiving excellent on-the-job training. The firm's attorneys worked eighty- to ninety-hour weeks. Slowly they acquired a large percentage of the major corporate clients in their

region. Most of the attorneys who performed well became partners. In general, the firm was highly profitable, compensation for all workers was competitive, and job satisfaction was high.

Since 1980, however, the firm has experienced significant competition from several other firms in the area. Many of their clients have complained that Maconi, Smith, and Solomon's fees are too high, their work is often behind schedule, and their approaches to legal problems seem somewhat antiquated. The younger attorneys in the firm complain that the firm's quality control system, which requires review of all documents by at least one senior partner, slows down production and the attorneys' ability to respond quickly to client requests. In addition, the attorneys feel that their work is being unnecessarily scrutinized and that they do not receive financial rewards in proportion to their long hours or to the quality of their work— only as a function of the new clients they bring to the firm. They also feel that it is long past time to fully computerize the report preparation portion of their jobs. They have expressed increasing frustration and dissatisfaction with their jobs.

Several of the younger attorneys are now planning to leave Maconi, Smith, and Solomon to develop a new, more progressive company, one that will move forward rather than backward.

QUESTIONS

1. How have individual differences in personality impacted the situation at the law firm of Maconi, Smith, and Solomon? Discuss.
2. What is the "significance for performance" in the firm's current operation? Discuss.

EXPERIENTIAL EXERCISE

Due to a downward trend in business over the last two years, and the resulting financial constraints, Straight Manufacturing Company has been able to grant only cost-of-living increases to its employees. However, the firm has just signed a lucrative three-year contract with a major defense contractor. As a result, management has formed a salary review committee to award merit increases to deserving employees. Members of the salary review committee have only $13,500 in merit money, and deciding who will receive merit increases will be difficult. Louis Convoy, Sharon Kubiak, J. Ward Archer, Ed Wilson, C. J. Sass, and John Passante have been recommended for raises.

Louis Convoy, Financial Analyst, has an undergraduate business degree and is currently working on an MBA. His previous work experience has allowed him to develop several outstanding financial contacts. Sharon Kubiak, HRM Administrative Assistant, began as a secretary and after three years with the organization was promoted to her present position. Because her first position was that of secretary, her current salary is not at the range commensurate with her new position and responsibilities.

J. Ward Archer, Assistant Plant Manager, worked three years as a production foreman after obtaining his undergraduate degree in business. He then received an MBA degree from Harvard two years ago. He is viewed by many as a "successful fast-tracker."

Ed Wilson, Production Foreman, has been with the organization for nine years, the last two as production foreman. Last year he single-handedly prevented a wildcat strike. To become a member of management as Production Foreman, Ed took a substantial pay cut in comparison to his union wages.

C. J. Sass, Director of Computer Services, has a doctoral degree in computer sciences and was hired away from a business college at a leading eastern university three years ago. Two and a half years ago he introduced a corporatewide Human Resource Information System, which has refined the internal recruiting and promotion policies of the organization.

John Passante, District Sales Manager, has been with the organization for twelve and a half years. In his tenth year with the organization, John was promoted to District Sales Manager and has done a fine job in that position.

Six students will serve on the salary review committee. While the committee would like to award significant merit increases to all those who have been recommended, there are only limited funds available for raises. The committee must make a decision as to how the merit funds will be distributed. Your instructor will provide the participants with additional information necessary to participate.

NOTES

1. J. B. Rotter, "Generalized Expectancies for Internal versus External Control of Reinforcement," *Psychological Monographs* 1, no. 609 (1966): 80.
2. J. B. Rotter, "External Control and Internal Control," *Psychology Today* (June 1971): 37.
3. Rotter, "External Control," 37.

4. R. Christie and F. L. Geis, eds., *Studies in Machiavellianism* (New York: Academic Press, 1970).

5. Christie and Geis, *Machiavellianism.*

6. M. Friedman and R. Roseman, *Type A Behavior and Your Heart* (New York: Alfred A. Knopf, 1974).

7. Friedman and Roseman, *Type A Behavior;* M. T. Matteson and C. Preston, "Occupational Stress, Type A Behavior and Physical Well-being," *Academy of Management Journal* 25 (1982): 373–391.

8. C. C. Jung, *Collected Works,* ed. H. Read, M. Fordham, and G. Adler (Princeton, N.J.: Princeton University Press, 1953).

9. D. B. Myers and K. C. Briggs, *Myers-Briggs Type Indicator* (Princeton, N.J.: Educational Testing Service, 1962).

10. Myers and Briggs, *Type Indicator.*

11. A. Anastasi, *Psychological Testing* (New York: Macmillan, 1976).

12. See R. Gould, "Adult Life States: Growth Toward Self-tolerance," *Psychology Today,* February 1975; H. Levinson, *The Seasons of a Man's Life* (New York: Knopf, 1978); G. Sheehy, *Passages* (New York: Dutton, 1976).

13. E. G. C. Collins and P. Scott, "Everyone Who Makes It Has a Mentor," *Harvard Business Review* 56 (1978): 9–18.

14. See K. E. Kram, *Mentoring at Work: Developmental Relationships in Organizational Life* (Glenview, Ill.: Scott, Foresman, 1985).

15. S. C. Bushardt, R. N. Moore, and S. C. Debnath, "Picking the Right Person for Your Mentor," *SAM Advanced Management Journal* 47 (Summer 1982): 46–54.

16. K. E. Kram and L. A. Isabella, "Mentoring Alternatives: The Role of Peer Relationships in Career Development," *Academy of Management Journal* 28 (1985): 110–132.

17. G. R. Roche, "Much Ado About Mentors," *Harvard Business Review* 57 (January–February 1979): 17–28.

18. D. M. Hunt and C. Michael, "Mentorship: A Career Training and Development Tool," *Academy of Management Review* 8 (1983): 475–485; K. E. Kram, "Phases of the Mentor Relationship," *Academy of Management Journal* 26 (1983): 608–625.

19. See F. S. Hall and D. T. Hall, *Dual Career Couples* (Reading, Mass.: Addison-Wesley, 1979), for a more detailed discussion.

20. F. S. Hall and D. T. Hall, "Dual Careers—How Do Couples and Companies Cope with the Problems?" *Organizational Dynamics* 6 (1978): 57–77.

21. J. C. Latack, "Career Transitions Within Organizations: An Exploratory Study of Work, Nonwork, and Coping Strategies," *Organizational Behavior and Human Performance* 34 (1984): 296–322.

22. D. T. Hall, *Careers in Organizations* (Santa Monica, Cal.: Goodyear, 1976).

23. James W. Walker, *Human Resource Planning* (New York: McGraw-Hill, 1980), 331–332.

24. R. A. Webber, "Career Problems of Young Managers," *California Management Review* 18 (1976): 19–33.

25. See S. S. Dubin, *Professional Obsolescence* (New York: English University Press, 1972).

26. See T. P. Ference, "The Career Plateau: Facing Up to Life at the Middle," *MBA* 12 (1978); E. K. Warren, T. P. Ference, and J. A. C. Stoner, "The Case of the Plateaued Performer," *Harvard Business Review* 53 (1975): 30–38, 146–148.

27. D. J. Levinson, "The Mid-life Transition: A Period in Adult Psychological Development," *Psychiatry* 40 (1977): 99–112.

28. Levinson, "Mid-life Transition," 99–112.

29. Gould, "Adult Life States."

30. F. W. Dalton, P. H. Thompson, and R. L. Price, "The Four Stages of Professional Careers: A New Look at Performance by Professionals," *Organizational Dynamics* 6 (1977): 19–42.

31. Dalton, Thompson, and Price, "Professional Careers," 19–42.

32. Ference, "Career Plateau"; Warren, Ference, Stoner, "Plateaued Performer," 30–38, 146–148.

33. J. A. Raelin, C. K. Sholl, and D. Leonard, "Why Professionals Turn Sour and What to Do," *Personnel* 62 (October 1985): 28–41.

34. See J. Raelin, *Professional Careers* (New York: Praeger, 1983).

35. J. Raelin, "Examination of Deviant/Adaptive Behaviors in the Organizational Careers of Professionals," *Academy of Management Review* 9 (1984): 413–427.

36. E. H. Schein, "Organizational Socialization and the Profession of Management," *Sloan Management Review* 9 (1968): 1–16.

37. Schein, "Organizational Socialization," 1–16.

38. J. Van Maanen, "People Processing: Strategies of Organizational Socialization," *Organizational Dynamics* 7 (1978): 19–36.

39. Van Maanen, "People Processing," 19–36.

40. H. Selye, *The Stress of Life* (New York: McGraw-Hill, 1956).

41. H. Selye, *The Stress of Life,* 2d ed. (New York: McGraw-Hill, 1976).

42. C. N. Cofer and M. H. Appley, *Motivation: Theory and Research* (New York: John Wiley & Sons, 1964).

43. D. R. Frew, *Management of Stress* (Chicago: Nelson Hall, 1977), xix; see also A. P. Brief, R. S. Schuler, and M. Van Sell, *Managing Job Stress* (Boston: Little, Brown, 1981).

44. D. L. Nelson and J. C. Quick, "Professional Women: Are Distress and Disease Inevitable?" *Academy of Management Review* 10 (1985): 206–218; G. L. Cooper and M. J. Davidson, "The High Cost of Stress on Women Managers," *Organizational Dynamics* 10 (Winter 1982): 44–53.

45. The discussion of roles is based, in large part, on R. L. Kahn, D. M. Wolfe, R. P. Quinn, and J. D. Snoek, *Organizational Stress: Studies in Role Conflict and Ambiguity* (New York: John Wiley & Sons, 1964).

46. C. D. Fisher and R. Gitelson, "A Meta-analysis of the Correlates of Role Conflict and Ambiguity," *Journal of Applied Psychology* 68 (1983): 320–333; A. G. Bedeian and A. A. Armenakis, "A Path-analytic Study of the Consequences of Role Conflict and Ambiguity," *Academy of Management Journal* 24 (1981): 417–424; M. Van Sell, A. P. Brief, and R. S. Schuler, "Role Conflict and Role Ambiguity: Integration of the Literature and Directions for Future Research," *Human Relations* 34 (1981): 43–71.

47. Kahn et al., *Organizational Stress.*

48. S. V. Kasl, "Epidemiological Contributions to the Study of Work Stress," in *Stress at Work,* ed. G. L. Cooper and R. Payne (New York: John Wiley & Sons, 1978).

49. Kets de Vries, "Organizational Stress," 3–14.

50. R. Kreitner, "Personal Wellness: It's Just Good Business," *Business Horizons* 25 (May–June 1982): 28–35.

51. D. A. Whetten and K. S. Cameron, *Developing Management Skills* (Glenview, Ill.: Scott, Foresman, 1984).

52. T. D. Jick and R. Payne, "Stress at Work," *Exchange: The Organizational Behavior Teaching Journal* 5 (1980): 50–56.

53. J. C. Quick and J. D. Quick, *Organizational Stress and Preventive Management* (New York: McGraw-Hill, 1984).

54. J. M. Ivancevich and M. T. Matteson, "Employee Claims for Damages Add to the High Cost of Job Stress," *Management Review* (November 1983).

55. G. L. Cooper, *The Stress Check* (New York: Pitman, 1981).

56. K. Albrecht, *Stress and the Manager: Making It Work for You* (Englewood Cliffs, N.J.: Prentice-Hall, 1979).

57. J. W. Greenwood III and J. W. Greenwood, Jr., *Managing Executive Stress: A Systems Approach* (New York: John Wiley & Sons, 1979).

58. Herbert J. Freudenberger, *Burnout: The High Cost of High Achievement* (Garden City, N.Y.: Doubleday, Anchor Press, 1980), 13.

59. John G. Nelson, "Burn-Out—Business's Most Costly Expense," *Personnel Administrator* 25 (August 1980): 82.

60. Dick Friedman, "Job Burnout," *Working Woman* 5 (July 1980): 34.

61. Christina Meslack and Susan E. Jackson, "Burned-Out Cops and Their Families," *Psychology Today* 12 (May 1979): 59.

62. Beverly Norman, "Career Burnout," *Black Enterprise* 12 (July 1981): 45.

63. Cary Cherniss, "Job Burnout: Growing Worry for Workers, Bosses," *U.S. News & World Report* 88 (February 1980): 72.

64. Harry Levinson, "When Executives Burn Out," *Harvard Business Review* 59 (May–June 1981): 76.

REFERENCES

Bedeian, A. G., and A. A. Armenakis. "A Path-Analytic Study of the Consequences of Role Conflict and Ambiguity." *Academy of Management Journal* 24 (1981): 417–424.

Brief, A. P., R. S. Schuler, and M. Van Sell. *Managing Job Stress.* Boston: Little, Brown, 1981.

Bushardt, S. C., R. N. Moore, and S. C. Debnath. "Picking the Right Person for Your Mentor." *SAM Advanced Management Journal* 47 (Summer 1982): 46–54.

Christie, R., and F. L. Geis, eds. *Studies in Machiavellianism.* New York: Academic Press.

Collins, E. G. C., and P. Scott. "Everyone Who Makes It Has a Mentor." *Harvard Business Review* 56 (1978): 9–18.

Cooper, G. L., and M. J. Davidson. "The High Cost of Stress on Women Managers." *Organizational Dynamics* 19 (Winter 1982): 44–53.

Fisher, C. D., and R. Gitelson. "A Meta-Analysis of the Correlates of Role Conflict and Ambiguity." *Journal of Applied Psychology* 68 (1983): 320–333.

Friedman, M., and R. Roseman. *Type A Behavior and Your Heart.* New York: Alfred A. Knopf, 1974.

Garelik, Michael. "The Power Is in the People." *ABA Banking Journal* 79 (May 1987): 19–21.

Hunt, D. M., and C. Michael. "Mentorship: A Career Training and Development Tool." *Academy of Management Review* 8 (1983): 475–485.

Ivancevich, J. M., and M. T. Matteson. "Employee Claims for Damages Add to the High Cost of Job Stress." *Management Review* (November 1983).

Jones, G. R. "Psychological Orientation and the Process of Organizational Socialization: An Interactionist Perspective." *Academy of Management Review* 8 (1983): 464–474.

Jung, C. C. *Collected Works.* Edited by H. Read, M. Fordham, and G. Adler. Princeton, N.J.: Princeton University Press, 1953.

Kram, K. E. *Mentoring at Work: Developmental Relationships in Organizational Life.* Glenview, Ill.: Scott, Foresman, 1985.

———. "Phases of the Mentor Relationship." *Academy of Management Journal* 26 (1983): 608–625.

Kram, K. E., and L. A. Isabella. "Mentoring Alternatives: The Role of Peer Relationships in Career Development." *Academy of Management Journal* 28 (1985): 110–132.

Latack, J. C. "Career Transitions Within Organizations: An Exploratory Study of Work, Nonwork, and Coping Strategies." *Organizational Behavior and Human Performance* 34 (1984): 296–322.

Marsh, Cynthia E., and Val J. Arnold. "Address the Cause Not the Symptoms of Behavior Problems." *Personnel Journal* 87 (May 1988): 82.

Matteson, M. T., and C. Preston. "Occupational Stress, Type A Behavior and Physical Well-Being." *Academy of Management Journal* 25 (1982): 373–391.

Myers, D. B., and K. C. Briggs. *Myers-Briggs Type Indicator.* Princeton, N.J.: Educational Testing Service, 1962.

Ono, Karou, and James H. Davis. "Individual Judgement and Group Interaction: A Variable Perspective Approach." *Organizational Behavior & Human Decision Processes* 11 (April 1988): 211–232.

Quick, J. C., and J. D. Quick. *Organizational Stress and Preventive Management.* New York: McGraw-Hill, 1984.

Raelin, J. "Examination of Deviant/Adaptive Behaviors in the Organizational Careers of Professionals." *Academy of Management Review* 9 (1984): 413–427.

Raelin, J. A., C. K. Sholl, and D. Leonard. "Why Professionals Turn Sour and What to Do." *Personnel* 62 (October 1985): 28–41.

Schein, E. H. "Organizational Socialization and the Profession of Management." *Sloan Management Review* 9 (1968): 1–16.

CHAPTER
17

Chapter Outline

Group Performance, Intergroup Behavior, and Conflict

Learning Objectives

After completing this chapter students should be able to

1. Define groups, describe the various types of groups, and explain group formation and development.
2. Explain factors influencing group effectiveness and the means of increasing group effectiveness.
3. State how work-team effectiveness can be diagnosed.
4. Describe the types of interdependent groups.
5. Describe the influences on relationships between groups and the means for improving relationships between groups.
6. Discuss conflict in organizations and the means of managing conflict.

LINDA WATSON EXPRESSED excitement as she filled out the employment forms at the Derek Garment Factory in Barnwell, South Carolina. She told the personnel clerk she had been looking for a job for nearly six months and her unemployment pay had run out. Linda claimed to be especially pleased to be paid a set wage plus a piece rate for production above standard. Asked why incentive pay was so important to her, she said, "Wherever I have worked before I did more than most other people for the same pay."

Linda became attached to a group of new friends right away. During coffee breaks and lunch periods they could be overheard chatting about their husbands or ex-husbands, their children, and the problems of being working women. Later, Linda would tell of learning a lot from her new friends about Derek Garments, things that had not been covered during orientation. Among them were the personnel director's reputation for protecting workers from the operations manager, who was thought to be quite ruthless, and the fact that several of the plant manager's relatives, including two sons-in-law, had cushy jobs with Derek. Finally, she would give other workers credit for answering her frequent questions about the medical plan, sick leave, and so forth.

Within two weeks Linda was exceeding the production standard. Her third paycheck included a piece-rate bonus of nearly $50. Linda confided to friends that she was barely making ends meet and needed the extra money. She would later tell of a conversation she had with Charissa Gorman, one of the more experienced workers: "I was happy about my bonus and told Charissa so. But Charissa said, 'A bonus would be handy for any of us. But if you keep it up, they will just change the standard, and we will all be worse off.' Charissa also said I was making the rest of them look bad."

Though aware of Charissa's disapproval, Linda continued to work faster. But over the next few weeks a definite coolness toward her had developed. People avoided sitting with her in the lunchroom. When she joined the others, she saw strained smiles and heard little conversation—a couple of times when Linda approached, the group fell silent. One of the women, known for her gruffness, said to Linda as she was leaving the lunchroom one day, "If you don't stop trying to show off, you're not going to have a friend left around here."

The next week Linda's production fell back to just a little above standard. Within a few days, she could be seen pleasantly chatting with her friends again. But Linda's supervisor noticed how her work pace had slowed. He caught her in the lunchroom on Thursday and asked to see her in his office the next morning. That evening Linda came to the personnel office to call for help in repairing a flat tire. A clerk suggested that she use the telephone in the plant for future calls. The next morning she was back at the personnel office to say she was quitting. During an exit interview, routinely conducted by the personnel director, Linda told her story. ■

THE STORY OF Linda Watson's experience at Derek Garments raises a number of issues related to group performance. She experienced, firsthand, the influence of the informal group to enforce its norms on individuals. But it was also through the informal organization that she initially received emotional support and learned more about her employer.

In this chapter, we define groups first and then describe the various types of groups. The significant aspects of group formation and development will next be reviewed. Then, the factors influencing group effectiveness, the variables involved in increasing group effectiveness, and the aspects involved in diagnosing work-team effectiveness are all addressed. We then describe the types of interdependent groups. Next, influences on relationships between groups and ways of improving the relationships will be examined. The final portion of the chapter is devoted to conflict in organizations and ways of managing conflict.

GROUPS DEFINED

Group
Two or more people having a unifying relationship, such as common goals or physical proximity.

A **group** is defined as two or more people having a unifying relationship, such as common goals or physical proximity. At the LTV Steel plant in Cleveland, Ohio, teams of highly trained technicians manage a huge electrogalvanizing line practically by themselves and participate in hiring, work scheduling, and operations planning.[1] This is one example of a group effort that, so far, has been successful.

Although group members generally share certain similarities with one another, each individual member may have personal reasons for joining a group. According to Jewell and Reitz,[2] people join groups for security, affiliation, esteem, power, and goal accomplishment. Basically, individuals choose group membership to achieve an outcome that requires their association with other people.

Everyone belongs to many groups—at work, in the community, and even at home (the family is a group). There are formal work groups, of course, made up of managers and subordinates. Linda was assigned to a certain supervisor at Derek Garment Factory as part of a formal work group. As Linda soon realized, there are also informal groups, which have significant influence on group members. To increase individual and group job performance, managers need to understand all of the kinds of groups that exist both within and outside the organization.

TYPES OF GROUPS

Primary groups
Small groups characterized by relatively close associations among members.

Secondary groups
Groups that are larger and less intimate than primary groups.

Groups are often categorized in a number of different ways. Understanding the characteristics of each type can affect a manager's expectations of relationships among group members. Initially, it is critically important that managers appreciate the difference between primary and secondary groups. **Primary groups** are small groups characterized by relatively close associations among members. As might be expected, the closeness of these associations directly influences the behaviors of individuals in the group. In contrast, **secondary groups** are larger and less intimate than primary groups. Relationships tend to be more impersonal and frequently are formalized.

Everyone participates in both types of groups. Primary groups exert a greater influence on individuals' day-to-day activities through the presence of other group members and their ability to reinforce member behavior. Secondary groups rely instead on sanctions, which are imposed through control systems (rules, regulations, policies, etc.) or exercised by designated individuals such as group leaders. Groups also can be classified according to their function or the circumstances under which they are formed. Three types of groups commonly encountered in organizations are task (or functional) groups, project groups, and informal groups.

Task/Functional Groups

Task or functional groups
Groups that are determined by prescribed job requirements.

Task or functional groups are determined by prescribed job requirements. They are brought together for the purpose of transforming certain inputs (raw materials, ideas, objects) into a distinguishable output such as a physical product, a decision, or some other "detectable environmental change."[3] Functional group members usually interact with one another on a daily basis, and they are often organized into departments or work teams to facilitate accomplishment of organizational objectives.

Project Groups

Project groups include formal, but temporary assignments to groups, committees, and special projects. All organizations have some activities requiring group cooperation across functional lines (e.g., an interdepartmental planning committee). After a project has been completed, project group members return to their routine work activities or go to another temporary project group. Examples of project groups include research and development teams and internal consultant groups. Possibly the best known organization that uses project groups is the National Aeronautics and Space Administration (NASA).

Informal Groups

Informal group
Two or more persons associated with one another in ways not prescribed by the formal organization.

An **informal group** is defined as two or more persons associated with one another in ways not prescribed by the formal organization. Informal groups are very common to everyone. In some cases, they arise because people find themselves in a common location. Informal groups can also result from the need to solve organizational problems or achieve formal goals; thus, similarities or differences within formal groups can lead to informal activities in organizations. Linda became a member of an informal group based on such common interests as husbands or ex-husbands and the problems of working women. The informal group included workers who were especially close friends and who had their own cliques. Informal groups can also take the form of two or three people who belong to the same church or baseball team, or who play racquetball or have parties together.

ETHICAL DILEMMA

Y OU ARE AN up-and-coming manager, and you have been employed with a major tobacco company for six years. Managers in the company have a fairly consistent path of movement up the corporate ladder to senior-level management positions. Most managers utilize their general expertise in a department for four to six years. They then serve as a member of one of the company's special committees for five to seven years. Ultimately they reach a senior management position. You are placed on the committee that handles legal suits made by customers who claim that they or their loved ones have gotten cancer from smoking your company's cigarettes. The committee is composed of yourself, one R&D manager, one marketing manager, and four attorneys. Initially, this committee reviews the merits of each case and takes actions to limit the financial and public relations impact on the company.

You have just finished reviewing documents used in a case against the Liggett Group, Inc. Liggett's scientist duplicated the experiments that suggested that the tar in cigarettes causes cancerous tumors to grow on mice. You have also come across memos used as evidence against R. J. Reynolds. R. J. R. lawyers wrote management several warnings, to the effect that marketing a "safer" cigarette could increase their vulnerability to charges that R. J. R. *knew* their conventional tobacco products were less safe than they had maintained. You then find several memos from your company's research scientist. The memos state that cigarettes *do actually cause cancer in humans, and do increase the likelihood of heart disease*. The memos further state that R&D has come up with a new, safer cigarette. Follow-up memos from company executives killed the project, for fear of severe legal action. When you review these documents you get a warm, sick feeling all over. You confront the chairman of the committee with the memos and express your disgust at company executives for not marketing a safer cigarette. You are told to forget what you saw and fall in line, or *flush* your career. You can either fall in line and protect the profitability and reputation of the company, and your career, or you can blow the whistle.

What would you do?

■ GROUP FORMATION

People join groups for a multitude of reasons. As previously mentioned, they may form informal groups—those that arise spontaneously in the organization or within formal groups, such as a clique or a network of professionals. Individuals may also join formal groups—those officially sanctioned and organized by managerial or other authority to accomplish organizational goals, such as departments in organizations or task forces.

As may be seen in Figure 17.1, groups form when individuals exhibit one or more of the following:[4]

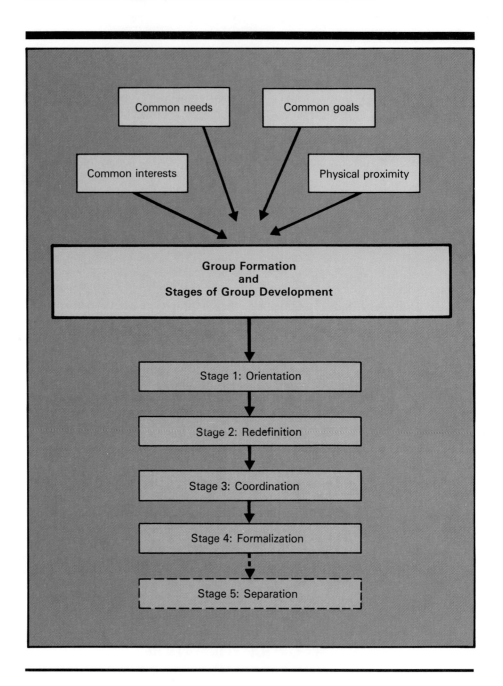

1. *Common needs.* Food cooperatives form because individuals want to satisfy their basic needs for food at a low cost.
2. *Common interests.* Engineers employed by different companies often join the same professional groups.
3. *Common goals.* A board of directors of a company forms to help the company reach its objectives.
4. *Physical proximity.* Employees in the same work area often join together as a social group.

The reason a group forms influences the nature and quality of the group's functioning. Studying the causes of group formation, then, helps predict and anticipate the ways a group is likely to act.

Coalitions *(counsel)*
Informal groups that form to influence the goals, policies, and allocation of resources in groups.

Extensive research has focused on the formation of informal groups known as **coalitions**[5] that form to influence the goals, policies, and allocation of resources in groups.[6] Recent research uses attribution theory to explain membership in coalitions.[7] As noted in Chapter 14, individuals attribute the cause of an event to either personal or situational factors, depending on the extent of their involvement in the event and its success or failure. Once a group forms, it must evolve into an effective collective unit through the process of group development.

■ GROUP DEVELOPMENT

Once a group forms, it must resolve a variety of issues before it can function effectively. Tracing the development of groups provides one perspective for assessing a group's performance. Bruce Tuchman,[8] among other theorists,[9] identifies four stages of development—orientation, redefinition, coordination, and formalization—which focus on two dimensions of group behavior: (1) task activity and (2) group structure process. **Task activity** refers to the steps used to perform a task, not including the procedures and materials required to accomplish it.[10] **Group structure process** refers to the interpersonal interactions needed to accompany and accomplish task activities.[11] Referring again to Figure 17.1, there are four stages of group development.

Task activity
The steps used to perform a task, not including the procedures and materials required to accomplish it.
Group structure process
The interpersonal interactions needed to accompany and accomplish task activities.

Orientation (Forming)

Orientation occurs when the group views the task and determines acceptable interpersonal behaviors (process).

> *Task: Orientation to Task.* The group members gather information about the nature of the group's task.
> *Process: Testing and Dependence.* Group members discover acceptable behaviors.

Redefinition (Storming)

broad Redefinition occurs when the group redefines the task, tries to agree on its objectives and strategy, and develops group structure. Conflict may result at this stage.

> *Task: Emotional Response to the Demands of the Task.* The group members then determine whether they like the task and their degree of commitment to it.
> *Process: Intragroup Conflict.* Disagreements by members of the group in their reactions to the demands of the task often lead to conflict. They may differ in the amount of time they are willing to devote to a

During the "norming" stage of group development, the group collects information and interprets it, in order to accomplish the group goals. (© Stacy Pick/Stock, Boston, Inc.)

particular task, the priority they assign to the task, or the means they feel will best accomplish it. The sharper these differences, the greater the intragroup conflict that results.

Coordination (Norming)

During the coordination stage, often the longest, the group collects information and interprets it in order to facilitate the accomplishment of group goals. Arguments over interpretation frequently occur.

> *Task: Open Exchange of Relevant Interpretation and Opinions.* Here, discussions about the nature of the task, different emotional responses to it, alternatives, and possible action occur. A group's discussion about the types and quality of existing programs, as well as its members' participation in the process of developing a new one, illustrate the activities of this stage.
> *Process: Development of Group Cohesion.* The members resolve their differences after an open exchange of relevant interpretations and opinions and begin to act as a group. Often groups do not reach this stage, and the group disintegrates.

Formalization (Performing)

The group specifies the final version of the decision during formalization.

> *Task: Emergence of a Solution.* At this stage, the final choice of task activities and their implementation occur.
> *Process: Functional Roles Emerge as a Way of Problem Solving.* At this time, the assignment of roles that match the group's needs for leadership and expertise, as well as the members' abilities and attitudes, occur.

Separation

Although Tuchman's four stages of group development have come to be accepted generally, a fifth stage also merits examination. In studies on group transformation in training groups at Harvard University, Mills found that preparing for and handling the reality of the group's death was an important issue for people committed to the group.[12] Mills labeled this final stage *separation*.

Additionally, William Schutz[13] observed that as groups develop, they pass through three intervals: (1) inclusion (member activities influenced by their needs to be included and their needs to include others), (2) control (activities influenced by member needs to control others or be controlled by them), and (3) affection (activities influenced by a liking for other people and a desire to be liked by them). However, as the group moves toward its anticipated termination, the sequence is reversed. Basically, the real significance of group development lies in the need for groups to mature in order to fulfill their potential within an organization.

Moving through the Developmental Stages

A group may recycle through the four stages of development, particularly as changes in the group's membership, its task, or the environment occur. For example, if a new member is added to the group, the group begins its development anew. Of course, movement through stages that the group has already resolved may occur more rapidly the second time. For example, orientation of a new member may require ten minutes rather than two hours. Instead of receiving new members, a group may change its goals. The extent and uniqueness of the personnel, task, or environmental changes will influence the speed with which the group moves through stages it has already resolved.

Some groups remain at one stage: they fail to resolve the issues associated with it. In normally functioning groups, the orientation stage is the shortest, followed in length by the redefinition and formalization stages; the coordination stage is longest.[14] Groups experiencing difficulties tend to have an elongated formation stage.[15] Failure to move beyond redefinition signals a group's lack of conflict-resolution mechanisms. Occasionally groups remain stuck at other stages. Remaining at the orientation stage suggests that the group lacks the skill to screen out irrelevant information and behavior. Inability to move beyond coordination often reflects a group with poor information, which hinders effective interpretation. Frequently, such dilemmas can remain unresolved when a group lacks clear goals, or when individual members have incompatible goals.

Research suggests a similarity between group development and organizational socialization.[16] These processes occur simultaneously for groups and help us diagnose their developmental progress. Like group development, organizational socialization, discussed in Chapter 16 with regard to career development, has been described as a four-step model.[17] Newcomers first confront and accept organizational reality by checking their own expectations and learning behaviors that are rewarded or punished; this corresponds to orientation to task and testing roles. Second, they attempt to clarify their roles and learn ways to deal with change and ambiguity; this corresponds to an emotional response and accompanying intragroup conflict. Third, they achieve role clarity in the socialization process, and exchange relevant information in the group development process.

F I G U R E   17.2   ■■   Comparison of Stages of Group Development to Stages of Socialization

	Group Development[a]	Organizational Socialization[b]
Stage 1: Orientation	**1. Forming** Establish interpersonal relationships Conform to organizational traditions and standards Boundary testing in relationships and task behaviors	**1. Getting In (Anticipatory socialization)** Setting of realistic expectations Determining match with the newcomer
Stage 2: Redefinition	**2. Storming** Conflict arising because of interpersonal behaviors Resistance to group influence and task requirements	**2. Breaking In (Accommodation)** Initiation on the job Establishing interpersonal relationships Congruence between self and organizational performance appraisal
Stage 3: Coordination	**3. Norming** Single leader emerges Group cohesion established New group standards and roles formed for members	**3. Settling In (Role managment)** The degree of fit between one's life interests outside of work and the demands of the organization Resolution of conflicts at the workplace itself
Stage 4: Formalization	**4. Performing** Members perform tasks together Establishing role clarity Teamwork is the norm	

[a]Based on B. Tuchman, Developmental sequence in small groups, *Psychological Bulletin* 63 (1965): 384–399.

[b]Based on D.C. Feldman, A contingency theory of socialization, *Administrative Science Quarterly* 21 (1976): 433–454; D.C. Feldman, A practical program for employee socialization, *Organizational Dynamics* 7 (1976): 64–80.

Source: Adapted from J. P. Wanous, A. E. Reichers, and S. D. Malik, Organizational socialization and group development: Toward an integrative perspective, *Academy of Management Review* 9 (1984): 670–683. Reprinted with permission.

Finally, they experience satisfaction and commitment to the organization; the group reaches a solution and develops functional role-related behavior.

Group development and organizational socialization thus show both temporal and conceptual parallels,[18] as reflected in Figure 17.2. Thus, to diagnose a situation completely and precisely, these frameworks should be used both separately and in concert. The processes that are dysfunctional must be identified and readied for correction.

■ FACTORS INFLUENCING GROUP EFFECTIVENESS

An effective group can attain, or make acceptable progress toward, its goals or the goals of its members. In an organization, this may mean getting a job done, providing group members with a sense of belonging, or successfully competing with another person or group. As Figure 17.3 suggests, many factors influence group effectiveness, including individual roles, group norms, leadership, group cohesiveness, group size, and synergism.

Role
The total pattern of expected behavior of an individual.

Task roles
Roles that focus on task or goal accomplishment.

Maintenance or group-building roles
Roles that direct the group toward positive member interaction and interpersonal behavior.

Individual Roles

A **role** consists of the total pattern of expected behavior of an individual. In the discussion of role conflict and role ambiguity in Chapter 16, it was noted that people have various roles that may conflict with each other, or that may be more or less clear. The idea of work roles is covered further here.

A widely used classification of roles describes the actual behaviors of various group members.[19] **Task roles** focus on task or goal accomplishment. **Maintenance or group-building roles** direct the group toward positive member interaction and interpersonal behavior. A trainee who lacks experience may act as an encourager by praising the ideas of other task force members, or as a gatekeeper by

F I G U R E 17.3 ■
Factors Influencing
Group Effectiveness

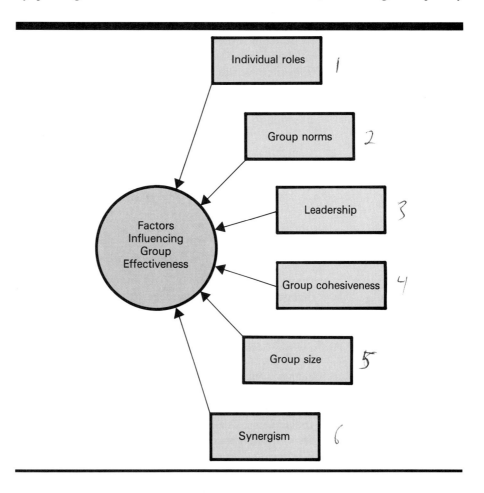

TABLE 17.1 ■ Classification of Group Roles		
Task roles	Initiator	Offers new ideas or suggests solutions to problems
	Information seeker	Seeks pertinent facts or clarification of information
	Information giver	Describes one's own experience or offers facts and information
	Coordinator	Coordinates activities, combines ideas or suggestions
	Evaluator	Assesses the quality of suggestions, solutions, or norms
Maintenance roles	Encourager	Encourages cohesiveness and warmth, praises and accepts others' ideas
	Harmonizer	Alleviates tension; resolves intragroup disagreements
	Gatekeeper	Encourages participation by others and sharing of ideas
	Standard setter	Raises questions about group goals; helps set goals and standards
	Follower	Agrees and pursues others' activities
	Group observer	Monitors group operations; provides feedback to group
Self-oriented roles	Blocker	Resists stubbornly; negative; returns to rejected issues
	Recognition-seeker	Calls attention to self by boasting, bragging, acting superior
	Dominator	Manipulates group; interrupts others; gains attention
	Avoider	Remains apart from others; resists passively

Source: Kenneth D. Benne and Paul Sheats, Functional roles of group members, *Journal of Social Issues* 4(2): 43–46.

Individual or self-oriented roles
Roles that focus on satisfying an individual's needs; such role behaviors frequently distract the group from effective functioning through individual dominance in the group.

encouraging others' participation. **Individual or self-oriented roles** focus on satisfying an individual's needs; such role behaviors frequently distract the group from effective functioning through individual dominance in the group. Two group members who repeatedly argue with each other likely take blocker roles—stubbornly resisting or reacting negatively—or recognition-seeker roles—calling attention to themselves by bragging or boasting. Table 17.1 lists examples of these three role types. A group member may perform more than one role, and several members may perform the same role.

Frequently a pattern of roles emerges for each group member. By tallying the nature and frequency of role behaviors and individuals' interactions in a group, an observer can identify roles played by the members. This diagnosis is prerequisite to the evaluation of group functioning and effectiveness.

2) Group Norms

Norm
A standard of behavior expected of informal group members.

Underlying group development and implicit in group functioning are expectations that guide behavior. A student, for example, is expected to attend classes, prepare homework, and take examinations. A worker is expected to be at work on time, miss work only in case of illness, put in a "good day's work for a good day's pay." These unwritten expectations, called norms, develop through interaction of group members and reinforcement of behaviors by the group. A **norm** is a standard of behavior expected of informal group members. Generally these expectations are in line with group goals, which in turn are helpful in accomplishing organizational goals; however, in some cases these expectations do not fit with the organization's goals. Some work groups, for example, insist that their members maintain a certain, often suboptimal, production level. In other organizations, arriving late is expected of certain management-level employees.

INSIDE BUSINESS

Teamwork, a Key to AFG Industries' Success

AN EFFECTIVE GROUP can attain, or make acceptable progress toward, its goals or the goals of its members. In the business of making glass, this often means getting the job done by providing group members with a sense of belonging. Teamwork contributes to the successful completion of the job of glass making and helps maintain profits in an extremely competitive business. A proponent of teamwork is Mr. R. D. Hubbard, Chairman of AFG Industries. The type of "team" concept that AFG Industries utilizes involves everybody in the plant learning every job in the plant. Employees get paid more based on the more jobs they know and the more jobs they can successfully perform. The competitive situation in the glass business is about to become even more intense than it was previously because the Japanese are now building some automotive glass plants in the United States. In the interview with Myron Kandel, CNN Financial Editor, Stuart Varney, CNN Senior Correspondent, and Jan Hopkins, CNN Correspondent, Mr. R. D. Hubbard describes his management philosophy and the need for teamwork in the glass business.

Group members may act to encourage certain behaviors, for example, by reinforcing a specific level of production. Members may also discourage certain behaviors by responding negatively to their occurrence, such as by rejecting very low or very high performance, as was the case with Linda Watson.

Norms generally develop for behaviors that group members view as important. Most norms develop in one of four ways.[20] First, supervisors or co-workers may explicitly state certain expectations. Second, critical events in the group's history may also establish norms. Third, the initial pattern of behavior may become a norm. Finally, group members may carry over behavior from other situations.

There are norms about attendance, performance, interpersonal interactions, and dress. But not all norms apply to everyone.[21] Different norms exist for managers and nonmanagerial employees, for professionals and nonprofessionals, for men and women. They might differ in the extent to which people are expected to be innovative on the job, follow organizational rules and regulations, or demonstrate loyalty to a specific department or supervisor. Members who are expected to demonstrate loyalty to their department might try to provide a larger role for that department than would an individual with more organizational loyalty.

Furthermore, norms are established and enforced only for selected behaviors.[22] A group enforces norms that facilitate its survival, help predict the behavior of group members, prevent embarrassing interpersonal problems from arising, express the group's central values, and clarify the group's identity.[23]

NORM CLASSIFICATION SCHEMES

Norms have been classified in several ways. **Pivotal norms** guide behavior essential to the core mission of the organization. Expectations about the level of

Pivotal norms
Norms that guide behavior essential to the core mission of the organization.

Peripheral norms
Norms that guide behaviors that are important, but not essential, to the performance of the organization's goals or mission.

Unattainable-ideal norm
A norm that describes behavior where "more is better."

Preferred-value norm
A norm that describes behavior where either too much or too little of the behavior receives disapproval from group members.

Attainable-ideal norm
A norm that describes behavior where approval occurs for increasing amounts of behavior until an attainable goal is reached, then, further goal-oriented behavior lacks value.

production or innovation required of workers fall into this category. **Peripheral norms** guide behaviors that are important, but not essential, to the performance of the organization's goals or mission. A dress code could be an example of a peripheral norm.[24] Those who violate pivotal norms are often chastised by superiors, ostracized by co-workers, or lose the loyalty of subordinates. A violation of peripheral norms typically has less negative consequences for the worker and the organization.

Another classification scheme describes a norm according to whether the behavior is acceptable to, or approved by, group members:

The **unattainable-ideal norm** describes behavior where "more is better." For example, among a group of policemen, the more criminals arrested the better; among salespeople, the more sales the better.

The **preferred-value norm** describes behavior where either too much or too little of the behavior receives disapproval from group members. For example, work groups often approve only a small range of output; assembly-line workers who work too fast or too slowly may violate this norm. Some groups of friends complain if their peers earn too many high grades or too many low ones.

The **attainable-ideal norm** describes behavior where approval occurs for increasing amounts of behavior until an attainable goal is reached, then, further goal-oriented behavior lacks value. For example, an advertising executive receives approval for each new campaign idea he or she generates until the client chooses one of the ideas.[25]

COMPLIANCE WITH NORMS

In any group, managers can diagnose which type of norm is in operation, and whether violation of it contributes to low group performance or dysfunctional attitudes. Diagnosing the norms in a group or organization must precede any action on them, since compliance contributes to group performance and group effectiveness. Compliance with norms increases as the group's size decreases, or as its homogeneity, visibility, or stability increases. The more the group's members are committed to the group's task, the more the group generates its own rules. Finally, the more a group controls information about its members, the greater the compliance with norms. Thus, altering the factors that affect compliance can also affect the group's performance.[26]

NORM-RELATED BEHAVIOR

The extent to which group members comply with norms delineates one set of roles in a group.[27] The *leader* adheres to group norms and generally makes a special contribution to their identification and enforcement. The *regular* follows most, if not all, group norms; the regular contributes as a "good member." For example, several members of a task force seem to act as regulars; they perform the tasks requested by the leader, attend meetings regularly, and contribute to the discussion based on their expertise. The *deviant* falls lower in the hierarchy; an individual deviates from the norms but is tolerated by others in the group. The very high producer may fall into the deviant category. Although this deviant breaks the production norms, the group still values the high level of performance. Finally, the *isolate* falls at the lowest level of the role hierarchy. The isolate does not meet group norms; therefore, the group rejects, and does not value, this member. Members who continually argue against other members' ideas without offering constructive ideas of their own may be viewed as isolates. By diagnosing roles in this way, managers can anticipate, to some degree, the extent and quality of interaction among particular group members and the group's effectiveness.

Leadership

In the formal organization, leaders (managers) are placed in their positions of authority by top management. By filling a particular management position, the individual is designated a leader. An entirely different process occurs in selecting a leader for the informal organization. The informal leader is usually chosen in one of two ways. First, people may appoint themselves informal leaders. A leadership vacuum may have existed, and the first person who takes charge may be automatically followed. Second, the informal leader may be chosen through consensus. In this case, the person who is closest to the norms of the group often becomes the leader. Charissa Gorman may have been such a leader at Derek Garment Factory. There may be no formal title attached to this individual. This person is the one who is looked to for guidance in achieving the group's goal. Should the leader begin to deviate from group norms, another leader who is closer to the group norms may take the leader's place. For instance, if Charissa began to increase her own output, she would probably lose her influence with the group.

Group Cohesiveness

Cohesiveness
The degree of attraction that the group has for each of its members.

The degree of attraction that the group has for each of its members is referred to as **cohesiveness.** Important to both the formal and the informal organization, group cohesiveness is identified by attitudes such as loyalty to the group, friendliness, and congeniality, a feeling of responsibility for group effort, and defense against outside attack. Cohesive informal work groups are powerful instruments; they can work for, or against, the formal organization. For instance, a highly cohesive group whose goals are in agreement with organizational objectives can use this strength to assist the firm in increasing productivity. On the other hand, a highly cohesive group that is not in agreement with organizational objectives can have an extremely negative effect on the accomplishment of the firm's goals. Because of this potential problem, some managers attempt to reduce cohesion in order to maintain control. The informal work group at Derek Garments is highly cohesive and also has goals that conflict with company goals.

Several factors will affect the degree of cohesiveness group members have for each other (see Figure 17.4). First, a group that works under dangerous conditions often develops great cohesiveness. The manager who is seen as a threat to workers can cause the workers to band together in opposition. Second, groups whose members seldom see each other are not likely to be as cohesive. Third, groups consisting of workers of one sex, race, or age are usually more cohesive than mixed groups. That is one of the reasons why women or minorities may not be readily accepted into a work group that consists of white males. The fact that most of the garment workers at Derek were women probably made the informal work group more cohesive. Group cohesiveness may break down as characteristics of group members become more diverse. Fourth, if being a member of the group satisfies members' needs, they will have a stronger desire to stay with the group.

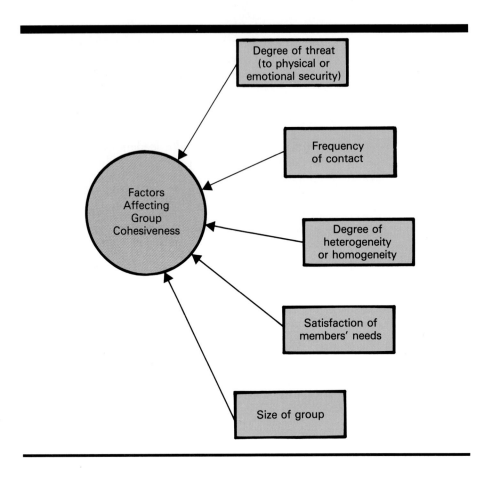

Finally, smaller groups tend to be more cohesive. Large groups have so many different relationships that cohesiveness is reduced.

Some managers oppose the existence of cohesive informal groups because they know they will have to implement unpopular decisions sooner or later. However, even for small companies—perhaps especially for them—a clear understanding of informal group characteristics such as cohesiveness can make implementing unpopular decisions easier.[28]

Group Size

The informal group tends to be small so that its members may interact frequently. But when groups get too small, difficulties arise. The dyad, or two-person group, provides a perfect example. When a decision is required and there is not a consensus, one group member must lose.

There has been considerable research devoted to determining the most effective group size. This research has led to the following conclusions:

- When quality of a complex group decision is important, the use of seven to twelve members under a formal leader is most appropriate.

- When consensus in a conflict situation is important, the use of three to five members with no formal leader will ensure that each member's view will be discussed.
- When both quality and consensus are important, five to seven members seems most appropriate.[29]

There tends to be greater group conflict in even-sized groups, and there is more conflict in groups of two and four members than there is in groups of six members. In seating arrangements, members who sit across from each other tend to engage in more frequent, and often argumentative, communication. If consensus is the goal, members with any conflict potential should be seated alongside each other.

Thus, when dealing with the subject of effective work groups, managers are primarily concerned that they be small ones. Obviously, many organizations consist of thousands of members. The initial approach to organization must therefore be formal in nature, resulting in the design of official units, jobs, and formal relationships of authority, responsibility, and accountability. Within this formal organization, a limitless number of small, informal work groups will be spontaneously established and, it is hoped, will be aligned with overall organizational objectives.

Synergism

Synergism
The cooperative action of two or more persons working together to accomplish more than they could working separately.

Synergism is the cooperative action of two or more persons working together to accomplish more than they could working separately. It implies the possibility of accomplishing tasks that could not have been done by two people working alone.[30] Managers need to recognize that greater effect may be achieved when two workers are placed together. Additional synergism can be gained by integrating multi-skilled, highly skilled, highly motivated employees and computer-driven technology.[31] The concept of synergism has implications for both formal and informal groups; however, through the synergistic effect, the informal group may become more powerful. People in groups often have much more influence outside the group than the same number of individuals have who are working alone. In addition to the factors discussed above, group members themselves can also significantly influence group effectiveness.

■ INCREASING GROUP EFFECTIVENESS

J. Richard Hackman and Charles Morris note that group members can enhance the effectiveness of their group by increasing the following three variables:[32]

1. The level of effort the group applies to carrying out its task.
2. The adequacy of the task performance strategies used by the group carrying out the task.
3. The level and appropriateness of the knowledge and skills brought to bear on the task by group members.

Organizational members can then manipulate (1) behavioral norms, (2) task design, or (3) group composition as ways of increasing these three variables.[33]

Changing existing norms is the most promising way of increasing the effort of group members. The group or its leader can require regular attendance at meetings, extensive time, three to five hours, say, spent preparing for them, or extension of the length of meetings until a particular goal is reached.

Second, members of the task force can redesign the task. This is the most promising way to improve task performance strategies. The group might, on the one hand, introduce greater specialization of responsibilities or, on the other hand, increase the amount of job enrichment. Each task force member could be given responsibility for a single, integral part of the task, one that best fits the person's expertise or experience. Third, changing the composition of the group by using volunteers rather than appointed employees, representatives of different departments, or only experienced workers would affect the knowledge and skills brought to bear on the task.

■ DIAGNOSING WORK-TEAM EFFECTIVENESS

Teams are "collections of people who must rely on group collaboration if each member is to experience the optimum of success and goal achievement."[34] They generally have specific projects with specified (short- or long-term) duration. Management groups, committees, task forces, and other work units strive to act as teams, because they recognize the importance of concerted effort in accomplishing group goals.

Characteristics of Effective Teams

Table 17.2 summarizes one view of the characteristics of an effective work team. A team-building program can begin when a new team is formed or when an

---

TABLE 17.2 ■■ Characteristics of an Effective Work Team

Goals are clear to all, shared by all, and all care about and feel involved in the goals.

All members participate and are listened to.

Members freely express themselves and receive empathetic responses.

When problems arise, the situation is carefully diagnosed before action is proposed; remedies attack basic causes.

As needs for leadership arise, various members meet them; anyone feels free to volunteer as he or she sees a group need.

Consensus is sought and tested; decisions, when made, are fully supported.

Members trust one another; they reveal to the group what they would be reluctant to expose to others; they respect and use the responses they get; they can freely express negative reactions without fearing reprisal.

The group is flexible and seeks new and better ways of acting; individuals change and grow; they are creative.

Source: Edgar Schein, *Process Consultation,* © 1969, Addison-Wesley Publishing Co., Inc., Reading, Massachusetts. Adapted from pages 42–43. Reprinted with permission.

existing team stops functioning effectively. In forming a new team, members should ideally follow four steps:[35]

1. Each member must determine the priority he or she attaches to participating in the team's activities and assess the personal importance of these activities.
2. The members must share their expectations about working on the team.
3. Members must clarify the team's objectives.
4. The team must formulate operating guidelines about the process of decision making, basic work methods, the extent and nature of member participation in discussion, ways of resolving differences, ways of ensuring that work is completed, and how to change nonproductive activities.

To ensure the effectiveness and productivity of a task force, managers must carefully form the task force, define and allocate resources, and manage day-to-day activities.[36] To do this, a manager might choose individuals whose job performance will be affected by the goals of the task force. Generally, the person who organizes the task force selects a leader or requests that task force members participate in selecting one. Once the leader has been selected, he or she should set agendas for group meetings, help reduce members' hidden agendas, and build members' commitment to the task and to other group members. The individual who forms a task force must select members who have a vested interest in its mission, will be challenged by its task, and who have complementary skills.

Procedures are available to assess which steps a team has not handled well. It can also be determined whether or not the team needs to demonstrate greater imagination and creativity. In this regard, Table 17.3 provides a checklist for scoring work-team creativity. Lower scores suggest a need for additional team-building activities.

Strategies for Team Building

To improve the performance of work teams, managers (or outside consultants) may prescribe a variety of team-building activities. Data collection is an essential activity. Managers, group members, or outside parties may use group process observation as one means of data collection.[37] The observer collects data about the communication, decision making, and leadership in a team. This individual records information about group norms and roles by tabulating who talks to whom, how frequently, and about what topics, then feeds this information back to team members. A group process consultant may also be called in to help set agendas, coach the group or its members individually in effective interpersonal processes, and offer recommendations for more effective performance.

For effective team building to occur:[38]

1. The primary objective of a team development meeting must be explicit and well articulated.
2. This primary objective must be held by the leader of the group and understood (hopefully, agreed to) by the work-group members.

TABLE 17.3 ■ Checklist for Scoring Work-Team Creativity

This scale will help you see to what extent the type of management and the organizational conditions support and encourage creative effort.

1. My ideas or suggestions never get a fair hearing.   1 2 3 4 5 6 7 ←→   My ideas or suggestions get a fair hearing.

2. I feel like my boss is not interested in my ideas.   1 2 3 4 5 6 7 ←→   I feel like my boss is very interested in my ideas.

3. I receive no encouragement to innovate on my job.   1 2 3 4 5 6 7 ←→   I am encouraged to innovate on my job.

4. There is no reward for innovating or improving things on my job.   1 2 3 4 5 6 7 ←→   I am rewarded for innovating and improving on my job.

5. There is no encouragement for diverse opinions among subordinates.   1 2 3 4 5 6 7 ←→   There is encouragement of diversity of opinion among subordinates.

6. I'm very reluctant to tell the boss about mistakes I make.   1 2 3 4 5 6 7 ←→   I feel comfortable enough with my boss to tell about mistakes I make.

7. I'm not given enough responsibility to do my job right.   1 2 3 4 5 6 7 ←→   I am given enough responsibility to do my job right.

8. To really succeed in this organization, one needs to be a friend or a relative of the boss.   1 2 3 4 5 6 7 ←→   There is no favoritism in the organization.

9. There are other jobs in this organization that I would prefer to have.   1 2 3 4 5 6 7 ←→   I have the job in this organization that I think I do best.

10. They keep close watch over me too much of the time.   1 2 3 4 5 6 7 ←→   They trust me to do my job without always checking on me.

11. They would not let me try other jobs in the organization.   1 2 3 4 5 6 7 ←→   I could try other kinds of jobs in the organization if I wanted to.

12. The management is made very uptight by confusion, disorder, and chaos.   1 2 3 4 5 6 7 ←→   The management deals easily with confusion, disorder, and chaos.

13. There is a low standard of excellence on the job.   1 2 3 4 5 6 7 ←→   There is a high standard of excellence on the job.

14. My boss is not open to receive my opinion of how he/she might improve his/her own performance on the job.   1 2 3 4 5 6 7 ←→   My boss is very open to suggestions on how he/she might improve his/her own performance.

15. My boss has a very low standard for judging his/her own performance.   1 2 3 4 5 6 7 ←→   My boss has a very high standard of excellence for judging his/her own performance.

16. I am not asked for suggestions on how to improve service to the customers.   1 2 3 4 5 6 7 ←→   The management actively solicits my suggestions and ideas on how to improve service to the customers.

17. My boss shows no enthusiasm for the work we are engaged in.   1 2 3 4 5 6 7 ←→   My boss exhibits lots of enthusiasm for the work we are engaged in.

18. Mistakes get you in trouble; they aren't to learn from.   1 2 3 4 5 6 7 ←→   Around here mistakes are to learn from and not to penalize you.

19. Someone else dictates how much I should accomplish on my job.   1 2 3 4 5 6 7 ←→   I'm allowed to set my own goals for my job.

20. The organization has too many rules and regulations for me.   1 2 3 4 5 6 7 ←→   The organization has adequate rules and regulations for me.

Source: William Dyer, *Team Building,* © 1977, Addison-Wesley Publishing Co., Inc., Reading, Massachusetts. Chart on pages 108–109. Reprinted with permission.

3. The leader's objective should be the conditions within which third parties (consultants) work; that is, the primary purpose is defined by the leader who sets the agenda and activities of the meeting.
4. If the consultant is working with the team directly, he or she should help the leader to explicitly define and share the primary purpose with team members.

■ TYPES OF INTERDEPENDENT GROUPS

Transactions
The exchange of resources, such as budgeted funds, support services, products, and information, between two work units.

Because an organization is a system, no two groups in it can exist truly independently. Rather, one group may depend on another for raw materials, resources, information, or assistance in performing a task. This interdependence can be described in transactional terms.[39] **Transactions** refer to the exchange of resources, such as budgeted funds, support services, products, and information, between two work units. Work units are perceived as increasingly interdependent in several circumstances. As a greater variety of resources is exchanged, interdependence increases. As more resources are exchanged in a given amount of time, or more exchanges occur in a given amount of time, interdependence increases. The sooner a loss of a resource has significant consequences for the two groups, the more the resource is valued by the work units. Also, the extent to which the resource flowed both ways between the units affects their interdependence. Such interdependence occurs in one of four ways: (1) pooled, (2) sequential, (3) reciprocal, and (4) team, as shown in Figure 17.5.[40] Although any group can demonstrate any of these types of interdependence at specific times, one type usually characterizes the group's relationship with other groups. Assessing the nature and extent of interdependence occurs through interviewing key organizational members, such as top and middle managers, about the nature of work flow, whom they interact with most frequently, or the types of decisions they make. Each of these types are examined in the next section.

FIGURE 17.5 ■ Types of Interdependence

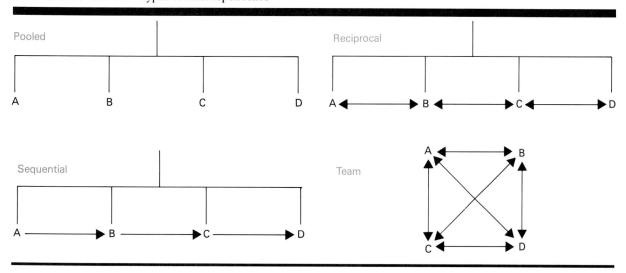

Pooled Interdependence

Pooled interdependence
Groups that rely on each other only because they belong to the same parent organization.

Groups that rely on each other only because they belong to the same parent organization show **pooled interdependence.** Two restaurants in a fast-food chain show pooled interdependence because their reputations depend on their identification with the parent organization. Two subsidiaries in a conglomerate, such as two department stores in the Federated Department Stores' chain, may show pooled interdependence because they share a common advertising agency or benefit from mass buying power. The maintenance workers and the cafeteria workers in a single organization are two departments that, for the most part, demonstrate pooled interdependence. Groups with pooled interdependence may obtain their reputation, staff resources, financing, or other services from corporate headquarters. Basically, however, they operate as separate groups or organizations. Because these groups have limited interactions, pooled interdependence has few potentially dysfunctional consequences for groups. Such groups may be required to compete for resources, but the interactions are limited.

Sequential Interdependence

Sequential interdependence
Occurs when one group's operations precede and act as prerequisites for the second group's.

Sequential interdependence occurs when one group's operations precede and act as prerequisites for the second group's. In a manufacturing plant, the assembly group and the packing group exhibit sequential interdependence. In the post office, the postal workers at the central office demonstrate sequential interdependence with the letter carriers in the local post offices: the postal workers must sort the mail before the local letter carriers can sort and deliver it. In a hospital, the nurses have sequential interdependence with the purchasing department: the purchasing department buys supplies that the nurses then use. But the nurses have more than sequential interdependence with the physicians, since the interaction does not stop when nurses receive directions from physicians; they also provide input to the physician's decisions about patient care.

Skip

The second group in the sequence may experience difficulty in accomplishing its tasks if it does not interact effectively with its predecessor. If the first group does not complete its job on time, the performance of the second group is jeopardized. This may cause members of the second group to resent the first group and limit their interactions with it. Where collaborative relations do not exist between these groups, sabotage may even occur. The purchasing department may change the nurses' requests for specific products or may delay their orders.

Reciprocal Interdependence

Reciprocal interdependence
Groups where the operations of each precede and act as prerequisites to the functioning of the other.

Groups where the operations of each precede and act as prerequisites to the functioning of the other have **reciprocal interdependence.** Sales and support staff typically have this type of interdependence; a salesperson selling computer hardware relies on technical support staff to handle installation problems; in turn, the support staff requires the sales staff's input in identifying customer problems. Union and management also have reciprocal interdependence. As the extent of group interdependence increases, the potential for conflict and other dysfunctional behavior increases correspondingly. Reciprocal interdependence may result in dysfunctional behaviors and attitudes. Because each group relies on the other to perform its own job effectively, any problems between them may result in reduced productivity or decreased worker satisfaction. Conflict is common when there is reciprocal interdependence.

Team Interdependence

Where multiple groups interact, reciprocal interdependencies may be multiplied and team interdependence results. In such cases the interdependence can be categorized as an analogue of the completely connected communication network.[41] In this case, each group's operations precede and act as prerequisites for every other group's operations when their functioning is considered over time. For example, the various departments supervised by a vice-president of marketing—sales support, advertising, and research—may exhibit this type of interdependence. Or we might characterize the overall interdependence of the nurses, physicians, and hospital administration in this way. Groups with team interdependence have the greatest potential for conflict and the highest requirements for effective communication.

■ INFLUENCES ON RELATIONSHIPS BETWEEN GROUPS

Many of the perspectives previously discussed can be used to understand intergroup relations. In this section two categories are used to diagnose intergroup dynamics: (1) the perceptual differences among groups and (2) the nature of task relations. Power differences between groups will be discussed in Chapter 19.

Perceptual Differences among Groups

It was noted in Chapter 14 that perception of events and attributions of their causes are subjective. The roles individuals hold, or the groups to which they belong, influence their perceptions. One study of unionized manufacturing workers over a three-year period traced the changes in attitudes associated with changes in roles.[42] Workers who were promoted to supervisor demonstrated significant pro-management and anti-union attitudes; those who later returned to worker roles reverted to their previous pro-union and anti-management attitudes. In contrast, those workers who became union stewards became only slightly more pro-union and anti-management, probably because of the greater similarity between their old and new roles.

In another study,[43] managers in a large organization received detailed descriptions about a company, and then were asked to describe its biggest problem. The majority of the managers identified the major problem as being in their own functional area. For example, sales managers cited sales problems as most important; production managers identified production problems. These differences in personal concerns may also influence the way each group views the other's actions. Perceptual differences between the groups create the resulting role conflict.

ORIENTATIONS

All groups evaluate events in terms of their own orientations. Differences in personal concerns and orientations often accompany differences in goals. Marketing departments typically concern themselves with the attractiveness of a product to consumers. Research and development groups focus on the product's innovative characteristics and its value to the advancement of scientific knowledge. Production departments emphasize a product's ease of production and susceptibility to cost controls.

Groups also differ in the extent to which they focus on events now and in the future. A research and development department, for example, has a long-term orientation, since new product formulation takes long periods of time. In contrast, a production department has a short-term orientation, since its goals emphasize meeting immediate inventory needs.

The social orientations of the groups, too, might differ. Consider what might occur if a hospital had unionized nurses and nonunionized physicians. The nurses would be more involved with union activities and would probably choose their friends from other nurses or union members. The physicians would be oriented toward their professional group, other physicians. What are the implications of these different orientations? What happens when the union confronts management, with whom physicians are closely allied, during a contract negotiation? The nurses and physicians may also differ in their stages of personal or career development; their social orientations and consequently their perceptions might then differ as a result.

ATTITUDINAL SETS

Attitudinal sets held by separate groups also contribute to perceptual differences. One such set reflects the extent to which a group has a competitive or cooperative attitude.[44] A group with a competitive attitude toward other groups may encourage its members to have negative attitudes toward the tasks the other groups perform, to distrust and dislike other group members, and to act without considering others. A group with a cooperative attitude toward other groups, in contrast, may encourage trust, mutual influence, coordination of effort, and acceptance of differences both within the group itself and between its members and the other group's members.

A second attitudinal set is the extent to which a group has a *cosmopolitan* versus a *local* orientation. Cosmopolitans are low on loyalty to the employing organization, high on commitment to specialized role skills, and likely to use an outer (professional) reference group orientation. Locals are those high on loyalty to the employing organization, low on commitment to specialized role skills, and likely to use an inner (organizational) reference group orientation.[45]

STATUS DIFFERENCES

Individuals' perceptions frequently influence their view of their own roles and status in an organization.[46] Often these perceptions lack clarity and validity. For effective performance, each interacting group must understand clearly what the organization and other groups expect of it. Each group must also assess whether these expectations fit with its own perceptions of its members' jobs and positions in the organization's hierarchy. Differences in education, experience, or background may influence perceptions of status. Either real or perceived differences about the relative status of two groups may influence their interactions.

The Nature of Task Relations

Task relations refer to the activities or processes that interdependent groups perform and the way these activities interrelate. Task relations fall into three categories: (1) independent, (2) dependent, and (3) interdependent. Not surprisingly, the nature of task relations generally resembles the nature of interdependence among groups described earlier.

TASK INTERACTION

Where one group's task can be done without any relationship to another group's task, the task relations are *independent*. Consider the tasks of a machine operator and an accountant. Each can perform their respective tasks without any assistance from the other. If one of these employees is absent, there is no effect on the other's job.

Where one group's task precedes and is prerequisite to another's task, the task of the latter group is *dependent* on the task of the former group. Company recruiters depend on line managers to identify the types of personnel they require. Truckers' tasks follow those of manufacturing workers. While most tasks performed by nurses follow the physicians' writing of orders, their implementation of tasks does not depend solely on the physicians. Nurses can also initiate some actions that only call for responses by physicians.

Where the tasks of two groups both follow and are prerequisite at some time to each other, the tasks are *interdependent*. The copy editor of a publishing firm works on a manuscript provided by an author, who then checks the changes made by the editor. For groups with independent tasks, the potential for problematic relations with other groups is much less than that for groups with dependent or interdependent task relations, because the more independent task groups have less interaction. Interdependent tasks most frequently contribute to problematic relations between interacting groups.

TASK CERTAINTY

The degree of certainty of the task relationships determines the extent to which the interacting groups have clear, predetermined processes of activity. Nurses, for example, have some clearly specified tasks detailed in the medical orders written by the physicians. Other tasks are less clearly specified and rely on the nurses' assessment of particular situations. In the case of the physicians, new technology, new research findings, and the changing demands for cost-effective medical care by the hospital administration often increase the uncertainty of the physician's task or the tasks of those interdependent groups. Often, too, a particular group does not understand its responsibilities and the requirements of its task; this situation also results in less task clarity and more task uncertainty. Consequently, role conflict and ambiguity may arise and contribute to dysfunctional interaction between two groups.

■■ IMPROVING THE RELATIONSHIPS BETWEEN GROUPS

When diagnosis indicates dysfunctional intergroup relations, a prescription for improving them will encourage greater *integration*,[47] or collaboration among

Skip

groups. "The three ongoing management tasks can be defined as (a) creating and maintaining shared appreciations of interdependencies, (b) reaching agreement about appropriate coordination and control strategies, and (c) implementing and maintaining these strategies."[48] Members may use process strategies, job redesign, and structural mechanisms for encouraging communication, correcting faulty perceptions or attributions, and changing task relations. Reducing power differences is discussed in Chapter 19.

Process Strategies

There are three intervention strategies that focus on improving the process of interactions between two or more groups: (1) confrontation meeting, (2) organizational mirror, and (3) third-party interventions.

CONFRONTATION MEETING

The confrontation meeting addresses problems experienced by two interacting groups that result in dysfunctional organizational performance. It is a one-day meeting where the two interacting groups share their problems and offer solutions for resolving them. The one-day meeting occurs as follows:[49] First, a top manager introduces the issues and goals that will be the focus of discussion during the day and that are causing the two groups to experience problems. The manager may identify these issues on the basis of prior discussions with group members. Then, in small groups of members drawn from the two interacting groups, the participants gather more detailed information about the problems they face. Next, representatives from each small group report on their list of items to the entire group. In natural work groups, participants set priorities and determine early action steps; then they set a concrete agenda for the steps they will take to resolve their problems. Implementation of the plan follows. A top management team continues to meet to plan and monitor follow-up action. Four to six weeks later the group reconvenes to report its progress.

The confrontation meeting is most effective in dealing with intergroup problems when

- The total management group needs to examine its own workings
- Very limited time is available for the activity
- Top management wishes to improve conditions quickly
- There is enough cohesion in the top team to ensure follow-up
- There is real commitment to resolving the issues on the part of top management
- The organization is experiencing, or has recently experienced, some major change[50]

Top management is the mediator

Organizational mirror
Describes a set of activities in which a particular organizational group, the host group, gets feedback from representatives of several other organizational groups about how it is perceived and regarded.

ORGANIZATIONAL MIRROR

The **organizational mirror** describes a set of activities in which a particular organizational group, the host group, gets feedback from representatives of several other organizational groups about how it is perceived and regarded.[51] A consultant begins by conducting preliminary interviews with all groups' members. Then that individual reports data from these interviews to all groups (invited and host groups). The groups then discuss the data presented. Small, heterogeneous groups of representatives from the diverse groups meet, discuss the data further if appropriate, and develop action plans for the identified problems. Implementation of the action plans should follow. Like the confrontation meeting, the organizational mirror requires top management commitment and follow-up for effective action to result.

THIRD-PARTY INTERVENTIONS

Third-party interventions are frequently used in labor-management interactions to resolve the intergroup conflict that occurs. The third party can act as a mediator, arbitrator, or fact-finder. Such third parties must demonstrate the following:[52]

- A high degree of professional expertise regarding social processes
- A low level of power over the fate of the principles
- A high level of control over confrontation-settling processes
- Moderate knowledge about the principles, issues, and background factors
- Neutrality or balance with respect to substantive outcomes, personal relationships, and conflict-resolution methodology

The confrontation meeting, organizational mirror, and third-party interventions are typical of process interventions used in most organizations today, but others are also available.[53] In addition, various diverse strategies are used for dealing with the conflict that often results between groups.[54] These are discussed in the final section of the chapter.

Job Redesign Strategies

Altering the nature of task relations between two groups may also improve intergroup behavior. Job enrichment, for example, reduces job specialization and likely reduces the dependence of one job-holder on another. Sociotechnical redesign considers the social implications of introducing new technologies to work units. In concert with job redesign, the organization must assign rewards that encourage collaborative and functional interdependencies and interactions between groups.

Structural Mechanisms

Structural strategies can also increase integration and coordination. They differ from process strategies in that they call for a change in the organization's formal reporting relationships—its structure—rather than a change in individuals' interpersonal behavior. Such structural strategies require adding at least one of the following formal managerial mechanisms to the problem situation:[55]

Hierarchy. A common superior is assigned to coordinate the work of two interacting groups. This approach works best when interacting groups are reasonably close in function or work on similar projects.

Plans. Plans direct the activities of interacting groups while minimizing their interaction. By using plans, even the integration of geographically distant groups can be effective. The use of common or superordinate objectives can have an influence similar to plans: they can refocus the efforts of conflicting groups and can rearrange group boundaries.[56]

Linking roles. Individuals are placed in informal positions and act as conduits between interacting groups. This expedites communication because issues are resolved through a person who is at the same level in the organization rather than by a common supervisor.[57]

Task forces. Special groups of representatives from all parties can be convened to work on problems faced by the interacting groups. Task forces integrate by presenting their ideas to the representatives of the interacting groups. Task forces typically include one representative from each group affected by, or involved in, a particular problem or task.

Integrating roles or units. Analogous to the informal linking roles, a permanent coordinating individual or group of people can be formally appointed to act as an interface between interacting groups. A project or product manager, for example, coordinates the decisions of such interdependent groups as sales representatives, R&D engineers, and the production line.

Project or product structure. This structure groups together individuals who work on the same product or project.

Matrix organization. This highly sophisticated organizational design integrates both functional departments and project groups through a dual authority and reporting system. In a matrix organization, each individual has two superiors.

When individuals are brought together in a highly structured environment, a potential for major disagreements exists. The following section deals with conflict in organizations.

■ CONFLICT IN ORGANIZATIONS

Conflict
Antagonism or opposition between or among persons.

Conflict refers to antagonism or opposition between or among persons. Conflict is the result of incongruent or incompatible relationships between members of a group or dyad.[58] It is a process that begins when one party perceives that the other has frustrated, or is about to frustrate, some concern of his (or hers).[59] It can also occur between and within individuals, groups, or organizations. Conflict occurs when

1. mutually exclusive goals or values exist in fact, or are perceived to exist, by the groups involved;
2. interaction is characterized by behavior designed to defeat, reduce, or suppress the opponent, or to gain a mutually designated victory;
3. the groups face each other with mutually opposing actions and counteractions;
4. each group attempts to create a relatively favored position vis-à-vis the other.[60]

The classic example of intercompany conflict may be the many union/management clashes that occurred in the 1980s. Of the many examples that could be cited, the most commonly referred to is probably the conflict between Frank

Lorenzo, chairman of Texas Air Corporation, and Eastern's three unions. Lorenzo demanded pay cuts from Eastern's three unions and threatened to transfer Eastern's jobs to nonunion Continental if the unions did not comply.[61] As might be expected, the unions were not in total agreement, and conflict resulted. Differences among interacting individuals or groups can increase the probability of conflict in organizations. So, too, can certain power configurations (discussed in Chapter 19), particularly where multiple coalitions compete for influence. These situations may cause conflict over appropriate organizational goals or reasonable ways of attaining them.

Conflict can have both positive and negative consequences. It can encourage organizational innovation, creativity, and adaptation.[62] In fact, the failure of organizations such as the Penn Central Railroad and Studebaker has been traced to too much harmony: complacency can cause a failure to occur.[63] Although some amount of conflict is beneficial, too often it produces dysfunctional consequences. It can reduce productivity, decrease morale, cause dissatisfaction, and increase tension and stress in the organization.

Levels of Conflict

Six levels of conflict are described: (1) intrapersonal, (2) interpersonal, (3) intragroup, (4) intergroup, (5) intraorganizational, and (6) interorganizational (see Figure 17.6).

INTRAPERSONAL CONFLICT

Intrapersonal conflict
Conflict that exists when an individual must choose between incompatible goals.

Conflict that exists when an individual must choose between incompatible goals is referred to as **intrapersonal conflict** (role conflict). Individuals who must decide whether to act in their own or in the organization's interest illustrates such conflict. Or a person may feel cognitive conflict. For example, if the superintendent of schools sends his children to one of the schools slated for closing, he may experience conflict over whether to make an objective choice or keep his own children's school open. Likewise, members of the school committee may be torn over the objective data that call for closing a school that their constituents' children attend. Intrapersonal conflict may cause an individual to secure additional information before acting, or it may paralyze evaluative activities altogether.

INTERPERSONAL CONFLICT

Interpersonal conflict
Conflict that results when two individuals disagree about issues, actions, or goals.

Interpersonal conflict results when two individuals disagree about issues, actions, or goals. As discussed later, latent (below the surface) conflict often exists because of differences in two individuals' perceptions, orientations, or status. Such conflict may cause additional relevant issues to surface; or it may prevent the two individuals from ever communicating effectively.

INTRAGROUP CONFLICT

Substantive conflict
Intragroup conflict that is based on intellectual disagreement among group members.

A group may experience either substantive or affective conflict. **Substantive conflict** is intragroup conflict that is based on intellectual disagreement among group members. When various members of a school committee draw different conclusions from the same data, they experience substantive conflict. In this situation, conflict often results in better information exchange and decision making. Another example is when the tasks of one group member interfere with the tasks of another. Two or more committee members who have goals of keeping

FIGURE 17.6 ■
Levels of Conflict

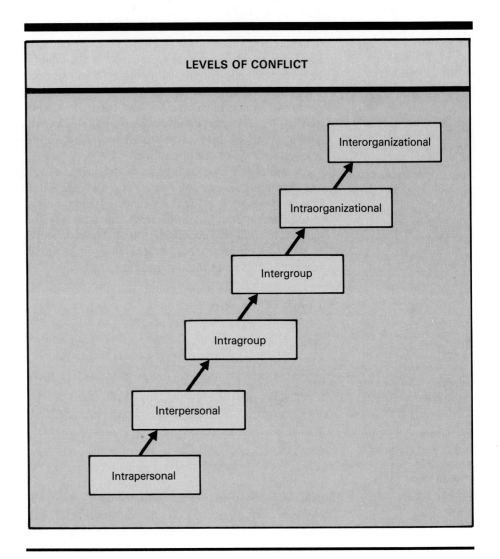

LEVELS OF CONFLICT

Interorganizational

Intraorganizational

Intergroup

Intragroup

Interpersonal

Intrapersonal

Affective conflict
Intragroup conflict that is based on emotional responses to a situation.

their own neighborhood schools open may also experience such conflict. **Affective conflict** is intragroup conflict that is based on emotional responses to a situation. If members of a school committee feel passionate (or even irrational) about the importance of neighborhood schools in general, or of one school in particular, this generates affective conflict. It may also result when interacting individuals have incompatible styles or personalities.

INTERGROUP CONFLICT

Intergroup conflict
Conflict that takes place between groups.

Intergroup conflict is conflict that takes place between groups. For example, the production department and the department of research may experience such conflict. It commonly exists between union and management negotiating teams, unless emphasis is placed on integrative problem solving. This type of conflict typically results in competitive, win-lose behavior and outcomes.

INTRAORGANIZATIONAL CONFLICT

This type of conflict within organizations encompasses three subtypes. **Vertical conflict** is conflict that exists between supervisors and subordinates, who may disagree about the best way to accomplish a task. The manager may experience such conflict with his subordinates. **Horizontal conflict** is conflict that exists between employees or departments at the same level. For example, the department of research may experience conflicts with the department of facilities management. **Line-staff conflict** is conflict that occurs over resources or the involvement of staff people in line decisions. Teachers and curriculum specialists may experience such conflict.

INTERORGANIZATIONAL CONFLICT

Interorganizational conflict is conflict that exists between organizations that are interdependent with the same suppliers, customers, competitors, and governmental agencies, among others. Organizations in conflict frequently demonstrate either cooperative or competitive relations, although other types of interactions are possible. The extent to which conflict arises may depend on the extent to which one organization creates uncertain conditions for the others, attempts to access or control the same resources, encourages communication with the others, attempts to balance power in the marketplace, and develops procedures for resolving existing conflict.[64]

Stages of Conflict

One way to understand conflict is to view it as dynamic rather than stable or static. In fact, as seen in Figure 17.7, it can be viewed as a sequence of conflict episodes with five stages: (1) latent, (2) perceived, (3) felt, (4) manifest, and (5) aftermath.[65]

> *Latent Stage.* Conflict begins when the conditions for conflict exist. Individuals or groups may have power differences, compete for scarce resources, strive for autonomy, have different goals, or experience diverse role pressures. These differences provide the foundation for disagreement, competition, and ultimately conflict.
>
> *Perceived Stage.* In the next stage individuals or group members know that conflict exists, for example, if one group misunderstands another group's position. Yet conflict can be denied by individuals or by whole groups who do not want to deal with it in any way.
>
> *Felt Stage.* When one or more parties feels tense or anxious, conflict has moved beyond the perceived stage to the felt stage. Here, the conflict becomes personalized to the individuals or groups involved. *~ or constructive*
>
> *Manifest Stage.* Observable behavior designed to frustrate another's attempts to pursue goals is the most overt form of conflict. Both open aggression and withdrawals of support illustrate manifest conflict. At this stage conflict must be resolved or used constructively in order for effective organizational performance to continue.
>
> *Aftermath Stage.* The final stage of conflict is the situation after it has been resolved or suppressed. Conflict aftermath describes the resulting relationship—supportive, paternalistic, or perhaps adversarial—between the parties in conflict.

Vertical conflict
Conflict that exists between supervisors and subordinates, who may disagree about the best way to accomplish a task.

Horizontal conflict
Conflict that exists between employees or departments at the same level.

Line-staff conflict
Conflict that occurs over resources or the involvement of staff people in line decisions.

Interorganizational conflict
Conflict that exists between organizations that are interdependent with the same suppliers, customers, competitors, and governmental agencies, among others.

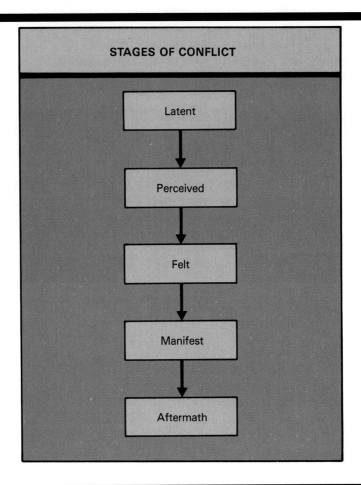

Ken Thomas describes the conflict process a little differently. According to his model, each conflict episode moves through four stages:[66]

1. *Frustration*—A group cannot accomplish a goal or complete a task.
2. *Conceptualization*—The individuals involved perceive that conflict exists and formulate ideas about the conflict issue. They frequently gather information and consider multiple points of view to gain a better understanding of the conflict issue.
3. *Behavior*—Those affected respond to the conflict.
4. *Outcome*—The conflict is resolved, or frustration continues and leads to another conflict episode.

Outcomes of Conflict

Conflict can have positive outcomes. There may be situations where conflict results in greater creativity, more worker enthusiasm, or better decisions. Perhaps during a disagreement a manager may come to hold a different perspective on an

Conflict within organizations can create anxiety and decrease productivity for individuals, or it can have positive outcomes including a clarification of individual views. (COMSTOCK, Inc.)

issue, or learn that a perception or information has been inaccurate. Other positive outcomes can include:[67]

- Improved ideas
- A tendency to search for new approaches
- A surfacing, then resolving, of long-standing problems
- Clarification of individual views
- Increased interest and creativity

But conflict is often viewed as dysfunctional for organizations. It can arouse anxiety in individuals, increase the tension in an organizational system and its subsystems, lower satisfaction, and decrease productivity. The following negative outcomes can also occur:[68]

- Some people feel defeated and demeaned
- The distance between people increases
- A climate of mistrust and suspicion arises
- Individuals or groups focus on their own narrow interests
- Resistance, rather than teamwork, develops
- Turnover increases

Recognizing that conflict exists, how can an organizational member deal with it most constructively? In the next section, ways of managing conflict are examined.

Interpersonal Conflict Management

There are numerous techniques for dealing with conflict between two or more individuals. They range from the use of force by a superior over a subordinate to a problem-solving approach. Possible ways of dealing with interpersonal conflict management are as follows:

Force. When conflict exists in an organization, a manager may compel one party to accept a certain solution. The expression, "He may not be right, but he's still the boss" applies in this instance. The party who is overruled may not agree with the result but must accept the directive if he or she wishes to stay in the organization.

Withdrawal. A solution that some individuals adopt in resolving conflict is to withdraw from or avoid the person with whom the conflict exists. Conflict is reduced, but the original cause remains. For example, suppose you see someone you don't want to speak to approaching you. You withdraw by walking around the block to avoid speaking to the person. This usually does not resolve the conflict; it merely prevents a confrontation or discussion of the problem.

Smoothing. When smoothing is used, a manager attempts to provide a semblance of peaceful cooperation by presenting an image such as *"we're one big happy family."* With this approach, problems are rarely permitted to come to the surface, but the potential for conflict remains.

Compromise. Neither party gets all it wants in a compromise. This is the most typical way of dealing with labor-management conflict. For example, management may offer to increase wages by 4 percent, while the union may be seeking a 6-percent pay hike. A compromise figure of a 5-percent pay increase may result in a reasonable settlement of the conflict.

Mediation and Arbitration. Both arbitration and mediation call for outside neutral parties to enter the situation to assist in resolving the conflict. *Arbitration* is a process in which a dispute between two parties is submitted to a third party to make a binding decision. Arbitration is frequently used in union-management grievance conflicts. The arbitrator is given the authority to act as a judge. The decision rendered is usually final because both union and management agree in advance that it will be. *Mediation* is a process in which a third party enters a dispute between two parties for the purpose of assisting them in reaching an agreement. A mediator can only suggest, recommend, and attempt to keep the two parties talking in hopes of reaching a solution.

Superordinate Goals. At times, a goal may be encountered that overshadows the separate interests of two opposing factions. For example, if the firm is in danger of going out of business, both union and management have been known to put aside minor conflict and work toward the common goal of survival. There have been instances where union members have taken a decrease in pay and benefits in order to assist in the survival of the firm. Union members and management at Chrysler and General Motors and other firms have cooperatively worked together to ensure the survival of their firms. Responding to major financial crises, such firms experienced significant reductions in their management ranks, as well as reductions in the work force, wages, and benefits.

Problem Solving. A recommended approach to conflict management is problem solving. Ideally, problem solving is characterized by an open and trusting exchange of views. Both parties realize that conflict is caused by relationships among people and is not within the person. With the problem-solving approach, an individual can disagree with your ideas and still remain your friend. It is a healthy approach that recognizes that one person is rarely completely right and the other person completely wrong. Granting a concession is not seen as a sign of weakness. Neither party feels that it has to win every battle to maintain self-respect.

A certain amount of conflict is healthy, when the problem-solving approach is taken. If a difference of opinion exists between two individuals and they openly discuss their difficulties, a superior solution often results. With problem solving, a person is encouraged to bring difficulties into the open without fear of reprisal. When this occurs, a situation that initially appeared to be a major problem may become only a minor one, which is easily resolved.

Structural Conflict Management

Conflict can often be managed by changing procedures, organizational structure, and physical layout. These methods for resolving conflict are discussed next.

PROCEDURAL CHANGES

Conflict can occur because a procedure is illogically sequenced. When a credit manager and a sales manager were both about to be fired because of an irreconcilable personality conflict, it was discovered that the processing of credit applications too late in the procedure was the cause of the difficulty. The credit manager was forced to cancel too many deals already made. When the credit check was placed earlier in the procedure, most of the conflict disappeared. In another instance, the personnel director and the production manager were in continuous disagreement. At times, the conflict almost caused them to come to blows. Then it was discovered that the production manager was not being permitted to review applications at an early stage of the hiring sequence and to make comments. When the procedure was changed, many of the difficulties were resolved.

ORGANIZATIONAL STRUCTURE CHANGES

Some degree of conflict is often desirable. For example, this is the case where a quality control department must inspect the work of the production department. Conflict between quality control and production can probably be minimized if the quality control director reports to the production manager. In this case, however, quality control loses its independence. This is why the quality control director typically reports to someone high in the organization, often even the president. The resulting potential conflict is justified by the quality improvement that results from such a structure.

In other cases, conflict between departments is unplanned and undesirable. In some firms, sales and distribution are in separate departments, each reporting to a senior manager. This division often creates conflict when individuals in sales expect quick delivery in response to customer requests. In an effort to keep costs down, the distribution department wants to make deliveries in full trucks and at scheduled intervals. To resolve this kind of conflict, it may be desirable to combine the two departments under a marketing manager who has experience in both sales and distribution. A marketing manager is likely to ensure that the organization's needs take priority over the preferences of sales and distribution personnel.

PHYSICAL LAYOUT CHANGES

Changes in the design of the physical workplaces have been used effectively to reduce or eliminate conflict. Office space can be designed either to force interaction or to make it difficult. Personnel can use desks as barriers and buffers. Some offices have dividers to separate workers. However, if a manager desires to stimulate a problem-solving atmosphere, a more open office arrangement may be permitted. When known antagonists are seated in conference directly across from each other, the amount of conflict increases. When they are seated side by side, the conflict tends to decrease. These principles can be applied in arranging workspaces.

A detrimental conflict involving physical layout existed between two groups of workers in a truck assembly plant. Working at different phases on the assembly line, the two groups came into conflict because both had to obtain parts from the same shelving unit. Each group felt the other was deliberately rearranging its supply of parts, which sometimes resulted in fights. The conflict was resolved by moving the shelving unit between the two groups so as to set up a barrier between them. Thus, each group had its own supply area or "territory." As a result of this change, mistakes were reduced by 50 percent within two days.[69]

4) Reward System

SUMMARY

Groups, defined as two or more people having a unifying relationship, are often categorized by size, function, or some other way. Task groups are determined by job requirements, and project groups include formal, but temporary assignments to groups, committees, and special projects. An informal group is two or more persons associated in ways not prescribed by the formal organization. Groups form when individuals exhibit common needs, common interests, common goals, and/or physical proximity, which influence the nature and quality of the group's functioning. Individual roles, group norms, leadership, group cohesiveness, group size, and synergism all influence group effectiveness.

Because an organization is a system, no two groups in it can exist truly independently. This interdependence, described in transactional terms, can be pooled, sequential, or reciprocal. Interdependent groups perform independent, dependent, or interdependent task relations that generally resemble the nature of the interdependence among the groups. When diagnosis indicates dysfunctional intergroup relations, managers must create and maintain shared appreciations of interdependencies, reach agreement about appropriate coordination and control strategies, and implement and maintain these strategies.

Conflict, the result of incongruent or incompatible relationships between group members occurs on six levels: intrapersonal, interpersonal, intragroup, intergroup, intraorganizational, and interorganizational. One way to understand conflict is to view it as dynamic rather than stable or static. In fact, conflict can be viewed as a sequence with five stages: latent, perceived, felt, manifest, and aftermath.

Conflict management may be classified as interpersonal or structural. Interpersonal conflict management deals with conflict between two or more individuals. Structural conflict management is concerned with changing the structures and processes that can have an effect on behavior.

REVIEW QUESTIONS

1. Define a group and describe the various types of groups.
2. Why do groups form?
3. Describe the typical developmental progression of a group.
4. Explain the factors that influence group effectiveness.
5. Define the following terms:
   a. role
   b. task roles
   c. maintenance roles
   d. individual roles
6. Define norms and explain the various norm classification schemes.
7. What are the various types of interdependent groups?
8. What are the means of improving the relationship between groups?
9. Define conflict. What are the various levels of conflict? Define each.
10. Identify and describe the various strategies for dealing with conflict.

KEY TERMS

group	norm	organizational mirror
primary groups	pivotal norms	conflict
secondary groups	peripheral norms	intrapersonal conflict
task or functional groups	unattainable-ideal norm	interpersonal conflict
informal group	preferred-value norm	substantive conflict
coalitions	attainable-ideal norm	affective conflict
task activity	cohesiveness	intergroup conflict
group structure process	synergism	vertical conflict
role	transactions	horizontal conflict
task roles	pooled interdependence	line-staff conflict
maintenance or group-building roles	sequential interdependence	interorganizational conflict
individual or self-oriented roles	reciprocal interdependence	

AS JAMES MITCHELL approached the table where Betty Fuller was seated, he asked, "Mind if I sit here?"

"Of course not," said Betty. "I've been wanting to talk to you anyway." James placed his tray on the table and sat down.

"James," Betty said, "you heard that Dave is being transferred?"

"Yes," said James. "I think he'll be leaving next month and going to the Jackson plant."

"Well," said Betty, "I've decided to apply for the job. I don't really have much hope, though. A woman doesn't have much chance for promotion, no matter how hard she works. Even if a woman did get promoted, she would probably be paid less."

"You have the same chance that everyone else does," James said. "I'm going to apply for that job myself."

"Well, that pretty well settles it," said Betty. "I don't really have a chance. But I am still going to apply."

"Don't you think that's a little unfair, Betty?

Now, if you don't get promoted, you are going to think that it's because you're a woman."

"Well," said Betty, "don't you think it will be?"

"Of course not," James said. "I don't think you're so obviously superior to me. Of course, if you make a big issue of this sex thing, they might promote you just to show how open-minded they are."

"Look, James," said Betty, "I've earned everything I've gotten. Not only have I worked hard here and made a real effort to get along with everybody, I also went to night school and got my degree."

"Having a degree in management doesn't make you a manager, Betty. Anyway, I think I'm about to lose my temper. I'd just as soon not talk about this anymore." James took his half-eaten lunch and moved across the lunchroom to another table.

QUESTIONS
1. At what stage is this conflict situation in? Discuss.
2. What means of resolving this conflict situation would you recommend? Explain.

SPRINGFIELD PRODUCTS COMPANY in Springfield, Missouri, is a medium-sized manufacturer of small outboard motors. The motors are supplied to major retailing chains, which sell them under their own brand names. For the past few years, sales at Springfield Products has been falling. The decline was industrywide. In fact, Springfield was faring better than its competitors and had actually been able to increase its share of the market slightly. While forecasts indicated that the demand for the company's outboards would improve in the future, Anne Goddard, the company's president, believed that something needed to be done immediately to help the company maintain its financial health through this temporary slump. As a first step, she employed a consulting firm to determine if a reorganization might be helpful.

A team of three consultants arrived at the firm. They told Goddard that they first had to gain a thorough understanding of the current situation prior to making any recommendations for action. After informing them that the company was open to them, she told her supervisors to refrain from informing anyone of the purpose of the investigation, because this might cause employees to perform differently.

The grapevine was full of rumors almost from the day the consulting group arrived, however. Some employees heard that the company may be shut down, others heard that massive transfers were possible, and others heard that forced retirements were probable. The work groups at Springfield Products Company are very close knit and these rumors upset virtually everyone. Matters were made even worse when workers received no explanation from their supervisors. The climate quickly changed from one of concern to one of fear. Rather than being concerned about their daily work, employees worried about what was going to happen to the company and their jobs. Productivity dropped drastically as a result.

Three weeks after the consultants left, a memorandum was circulated throughout the company, which stated that the consultants had recommended a slight modification in the top levels of the organization; no one would be terminated,

and any reductions would be the result of normal attrition. By that time, however, some of the best workers had already found other jobs, and company operations were severely disrupted for several months.

QUESTIONS

1. What part did the informal organization play in what happened at Springfield Products?
2. Explain what happened in relation to the "Nature of Task Relations."

EXPERIENTIAL EXERCISE

You are Judy Mills, and you have just come to a startling revelation. Two of your best employees, Josephine Johnston and Joan Jones, are having serious difficulty getting along on the job. Since this is a special project, neither has worked for you previously; instead, they were each "hand-picked" for the project. Until now, you thought they were working well together. You knew they came from different backgrounds and are of different races, but you felt they would make a good team.

Josephine Johnston, a black employee with a degree in industrial technology from a black university, has always gotten along with every employee she has ever worked with. Josephine has developed expertise with a piece of specialized equipment and has been selected to operate it on a major project under the new supervisor. Yesterday, she overheard a conversation in which she was referred to as "the darkie from the colored university." When she confronted the co-worker, she was accused of being "overly sensitive."

Joan Jones, a white employee with a degree in industrial engineering from a major state university, has also always gotten along with everyone she has worked with. However, she is now working with people she has never worked with before. Joan does not believe that she is prejudiced, but her professors at the university always cut down the black schools for turning out "glorified machine operators." Now she has to work with one on an important project. Joan had a run-in with Josephine, when Josephine overheard Joan telling another engineer that she hoped that he didn't get "burned working with that darkie from that colored institution."

You believe conflicts should be addressed directly, so you have decided to talk to each person individually, and then bring them together. You are not sure what triggered the problem, but you are determined to resolve it. Select three individuals; one to serve as Judy Mills, the supervisor, one to play the role of Josephine Johnston, the black employee, and one to serve as Joan Jones, the white employee. The instructor will provide more information to participants.

NOTES

1. John Hoerr, "Is Teamwork a Management Plot? Mostly Not," *Business Week,* 20 February 1989, 70.
2. L. N. Jewell and H. J. Reitz, *Group Effectiveness in Organizations* (Glenview, Ill.: Scott, Foresman, 1981), 8–9.
3. D. M. Herold and S. Kerr, "The Effectiveness of Work Groups," *Organizational Behavior* (Columbus, Oh.: Grid Publishing, 1979), 96.
4. R. W. Napier and M. K. Gershenfeld, *Groups: Theory and Experience,* 2d ed. (Boston: Houghton Mifflin, 1981).
5. See J. K. Murningham, "Models of Coalition Behavior: Game Theoretic, Social Psychological, and Political Perspectives," *Psychological Bulletin* 85 (1978): 1130–1153.

6. W. A. Gamson, "A Theory of Coalition Formation," *American Sociological Review* 26 (1961): 372–382.

7. J. A. Pearce II and A. S. De Nisi, "Attribution Theory and Strategic Decision-making: An Application to Coalition Formation," *Academy of Management Journal* 26 (1983): 119–128.

8. B. W. Tuchman, "Developmental Sequences in Small Groups," *Psychological Bulletin* 63 (1965): 384–399; N. R. F. Maier, *Problem Solving and Creativity in Individuals and Groups* (Belmont, Cal.: Brooks/Cole, 1970); R. F. Bales and F. L. Strodtbeck, "Phases in Group Problem Solving," *Journal of Abnormal and Social Psychology* 46 (1951): 485–495.

9. See, for example, Maier, *Problem Solving;* Bales and Strodtbeck, "Problem Solving," 485–495.

10. Tuchman, "Sequences," 384–399; Maier, *Problem Solving;* Bales and Strodtbeck, "Problem Solving," 485–495.

11. A. C. Kowitz and T. J. Knutson, *Decision-Making in Small Groups: The Search for Alternatives* (Boston: Allyn and Bacon, 1980); Tuchman, "Sequences," 384–399.

12. T. M. Mills, *Group Transformation* (Englewood Cliffs, N.J.: Prentice-Hall, 1964), 67–80.

13. W. C. Schutz, *FIRO: A Three-Dimensional Theory of Interpersonal Behavior* (New York: Holt, Rinehart, 1958), 168.

14. Schutz, *FIRO,* 168.

15. Schutz, *FIRO,* 168.

16. J. P. Wanous, A. E. Reichers, and S. D. Malik, "Organizational Socialization and Group Development: Toward an Integrative Perspective," *Academy of Management Review* 9 (1984): 670–683.

17. J. P. Wanous, *Organizational Entry: Recruitment, Selection, and Socialization of Newcomers* (Reading, Mass.: Addison-Wesley, 1980).

18. Wanous, *Organizational Entry.*

19. K. D. Benne and P. Sheats, "Functional Roles of Group Members," *Journal of Social Issues* 4 (1948): 41–49.

20. D. C. Feldman, "The Development and Enforcement of Group Norms," *Academy of Management Review* 9 (1984): 47–53.

21. J. W. Thibaut and H. H. Kelley, *The Social Psychology of Groups* (New York: John Wiley & Sons, 1959).

22. M. E. Shaw, *Group Dynamics,* 3d ed. (New York: Harper & Row, 1980).

23. Feldman, "Group Norms," 47–53.

24. E. F. Huse and J. L. Bowditch, *Behavior in Organizations: A Systems Approach,* 2d ed. (Reading, Mass.: Addison-Wesley, 1977).

25. J. Jackson, "A Conceptual and Measurement Model for Norms and Values," *Pacific Sociological Review* 9 (1966): 35–47.

26. R. W. Napier and M. K. Gershenfeld, *Groups: Theory and Experience,* 1st ed. (Boston: Houghton Mifflin).

27. A. Zaleznik, C. R. Christensen, and F. J. Roethlisberger, *The Motivation, Productivity, and Satisfaction of Workers* (Boston: Harvard University Graduate School of Business, Division of Research, 1958).

28. S. D. Malik and Kenneth N. Wexley, "Improving the Owner/Manager's Handling of Subordinate Resistance to Unpopular Decisions," *Journal of Small Business Management* 24, no. 3 (July 1986): 22–28.

29. L. L. Commings, George P. Huber, and Eugene Arendt, "Effects of Size and Spatial Arrangements in Group Decision Making," *Academy of Management Journal* 17 (September 1974): 473.

30. Arthur D. Sharplin, "Synergism in Action" (Northeast Louisiana University, December 1981).

31. John Hoerr, "Getting Man and Machine to Live Happily Ever After," *Business Week,* 20 April 1987, 61.

32. J. R. Hackman and C. G. Morris, "Improving Group Performance Effectiveness," in *Advances in Experimental Social Psychology,* vol. 8, ed. L. Berkowitz (New York: Academic Press, 1975), 345.

33. Hackman and Morris, "Group Performance," 350.

34. W. G. Dyer, *Team Building: Issues and Alternatives* (Reading, Mass.: Addison-Wesley, 1979).

35. Dyer, *Team Building.*

36. S. D. Van Raalte, "Preparing the Task Force to Get Good Results," *Advanced Management Journal* 47 (Winter 1982): 11–19.

37. E. H. Schein, *Process Consultation* (Reading, Mass.: Addison-Wesley, 1969).

38. R. Beckhard, "Optimizing Team Building Effort," *Journal of Contemporary Business* (Summer 1972): 23–32.

39. J. E. McCann and D. L. Ferry, "An Approach for Assessing and Managing Interunit Interdependence," *Academy of Management Review* 4 (1979): 113–119.

40. J. D. Thompson, *Organizations in Action* (New York: McGraw-Hill, 1967); A. H. Van de Ven, A. L. Delbecq, and R. Koenig, Jr., "Determinants of Coordination Modes Within Organizations," *American Sociological Review* 41 (1976): 322–338.

41. Van de Ven, Delbecq, and Koenig, Jr., "Coordination Modes," 322–338.

42. S. Lieberman, "The Effects of Changes in Roles on the Attitudes of Role Occupants," *Human Relations* 9 (1956): 385–417.

43. D. C. Dearborn and H. A. Simon, "Selective Perception: A Note on the Departmental Identifications of Executives," *Sociometry* 21 (1958): 290.

44. D. W. Johnson and F. P. Johnson, *Joining Together: Group Theory and Group Skills* (Englewood Cliffs, N.J.: Prentice-Hall, 1975).

45. A. W. Gouldner, "Cosmopolitans and Locals: Toward an Analysis of Latent Social Roles," *Administrative Science Quarterly* 2 (1958): 290.

46. R. L. Kahn, D. M. Wolfe, R. P. Quinn, and J. D. Snoek, *Organizational Stress: Studies in Role Conflict and Ambiguity* (New York: John Wiley & Sons, 1964).

47. P. Lawrence and J. Lorsch, *Organization and Environment: Managing Differentiation and Integration* (Homewood, Ill.: Irwin, 1969).

48. J. McCann and J. R. Galbraith, "Interdepartmental Relations," in *Handbook of Organizational Design,* vol. 2, ed. P. C. Nystrom and W. H. Starbuck (New York: Oxford University Press, 1981), 68.

49. R. Beckhard, "The Confrontation Meeting," *Harvard Business Review* 45 (1967): 154.

50. Beckhard, "Confrontation Meeting," 154.

51. W. L. French and C. H. Bell, Jr., *Organization Development: Behavioral Science Interventions for Organization Improvement,* 2d ed. (Englewood Cliffs, N.J.: Prentice-Hall, 1978).

52. R. E. Walton, *Interpersonal Peacemaking: Confrontation and Third-Party Consultations* (Reading, Mass.: Addison-Wesley, 1969), 150.

53. See J. Gordon, "A Brief Dictionary of Intervention Strategies," in *A Diagnostic Approach to Organizational Behavior,* 1st ed. (Boston: Allyn and Bacon, 1983); and French and Bell, *Organization Development,* for discussion of other strategies.

54. A. C. Filley, *Interpersonal Communication* (Glenview, Ill.: Scott, Foresman, 1975), 52.

55. J. Galbraith, *Designing Complex Organizations* (Reading, Mass.: Addison-Wesley, 1973).

56. M. Sherif and C. W. Sherif, *Groups in Harmony and Tension* (New York: Harper & Row, 1953).

57. R. Likert and J. Likert, *New Ways of Managing Conflict* (New York: McGraw-Hill, 1976).

58. B. Kabanoff, "Potential Influence Structures as Sources of Interpersonal Conflict in Groups and Organizations," *Organizational Behavior and Human Decision Processes* 36 (February 1986): 115.

59. K. W. Thomas, "Conflict and Conflict Management," in *Handbook of Industrial and Organizational Psychology,* ed. M. D. Dunnette (Chicago: Rand McNally, 1976), 889–935.

60. A. C. Filley, *Interpersonal Conflict Resolution* (Glenview, Ill.: Scott, Foresman, 1975).

61. Jo Ellen Davis and Pete Engardio, "What It's Like to Work for Frank Lorenzo," *Business Week,* 18 May 1987, 76.

62. K. W. Thomas, "Organizational Conflict," in *Organization Behavior,* ed. S. Kerr (Columbus, Ohio: Grid, 1979).

63. S. P. Robbins, *Managing Organizational Conflict: A Non-Traditional Approach* (Englewood Cliffs, N.J.: Prentice-Hall, 1974).

64. J. Pfeffer, "Beyond Management and the Workers: The Institutional Function of Management," *Academy of Management Review* 1 (January 1976): 36–46; H. Assael, "Constructive Role of Interorganizational Conflict," *Administrative Science Quarterly* 12 (June 1967): 296–320.

65. L. R. Pondy, "Organizational Conflict: Concepts and Models," *Administrative Science Quarterly* 12 (June 1967): 296–320.

66. Thomas, "Organizational Conflict."

67. W. H. Schmidt, "Conflict: A Powerful Process for (Good or Bad) Change," *Management Review* 63 (December 1974): 4–10.

68. Schmidt, "Conflict," 4–10.

69. H. Kenneth Bobele and Peter J. Buchanan, "Building a More Productive Environment," *Management World* 8 (January 1979): 8.

REFERENCES

Alderfer, C. P., and K. K. Smith. "Studying Intergroup Relations Embedded in Organizations." *Administrative Science Quarterly* 27 (1982): 35–65.

Aldrich H., and D. Herker. "Boundary Spanning Roles and Organization Structure." *Academy of Management Review* 2 (1977): 217–230.

Bales, R. F., and F. L. Strodtbeck. "Phases in Group Problem Solving." *Journal of Abnormal and Social Psychology* 46 (1951): 485–495.

Barkman, Donald F. "Team Discipline: Put Performance on the Line." *Personnel Journal* 66 (March 1987): 58–63.

Barrett, F. D. "Teamwork—How to Expand Its Power and Punch." *Business Quarterly* 52 (Winter 1987): 24–31.

Benne, K. D., and P. Sheats. "Functional Roles of Group Members." *Journal of Social Issues* 4 (1948): 41–49.

Brightman, Harvey J., and Penny Verhoeven. "Running Successful Problem-Solving Groups." *Business* 36 (April–June 1986): 15–23.

Briscoe, Dennis R. "Organizational Design: Dealing with the Human Constraint." *California Management Review* 23 (Fall 1980): 71–80.

Brockner, Joel, and Todd Hass. "Self-Esteem and Task Performance in Quality Circles." *Academy of Management Journal* 29 (September 1986): 17–22.

Bushe, Gervase R. "Temporary or Permanent Middle-Management Groups?" *Group & Organization Studies* 12 (March 1987): 23–37.

Caruth, D., and H. N. Mills, Jr. "Working Toward Better Union Relations." *Supervisory Management* 30 (February 1985): 11.

Cotton, John L., David A. Vollrath, Kirk L. Froggatt, Mark L. Lengnick-Hall, and Kenneth R. Jennings. "Employee Participation: Diverse Forms and Different Outcomes." *Academy of Management Review* 13 (January 1988): 8–22.

Feldman, D. C. "The Development and Enforcement of Group Norms." *Academy of Management Review* 9 (1984): 47–53.

Fiegenbaum, Avi, John McGee, and Howard Thomas. "Exploring the Linkage Between Strategic Groups and Competitive Strategy." *International Studies of Management & Organization* 18 (Spring 1988): 6–25.

Fiorelli, Joseph S. "Power in Work Groups: Team Member's Perspectives." *Human Relations* 11 (January 1988): 1–12.

Fisher, R., and W. Uri. *Getting to Yes: Negotiating Agreement Without Giving In.* Boston: Houghton Mifflin, 1981.

Gamson, W. A. "A Theory of Coalition Formation." *American Sociological Review* 26 (1961): 372–382.

Garelik, Michael. "The Power Is in the People." *ABA Banking Journal* 79 (May 1987): 19–21.

Gersick, Connie J. G. "Time and Transition in Work Teams: Toward a New Model of Group Development." *Academy of Management Journal* 31 (March 1988): 9–41.

Gist, Marilyn E., Edwin A. Locke, and M. Susan Taylor. "Organizational Behavior: Group Structure, Process, and Effectiveness." *Journal of Management* 13 (Summer 1987): 237–257.

Gobor, Beverly. "Quality Circles: The Second Generation." *Training: The Magazine of Human Resources Development* 23 (December 1986): 54–60.

Gouldner, A. W. "Cosmopolitans and Locals: Toward an Analysis of Latent Social Roles." *Administrative Science Quarterly* 2 (1958): 290.

Hart, S., M. Boroush, G. Enk, and W. Hornick. "Managing Complexity Through Consensus Mapping: Technology for the Structuring of Group Decisions." *Academy of Management Review* 10 (1985): 587–600.

Henderson, Monika, and Michael Argyle. "The Informal Rules of Working Relationships." *Journal of Occupational Behavior* 7 (October 1986): 259–275.

Hodge, John. "Getting Along with the Informal Leader." *Supervisory Management* 25 (October 1980): 41–43.

Hunt, Bradley D., and Judith F. Vogt. "What Really Goes Wrong with Participative Work Groups?" *Training & Development Journal* 42 (May 1988): 96–100.

Hyde, W. D. "How Small Groups Can Solve Problems and Reduce Costs." *Industrial Engineering* 18 (December 1986): 42–47.

Jackson, S. E. "Participation in Decision Making as a Strategy for Reducing Job-Related Stress." *Journal of Applied Psychology* 68 (1983): 3–19.

Jewell, L. N., and H. J. Reitz. *Group Effectiveness in Organizations.* Glenview, Ill.: Scott, Foresman, 1981.

Katz, R., and M. L. Tushman. "A Longitudinal Study of the Effects of Boundary Spanning Supervision on Turnover and Promotion in Research and Development." *Academy of Management Journal* 26 (1983): 437–456.

Keller, Robert T. "Cross-Cultural Influences on Work and Nonwork Contributors to Quality of Life." *Group & Organization Studies* 12 (September 1987): 304–318.

Kinlaw, Dennis C., and Donna R. Christensen. "Management Education: The Wheat and the Chaff." *Training: The Magazine of Human Resources Development* 23 (December 1986): 45–50.

Lieberman, S. "The Effects of Changes in Roles on the Attitudes of Role Occupants." *Human Relations* 9 (1956): 385–417.

Lynch, Robert. "The Shoot Out Among Nonteam Players." *Management Solutions* 32 (May 1987): 5–12.

McCann, J. E., and D. L. Ferry. "An Approach for Assessing and Managing Inter-Unit Interdependence." *Academy of Management Review* 4 (1979): 113–119.

Miljus, Robert C. "Key Ingredients in Cooperative Initiatives." *Personnel* 63 (April 1986): 69–73.

Mintzberg, H. *The Structuring of Organizations.* Englewood Cliffs, N.J.: Prentice-Hall, 1978.

Napier, R. W., and M. K. Gershenfeld. *Groups: Theory and Experience.* 2e ed. Boston: Houghton Mifflin, 1981.

———. *Making Groups Work: A Guide for Group Leaders.* Boston: Houghton Mifflin, 1983.

Nicholson, P. J., Jr., and S. C. Goh. "The Relationship of Organization Structure and Interpersonal Attitudes to Role Conflict and Ambiguity in Different Work Environments." *Academy of Management Journal* (March 1983): 148.

Ono, Karou, and James H. Davis. "Individual Judgement and Group Interaction: A Variable Perspective Approach." *Organizational Behavior & Human Decision Processes* 11 (April 1988): 211–232.

Pearce, J. A., III, and A. S. De Nisi. "Attribution Theory and Strategic Decision-Making: An Application to Coalition Formation." *Academy of Management Journal* 26 (1983): 119–128.

Quinn, R. E. "Coping with Cupid: The Formation, Impact, and Management of Romantic Relationships in Organizations." *Administrative Science Quarterly* 22 (March 1980): 57–71.

Sashkin, M. "Participative Management Is an Ethical Imperative." *Organizational Dynamics* 12 (Spring 1984): 4–22.

Smith, Kenwyn K., and David N. Berg. "A Paradoxical Conception of Group Dynamics." *Human Relations* 10 (October 1987): 633–657.

Srivastva, Suresh, and Frank J. Barrett. "The Transforming Nature of Metaphors in Group Development: A Study in Group Theory." *Human Relations* 11 (January 1988): 31–63.

Thibaut, J. W., and H. H. Kelley. *The Social Psychology of Groups.* New York: John Wiley & Sons, 1959.

Thompson, J. D. *Organizations in Action.* New York: McGraw-Hill, 1967.

Tushman, M. L., and T. J. Scanlan. "Characteristics and External Orientations of Boundary Spanning Individuals." *Academy of Management Journal* 24 (1981): 83–98.

Vroom, V. H., and P. Yetton. *Leadership and Decision-Making.* Pittsburgh, Pa.: University of Pittsburgh Press, 1973.

Wanous, J. P. *Organizational Entry: Recruitment, Selection, and Socialization of Newcomers.* Reading, Mass.: Addison-Wesley, 1980.

Wanous, J. P., A. E. Reichers, and S. D. Malik. "Organizational Socialization and Group Development: Toward an Intergrative Perspective." *Academy of Management Review* 9 (1984): 670–683.

Wultman, Kenneth E. "Behavior Modeling for Results." *Training & Development Journal* 10 (December 1986): 60.

Yetton, P. W., and P. C. Bottger. "Individual versus Group Problem Solving: An Empirical Test of a Best-Member Strategy." *Organizational Behavior and Human Performance* 29 (1982): 307–321.

Zaleznik, A., C. R. Christensen, and F. J. Roethlisberger. *The Motivation, Productivity, and Satisfaction of Workers.* Boston: Harvard University Graduate School of Business, Division of Research, 1958.

CHAPTER 18

Leadership

Learning Objectives

After completing this chapter students should be able to

1. Define leadership and state the importance of good leadership in an organization.
2. Describe the trait approach to the study of leadership.
3. Identify and describe the major behavioral theories that focus on the search for an appropriate style.
4. Describe major situational leadership theories.
5. Explain the attributional model and describe substitutes for leadership.

IN THE CORPORATE turnaround story of the century, the mammoth Wickes Companies, a marketer of building products, went from a $258 million loss in 1982 to a modest profit in the 1983–1984 fiscal year. By 1987 Wickes was not only solidly in the black but had hit the corporate-acquisition trail. Wickes paid over $1 billion for a Gulf + Western Corporation division and made millions in attempts to take over other companies. Most authorities give the credit to one man, Sanford Sigoloff. When Sigoloff took over the chairmanship of Wickes in 1982, the company had lost more than $400 million in just fifteen months. Money was flowing out, shelves and showrooms in thousands of Wickes stores were bare or stocked with inferior goods, and customers were staying away in droves.

Sanford Sigoloff—"Flash Gordon" or "Ming the Merciless," depending on whom you ask—had earned his reputation turning around disabled companies. In Wickes, the fifty-two-year-old former nuclear physicist faced his greatest challenge ever. He accepted what he called "a very, very tough challenge" because "I couldn't resist it. How many times in a lifetime do you get the opportunity to put your stamp on a business of this magnitude in the American system?" The Sigoloff stamp means total commitment throughout the organization. Sigoloff expects fourteen-hour days out of his corporate staff. Almost the entire financial department at Wickes quit when he told them this. Many other employees left involuntarily as he fired nearly a quarter of Wickes's 40,000-member work force. The managers who chose, and were permitted to remain with, Wickes were supplemented with Sigoloff lieutenants who had worked with him in the past.

Sigoloff practiced a team approach to problem solving. He demanded and got not only personal loyalty from top executives, but also their help in making difficult decisions. The frequent trips he and his senior managers made to far-flung stores and offices served to encourage and inform workers and managers at every level. Wickes employees who came to know Sigoloff during the turnaround recall his snappy stride, his neat, trim appearance, his ready smile, and his reputation for personal integrity.

Early in his turnaround effort at Wickes, Sigoloff chose to file for protection under Chapter 11 of the U.S. Bankruptcy Code. This staved off creditors and gave him time to make necessary changes. But it also discouraged employees and customers, many of whom knew that most companies never successfully emerge from Chapter 11. Sigoloff had to convince all of them that Wickes would emerge. "We developed an efficient nomenclature," explains Sigoloff, "a way for top management to communicate with middle management and with creditors." The "efficient nomenclature" involved the use of charts, graphs, and tables to simplify presentations inside and outside the organization.

In conjunction with his efforts inside the company to refurbish stores and restore optimism, Sigoloff launched a national TV ad campaign, with the serious-looking chairman in front of the camera personally guaranteeing Wickes's products and services. "There are a lot of tough decisions that have to be made to ensure this company's survival," Sigoloff says. "It isn't a game for the fainthearted."[1]

Sigoloff is recognized worldwide as an effective leader. Because of his leadership, Wickes Companies and two other companies he previously saved continue in operation, and thousands of jobs have been saved. Many who know Sigoloff say he has "charisma," a characteristic that seems to have marked many other well-known leaders. Others comment on his apparent energy and enthusiasm, his honesty, his ready smile, or his neat appearance. ■

W HAT DOES IT TAKE to be a good leader, and what is the most effective leadership style? These questions have perplexed and challenged managers for generations. Literally thousands of research studies concerning leadership have been conducted to provide greater insight into these questions. Such studies of leaders and the leadership process have not yielded any set of traits or qualities that are consistently related to effective leadership. The only conclusion we can draw from these studies is that there is *no one* most effective leadership style. What we do know is that effective leadership is absolutely essential to the survival and overall growth of every organization.

In this chapter, we first define leadership and examine the relationship between leadership and management. Then we examine the nature of effective leadership and discuss five perspectives that have been used to define effective leadership—(1) trait, (2) behavioral, (3) situational, (4) attributional, and (5) substitutes for leadership. We conclude the chapter by examining the relationship between leadership and management.

■■■ LEADERSHIP DEFINED

A variety of definitions of leadership exist:

1. Leadership is "the behavior of an individual when he (or she) is directing the activities of a group toward a shared goal."[2]
2. Leadership is "interpersonal influence, exercised in a situation, and directed, through the communication process, toward the attainment of a specified goal or goals."[3]
3. Leadership is "the initiation and maintenance of structure in expectation and interaction."[4]
4. Leadership is "an interaction between persons in which one presents information of a sort and in such a manner that the other becomes convinced that his (or her) outcomes (benefits/costs ratio) will be improved if he (or she) behaves in the manner suggested or desired."[5]
5. Leadership is "the influential increment over and above mechanical compliance with the routine directives of the organization."[6]

Leadership
The influencing of others to do what the leader wants them to do.

In this context, **leadership** is defined as influencing others to do what the leader wants them to do. Highly regarded companies that have been around for a long time usually have a history of excellent leadership. For example, for seventy-five years IBM has had one extraordinary boss after another. The leadership of such notables as founder Thomas J. Watson, his son Thomas, Jr., followed by T. Vincent Learson, Frank Cary, and then John Opel, has built and

F I G U R E 18.1 ■■■ Four Basic Leadership Styles and Their Relation to Types of Workers

Autocratic	Participative	Democratic	Laissez-Faire
Leader tells workers what to do.	Leader allows and expects worker participation.	Leader seeks majority rule from workers.	Leader lets group members make all decisions.
McGregor's Theory X Workers	McGregor's Theory Y Workers		Expert-Specialist Workers

Autocratic leader
A person who tells subordinates what to do, and expects to be obeyed without question.

Participative leader
A person who involves subordinates in decision making but may retain the final authority.

Democratic leader
A person who tries to do what the majority of subordinates desire.

Laissez-faire leader
A person who is uninvolved in the work of the unit.

protected IBM's position as number one in the computer business.[7] Four basic leadership styles have been identified: autocratic, participative, democratic, and laissez-faire (see Figure 18.1). An **autocratic leader** is a person who tells subordinates what to do, and expects to be obeyed without question. Real estate mogul Donald Trump appears to singularly determine his destiny and then direct others to carry out his mandates. SCI president Eugene Sapp is so autocratic that he actually inspects travel requests and approves all personnel changes. This style is typical of a person who accepts McGregor's Theory X assumptions, described in Chapter 15. A **participative leader** is a person who involves subordinates in decision making but may retain the final authority. Sam Walton, the flamboyant founder of Wal-Mart Stores, has established a management team that keeps employees closely informed about company plans and practices and includes them in corporate decision making.[8] A **democratic leader** is a person who tries to do what the majority of subordinates desire. Participative and democratic leaders tend to be those who make Theory Y assumptions. Democratic leaders are becoming more and more important as the team approach expands. Russell A. Nagel, general manager of Westinghouse Furniture Systems, appears to be a democratic leader. He has supported the existence of an elaborate system of committees and ad hoc task forces to discuss issues ranging from business strategy to constant redesign of work areas for product innovation. This high degree of worker participation has produced a 74-percent increase in productivity from 1983 to 1986.[9] The **laissez-faire leader** is a person who is uninvolved in the work of the unit. It is difficult to defend this leadership style, unless the leader is a supervising expert and a well-motivated specialist, such as a scientist. In fact, practically every leader who has attained recognition for effectiveness—from political leader Mahatma Gandhi in India to business leader Sanford Sigoloff at Wickes—has done so by being deeply involved and active.

■■ LEADERSHIP VERSUS MANAGEMENT

In Chapter 1 *management* was defined as the process of getting things done through the efforts of other people. Obviously, the definitions of leadership and management overlap. Managers get all sorts of things done through the efforts of

Perspectives for Defining
Effective Leadership

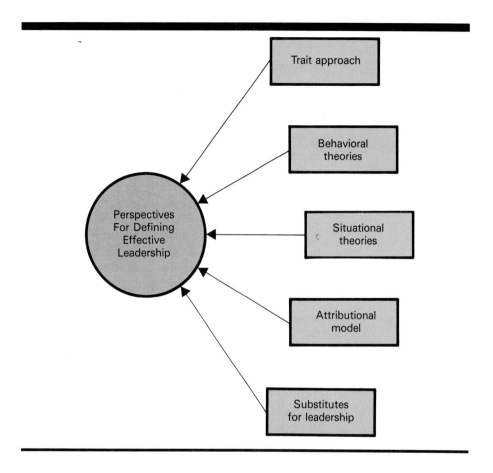

other people, so they must lead. The main distinction between the two terms is
one of focus. *Leadership* focuses on human interactions, "influencing others."
Management is more concerned with procedure and results, "the process of
getting things done." Also, *management* suggests more formality. *Manager* often
refers to a position in an organization. On the other hand, a *leader* may have no
formal title at all and rely on personal traits and style to influence followers.

There are several perspectives for defining effective leadership. As may be
seen in Figure 18.2, they include the trait approach, behavioral theories, situational
theories, the attributional model, and substitutes for leadership.

■■ THE TRAIT APPROACH TO LEADERSHIP

**Trait approach to
leadership**
The evaluation and
selection of leaders based
on their physical, mental,
and psychological
characteristics.

The leader has always occupied a strong and central role in traditional management
theory. Most of the early research on leadership attempted (1) to compare the
traits of people who become leaders with those who remain followers and (2) to
identify characteristics and traits possessed by effective leaders. The **trait
approach to leadership** is the evaluation and selection of leaders based on their
physical, mental, and psychological characteristics. Research studies comparing

BUSINESS
BRIEFS

PINNACLE

A Born Leader

LEADERSHIP IS DEFINED as influencing others to do what the leader wants them to do. Highly regarded companies usually have a history of excellent leadership. Six of the most commonly accepted leadership traits are supervisory ability, need for occupational achievement, intelligence, decisiveness, self-assurance, and initiative. One individual who has such leadership traits, and whose effectiveness as a leader is enviable, is Mr. Richard Snyder, Chairman of Simon & Schuster. He is the man in charge of Gulf + Western's publishing empire. Snyder's tough business instincts are legend, critics respect him, and *Fortune Magazine* called him one of America's ten toughest bosses. Even though this individual was lucky to get a "C" average at Tufts University, and spent study time playing the horses, he became a respected, effective leader. He started his quest for greatness with $50, encouragement from his father, and a meager job at Doubleday. Snyder was described by his father as an individual with the "better stuff"—evidently the stuff of which leaders are made. Mr. Richard Snyder, Chairman of Simon & Schuster, shares these and other views with CNN correspondent, Tom Cassidy.

the traits of leaders and nonleaders have found that leaders tend to be somewhat taller, more outgoing, more self-confident, and more intelligent than nonleaders. Even within an organization, leaders often have far different beliefs, depending in part on the type of work they supervise.[10] But a specific combination of traits has not been found that can differentiate leaders or potential leaders from followers. Clearly it is difficult to identify a leader from only an initial impression.

Considerable research has been conducted to compare the traits of effective and ineffective leaders. Aggressiveness, ambition, decisiveness, dominance, initiative, intelligence, physical characteristics (looks, height, and weight), self-assurance, and other traits were studied to determine if they were related to effective leadership. The major question was, "Could such traits differentiate effective from ineffective leaders?" Perhaps the underlying assumption of some trait research has been that leaders are born, not made, that is, the "Great Man" theory. Although research has demonstrated that this is not the case, some people still believe there are certain inborn or acquired traits that make a person a good leader. Research has clearly not shown that *physical traits* can distinguish effective from ineffective leaders.

The trait approach to the study of leadership is not dead, however. Edwin Ghiselli has conducted research in an effort to identify personality and motivational traits related to effective leadership.[11] Ghiselli identified thirteen trait factors. The six most significant traits are defined as follows:

1. *Supervisory ability.* The performance of the basic functions of management, including planning, organizing, influencing, and controlling the work of others.
2. *Need for occupational achievement.* The seeking of responsibility and the desire for success.

3. *Intelligence.* Creative and verbal ability, including judgment, reasoning, and thinking capacity.
4. *Decisiveness.* Ability to make decisions and solve problems capably and competently.
5. *Self-assurance.* Extent to which the individual views himself or herself as capable of coping with problems.
6. *Initiative.* Ability to act independently and develop courses of action not readily apparent to other people. Self-starter—able to find new or innovative ways of doing things.

Warren Bennis offers the following protocol for effective leadership:

1. Leaders must develop the vision and strength to call the shots.
2. The leader must be a "conceptualist" (not just someone to tinker with the "nuts and bolts").
3. The leader must have a sense of continuity and significance in order . . . to see the present in the past and the future.
4. Leaders must get their heads above the grass and risk the possibility, familiar to any rooster, of getting hit by a rock.
5. The leader must get at the truth and learn how to filter the unwieldy flow of information into coherent patterns.
6. The leader must be a social architect who studies and shapes what is called "the culture of work."
7. To lead others, leaders must first know themselves.[12]

Individuals can cultivate these qualities as the basis for building their leadership effectiveness.

A recent revival of trait theory emphasizes the importance of a leader's charisma to effective leadership. Robert House has proposed a theory of charismatic leadership. House's theory suggests that such leaders employ four personal characteristics—dominance, self-confidence, a need for influence, and conviction of moral righteousness—to increase their effectiveness.[13]

Transformational leader
A person who has the ability to take an organization through a major strategic change such as revitalization.

A transformational leader has these and other characteristics. Thus, a **transformational leader** is a person who has the ability to take an organization through a major strategic change such as revitalization. Such leaders have the ability to make necessary changes in the organization's mission, structure, and human resource management. Using charisma to inspire followers, this type of leader talks to followers about how essential their performance is, how confident the leader is in the followers, how exceptional the followers are, and how the leader expects the group's performance to break records.[14]

Basically, this type of leader attempts to motivate followers (primarily subordinates or peers) to perform better. Recall our discussion of motivation in Chapter 15. It was noted that individuals work to satisfy certain needs and achieve desired outcomes. A boss who is a transformational leader has three ways to motivate subordinates to do better than they expected. The leader (1) raises their consciousness about the importance of certain outcomes, such as high productivity or efficiency, (2) shows the value of workers' concentrating on their work team's good rather than on their personal interest, and (3) raises the workers' need levels so that they value challenges, responsibility, and growth.[15]

To be effective, a leader must take a developmental orientation toward his or her followers—by elevating their potential, setting examples, assigning tasks on

Leadership is influencing others to do what the leader wants them to do. (COMSTOCK, Inc.)

an individual basis, increasing subordinate responsibilities, delegating challenging work, serving as a role model, keeping subordinates informed, providing intellectual stimulation, seeking ways of acting, and being more proactive.[16]

In spite of the contributions of trait researchers, the trait approach to the study of leadership effectiveness has left many questions unanswered. This has led to a continuing search for an appropriate leadership style. A major limitation of trait theory is that traits associated with leadership in one situation do not predict leadership in another.[17]

████ BEHAVIORAL LEADERSHIP THEORIES

Dissatisfaction with the trait approach has caused most leadership researchers to focus attention on how leaders should behave, as opposed to the traits or characteristics they should possess. The result has been several theories and studies on the effectiveness of leader styles and behaviors. These are discussed below.

University of Iowa Studies

In 1938, the first of several studies examining the impact of leadership style was conducted at the University of Iowa.[18] Researchers Kurt Lewin, Ronald Lippitt, and Ralph White conducted a controlled experiment in which they observed the impact of three separate leadership styles—autocratic, democratic, and laissez-faire—on the behavior of adolescent boys.

The basic difference in the three styles was the location of the decision-making function in the group. Authoritarian leaders made decisions for their groups and communicated those decisions to group members. Democratic leaders allowed the group to make decisions that would affect their activities; the leader merely helped the group arrive at a decision point. Laissez-faire leaders limited their interaction with group members to answering questions and providing materials when requested. Group members made decisions independent of this virtual nonleader and each other.

Data was gathered on the behavioral reactions of group members to each of the three leadership styles during two separate experiments. The implications of this research were that (1) group members preferred democratic over autocratic leaders and (2) incidents of intragroup hostility were significantly higher in autocratic and laissez-faire groups than in democratic groups. Additionally, the productivity of the groups with democratic leaders was higher than either the autocratic or laissez-faire groups.

Findings of the Iowa studies generally supported the effectiveness of a democratic leadership style and no doubt contributed further to the human relations movement. However, the sample used (twenty adolescent boys), along with the narrow scope of the research, severely limited the application of the findings beyond the sample studied. Nevertheless, the Iowa Leadership Studies ushered in an era in which leadership behaviors rather than traits received increased research attention.

Ohio State Leadership Studies

Initiating structure
The extent to which leaders establish goals and structure their roles and the roles of subordinates toward the attainment of the goals.

Consideration
The extent to which leaders have relationships with subordinates characterized by mutual trust, respect, and consideration of employees' ideas and feelings.

Beginning in 1945, researchers in the Bureau of Business Research at Ohio State University made a series of in-depth studies of the behavior of leaders in a wide variety of organizations. The key concern of the Ohio State leadership studies was the leader's behavior in directing the efforts of others toward group goals. After a considerable number of studies had been completed, two separate and distinct dimensions of leader behavior were identified: **initiating structure**—the extent to which leaders establish goal and structure their roles and the roles of subordinates toward the attainment of the goals, and **consideration**—the extent to which leaders have relationships with subordinates characterized by mutual trust, respect, and consideration of employees' ideas and feelings.

As illustrated in Figure 18.3, four basic leadership styles, which represent different combinations of the two dimensions of leadership behavior, emerged from the Ohio State studies. A manager can be high in both consideration and initiating structure, low in both, or high in one and low in the other. Although the Ohio State model describes two important elements of leadership behavior, it does not suggest the *one* most effective combination that will meet the needs of all situations. Rather, the combination, or appropriate level, of initiating structure and consideration is determined by the demands of the situation.

Among the many situational variables that must be related to leadership behavior are the following:

FIGURE 18.3 ■
Ohio State Leadership
Model

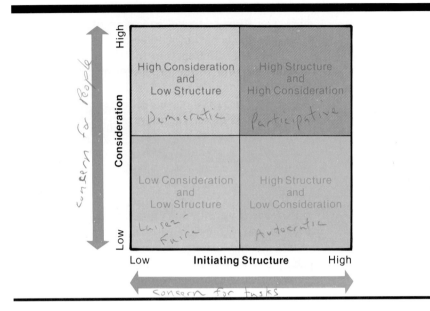

- Expectations of the led
- Degree of task structuring imposed by technology
- Pressures of schedules and time
- Degree of influence of the leader outside of the group
- Congruency of style with that of one's superior
- Degrees of interpersonal contact possible between leader and the led

The following observations can be made with regard to the type of leadership styles proposed in the Ohio State model:

- If a group expects and wants authoritarian leadership behavior, it is more likely to be satisfied with that type of leadership.
- If group members have less authoritarian expectations, a leader who strongly emphasizes initiating structure will be resented.
- If the work situation is highly structured by technology and the pressures of time, the supervisor who is high in consideration is more likely to meet with success, as measured by absenteeism, turnover, and grievances.
- If task structuring precludes individual and group self-actualization, it will be useless to look for motivation from this source.
- When subordinates have little contact with their supervisor, they tend to prefer a more autocratic style.
- If employees must work and interact continuously, they usually want the superior to be high in consideration.

University of Michigan Studies

A series of leadership studies at the University of Michigan, which looked at managers with an employee orientation and a production orientation, yielded results similar to those of the Ohio State studies.[19] In the Michigan studies, differences in high-productivity and low-productivity work groups were related to differences in supervisors. It was found that highly productive supervisors spent more time planning departmental work and supervising their employees and less time working alongside and performing the same task performance; and they tended to be employee-oriented.[20]

Managerial Grid®
A two-dimensional matrix developed by Robert Blake and Jane Mouton that shows concern for people on the vertical axis and concern for production on the horizontal axis.

Blake and Mouton's Managerial Grid®

One of the most widely known leadership theories is that based on the Managerial Grid.[21] The **Managerial Grid®** is a two-dimensional matrix developed by Robert Blake and Jane Mouton that shows concern for people on the vertical axis and concern for production on the horizontal axis. The Managerial Grid is illustrated in Figure 18.4. The two dimensions of the 9 × 9-grid are labeled "concern for

FIGURE 18.4 ■
The Managerial Grid®

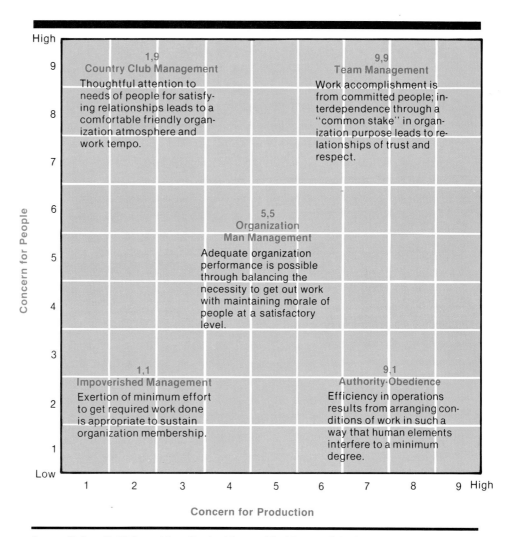

Source: Robert R. Blake and Jane Srygley Mouton, *The Managerial Grid III: The Key to Leadership Excellence* (Houston: Gulf Publishing Company, 1985), p. 12. © 1985. Used with permission.

people" and "concern for production." A score of 1 indicates a low concern, and a score of 9 shows a high concern. The grid depicts five major leadership styles, each of which represents a degree of concern for "people" and "production."

- **1,1** *Impoverished Management.* The manager has little concern for either people or production.
- **9,1** *Authority-Obedience.* The manager stresses operating efficiently through controls in situations where human elements cannot interfere.
- **1,9** *Country Club Management.* The manager is thoughtful, comfortable, and friendly, and has little concern for output.
- **5,5** *Organization Man Management.* The manager attempts to balance and trade off concern for work in exchange for a satisfactory level of morale—a compromiser.
- **9,9** *Team Management.* The manager seeks high output through committed people, achieved through mutual trust, respect, and a realization of interdependence.[22]

According to Blake and Mouton, the first four styles are not the most effective. They say that the 9,9 position of maximum concern for both output and people, the team management approach, is the leadership style that will most effectively result in improved performance, lower employee turnover and absenteeism, and greater employee satisfaction. Job enrichment and subordinate participation in managerial decision making contribute to this 9,9 situation, where both the organization and its members are accorded maximum and equal concern. The Managerial Grid concept has been introduced to many managers throughout the world since its development in the early 1960s and has influenced the management philosophies and practices of many of them. Blake and Mouton have conducted Grid training seminars around the world.

■ SITUATIONAL LEADERSHIP THEORIES

Contingency or situational models assert that no single way of behaving works in *all* situations. Rather, appropriate behavior depends on the circumstances at a given time. The development of contingency theories was a response to the failure of earlier, more universalist theories to explain or predict effective behavior.

House's Path-Goal Theory of Leadership

Path-goal theory
The proposition that managers can facilitate job performance by showing employees how their performance directly affects their receiving desired rewards.

Robert House developed what he termed the path-goal theory of leadership.[23] This approach to leadership is closely related to the expectancy theory of motivation discussed in Chapter 15. **Path-goal theory** is the proposition that managers can facilitate job performance by showing employees how their performance directly affects their receiving desired rewards. In other words, a manager's behavior causes or contributes to employee satisfaction and acceptance of the manager if it increases employees' goal attainment. According to the path-goal approach, effective job performance results if the manager clearly defines the job, provides training for the employee, assists the employee in performing the job effectively, and rewards the employee for effective performance.

ETHICAL DILEMMA

THE MILLING COMPANY you run has developed a special milling process that yields a wheat flour which, when used for bread, provides a lighter, more uniform texture than conventionally milled wheat flour. Unfortunately, the process gives off more dust than the emissions control equipment presently installed can handle and still maintain emissions within legal limits. Due to lack of availability, your company will be unable to install new emissions control equipment for at least two years; however, if it waits that long to introduce the new process, its competitors would very likely beat it to the market. You can process the new type of flour during the third shift, which runs from 10 P.M. to 6 A.M., or you can shut down the unit. By using the special milling process during the third shift, you can introduce the new type of flour, and the excess pollution, which is released after dark, will not be detected. By the time demand becomes great enough to utilize a second shift, new emissions control equipment should be available.

What would you do?

According to House, effective leadership facilitates the accomplishment of a particular goal by clarifying the path to that goal in the subordinates' minds. The following four distinct leadership behaviors are associated with the path-goal approach:

- *Directive.* The manager tells the subordinate what to do, and when to do it (no employee participation in decision making).
- *Supportive.* The manager is friendly with, and shows interest in, employees.
- *Participative.* The manager seeks suggestions and involves employees in decision making.
- *Achievement oriented.* The manager establishes challenging goals and demonstrates confidence in employees in achieving these goals.

Following the path-goal theory, a manager may use all four of the behaviors for four different situations. For instance, a manager may use directive behavior when supervising an inexperienced employee and supportive behavior when supervising a well-trained, experienced worker aware of the goals to be attained.

In addition to utilizing the most appropriate leadership style, managers need to consider two groups of contingency factors that influence the nature of the leadership situation. *Subordinate characteristics,* the first group, include such factors as authoritarianism of the subordinate, locus of control, and ability. The second group are the *environmental factors,* which include the nature of the task, the formal authority system, and the primary work group. Subordinate characteristics influence job satisfaction and the subordinates' acceptance of the leader. Environmental factors affect the motivational behavior of the subordinate. An appropriate leadership style and a proper accounting of the two groups of contingency factors can increase employee motivation and job satisfaction by clarifying performance goals and the path to achieving those goals.[24]

F I G U R E 18.5 ■ Continuum of Leadership Behavior

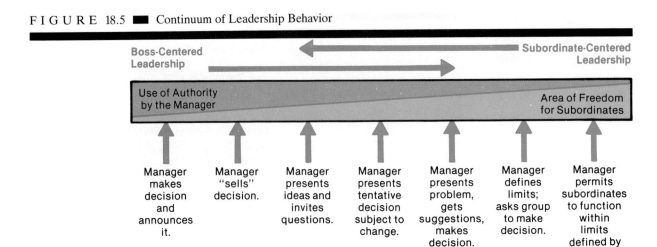

Tannenbaum and Schmidt's Leadership Continuum

Leadership continuum
The graphical representation developed by Robert Tannenbaum and Warren H. Schmidt showing the trade-off between a manager's use of authority and the freedom that subordinates experience as leadership style varies from boss centered to subordinate centered.

The **leadership continuum** is the graphical representation developed by Robert Tannenbaum and Warren H. Schmidt showing the trade-off between a manager's use of authority and the freedom that subordinates experience as leadership style varies from boss centered to subordinate centered. Tannenbaum and Schmidt described a series of factors that they thought influenced a manager's selection of the most appropriate leadership style. Their approach advocated a continuum of leadership behavior supporting the notion that choosing an effective leadership style depends on the demands of the situation. As illustrated in Figure 18.5, leadership behavior ranges from boss centered to subordinate centered, which is similar in concept to initiating structure and consideration. Tannenbaum and Schmidt emphasized that a manager should give careful consideration to the following factors before selecting a leadership style:

- *Characteristics of the manager.* Background, education, experience, values, knowledge, goals, and expectations.
- *Characteristics of the employees.* Background, education, experience, knowledge, goals, values, and expectations.
- *Requirements of the situation.* Size, complexity, goals, structure, and climate of the organization, as well as the impact of technology, time pressure, and nature of the work.

According to the Tannenbaum and Schmidt leadership continuum, a manager may engage in a more participative leadership style when subordinates

- Seek independence and freedom of action
- Are well educated and experienced in performing the jobs
- Seek responsibility for decision making
- Expect a participative style of leadership
- Understand and are committed to the goals of the organization

According to Tannenbaum and Schmidt, a manager must be able to diagnose existing situations and then choose a leadership style that will improve his or her chances for effectiveness. (COMSTOCK, Inc.)

If the above conditions do not exist, managers may need to adopt a more autocratic, or boss-centered, leadership style. Thus, in essence, managers must be able to diagnose the situations confronting them and then attempt to choose a leadership style that will improve their chances for effectiveness. The most effective leaders are neither task centered nor people centered; rather, they are flexible enough to select a leadership style that fits their needs as well as the needs of their subordinates and the situation.

When Sigoloff first took over at Wickes, the situation demanded that his leadership style be boss centered. The company was failing, and no one would have expected him to give subordinates a free rein. Also, his recognized knowledge of what is needed to save a failing company marked him as the one who should determine what to do. Later, as he learned the capabilities of subordinates and as they learned from him, he could relinquish some authority.

Fiedler's Contingency Theory

Fred Fiedler and his colleagues at the University of Illinois developed the first leadership theory explicitly called a contingency model. He stated that the most effective leadership style depends on the nature of the situation.[25] According to Fiedler, a leader can only be effective if that individual's personality style is appropriately matched to a given set of situational variables. Personality style is measured by the Least-Preferred Coworker Scale.

THE LEAST-PREFERRED COWORKER SCALE

Fiedler developed a Least-Preferred Coworker Scale (LPC) to measure the two basic styles he identified: (1) task-oriented, or controlling, active, structuring leadership, and (2) relationship-oriented, or permissive, passive, considerate leadership. Research has suggested that low-LPC leaders emphasize completing tasks successfully, even at the expense of interpersonal relationships, gaining self-esteem through task completion, and valuing job performance. High-LPC leaders emphasize good interpersonal relationships, are more considerate, derive major satisfaction from relationships with others, and are not influenced by success or task accomplishment.[26] Fiedler argued that a correlation exists between high-versus low-LPC score and type of leadership. Low LPC reflects task-oriented leadership, because the leader cannot overlook the negative traits of a follower that likely infringe on task accomplishment. High LPC reflects relationship-oriented leadership, because the leader can overlook negative traits and retain a strong interpersonal relationship regardless of its effect on task accomplishment.

Fiedler argued that changing an individual's leadership style is quite difficult. He thus proposed that organizations "engineer the job to fit the manager."[27] Fiedler identified three features of any circumstances that determine whether high-LPC (relationship-oriented) or low-LPC (task-oriented) managers are more likely to be effective:

1. *Leader-member relations.* The extent to which the group trusts and respects the leader and will follow the leader's directions; that is, has *good* leader-member relations. A leader who has subordinates who willingly follow instructions, set goals, or take initiative has good leader-member relations; a leader who has difficulty getting cooperation from workers does not.

2. *Task structure.* The degree to which the task is clearly specified and defined or *structured,* as opposed to ambiguous or unstructured. Putting a wheel assembly on an automobile or disbursing cash in a bank are structured tasks; determining the contents of an investment portfolio or selecting a new chief operating officer are unstructured tasks.

3. *Position power.* The extent to which the leader has official power, or the potential or actual ability to influence others in a desired direction due to the position held in the organization. A manager, chief executive officer, or other supervisor has position power; a staff member or nonmanagerial employee does not.[28]

Fiedler considered leader-member relations, followed by task structure and then position power, to have the greatest weight in determining effective leadership style. Table 18.1 shows the style recommended for each combination of these three situational factors. The recommendations are based on the degree of control or influence leaders can exert in their leadership position. In general, high-control situations (I, II, and III) call for task-oriented leadership because they allow the leader to take charge. The President of the United States typically faces such a situation; he can use task-oriented leadership because, among other reasons, he has to spend relatively little time developing relationships with his subordinates. A low-control situation (VIII) also calls for task-oriented leadership because it requires the leader to take charge. In a task force of peers with the responsibility for determining their company's strategic plan, when the appointed leader has a

30 ∧ 8
3 0 ∧ !
3² = 8 octants

TABLE 18.1 ■ Fiedler's Model of Effective Leadership

	Description of the Situation			Effective Leadership Style
	Leader-Member Relations	Task Structure	Power Position	
I	Good	Structured	Strong	Task-oriented
II	Good	Structured	Weak	Task-oriented
III	Good	Unstructured	Strong	Task-oriented
IV	Good	Unstructured	Weak	Relations-oriented
V	Poor	Structured	Strong	Relations-oriented
VI	Poor	Structured	Weak	Relations-oriented
VII	Poor	Unstructured	Strong	Either
VIII	Poor	Unstructured	Weak	Task-oriented

Source: Adapted from F. E. Fiedler, *A Theory of Leadership Effectiveness* (New York: McGraw-Hill, 1967), p. 37. Reprinted with permission of the author.

Know 3 situational variables

2 possible classes of each Good/Poor

high control or low control

history of poor relationships with the rest of the task force, task-oriented leadership allows the manager to focus the group's activities, and the leader has nothing to lose by this stance. Moderate control situations (IV, V, VI, and VII), in contrast, call for relationship-oriented leadership because the situations challenge leaders to get the cooperation of their subordinates.[29] If the task force leader has good relations with peers, then relations-oriented leadership is more appropriate. One research study has suggested that middle-LPC leaders—those receiving scores in the middle 25 percent of the distribution—may be more effective in all leadership situations because of their greater flexibility.[30]

Although Fiedler and Martin Chemers cite extensive research to support the theory, critics suggest that it may be too methodology-bound and limiting in the number of situational variables it incorporates.[31] More specifically, critics question the reliability of the LPC and the quality of measurement of the situational components.[32] These extend to more general doubts about such aspects as the validity of a theory based on a measurement such as the LPC and the ability of Fiedler's theory to predict effective leadership. Although questions about extensive reliance on the LPC detract from the power of Fiedler's theory, the overall approach offers significant insights for evaluating leadership effectiveness.

Vroom and Yetton's Normative Theory

Victor Vroom and Philip Yetton introduced a normative theory of leadership and decision making.[33] It focuses on decision making by managers with a defined group of subordinates and consists of a procedure for determining the extent to which leaders should involve subordinates in the process. In any decision-making situation, the manager has some freedom to determine the solution, the impact of which will affect one or more of the subordinates. According to this theory, the manager can choose one of the five basic processes for involving subordinates

TABLE 18.2 ■ Decision-Making Processes

For Individual Problems	For Group Problems
AI You solve the problem or make the decision yourself, using information available to you at that time.	**AI** You solve the problem or make the decision yourself, using information available to you at that time. *autocratic*
AII You obtain any necessary information from the subordinate, then decide on the solution to the problem yourself. You may or may not tell the subordinate what the problem is, in getting the information from him. The role played by your subordinate in making the decision is clearly one of providing specific information which you request, rather than generating or evaluating alternative solutions. *Participative*	**AII** You obtain any necessary information from subordinates, then decide on the solution to the problem yourself. You may or may not tell subordinates what the problem is, in getting the information from them. The role played by your subordinates in making the decision is clearly one of providing specific information which you request, rather than generating or evaluating solutions.
CI You share the problem with the relevant subordinate, getting his ideas and suggestions. Then *you* make the decision. This decision may or may not reflect your subordinate's influence.	**CI** You share the problem with the relevant subordinates individually, getting their ideas and suggestions without bringing them together as a group. Then *you* make the decision. This decision may or may not reflect your subordinates' influence.
GI You share the problem with one of your subordinates and together you analyze the problem and arrive at a mutually satisfactory solution in an atmosphere of free and open exchange of information and ideas. You both contribute to the resolution of the problem with the relative contribution of each being dependent on knowledge rather than formal authority.	**CII** You share the problem with your subordinates in a group meeting. In this meeting you obtain their ideas and suggestions. Then, *you* make the decision which may or may not reflect your subordinates' influence.
DI You delegate the problem to one of your subordinates, providing him with any relevant information that you possess, but giving him responsibility for solving the problem by himself. Any solution which the person reaches will receive your support. *Democratic*	**GII** You share the problem with your subordinates as a group. Together you generate and evaluate alternatives and attempt to reach agreement (consensus) on a solution. Your role is much like that of chairman, coordinating the discussion, keeping it focused on the problem, and making sure that the critical issues are discussed. You do not try to influence the group to adopt "your" solution and are willing to accept and implement any solution which has the support of the entire group.

Slip

Source: V. H. Vroom and A. G. Jago, Decision-making as a social process: Normative and descriptive models of leader behavior, *Decision Sciences* 5 (1974): 745. Reprinted with permission.

13 possible ways
only 5 amounted + mattered to anyone

in the decision making listed in Table 18.2. For individual problems, managers choose from solving the problem themselves with available information, jointly solving the problem with subordinates, or delegating problem-solving responsibility. For group problems, managers choose from making the decision themselves with available information, solving the problem themselves with information or ideas from subordinates, or solving the problem with the subordinates as a group.

CHOOSING A PROBLEM-SOLVING APPROACH
Selection of the appropriate decision process involves assessing the characteristics of the particular problem. Matching the process and problem characteristics results from the application of ten rules underlying the model, shown in Table 18.3. These rules identify the process for each case that will improve one

TABLE 18.3 ■ Rules Underlying the Normative Model

1. *The Leader Information Rule: $A \cap \overline{B} \to \overline{AI}$*
   If the quality of the decision is important and the leader does not possess enough information or expertise to solve the problem by himself, then AI is eliminated from the feasible set.

2. *The Subordinate Information Rule: $A \cap \overline{H} \to \overline{DI}$*
   (applicable to individual problems only)
   If the quality of the decision is important and the subordinate does not possess enough information or expertise to solve the problem himself, then DI is eliminated from the feasible set.

3a. *The Goal Congruence Rule: $\overline{A} \cap \overline{F} \to \overline{GII}, \overline{DI}$*
   If the quality of the decision is important and the subordinates are not likely to pursue organization goals in their efforts to solve this problem, then GII and DI are eliminated from the feasible set.

3b. *The Augmented Goal Congruence Rule: $A \cap (\overline{D} \cup E) \cap \overline{F} \to \overline{GI}$*
   (applicable to individual problems only)
   Under the conditions specified in the previous rule (i.e., quality of decision is important, and the subordinate does not share the organizational goals to be attained in solving the problem) GI may also constitute a risk to the quality of the decision taken in response to an individual problem. Such a risk is a reasonable one to take only if the nature of the problem is such that the acceptance of the subordinate is critical to the effective implementation and prior probability of acceptance of an autocratic solution is low.

4a. *The Unstructured Problem Rule (Group): $A \cap \overline{B} \cap \overline{C} \to \overline{AI}, \overline{AII}, \overline{CI}$*
   In decisions in which the quality of the decision is important, if the leader lacks the necessary information or expertise to solve the problem by himself and if the problem is unstructured, the method of solving the problem should provide for interaction among subordinates. Accordingly, AI, AII and CI are eliminated from the feasible set.

4b. *The Unstructured Problem Rule (Individual): $A \cap \overline{B} \cap \overline{C} \to \overline{AI}, \overline{AII}$*
   In decisions in which the quality of the decision is important, if the leader lacks the necessary information to solve the problem by himself and if the problem is unstructured, the method of solving the problem should permit the subordinate to generate solutions to the problem. Accordingly, AI and AII are eliminated from the feasible set.

5. *The Acceptance Rule: $D \cap \overline{E} \to \overline{AI}, \overline{AII}$*
   If the acceptance of the decision by subordinates is critical to effective implementation and if it is not certain that an autocratic decision will be accepted, AI and AII are eliminated from the feasible set.

6. *The Conflict Rule: $D \cap \overline{E} \cap G \to \overline{AI}, \overline{AII}, \overline{CI}$*
   (applicable to group problems only)
   If the acceptance of the decision is critical, an autocratic decision is not certain to be accepted and disagreement among subordinates in methods of attaining the organizational goal is likely, the methods used in solving the problem should enable those in disagreement to resolve their differences with full knowledge of the problem. Accordingly, AI, AII and CI, which permit no interaction among subordinates, are eliminated from the feasible set.

7. *The Fairness Rule: $\overline{A} \cap D \cap \overline{E} \to \overline{AI}, \overline{AII}, \overline{CI}, \overline{CII}$*
   If the quality of the decision is critical and not certain to result from an autocratic decision, the decision process used should permit the subordinates to interact with one another and negotiate over the fair method of resolving any differences with full responsibility on them for determining what is equitable. Accordingly, AI, AII, CI and CII are eliminated from the feasible set.

8. *The Acceptance Priority Rule: $D \cap \overline{E} \cap F \to \overline{AI}, \overline{AII}, \overline{CI}, \overline{CII}$*
   If acceptance is critical, not certain to result from an autocratic decision and if (the) subordinate(s) is (are) motivated to pursue the organizational goals represented in the problem, then methods which provide equal partnership in the decision-making process can provide greater acceptance without risking decision quality. Accordingly, AI, AII, CI, and CII are eliminated from the feasible set.

9. *The Group Problem Rule: Group $\to \overline{GI}, \overline{DI}$*
   If a problem has approximately equal effects on each of a number of subordinates (i.e., is a group problem) the decision process used should provide them with equal opportunities to influence that decision. Use of a decision process such as GI or DI which provides opportunities for only one of the affected subordinates to influence that decision may in the short run produce feelings of inequity reflected in lessened commitment to the decision on the part of those "left out" of the decision process and, in the long run, be a source of conflict and divisiveness.

10. *The Individual Problem Rule: Individual $\to \overline{CII}, \overline{GII}$*
   If a problem affects only one subordinate, decision processes which *unilaterally* introduce other (unaffected) subordinates as equal partners constitute an unnecessary use of time of the unaffected subordinates and can reduce the amount of commitment of the affected subordinate to the decision by reducing the amount of his opportunity to influence the decision. Thus, CII and GII are eliminated from the feasible set.

Source: V. H. Vroom and A. G. Jago, Decision-making as a social process: Normative and descriptive models of leader behavior, *Decision Sciences* 5 (1974): 749. Reprinted with permission.

FIGURE 18.6 ■
Decision Process Flow
Chart for Both Individual
and Group Problems

Słóp

A. Is there a quality requirement such that one solution is likely to be more rational than another?
B. Do I have sufficient information to make a high quality decision?
C. Is the problem structured?
D. Is acceptance of decision by subordinates critical to effective implementation?
E. If I were to make the decision by myself, is it reasonably certain that it would be accepted by my subordinates?
F. Do subordinates share the organizational goals to be attained in solving this problem?
G. Is conflict among subordinates likely in preferred solutions? (This question is irrelevant to individual problems.)
H. Do subordinates have sufficient information to make a high quality decision?

Don't need to know

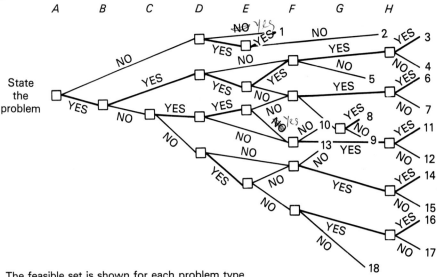

The feasible set is shown for each problem type
for Group (G) and Individual (I) problems.

1 {G: A1, A11, C1, C11, G11
{I: A1, D1, A11, C1, G1

2 {G: G11
{I: D1, G1

3 {G: A1, A11, C1, C11, G11
{I: A1, D1, A11, C1, G1

4 {G: A1, A11, C1, C11, G11
{I: A1, A11, C1, G1

5 {G: A1, A11, C1, C11
{I: A1, A11, C1

6 {G: G11
{I: D1, G1

7 {G: G11
{I: G1

8 {G: C11
{I: C1, G1

9 {G: C1, C11
{I: C1, G1

10 {G: A11, C1, C11
{I: A11, C1

11 {G: A11, C1, C11, G11
{I: D1, A11, C1, G1

12 {G: A11, C1, C11, G11
{I: A11, C1, G1

13 {G: C11
{I: C1

14 {G: C11, G11
{I: D1, C1, G1

15 {G: C11, G11
{I: C1, G1

16 {G: G11
{I: D1, G1

17 {G: G11
{I: G1

18 {G: C11
{I: C1, G1

G= group

Source: V. H. Vroom and A. G. Jago, Decision-making as a social process: Normative and descriptive models of leader behavior, *Decision Sciences* 5(1974): 748. Reprinted with permission.

or more of the following: (1) "the quality or rationality of the decision; (2) the acceptance or commitment of the subordinates to execute the decision effectively; or (3) the amount of time required to make the decision."[34] A manager who has to decide in the next week which of three subordinates to promote must choose a process that ensures a high-quality decision, a decision that subordinates will accept and be committed to executing, and that will take relatively little time.

Figure 18.6 illustrates the normative model, expressed as a decision tree. To make a decision, the leader asks each question, A through H, corresponding to each box encountered from left to right, unless a question may be skipped because the response to the previous question leads to a later one. For example, a No response to question A allows questions B and C to be skipped. When the set of feasible methods for group problems includes more than one process (e.g., a No response to each question results in problem type 1, for which every decision style is feasible), final selection of the single approach can use either minimum number of hours (AI, AII, CI, CII, or GII) or maximum subordinate involvement (GII, CII, CI, AII, or AI) as secondary criteria. A manager who wishes to make the decision in the shortest time possible, and for whom all processes are appropriate, will choose AI (solving the problem himself or herself using available information) over any other process. A manager who wishes to maximize subordinate involvement in the decision making, for example, as a training and development tool, will choose DI or GII (delegating the problem to the subordinate, or working together with subordinates to reach a decision) if all processes are feasible. A process using the former criterion is called Model A behavior; the latter, Model B.[35] Similar choices can be made when analyzing individual problems. Research has shown that decisions made using processes from the feasible set result in more effective outcomes than those not included.[36]

LIMITATIONS

The normative model provides a set of diagnostic questions for analyzing a problem, yet its narrow focus—on the extent of subordinate involvement in decision making—probably limits its usefulness. To test whether behavior actually conforms to the specified decision rules, most research on the model has compared predicted outcomes to managers' reports of successful and unsuccessful decisions. Some of the results question the model's validity as well as its reliability.[37] A manager's view of a situation as a crisis, challenging problem, or minor issue may affect the choice of a decision style, as well as the precise nature of interaction with subordinates when using any of the problem-solving approaches.[38]

Hersey and Blanchard's Situational Leadership Theory

Paul Hersey and Kenneth Blanchard have developed a situational leadership theory that has attracted considerable attention on the part of managers.[39] Hersey and Blanchard's situational leadership theory is based on the notion that the most effective leadership style depends on the level of readiness of the followers and the demands of the situation. Their model uses two dimensions of leadership behavior—task and relationship. These are similar to the classifications used in the leadership models developed by Ohio State and the Managerial Grid. Hersey and Blanchard argue that an effective leader is one who can diagnose the demands of the situation and the level of readiness of the followers and use a leadership style that is appropriate. Their theory is based on a relationship between these factors:

1. The amount of task behavior the leader exhibits (providing direction and emphasis on getting the job done).
2. The amount of relationship behavior the leader provides (consideration of people, level of emotional support for people).
3. The level of task-relevant readiness followers exhibit toward the specific goal, task, or function that the leader wants accomplished.

The key concept of their leadership theory is the level of task-relevant readiness of the followers. The readiness level of the followers is not defined as age or psychological stability but as

- *A desire for achievement*—level of achievement motivation based on the need to set high but attainable goals
- *The willingness and ability to accept responsibility*
- *Education and/or experience and skills* relevant to the particular task

A leader should consider the level of readiness of followers only in relation to the work or job to be performed. Certainly employees are "ready" on some tasks—when they have the experience and skills as well as the desire to achieve and are capable of assuming responsibility. For example, Dianne Crawford, an accountant, may be very "ready" in the manner in which she prepares accurate quarterly IRS tax reports, but she may not exhibit the same level of readiness when preparing written audits of the company's operations. Dianne needs very little direction on task-related behavior from her manager in preparing the tax reports but may require considerably closer supervision and direction over the preparation and writing of audits. Dianne may not have the skills and/or motivation to prepare audits, but with proper training, direction, and encouragement from her manager she can assume greater responsibility in this area.

As illustrated in Figure 18.7, the appropriate leadership style used by a manager varies according to the readiness level (represented by R1 through R4) of the followers. There are four distinct leadership styles that are appropriate, given different levels of readiness. As the task-relevant readiness level of followers increases, the manager should reduce task behavior and increase relationship behavior. These are illustrated by the classifications of the styles as

S1—Telling	High task, low relationship
S2—Selling	High task, high relationship
S3—Participating	High relationship, low task
S4—Delegating	Low relationship, low task

With the S1 (Telling) high-task, low-relationship leadership style, the leader uses one-way communication, defines the goals and roles of employees, and tells them what, how, when, and where to do the work. This style is very appropriate when dealing with subordinates who lack task-relevant readiness. For example, in supervising a group of relatively new, inexperienced employees, a high level of task-directed behavior and low-relationship behavior may be an appropriate

FIGURE 18.7 ■
Hersey and Blanchard's
Situational Leadership
Theory

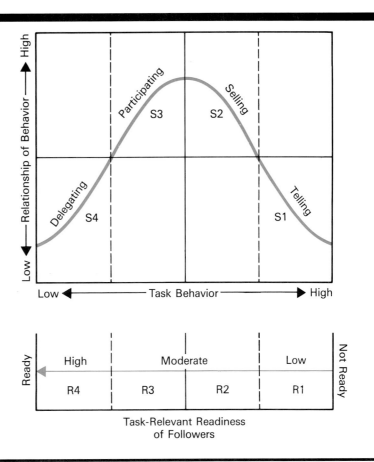

Source: Paul Hersey and Kenneth Blanchard. Center for Leadership Studies. California American University, 1989. Reprinted with permission.

leadership approach. Inexperienced employees need to be told what to do and how to accomplish their jobs.

As employees learn their jobs, the manager begins to use an S2 leadership style. There still is a need for a high level of task behavior, because the employees do not yet have the experience or skills to assume more responsibility, but the manager provides a higher level of emotional support—high-relationship behavior. The manager encourages the employees and demonstrates greater trust and confidence in them.

In the S3 leadership style, the employee begins to exhibit an increase in task-relevant readiness. As employees become more experienced and skilled, as well as more achievement motivated and more willing to assume responsibility, the leader should reduce the amount of task behavior but continue the high level of emotional support and consideration. A continuation of a high level of relationship behavior is the manager's way of reinforcing the employees' responsible performance. Thus, S3—high-relationship and low-task behavior—becomes the appropriate leadership style.

The S4 leadership style represents the highest level of follower readiness. In this stage, the employees possess a very high level of task readiness. They are very skilled and experienced, possess high achievement motivation, and are capable of exercising self-control. Thus, the leadership style that is most appropriate for this situation is S4—low relationship and low task. At this point the employees no longer need or expect a high level of supportive or task behavior from their leader.

It would, however, be inappropriate to conclude from this discussion that Hersey and Blanchard consider determining appropriate leadership style to be a simple matter. Diagnosing the readiness level of the followers as well as the specific needs of the situation is a complex undertaking. The leader must have insight into the abilities, needs, demands, and expectations of followers and be aware that these can and do change over time. Also, managers must recognize that they must adapt or change their style of leadership whenever there is a change in the level of readiness of followers for whatever reason—change in jobs, personal or family problems, or change in complexity of present job due perhaps to new technology. For example, suppose that Bill Woodall, a sales manager, has been using an S4 leadership style in supervising John Chriswell, a normally highly productive sales representative. But suppose that John's pending divorce has recently been adversely affecting his performance. In this situation, Bill might increase the level of both task and relationship behavior in order to provide John with the direction, support, and confidence he may need to cope with his problems and improve his performance.

In summary, Hersey and Blanchard's theory provides a useful and understandable framework for situational leadership. In essence, their model suggests that there is *no one* best leadership style that meets the needs of all situations. Rather, a manager's leadership style must be adaptable and flexible enough to meet the changing needs of employees and situations. More recent evidence indicates that a given individual might respond differently to a certain leadership strategy at different times.[40] The effective manager is one who can change styles as employees develop and change or as required by the situation.

In other research on the theory, Blake and Mouton pitted their proposition against the Hersey and Blanchard situational theory. They found that the professional managers they surveyed consistently chose the 9,9 style, rather than varying their styles as Hersey and Blanchard advocate.[41]

■ ATTRIBUTIONAL MODEL

Attribution theory suggests that leadership exists only as an individual's perception of a situation rather than as objective fact. Recall that attributions are influenced by an individual's viewpoint and involvement in the situation—whether the person is an actor in or observer of the event, whether an action or event succeeds or fails, and whether the action is intentional or accidental. A leader's judgment about his or her followers is thus influenced by the leader's attribution of the causes of the followers' behavior.[42] Effective leaders link themselves with successes in the group, and remove themselves from failures, by manipulating their attributions of subordinates' behavior in the desired direction.[43] One study has shown, for example, that leaders more often attributed poor performance to a subordinate when that person had a poor work history than when the worker had a good one.[44] The leader thus makes attributions about the cause of performance before deciding what action to take.[45]

FIGURE 18.8 ■■ An Attributional Leadership Model

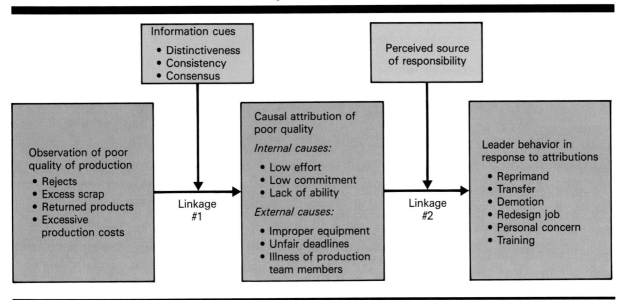

Source: Adapted from Terence R. Mitchell and Robert E. Wood, An empirical test of an attributional model of leader's responses to poor performance. In Richard C. Huseman (ed.), *Academy of Management Proceedings,* 1979, p. 94.

In determining whether personal or situational factors cause a subordinate's behavior, such as poor performance, a leader processes three types of information about the action: (1) its distinctiveness or uniqueness to a particular task; (2) its consistency or frequency; and (3) its consensus or lack of unique occurrence by other followers.[46] Behavior viewed as distinctive, inconsistent, and of high consensus is more likely attributed to characteristics of the situation than to the person. Figure 18.8 summarizes this attributional model of leadership.

Followers, too, attribute certain causality to the leader's behavior. "Whether or not leader behavior actually influences performance or effectiveness, it is important because people believe it does."[47] Thus, subordinates tend to view leaders as the cause of group behavior and, depending on members' attitudes toward group behavior, they develop either positive or negative attitudes about and reactions to the leader. A group's previous performance will affect members' ratings of the leader. In a laboratory study, when individuals were told that a group had performed well, they rated the leader as behaving more consistently and providing somewhat more task structure.[48] Their bias is to attribute failures to the situation, in this case to their supervisor, rather than to their personal characteristics.

■■ SUBSTITUTES FOR LEADERSHIP

While previous theories assume that some leadership style will be effective in each situation, Steven Kerr and John Jermier argue that certain individual, task, and organizational variables prevent leaders from affecting subordinate attitudes and behaviors at all.[49] Substitutes for leadership, or characteristics that negate or substitute for leadership influence, are those that structure tasks for followers or give them positive strokes (support) for their actions—functions that, according to path-goal theory, for example, leadership style performs.

The following features of a leadership situation may provide structuring or stroking behavior:[50]

1. *Characteristics of subordinates:* (a) ability, knowledge, experience, training; (b) need for independence; (c) professional orientation; and (d) indifference toward organizational rewards.
2. *Characteristics of the task:* (a) clarity and routinization; (b) invariant methodology; (c) provision of own feedback concerning accomplishment; and (d) intrinsic satisfaction.
3. *Characteristics of the organization:* (a) formalization (explicit plans, goals, and areas of responsibility); (b) inflexibility (rigid, unbending rules and procedures); (c) highly specified and active advisory and staff functions; (d) closely knit, cohesive work groups; (e) organizational rewards not within the leader's control; and (f) spatial distance between superior and subordinates.

These substitutes may replace leadership. One study of nursing work indicated that the staff nurses' education, the cohesion of the nurses, and work technology substituted for the head nurse's leadership behaviors in determining the staff nurses' performance.[51] For example, the administration had a strong performance orientation and rewarded nurses' accomplishments of performance objectives. The research findings also indicated that the leader's behavior—in this case assertiveness by the head nurse—interacted with characteristics of the organization—the performance-reward contingency—to negatively influence performance. The leader's behavior may even have affected the dysfunctional characteristics of other substitutes.

SUMMARY

Leadership is defined as influencing others to do what the leader wants them to do. Four basic leadership styles have been identified: autocratic leaders tell subordinates what to do and expect to be obeyed without question; participative leaders involve subordinates in decision making but may retain final authority; democratic leaders try to do what the majority of subordinates desire; and laissez-faire leaders are uninvolved in the work of the unit.

The trait approach to leadership is the evaluation and selection of leaders based on their physical, mental, and psychological characteristics. Dissatisfaction with the trait approach has caused most leadership researchers to focus attention instead on how leaders should behave. In 1938 Kurt Lewin and his colleagues conducted an experiment on autocratic, democratic, and laissez-faire leadership styles. The basic difference in the three styles was the location of the decision-making function in the group. In the Ohio State leadership studies, the key concern was the leader's behavior in directing the efforts of others toward group goals. Two important dimensions of leader behavior were identified: initiating structure and consideration. The Managerial Grid®, a two-dimensional matrix developed by Robert Blake and Jane Mouton, depicts five leadership styles, each representing degrees of concern for people and concern for production. A series of leadership studies at the University of Michigan related differences in high-productivity and low-productivity work groups to differences in supervisors.

Contingency or situational models assert that no single way of behaving works in all situations. Robert House's path-goal theory proposes that managers can facilitate job performance by showing employees how their performance directly affects their receiving desired rewards. The leadership continuum, developed by Robert Tannenbaum and Warren Schmidt, shows the trade-off between a manager's use of authority and the freedom that subordinates experience as leadership style varies from boss centered to subordinate centered. Fred Fiedler and his colleagues at the University of Illinois developed the first leadership theory explicitly called a contingency model. He stated that the most effective leadership style depends on the nature of the situation.

Victor Vroom and Philip Yetton introduced a normative theory of leadership and decision making. Managers determine the extent to which they should involve subordinates in the decision-making process. In Paul Hersey and Kenneth Blanchard's situational leadership theory, effective leadership depends on the level of readiness of the followers and the demands of the situation.

Attribution theory suggests that leadership exists only as an individual's perception of a situation rather than as objective fact. Effective leaders manipulate their attributions of subordinates' behavior in the desired direction. Steven Kerr and John Jermier argue that certain individual, task, and organizational variables prevent leaders from affecting subordinate attitudes and behaviors at all. In conclusion, *no one* leadership style is most effective. Managers, as leaders, will choose a style that best contributes to the survival and growth of the organization.

REVIEW QUESTIONS

1. Define leadership. What are the basic leadership styles?
2. What is the trait approach to leadership? Discuss.
3. List and briefly describe the various behavioral leadership theories.
4. Describe each of the following situational leadership theories:
   a. House's path-goal theory of leadership
   b. Tannenbaum and Schmidt's leadership continuum
   c. Fiedler's contingency theory
   d. Vroom and Yetton's normative theory
   e. Hersey and Blanchard's situational leadership theory
5. Describe what is meant by the attributional model.
6. According to the text, what are substitutes for leadership?
7. Distinguish between leadership and management.

KEY TERMS

leadership	trait approach to	consideration
autocratic leader	leadership	Managerial Grid®
participative leader	transformational leader	path-goal theory
democratic leader	initiating structure	leadership continuum
laissez-faire leader		

CASE STUDY   A CAUSE FOR DISMISSAL

DWAYNE SANDERS WAS the Dallas-area supervisor for Quik-Stop, a chain of convenience stores. There were seven Quik-Stop stores in Dallas, and Dwayne had full responsibility for managing them. Each store operated with only one person on duty at a time. Several of the stores stayed open all night every night. The Center Street store was open Monday through Thursday all night but only from 6:00 A.M. to 10:00 P.M. Friday through Sunday. Because the store was open fewer hours during the weekend, the money pickup was not done on Saturday and Sunday. Therefore, on Monday, the time it took to complete a money count was greater than normal.

The company had a policy that, when emptying the drop safe, the manager must be with the employee on duty, and the employee must place every $1,000 in a brown bag, mark the bag, and leave the bag on the floor next to the drop safe until the manager verified the amount in each bag. Bill Catron worked the Sunday night shift at the Center Street store and was trying to save the manager time by counting the money prior to his arrival. The store got very busy, and when bagging a customer's groceries, Bill accidentally placed the money bag in the customer's grocery bag instead of

the bag containing his three sandwiches as he had intended. Twenty minutes later the manager arrived, and both men began to search for the money. A minute later the customer came back with the bag of money. The company has a policy that anyone violating this money counting procedure must be fired immediately.

Bill was very upset. "I really need this job," Bill exclaimed. "With the new baby and all the medical expenses we have had, I sure can't stand to be out of a job."

"You knew about the policy, Bill," said Dwayne.

"Yes, I did, Dwayne," said Bill, "and I really don't have any excuse. If you don't fire me, though, I promise you that I'll be the best store manager you've got."

While Bill waited on a customer, Dwayne called his boss at the home office in Houston. With the boss's approval, Dwayne decided not to fire Bill.

QUESTIONS
1. Discuss Dwayne's leadership style in terms of the Managerial Grid®.
2. Evaluate the action Dwayne took. Take particular note of how the events in the case might affect other store managers.

CASE STUDY   A NATURAL-BORN LEADER

"PHIL IS A natural-born leader," said Jim Hollis, the plant manager, as he looked out over the factory floor from the production manager's office.

"Yes," said the production manager. "I believe those carpenters would follow him off the end of the earth."

Phil Granger is the carpentry supervisor in the shipping department at the Jacobs Castings Company. He is a big man, six-foot-four, 240 pounds. He has a booming voice. His size and the steel-blue sternness of his eyes belie a gentle spirit. He avoids confrontations and is known to be patient and lenient with subordinates. Phil and his crew of six make wooden boxes for packaging the

several hundred custom-made castings that Jacobs ships every day. The work requires little skill, but is vital to the plant.

Before Phil took over, the carpentry division was a bottleneck. Shipments were often delayed for days because the carpentry work just did not seem to get done. Turnover in the department had been high. The carpenters seemed to have more personal problems than other workers in the plant.

When Phil took over, everything seemed to change almost immediately. The work was caught up within a few days, and castings no longer had to wait for more than a day to be shipped. The carpenters also seemed happier. During the first two months that Phil was in charge, there was not a single complaint, and only one day was lost because of absenteeism.

As Phil sketched the boxes to be made the next morning, he thought, "I sure would like to go home a little early today, but I want the others to know I'm trying as hard as they are. Anyway, I need to finish these sketches so I'll have time to help with the boxes in the morning. I also want to check with Brad about his new baby before he leaves today. Since I took him around and showed him how our work affected the rest of the plant, he sure has done a great job."

QUESTIONS

1. Is Phil a natural-born leader? Explain.
2. What do you believe accounts for the success of the carpentry division? Defend your answer.

EXPERIENTIAL EXERCISE

The assessment that you will complete really reveals some critical aspects concerning your leadership style. The results of this assessment cannot be interpreted exactly, but they will be revealing. Your results will be translated into a rough indication of the way you would tend to lead people.

Read each of the statements given below and mark them according to the following code:

3—You nearly always agree
2—You agree about half the time
1—You seldom agree
0—You never agree

____ 1. Good supervisors do not get very close to their workers.

____ 2. Workers perform best when they are afraid of losing their jobs.

____ 3. Workers should be dealt with only as individuals, never as groups.

____ 4. Workers are being paid to get out the work and have no business being involved in the supervisor's decisions.

____ 5. Effective supervisors are usually tough.

____ 6. Workers do not question or disagree with effective supervisors.

____ 7. Supervisors who handle most of the details themselves make the best managers.

____ 8. Most workers are careless and lazy by nature.

____ 9. Most workers are out to get what they can for the least amount of effort.

____ 10. Supervisors should realize that workers usually have little ambition and want security more than anything else.

____ 11. Workers should never participate in making decisions for which their supervisor will be held responsible.

____ 12. Supervisors' ideas are better than those of their workers.

____ 13. To ensure fairness, supervisors should treat every worker exactly the same and never make allowances for individual differences.

____ 14. A worker's mistake should be emphasized by bringing it up from time to time.

____ 15. To be effective, supervisors should demonstrate their superiority from time to time.

____ 16. To win workers' support, all the supervisor has to do is be nice to them.

____ 17. A sure sign of a hard worker is the willingness to do a dirty, unimportant job.

____ 18. Workers will not respect company rules if the supervisor ever allows an exception.

____ 19. When employees are uncooperative, the supervisor should give them a "pep talk."

____ 20. A good way to get the new worker started right is through a show of authority by the supervisor.

____ 21. Supervisors have found that a good "chewing out" every now and then helps to keep workers on their toes.

____ 22. A good supervisor must be tough and let everyone know it.

___ 23. When talking to a worker about job performance, the supervisor should emphasize a worker's weaknesses.

___ 24. Individuals have to stick up for their own rights to get ahead in today's world.

___ 25. Supervisors should remember that happy employees are seldom very productive.

The results of this assessment cannot be interpreted exactly. However, the instructor has information that will help you translate your results into a rough indication of the way you would tend to lead people.

NOTES

1. Roger Skrentny, "Sandy Sigoloff: The Man Who Threw Wickes a Life Raft," *California Business,* February 1983, 18–23; Mark Liff, "Ming Shows Wickes Cos. No Mercy," *Advertising Age,* 23 January 1984, M-27–28; "On the Comeback Trail," *Time,* 12 March 1984, 52–53; and Jennifer Fendleton, "Sigoloff Finds Star Status Is Hard Work," *Advertising Age,* 19 September 1983, 47; numerous articles from *The Wall Street Journal;* and Wickes Companies Annual Report (various years).
2. J. K. Hemphill and A. E. Coons, "Development of the Leader Behavior Description Questionnaire," in *Leader Behavior: Its Description and Measurement,* ed. R. M. Stogdill and E. A. Coons (Columbus: Ohio State University, Bureau of Business Research, 1957), 7.
3. R. Tannenbaum, I. R. Weschler, and F. Massarik, *Leadership and Organization* (New York: McGraw-Hill, 1961), 24.
4. R. M. Stogdill, *Handbook of Leadership: A Survey of Theory and Research* (New York: Free Press, 1974), 411.
5. T. O. Jacobs, *Leadership and Exchange in Formal Organizations* (Alexandria, Va.: Human Resources Research Organization, 1970), 232.
6. D. Katz and R. L. Kahn, *The Social Psychology of Organizations,* 2d. ed. (New York: John Wiley & Sons, 1978).
7. Geoff Lewis, Anne R. Field, John J. Keller, and John W. Verity, "Big Changes at Big Blue," *Business Week,* 15 February 1988, 92.
8. Thomas J. Murry, "Wal-Mart Stores Penny Wise," *Business Month,* December 1988, 42.
9. John Hoerr, "Getting Man and Machine to Live Happily Ever After," *Business Week,* 20 April 1987, 61.
10. Paul C. Nystrom, "Comparing Beliefs of Line and Technostructure Managers," *The Academy of Management Journal* 26, no. 4 (December 1986): 816.
11. Edwin Ghiselli, *Explorations in Managerial Talent* (Pacific Palisades, Calif.: Goodyear, 1971).
12. W. Bennis, "Leadership: A Beleaguered Species?" *Organizational Dynamics* 5 (1976): 13–14.
13. R. J. House, "A 1976 Theory of Charismatic Leadership," in *Leadership: The Cutting Edge,* ed. J. G. Hunt and L. L. Larson (Carbondale: Southern Illinois University Press, 1977), 205, 207.
14. B. M. Bass, "Leadership: Good, Better, Best," *Organizational Dynamics* 13 (Winter 1985): 26–40.
15. Bass, "Leadership," 26–40.
16. Bass, "Leadership," 26–40.
17. R. M. Stogdill, "Personal Factors Associated with Leadership: A Survey of the Literature," *Journal of Psychology* 25 (1948): 35–71.

18. K. Lewin, R. Lippitt, and R. White, "Patterns of Aggressive Behavior in Experimentally Created 'Social Climates,'" *Journal of Social Psychology* 10 (February 1939): 271–299.

19. E. Fleishman, E. F. Harris, and R. D. Burtt, *Leadership and Supervision in Industry* (Columbus: Ohio State University Press, 1955); E. Fleishman and E. F. Harris, "Patterns of Leadership Behavior Related to Employee Grievances and Turnover," *Personnel Psychology* 1 (1959): 45–53.

20. R. L. Kahn and D. Katz, "Leadership Practices in Relation to Productivity and Morale," in *Group Dynamics,* ed. D. Cartwright and A. Zander (Evanston, Ill.: Row, Peterson, 1953), 585–611.

21. Robert R. Blake and Jane S. Mouton, *The New Managerial Grid* (Houston: Gulf Publishing, 1985), 11.

22. Blake and Mouton, *Managerial Grid,* 11.

23. Robert House, "A Path-Goal Theory of Leadership Effectiveness," *Administrative Science Quarterly* 16 (September 1971): 321–338.

24. Alan C. Filley, Robert House, and Steven Kerr, *Managerial Process and Organizational Behavior* (Glenview, Ill.: Scott, Foresman, 1976), 256–260.

25. F. E. Fiedler, *A Theory of Leadership Effectiveness* (New York: McGraw-Hill, 1967), 45–46.

26. R. W. Rice, "Construct Validity of the Least Preferred Co-worker Score," *Psychological Bulletin* 85 (1978): 1199–1237.

27. F. E. Fiedler, "Engineer the Job to Fit the Manager," *Harvard Business Review* 43 (1965): 115–122.

28. Fiedler, "Engineer the Job," 115–122.

29. F. E. Fiedler and M. M. Chemers, *Leadership and Effective Management* (Glenview, Ill.: Scott, Foresman, 1974), 78–87.

30. J. A. Kennedy, Jr., "Middle LPC Leaders and the Contingency Model of Leader Effectiveness," *Organizational Behavior and Human Performance* 30 (1982): 1–14.

31. See J. C. Barrow, "The Variables of Leadership: A Review and Conceptual Framework," *Academy of Management Review* 2 (1977): 214–235.

32. R. Singh, "Leadership Style and Reward Allocation: Does Least Preferred Co-worker Scale Measure Task and Relationship Orientation?" *Organizational Behavior and Human Performance* 32 (1983): 178–197.

33. V. H. Vroom and P. W. Yetton, *Leadership and Decision-Making* (Pittsburgh, Pa.: University of Pittsburgh Press, 1973).

34. V. H. Vroom and A. J. Jago, "Decision-making as a Social Process: Normative and Descriptive Models of Leader Behavior," *Decision Sciences* 5 (1974): 743–769.

35. Vroom and Jago, "Decision-making," 743–769.

36. R. H. G. Field, "A Test of the Vroom-Yetton Normative Model of Leadership," *Journal of Applied Psychology* 67 (1982): 523–532.

37. R. H. G. Field, "A Critique of the Vroom-Yetton Contingency Model of Leadership Behavior," *Academy of Management Review* 4 (1979): 249–253.

38. D. Tjosvold, "Effects of Crisis Orientation on Managers' Approach to Controversy in Decision-making," *Academy of Management Journal* 27 (1984): 130–138.

39. See Paul Hersey and Kenneth Blanchard, "So You Want to Know Your Leadership Style?" *Training and Development Journal* (February 1974): 22–32. This article contains the Leader Adaptability and Style Inventory (LASI), an instrument that can be used to examine leadership behavior, style adaptability, and effectiveness. Since this article, the LASI has been renamed as the Leader Effectiveness and Adaptability Description (LEAD). Information, LEAD inventories, and training materials may be obtained from the Center for Leadership Studies, 17253 Caminito Canasto, Rancho Bernardo, San Diego, California 92127.

40. S. D. Malik and Kenneth N. Wexley, "Improving the Owner/Manager's Handling of Subordinate Resistance to Unpopular Decisions," *Journal of Small Business Management* 24, no. 3 (July 1986): 27.

41. Blake and Mouton, *The New Managerial Grid,* 282.
42. J. Bartunek, "Attribution Theory: Some Implications for Organizations," *Business Horizons* 24 (1981): 66–71.
43. B. Calder, "An Attribution Theory of Leadership," in *New Directions in Organizational Behavior,* ed. B. H. Staw and G. R. Salancik (Chicago: St. Clair Press, 1977).
44. T. R. Mitchell and R. Wood, "Supervisor Responses to Subordinates' Poor Performance: A Test of the Attributional Model," *Organizational Behavior and Human Performance* 25 (1980): 123–138.
45. S. G. Green and T. R. Mitchell, "Attributional Processes of Leaders in Leader-member Interactions," *Organizational Behavior and Human Performance* 23 (1979): 429–458.
46. See H. H. Kelley, "Attribution Theory in Social Psychology," in *Nebraska Symposium on Motivation,* ed. D. Levine (Lincoln: University of Nebraska Press, 1967); Green and Mitchell, "Attributional Processes"; T. R. Mitchell and R. E. Wood, "An Empirical Test of an Attributional Model of Leader's Responses to Poor Performance," *Academy of Management Proceedings* (1979): 94.
47. J. Pfeffer, "The Ambiguity of Leadership," *Academy of Management Review* 2 (1977): 104.
48. J. R. Larson, Jr., J. H. Lingle, and M. M. Scerbo, "The Impact of Performance Cues on Leader-behavior Ratings: The Role of Selective Information Availability and Probalistic Response Bias," *Organizational Behavior and Human Performance* 33 (1984): 323–349.
49. S. Kerr and J. M. Jermier, "Substitutes for Leadership: Their Meaning and Measurement," *Organizational Behavior and Human Performance* 22 (1978): 375–403.
50. Kerr and Jermier, "Substitutes for Leadership," 375–403.
51. J. E. Sheridan, D. J. Vredenburgh, and M. A. Abelson, "Contextual Model of Leadership Influence in Hospital Units," *Academy of Management Journal* 27 (1984): 57–78.

.

REFERENCES

Barnes, Louis B., and Mark P. Kriger. "The Hidden Side of Organizational Leadership. *Sloan Management Review* 28 (Fall 1986): 15–25.
Barrow, J. C. "The Variables of Leadership: A Review and Conceptual Framework." *Academy of Management Review* 2 (1977): 231–235.
Batten, Joe D. "Leading by Expectation." *Management World* 17 (January–February 1988): 35–36.
Bellman, Geoffrey M. "The Quest for Staff Leadership." *Training & Development Journal* 10 (January 1986): 36–41.
Bennis, W. "Leadership: A Beleaguered Species?" *Organizational Dynamics* 5 (1976).
Blake, R. R., and J. S. Mouton. *Building a Dynamic Corporation Through Grid Organization Development.* Reading, Mass.: Addison-Wesley, 1969.
———. "A Comparative Analysis of Situationalism and 9,9 Management by Principle." *Organizational Dynamics* 10 (Spring 1982): 20–43.
———. "Theory and Research for Developing a Science of Leadership." *Journal of Applied Behavioral Science* 18 (1966): 275–291, 349–361.
Burke, W. W. "Leadership: Is There One Best Approach?" *Management Review* 69 (November 1980): 54–56.
Byrd, Richard E. "Corporate Leadership Skills: A New Synthesis." *Organizational Dynamics* 16 (Summer 1987): 31–40.
Carbone, T. C. "Theory X and Theory Y Revisited." *Managerial Planning* 29 (May–June 1981): 24–27.

Davis, T. R. V., and F. Luthans. "Leadership Reexamined: A Behavioral Approach." *Academy of Management Review* 4 (1979): 237–248.

Fiedler, F. E. *A Theory of Leadership Effectiveness.* New York: McGraw-Hill, 1967.

——— . "Engineer the Job to Fit the Manager." *Harvard Business Review* 43 (1965): 115–122.

Fiedler, F. E., and M. M. Chemers. *Leadership and Effective Management.* Glenview, Ill.: Scott, Foresman, 1974.

Field, R. H. G. "A Critique of Vroom-Yetton Contingency Model of Leadership Behavior." *Academy of Management Review* 4 (1979): 249–253.

Glassman, Edward. "Leadership Style's Effect on the Creativity of Employees." *Management Solutions* 31 (November 1986): 18–25.

Graeff, C. L. "The Situational Leadership Theory: A Critical View." *Academy of Management Review* (April 1983): 285–291.

Griffin, R. W. "Relationships among Individual, Task Design and Leader Behavior Variables." *Academy of Management Journal* 23 (December 1980): 665–683.

Handy, Charles. "Management Training: Perk or Prerequisite?" *Personnel Management* (May 1987): 28–31.

Heilman, M. E., H. A. Hornstein, J. H. Cage, and J. K. Herschdag. "Reaction to Prescribed Leader Behavior as a Function of Role Perspective: The Case of the Vroom-Yetton Model." *Journal of Applied Psychology* (February 1984): 50–60.

Hennecke, Matt. "How Do You Know It Works?" *Training: The Magazine of Human Resources Development* 25 (April 1988): 49–51.

Hersey, P., and K. H. Blanchard. *Management of Organizational Behavior.* 4th ed. Englewood Cliffs, N.J.: Prentice-Hall, 1982.

Himes, G. K. "Management Leadership Styles." *Supervision* 42 (November 1980): 9–11.

Hodge, John. "Getting along with the Informal Leader." *Supervisory Management* 25 (October 1980): 41–43.

House, R. J. "A Path-Goal Theory of Leader Effectiveness." *Administrative Science Quarterly* 16 (1971): 321–338.

Kinlaw, Dennis C., and Donna R. Christensen. "Management Education: The Wheat and the Chaff." *Training: The Magazine of Human Resources Development* 23 (December 1986): 45–50.

Klimoski, R. J., and N. J. Hayes. "Leadership Behavior and Subordinate Motivation." *Personnel Psychology* 33 (Autumn 1980): 543–545.

Lee, Dixie, and Richard Brostrom. "Managing the High-Tech Professional." *Personnel* 65 (June 1988): 12–17.

Lippitt, R. "The Changing Leader-Follower Relationships of the 1980s." *Journal of Applied Behavioral Science* 18 (March 1982): 395–403.

Lueder, D. C. "Don't be Misled by LEAD." *Journal of Applied Behavioral Science* 21 (1985): 143–151.

McGregor, D. *The Human Side of Enterprise.* New York: McGraw-Hill, 1961.

Malik, S. D., and Kenneth N. Wexley. "Improving the Owner/Manager's Handling of Subordinate Resistance to Unpopular Decisions." *Journal of Small Business Management* 24, no. 3 (July 1986): 22–28.

Mann, Carl P. "Transformational Leadership in the Executive Office." *Public Relations Quarterly* 33 (Spring 1988): 19–23.

Nystrom, Paul C. "Comparing Beliefs of Line and Technostructure Managers." *Academy of Management Journal* 26, no. 4 (December 1986): 812–819.

Rice, R. W., D. Instone, and J. Adams. "Leader Sex, Leader Success, and Leadership Process: Two Field Studies." *Journal of Applied Psychology* (February 1984): 12–31.

Sinetar, M. "Developing Leadership Potential." *Personnel Journal* 60 (March 1981): 193–196.

Targowski, Andrew S. "The Management Wheels: A Technique of Applying Management Philosophies." *Data Management* 25 (October 1987): 12–14.

Vroom, V. H., and A. J. Jago. "Decision-Making as a Social Process: Normative and Descriptive Models of Leader Behavior." *Decision Sciences* 5 (1974): 743–769.

Vroom, V. H., and P. W. Yetton. *Leadership and Decision-Making.* Pittsburgh, Pa.: University of Pittsburgh Press, 1973.

Wagel, William H. "An Unorthodox Approach to Leadership Development." *Personnel* 63 (July 1986): 1–3.

Wolff, Michael F. "Leadership and R&D Productivity. *Research Management* 29 (November–December 1986): 9–11.

Zierden, William E. "Leading Through the Follower's Point of View." *Organization Dynamics* 8, no. 4 (Spring 1980): 27–46.

CHAPTER
19

Chapter Outline

Power
and
Organizational
Politics

Learning Objectives

After completing this chapter students should be able to

1. Define power and explain reasons for exerting power.
2. Describe sources of power and power differences.
3. Explain strategies for obtaining power, some special cases of power relations, and the significance of power to the manager.
4. Define politics and describe political action in organizations.

THE LAKEDALE PUBLIC SCHOOLS had experienced declining enrollment for ten years. Under tightening budget constraints, members of the school committee and the superintendent of schools had agreed that closing schools was the only way to meet the budget and still provide quality education. During the past eight years the committee closed five elementary schools, two junior high schools, and a high school. The superintendent asked the Director of Research to analyze the seventeen schools in the community and offer four alternative plans for school closings.

The Director of Research had been employed by the school department for fifteen years. During that time he repeatedly offered projections of the number of schoolchildren that would be enrolled at specified times in the future. His projections were extremely accurate, generally varying by, at most, 3 percent. As requested, he formulated four possible scenarios of school closings. Each scenario paired two of five schools. The remaining twelve schools were eliminated from consideration for various reasons (e.g., they had been involved in previous closings, or their students could not easily be consolidated into other schools without costly bus transportation). In private conversations with the superintendent and other individuals in and out of the school department, the director stated that his data suggested that the Adams and McKinley Schools should be closed. He submitted the report to the school committee, who made it available to the entire community.

The superintendent of schools reviewed the formal recommendations and ranked them according to his priorities for closing. Since many of the schools were geographically near each other, he preferred that adjacent schools not be closed. He also preferred to close smaller schools so that the system would have more flexibility in the future in case enrollments were greater than projected. He distributed an addendum to the report with his recommendations.

Members of the community from the various schools slated for closing scrutinized the report. They began by questioning the director's logic in removing twelve schools from consideration. Many called for the school committee to consider all seventeen schools for potential closing. Each local school's constituency then built a case for keeping its school open. The community members found factual errors in the data that they felt affected the validity of the recommendations. They called the school committee's attention to these errors in public and private meetings. In addition, they lobbied for their causes both in public and in private.

The ultimate choice of which schools to close was the responsibility of the school committee. A majority vote of the eight-person committee closed a school. Several of the committee members had clear favorites among the schools to be closed. Their priorities did not match those of the superintendent. The superintendent recommended the Madison and McKinley Schools be closed because they were the smallest and together had the highest yearly cost savings. Three members of the school committee, because they represented the Madison and McKinley communities, strongly advocated closing the Washington and Taft Schools. Community members who spoke with these school committee representatives expressed concern that they were not considering the good of the entire community, but solely that of their own limited constituencies. Conversations with three other committee members indicated that they planned to support the Director of Research's recommendations, because he had the most objective knowledge of enrollments, costs, and savings in each alternative. The remaining two members stated that they leaned toward the superintendent's recommendations.

School committee meetings regarding the school closings were characterized by noisy arguments among committee members and community representatives about whose recommendations should be adopted. After five such meetings, the committee was no closer to an agreement than they had been at the first meeting. ■

W HICH SCHOOLS WERE CLOSED? Why? Who had the most influence over the decision to close schools? As will be seen in this chapter, both power and politics were involved. The chapter begins by defining power and providing reasons individuals or groups exert power. Then, power differences and strategies for obtaining power will be discussed. Next, we present some special cases in power relations and consider the significance of power to the manager. The chapter concludes with a discussion of political action in organizations.

▨ POWER DEFINED

Power
The potential or actual ability to influence others in a desired direction.

Power is the potential or actual ability to influence others in a desired direction. It is the ability to get things done the way one wants them to be done.[1] *Power* is an emotionally laden term, particularly in cultures that emphasize individuality and equality. To call a manager a "power seeker" is to cast doubt on that manager's motives and actions. Some of these negative views are from older analyses that suggest power is evil and corrupts people, it is largely composed of naked force, and the amount of power available is fixed. Certainly, modern business corporations constitute major concentrations of economic power. These concentrations have materially improved the standard of living of millions of people; but when they lead to abuse, control rather than elimination would appear to be the more desirable course of action.

Power can be a highly effective instrument for good, or it can be an instrument of evil. Frequently there is disagreement regarding the exact nature of power. For instance, there is little doubt that Frank Lorenzo has substantial power. Frank Lorenzo, chairman of Texas Air Corporation, has power that emanates from business savvy and what one twenty-year company veteran characterized as "subtle intimidation."[2] However, some individuals, such as the union members who struck Eastern in March 1989, might view Lorenzo's power as evil. On the other hand, fellow managers in the airline industry may view his accumulation of power, and his subsequent use of such power to drive down operating cost, as good management and therefore a good application of power.

H. Ross Perot of EDS fame had loyal followers at EDS who respected the man and his actions, and from their high regard for him came his power over them. Even though Perot had immense power, he was rarely, if ever, criticized as evil, probably because his application of power was virtually always seen as good for employees and/or humanity. Organizational researchers increasingly cite the value of identifying and using power to improve individual and organizational performance.[3] Theorists and practitioners have translated an early view of power, which considered it evil and as mainly stemming from coercion,[4] into a model of viable political action in organizations. Yet, while functional and advantageous in many situations, aggressive power behavior can also create conflict, which frequently is dysfunctional for the organization, as it was in the introductory case.

Different individuals and groups within and outside the organization can exert power. Individual employees, including top and middle management, technical analysts and specialists, support staff, and other nonmanagerial workers can influence the actions an organization takes to reach its goals. Formal groups of employees such as various departments, work teams, management councils, and task forces as well as informal groups, such as those with offices near each other or those who see each other socially, can similarly exercise power. In addition to individuals or groups within the organization, nonemployees may try to influence the behavior of an organization and its members. Owners, suppliers, clients, competitors, employee associations (e.g., unions and professional associations), the general public, and directors of the organization may all exert power.[5] Power is an inescapable part of a well-functioning organization and a definite result of human interaction. Therefore, it must be carefully managed to best benefit everyone involved.

■■ REASONS FOR EXERTING POWER

Why do individuals initiate an act of power? The reasons why individuals in organizational situations must develop a power base, and then apply that power, vary according to individual and organizational situations. In the case of job-related dependence—how dependent a person's position is on other positions—an individual may exercise power because of a job-related necessity. In other cases, the basic needs of individuals may motivate them to exert power. Power/dependence relationships and individual needs for power are two of the more common reasons for exerting power.

Power and Dependence

Recent definitions of power describe it as a property of a social relationship. Historically, power has been defined in terms of exchange processes,[6] where a person who commands services needed by others exchanges them for compliance with his or her requests. Power is often thought of as a situation where one person or a group is in compliance with the power holder's request. For example, the supervisor exchanges time off for high-quality performance by workers. In such a relationship, power has been alternatively viewed as a function of the ties of dependence.[7] For example, supervisors often have power because subordinates depend on them for rewards. In the same way, subordinates may have power if their supervisor's performance is linked to their own.

YOU ARE A VERY successful salesperson and have just been rewarded by being appointed the regional sales manager for the company's most successful region. This operation is in a mid-sized city. The close-knit community places a high value on local basketball. In fact, you soon realize that to most people in the community local basketball is much more important than the Super Bowl. While watching a local game with a buyer who purchases almost 40 percent of your yearly volume, you learn that the star of the team may leave town because his father was laid off. The buyer heard that you have an opening for a sales manager, and he asks you to hire the boy's father. You tell him that you will be glad to review the individual's resumé, but you have already found an extremely qualified person. The next day the woman you are replacing explains that in this town we do each other favors, and that is how we build trust. She also tells you that if the boy's father is not hired you may lose all of the buyer's business. You receive the individual's resumé and soon realize that he has no sales experience. You can hire the extremely qualified individual, or you can capitulate to the demands of your primary buyer.

What would you do?

Source: Adapted from a case presented in the video, *A Matter of Judgment,* which depicts five such conflicts of interest.

In the opening case, what types of dependence does the Director of Research have? Among others, he relies on the superintendent and the school committee for his continued employment and compensation. What dependencies does the superintendent show? He depends on the goodwill of the community in supporting his programs and curricular changes in the schools. He relies on the school committee to fund projects he and his staff propose; and he depends on the teachers to implement those projects. He also depends on teachers to implement the curriculum effectively. The school committee members, at a minimum, depend on the community members for their election to office.

According to John Kotter, individuals engage in power-oriented behavior to reduce their dependence on others.[8] In such situations, individuals may seek to increase the size of their power bases in order to decrease their dependence on current power holders. A technician who must rely on the supervisor for pay increases may reduce dependence by acquiring expertise in an area that no one else in the firm has. Similarly, the Director of Research may attempt to reduce his dependence on the superintendent by demonstrating additional expertise and by expanding his connections in the community, especially among those who will directly benefit from his recommendations. As the number of job-related dependencies increase, the manager (or other employee), as a way of coping with the dependencies, increases the time and energy individuals devote to power-oriented behavior.[9] Managers use several bases of power—the position they hold, their personal characteristics, and the resources or information they can access and control. The technician, for example, may attempt to acquire unique knowledge, charisma, or special information as a base of power; the Director of Research acts in this way by collecting, analyzing, and controlling information

Managers may have a number of bases of power, such as their position, their personal characteristics, and the resources or information they control.
(© COMSTOCK, Inc.)

about future school enrollments. Alternatively, a manager generates power over others by creating in them a sense of obligation, building their belief in his or her expertise, encouraging others to identify with the manager, and making others feel—or in fact be—dependent on—the manager for resources.[10] By creating such a dependence situation, managers can create a web of control that will result in an enhanced degree of power.

Diagnosing dependence is a first step in properly understanding and using power. To do this, one can perform a power/dependence analysis, which involves asking the following questions:

1. On whom does the incumbent really depend? How important is each dependency? What is the basis of each dependency?
2. Are any of these dependencies obviously inappropriate or dysfunctional? If so, what has created that pattern of dependence?
3. In how much effective power-oriented behavior does the incumbent engage? Is it enough to cope well with the dependencies in the job?
4. Does the manner in which the incumbent generates or uses power have any negative consequences for the organization? If so, exactly what are they?[11]

Consider once more the introductory scenario and conduct a power/dependence analysis for this situation. The data presented are limited; but then, a manager's information at hand is also frequently incomplete and imperfect in real

F I G U R E 19.1 ▉
Dependence Diagrams for
Lakedale Schools

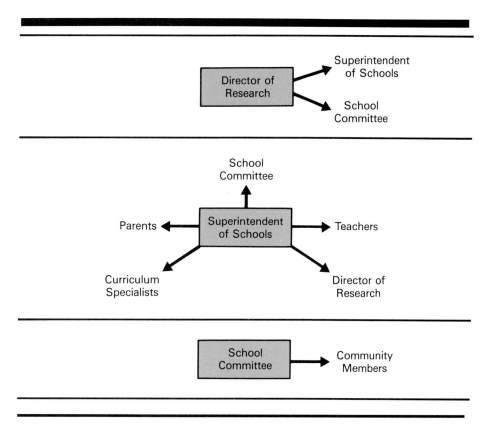

life. Figure 19.1 offers examples of possible dependence diagrams in the introductory scenario. According to these diagrams, who has the greatest need to exert power? The superintendent, as shown here, relies on the most constituencies. He likely uses many sources as bases of power and therefore has a broad and diverse power base.

Consider other people to whom power is typically attributed: the president of the United States, for example, or the head of a large corporation. What would their dependence diagrams look like? What would their power/dependence analyses reveal? The president of the United States is viewed as extremely powerful, but he can be severely stifled by uncooperative individuals in Congress. In order to limit such occurrences, a republican president often builds a power base of support, first among those of his own party, and then among those who are more conservative than liberal, and finally among those who need his support to accomplish their political agendas. This type of dependence analysis essentially derives from the association of power with mutual dependence in social relationships.

Individual Needs for Power

David McClelland and his associates identified the *need for power* as an individual motivator that causes a person to wield power.[12] Individuals with a high need for

PINNACLE

The Cincinnati Reds Power Person

INDIVIDUALS WITH A HIGH NEED for power try to influence and control others, seek leadership positions in groups, enjoy persuading others, and are perceived by others as outspoken, forceful, and demanding. Often politicians, top managers, or informal leaders are perceived as having a high need for power. Probably most observers would view Marge Schott, owner of the Cincinnati Reds, as a power person. Whether she is checking in at her car dealerships, or checking the team's line-up, one thing is for sure, Marge Schott is in charge. She is a powerful businesswoman and she knows how to use her power. The Reds were down and almost out, and the new Reds owner was faced with a challenge, but that is nothing new for this tenacious woman. Her philosophy is to live life as it comes and do your best and just keep going, and stay prepared. Marge Schott discusses her latest challenge, turning the Reds around, and other aspects of her business career with CNN correspondent Jan Hopkins.

power try to influence and control others, seek leadership positions in groups, enjoy persuading others, and are perceived by others as outspoken, forceful, and demanding.[13] Often politicians, top managers, or informal leaders are perceived as having a high need for power. Probably most observers would assume that former president Richard M. Nixon and Texas Air CEO Frank Lorenzo are individuals who have a high need for power. Do any individuals in the opening case have a high need for power? The case does not provide sufficient data for us to answer this question, but it may be inferred that on the basis of their holding elective office, some members of the school committee have (among other needs) a need for power. Additional data must be gathered to verify their needs, as well as those of the superintendent of schools, Director of Research, and community members.

David McClelland identified two types of men that demonstrate this need (although the research did not include women, realistically either sex could be either type):

1. The first type strives for dominance. He is the impulsive tough guy. He may be rude, fight with others, boast of sexual conquest, and try to exploit women. Such men tend to reject institutional responsibility and hate to join organizations.[14] These individuals influence subordinates to be responsible to them personally.
2. The second type, in contrast, is more successful at creating a good climate for regular work. His subordinates have both a sense of responsibility and a clear knowledge of the organization. Loyal to the organization, they are less defensive and more willing, when they need it, to seek expert advice in personal matters. They collect fewer status symbols.[15] This kind of maturity improves their performance from the organization's viewpoint.

Studying the specific types of individuals in an organization may allow a manager to predict their power behavior and its consequences for organizational performance. Such preparation could be extremely beneficial for the manager who must manage different power types. It could be predicted, for example, that individuals high in the need for power would more likely look for opportunities to exert it than individuals high in other needs. For example, one study of first-line supervisors showed that need for affiliation, not need for power, related to favorable job performance and favorable subordinate attitudes.[16] Similarly, the school committee would work more effectively if it included primarily social- or institutional-power types rather than personal-power types.

But power is not limited to individuals. Subunits, such as organizational departments or work teams, can also exercise power. The power of subunits can be analyzed the same way as the power of individuals. For both individuals and subunits, the sources of power are also the same.

■■ SOURCES OF POWER

What gives certain individuals in the introductory case the ability to influence others in the direction they desire? They derive their power from three sources, listed in Figure 19.2: (1) the position they hold (position power), (2) their personal characteristics (personal power), and (3) the information or resources they can access and control (information and resource-based power).

Position Power

Position power
Power that results from one's official place in an organization.

Position power is power that results from one's official place in an organization. As may be seen in Figure 19.3, the types of power that are positionally determined

FIGURE 19.2 ■
Sources of Power

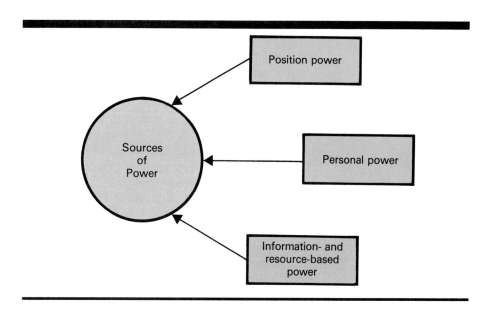

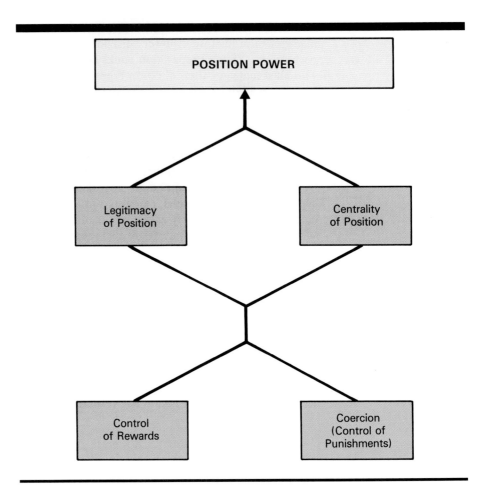

Legitimate power
Power that is derived from the position or job individuals hold in an organization.

Centrality
The degree to which the activities of the position are linked and important to those of other individuals or subunits.

include legitimate power, centrality power, reward power, and coercive power. **Legitimate power** is power that is derived from the position or job individuals hold in an organization. Possessing legitimate power means that managers can exert influence over others simply because of the authority associated with their jobs. The superintendent of schools has such power. It results in his subordinates obeying his rules or orders because they view them as legitimate due to the position he holds. Regardless of the performance level of the person holding a position, that individual has legitimate power simply because of the position held. For instance, even though Roger Smith, chairman of GM, has as yet not turned GM around, and has just recently realized that slashing capacity is necessary for GM to recover, he still has legitimate power. Among the most powerful individuals in business circles are those who possess both legitimate power and expertise, such as Chrysler CEO Lee Iacocca. Other positions accrue power because of their centrality. **Centrality** is the degree to which the activities of the position are linked and important to those of other individuals or subunits.[17] The superintendent, for example, has greater centrality than the school committee, thus he draws power from this characteristic of his job.

Individuals with position power frequently couple their authority with power due to their control of rewards and/or punishments. An individual who has control over organizational rewards, including pay raises, status, and desirable work assignments, as well as praise, recognition, or group sanctions, may use the rewards to encourage others' compliance with desired behaviors or goals. Managers effectively use this power if their subordinates believe that complying with the managers' requests will result in extrinsic or intrinsic rewards. Both the superintendent of schools and the school committee have some reward power, since they influence the hiring, promoting, and compensation of various employees. Caution must be used when rewarding employees. Providing virtually the same reward to all employees regardless of their performance frequently causes high-level performers to become disenchanted with the reward system, and subsequently they produce less.

Coercive power is power derived from the ability to punish or to recommend punishment. A manager with coercive power can force individuals to behave in certain ways, such as by demoting or dismissing them or by increasing the direction provided to them. For instance, when dealing with union problems in 1987, the founder/chairman of SCI Systems Inc., Olin King, used coercive power. His attitude toward the union was probably best summed up when he referred to union people as criminals and outlaws from the North. He used everything in his power to demoralize and cause problems for those affiliated with the union. Such a supervisor can exert power over a person who fears punishment for violation of a rule or policy. The superintendent of schools can recommend the termination or transfer of employees and thus has coercive power. The school committee gives final approval for the termination of any employee and therefore has coercive power. Coercive power must be used with extreme caution. Misapplied coercion can negatively affect the manager's effectiveness.

Coercive power
Power derived from the ability to punish or to recommend punishment.

Personal Power

Personal power
Power based on the contacts individuals have developed over time that allow them to influence the behavior of others.

Personal power is power based on the contacts individuals have developed over time that allow them to influence the behavior of others (see Figure 19.4). Some managers, for example, develop a network of individuals (subordinates, peers, or superiors) for whom they have done favors or provided special information or assistance. They establish a "quid pro quo" with these people, which allows them to influence their behavior. Such a web of influence can prove to be extremely effective, because to attain goals, managers can solicit the assured assistance of those in power positions.

An individual who has unique or special knowledge and experience may use this expertise as a source of influence and as a manner of building personal power. Physicians can influence patients to act in certain ways, because when giving advice based on medical knowledge, they are exerting expert power. As organizations become increasingly technology oriented, computer specialists and other technical workers acquire increased power. The Director of Research in the Lakedale Schools may use his unique knowledge about enrollment trends to influence closing decisions. Expertise in an area, especially in a firm where few others possess similar knowledge, can result in significant power for the experienced person.

Some individuals influence others because they have charisma or referent power—when one person identifies with or is attached to another and thus is influenced by that person. Individuals with charisma often exert referent power

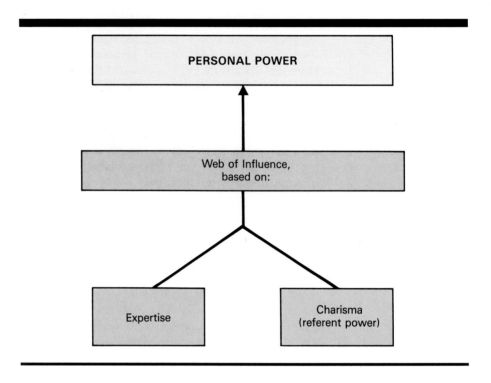

because they attract others to follow. A movie star, politician, or any organizational member with a charismatic personality may use this base of power. John F. Kennedy was said to have the power to hold a crowd spellbound when he spoke. Many who meet H. Ross Perot, founder of EDS, claim that he has referent power. To precisely assess someone's use of referent power, one must observe the individual in person or gather additional data on his or her behavior.

Information and Resource-Based Power

Access to information or resources provides a source of influence by helping individuals or subunits cope with uncertainty. An employee who has obtained information that others do not possess, but desire, has a certain degree of power. For example, the first individuals to learn how to operate a new software package has the power to share or not share the information. If other workers also have to learn how to use the software, this individual has the power to reduce the other workers' uncertainty.

Power may also come from the control of scarce resources or information, such as money or staff. Individuals who formulate rules to regulate the possession of resources, as well as those who actually possess, allocate, and use the resources, will acquire power.[18] Those who determine or administer the budget control resources. Employees who spend the budgeted funds access the resources.

Productive power is power that occurs when a job-holder has open channels to resources. It results from job activities that are relevant to, and that receive recognition from others, as well as from political alliances with sponsors, peers, and subordinates. In the introductory case, which job-holders have access to

Productive power
Power that occurs when a job-holder has open channels to resources.

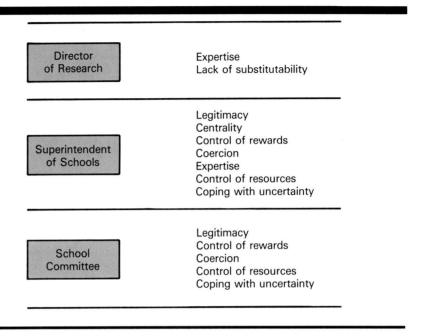

resources? Certainly the Director of Research has unique information about projected enrollments and costs of various school closing alternatives. He shares this with his supervisor, the superintendent. The superintendent, if he is to make quality decisions, relies on the director's providing accurate and complete information.

The power of an organizational subunit, such as the research department or the school committee, is a function of its unique capacity to fulfill the requirements of other subunits. In other words, its power derives from its *lack of substitutability* and the extent to which it *copes with uncertainty* for the other subunits.[19] In general, the less substitutable its activities, and the more it copes with uncertainty, the more power the subunit has. Also, a unit's ability to bring in resources from outside the organization influences the internal resources it acquires from the rest of the organization, thus further reinforcing its power.[20] Power can feed on power.

Returning to the introductory scenario, consider the information and resource-based power of the school committee. This unit lacks substitutability; no other unit has the same legal power. The committee can cope with uncertainty for other subunits by passing rules and regulations, allocating additional funds, and clarifying procedures for decisions such as school closings.

What types of social power do the people have in the introductory scenario? Figure 19.5 summarizes the source of power each person or group probably uses. Note that the individuals and groups use multiple sources of power. Although some sources are viewed as having a greater effect than others, typically, the more bases of power an individual can draw on, the more powerful the person is.[21]

To properly diagnose power, it is necessary to recognize the characteristics of the power-holder, his or her subordinates, and the organization. By doing so, managers may choose the appropriate source of influence from which to draw power. These power configurations may be either internal or external.

Power Configurations

Until now, we have addressed the concept of power as if it were absolute; however, there are various configurations of power. Henry Mintzberg identified eight power configurations, based on the nature of influence either inside or outside of the organization.[22] He describes the external influencers as *dominated,* where one individual or group has most power; *divided,* where a few competing groups or individuals share power; or *passive,* where no one outside the organization tries to exert power. The influence of those inside the organization is of five types: *personalized,* where the leader relies on personal control; *bureaucratic,* where formal standards are key; *ideologic,* where the norms created by the organization's ideology dominate; *professional,* where technical skills and knowledge are used; or *politicized,* where the political system is key.

Table 19.1 shows the basic ways influencers act to form power configurations. A closely held corporation (one where a few individuals—often family members—own all the stock), is an example of an instrument configuration. In it, an external owner, combined with formal standards, exerts primary influence. In a closed system, such as a large, mature organization, no external individuals or groups exert pressure. In entrepreneurial firms and others with the autocratic power configuration, primary influence comes from inside, but from the leader's own control and actions. Missionary organizations, such as charitable agencies and religious orders, also have only internal influence, by their predominant ideology. Meritocracies, such as universities and hospitals, experience power from internal

TABLE 19.1 ■ Major Power Configurations

Power Configuration	Example	External Influencers	Internal Influencers
Instrument	Closely held corporation Fire department Post Office	Dominated (one—e.g., external owner or the public)	Bureaucratic (formal standards)
Closed system	Large, mature organization Revolutionary political party Large government	Passive (no one)	Bureaucratic (formal standards)
Autocracy	Small organization Entrepreneurial firm Organization facing crisis	Passive (no one)	Personalized (leader control)
Missionary	Charitable organization Religious order	Passive (no one)	Ideologic (ideology)
Meritocracy	University Hospital Accounting firm	Passive (no one)	Professional (technical skills and knowledge)
Political arena	Organization experiencing a takeover Controversial public agency	Divided (several competing)	Politicized (political

Source: Henry Mintzberg, POWER IN AND AROUND ORGANIZATIONS, © 1983, p. 307. Adapted by permission of Prentice-Hall, Inc., Englewood Cliffs, New Jersey.

sources that have technical skills and knowledge. Finally, in organizations characterized as political arenas, a few competing external influences interact with the internal policies system to influence action. This typology can be used to help diagnose power attempts in an organization and then consider the likely consequences for the organization's performance and survival. By appreciating the nature of power configurations, managers are better able to understand and appreciate the nature of organizational power. It is also important that managers appreciate the impact of power differences on organizational effectiveness. When interacting groups experience performance difficulties, power differences are frequently the source of the problem.

■■ POWER DIFFERENCES

Performance difficulties occur when interacting groups differ in the power they have. These power differences could create managerial problems, and managers must be prepared to deal with the differences effectively. We discuss three causes of power differences: perceptions of substitutability, the ability to cope with uncertainty, and control of resources.

PERCEPTIONS OF SUBSTITUTABILITY

If the activities of a group are replaceable, or if another group can perform the same work, the group is considered substitutable. The less a group performs substitutable tasks, the more power it possesses. Top management frequently has unique knowledge and experience, which reduces its substitutability and results in its greater power. Those with technical knowledge in companies that have a computerized operation may be perceived by the less technically knowledgeable as essential to the organization's functioning, and subsequently they assume greater power. Basically, as the degree of substitutability increases, the degree of power a group possesses decreases, and vice versa.

ABILITY TO COPE WITH UNCERTAINTY

How well a group can deal with, and compensate for, a rapidly changing environment influences its power.[23] Typically, engineers can cope with uncertainty better than technicians because of their broader professional training and more diverse experiences; hence, they have greater power. Systems analysts can cope with uncertainty better than computer operators or computer programmers. It might be hypothesized that physicians can cope with a changing, complex environment and its demands better than nurses because physicians have a wider range of knowledge and experience to draw on. As nurses increase their professional training, however, this power difference is reduced. Basically, as the ability to cope with uncertainty increases, so does the degree of power a group possesses, and vice versa.

CONTROL OF RESOURCES

The amount of money, people, and time a group controls influences its power. The greater the amount of resources the group controls, the more power it has. Managers who control budgets often have greater power than those who do not.

Similarly, managers of line functions may have greater power than those who manage staff functions. Further, when two groups must divide resources, disagreements often arise about their optimal allocation, creating conflict between them. Communication between groups can increase or reduce these differences. Basically, however, as a group's control of resources increases, so does the degree of power a group possesses, and vice versa.

Perceptions of substitutability, the ability to cope with uncertainty, and control of resources are three common power differences that result in performance difficulties. By understanding and appreciating the nature of power differences among interacting groups, managers stand ready to effectively deal with performance difficulties.

■■■ STRATEGIES FOR OBTAINING POWER

Power is an inescapable element of management; when properly utilized, power enhances a manager's ability to attain organizational goals. Because of the usefulness of power, individuals and groups constantly seek a more favorable power position in organizations. There are numerous means by which a manager may secure power (see Figure 19.6). Among the most common are networking,

F I G U R E 19.6 ■■
Strategies for Obtaining
Power

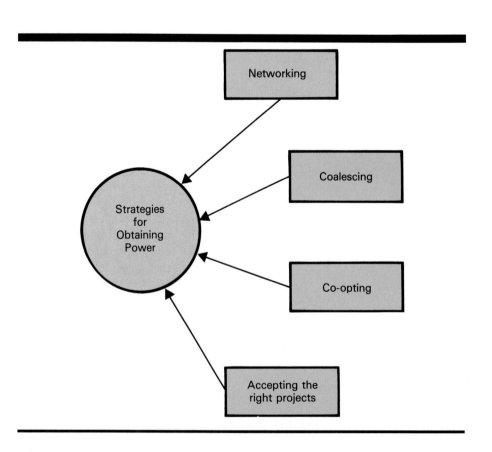

coalescing, co-opting, and accepting the right projects. This list should not be considered all inclusive, but it does provide insight into how power may be obtained.

Networking

Networking
The cultivating of relationships with the right people for the purpose of obtaining power.

Anyone who has worked in an organization for any length of time has likely heard the expression, "It's not what you know but who you know." At times, there is more than a smattering of truth to this statement. **Networking** is the cultivating of relationships with the right people for the purpose of obtaining power. As an example, a lower-level manager may meet an upper-level manager at the golf course. A friendship may develop as they build a social relationship at the golf club. This friendship may enhance the lower-level manager's personal power at the company. Networking relationships, however, do not necessarily involve upper-level management. They may also involve powerful peers and even subordinates. Influential peers or competent subordinates can enhance an individual's personal power and thereby facilitate an individual's ability to perform.

Research has shown that informal influence expressed among peers in a work unit and formal influence up the chain of command correlate positively with positional and personal bases of power.[24] For example, the informal network may result in the transfer of legitimate authority from a supervisor to an influential subordinate. The informal network can be utilized to build a power base.

Networking means cultivating relationships with people that may enhance one's personal power.
(© Daemmrich/Stock, Boston, Inc.)

To identify an informal network, the following questions can be asked:

1. Who has relevant information?
2. To whom does that person communicate the information?
3. How many others have access to it?
4. What potential sources of power exist in the team?

Rosabeth Moss Kanter argues that women in management experience powerlessness because of a combination of formal and informal practices that put them into low-power positions;[25] but these same practices can extend to men. Symptoms of powerlessness include receiving overly close supervision, being rules-minded and overly concerned with routines, and doing all the work oneself.[26]

Managers contribute to the powerlessness of both male and female job-holders. They particularly contribute to the powerlessness of a woman by

1. patronizingly overprotecting her—not suggesting her for high-risk, visible assignments, for example;
2. failing to provide managerial support—possibly by listening to all negative comments about her and thus inviting others to look for the woman's failings;
3. assuming that she does not know the ropes;
4. ignoring women in informal social situations; and
5. failing to provide organizational support by not sharing power with her.[27]

Boundary-spanner roles, in contrast, have significant power potential; for example, public relations directors and purchasing agents who deal with the outside environment for the benefit of the organization's members. Their ability to cope with uncertainty for others is one source of their power; the ability to channel or control information going to the organization's members is another. A study of power in a university concluded that the best predictor of the relative power of the different departments was the proportion of outside grant and contract money earned. The department's graduate program size, and even their national prestige, were less important factors.[28] Identification of boundary-spanners and diagnosis of their effectiveness in this role, then, are important means of assessing power in organizations.

Coalescing

Coalescing
The process of individuals or groups combining their resources to pursue common objectives.

The process of individuals or groups combining their resources to pursue common objectives is referred to as **coalescing.** The purpose of individuals or groups creating such alliances is to increase their ability to influence others and to secure greater control over resources. Labor leaders and members have long recognized the value of coalescing. "If I don't get a raise, I'll quit" will provoke little or no action on the part of management unless all workers issue the same statement in unison. By coalescing, the groups have considerably more influence with management. Even competing companies may coalesce and lobby for or against certain proposed legislation. Normally, the greater the influence of the individuals or groups combining their resources to pursue common objectives, the more significant the coalescing effort.

Co-opting

A method of increasing power and creating alliances in which individuals or groups whose support is needed are absorbed into another group is referred to as **co-opting.** Co-opting is used for the purpose of eliminating or reducing threats and opposition to an individual's power base. Suppose, for instance, that a manager desires to implement a particular project, but another manager of similar status has been known to have some reservations concerning the project. Perhaps the manager with the concerns may be invited to participate on the team responsible for the implementation of the project. Should the invitation be accepted, there is the likelihood that the resistance will be neutralized.

Co-opting
A method of increasing power and creating alliances in which individuals or groups whose support is needed are absorbed into another group.

Accepting the Right Projects

Individuals can obtain power in organizations by engaging in activities that are highly visible, extraordinary, and related to accomplishing organizational objectives.[29] For example, a faculty member may request and obtain the task of developing a very important accreditation report. In obtaining data for the report, he or she must work with the president, vice-presidents, deans, department heads, and other administrators across campus. If the faculty member accomplishes this task in an exceptional manner and accreditation results, then significant power has been obtained. As might be expected, there is risk involved. Should the project fail, everyone on campus will know who was in charge, and the faculty member may have less power than before.

Since power is an inescapable element of management, those with substantial power often have an edge in accomplishing organizational goals. An individual who uses networking, coalescing, or co-opting, who accepts the right projects, or who uses other similar ways to obtain power, can gain additional influence to facilitate accomplishment of organizational objectives. In many, possibly all, organizations, only those with a reasonable degree of power can operate effectively. To maximize their effectiveness, therefore, managers should first obtain a reasonable power base.

■ SPECIAL CASES OF POWER RELATIONS

Although groups of all types interact in organizations, two types of power relationships pose particular dilemmas and concerns. In this section, the power relations between union and management and between planners and implementers are examined. Knowing how to deal with these two types of power relationships serves as a framework for handling similar relationships.

The Power Relationship between Union and Management

Union and management groups work under collective bargaining agreements, which specify the rules of the workplace, amounts of compensation, and methods for settling disputes. Representatives of union and management negotiate a contract acceptable to both sides; the ease of reaching agreement may provide a backdrop for subsequent labor-management relations.

Traditionally, these groups have demonstrated an adversarial relationship. Distributive bargaining, where one party's gain is another's loss, has always characterized the bargaining process. To ensure that its demands will be met, each party tries to increase its power relative to the power of the other. This kind of bargaining frequently results in conflict between the two groups.

More recently, union and management have taken an integrative, or problem-solving, approach to negotiations. This approach assumes that both parties can win in the formulation of a contract.[30] Because one party's gain does not lead to another's loss, this type of bargaining tends to result in more effective interactions between the groups. A study of contracts in the 1980s showed some movement toward accommodation and cooperation, especially for those parties who re-opened contracts for renegotiations before they had expired.[31]

The tone set during negotiations and the satisfaction of both sides with the contract influence the subsequent relations between union and management during the contract period. Where adversarial relations persist, union members may seek any opportunity to challenge the actions of management. They may file grievances about their job assignments, work schedule, or compensation. As much as possible, both union and management should strive to maintain collaborative relationships that focus on accomplishing organizational goals.

Managers must also handle grievances and work with union representatives effectively. In handling a grievance, a supervisor should know the negotiated agreement, get all the facts, listen to the problem with interest, consider the matter important, remain calm, consider seeking a third party's assistance, give an answer as soon as possible, sell the decision to the workers, and document the outcomes.[32] In working with union representatives, supervisors must also understand the agreement, uphold it, be concerned for employee welfare, represent employers and management fairly, handle grievances promptly and fairly, keep current about solutions to similar grievances, develop good working relationships, protect management rights, respect and show an understanding of the union's position, provide a fair hearing, and keep the union informed about changes in the work situation.[33]

The Power Relationship between Planners and Implementers

Problems often arise between the individuals who plan and the individuals who implement the plans; for example, designers and manufacturing personnel, copy designers and copy setters, strategic planning groups and top management, and physicians and nurses. Too frequently these groups operate in isolation rather than in a collaborative fashion.

Planners and implementers may define their roles narrowly. Planners may exclude implementers from participating in the planning activity; implementers may similarly exclude planners. Each may feel accountable for accomplishing only their own part of the project; they may lack superordinate goals. To preserve their reputation, planning group members may feel they have to complete their part of the task perfectly before they hand the plans and responsibility over to the implementers.

In the power relationship between staff and line positions, the issues are similar to those of the power relationship between planners and implementers.

Line job-holders such as foremen, vice-presidents, and general managers produce the final product or service of an organization directly; they generally have legitimate, direct command over others. Staff job-holders such as accountants, quality-control managers, and assistants to the president, in contrast, provide advice and assistance to the line in getting the work done. Confusion over the roles they play may contribute to communication and operations difficulties.

In studying the relationship between these groups, one must assess the extent of their joint collaboration during both planning and implementation. Planners must establish communication with implementers early in the project. The two groups must use a common communication language and recognize that ongoing communication is essential. They must also identify and work toward a common goal.

■ SIGNIFICANCE OF POWER TO THE MANAGER

Research has shown that a good manager must have a concern for acquiring and using power. In a number of studies it was found that over 70 percent of managers have a higher need for power than does the general population.[34] Among better managers, the need for power is stronger than the need to be liked by others. This need for power is not normally a desire to be dictatorial, nor is it necessarily a drive for personal enhancement. Rather, it reflects a manager's concern for influencing others on behalf of the organization. Better managers probably have a need for socialized power rather than personal power. Managers who feel a greater need to be liked than to influence others tend to be less effective.

The control of situational factors, both in and out of the organization, is of significant concern to modern managers. It has been noted that when organizations grow so large and complex that no one individual has the capacity to manage all of the interdependencies, a dominant managing group will develop. This coalition is sometimes formalized into a presidential or executive office; normally, however, it is not actually so recorded on a formal organizational chart. If the president of the firm depends heavily on the vice-president of finance to develop crucial programs, that vice-president will likely be a member of the dominant coalition and therefore have power in excess of that suggested by the official chart. Within the organization, smaller and sometimes more temporary coalitions are formed to execute tasks involving significant interdependencies.

■ POLITICAL ACTION IN ORGANIZATIONS

In everyday conversations with the general public, the politician often receives low marks of approval. Political scandals regularly hit the front page of daily newspapers. Politics and politicians exist in all forms of organized society, not just government. In these, political-type action can and does provide positive values in promoting cooperation among individuals and groups with different interests and objectives.

Politics
A network of interactions by which power is acquired, transferred, and exercised on others.

Politics can be described as a "network of interactions by which power is acquired, transferred, and exercised on others."[35] Individuals and units in organizations use power to take political action. Let us think about this definition in order to gain a thorough appreciation of what it means. The politician is working with and through many people, hence the term *network*. As such, politics transcend the traditional organizational boundaries. The medium of exchange in politics is power, just as the dollar is used as the medium of exchange in economics. Shrewd politicians acquire power. They transfer it to others when it can *purchase* something of value. Just like a banker, a politician must keep a balance sheet. When power is transferred, something is expected in return. To the politician, a favor given now is often power to be extracted in the future.

Managers must at least recognize the political forces in their organizations. Some may choose to behave essentially as politicians. In fact, management theorists have attempted to apply political science techniques to their analysis of organizations.[36]

The degree of politicking a manager does is limited not only by the formal organizational restrictions but also by that manager's personal code of ethics and conscience. The fact that at times politics may be unethical should not preclude material attention to the subject. That politics does exist in various business organizations is undeniable. No business can be so completely and rigidly run by the book, and such politicking cannot be condemned per se. Some politically based accommodations are constructive; others perhaps are destructive, both of organized activity and of individual morals.

It is apparent that some degree of politics is a fact of organized life, regardless of the caliber of people involved or the degree of formalization of organization rules and regulations. No doubt some political maneuvering can make a new contribution toward an organization's effectiveness. Where there is head-on conflict, and where interdependencies make some degree of cooperation essential, concessions worked out between parties often involve some bending or reinterpretation of the rules. On many occasions, the various conflicting interests are all highly legitimate and rest on solid ground.

For the basic work of the organization to continue, some degree of reconciliation is required, necessitating some type of informal accommodation, compromise, or exchange. In the next section we will consider means of influence and the means of improving political action.

Means of Influence

As discussed above in the section on power configurations, individuals can exert influence in a variety of ways. Such influence may be regular or episodic, general or focused, detached or personal, supportive or obstructive, formal or informal.[37] Society or individuals outside the organization attempt to influence organizational behavior by using existing or developing social norms, imposing formal constraints on the organization, conducting pressure campaigns, instituting direct controls on the organization, or obtaining membership on the board of directors.[38]

Those inside the organization, in contrast, use authority, ideology, expertise, or politics, among others, to influence.[39] The superintendent of schools uses each of these four behaviors, and probably others; the Director of Research relies most on expertise; the school committee uses authority, ideology, or politics. The legitimacy of each type of influence might be argued, but each can affect decision making.

Most influence attempts described occur downward in the organization. Managers, for example, can give direct orders to subordinates, establish guidelines for their decision making, approve or reject subordinates' decisions, or allocate resources to them.[40] But lateral influence can also occur. Peers can offer advice or provide service; however, they can also use these roles to control others. They can audit or determine the acceptability of others' work, and they can stabilize or specify what will be permitted from others.[41]

Individuals can also exert upward influence, typically to promote or protect their self-interests.[42] They can control the type of information passed to superiors, and they may consciously withhold information they feel is detrimental to themselves. Occasionally workers punish or reward their superiors, by withholding or providing a quality work effort, for example. Managing the boss effectively requires understanding and responding to this individual's needs.[43]

Individuals who must identify and use resources implement their political influence along one of three dimensions: (1) internal-external, (2) vertical-lateral, or (3) legitimate-illegitimate.[44] Along the internal-external dimension, people may rely on resources internal to the organization. They exchange favors or form networks with other employees. When internal resources fail or become inadequate, these individuals may turn outside the organization, by joining professional organizations or forming alliances elsewhere. On the vertical-lateral dimension, individuals exert influence either by relating to superiors or subordinates or by relating to peers. Mentor-protégé activities occur vertically. Coalition formation occurs laterally. The third dimension contrasts normal to extreme behavior. For example, most organizational members view forming coalitions as legitimate and sabotaging production as illegitimate.

Means of Improving Political Action

Exchange theories discuss power in terms of bargaining and negotiations, rather than in terms of social networks.[45] Labor negotiations, in particular, often involve power acts that can significantly influence bargaining outcomes.[46] Labor-management relations increasingly emphasize integrative, rather than distributive, bargaining. Coalitions often form as a way of increasing an individual's or group's power in a bargaining situation; that is, members of coalitions frequently muster sufficient resources to resolve a negotiating problem.

In the political arena bargaining and negotiations are particularly important. Interest groups and political parties use power to influence authorities to give them what they want.[47] A party will choose among inaction, problem-solving, yielding, and contending strategies, depending on its level of concern for its own and another party's outcomes. A party with low concern for both its own and the other's outcome will not act—inaction strategy. A party with high concern for both parties' outcomes will take a problem-solving approach. A party with low concern for its own outcomes and high concern for the other's will yield to the other party. It will not if concern for its own outcomes is high and concern for the other's is low.[48] An effective negotiator is aware of negotiation's tightropes, avoids the need to impress others, develops interpersonal sensitivity, helps induce the other party's sense of negotiating competence, avoids commitments to intransigent positions, and is sensitive to conflict intensity and the necessary coping strategies.[49]

Conflict is often created by the exercise of political power. To reduce conflict, formal leaders of both private and public organizations frequently seek ways to exert power without generating conflict, to limit power, and to restore an organization to equilibrium after the exercise of power.[50]

SUMMARY

Power is the potential or actual ability to influence others in a desired direction. To get things done the way they want them to be done, individuals develop a power base and then apply that power to individual and organizational situations. Two common reasons for exerting power are power/dependence relationships and individual needs for power. Sources of power include position held, personal characteristics, and the resources or information individuals can access and control. Position power includes legitimate, reward, and coercive power. Personal power is based on contacts individuals develop over time that allow them to influence the behavior of others. Access to resources or information allows individuals to help others cope with uncertainty.

Today, various power configurations impact what was once a rather absolute concept of power. Knowledge of power configurations leads to a better understanding of the nature of organizational power. Also, managers need to understand how organizational effectiveness is affected by power differences, frequently a problem when interacting groups experience performance difficulties. To deal with such differences managers must understand their causes. Perceptions of substitutability, the ability to cope with uncertainty, and control of resources are three causes of power differences.

Power is an inescapable element of management. When properly utilized, power enhances a manager's ability to attain organizational goals. Individuals and groups are constantly seeking a more favorable power position. To secure power, managers may resort to networking, coalescing, co-opting, and accepting the right projects.

In a number of studies it was found that, in over 70 percent of managers, the need for power was higher than in the general population. Also, among better managers, the need for power is stronger than the need to be liked by others. Not normally a desire to be dictatorial, nor a drive for personal enhancement, this need for power reflects a concern for influencing others on behalf of the organization. Perhaps the need is for socialized power rather than personal power. Managers who feel a greater need to be liked than to influence others tend to be less effective in many organizations.

Politics is a network of interactions. In politics, power is acquired, transferred, and exercised on others. In organizations, individuals and units use power to take political action. Conflict is often created by the exercise of political power, and formal leaders of both private and public organizations frequently seek ways of exerting power without generating conflict. Properly utilized, political networks are extremely effective in accomplishing organizational goals.

REVIEW QUESTIONS

1. Define power.
2. Define the following terms:
   a. legitimate power
   b. centrality
   c. coercive power
   d. personal power
   e. productive power
3. What are the causes of power differences? Briefly discuss each.
4. What are the means a manager may use to secure power?
5. Describe how knowledge of power may be used in labor/management negotiations.
6. What is the significance of power to a manager?
7. Define politics. What is the importance of an understanding of politics to a manager?

KEY TERMS

power	coercive power	coalescing
position power	personal power	co-opting
legitimate power	productive power	politics
centrality	networking	

CASE STUDY   WHO'S IN CHARGE AROUND HERE?

WHEN DOUG SELF came to work in the accounting department at Ritger Paper Products Company, James Norris considered it a personal victory. Doug was the top business school graduate at nearby Wichita State College the previous year. For two years he was president of the Student Government Association and had been active in every aspect of campus life.

James was the comptroller at Ritger. He supervised nine accountants and clerks. James was pleased to have attracted such an outstanding young man, and he made sure his superiors knew of the excellent recruiting job he had done.

Within a short while it was clear to everyone in the department that Doug was not only friendly, outgoing, and easy to talk to but also well informed about accounting. Before long Doug had made friends with everyone in the office, and James noticed that a number of the accountants began to take their questions and problems to Doug for solution. He always seemed to have the right answer and to enjoy taking time to help. He also did an excellent job on all his own work.

Doug's presence in the accounting department made James's job easier. In fact, most of the problem-solving duties that James used to handle were brought to Doug. Only when a decision was required from outside the department would James be consulted. In a way, James was pleased with the

way things were turning out. But two things bothered him. First, the accountants and clerks began to consult with Doug even about personal matters. James was twenty years older than Doug, and he felt more qualified in that respect. Second, Doug had developed a number of fast friendships outside the department, especially with two of the company's senior officials. James felt very insecure about this. He thought it was only a matter of time until Doug began to bypass him on official matters.

James decided to take action. Although he was not really sure how to handle the situation, he began to look for chances to criticize Doug in front of his peers. He also began to check with others in the department. Anyone who took a problem or question to Doug was reminded that he was their direct superior, and he looked for ways to change or demean the advice Doug had given. It was not long before the other employees got the signal. Ultimately, James's strategy worked; Doug quit. But within a week, three other of James's best accountants turned in their resignations, and the department was thrown into complete confusion.

QUESTIONS
1. What sources of power did Doug possess? What sources of power did James possess?
2. To what extent was Doug a threat to James? Explain in relation to power differences.

CASE STUDY   POWER ANYONE?

JIM PERRY WAS the director of special projects at the Main Street Bank and Trust Company. He had recently been made an officer of the bank and reported directly to the president. During his five years at Main Street, Jim has been involved in the investigation, development, and implementation of several new products and services. Typically, he was assigned one other employee to help him with the special projects.

Recently, however, Jim was presented with what he considered to be the biggest challenge of his

career. Partnership banking had become the "hot product" in the banking industry. In partnership banking, each customer is assigned a liaison at the bank. This person coordinates the services provided and acts as an advocate for that customer within the bank. Main Street Bank and Trust was ready to jump on the bandwagon. Jim was made responsible for developing and implementing the new service. Because of the size of the project, he was assigned five bank employees to assist him, selected from five departments identified by the president. The manager of each department selected one employee. Together, the five employees would form what was being called the "partnership task force."

Interviews with the five managers indicated that they had chosen workers who could easily be freed from their current duties. The following comprised the team: (1) Paul Goodman, an administrative assistant to the vice-president of operations; (2) Jenny Jackson, a newly appointed senior loan officer; (3) Michael Tracy, a recently promoted branch manager of a small suburban branch; (4) Anne Richards, a marketing staff member; and (5) Jeffrey Wilson, a trainee assigned to the office of the president.

At the first weekly meeting of the task force, Jim outlined his goals for the project and a tentative timetable. There was little discussion, and the meeting was quickly adjourned. At the second meeting, Anne Richards presented a list of ideas. These elicited no interest or discussion from the other members. Subsequent weekly meetings followed similar patterns. Either Jim offered suggestions, ideas, and comments, with little discussion, or discussions were reduced to verbal

battles between Michael Tracy and Anne Richards, who each seemed to feel that he or she had the most, indeed the only expertise for designing the partnership banking program. Occasionally task force members seemed to agree that they had identified some viable components of the new program. However, no one worked on the project outside the group meeting time, and at the start of the following meeting, previous progress was ignored.

Jim expressed considerable frustration over the slow progress of the task force's efforts toward developing a viable program. He felt they were not working as a team and that individual agendas were surfacing too frequently. After two months of weekly meetings, Jim told the president he thought the group should be reconstituted if partnership banking were ever to be introduced at Main Street Bank and Trust.

QUESTIONS

1. From this case, identify any power positions that have developed or are developing.
2. Could politics be used to assist in this situation? Discuss.

EXPERIENTIAL EXERCISE

Ed Gray is a recently promoted supervisor, and he is about to meet with his boss, Gloria Manton, to discuss a problem relating to uncooperative employees. Ed reasons, "I need more coercive power in order to bring the employees in line. The only thing some of these people respect is force. Once they fear me, they will produce for me. I really want to come down hard on John Johnson, who is turning some of the other employees against me. Once I put the 'hammer down' on Johnson, the others will fall in line, and all I will need from that point on is the fear of force."

Gloria Manton, the manager, has been affiliated with the company for several years and has seen this problem before. She ponders, "Ed has become irritated with some employees who are intent on providing irritation. The main irritant is John, who is the group leader, and other people do follow his lead. John is excellent at his job and has helped almost everyone on the line. But, when an overanxious supervisor comes on too strong, John believes it is his duty to provide helpful insight. Harshly punishing John may actually cause more problems and severely upset the harmony of the work group. Putting the 'hammer down' on John would probably make Ed feel good, but it may adversely impact work-group productivity. Ed must be made to appreciate the total gravity of this situation."

It is fairly obvious that Gloria and Ed will have difficulty working out the proper method of dealing with John. Do you want to be Gloria or Ed? This exercise will require only two of you to actively participate, so don't miss out. The rest of you observe carefully. Your instructor will provide participants with additional information.

NOTES

1. G. R. Salancik and J. Pfeffer, "Who Gets Power—and How They Hold on to It: A Strategic-contingency Model of Power," *Organizational Dynamics* 5 (Winter 1977): 3–21.
2. Jo Ellen Davis and Pete Engardio. "What It's Like to Work for Frank Lorenzo," *Business Week,* 18 May 1987, 76.
3. R. M. Kanter, "Power Failures in Management Circuits," *Harvard Business Review* 57 (1979): 65–75.
4. A. Kaplan, "Power in Perspective," in *Power and Conflict in Organizations,* ed. R. L. Kahn and E. Boulding (London: Tavistock, 1964); M. Weber, *The Theory of Social and Economic Organization* (Glencoe, Ill.: Free Press, 1947).
5. H. Mintzberg, *Power In and Around Organizations* (Englewood Cliffs, N.J.: Prentice-Hall, 1983).
6. P. M. Balu, *Exchange and Power in Social Life* (New York: John Wiley & Sons, 1964).
7. R. M. Emerson, "Power-dependence Relations," *American Sociological Review* 27 (1962): 31–41.
8. J. P. Kotter, "Power, Dependence, and Effective Management," *Harvard Business Review* 55 (1977): 125–136.

9. Kotter, "Effective Management," 125–136.

10. J. P. Kotter, "Power, Success, and Organizational Effectiveness," *Organizational Dynamics* 6 (1978): 27–40.

11. Kotter, "Organizational Effectiveness," 27–40.

12. D. McClelland and D. H. Burnham, "Power Driven Managers: Good Guys Make Bum Bosses," *Psychology Today,* December 1975.

13. R. M. Steers and L. W. Porter, *Motivation and Work Behavior* (New York: McGraw-Hill, 1979).

14. McClelland and Burnham, "Power Driven Managers."

15. McClelland and Burnham, "Power Driven Managers."

16. E. T. Cornelius III and F. B. Lane, "The Power Motive and Managerial Success in a Professionally Oriented Service Industry Organization," *Journal of Applied Psychology* 69 (1984): 32–39.

17. D. J. Hickson, C. R. Hinings, C. A. Lee, R. E. Schneck, and J. M. Pennings, "A Strategic Contingencies Theory of Intraorganizational Power," *Administrative Science Quarterly* 16 (June 1971): 216–227; note that resource control and network centrality interact with hierarchical authority to create structural sources of power, as described by W. G. Astley and P. S. Sachdeva, "Structural Sources of Intraorganizational Power: A Theoretical Synthesis," *Academy of Management Review* 9 (1984): 104–113.

18. J. Pfeffer and G. R. Salancik, *The External Control of Organizations* (New York: Harper & Row, 1978).

19. Hickson et al., "Contingencies Theory," 216–227.

20. J.D. Hackman, "Power and Centrality in the Allocation of Resources in Colleges and Universities," *Administrative Science Quarterly* 30 (March 1985): 61–77.

21. D. H. Fenn, Jr., "Finding Where the Power Lies in Government," *Harvard Business Review* 57 (1979): 144–153; Y. K. Shetty, "Managerial Power and Organizational Effectiveness," *Journal of Management Studies* 15 (May 1978): 176–186.

22. H. Mintzberg, "Power and Organization Life Cycles," *Academy of Management Review* 9 (April 1984): 207–224; Mintzberg, *Power In and Around Organizations.*

23. D. Hickson, C. Hinings, C. Lee, R. Schneck, and J. A. Pennings, "A Strategic Contingencies Theory of Intraorganizational Power," *Administrative Science Quarterly* 23 (1978): 65–90.

24. A. Cobb, "Informal Influence in the Formal Organization: Perceived Sources of Power among Work Unit Peers," *Academy of Management Journal* 23 (March 1980): 155–161.

25. Kanter, "Power Failures," 65–75.

26. Kanter, "Power Failures," 65–75.

27. R. E. Spekman, "Influence and Information: An Exploratory Investigation of the Boundary Person's Bases of Power," *Academy of Management Journal* 22 (March 1979): 104–117.

28. G. R. Salancik and J. Pfeffer, "The Bases and Use of Power in Organizational Decision-making: The Case of a University," *Administrative Science Quarterly* 19 (December 1974): 453–473.

29. R. M. Kanter, *Men and Women of the Corporation* (New York: Basic Books, 1977).

30. R. Fisher and W. Uri, *Getting to Yes: Negotiating Agreement without Giving In* (Boston: Houghton Mifflin, 1981).

31. W. E. Fulmer, "Labor-management Relations in the '80s: Revolution or Evolution?" *Business Horizons* 27 (January–February 1984): 26–31.

32. D. Caruth and H. N. Mills, Jr., "Working Toward Better Union Relations," *Supervisory Management* 30 (February 1985): 11.

33. Caruth and Mills, Jr., "Union Relations," 12–13.

34. David C. McClelland and David H. Burnham, "Power Is the Great Motivator," *Harvard Business Review* 54 (March–April 1976): 102.

35. John M. Pfiffner and Frank P. Sherwood, *Administrative Organization* (Englewood Cliffs, N.J.: Prentice-Hall, 1960), 311.

36. Rob Lucas, "Political-Cultural Analysis of Organizations," *Academy of Management Journal* 12, no. 1 (January 1987): 144–156.
37. H. Mintzberg, "Power and Organization Life Cycles," *Academy of Management Review* 9 (April 1984): 207–224; Mintzberg, *Power In and Around Organizations.*
38. Mintzberg, "Power and Organization Life Cycles," 207–224.
39. Mintzberg, "Power and Organization Life Cycles," 207–224.
40. Mintzberg, "Power and Organization Life Cycles," 207–224.
41. L. Sayes, *Leadership: What Effective Managers Really Do and How They Do It* (New York: McGraw-Hill, 1979).
42. R. Allen, D. Madison, L. Porter, P. Renwick, and B. Mayes, "Organizational Politics: Tactics and Characteristics of Its Actors," *California Management Review* 22 (Fall 1979): 77–83.
43. J. Gabarro and J. Kotter, "Managing Your Boss," *Harvard Business Review* 58 (January–February 1980): 92–100.
44. D. Farrell and J. C. Petersen, "Patterns of Political Behavior in Organizations," *Academy of Management Review* 7 (July 1982): 403–412.
45. D. Kipnis, *The Powerholders* (Chicago: University of Chicago Press, 1976).
46. R. E. Walton and R. B. McKersie, *A Behavioral Theory of Labor Negotiations* (New York: McGraw-Hill, 1965).
47. W. A. Gamson, *Power and Discontent* (Homewood, Ill.: Dorsey Press, 1968).
48. D. G. Pruitt, "Strategic Choice in Negotiation," *American Behavioral Scientist* 27 (November–December 1983): 167–194
49. J. Z. Rubin, "Negotiation," *American Behavioral Scientist* 27 (November–December 1983): 136–148.
50. R. L. Kahn and E. Boulding, *Power and Conflict in Organizations* (New York: Basic Books, 1964).

REFERENCES

Brown, J. L., and N. M. Agnew. "The Balance of Power in a Matrix Structure." *Business Horizons* 25 (November–December 1982): 51–54.

Clegg, Stewart R. "The Language of Power and the Power of Language." *Organization Studies* 8 (Winter 1987): 60–69.

Cobb, A. "Informal Influence in the Formal Organization: Perceived Sources of Power among Work Unit Peers." *Academy of Management Journal* 23 (March 1980): 155–161.

Cornelius, E. T., III, and F. B. Lane. "The Power Motive and Managerial Success in a Professionally Oriented Service Industry Organization." *Journal of Applied Psychology* 69 (1984): 32–39.

Farrell, D., and J. C. Petersen. "Patterns of Political Behavior in Organizations." *Academy of Management Review* 7 (July 1982): 403–412.

Fenn, D. H., Jr. "Finding Where the Power Lies in Government." *Harvard Business Review* 57 (1979): 144–153.

Fiorelli, Joseph S. "Power in Work Groups: Team Member's Perspectives." *Human Relations* 11 (January 1988): pp. 1–12.

Gabarro, J., and J. Kotter. "Managing Your Boss." *Harvard Business Review* 58 (January–February 1980): 92–100.

Gist, Marilyn E., Edwin A. Locke, and M. Susan Taylor. "Organizational Behavior: Group Structure, Process, and Effectiveness." *Journal of Management* 13 (Summer 1987): 237–257.

Hackman, J. D. "Power and Centrality in the Allocation of Resources in Colleges and Universities." *Administrative Science Quarterly* 30 (March 1985): 61–77.

Hickson, D. J., C. R. Hinings, C. A. Lee, R. E. Schneck, and J. M. Pennings. "A Strategic Contingencies Theory of Intraorganizational Power." *Administrative Science Quarterly* 16 (June 1971): 216–227.

Kahn, R. L., and E. Boulding. *Power and Conflict in Organizations.* New York: Basic Books, 1964.

Kipnis, D. *The Powerholders.* Chicago: University of Chicago Press, 1976.

Kotter, J. P. "Power, Dependence, and Effective Management." *Harvard Business Review* 55 (1977): 125–136.

Lucas, Rob. "Organizational Diagnostics: Translating the Political into the Technical." *Journal of Management* 13 (Spring 1987): 135–148.

McClelland, D., and D. H. Burnham. "Power Driven Managers: Good Guys Make Bum Bosses." *Psychology Today* (December 1975).

Mainiero, Lisa A. "Coping with Powerlessness: The Relationship of Gender and Job Dependency to Empowerment-Strategy Usage." *Administrative Science Quarterly* 31 (December 1986): 633–653.

Mintzberg, H. *Power in and Around Organizations.* Englewood Cliffs, N.J.: Prentice-Hall, 1983.

——— . "Power and Organization Life Cycles." *Academy of Management Review* 9 (April 1984): 207–224.

Morley, Donald Dean, and Pamela Schockley-Zalabak. "Conflict Avoiders and Compromisers: Toward an Understanding of Their Organizational Communication Style." *Group & Organization Studies* 11 (December 1986): 387–402.

Pruitt, D. G. "Strategic Choice in Negotiation." *American Behavioral Scientist* 27 (November–December 1983): 167–194.

Roos, L. L., Jr., and R. I. Hall. "Influence Diagrams and Organizational Power." *Administrative Science Quarterly* 25 (March 1980): 57–71.

Smith, Kenwyn K., and David N. Berg. "A Paradoxical Conception of Group Dynamics." *Human Relations* 10 (October 1987): 633–657.

Van de Vliert, E. "Escalative Intervention in Small-Group Conflicts." *Journal of Applied Behavioral Science* 21 (February 1985): 19–36.

Weber, M. *The Theory of Social and Economic Organization.* Glencoe, Ill.: Free Press, 1947.

CHAPTER

20

Corporate Culture, Change, and Development

Learning Objectives

After completing this chapter students should be able to

1. Explain the concept of corporate culture, describe the factors that impact it, and state evidence of culture.
2. Distinguish between a participative and a non-participative culture and identify the values and limitations of participation.
3. Identify and describe the change sequence and relate sources of resistance to change and the approaches that can be used in reducing resistance to change.
4. Describe the organizational development techniques that are available to implement change.

IBM HAS LONG been recognized as having a distinctive corporate culture. The main elements of that culture are a service orientation, conservative dress, incentive-type compensation, internal competition among employees, and new ideas. Most of these principles have been reasonably constant for several decades, having grown out of the personal philosophies of Thomas J. Watson, who became president of IBM in 1914. Those philosophies were continued by Thomas, Jr., who took over from his father in the 1960s.

IBM purposely initiated radical change in the early 1980s. Writing about the "lean, mean new IBM," *Fortune* reported:

> Competitors have felt [the] ground tremble. Their nemesis from Armonk [Armonk, New York where IBM was headquartered] has revolutionized the way it does business, from grand strategy to the finest tactical detail, and has emerged a tougher opponent than ever before. IBM now speeds products to market faster than in the past, attacks its rivals with unprecedented price cuts, and outraces competitors to emerging new businesses. . . . To its old motto "Think" IBM seems to have appended the word "Differently."[1]

Since 1981, IBM has started fourteen new companies, which can more or less independently seek opportunities in areas such as robotics, medical technology, and communications equipment.

Finally, the company's dependency on people has been changed somewhat by the $10 billion sunk into plant and equipment since 1977. John Opel, IBM's chairman and chief executive, says, "Dominance may be a very transitory thing." By changing its culture rather than clinging to tradition, IBM has improved its chances of remaining number one. *Fortune* magazine concludes, "When a dominant company's advantage wanes, seemingly perilous, tradition-shattering change can be the course of least risk."

But despite the changes, many continued to criticize the IBM system. In 1987, the company was under attack from within and viewed with decreasing awe from without. Several hundred of the company's 288,000 U.S. workers had organized themselves into two groups, IBM Workers United and the Black Workers Alliance, to confront management about employee rights. A former IBM employee complained, "IBM is a total-control company. IBM's management style is from the top down. It's quasi-military." And after four years at the top of *Fortune* magazine's "most-admired company" list, IBM dropped to number seven.[2] ∎

T HE TRADITIONAL CORPORATE CULTURE at IBM sprang in large measure from the philosophies of Thomas Watson. Steve Jobs is credited with having created a looser, more informal climate at Apple Computer. Other examples of executives who shaped the character of their organizations are Harold Geneen of ITT Corporation, Sam Walton of Wal-Mart Stores, Harry Gray of United Technologies, and James Lincoln of Lincoln Electric Company. Every organization has a distinct culture, though, whether blessed with an influential chief executive or not.

Business scholars often treat corporate culture as a *constraint,* within which the management job must be done. However, recent research has shown that it is desirable—and to some degree possible—to modify culture to help accomplish company goals. Culture can foster commitment to the organization and provide an identity for organization members. It is clearly best for managers to understand the cultures that exist in their firms, whether they seek to change them or not. This is all the more important as Western countries try to match the Japanese devotion to quality and output.[3]

In this chapter we discuss the factors that help determine the nature of an organization's culture. Then, a model of the change sequence is presented and technological change addressed. Next, the sources of resistance to change and ways to overcome it are explored. The final section of the chapter addresses organizational development.

■ CORPORATE CULTURE DEFINED

Corporate culture

The system of shared values, beliefs, and habits within an organization that interacts with formal structure to produce behavioral norms.

Corporate culture is the system of shared values, beliefs, and habits within an organization that interacts with formal structure to produce behavioral norms.[4] According to Howard M. Schwartz, vice-president of Management Analysis Center, Inc., a leader in corporate culture consulting, "Culture gives people a sense of how to behave and what they ought to be doing."[5] It is similar in concept to meteorological climate. Just as the weather is described by such variables as temperature, humidity, and precipitation, corporate culture is composed of such factors as friendliness, supportiveness, and risk-taking. For instance, the weather of the southwestern United States may be described as "warm and pleasant," and the employees of an organization may characterize their organization as being "open and supportive." Such perceptions are gradually formed for each individual over a period of time as they perform their assigned activities under the general guidance of a superior and a set of organizational policies.

The culture existing within a firm has an impact on the employees' degree of satisfaction with the job as well as on the level and quality of their performance. For example, if an employee seeks an environment where the employees' input is important, Wal-Mart may be just that environment. Employee suggestions for improvements and changes are made on a weekly basis, and these ideas are taken very seriously at Wal-Mart headquarters.[6] If a person is anti-union, the corporate culture surrounding Texas Air Corporation may prove satisfying. The assessment of how good or poor the organization's culture is may differ for each employee. One person may perceive the environment as bad, and another may see the same environment as good. An employee may actually leave an organization in the hope of finding a more compatible culture.

ETHICAL DILEMMA

Y OUR COMPANY HAS recently adopted the Mead Corporation approach to ethics. The recently appointed CEO worked at Mead for several years and was determined to make your company the ethical leader in the industry. Mead Corporation has incorporated ethics into the total corporate culture as an effective and enforceable control for workplace behavior. Mead encourages line managers and other workers to spot potential problem areas and initiate appropriate responsive policies. One of the key aspects of this program is Project Hotline, a telephone hot line maintained by the company's corporate security department. Employees who believe that they have observed unethical behavior in a fellow employee or supervisor can use the hot line to report the details of the unethical behavior.[7] You are aware that the company that disposes the waste your plant generates is not following EPA guidelines. The less toxic waste is being dumped at night in a closed landfill six miles from the plant. To make matters worse, the company is operated by your brother-in-law. You have already warned him once, and you have just learned that he is still illegally dumping. You confront him and tell him that you are going to use the hot line and report him if he illegally dumps one more time. Your brother-in-law threatens to implicate you if you ever blow the whistle. You are now sure he will continue to dump illegally. You can call and report your brother-in-law, or you can let him continue to dump illegally.

What would you do?

Source: Adapted from a case presented in the video, *A Matter of Judgment,* which depicts five such conflicts of interest.

Writing in 1967, Antony Jay stated, "It has been known for some time that corporations are social institutions with customs and taboos, status groups and pecking orders, and many sociologists and social scientists have studied and written about them as such. But they are also political institutions, autocratic and democratic, peaceful and warlike, liberal and paternalistic."[8] What Jay was writing about, although the term had not then achieved broad usage, was corporate culture. In the early 1980s, several best-selling books on corporate culture appeared, including *In Search of Excellence, Theory Z: How American Business Can Meet the Japanese Challenge,* and *Corporate Culture.*[9] In 1981, Harvard University introduced its first course on corporate culture.

■ FACTORS THAT IMPACT CORPORATE CULTURE

Among the factors that affect corporate culture are work groups, organizational characteristics, supervision, and administration.[10] These factors are shown in

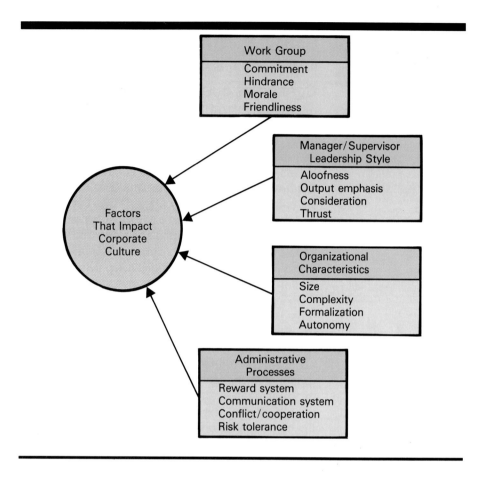

Figure 20.1. As can be seen, it would be difficult to discuss these topics without a reasonable understanding of the concepts of organizational behavior. Since culture permeates virtually every aspect of the organization, it is essential that the nature of culture be understood and appreciated.

Work Group

After reviewing each of the factors shown in Figure 20.1, it becomes fairly obvious that the nature of the immediate work group will affect one's perception of the nature of corporate culture. Commitment to the mission of the work group directly impacts cultural perceptions. Commitment refers to whether or not the group is just going through the motions of work. If people are just going through the motions, it is difficult for a particular individual to obtain high levels of output and satisfaction. Hindrance may also occur when individuals work together as a group. Hindrance is concerned with the degree to which a great deal of busywork of doubtful value is given to the group. Morale and friendliness within the group also affects the environment of the work group and the perceived nature of the corporate culture.

PINNACLE

Playboy's Corporate Culture Change

CORPORATE CULTURE IS the system of shared values, beliefs, and habits within an organization that interacts with formal structure to produce behavioral norms. Culture gives people a sense of how to behave and what they should be doing. The original corporate culture of Playboy Enterprises was the result of one man's dream, Hugh Hefner. This image and the values, beliefs, and habits of Hugh Hefner interacted to develop a unique corporate culture of an organization that was quite successful throughout the sixties and seventies. However, in fiscal year 1986, Playboy Enterprises lost $60 million, and the existing corporate culture was a prime contributor.

Christie Hefner inherited control of the troubled Playboy empire and turned it around. The corporate culture Christie developed was one of a business organization, where her father's living symbolism no longer permeated the corporate environment. She is now one of the most influential women in American publishing, a woman who's only a year older than the company she runs. Her strategy for revival meant venturing into new territory. She spearheaded home videocassettes and the Playboy channel and developed licensing agreements, attaching the famous bunny logo to clothing and accessories around the world. Playboy is now run by a Phi Beta Kappa graduate of Brandeis University, who describes herself as an accessible and informal manager, holding meetings at headquarters and her apartment near Lake Michigan. The style has changed, the image has changed, and so has the corporate culture at Playboy Enterprises. William Hartley, CNN Business News correspondent, interviews this fascinating individual.

Manager/Supervisor Leadership Style

The leadership style of the immediate supervisor will have a considerable effect on the culture of the group, and vice versa. If the manager is aloof and distant in dealing with subordinates, this attitude could have a negative impact on the organization. If the supervisor is always pushing for output, this alters the environment. Consideration is a desirable leadership characteristic, which can positively impact group effectiveness. Thrust refers to supervisory behavior characterized by personally working hard and setting an example.

Organizational Characteristics

Organizational characteristics may also affect the type of culture that develops. Organizations vary on such attributes as size and complexity. Large organizations tend toward higher degrees of specialization and greater impersonalization. Labor unions often find that large firms are easier to organize than smaller ones because smaller firms tend to be closer and have more informal relationships between employees and management. Complex organizations tend to employ a greater number of professionals and specialists, which alters the general approach to solving problems. Organizations also vary in the degree to which they write things down and attempt to program behavior through rules, procedures, and regulations. They can also be distinguished on the basis of the degree of decentralization of decision-making authority, which affects the degree of autonomy and employee freedom of personnel within the organization.

Administrative Processes

Corporate culture can be affected by administrative processes. Firms that can develop a direct link between performance and rewards tend to create cultures conducive to achievement. Communication systems that are open and free-flowing tend to promote participation and creative atmospheres. The general attitudes that exist toward the handling of risk and the tolerance of conflict will, in turn, have considerable impact on teamwork. They also affect the amount of organizational innovation and creativity that results. From these and other factors, organization members will develop a subjective impression of "what kind of place this is to work in." This general impression will affect performance, satisfaction, creativity, and commitment to the organization.

Classification of Culture

Dominant cultures
Those cultures that express the shared views of the majority of the organization's members.
Subcultures
Cultures characteristic of various subunits within an organization.

Strong culture
An organization's dominant culture that is widely and ardently held by members of the organization.

The above discussion focused on factors that impact corporate culture. It should be recognized, however, that within most large organizations both a dominant culture and many subcultures exist.[11] **Dominant cultures** are those that express the shared views of the majority of the organization's members. Our previous discussion focused on dominant cultures. However, existing within most organizations of any size are **subcultures**—cultures characteristic of various subunits within an organization. For instance, the marketing department may have a culture that is uniquely different from that of production. Although members from both departments share the dominant culture, they may also develop other views unique to their particular unit.

Another classification of cultures is whether or not they are strong or weak.[12] If the organization's dominant culture is widely and ardently held by members of the organization, it is said to possess a **strong culture.** Many Japanese firms are said to have a strong culture. IBM is also an example of a strong corporate culture. In addition, an organization's culture may be seen as participative or non-participative. We discuss this dimension of corporate culture below.

■■■ PARTICIPATIVE VERSUS NON-PARTICIPATIVE CULTURES

Culture is often viewed in terms of the level of participation that exists within the organization. On a continuum scale, involvement may range from highly participative to completely non-participative. And there are many degrees in between.

Most behaviorists advocate an open and participative culture, characterized by such attributes as:

- Trust in subordinates
- Openness in communications
- Considerate and supportive leadership
- Group problem solving
- Worker autonomy
- Information sharing
- High-output goals

Some behaviorists contend that this type of culture is the only viable one for all situations.

The opposite of the open and participative culture is a closed and autocratic one. Both may be characterized by high-output goals, but in a closed culture, such goals are more likely to be declared and imposed on the organization by autocratic and threatening leaders. There is greater rigidity in this culture, resulting from strict adherence to the formal chain of command, shorter spans of management, and stricter individual accountability. The emphasis is on the individual rather than on teamwork. Workers often simply go through the motions, doing as they are told.

Despite criticism of traditional organizational cultures by behaviorists, a more participative philosophy may not always work. In one instance involving packaging low-priced china, low productivity of the work group was caused by excessive and unnecessary interaction between employees during working hours. Management found that the threat of termination did not prevent the unproductive talking, because these low-skilled and low-paid employees were eligible for government subsidy programs. Management resolved the problem by redesigning the space allocated to the china-packaging process. Cubicles constructed of soundproofing material were built for each worker. The cubicles virtually eliminated the unproductive conversation between workers. As a result, productivity increased substantially, and employee turnover was reduced. The total cost was $3,200, which was recovered during the first three weeks.[13]

From the story at the beginning of the chapter, it is clear that the culture at IBM is neither purely open and participatory nor completely closed and autocratic. Although IBM employees are expected to dress conservatively and otherwise follow company rules, new ideas are encouraged and rewarded through incentive compensation. IBM is now a leaner, and more open-minded and fast-moving company. These changes have altered IBM's corporate culture, which now places greater emphasis on bringing an entrepreneurial spirit to their lines of business.[14] But even changes such as these may not return IBM to its former dominance.

Developing a Participative Culture

The prevailing managerial approach in most organizations has been characterized as highly structured. Consequently, most attempts to alter organizational culture have been directed toward creating a more open and participative culture. The theme of participation developed by McGregor, Herzberg, and Maslow, among others, relates primarily to self-actualization, motivator factors, consultative and democratic leadership, job enrichment, and management by objectives.

Values of Participation

The possible values of involving more people in the decision-making process within a firm relate primarily to productivity and morale. What makes the manufacturing successes possible at the Grand Rapids plant of Westinghouse Furniture Systems is a high degree of worker involvement in decision making.[15] Increased productivity can result from the stimulation of ideas and from the encouragement of greater effort and cooperation. Psychologically involved employees will often respond to shared problems with innovative suggestions and unusual efforts.

Open and participative cultures are often used to improve the levels of morale and satisfaction. Specific values in the area include:

- Increased acceptability of management's ideas
- Increased cooperation with members of management and staff
- Reduced turnover
- Reduced absenteeism
- Reduced complaints and grievances
- Greater acceptance of changes
- Improved attitudes toward the job and the organization

In general, the development of greater employee participation appears to have a direct and immediate effect on employee morale. Employees take a greater interest in the job and the organization. They tend to accept, and sometimes initiate, changes, not only because they understand the necessity for change but also because knowing more about the change reduces their fear or insecurity. Thus, though there is some question about the relationship between degree of participation and productivity, most experience and research indicate a positive relationship between employee participation and measures of morale, turnover, and absenteeism. Also, there has been little evidence of a positive relationship between job satisfaction and productivity. Still, if productivity is not harmed by participation, it would appear that these supplementary benefits would make participative management worthwhile. If management feels productivity is actually decreased in a particular situation, then serious decisions will have to be made concerning the trade-off between organizational needs and human needs.

Limitations of Participation

Despite the values of a participative approach to management, there are some limitations. The requirements for greater participation in decision making are (1) sufficient time, (2) adequate ability and interest on the part of the participants, and (3) restrictions generated by the present structure and system.

If immediate decisions are required, time cannot be spared for group participation. Because of rapid changes in the computer industry, IBM managers often find it difficult to take the time to involve workers in decisions. The manager frequently decides what to do and issues the order accordingly. Should management decide to switch from a practice of autocracy to one of increased participation, some time for adjustment on the part of both parties will be required. Participation calls for some measure of ability to govern oneself instead of leaning on others. In addition, it requires time for the subordinate to learn how to handle this new-found freedom and time for the supervisor to learn to trust the subordinate.

Whether greater involvement in decision making can be developed largely depends on the ability and interest of the participants, both subordinates and managers. This is not an easy concept to implement. Obviously, if the subordinate has neither knowledge of nor interest in a subject, there is little need to consult that person. As organizations and technology become increasingly complex, and as management becomes more professionalized, it is likely that employee participation will become more characterized by cooperation seeking or information gathering. It should also be noted that not all employees are equally desirous of participation. Managers must face the fact that some workers do not seek more responsibility and greater involvement in their job.

Finally, as indicated in Figure 20.2, the area of job freedom left to the individual may be quite restricted, but it can be expanded. For example, an individual's task is governed by management directives, organizational policies and procedures, the union contract, relations with the union steward, staff specialists, and the degree to which one can obtain the cooperation of subordinates. The greater the area in the Freedom to Do Job section, the greater the

F I G U R E 20.2 ■
Limits to Participative Freedom

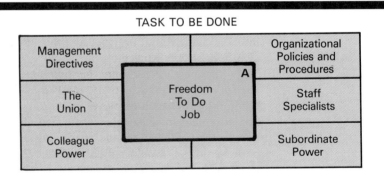

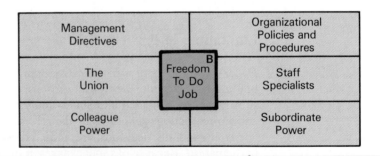

Source: Adapted from Edwin B. Flippo and Gary M. Munsinger, *Management*, 5th ed. (Boston: Allyn and Bacon, 1982), p. 360.

degree of participative freedom that is available. In the illustration, A would have more freedom to accomplish the job than B.

Measuring the Participation Level— Likert's Systems of Management

Rensis Likert, former director of the Institute for Social Research at the University of Michigan, developed a theory that keyed on a continuum of styles ranging from autocratic to participative. Likert's systems of management are System I, Exploitative Autocratic; System II, Benevolent Autocratic; System III, Consultative; and System IV, Participative Team. According to Likert, only the last style was deemed best in the long run for all situations.[16]

SYSTEM I—EXPLOITATIVE AUTOCRATIC
Managers make all decisions. They decide what is to be done, who will do it, and how and when it is to be accomplished. Failure to complete work as assigned results in threats or punishment. Under this system, management exhibits little confidence or trust in employees. A typical managerial response with this system is, "You do it my way or you're fired." According to Likert, there is a low level of trust and confidence between management and employees. In dealing with organized labor, Frank Lorenzo exhibits little confidence in those affiliated with organized labor. Lorenzo's threats, such as transferring Eastern's union jobs to Continental's non-union workers if Eastern employees refuse to take pay cuts, may be the actions of an exploitative autocratic.[17]

SYSTEM II—BENEVOLENT AUTOCRATIC
Managers still make the decisions, but employees have some degree of freedom and flexibility in performing their jobs so long as they conform to specific procedures. Under this system, managers take a very paternalistic attitude—"I'll take care of you if you perform well." With System II, there is a fairly low level of trust between management and employees, which causes employees to use caution when dealing with management.

SYSTEM III—CONSULTATIVE
Managers consult with employees prior to establishing the goals and making decisions about work. Employees of Wal-Mart Stores are encouraged to make suggestions for improvements and changes, which are forwarded to Wal-Mart headquarters weekly. Wal-Mart management also includes them in corporate decision making.[18] Employees have a considerable degree of freedom in making their own decisions as to how to accomplish the work. A manager using System III might say to an employee, "Charlie, I'd like your opinion on this before I make the decision." Management tends to rely on rewards rather than punishments to motivate employees. Also, the level of trust between the employees and management is fairly high. This creates a culture in which employees feel relatively free to openly discuss work-related matters with management.

SYSTEM IV—PARTICIPATIVE TEAM
This is Likert's recommended system or style of management. The emphasis of System IV is on a group participative role with full involvement of the employees in the process of establishing goals and making job-related decisions. In the

Grand Rapids plant of Westinghouse Furniture Systems, a unit of Westinghouse Electric Corporation, employees are highly involved in decision making in all areas, including business strategy aspects such as goal setting. Employees are even involved in hiring, the scheduling of work and hours, and operations planning. Subsequently, goals are better accepted and attained, even though the objectives originally seemed quite difficult to achieve. From 1983 to 1986, productivity increased by 74 percent.[19]

Employees involved in a participative team system feel free to discuss matters with their manager, who displays supportive rather than condescending or threatening behavior. It is contended that an entire organization should be designed along System IV lines, with work being performed by a series of overlapping groups. The leader provides a link between the group and other units at higher levels in the organization. This concept is often referred to as the *linking-pin theory.* Decision making is widespread throughout the enterprise, with the power of knowledge usually taking precedence over the power of authority.

FIGURE 20.3 ■■■ Sample of Questions on the Likert Scale Relating to Communications within the Organization

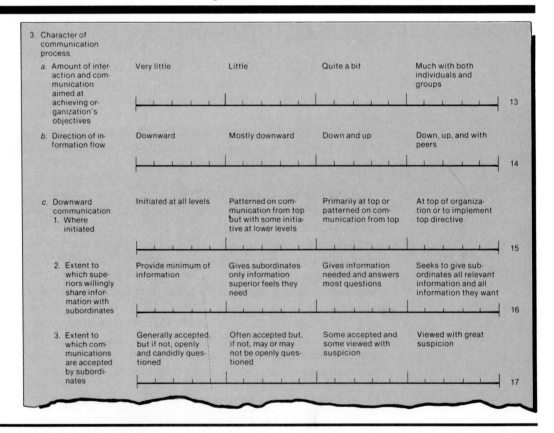

Measurement of the type of style in the Likert framework is usually accomplished by having the employees assess the organizational culture and management system on a Likert scale. For example, when the question, "Extent to which superiors are willing to share information with subordinates?" is asked, the employee can answer on the continuum from "provide minimum information" all the way to "seeks to give subordinates all relevant information and all information they want" (see question 3c2 in Figure 20.3). It has been found that the positions on these scales can be significantly altered through organizational and management development programs.

■■■ EVIDENCE OF CULTURE

Determining exactly what type of culture exists in an organization can be difficult. But if a person truly desires to do so, there are means available. The evidence of an organization's culture can be found in its status symbols, traditions, history, rituals, jargon, and physical environment (see Figure 20.4).

F I G U R E 20.4 ■■
Evidence of Culture in an
Organization

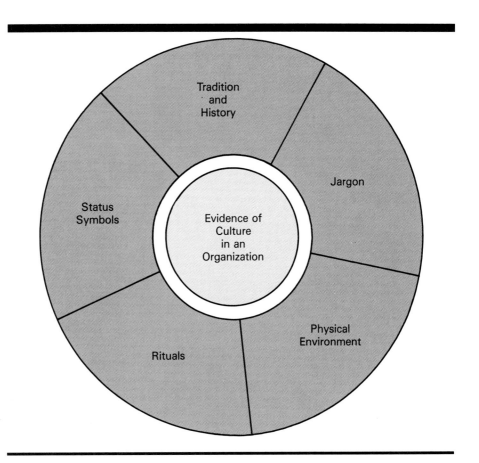

Status Symbols

Status symbol
A visible, external sign of
one's social position.

A visible, external sign of one's social position is referred to as a **status symbol.** A stranger can enter an organization and, if aware of status hierarchies, obtain a social fix quickly by reading the various symbols. Much regarding a firm's corporate culture can be gained through understanding the meaning of various status symbols as they vary from firm to firm. For example, one would usually expect that higher-status positions are accompanied by newer office furnishings. In one organization, however, the high-status positions were given antique roll-top desks, whereas the lower jobs were equipped with new, shiny, modern furniture. Symbols sometimes change with the times. Some typical status symbols in business are the following:

- Titles
- Pay
- Bonus/stock plans
- Size and location of desk or office
- Location of parking space or reserved parking
- Type of company car assigned
- Secretaries
- Privacy
- Use of executive clubs

An individual's mode of transportation to and from work can be an indication of that person's status within the organization.
(© COMSTOCK, Inc.)

- Cocktail party invitations
- Furnishings, including rugs, pictures, tables, and similar items
- Posted certificates
- Privileges, including freedom to move about, not punching the time clock, and freedom to set own working hours and to regulate coffee breaks
- Number of windows in office

Within the company, however, many of the symbols are not within the control of management and may be the basis of unwarranted preoccupation. Executives have gotten down on their hands and knees to measure the comparative size of their offices. Windows are counted, steps from the president's office are paced off, secretaries who can use a word processor are sought, parking space is fought for, and company cars are wangled. In some organizations, having a window office is a major status symbol.

Traditions and History

Within every organization there are certain traditions or ways of life that tend to distinguish one firm from another. Even firms that produce essentially the same product will be somewhat different because of certain traditions. In the opening case, IBM has a tradition of conservative dress, incentive-type compensation, internal competition among employees, and new ideas. Workers act and react on a daily basis because of past events that have become traditional. Typically, it is an unconscious action. Workers just know what is expected of them in certain situations.

Rituals

Closely related to tradition and history, but perhaps slightly different, are company rituals. Many Japanese firms have their employees begin the day by doing morning exercises. The Mary Kay Cosmetics Company provides an excellent example of the use of rituals. During high-profile and embellished meetings, saleswomen are awarded gold and diamond pins, fur stoles, and the use of pink Cadillacs. These awards are presented in an environment easily reminiscent of a Miss America pageant. There is a cheering audience, in a large auditorium, and all the participants are dressed in glamorous evening clothes.

Jargon

Jargon
A special language that group members use in their daily interaction.

Jargon refers to a special language that group members use in their daily interaction. The jargon that is used in one firm is often quite different from another. Sales representatives are keenly aware of this, and they train themselves to recognize the sales jargon of competing firms. Then, when calling on a new prospect, they are better able to recognize which other sales representatives had already visited this prospect, through the terminology the prospect uses when asking questions. Even within a single firm jargon separates one group or unit from another. Accountants may have one set of jargon and salesworkers another.

The Physical Environment

The firm's actual physical environment often makes a statement about its type of culture—for example, the office building itself. Offices that are closed in with few common areas for organization members to meet in creates an image of a closed form of culture. An office building with open offices and considerable common areas for employees to interact indicates a different culture. Whether office doors are consistently opened or closed is another clue as to the type of formality that exists in an organization. Even the type of furniture used can tell much about an organization's culture. For instance, round tables suggest more equality than do long, highly polished ones.

■ THE CHANGE SEQUENCE

Change sequence
The sequence of events that is needed to bring about change in an organization.

The **change sequence** is the sequence of events that is needed to bring about change in an organization. Whether the intended change is from a less participative to a more participative corporate culture or along some other dimension, the process tends to follow a certain pattern. The sequence of events needed to bring about change in an organization is shown in Figure 20.5. Management must first

F I G U R E 20.5 ■
The Change Sequence

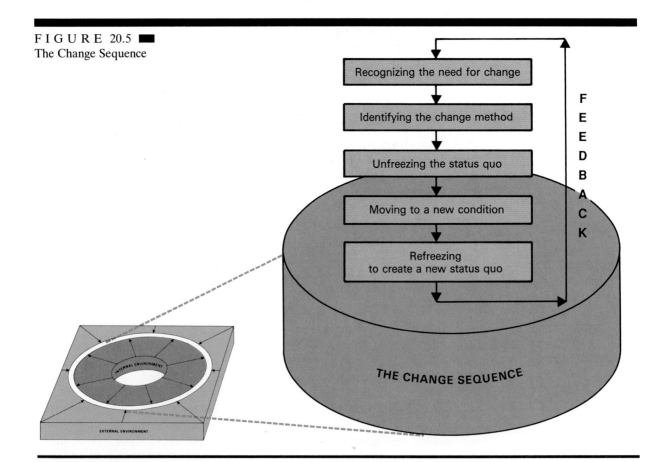

Recognizing the need for change

Identifying the change method

Unfreezing the status quo

Moving to a new condition

Refreezing
to create a new status quo

FEEDBACK

INTERNAL ENVIRONMENT

EXTERNAL ENVIRONMENT

THE CHANGE SEQUENCE

recognize a need for change. Then the specific change method(s) must be chosen. Finally, the following steps are carried out: (1) unfreezing the status quo, (2) moving to the new condition, and (3) refreezing to create a new status quo.

Recognizing the Need for Change

Perhaps the most important question to ask regarding the subject of change is "Is this change necessary?" There are some who unwisely believe that changes should be made merely for the sake of change. Managers who make a change merely to satisfy a desire for change may create a disruptive effect on their section. When one of the authors was working as a consultant for a manufacturing firm, he inadvertently noticed a note on the desk of a new vice-president, brought in from the outside to improve the performance of a division that was doing poorly. The note said, "Do not make any major changes for three months." The new executive obviously wanted to be aware of the total situation before making changes and perhaps further damaging an entire division. Organizations and people want some degree of stability in order to accomplish their assigned tasks. Yet there are times when changes are necessary, and failure to be quick and decisive can have disastrous effects.

A number of major companies, particularly in the fast-moving computer industry, have found that cultural change is not only feasible but necessary. One expert writes about Apple Computer, "Things have changed since its salad days before IBM entered the market in August 1981 (when IBM became an Apple competitor by introducing its personal computer, a time when Apple was seen as a kind of playground for ambitious and idealistic computer wizards)."[20] There are rumblings among some Apple staffers that the company is becoming regimented and losing its entrepreneurial soul. Apple is noted for a corporate culture that emphasizes blue jeans and tennis shoes, video games outside the executive offices, free thinking, and a flexible organizational structure. On the other hand, IBM traditionally has emphasized white shirts and gray suits and conservative thinking. But IBM is changing, too. That company's new strategy appears to be aimed at becoming more like Apple—whereas Apple is becoming more like IBM. Other companies that have accomplished broad-scale cultural change include AT&T, PepsiCo, Chase Manhattan, and Twentieth Century Fox.[21]

Donaldson and Lorsch argue that, at times, all companies must change their culture or die. The change may be revolutionary or evolutionary.[22] There are five possible reasons for imposing rapid cultural change:

1. If your company has strong values that don't fit a changing environment.
2. If the industry is very competitive and moves with lightning speed.
3. If your company is mediocre or worse.
4. If the company is about to join the ranks of the very largest companies.
5. If it's smaller, but growing rapidly.[23]

Identifying the Change Method

Management has at its disposal numerous methods and techniques for organizational development, or change. Specific techniques, discussed later in this chapter, are survey feedback, team building, sensitivity training, management by objectives, job enrichment, and the grid approach. The technique a firm chooses should meet its needs in reacting to the external environment and identifying the type of culture that will provide the greatest productivity.

Unfreezing the Status Quo

If individuals are to change their present attitudes, current beliefs must be altered or unfrozen.[24] Resistance to change must be eliminated or reduced if a change is to be effective. Reducing resistance to change may be accomplished by building trust and confidence, developing open communication, and encouraging employee participation. Once resistance to change has been reduced, the manager is in a position to implement the desired change. Sources of resistance to change and some approaches to reducing resistance are discussed later in the chapter.

Unfreezing in the change process generates self-doubt and provides a means of remedying the situation. Employees must be made to feel that ineffectiveness is undesirable, but it can be remedied. If organization members are to be receptive to change, they must feel that they *can* change.

Moving to the New Condition

The initiation of a change can come from an order, a recommendation, or a self-directed impetus. A manager with authority can command that a change be made and enforce its implementation by threats, punishments, and close supervision. If this path of implementing change is taken, the manager will likely find that the change must be constantly monitored. Change is more permanent and substantial if a person truly wants and feels a need to change.

The most effective approach to initiating change is a two-way relationship between the person who is attempting to implement the change and the person(s) who will be changed. The person implementing the change should make suggestions, and the person or persons who will be changed should be encouraged to contribute and participate. Those initiating the change should be responsive to suggestion, either by reformulating the change or by providing explanations as to why the suggestions cannot be incorporated.

Refreezing to Create a New Status Quo

If a person changes to a new set of work habits for a week and then reverts to former practices, the change has not been effective. Too often changes that are introduced do not stick. If the change is to be permanent, the person or persons changed must be convinced that the change is in their own and the organization's best interest. One of the best ways to accomplish this is to collect objective evidence of the success of the change. A manager who sees production increase because of a change in leadership style has excellent evidence of the success of the change. People should feel competent and take pleasure in using the new behavior. But the change will be completely accepted only if the reward system of the organization is geared to the new form of behavior. If a university states that all its faculty must begin to publish articles, and there is no reward attached to publishing, it is likely that few faculty members would be motivated to make this change. An employee's job may be substantially enriched in terms of content and self-supervision, but if the change is not accomplished by properly enriched pay and status symbols, dissatisfaction is likely to result. People tend to repeat behavior that they find rewarding.

■ TECHNOLOGICAL CHANGE

The tremendous impact of technological change was first discussed in Chapter 3. There it was highlighted that more than half of all existing jobs will be changed within the next decade, and an estimated 30 percent will be eliminated as a result of technological advances.[25] High technology is one of the most important causes of organizational change today.

The factories of yesteryear have been virtually reinvented through changes in technology. Rapidly moving into oblivion is the once-familiar scene of the blue-collar worker with grease-stained hands in front of a drill or stamping machine. Now there is an almost antiseptic atmosphere: robots and other computer-controlled machinery manufacture items while technicians stand by computer controls monitoring activities. For example, at the General Electric diesel locomotive factory in Pennsylvania, the modernization program has resulted in a reduction in production time for the heaviest motor frame from sixteen days to sixteen hours. However, the change that the employees underwent was also considerable. All 7,500 employees at the Erie, Pennsylvania, plant were required to attend communication sessions. Some continued in the training center as instructors. Others received special training in operating and servicing the 300 numerically controlled machines in the plant.

The General Electric plant in Erie, Pennsylvania, provides an ideal example of flexible manufacturing systems and the change that has resulted. One flexible manufacturing system machines ten different locomotive components, ranging from a small gearbox weighing only 150 pounds to large castings of more than a ton and containing as many as 140 machined surfaces. When a casting or welded frame enters the machining process, it is turned over to the central computer. This "executive computer" then orders the automatic transporter to take the piece to its first machining station. The executive computer loads the proper program into the individual machine computer. The various parts being manufactured are shuffled among the various machines to make sure each machine is used efficiently. Not a single nonrobotic hand works on the frames until the computer is satisfied with the work and summons a human to take them away. Even though it was in the best interest of the organization, the technological change certainly met with some resistance. Events such as these are occurring virtually daily in organizations around the world.

■ SOURCES OF RESISTANCE TO CHANGE

In the General Electric example, there was some resistance to change, even though the change was necessary. Sources of resistance may be individual or organizational. A change may cause some loss to the person or organization that

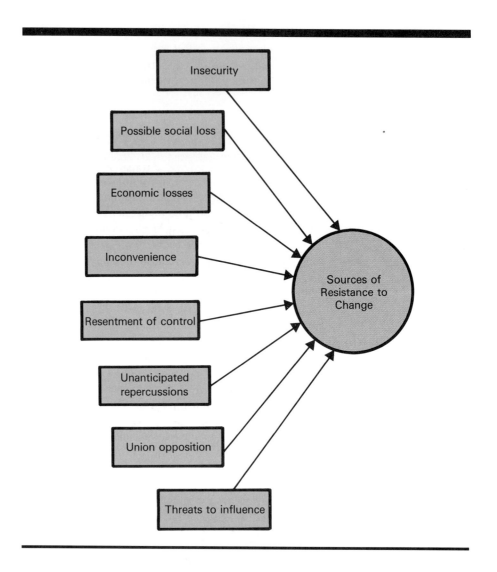

is affected by it. Attachments to old and familiar habits, places, and people must be given up. In major and unexpected changes, employees, groups, and even divisions often experience daze, shock, recoil, and turmoil.[26] Some of the many sources of resistance to change are shown in Figure 20.6 and discussed below.

Insecurity

Once people have operated in a particular environment for a long time, they begin to feel comfortable. A change of environment often brings about uncertainty; they do not know exactly what to expect. The feeling of insecurity surrounded virtually all of us as we made the transition from high school to college. The same sense of insecurity continues as the move is made from undergraduate to graduate work or when individuals move from one job to another or to a new city. Apparently some people become perpetual students because of such feelings of insecurity.

Possible Social Loss

A change has the potential to bring about social losses. As previously discussed, the informal work group may be extremely powerful. If change causes individuals in the group to be transferred, the power of the group is likely diminished. A change may cause established status symbols to be destroyed, or an individual of lower status may even be awarded a high-status symbol.

The impact that a change can have on the social environment was vividly illustrated when one of the authors was doing a consulting job for a regional medical center. The hospital had been a small, local, 100-bed hospital, but because industry was moving rapidly into the area, the board of directors decided to expand the hospital to 300 beds. In one department all personnel reported directly to the department head, and a close rapport developed among the members. On a rotating shift, staff members sometimes had to work the evening and night shift, but they could still maintain close contact with the other department members.

Because of the great increase in work load, the work force was expanded, and a decision was made to have three shifts with a shift supervisor for each shift. The department head now had only three people reporting directly to him, and it was believed that the work could be performed much more efficiently. But the social loss was drastic. Subordinates no longer had a close relationship with the department head; some, because they were on a different shift, rarely saw the department head. This created a tremendous social loss to several long-term employees and resulted in over 50 percent of the personnel quitting in six months.

Economic Losses

Technology that can produce the same amount of output with fewer personnel may be introduced. While most companies make an honest attempt to transfer or retain employees who have been affected by the change, the fear of being laid off remains. When the computer was first introduced, the number of clerical personnel needed was often drastically reduced. Firms attempted to lessen employees' fear of losing their jobs by claiming that the number of jobs needed had actually increased through the use of the computer. This explanation did not help the employee who was capable only of accomplishing the clerical work. For this individual, it was a major economic loss.

Inconvenience

Any change represents a new way of doing things, even when it is not associated with a social or economic loss. New procedures and techniques may have to be learned. Physical and mental energy must be expended (for some people this is not an enjoyable task). When a new telephone system was installed at a university, initially there were many complaints. The new system meant that time and effort had to be expended in learning how to use the system. It took approximately one year for the system to be accepted by a majority of the university personnel.

Resentment of Control

As a whole, Americans are very independent. When employees are told that a change must take place, they are made to realize that they do not have control over their destiny. Although the change may be for the better, a certain amount of resentment may develop. IBM's Tom Watson was convinced that conservative dress would help sustain the company's image and, indirectly, increase profitability. Some within the company, however, resented being told how to dress. This might be true even for persons who normally dress conservatively.

Unanticipated Repercussions

Because the organization is a system, a change in one part is likely to have unforeseen repercussions in another. For example, a newly enriched job is likely to demand a change in supervisory behavior. Supervisors may resist this change in behavior, although initially they supported the concept of job enrichment.

Union Opposition

Labor union representatives are often accused of opposing any change suggested by management. Employees are often more comfortable with a fighting union than they are with one inclined to cooperate with management on changes designed to promote organizational interest. There are indications, however, that the old adversarial relationship is being replaced by a more cooperative one between companies and unions. Sometimes joint collaboration is the result of a new regard for improving productivity and enhancing the quality of work life. Recent surveys indicate that many rank-and-file workers want something more from their jobs and their unions than wages, benefits, and job security.[27]

Threats to Influence

There are times when a change will reduce the power base of a group, department, or even a division. Even when the change is best for the organization as a whole, resistance may persist. This scene has often been enacted as state boards of education attempt to reduce duplication of programs. Should one university give up a program, its personal influence in the total system is diminished. Calls are made to alumni and supporters throughout the state to keep this dastardly deed from occurring, even though a reduction in duplication of programs would improve the overall quality of the educational program in the state.

■■■ APPROACHES TO REDUCING RESISTANCE TO CHANGE

Change is often necessary, despite the resistance that might arise. One of the authors, while working as a personnel administrator for a large insurance company, observed that an anticipated change in computers brought about considerable employee resistance. Management of the company had announced that a new computer system with greatly increased capacity would be installed in about six

FIGURE 20.7 ■■
Approaches to Reducing
Resistance to Change

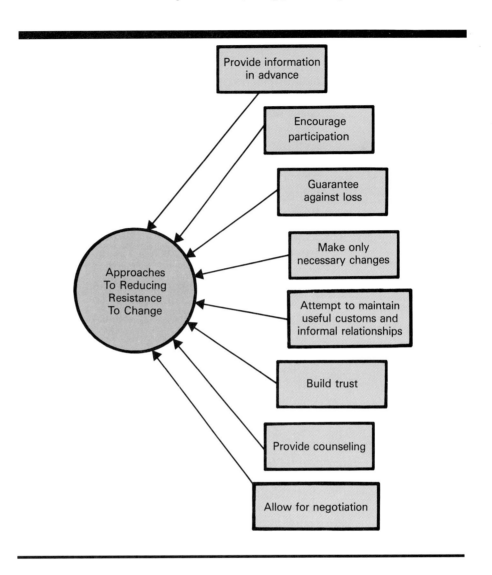

months. The new computer would cause substantial changes in many of the clerical jobs being performed by office personnel. Uncertainty resulting from not knowing what to expect from the change in computer systems caused numerous employees to express fear and concern about the impact of the change.

Before management took any action, the employees caused a rather severe slowdown of the work flow in the office. Customer and agent complaints rose substantially during the six-week period after the announced change. Management took action to correct the situation by holding a series of small group meetings to explain the new computer system and how it would affect each job and each work group. While there would be several major changes in job functions affecting some individuals and work groups, management made a commitment to all employees that no one would be dismissed as a result of the installation of the new computer. The company would provide retraining programs to increase the affected employees' skills, thereby improving their adaptability to the new system. Some of the approaches designed to reduce resistance to change are shown in Figure 20.7 and discussed below.

Provide Information in Advance

Whenever possible, managers should provide the reasons for the change, its nature, planned timing, and the possible impact on the organization and its personnel. They should avoid, if possible, the withholding of information that could seriously affect the lives and futures of particular individuals, such as keeping secret the planned closure of a plant in order to preserve the workforce level until the last possible moment. The firm that gains a reputation for such actions will have difficulty making future changes. There are, however, occasions when competitive survival requires that information be closely held until shortly before introduction. In these cases, the information should be provided on an *as required* basis.

Encourage Participation

When possible, subordinate participation should be encouraged in establishing the change. A person who is involved in implementing change procedures will likely be more supportive of the change. It will be recalled that Theory Y assumes that abilities are widespread in the population. Thus, many valuable ideas may be gained by permitting employees a degree of participation in implementing the change. A company that has gained a reputation for participative management is Xerox Corporation. David T. Kearns, president, said to his employees, "I pledge to you that management of this company at all levels will listen to you and put your ideas to work."[28]

Guarantee Against Loss

To promote acceptance of technological changes, some organizations guarantee no layoffs as a result of such changes. In cases of a change in methods and output standards, employees are often guaranteed retention of their present level of earnings during the learning period.

Make Only Necessary Changes

Changes should be made only when the situation demands, not because of a whim on the part of a manager. A manager who gains a reputation for making change for the sake of change will discover that any change, beneficial or not, will receive only minimum acceptance.

Attempt to Maintain Useful Customs and Informal Relationships

As previously mentioned, the informal work group has real value from the standpoint of interpersonal understanding and cooperation. When possible, changes should be made to coincide with the culture of the personnel within the organization. When safety shoes were first introduced, few would wear them willingly because of their appearance. When they were redesigned to resemble normal shoes, resistance faded. Civilian consultants who are to work with military personnel are granted fictional rank, to make their integration into ongoing operations more understandable and acceptable. A staff expert who wants a change introduced may find it advisable to have the announcement made by a line executive, with some sharing of the credit. Changes that go against established customs and informal norms will likely create resistance and have little chance of being readily accepted.

Build Trust

If a manager has a reputation for having provided reliable and timely information to employees in the past, his or her explanation as to why a change is to be made will likely be believed. The change may still be resisted, but if the manager is trusted by the employees, problems will be minimized. On the other hand, managers who have gained a reputation for providing incomplete or inaccurate information will often have difficulty convincing employees that a proposed change is good for them. IBM's management has tended to maintain open communication with employees and to honor the commitments made to them. Undoubtedly, their trust played a large part in the company's successful change efforts.

Provide Counseling

At times some form of nonthreatening discussion and counseling may not only prevent rebellion but have some chance of stimulating voluntary adaptation. Nondirective counseling has been used effectively in many change situations. The approach rests on a fundamental belief that people have the ability to solve their own problems with the aid of a sympathetic listener. The role of a counselor is one of understanding and perhaps advising rather than passing judgment. This requires a somewhat permissive, friendly atmosphere, with actions and statements that exhibit continuing interest but not judgment. In most instances, managers with authority are unable to establish this type of atmosphere. To be successful, nondirective counseling usually must be undertaken by staff psychologists. What the manager can do is to permit some subordinate ventilation of feelings, particularly those of frustration and anger. Just talking about the "good old days" will assist in the transition process. Discovering that others have similar feelings and doubts will often make the transition less painful; as the saying goes, "misery loves company."

Allow for Negotiation

Resistance to change can be reduced by the process of negotiation. Negotiation is the primary method used by labor unions to effect modification of proposed managerial changes. For example, in return for accepting many changes in work rules, a West Coast employer at one time provided a $29 million benefit fund to aid longshoremen through early retirement and provide a type of annual wage guarantee. Several years ago when wage reductions were necessary at Eastern Airlines, President Frank Borman agreed to give employees company stock in exchange for the cuts.

■ ORGANIZATIONAL DEVELOPMENT

Several change efforts that affect the entire organization will be described next (see Figure 20.8). They are basically techniques of organizational development (OD). The organizational development movement has been strongly advocated by such researchers as Chris Argyris and Warren Bennis. **Organizational development** (OD) is a planned and systematic attempt to change the organization, typically to a more behavioral environment. OD education and training strategies are designed to develop a more open, productive, and compatible workplace, despite existing differences in personalities, culture, or technologies.[29]

Change Agents

The person who is responsible for ensuring that the planned change in OD is properly implemented is referred to as a **change agent.** This individual or group may be either an external or an internal consultant. Change agents have knowledge in the OD techniques described below. They use this knowledge to assist in organizational change.

When an organization first attempts to change, outside consultants are often used. An outside expert may bring more objectivity to a situation and be better

Organizational development
A planned and systematic attempt to change the organization, typically to a more behavioral environment.

Change agent
The person who is responsible for ensuring that the planned change in OD is prcperly implemented.

F I G U R E 20.8 ■
Techniques of
Organizational
Development

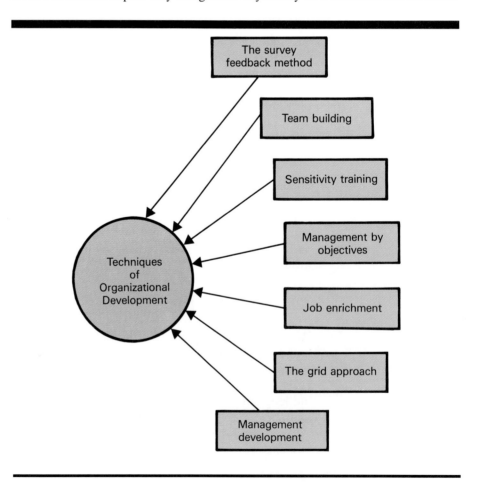

F I G U R E 20.9 ■ The Survey Feedback Method

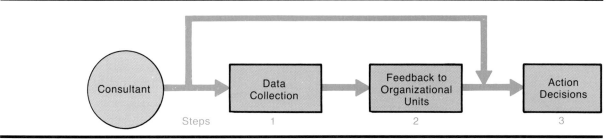

able to obtain the acceptance and trust of organizational members. With time, internal consultants may move into the role of a change agent. It is vitally important to understand and appreciate the following techniques for implementing change.

The Survey Feedback Method

Survey feedback method
The method of basing organizational change efforts on the systematic collection and measurement of subordinate attitudes by anonymous questionnaires.

The method of basing organizational change efforts on the systematic collection and measurement of subordinate attitudes by anonymous questionnaires is referred to as the **survey feedback method.** The three basic steps in the process are shown in Figure 20.9. First, data are collected from members of the organization by a consultant. Survey questions typically require either objective multiple-choice responses (see Table 20.1) or scaled responses (see Table 20.2), to suggest agreement or disagreement with a particular question. Normally, anonymously answered questionnaires are used. If truthful information is to be obtained concerning attitudes, the employee must feel comfortable, secure, and confident in responding.

In the second step, the results of the study are presented to concerned organizational units. In the final step, the data are analyzed and decisions are made. Some means by which the data may be compared and analyzed include

- Scores for the entire organization now and in the past
- Scores for each department now and in the past

TABLE 20.1 ■ Examples of Multiple-Choice Responses to Survey Questions

Why did you decide to do what you are now doing?	What do you like least about your job?
a. Desire to aid or assist others	a. Nothing
b. Influenced by another person or situation	b. Pay
c. Always wanted to be in this vocation	c. Supervisor relations
d. Lack of opportunity or interest in other vocational fields	d. Problems with fellow workers
e. Opportunities provided by this vocation	e. Facilities
f. Personal satisfaction from doing this work	f. Paperwork and reports

---

TABLE 20.2 ■ Examples of Scaled Responses to Survey Questions

Considering all aspects of your job, evaluate your compensation with regard to your contributions to the needs of the organization. Circle the number that best describes how you feel.

Pay Too Low		Pay Low		Pay Average		Pay Above Average		Pay Too High	
1	2	3	4	5	6	7	8	9	10

What are your feelings about overtime work requirements? Circle the number that best indicates how you feel.

Unnecessary				Necessary on Occasion				Necessary	
1	2	3	4	5	6	7	8	9	10

Source: R. Wayne Mondy and Robert M. Noe, III, *Personnel: The Management of Human Resources,* 3d ed. (Newton, Mass.: Allyn and Bacon, 1987), p. 678.

- Scores by organizational level
- Scores by seniority
- Relative scores on each question
- Scores for each question for each category of personnel cited above

The decisions are directed at improving relationships in the organization. This is accomplished by revealing problem areas and dealing with them through straightforward discussion.

Team Building

Team building
A conscious effort to develop effective work groups throughout the organization.

One of the major techniques in the arsenal of the organizational development consultant is **team building,** a conscious effort to develop effective work groups throughout the organization.[30] These work groups focus on solving actual problems in building efficient management teams. The team-building process begins when the team leader defines a problem that requires organizational change. Next, the group analyzes the problem to determine the underlying causes. These factors may be related to such areas as communication, role clarifications, leadership styles, organizational structure, and interpersonal frictions. The next step is to propose alternative solutions and then select the most appropriate one. Through this process, the participants are likely to be committed to the solution. Interpersonal support and trust develops. The overall improvement in the interpersonal support and trust of group members enhances the implementation of the change.[31] The concept of the quality circle, imported from Japan, is a modern example of team building.

Sensitivity Training

Sensitivity training
An organizational development (OD) technique that uses leaderless discussion groups.

An organizational development technique that uses leaderless discussion groups is referred to as **sensitivity training** (also called T-group training or laboratory training). The general goal of sensitivity training is to develop awareness of, and

Team building is a technique for creating effective work groups throughout the organization. (© 1987 Lawrence Migdale/Stock, Boston, Inc.)

sensitivity to, oneself and others. More specifically, the goals of sensitivity training include the following:

- Increased openness with others
- Greater concern for needs of others
- Increased tolerance for individual differences
- Less ethnic prejudice
- Awareness and understanding of group processes
- Enhanced listening skills
- Greater appreciation of the complexities of behaving competently
- Establishment of more realistic personal standards of behavior

Sensitivity training is not widely used in business today as an OD technique.[32] It has been labeled "psychotherapy" rather than proper business training. Leaders of T-groups have been criticized for having an insufficient background in psychology. Detractors suggest that individual defense mechanisms—built up to preserve the personality over a period of years—may be destroyed, with little help provided in replacing them with more satisfactory behavioral patterns. It is contended that one cannot exist without ego defense mechanisms.

Also, in business organizations, managers frequently must make unpleasant decisions that work to the detriment of particular individuals and groups. Excessive empathy and sympathy will not necessarily lead to a better decision and may exact an excessively high emotional cost for the decision maker. Many business organizations have internal environments characterized by competition and autocratic leadership. The power structure may not be compatible with openness and trust. In some instances, an effective manager may practice "diplomacy" by telling only part of the truth, or perhaps even telling different stories to two different persons or groups. Truth is not always conducive to effective interpersonal and group relations. Sensitivity training would also tend to ignore organizational values that are derived from aggressiveness, initiative, and the charismatic appeals of a particular leader.

Management by Objectives

As described in Chapter 5, management by objectives is a systematic approach to change that facilitates achievement of results by directing efforts toward attainable goals. MBO encourages managers to plan for the future. Because MBO emphasizes participative management, it is considered a philosophy of management. Within this broader context, MBO becomes an important method of organizational development. The participation of individuals in setting goals and the emphasis on self-control promote not only individual development but also the development of the entire organization.

Job Enrichment

Job enrichment
Refers to basic changes in the content and level of responsibility of a job so as to provide greater challenge to the worker.

In the past two decades, there has been considerable interest in, and application of, job enrichment in a wide variety of organizations. Strongly advocated by Frederick Herzberg, **job enrichment** refers to basic changes in the content and level of responsibility of a job so as to provide greater challenge to the worker. Job enrichment basically provides an expansion of responsibilities. The individual is provided with an opportunity to derive a feeling of greater achievement, recognition, responsibility, and personal growth in performing the job. Although job enrichment programs have not always achieved positive results, such programs have demonstrated improvements in job performance and in the level of satisfaction of personnel in many organizations.

AT&T, Polaroid, Texas Instruments, Monsanto, Weyerhaeuser, General Motors, Corning Glass, and many other firms have achieved excellent results after implementing job enrichment programs. In most instances productivity and job satisfaction increased, accompanied by reduction in employee turnover and absenteeism.[33]

According to Herzberg, there are a number of principles applicable for implementing job enrichment:

1. *Increasing job demands:* Changing the job in such a way as to increase the level of difficulty and responsibility of the job.
2. *Increasing a worker's accountability:* Allowing more individual control and authority over the work while retaining accountability of the manager.
3. *Providing work scheduling freedom:* Within limits, allowing individual workers to schedule their own work.
4. *Providing feedback:* Making timely periodic reports on performance to employees (directly to the worker rather than to the supervisor).
5. *Providing new learning experiences:* Work situations should encourage opportunities for new experiences and personal growth of the individual.[34]

The Grid Approach to OD

One of the best-known predesigned OD programs is the Managerial Grid® developed by Robert Blake and Jane Mouton. As we discussed earlier in Chapter 18, Blake and Mouton suggest that the most effective leadership style is the one that stresses maximum concern for both output and people. The Managerial Grid provides a systematic approach for analyzing managerial styles and assisting the organization in moving to the best style.

Management Development

Management development programs
Formal efforts to improve the skills and attitudes of present and prospective managers.

Organizational development techniques are designed to change the entire organization. **Management development programs** (MDP) are formal efforts to improve the skills and attitudes of present and prospective managers. Managers learn more effective approaches to managing people and other resources. With MDP, specific areas that have been identified as possible organizational weaknesses are included in the program. Some of these areas might relate to leadership style, motivation approaches, or communication effectiveness.

The training programs may be administered by either in-house or external personnel. An illustration of a management development program that was utilized by a major independent telephone company is provided in Table 20.3.

TABLE 20.3 ■ Course Content for a Management Development Program

I. Management Development Program Title:
"Improving Group Effectiveness and Team Building"

II. Objectives:
(1) To identify the reasons for group formation
(2) To understand the types of groups and their attributes
(3) To discover the implications of research on group dynamics
(4) To acquire an understanding as to forces in intra- and inter-group processes
(5) To learn the characteristics of teamwork and ways to achieve it
(6) To provide experience in analyzing and diagnosing work group dimensions
(7) To acquire an appreciation for various team-building techniques

III. Description and Evaluation:
The course is designed to provide greater understanding of, and ability to work with and through, groups. Special emphasis is given to understanding the various need levels of groups and what can be done to appeal more effectively to those levels. Actual practice in team-building techniques is given, as well as experience in analyzing work groups. Evaluation is made of the major contingencies affecting groups. Observing group behavior through various media is a portion of the course content.

IV. Size of Class:
The class should have a maximum enrollment of 20 participants so as to allow the group process to be seen in action in the group itself, yet small enough to allow for active participation.

V. Assignment of Instructor:
The instructor allocates an equal amount of time to lecture and active class discussion with approximately one-third of the time devoted to various media presentations and group involvement. The course is designed for a 2- or 3-day session.

VI. Enrollment Requirements:
Middle- and upper-level managerial experience desired.

The intent of MDP is not only to learn new methods and techniques but to develop an inquisitive thought process. Too often personnel within a firm become so accustomed to performing the same task day after day that they forget how to think. A properly designed management development program places a person in a frame of mind to analyze problems and is often used to provide the foundation for a change to occur.

SUMMARY

Corporate culture, the system of shared values and beliefs, impacts employees' degree of satisfaction and the quality of their performance. The assessment of how good or poor the corporate culture is may differ for each employee. Work groups, organizational characteristics, supervision, and administration affect corporate culture.

Most attempts to change an organization have been directed toward creating a more open and participative culture. Involving more people in the decision-making process improves productivity and morale. Still, there are some limitations.

Rensis Likert developed a systems theory that uses a continuum of styles ranging from autocratic to participative. System IV, Participative Team, was deemed best in the long run for all situations regarding organizational change.

No matter what the intended change, the change process tends to follow a pattern. Management first recognizes a need for change and then chooses a specific change method. The following steps are carried out: (1) unfreezing the status quo, (2) moving to the new condition, and (3) refreezing to create a new status quo. A change may cause a social and/or economic loss to the person who is affected by it. Despite the resistance that might arise, change is often necessary.

Organizational development (OD) is a planned and systematic attempt to change the organization, typically to a more behavioral environment. A major technique in the arsenal of the organizational development consultant is team building, a conscious effort to develop effective work groups throughout the organization. Another, which uses leaderless discussion groups, is referred to as sensitivity training. The general goal is to develop awareness of, and sensitivity to, oneself and others. Management by Objectives (MBO) is a philosophy of management that encourages managers to plan for the future and emphasizes participative management approaches. Within this broader context, MBO becomes an important method of organizational development. The deliberate restructuring of a job to make it more challenging, meaningful, and interesting is referred to as job enrichment.

One of the best-known predesigned OD programs is the Managerial Grid®. Blake and Mouton suggest that the most effective leadership style is that which stresses maximum concern for both output and people. The Managerial Grid provides a systematic approach for analyzing managerial styles and assisting the organization in moving to the best style. Management development programs are formal efforts to improve the skills and attitudes of present and prospective managers. Managers learn more effective approaches to managing people and other resources.

REVIEW QUESTIONS

1. Define corporate culture. What are the factors that interact to determine the type of corporate culture that exists in a firm?
2. Identify the values and limitations of a participative climate.
3. List and describe the change sequence discussed in the text.
4. What are the sources of resistance to change as described in the text?
5. Describe the approaches that may be used in reducing resistance to change.
6. Define each of the following terms:
   a. Organizational development
   b. Team building
   c. Sensitivity training

KEY TERMS

corporate culture	change sequence	sensitivity training
dominant cultures	organizational	job enrichment
subcultures	development	management
strong culture	change agent	development
status symbol	survey feedback method	programs
jargon	team building	

CASE STUDY

A CHANGE IN COMPANY CULTURE

UNTIL ONE YEAR AGO Wayne, Don, and Robert had been supervisors with a small chain of thirty-nine grocery stores. Each supervisor had responsibility for thirteen stores and reported directly to the company president. All three supervisors worked well together, and there was a constant exchange of information, which was quite useful in coordinating the activities of the stores. Each supervisor had specific strengths that were useful in helping the others. Wayne coordinated the deployment of the part-time help at all thirty-nine stores. Don monitored the inventories, and Robert interviewed prospective new employees before sending them to Wayne and Don for review. It was a complete team effort directed toward getting the job done.

One year later a completely different environment existed at the chain. The president, wishing to relieve himself of many daily details, decided to promote Robert to vice-president. Another supervisor, Phillip, was hired for Robert's position. Robert had a completely different idea of how the activities of the supervisors should be conducted. Under Robert's leadership, each supervisor was now responsible for the activities at only his stores. If a problem occurred, the supervisor was to discuss it with Robert, and he would provide the solution. When either Wayne, Don, or Phillip attempted to solve problems on their own, they were reprimanded by Robert. After a few "chewing outs," Wayne, Don, and Phillip decided not to fight the system and did as

Robert wanted; they rarely saw each other any more. If Don had a problem at his stores that caused him to work all night, that was not any concern of Wayne or Phillip.

The only problem with the new system was that efficiency dropped drastically. For instance, Wayne was a good coordinator of part-time help. He had the type of personality that could talk a person into coming to work at 5:00 P.M. on Saturday when the individual had a date at 6:00 P.M. Wayne's stores remained well staffed with part-time help, but the others suffered. Many times the part-time help did not show up, and either Don or Phillip had to act as the replacement if the store manager could not be convinced to work overtime. On the other hand, Wayne's inventory control suffered because Don was best qualified in this area.

Robert accused the three supervisors of working against him and threatened them with dismissal if operations did not get better. Wayne, Don, and Phillip felt that they could not be productive in this environment and found other positions. When the president discovered what had occurred, Robert was fired.

QUESTIONS
1. What different organizational environment was created as a result of promoting Robert to vice-president?
2. How do you think this situation could have been avoided? Discuss the possibility of the use of the participative approach in this instance.

CASE STUDY

RUMORS AT DUNCAN ELECTRIC

DONNA GARCIA IS a supervisor for Duncan Electric Corporation, a manufacturer of high-quality electrical parts. Donna has been with the firm for five years and has a reputation for having one of the best teams in the plant. Donna had picked the majority of these employees and was proud of the reputation they had achieved. But a problem was now brewing that had the potential to destroy her department.

For weeks, rumors of a substantial reduction in personnel at Duncan Electric have been circulating. Donna has not received any confirmation from the corporate office regarding the reduction. The rumors, all seeming to be from reliable sources, range from minor reductions to a large-scale reduction in personnel. Every day someone claims to have the inside story, and every day the story changes. Donna, who has a reputation for leveling with her people, successfully discounted the rumors for awhile. But as the doubts began to grow, work output began to suffer. Her employees were now spending time trying to verify the latest rumor. Speculation increased to the point where the best-qualified employees were starting to shop around. Donna was convinced that a minor layoff was the worst that could possibly happen, and she was demoralized to see things falling apart for no good reason.

On Friday, Bob Phillips and Henry Barham, two of the most skilled employees in the department, told Donna that they had taken jobs with a competitor. This situation was what she had feared the most; the most qualified workers would leave and the least qualified workers would remain. Instead of having one of the best departments at Duncan Electric, she may now have the worst.

QUESTIONS

1. To what extent have the rumors of the anticipated change in the work force damaged the morale of the employees?
2. What should management do to reduce the fear of the anticipated change?
3. What should Donna do in a situation like this?

EXPERIENTIAL EXERCISE

The type of corporate culture existing within an organization can have a major influence on whether or not a union is able to organize the work force. With certain cultures, unions have experienced considerable difficulty in their unionizing attempts. With other cultures, it is much easier. This exercise is designed to give participants an opportunity to experience the kinds of things that go on when a union is being considered in a company. Quite possibly the corporate culture will affect the fate of unionism in the company.

Two groups, one employee group and one manager group, will discuss the prospects of unionization. Each committee must come up with a recommendation for or against unionization and the reasons for their recommendation. The spokesperson for the employee group is Bob Jones, and the group members are Gerald Young, Julie Faire, and Tony Wells. Bob Jones is a very outspoken union advocate. He has always believed this company should have a union. He believes wages are lower here than at unionized firms in the area, and he sees too much "brother-in-lawing" going on. Besides, he was denied a raise recently. He was told that the boss just did not "feel" he deserved one.

This is Gerald Young's first job. His father, the union steward of another company, often says, "What you guys need over there is a good union." Last month when production standards were raised, Gerald's piece-rate bonus was wiped out. His dad says they do not pull that in a unionized firm.

Julie Faire has been working here for several years, and the company has always been good to her. She had some family problems last year, and her boss let her off for several days. Could a union be better than her understanding boss?

Tony Wells is an old hand here, and has seen lots of things come and go over the years. Tony's experience has been that if employees have enough guts to go to their supervisors directly, they can usually get satisfaction. It seems that too many people today are looking for a "free lunch."

The spokesperson for the supervisor group, Charlie Neal, is very anti-union. Charlie is really fed up with all this union talk and believes that these people do not seem to know when they are well off. Charlie has been with the company for nearly twenty years and does not intend to put up with a union now. He believes the company should "get tough." Charlie has a pretty good idea of who is leading the unionizers. If the other supervisors will listen, it will be easy enough to find reasons to get rid of the troublemakers.

Beverly Woods has only been a supervisor for a few years, previously in a unionized company. Beverly has a healthy respect for unions and some feeling for how they get their power. It seems that this is a great opportunity for the supervisors to get together with the employees and solve the employees' legitimate complaints. She believes this would be all it would take to convince employees that they do not need a union.

According to what is determined in the conference, there may be an agreement proposed that will prevent unionizing, or some delaying action such as a joint committee. There may be hard lines drawn leading to a showdown, or even an immediate call for a union election. The groups will decide, and the spokespersons will report their decisions. Your instructor will provide the participants with additional information necessary to participate.

NOTES

1. Peter D. Petre, "Meet the Mean, Lean New IBM," *Fortune* 107 (13 June 1983): 69.

2. This story is a composite of a number of published accounts, including: Peter D. Petre, "Meet the Mean, Lean New IBM," *Fortune* 107 (13 June 1983): 69–82; Thomas J. Watson, Jr., *A Business and Its Beliefs: The Ideas That Helped to Build IBM* (New York: McGraw-Hill, 1963); Thomas J. Peters and Robert H. Waterman, Jr., *In Search of Excellence: Lessons from America's Best Run Companies* (New York: Harper & Row, 1982); Marylyn A. Harris, "How IBM Is Fighting Back," *Business Week,* 17 November 1986, 152–157; and a number of articles from *The Wall Street Journal.*

3. David A. Garvin, "Quality Problems, Policies, and Attitudes in the United States and Japan: An Exploratory Study," *The Academy of Management Journal* 29, no. 4 (December 1986): 653.

4. Arthur Sharplin, *Strategic Management* (New York: McGraw-Hill, 1985), 102.

5. "Corporate Culture: The Hard-to-Change Values That Spell Success or Failure," *Business Week,* 27 October 1980, 148–160.

6. Thomas J. Murry, "Wal-Mart Penny Wise," *Business Month,* December 1988, 42.

7. Barbara Jean Gray. "Taking a Stand on Ethics," *Human Resource Executive* (May 1988): 34–35.

8. Anthony Jay, *Management and Machiavelli* (New York: Holt, Rinehart, and Winston, 1967).

9. Peters and Waterman, *In Search of Excellence;* William G. Ouchi, *Theory Z: How American Business Can Meet the Japanese Challenge* (New York: Avon Books, 1982); Terrence E. Deal and Allan A. Kennedy, *Corporate Culture* (Reading, Mass.: Addison-Wesley, 1981).

10. Many of the factors were taken from the Organizational Climate Description Questionnaire generated by Halpin and Croft as described in Andrew W. Halpin, *Theory and Research in Administration* (New York: Macmillan, 1966), chap. 4. Another widely used measure is that of Litwin and Stringer found in G. Litwin and R. Stringer, *Motivation and Organizational Climate* (Cambridge: Harvard University Press, 1968).

11. K. L. Gregory, "Native-View Paradigms: Multiple Cultures and Culture Conflicts in Organizations," *Administrative Science Quarterly* (September 1983): 359–376.

12. T. E. Deal and A. A. Kennedy, *Corporate Cultures: The Rites and Rituals of Corporate Life* (Reading, Mass.: Addison-Wesley, 1982), 65–66.

13. H. Kenneth Bobele and Peter J. Buchanan, "Building a More Productive Environment," *Management World* 1 (January 1979): 8.

14. Geoff Lewis, Anne R. Field, John J. Keller, and John W. Verity, "Big Changes at Big Blue," *Business Week,* 15 February 1988, 92.

15. John Hoerr, "Getting Man and Machine to Live Happily Ever After," *Business Week,* 20 April 1987, 61.

16. Rensis Likert, *The Human Organization* (New York: McGraw-Hill, 1967).

17. Jo Ellen Davis, and Pete Engardio, "What It's Like to Work for Frank Lorenzo," *Business Week,* 18 May 1987, 76.

18. Thomas J. Murry, "Wal-Mart Penny Wise," *Business Week,* December 1988, 42.

19. Hoerr, "Man and Machine," 61.

20. Petre, "New IBM," 69–82.

21. "Corporate Culture," 148–160.

22. Gordon Donaldson and Jay Lorsch, *Decision Making at the Top* (New York: Basic Books, 1983).

23. Bro Uttal, "The Corporate Culture Vultures," *Fortune* 17 (October 1983): 66–72.

24. Kurt Lewin, *Field Theory and Social Science* (New York: Harper, 1964), chaps. 9, 10.

25. Eric G. Flanholtz, Yvonne Randle, and Sonja Sackmann, "Personnel Management: The Tenor of Today," *Personnel Journal* (June 1987): 64.

26. Ralph G. Huschowitz, "The Human Aspects of Managing Transition," *Personnel* 51 (May–June 1974): 13.

27. "The New Industrial Relations," *Business Week,* 11 May 1981, 98.

28. "Industrial Relations," 98.

29. Portions of the following discussion were adapted from R. Wayne Mondy and Robert M. Noe III, *Personnel: The Management of Human Resources,* 2d ed. (Newton, Mass.: Allyn and Bacon, 1984), 224–240.

30. Edgar F. Huse, *Organization Development and Change* (St. Paul, Minn.: West, 1975), 230.

31. Michael A. Hitt, R. Dennis Middlemist, and Robert Q. Mathis, *Effective Management* (St. Paul, Minn.: West, 1979), 462–464.

32. For a detailed review of one hundred research studies on sensitivity training, see P. B. Smith, "Control Studies on the Outcome of Sensitivity Training," *Psychological Bulletin* (July 1975): 597–622.

33. See "Case Studies in the Humanization of Work," in *Work in America: Report of Special Task Force to the Secretary of Health, Education and Welfare* (Cambridge, Mass.: MIT Press, 1973), appendix 188–200.

34. Frederick Herzberg, "One More Time: How Do You Motivate Employees?" *Harvard Business Review* 22, no. 2 (Winter 1979).

REFERENCES

Albert, Michael. "Transmitting Corporate Culture Through Case Stories." *Personnel* (August 1987): 71–73.

Albrecht, K. *Organization Development: A Total Systems Approach to Positive Change in Any Business Organization.* Englewood Cliffs, N.J.: Prentice-Hall, 1983.

Arogyaswamy, Bernard, and Charles M. Byles. "Organizational Culture: Internal and External Fits." *Journal of Management* 13 (Winter 1987): 647–658.

Baird, John E., Jr. "Supervisory and Managerial Training Through Communication by Objectives." *Personnel Administrator* 26 (July 1981): 28–32.

Barley, Stephen R. "Cultures of Culture: Academics, Practitioners and the Pragmatics of Normative Control." *Administrative Science Quarterly* 3 (March 1988): 24–60.

Barrett, F. D. "Teamwork—How to Expand Its Power and Punch." *Business Quarterly* 52 (Winter 1987): 24–31.

Baysinger, Rebecca T., and Richard W. Woodman. "The Use of Management by Objectives in Management Training Programs." *Personnel Administrator* 25 (February 1981): 83–86.

Bernhard, Harry B., and Cynthia A. Ingols. "Six Lessons for the Corporate Classroom." *Harvard Business Review* (September–October 1988): 40–47.

Coch, L., and J. French, Jr. "Overcoming Resistance to Change." *Human Relations* 1 (1984): 512–532.

Cotton, John L., David A. Vollrath, Kirk L. Froggatt, Mark L. Lengnick-Hall, and Kenneth R. Jennings. "Employee Participation: Diverse Forms and Different Outcomes." *Academy of Management Review* 13 (January 1988): 8–22.

Davis, L. E. "Individuals and the Organization." *California Management Review* 22 (Spring 1980): 5–14.

Deal, Terrence E., and Allan A. Kennedy. *Corporate Culture.* Reading, Mass.: Addison-Wesley, 1981.

Donaldson, Gordon, and Jay Lorsch. *Decision Making at the Top.* New York: Basic Books, 1983.

Feldman, Steven P. "How Organizational Culture Can Affect Innovation." *Organizational Dynamics* 17 (Summer 1988): 57–68.

Freudenberger, Herbert J. *Burnout: The High Cost of High Achievement.* Garden City, N.Y.: Doubleday, Anchor Press, 1980. 13.

Garvin, David A. "Quality Problems, Policies, and Attitudes in the United States and Japan: An Exploratory Study." *The Academy of Management Journal* 29, no. 4 (December 1986): 653–666.

Gersick, Connie J. G. "Time and Transition in Work Teams: Toward a New Model of Group Development." *Academy of Management Journal* 31 (March 1988): 9–41.

Gordon, Jack. "Organizational Development: Next Time, Just Smile and Nod." *The Oil Daily* (9 March 1987): 12–13.

Hamilton, Rosemary. "Facing, Welcoming, Implementing Change." *Computerworld* 22 (19 September 1988): 95–96.

Hunt, Bradley D., and Judith F. Vogt. "What Really Goes Wrong with Participative Work Groups?" *Training & Development Journal* 42 (May 1988): 96–100.

Ivancevich, John M., and Michael T. Matteson. *Stress and Work: A Managerial Perspective.* Glenview, Ill.: Scott, Foresman, 1980.

Jennings, Eugene E. "How to Develop Your Management Talent Internally." *Personnel Administrator* 26 (July 1981): 20–23.

Joiner, C. W., Jr. "Making the 'Z' Concept Work." *Sloan Management Review* 26 (September 1985): 57–63.

Keil, E. C. "Corporate Culture; Fashion or Fact?" *Colorado Business Magazine* 15 (May 1988): 105–109.

Kelly, Joe, and Kamiran Khozan. "Participative Management: Can It Work?" *Business Horizons* (August 1980): 74–79.

Kuhlmann, Torsten M. "Adapting to Technical Change in the Workplace." *Personnel* 65 (August 1988): 67–69.

Levinson, Harry. "When Executives Burn Out." *Harvard Business Review* 59 (May–June 1981): 76.

Lewis, Geoff. "The Portable Executive: From Faxes to Laptops, Technology Is Changing Our Work Lives." *Business Week* (10 October 1988): 102–112.

Liebowitz, S. Jay, and Aubrey L. Mendelow. "Directions for Development; Long-Term Organizational Change Requires Corporate Vision and Patience." *Personnel Administrator* 33 (June 1988): 116–124.

Litton, Moneca. "Reducing the Risk." *Executive Female* 11 (March–April 1988): 11.

Lucas, Rob. "Political-Cultural Analysis of Organizations." *Academy of Management Journal* 12, no. 1 (January 1987): 144–156.

MacDougall, Neil. "How You Should Evaluate Company Culture." *CMA Magazine* (September–October 1986): 71.

Margerison, Charles, and Colin New. "Management Development by Intercompany Consortiums." *Personnel Management* 12 (November 1980): 42–45.

Miles, James M. "How to Establish a Good Industrial Relations Climate." *Management Review* 67 (August 1980): 42–44.

Miller, Danny, and Peter H. Friesen. "Momentum and Revaluations in Organizational Adaptation." *Academy of Management Journal* 23 (December 1980): 591–614.

Mintzberg, Henry. "Organizational Design: Fashion or Fit?" *Harvard Business Review* 59 (January–February 1981): 103–116.

Monat, Jonathan S. "A Perspective on the Evaluation of Training and Development Programs." *Personnel Administrator* 26 (July 1981): 47–52.

Mondy, R. Wayne, and Robert M. Noe III. *Personnel: The Management of Human Resources.* 3rd ed. Newton, Mass.: Allyn and Bacon, 1987.

Morey, N. C., and F. Luthans. "Refining the Displacement of Culture and the Use of Scenes and Themes in Organizational Studies." *Academy of Management Review* 10 (1985): 219–229.

Morris, Richard M., III. "Management Control and Decision Support Systems—An Overview." *Industrial Management* 28 (January–February): 8–15.

Moskowitz, J. "Lessons from the Best Companies to Work For." *California Management Review* 27 (Winter 1985): 42–47.

Nelton, Sharon. "Cultural Changes in a Family Firm." *Nation's Business* (January 1989): 62–65.

Nurick, A. J. "The Paradox of Participation: Lessons from the Tennessee Valley Authority." *Human Resource Management* 24 (1985): 341–356.

Olivas, Louis. "Using Assessment Centers for Individual and Organizational Development." *Personnel* 57 (May–June 1980): 63–67.

O'Toole, J. "Employee Practices at the Best Managed Companies." *California Management Review* 28 (Fall 1985): 35–66.

Reimann, Bernard C., and Yoash Wiener. "Corporate Culture: Avoiding the Elitist Trap." *Business Horizons* (March–April 1988): 36–42.

Sandwith, Paul. "Absenteeism: You Get What You Accept." *Personnel Journal* (November 1987): 88–93.

Schein, E. H. *Organizational Culture and Leadership.* San Francisco: Jossey-Bass, 1985.

Schied-Cook, Teresa L. "Mitigating Organizational Contradictions: The Role of Mediatory Myths." *Journal of Applied Behavioral Science* 24 (May 1988): 161–171.

Schneider, Susan C., and Paul Shrivastava. "Basic Assumptions Themes in Organizations." *Human Relations* 41 (July 1988): 493–515.

Schriber, Jacquelyn, and Barbara A. Gutck. "Some Time Dimensions of Work: Measurement of an Underlying Aspect of Organization Culture." *Journal of Applied Psychology* 72 (November 1987): 642–650.

Trice, H. M., and J. M. Beyer. "Studying Organizational Cultures Through Rites and Ceremonials." *Academy of Management Review* 9 (October 1984): 653–669.

Weiss, Richard M., and Lynn E. Miller. "The Concept of Ideology in Organizational Analysis: The Sociology of Knowledge or the Social Psychology of Beliefs?" *The Academy of Management Review* 12, no. 1 (January 1987): 104–116.

CHAPTER
21

Chapter Outline

History and Development of Multinationals

The Multinational Environment

Management in a Multinational Environment

Human Resources and the Multinational Environment

Summary

Managing the Multinational Enterprise

Learning Objectives

After completing this chapter students should be able to

1. Explain the history and development of multinationals.
2. Describe the multinational environment.
3. Explain management in a multinational environment.
4. Describe human resources in the multinational environment.

WHEN THE AMC ALLIANCE was named *Motor Trend Magazine's* "Car of the Year" in 1983, it was a compliment not only to the car but to a much broader alliance—that between the French company Renault and American Motors Corporation. Renault had purchased a small percentage of AMC's common stock in 1978. At that time, Renault had a meager 14 percent of the U.S. market. Over the following five years, Renault slowly increased its percentage of ownership in AMC to almost 50 percent. The cost: $450 million.

When the alliance with Renault began, AMC seemed an unlikely choice for the famous French automaker. Renault was the sixth largest car manufacturer in the world, with plants in France and ten other countries. The company's marketing network extended to practically every country on the globe. Under France's socialist government, Renault was accustomed to being propped up whenever the need arose. American Motors Corporation, on the other hand, was by far the smallest of the big four U.S. automakers. AMC sales were sagging. The company was losing money, and there had not been a really successful American Motors car in over twenty years. Despite its name, American Motors was not an American favorite, and there was little sentiment for government support or public concern over the company's decline.

But American Motors did have some things Renault wanted. In order to maintain its position in the world auto industry, Renault needed to sell 2.5 million cars by 1985. But the European car market grew at only 4 percent a year in the 1970s, and it was expected to grow even more slowly in the 1980s. American Motors Corporation provided Renault with an entry into the largest and fastest-growing auto market in the world. Bernard Hanon, Renault's chairman, saw another advantage, calling the United States "a fertile ground for new ideas and concepts that no car manufacturer can ignore." AMC's network for 2,000 dealers and three auto assembly plants, all operating at far below capacity, were also a major plus.

Despite its declining sales, AMC had solid name identification in the United States. Company executives understood the culture of the United States and thus offered the capability of being able to eliminate many of the barriers foreign companies face. AMC managers were highly respected as marketers. Past failures were considered to have been for engineering and technological reasons, not because of marketing deficiencies.

The marriage was not an immediate success. There were a number of threats by U.S. lawmakers trying to prevent Renault from "taking over" an important U.S. company. Other U.S. automakers complained that the government subsidies France gave Renault would translate into an unfair advantage for American Motors. Unions complained that before long AMC cars would only be assembled in the United States—the parts, they said, would be made in France, at the cost of U.S. jobs. These objections seemed less significant after AMC lost $136.6 million in 1981. But they were still matters of concern to company executives.

At first, Renault stressed its desire to "support and not manage" its U.S. partner. After investing the $450 million, however, Renault began to increase its hold over AMC management. By 1984, a French vice-president had taken charge of most of AMC's manufacturing and marketing activities, including research and development and quality control. In 1986 Renault vetoed a new U.S. plant planned by AMC executives.

All of AMC's traditional car designs were phased out in favor of French-designed front-wheel-drive cars. The French technology required retraining of U.S. workers. And the ingrained attitudes and abilities of U.S. workers required some adaptation to the French designs and work methods. Because of the overwhelming success of the Alliance, Renault came to control a healthy slice of the U.S. auto market. Renault's U.S.A. president, Pierre Gazarian, remained optimistic. "Renault has a lot of confidence in what AMC can become," he said.

But as 1987 began, no hot replacement for the Alliance was in sight, and AMC sales crashed. It became increasingly clear that Renault would have to give up on its effort to become a major United States automaker. In March of 1987, Chrysler Corporation announced that it had agreed to purchase Renault's controlling interest in AMC.[1] ■

A COMPANY ENGAGES IN international business typically because of significant opportunities beyond the home country's borders. These opportunities are usually partly offset by the well-known problems of international business: cultural differences, legal restrictions, language barriers, monetary effects, and the distances over which information and materials must travel. This is no less true for a foreign company like Renault doing business in the United States than it is for a U.S. company going abroad. The methods Renault used in attempting to minimize the problems of the U.S. market are typical of those found effective by companies engaged in international business all over the world.

As recently as the 1950s and 1960s, the need for adapting business practices to different national environments was not fully appreciated. Some thought that international businesses could simply force the foreign country situation to conform to the international company's usual way of operating.[2] Today it is recognized that the challenge of engaging in multinational operations is not this simply met.

This chapter begins by describing the history and development of multinational enterprises. Then, environmental factors confronting multinationals are described. Next, management in a multinational environment is addressed. The final section of the chapter focuses on human resources and the multinational environment.

Multinational company (MNC)
An organization that conducts a large part of its business outside the country in which it is headquartered and has a significant percentage of physical facilities and employees in other countries.

■ HISTORY AND DEVELOPMENT OF MULTINATIONALS

A **multinational company (MNC)** is an organization that conducts a large part of its business outside the country in which it is headquartered and has a significant percentage of physical facilities and employees in other countries. With operations in many countries, Renault is clearly an MNC. Some experts in the field of multinational enterprises believe that organizations designated as multinationals should meet the following criteria:

1. Conduct operations in at least six different countries.
2. Have at least 20 percent of the firm's assets and/or sales from business in countries other than that where the parent company is located.
3. Have and demonstrate an integrated, global managerial orientation:
    a. Resources of the enterprise are allocated without regard to national boundaries.
    b. National boundaries are merely a constraint that enters into the decision-making process; they are not part of the definition of the company itself.
    c. The firm's organizational structure cuts across national boundaries.
    d. Personnel are transferred throughout the world.
    e. Management takes on a broad, global perspective; they view the world as interrelated and interdependent.

To illustrate the impact of the multinational, a Massey-Ferguson executive states, "We combine French-made transmissions, British-made engines, Mexican-made axles, and United States-made sheet metal parts to produce in Detroit a tractor for sale in Canada."[3]

The first MNC established with a global orientation grew out of a merger in 1929 between Margarine Unie, a Dutch firm, and Lever Brothers, a British company. The company became Unilever, and it has since become one of the largest companies in the world with approximately 500 subsidiaries operating in

A multinational corporation creates interrelationships between countries and cultures, and between different economic and political systems.
(© Derek Berwin, The Image Bank)

about sixty nations. Unilever has two headquarters units, one located in Rotterdam and the other in London.

Multinationals usually operate through subsidiary companies in countries outside their home nation. Some of the names of the largest multinationals have become household words: General Motors, Ford, IBM, General Electric, and Exxon. The worldwide impact of these companies is significant. Their operations create interrelationships between countries and cultures as well as between economic and political systems.

The economic output of MNCs is a significant portion of the total economic output of the world. Some economists have estimated that by the year 2000, about 200 to 300 multinationals will account for one half of the world's total output of goods and services. In recent years, there has been a rapid growth of direct investment by multinational firms averaging about 10 percent per year. MNCs based in the United States account for more than half of this worldwide investment.

One of the most aggressive countries whose multinationals appear to be quickly expanding into more and more countries is Japan. Recently, Japanese manufacturers have been fighting to establish a solid presence in Europe, and their entry point appears to be Britain. Japanese companies fear they will face increased protectionism if they are not entrenched in Europe as the Economic Community reduces its barriers to internal trade.[4]

■■■ THE MULTINATIONAL ENVIRONMENT

Today it is commonly recognized that the challenge of engaging in multinational operations is not easily met. This is especially true with regard to the challenges

BUSINESS BRIEFS

INSIDE BUSINESS

Competing in the Multinational Environment

GLOBAL COMPETITION, air travel, and satellite communication technology have made doing business abroad both necessary and feasible, and companies have responded by establishing operations overseas. Unfortunately, American managers have tended to fall back on their own limited experiences and to treat an assignment in Hong Kong, Sydney, or Paris much like a stint in Dallas or Atlanta. Some managers have incorrectly assumed that international businesses can simply force foreign countries to conform to the international company's usual way of operating. One man constantly dealing with the complexities involved in operating in the multinational environment is Cornelius Van Der Klugt, President and Chairman of the Dutch electronics giant, Philips NV. Van Der Klugt discusses some of the facts of life that managers must face when competing in the global economy. He shares his perspectives regarding certain realities of the multinational environment with the CNN business news team of Kandel, Hartley, and Young.

F I G U R E 21.1 ■■■ Management in the Multinational Environment

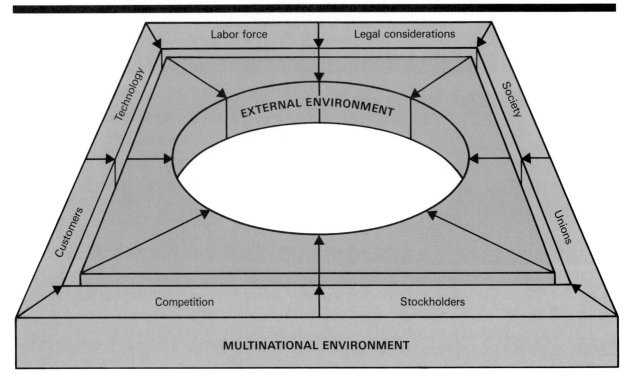

of management. In Chapter 3 the discussion was primarily focused on environmental factors of organizations located in the United States. However, the external environment that confronts multinational enterprises is even more diverse and complex than that confronted by domestic firms.

As is illustrated in Figure 21.1, another layer has been added to the external environment (described in Chapter 3) that management must contend with in a multinational climate. Although the basic tasks associated with management remain essentially the same, the manner in which the tasks are accomplished may be altered substantially by the multinational's external environment. Additionally, the organizational behavior considerations of multinational corporations are usually more complex than those of domestic organizations. As Figure 21.1 suggests, the MNC must deal with the environment not only of the parent country, but of the host country as well. The **parent country** is the country in which the headquarters of the multinational corporation is located. The **host country** is the country in which resides the operational unit of the multinational corporation.

Parent country
The country in which the headquarters of the multinational corporation is located.

Host country
The country in which resides the operational unit of the multinational corporation.

Legal Considerations

Not only must the multinational corporation adhere to the federal, state, and local legislation of the parent country, the laws of the host country must also be obeyed. However, there is no comprehensive system of international law or courts requiring that the MNC understand in detail the laws of each host country. The

YOUR COMPANY, Empire Southwest, a distributor of Caterpillar equipment in Phoenix, wants to trade in the Mexican market where cash under the table, *mordita* (a "little bite"), is part of doing business. This payoff practice is so ingrained in the Spanish culture that a business virtually cannot open a Mexican operation without going along. You can continue to raise your stature with mining companies, farmers, and contractors, and encourage them to lobby the government to freely open the market, or you can pay the bribe.
What would you do?

Source: Adapted by permission, *Nation's Business,* August 1987. Copyright 1987, U.S. Chamber of Commerce.

United States, England, Canada, Australia, and New Zealand have developed their legal requirements by means of English common law. Under English common law, judges and courts are extremely important, for they are guided by principles declared in previous cases. In most of continental Europe, Asia, and Africa, the approach is one of civil law. Judges play a lesser role because the legal requirements are codified. The civil servant or bureaucrat has greater power under civil law than under the common law.

Although the United States is a highly legalistic country, and American MNCs tend to carry U.S. law with them, managers must realize that the legal systems of other countries can differ considerably. For example, the Japanese dislike laws, lawyers, and litigation. In France, lawyers are prohibited from serving on boards of directors by codes of the legal profession. The vastness and sheer complexity of various legal systems throughout the world demonstrates clearly the intricate and demanding legal environment of the MNCs. In order to function in a manner consistent with the host country, managers should become familiar with its legal considerations. Failure to carefully consider legal considerations could have a drastic effect on multinational success.

Frederick W. Smith, founder of Federal Express Corporation, soon realized that not properly preparing for legal considerations can cause severe problems. Smith is usually a winner, but one victory has eluded him over the past three years. Federal has struggled to become a major player in international deliveries, but since 1985, Federal has lost approximately $74 million. Because of entrenched overseas rivals and foreign regulations, he has been stifled. In December 1988 he announced plans to buy Tiger International Inc., the world's largest heavy-cargo airline. Smith had to spend $880 million to possibly crack the market. He purchased Tiger's delivery routes, painstakingly acquired over forty years, and now appears to have a reasonable foothold in the international delivery market.[5]

Businesses in the United States are heavily impacted by government legislation, Executive Orders, and court decisions. Firms operating in the United States must abide by these actions. But, when an organization headquartered in the United States goes multinational, the laws of the host country must be obeyed. United States firms operating in the multinational environment often find their human resource policies in conflict with the accepted norm of the host country.

For instance, the influence of Title VII of the Civil Rights Act of 1964, as amended, has been felt by virtually all firms operating in the United States. But most countries in the world do not have such laws prohibiting discrimination. In fact, in some countries there is overt discrimination against certain groups, who would be protected if they were employed in the United States. In certain Middle East countries, the status of women is below that of men. Should a U.S. firm desire to conduct business within those countries, women would have a difficult time being accepted. The firm may have a strong affirmative action program in the United States, yet it might have to make a decision to place women managers in foreign countries where the climate is more conducive to organizational success. With regard to law, multinational firms may have to abide by the old expression, "When in Rome, do as the Romans."

Labor Force

In filling key managerial, technical, or professional positions abroad, multinationals can choose among three basic types of employees: (1) parent country nationals (PCN), (2) host country nationals (HCN), and (3) third country nationals (TCN). Until the 1950s, it was common for MNCs to fill foreign key posts with trusted and experienced employees from the parent company (PCNs). Recently, stronger nationalistic feelings have led companies to alter their policies and employ more people from host countries (HCNs). Additionally, some firms have used workers from countries other than the parent country or host country (TCNs). For example, one U.S.-based firm received a contract to build highways in Saudi Arabia using workers from Turkey and Italy. Still, many companies attempt to keep parent country employees in at least half of the identified key positions, particularly in the financial area.

Using workers from the parent nation of the multinational ensures a greater degree of consistency and control in the firm's operations around the world. However, this approach is not without its costs, because these workers may experience considerable difficulty in understanding cultural differences and adapting to life in the host country. In an attitude survey of workers in forty-nine multinationals, employees from the host country contended that parent country workers tended not to question orders from headquarters even when it was appropriate to do so.[6] Unquestioned actions enabled these individuals to advance their own long-term interests in the firm by getting better headquarters evaluations and facilitating repatriation at the end of their tour of duty. In addition, the common practice of frequent rotation of key employees intensified the problem of understanding and adapting to local cultures. However, using PCNs facilitates communications with headquarters because both parties are of the same culture.

Utilizing workers from the host country in key positions will usually improve the MNC's relations with the host country government. It will also enable a quicker and more accurate adaptation to the requirements of the host country. Disadvantages include a lessened degree of centralized control and increased communication problems with headquarters. In addition, if the HCNs perceive that the opportunity for higher-level positions is blocked for ethnic reasons, they will use the MNC to gain experience so they may transfer to local national firms at higher positions. Properly balancing the type of key employees stationed in the host country is often a complex and difficult task, but one that is critical to the success of the MNC.

Society

It is apparent that the significant societal considerations of one nation will differ to some extent from those of other countries. Customs, beliefs, values, and habits of each society will vary. If the multinational corporation is to operate in many nations, it will be required to adapt some of its managerial practices to the specific and unique expectations and situations of each nation. Attitudes will differ concerning such subjects as work, risk-taking, change introduction, time authority, and material gain. It is dangerous for managers to assume that the attitudes within the parent country will be similar in all other countries. However, it is sometimes possible for successful multinationals to change the way those in the parent countries do business. According to Barry Wilkinson, lecturer at Cardiff Business School and co-author of *The Japanization of British Industry,* the British are looking at the Japanese organization as the model for success.[7]

Lack of cultural sensitivity has limited the transfer of successful U.S. management practices to European countries. The same is true for some foreign MNCs doing business in the United States. For example, when Renault built plants in the United States, they found it necessary to adapt to the U.S. work ethic. Primarily, U.S. workers tend to prefer less direct supervision than do the French, so Renault adapted their management style to better accommodate U.S. employees.

In certain societies, authority is viewed as a natural right and is not questioned by subordinates. In other cultures, authority must be earned and is provided to those who have demonstrated their ability to lead. In some cultures, work is good and moral; in others it is to be avoided. Building up wealth in some nations is indicative of good and approved behavior. In others, riches are to be avoided. David McClelland discovered that the fundamental attitude toward achievement is somewhat correlated with rates of economic development. If a nation's citizens are willing to commit themselves to the accomplishment of tasks deemed worthwhile and difficult, a country will benefit economically. McClelland contends that one's ability to influence the future will have a definite impact on the behavior of a country's work force.[8] If the basic belief is one of fatalism—what will be, will be—then the importance of planning and organizing for the future is downgraded.

Societies also vary as to interclass mobility and sources of status. If there is little hope of moving up to higher classes in a society, then fatalism and an absence of a drive for achievement are likely. In many instances, the MNC will have to adapt and conform to the societal requirements of the host country in order to successfully operate as a multinational corporation. Obviously, management is directly impacted by societal concerns; therefore, such concerns must be carefully considered by MNC managers.

Unions

The prospect for future unionism throughout the world is not good. Factors such as the decline in union membership in the U.S. since the 1950s, the lack of government support for employee organizations in non-free countries, and the troubled labor movements in other industrialized free nations dims the prospects for worldwide unionism.[9] During the past decade, many Western democracies have experienced a political movement toward conservatism and against unionism.

Conservative legislation and administration of this legislation may also limit growth in union organizing efforts.[10]

Unions in industrialized free nations seem to be yielding to management demands for enhanced productivity, often without the benefit of increased compensation. In most industrialized free countries, union demands for higher wages are gradually taking a backseat to concerns for retraining and improved working conditions. West Germany is a perfect example of an industrialized nation that has seen many employees quitting unions, because of the union's lack of flexibility in dealing with management.[11] Surprisingly, British labor relations has been another inducement for the Japanese to come in force to Britain. Japanese companies have obtained flexible work rules and no-strike deals from the once-hidebound British unions.[12]

The pressures of a global economy are creating the need for greater productivity at reduced or capped wage levels, which greatly limits a union's attractiveness to employees. The state of unionism worldwide can have a dramatic impact on the competitiveness of MNCs. Therefore, the impact of unionism throughout the world must be taken into account when making many management decisions.

Stockholders

Stockholders must be satisfied with their return on investment or they will seek other investment opportunities. An MNC seeks to produce and distribute products and services throughout the world in return for a satisfactory return on its invested capital. A multinational corporation survives, grows, and remains attractive to stockholders by maintaining its technological advantages and minimizing risks.

Competition

Competition impacting firms operating in a multinational environment typically comes from many directions. In the past, United States firms had the luxury of viewing the competition as primarily American. This is no longer true, however. Now these same firms find themselves competing with corporations in many countries. According to many experts, United States firms have a difficult time competing on a worldwide basis, primarily because of poor product quality.[13] Furthermore, firms may now find themselves competing with other multinationals and host country firms for the same personnel. This situation further compounds the problems associated with management and creates a need for greater emphasis on the importance of managers in multinational corporations.

Customers

In this new environment, customers may exist in any country in the world. Cultivating these potential customers often requires new, and sometimes innovative, management approaches. For example, fundamental selling skills transcend cultural barriers. However, the perception of the salesperson differs from country to country, and the manner in which the sale is culminated often differs.[14] Subsequently, it is the proper preparation of the sales force that could mean the difference between success and failure. Therefore, managers must make every attempt to assure that critical personnel who directly influence customers are properly prepared to represent the MNC.

Technology

Although the host country has power as a result of national sovereignty, multinationals are not helpless. Multinationals' power lies primarily in their ability to grant or withhold needed economic resources and technological knowledge. Other MNCs will observe the nature of treatment accorded by the host country, and this will affect their decision to invest in that country. Should the host country have enterprises with investments in the parent country, retaliation could occur. If the parent country provides foreign economic aid, this can also be used as leverage in promoting equitable treatment for the MNC subsidiary.

Transfer of technological expertise is the primary advantage of the multinational enterprise. Many MNCs operate in high-technology industries such as petroleum, pharmaceutical, tires, electronics, and motor vehicles. There are fewer MNCs in such fields as cotton, textiles, and cement. The technological gap that exists in some nations provides the unique opportunity for the MNC to transfer high technology from the parent company. The reverse can also be true. The situation existing within a country will dictate the nature of the technology required to accomplish work. There is obviously a wide range of environments, objectives, and technologies that would preclude any significant general statements that would apply to all multinationals. It should be noted, however, that the strength of most MNCs lies in their ability to operate highly complex technologies.

Of course, transferring technologies profitably requires specially designed strategies. Among the factors that must be considered are host country laws, the stability of the region, and financial incentives.[15] Obviously, the technological nature of the operation will have a direct bearing on certain aspects of management. Basically, managers must maintain the personnel needed to support the level of technology employed by the MNC and provide assistance to those who must adapt to a high-tech work environment.

■■ MANAGEMENT IN A MULTINATIONAL ENVIRONMENT

Each of the management functions is quite important in the multinational environment. In order to effectively manage a multinational firm, proper utilization of each of the management functions is essential. However, there are some differences that should be recognized when planning, organizing, influencing, and controlling in the multinational environment (see Figure 21.2).

Planning

At first glance, the objectives of MNCs may not appear to be any different from the objectives of businesses operating exclusively within the United States. The typical MNC goals of survival, profit, and growth are indeed similar to companies

F I G U R E   21.2   ■■   Management in a Multinational Environment

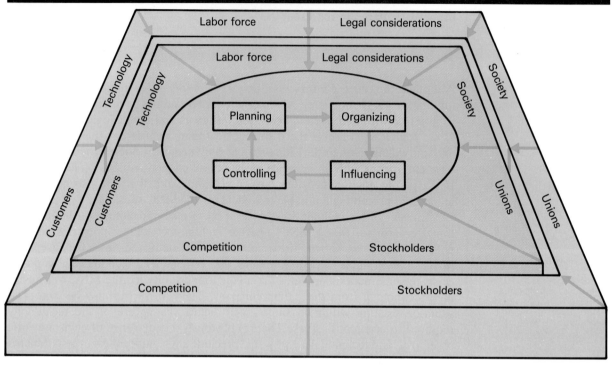

operating in the United States. However, there is a major difference. The goals of the MNC may clash with the objectives of the economic and political systems of the various countries within which they operate. Some of the objectives of countries may coincide with the objectives of the MNC, and some may not. Most countries want improved standards of living for their people, and such goals as a trained labor force, full employment, reasonable price stability, a favorable balance of payments, and steady economic growth are fairly common.

In achieving some of these goals, therefore, there is an overlapping of interests between the MNC and the host country. For example, a new MNC in a country will usually create new jobs, thereby contributing to a higher level of employment, increased income, and economic growth. By doing so, MNCs often reduce the pressure on political leaders accused of having contributed to unemployment in their countries.[16] Although the MNC usually contributes to the accomplishment of such goals, it may not do so at the rate expected by the host country, and this can create problems. The bottom line, in relation to objectives, is that the interest of stockholders must be protected, regardless of whether the firm is a domestic or a multinational corporation.

A pattern has recently developed whereby strategic plans tend to originate in the home office but are formulated using intensive communication with international divisions. On the other hand, tactical planning tends to be delegated to the individual international branches.[17] To facilitate tactical planning at American Motors and to ensure consistency, Renault appointed Pierre Gazarian, a Frenchman, to head its U.S. subsidiary.

Organizing

The organizational structure of a multinational firm must be designed to meet the needs of the international environment. Typically, the first effort of a firm to become a multinational is the creation of an export unit in the domestic marketing department. At some point, the firm may perceive a need to locate manufacturing units abroad. After a time, these various foreign units are grouped into an international division. This is the typical structure for the U.S. multinational.

The international division becomes a centralized profit center, equal in status to other major domestic divisions. It is typically headed by a vice-president and operates on a fairly autonomous basis independent of the domestic operations. The reasons for this approach are (1) the necessity of obtaining managerial and technical expertise in the diverse environments of many countries and (2) the reduction of control from the often larger domestic divisions. The disadvantage is the decreased coordination and cohesion of the international division with the rest of the company.[18]

As the international division grows, it usually becomes organized on either a geographical or product base of specialization. In giant MNCs, the international division is often a transitional stage in moving toward a worldwide structure that discounts the importance of national boundaries. As portrayed in Figures 21.3, 21.4, and 21.5, any such global structure requires a careful balance of three types of specialization: functional, area (geographical), and product. When the primary base is any one of the three, the other two must be present in the form of specialized staff experts or coordinators. A clear-cut decision that is heavily in favor of any one base is usually inappropriate.

Figure 21.3 illustrates a global functional organizational structure for a multinational. The executive in charge of the production function has worldwide responsibility. Together with the presidents and executives in charge of sales and

FIGURE 21.3 ■■
MNC: Global-Functional
Organizational Structure

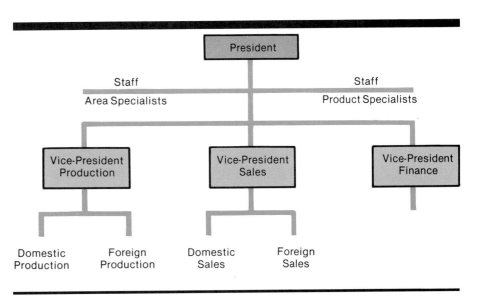

Source: Edwin B. Flippo and Gary M. Munsinger, *Management,* 5th ed. (Newton, Mass.: Allyn and Bacon, 1982), p. 212.

FIGURE 21.4 ■ MNC: Global-Area Structure

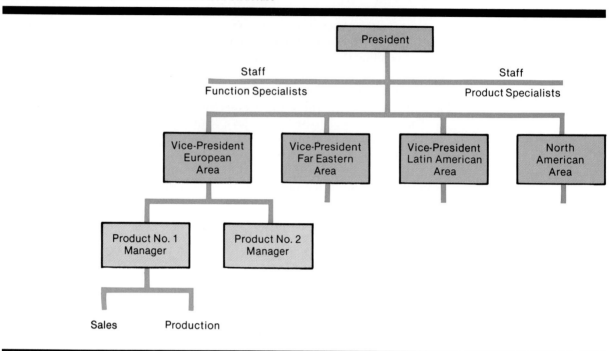

Source: Edwin B. Flippo and Gary M. Munsinger, *Management,* 5th ed. (Newton, Mass.: Allyn and Bacon, 1982), p. 213.

finance, a small group of managers enables worldwide centralized control of the MNC to be maintained.

MNCs with widely diversified lines of products requiring a high technology to produce and distribute tend to use the area base in their global structures. This form is portrayed in Figure 21.4. During the 1960s, General Electric moved from the international division form to the global-area structure. Primary responsibility for worldwide operations was assigned to the fifty to sixty general managers in charge of product divisions. International specialists, formerly in the international division, were reassigned to the various product divisions to provide aid in adapting to a multitude of national environments. To ensure that the product orientation did not dominate to the exclusion of area emphasis, four regional managers were established in Europe, Canada, Latin America, and the rest of the world. These executives were General Electric's eyes and ears in the countries assigned. They advised on the most suitable approach in each country for the product executives, identified potential partners, and aided in establishing locally oriented personnel programs. The area executive might be given line authority when a product division had not yet sufficient skill in the region or when a subsidiary unit reported to many product divisions. Though the basic emphasis is on product, the addition of the geographical concept produced a type of matrix organizational structure.

Finally, when the range of products is somewhat limited, or when the product is highly standardized, MNCs tend to use the global-product structure, as shown in Figure 21.5. Executives with true line authority are placed over major regions

FIGURE 21.5 ■■ MNC: Global-Product Structure

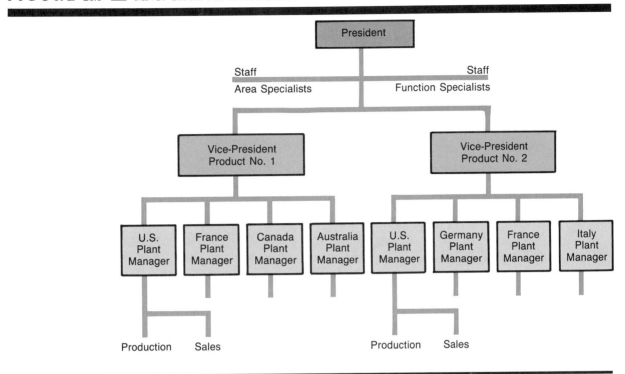

Source: Edwin B. Flippo and Gary M. Munsinger, *Management,* 5th ed. (Newton, Mass.: Allyn and Bacon, 1982), p. 213.

throughout the world. This type of structure is used by international oil companies (limited variety of products) and soft-drink producers (highly standardized product). As in other instances, some supporting staff is necessary in the product and functional areas.

In all forms of MNC structures, one makes sure (1) that the product is properly managed and coordinated throughout the world, (2) that the functional processes of production, sales, and finance are executed efficiently, and (3) that proper and efficient adaptations are made in response to the environments in the host country.

Influencing

Many aspects of the influencing function may be altered when operating in a multinational environment. Of particular significance in the operation of a multinational firm are the topics of leadership, motivation, and communication.

LEADERSHIP

Successful management of an MNC requires that the manager understand the needs, values, and problems of employees in the countries where the company operates. A study of 300 managers in fourteen countries found that parent country managers had a low opinion of their subordinates' abilities to take an active role in the management process.[19]

To successfully manage a multinational corporation, leaders must understand the needs, values, and problems of employees at each location where the company will be operating. (COMSTOCK, Inc.)

The requirements for effective leadership of personnel in the United States, Canada, Great Britain, Australia, or many of the Western European countries differ significantly from such countries as Turkey, Mexico, Malaysia, Taiwan, Thailand, or certain African, Asian, or South American countries. Research has shown that the needs and values of people vary from nation to nation, often the result of differences in economic living standards or cultural or religious influences.

In selecting individuals for overseas assignments, management must recognize that no one style of leadership will be equally effective in all countries. People in the various countries have widely divergent backgrounds, education, cultures, and religions and live within a variety of social conditions and economic and political systems. Managers must consider all of these factors, because they all can have a rather dramatic effect on the working environment.

Much that is said concerning the appropriate management approach for international businesses must be based on common sense and informed conjecture. It seems reasonable that a successful international manager should possess the following qualities, among others:

- A knowledge of basic history, particularly in countries of old and homogeneous cultures
- A social background in basic economics and sociological concepts as they differ from country to country
- An interest in the host country and a willingness to learn and practice the language
- A genuine respect for different philosophical and ethical approaches

Basically, individuals transferred overseas should have a desire to function, as well as possible, in the host country environment.

MOTIVATION

Unsatisfied needs motivate behavior. In the United States and other highly developed countries, people's basic needs—physiological, security, and social—are fairly well satisfied. Research on the application of Maslow's hierarchy of needs theory of human behavior has shown considerable differences concerning the dominant needs of people in different countries. Thus, in some advanced countries, managers must try to satisfy the needs for esteem and self-actualization. In developing countries with lower standards of living, appeals to basic human needs may prove to be not only appropriate, but the primary means for motivating desired behavior.

COMMUNICATION

Communication is the transfer of information, ideas, understanding, or feelings between people. When operating in a multinational environment, a major difficulty one often encounters is ineffective communication. The meanings of words may be understood as defined. However, their interpretation may elicit other meanings. Even a tone of voice may be misinterpreted when two different cultures attempt to communicate.

Controlling

Controlling has been defined as the process of comparing actual performance with standards and taking any necessary corrective action. The more multinational a firm becomes, the more important its control system. The need to effectively control inputs, the process, and outputs is certainly applicable in the multinational environment. However, certain aspects of controlling may not be the same as in the United States. For example, as a control mechanism, disciplinary action may take different forms in some countries.

Standards are established levels of quality or quantity used to guide performance. In establishing standards in the multinational environment, both corporate objectives and the local environment must be taken into consideration. Often host country managers need to be consulted with regard to the feasibility of a particular standard.

Evaluating performance is a critical but often more difficult task to accomplish when operating in a multinational environment. Often an extensive management information system is needed to provide managers in the parent country with the knowledge they need to make timely and proper decisions. At times, too much or too little information is fed into the system. This factor, combined with the distance factor, places increased pressure on the evaluation of performance of a multinational organization.

■■ HUMAN RESOURCES AND THE MULTINATIONAL ENVIRONMENT

By and large, the success of a multinational corporation hinges on the human component of the organization (see Figure 21.6). Selection and training and

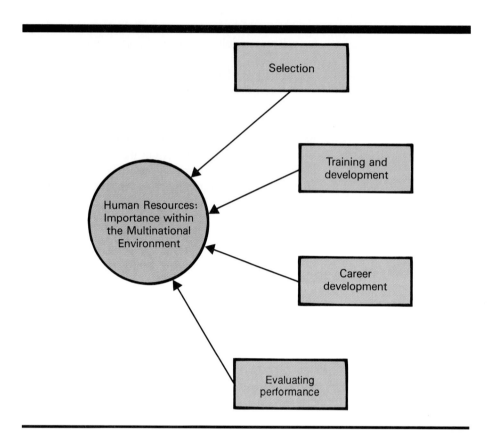

development needs are often quite different in the multinational climate. Career development of individuals may also be helped or hindered, depending on the internal and external factors affecting the multinational. The process of performance appraisal should reflect the unique culture of the host country as well as the needs of the multinational firm.

Selection

One of the most difficult management problems for the multinational organization is that of selecting suitable people to be sent on foreign assignments. Inappropriate selections are often made that negatively impact the multinational operation. A National Industrial Conference Board survey has called staffing overseas executive positions the second most serious problem facing multinational corporations.[20] Although specific failure rates vary by country and by company, most researchers agree that about one fourth of Americans selected for overseas operations are obvious failures who, in many cases, return home prematurely. A similar percentage are hidden failures or marginal performers.[21] However, some firms have experienced a 60- to 90-percent failure rate in certain countries.[22]

After being carefully selected for the assignment and briefed on the new job and locale, employees based in the United States are sent to do business in familiar surroundings. However, the multinational environment is often unfamiliar, and doing business as it's always been done may no longer be effective. The daily tasks of everyday living may also be very different and difficult.[23] Poor selection, coupled with the stress of living and working overseas, have been documented as factors contributing to mental breakdown, alcoholism, and divorce.

There are three common reasons why United States workers sent overseas fail: (1) Their family is misjudged, or is not considered at the time of selection; (2) managers are selected solely on the basis of their domestic track records; or (3) they lack adequate cross-cultural training.[24] To overcome this situation, careful plans should be made to assure that selectees possess certain basic characteristics. Certainly, they must possess the technical ability to get the job done.[25] Unfortunately, however, U.S. firms seem to focus their selection efforts on the single criterion "technical competence"—at the expense of attention to other criteria. For example, few firms administer tests to determine the relational/cross-cultural/ interpersonal skills of their candidates. Other factors such as the following are also needed:

- A real desire to work in a foreign country
- Spouses and families who have actively encouraged the person to work overseas
- Cultural sensitivity and flexibility
- A sense for politics

Several surveys of overseas managers have revealed that the spouse's opinion and attitude should be considered the most important screening factor. Cultural sensitivity is also essential to avoid antagonizing host country nationals unnecessarily.

The selection process for the expatriate should focus on the measurement and evaluation of the candidate's current levels of expertise. Psychological tests, stress tests, evaluations by the candidate's superiors, subordinates, peers, and acquaintances, and professional evaluations from licensed psychologists can all aid in ascertaining the candidate's current level of ability in interpersonal and cross-cultural skills. The candidate's spouse and children should undergo modified versions of the selection process, since the family members confront slightly different challenges overseas than do employees.[26]

Training and Development

Only a few multinational corporations offer formal training programs to prepare people to live and work overseas. People who were regarded as superior employees often fail because they are ill-equipped to cope with the complexities and dangers of intercultural management.[27] A review of the placement decisions of some American multinational companies found that the companies reported 30 percent of their placements to be mistakes—primarily due to the employees' failure to adjust properly to a new culture.[28] Some companies do offer training to expatriate employees, but the training is generally not comprehensive in nature.[29] The duration of cross-cultural training programs tends to be relatively short, considering the amount of knowledge and skills that need to be taught to the expatriates. Also, spouses tend to be left out of whatever training is offered by the company. However, multinational corporations are beginning to study culture to determine how different cultures communicate and work with each other.[30]

A major objective of intercultural training is to help people cope with unexpected events in a new culture. Once an expatriate is selected, the essential thing is to ensure that the person chosen is suitable for cross-cultural work. Such skills may not be present in the most senior person—or in the person with the most technical competence.[31] An individual overwhelmed by a new culture will be unable to perform required work duties effectively. Further, an ill-prepared individual may inadvertently offend or alienate a foreign host and perhaps jeopardize the MNC's existing long-term relations with that country.[32] Training should be sufficient to permit the manager (and spouse) to understand the new culture and adapt to their anticipated roles.[33]

Career Development

Foreign assignments have often been thought to provide career advancement opportunities. However, the relationship between expatriation and career development/advancement is often not clear. With varying results in terms of advancement, it appears as though there is no standard interpretation of the importance of an overseas assignment. The impetus for overseas staffing seems to be more to meet immediate human resource needs than to create an integrated career development strategy for future corporate executives.[34]

Whatever the case, without generous support during the overseas assignment, employees can become demoralized, frustrated, and anxious.[35] Despite a company's intention to provide career advancement opportunities, there is still some danger that skilled managers assigned to foreign operations will ultimately perceive that their career progress has suffered. Some managers have returned from foreign assignments to find no job available, or they are given jobs that do not utilize skills obtained overseas. To solve this problem, a godfather system has been set up in companies such as Control Data Corporation.[36] Before the person leaves on assignment, a specific executive is appointed as the "godfather"—to look after the person's interests while in a foreign country, and to assist the executive in achieving a smooth transition when returning home. A repatriation plan is worked out, including the duration of the assignment and to what job the appointee will return. Ordinarily the godfather is the person's future boss on return to the parent country. During the overseas assignment, the individual is kept informed of major events occurring in the unit that this person will be assigned to in the future. In this way, not only is there a logical career plan worked out, there is no feeling of being lost in the vast international shuffle of the company.

Some repatriated managers report that the overseas assignment is a haphazard, ill-planned affair that is usually accompanied by vertical advancement. Upon return, many have difficulty in readjusting to domestic operations, experience lowered self-efficacy in their domestic position, and on occasion find themselves without a job. Managers may be unaware of the challenges facing the repatriated employee, thus career obstacles persist for the expatriate.

There is a need to assist the expatriate manager in career development. By putting in place policies and procedures toward that end, an organization can more efficiently manage human resources globally and encourage more employees to accept foreign assignments. The fundamental nature of such a system must be comprehensive; that is, the emphasis should not solely be on predeparture activities. The ideal international career management program should assess (and give feedback and preparation on) career and skill issues prior to departure, during the assignment, and subsequent to repatriation.[37]

Evaluating Performance

Failure to develop highly flexible standards for the performance evaluations of the expatriate manager may result in the manager viewing his or her role as undefined and dysfunctional. Present performance evaluations focus on personality traits, communication skills, belief in mission, and organizational structure, but lack focus on evaluation of an expatriate manager upon arrival in a host country.[38] The performance evaluation system may need to be completely rethought and rewritten with regard to individuals working in multinational organizations.

SUMMARY

Multinational Corporations (MNC), organizations that conduct a large part of their business outside their home country, usually operate through subsidiary companies abroad. Their operations create interrelationships between countries and cultures as well as between economic and political systems.

The external environment is extremely diverse and complex, and the manner in which managers' tasks are accomplished may be altered substantially. Additionally, organizational behavior considerations are much more complex. The MNC must deal with the environment of the parent country, in which the headquarters is located, and the host country, in which the operational unit resides.

The same management functions are important in the multinational environment. However, there are some differences. The MNC objectives differ from those of domestic firms because of their potential clash with the objectives of the economic and political systems of the host countries. Strategic plans tend to originate in the home office. Tactical plans tend to be delegated to the individual international branches. Further, the organizational structure of a multinational firm must be designed to meet the needs of the international environment.

Many aspects of the influencing function may be altered when operating in a multinational environment. Successful management of an MNC requires that managers understand the needs, values, and problems of employees in the host countries. In selecting individuals for overseas assignments, management must recognize that no one style of leadership will be equally effective in all countries. People's basic needs may differ, and there may be problems in communication. A firm's control system is extremely important, the more multinational it becomes.

By and large, the success of a multinational corporation hinges on the human component. Selection and training and development needs are often quite different, and career development may be helped or hindered, depending on internal and external factors. The process of performance appraisal should reflect the unique culture of the host country as well as the needs of the multinational firm.

REVIEW QUESTIONS

1. What is a multinational corporation? List the major criteria used to classify multinationals.
2. Briefly describe the major environmental factors affecting the management of multinationals.
3. Why do many American workers who are sent overseas fail?
4. What types of organizational structures are used for multinational firms?
5. How are human resource needs different for multinational firms?

KEY TERMS

multinational company (MNC)   parent country   host country

CASE STUDY

A JAPANESE VIEW OF THE TRADE IMBALANCE

THROUGHOUT THE MID-EIGHTIES the U.S. trade deficit with Japan grew worse. Especially in automobiles and electronics, the Japanese share of American markets steadily increased. But very few products or services flowed the other way. The steadily growing stock of United States dollars in Japanese hands was used to buy up increasing shares of United States companies. Labor unions and politicians complained about the loss of American jobs. Citizens expressed fear that the Japanese would come to own too much of American industry. And corporations griped that they were shut out of potentially profitable foreign markets.

United States managers accused the Japanese of "dumping" products in the States (that is, selling items in the United States for less than the costs of production). Another frequent complaint was that the Japanese government erected every conceivable trade barrier to keep American products out of Japan. At the same time, it was argued, American markets were essentially open to Japanese companies.

But George Tanaka, Senior Vice-President of Toyonoka Electronics, said the problems were the Americans' own fault. Tanaka described what he saw as the "real" source of United States trade balance problems:

"In a nutshell, in Japan we treat customers as God and you only say, 'The customer is king.' Let me explain. Toyonoka sells microwave ovens in the United States. I have been trying for over a year to find an American company to make some of the parts we need. We want to have the parts shipped to Japan for installation in United States-bound ovens. That would improve your trade balance. It would also allow us to take advantage of present favorable exchange rates.

"But I cannot find anyone who will produce the quality we need to stay competitive. American managers tell me, 'This is as good as we can do.

You will have to change your operation to make the parts work.' In Japan, of course, suppliers value contracts like this and do all they can to meet our specifications. I am under a great deal of pressure to buy American. But American firms just do not seem to care about our needs.

"The same kind of attitude surfaces when I ask about shipping schedules. In our factories, we practice 'just-in-time' inventory control. Japanese suppliers deliver the parts we need just when we need them—and in small quantities. I know United States companies have to ship long distances. So we are willing to accept larger shipments and be somewhat flexible about delivery dates. But no American firm I have talked to will guarantee even the *week* of delivery. They say there are too many variables involved—strikes, raw materials shortages, shipping problems. In Japan, a supplier would not ask *me* to worry about those things. I am the customer.

"The language also presents a problem. United States firms will not bother to use Japanese. They refuse to even print installation instructions and invoices in any language but English. This is especially grating since we take the time to learn even the American dialect of English. Can any American imagine buying a Toyonoka stereo or a Mazda automobile with the owner's manual written in Japanese? We take care of those problems because Americans are our valued customers."

Mr. Tanaka went on to reemphasize that American companies could sell as much in Japan as Japan sells in the United States if they gave Japanese customers proper regard.

QUESTIONS

1. Does Mr. Tanaka's "ugly American" argument have some validity?
2. What are the cultural factors that may account for the difference in perspectives on the balance of trade issue?

CASE STUDY

MARK IS TRANSFERRED OVERSEAS

IN COLLEGE, MARK Brinson majored in industrial management and was considered by his teachers and peers to be one of the best all-around students to graduate from Memphis State University. Mark not only took the required courses in business, he also acquired a minor in foreign language. The language that Mark concentrated on the most was French, and he became quite fluent in the language.

After graduation, Mark took an entry-level management training position with Tuborg International, a multinational corporation with offices and factories in thirty countries, including the United States. Mark's first assignment was in a plant in New York. His supervisors quickly identified Mark for his ability to get the job done and still maintain rapport with subordinates, peers, and superiors. In only three years Mark had advanced from manager trainee to the position of assistant plant superintendent.

After two years in this position, Mark was called into the superintendent's office one day and told that he had been identified as being ready for a foreign assignment. The move would mean a promotion, and the location of the plant was in a small industrialized region in France. Mark was excited, and he wasted no time in making the necessary preparations for the new assignment.

Before arriving at the plant in France, Mark took considerable time to review his books in the French language. He was surprised at how quickly the use of the language came back to him. He didn't think there would be any major difficulties in making the transition from the United States to France. But on arriving, Mark rapidly discovered that there were to be problems. The small industrialized community where Mark's plant was located did not speak the "pure" French that he had learned. There were many slang expressions that meant one thing to Mark but had an entirely different meaning to the employees of the plant.

While meeting with several of the employees a week after arriving, one of the workers said something to Mark that he interpreted as very uncomplimentary (in actuality, the employee had greeted him with a rather risqué expression but in a different tone than he had known before). All of the other employees interpreted the expression to be merely a friendly greeting. Mark's disgust was evident, and as time went by, this type of instance occurred a few more times, and the other employees began to limit their conversation with Mark. In only one month, Mark managed to isolate himself from the workers within the plant. He became disillusioned and thought about asking to be relieved from the assignment.

QUESTIONS

1. What problems had Mark not anticipated when he took the assignment?
2. How could the company have assisted Mark to reduce the difficulties that he confronted?
3. Do you believe the situation that Mark confronted is typical of an American going to a foreign assignment? Discuss.

EXPERIENTIAL EXERCISE

One of the most difficult management problems for the multinational organization is selecting suitable people to be sent on foreign assignments. Inappropriate selections are often made, which negatively impact the multinational operation. Although specific failure rates vary by country and by company, most researchers agree that about one fourth of Americans selected for overseas operations are obvious failures who, in many cases, return home prematurely. A similar percentage are hidden failures or marginal performers.

Multi-Corp has experienced a 68-percent failure rate in their Asian operations over the last five years. The boss has instructed Gordon Liddy to come up with a procedure to resolve the problem. He will call in two successful managers from the firm to discuss the matter. Dick Nixon has been a highly successful overseas manager in China, Japan, and Korea for over thirteen years and should offer valuable insights. Margaret Mitchell, personnel director, has never been overseas, but she has had input into the selection process in the past.

According to Margaret Mitchell, the company needs to expand the pool of employees who can be sent to the multinational operations. These individuals must be better briefed on their new jobs, and managers must be selected based primarily on their domestic track records.

According to Dick Nixon, the focus should be on the measurement and evaluation of the candidate's current levels of expertise. In addition, psychological tests, stress tests, and evaluations by the candidate's superiors, subordinates, peers, and acquaintances should be administered to assess the candidate's current level of ability in interpersonal and cross-cultural skills. Also, the candidate's spouse and children should undergo modified versions of the selection process, since the family members confront slightly different challenges overseas than do employees.

Select three individuals: one to serve as Gordon Liddy, the senior supervisor; one to play Dick Nixon, an experienced overseas manager; and Margaret Mitchell, personnel director. All students not participating in the role-playing exercise should carefully observe the behavior of the participants. The instructor will provide more information to participants.

NOTES

1. This story is a composite taken from a number of published sources, including: "Battling for Survival," *Time,* 1 February 1982, 57; "AMC Turns to Renault for More," *New York Times,* 29 January 1984, F1; *American Motor Corporation, Annual Report—1981;* "France Makes Renault Its Model," *Business Week,* 31 May 1982, 48–57; "French Automakers' Lonely Slump," *Fortune,* 28 November 1983, 121–126; Richard Johnson, "AMC Plant is Opposed by Renault," *Automotive News,* 14 April 1986, 1; and several articles from *The Wall Street Journal.*
2. Geert Hofstede, "The Cultural Relativity of Organizational Practices and Theories," *Journal of International Business Studies* 24 (Fall 1983): 75.

3. Robert W. Stevens, "Scanning the Multinational Firm," *Business Horizon* 14 (June 1971): 53.
4. Richard A. Melcher, Mark Maremont, Amy Borrus, and Thane Peterson, "The Japanese Are Coming—And Thatcher Is All Smiles," *Business Week,* 20 February 1989, 46.
5. Dean Foust, Pia Kapstein Farrell, Peter Finch, and Chris Power, "Mr. Smith Goes Global," *Business Week,* 13 February 1989, 66.
6. Yoram Zeira, "Overlooked Personnel Problems of Multinational Corporations," *Columbia Journal of World Business* 10 (Summer 1975): 96–103.
7. Melcher, et al., "Japanese Are Coming," 46.
8. Peter Wright, David Townsend, Jerry Kinard, and Joe Iverstine, "The Developing World to 1990: Trends and Implications for Multinational Business," *Long Range Planning* 15 (1982): 122.
9. Joseph Krislov, "Unions in the Next Century: An Exploratory Essay," *Journal of Labor Research* 7 (Spring 1986): 165–166.
10. Krislov, "Unions," 160.
11. Gail Schares, "Are Labor Leaders Asking for the Moon?" *Business Week,* 19 September 1988, 50.
12. Melcher, et al., "Japanese Are Coming," 46.
13. Otis Port, "The Push for Quality," *Business Week,* 8 June 1987, 132.
14. Brian H. Flynn, "The Challenge of Multinational Sales Training," *Training and Development Journal* (November 1987): 54.
15. Wright, et al., "Developing World," 119.
16. J. O. Enitame, "Do Multinationals Create Wealth?" *International Management* 37 (January 1983): 48.
17. Narendra K. Sethi, "Strategic Planning System for Multinational Companies," *Long Range Planning* 15 (June 1982): 81–82.
18. L. Drake Rodman and Lee M. Caudill, "Management of Large Multinationals: Trends and Future Challenges," *Business Horizons* 19 (December 1976): 19.
19. Abdulrahman Al-Jafary and A. T. Hollingsworth, "Practices in the Arabian Gulf Region," *Journal of International Business Studies* 14 (Fall 1983): 144.
20. Philip R. Harris, "Employees Abroad: Maintain the Corporate Connection," *Personnel Journal* 65 (August 1986): 107–108.
21. Allen L. Hixon, "Why Corporations Make Haphazard Overseas Staffing Decisions," *Personnel Administrator* 31 (March 1986): 91.
22. Prabhu Guptara, "Searching the Organization for the Cross-Cultural Operators," *International Management* (August 1986): 39–40.
23. Harris, "Employees Abroad," 107–108.
24. Hixon, "Staffing Decisions," 91.
25. Gurudutt M. Baliga and James C. Baker, "Multinational Corporate Policies for Expatriate Managers: Selection, Training, Evaluation," *SAM Advanced Management Journal* 50 (Autumn 1985): 32.
26. Mark E. Mendenhall, Edward Dunbar, and Gary R. Oddou, "Expatriate Selection, Training and Career-Pathing: A Review and Critique," *Human Resource Management* 26 (Fall 1987): 331–345.
27. Michael Berger, "Building Bridges over the Cultural Rivers," *International Management* (July–August 1987): 61.
28. Christopher Earley, "Intercultural Training for Managers: A Comparison of Documentary and Interpersonal Methods," *Academy of Management Journal* 30, no. 4 (1987): 685.
29. Mendenhall, Dunbar, and Oddou, "Expatriate Selection," 331–345.
30. Berger, "Building Bridges," 61.
31. Guptara, "Searching the Organization," 40.
32. Earley, "Intercultural Training," 685.

33. Earley, "Intercultural Training," 685.
34. Mendenhall, Dunbar, and Oddou, "Expatriate Selection," 331.
35. Harris, "Employees Abroad," 108.
36. David M. Noer, "Integrating Foreign Service Employees to Home Organization: The Godfather Approach," *Personnel Journal* 53 (January 1974): 45–50.
37. Mendenhall, Dunbar, and Oddou, "Expatriate Selection," 331.
38. Baliga and Baker, "Multinational Corporate Policies," 36.

REFERENCES

Adler, Nancy J. "The Ostrich and the Trend." *Academy of Management Review* 8 (April 1983): 231.

Al-Jafary, Abdulrahman, and A. T. Hollingsworth. "Practices in the Arabian Gulf Region." *Journal of International Business Studies* 14 (Fall 1983): 144.

Baliga, Gurudutt M., and James C. Baker. "Multinational Corporate Policies for Expatriate Managers: Selection, Training, Evaluation." *SAM Advanced Management Journal* 50 (Autumn 1985): 32.

Bartlett, Christopher A., and Sumantra Ghoshal. "Managing Across Borders: New Organizational Responses." *Sloan Management Review* 29 (Fall 1987): 43–53.

Berger, Michael. "Building Bridges over the Cultural Rivers." *International Management* (July–August 1987): 61.

Earley, Christopher. "Intercultural Training for Managers: A Comparison of Documentary and Interpersonal Methods." *Academy of Management Journal* 30, 4 (1987): 685.

Enitame, J. O. "Do Multinationals Create Wealth?" *International Management* 37 (January 1983): 48.

Flynn, Brian H. "The Challenge of Multinational Sales Training." *Training and Development Journal* (November 1987): 54.

Frank, Victor H., Jr. "Living with Price Control Abroad." *Harvard Business Review* 62 (March–April 1984): 137.

Garland, John, and Richard N. Farmer. *International Dimensions of Business Policy and Strategy.* Boston: Kent, 1986.

Ghertman, Michel. "Foreign Subsidiary and Parents' Roles During Strategic Investment and Divestment Decisions." *Journal of International Business Studies* 19 (Spring 1988): 17–37.

Godiwalla, Yezdi H. "Multinational Planning—Developing a Global Approach." *Long Range Planning* 19, no. 2 (April 1986): 110–116.

Guptara, Prabhu. "Searching the Organization for the Cross-Cultural Operators." *International Management* (August 1986): 39–40.

Harris, Phillip R. "Employees Abroad: Maintain the Corporate Connection." *Personnel Journal* (August 1986): 108.

Herbert, Theodore T. "Strategy and Multinational Organization Structure: An Interorganizational Relationships Perspective." *Academy of Management Review* 9, no. 2 (1984): 259–271.

Hixon, Allen L. "Why Corporations Make Haphazard Overseas Staffing Decisions." *Personnel Administrator* 31 (March 1986): 91.

Hofstede, Geert. "The Cultural Relativity of Organizational Practices and Theories." *Journal of International Business Studies* 24 (Fall 1983): 75–90.

Jones, Louise H. "Information Systems, Organizational Change, and Quality Improvement Programs." *National Productivity Review* 7 (Spring 1988): 165–168.

Krislov, Joseph. "Unions in the Next Century: An Exploratory Essay." *Journal of Labor Research* 7 (Spring 1986): 165–166.

Mendenhall, Mark E., Edward Dunbar, and Gary R. Oddou. "Expatriate Selection, Training and Career-Pathing: A Review and Critique." *Human Resource Management* 26 (Fall 1987): 331–345.

Modic, Stanley J. "No Time for Gutless Decisions." *Industry Week* 232 (23 February 1987): 7.

Morton, David. "Why Multinationals Are Positive Links Between 'North' and 'South,' " *International Management* 37 (August 1982): 36.

"A New Ideology for Managers." *Multinational Business* (Winter 1986): 30–31.

Schares, Gail. "Are Labor Leaders Asking for the Moon?" *Business Week* (19 September 1988): 50.

Sethi, Narendra K. "Strategic Planning System for Multinational Companies." *Long Range Planning* 15 (June 1982): 81–82.

Stevens, Robert W. "Scanning the Multinational Firm." *Business Horizon* 14 (June 1971): 53.

Vinso, Joseph D. "Financial Planning for the Multinational Corporation with Multiple Goals." *Journal of International Business Studies* 13 (Winter 1982): 43–58.

Wright, Peter, David Townsend, Jerry Kinard, and Joe Iverstine. "The Developing World to 1990: Trends and Implications for Multinational Business." *Long Range Planning* 15, no. 4 (1982): 116–125.

CHAPTER

22

Management

Information

Systems

Learning Objectives

After completing this chapter students should be able to

1. Define the term *management information system (MIS)* and explain the types of informational needs firms have.
2. Describe the steps involved in developing the MIS.
3. Distinguish among the various types of computers.
4. Describe the various types of information subsystems that are available for use by management and discuss the advantages of an integrated system.
5. Describe major computer trends and how these trends can affect productivity.

"IT'S A MEDIUM for exchanging information that has proven to be an effective productivity tool." Charles D. Hollis, senior telecommunications analyst at J.P. Stevens, was describing the company's new "voice mail" system. With ten textile divisions, J.P. Stevens is the second-largest U.S. textile manufacturer, behind Burlington Industries. In 1986, 500 Stevens employees were using the system, and more were signing on every day. Essentially, the system (built around a Northern Telecom SL-1 PBX) allows recorded messages to be sent and accessed by telephone twenty-four hours a day. Each authorized user must enter a personal security code to send or check "mail."

One manager who uses the system regularly is John T. English, a customer service director in Stevens's Converter and Industrial Fabrics Division. "If I'm caught at a meeting," English said, "I'm confident that messages are accurate because they are what a person said, not a translation. I've detected in messages how strongly someone feels about something by his or her voice." English uses the system, for example, to pass along confidential information to his accounting group. "They need certain information from me, and voice messaging saves me from having to travel to a different part of the building, hoping the person is there to deliver confidential information to. Now I know the information remains confidential and I know when it's received." English concluded, "I'm sure there's a reduction of memo writing. I used to have a stack of pink confidential envelopes. I don't use them anymore—I use voice messaging."

The new voice mail system is just one element in Stevens's evolving management information system (MIS). The Stevens MIS has become progressively more automated since the company bought its first computer in 1957. In 1966, the Information Services Division (ISD) was formed and given a budget of one percent of sales, about the average amount spent for this purpose in the industry. The charter of ISD directed it to adopt standard hardware and a common programming language throughout the company and to develop an efficient, integrated MIS.

The ten textile divisions—Stevens Carpets, Cotton and Blended Fabrics, Woolen and Worsteds, and so on—were so accustomed to operating autonomously, that it was difficult to impose a companywide information system. It was six years before ISD was able to install its first full-fledged data base system. Even then, most data-processing systems within the company were initiated and controlled by division management, with ISD providing requested support rather than system design and coordination among divisions.

With Stevens's MIS still highly fragmented, company management employed IBM in 1975 to help ISD meet its original charter—an efficient, integrated MIS. A comprehensive plan, the Business System Plan, was adopted in 1976. ISD was charged with executing the plan. But by 1980 little had been accomplished in that direction, and ninety of ISD's 100 programmers stayed busy maintaining existing systems, leaving only ten involved in new systems development.

In 1980, George Langston was brought in from another textile company to direct ISD and belatedly implement the Business System Plan. He prioritized the various functions the MIS system was intended to serve (cost estimation and control, inventory accounting, customer order servicing, plant production reporting, etc.) and assigned seventy-five of his 100 programmers to develop the integrated system, leaving only 25 for maintenance (ISD had about 400 employees in all). He also decided to restrict access to the company data base. At the same time, he promoted use of terminals that behaved as personal computers but were tied into the company's mainframe. These were called "virtual PCs." Without access to the main data base, many managers built their own data bases in Stevens's centralized data-processing facility, and the system was continuously short of storage capacity and processing capability. In fact, by 1983 the use of virtual PCs was doubling every four months, and Langston was running out of resources to support them.

Still, there was no indication that management's expanding demand for information was going to recede any time soon so that Langston would have time and resources to put the Business System Plan into effect. Julius Pinkston, Stevens's assistant controller, said, "Of course the new BSP system will remove the need to use this program (virtual PCs), but the BSP won't be ready for two or three years. In the meantime you've got to keep running the business. You can't let development and design work get in your way. Hopefully, the systems can catch up. It's the businesses that make the money and you mustn't lose sight of that!"[1] ∎

T HE J.P. STEVENS story illustrates how one company has progressed into the information processing age. A multitude of similar stories may be told of businesses across the nation—in fact, the world is in the midst of both an information and a high-tech revolution. With regard to the information revolution, the total amount of scientific information available in the world doubles every twenty months. In a similar manner, information for use in business continues to expand rapidly. Managers now have various types of computers and technology that allow them to more effectively use this information. The high-tech revolution is creating unlimited possibilities for managers, and managers are now able to implement what had only been dreamed of before—an effective management information system.

Management information system (MIS)
Any organized approach for obtaining relevant and timely information on which to base management decisions.

A **management information system (MIS)** is any organized approach for obtaining relevant and timely information on which to base management decisions. In all probability, no attribute of an organization so significantly affects decision making as does the management information system. Remember that the Chrysler Corporation and Maserati joint venture to build the Chrysler TC automobile was continually hindered by lack of information needed for decision making.[2] Such occurrences are often very expensive and virtually always disruptive. An effective MIS typically employs computers and other sophisticated technologies to process information that reflects the day-to-day operations of a company, organized in the form of information to facilitate the decision-making process.

Because of the importance of the management information system, an entire chapter is needed to review the topic and discuss future information trends. This discussion focuses on a company's information needs and describes the characteristics of the MIS. Then, the different roles of the MIS at various organizational levels are examined, followed by a discussion of the development of an effective MIS. Because of its role in the MIS, we discuss various types of computers. We then review information subsystems available for use by management. Finally, MIS trends are examined with regard to their effect on productivity.

■ INFORMATION NEEDS OF A FIRM

The significant impact of both the external and internal environments on a firm was discussed in detail earlier in the text. Each component of the external and internal environment creates informational needs for managers. A properly designed MIS assists in satisfying these informational needs. As may be seen in Figure 22.1, both internal and external factors affect the organization and therefore must be accounted for in the MIS. For example, the Japanese are major competitors in the semiconductor industry. Representatives of U.S. firms allege that the Japanese copy microprocessor designs and then sell products based on these designs to users in the United States at a much lower price. Recent court rulings allow American developers to copyright these programs, thereby obtaining some protection.[3] Without a keen awareness of information flows in the external environment, domestic producers may have acted too slowly in stopping the unfair Japanese advantage.

Notice in Figure 22.1 that the MIS draws information from the various internal functional areas, such as marketing, production, and finance, and integrates this information with that of the external environment, resulting in creation of an information system. Both types of information are needed if managers are to perform effectively. For example, the marketing function will probably not operate properly without knowledge of the types of customers the firm is attempting to serve. Certainly J.P. Stevens wants to know the types of customers that will ultimately purchase their products. And production may be hampered without an appreciation of the nature of the labor force that is available in certain areas. A multitude of internal and external interrelationships exist and

FIGURE 22.1 ■
Management Information
Needs

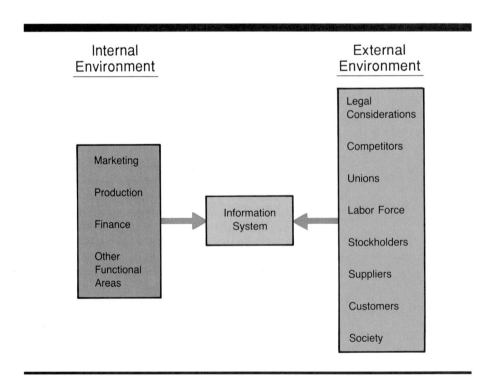

therefore must be reflected in the information system in order to satisfy the informational needs of managers. In order to provide maximum benefit, however, the MIS must be designed in such a manner that results in the most beneficial information possible.

▨ CHARACTERISTICS OF AN EFFECTIVE MIS

Any MIS, whether computerized or manual, should be designed to provide information with the following characteristics in order to afford managers the maximum utility from such information. Information should be:

> *Timely*—up to date. Sound decisions cannot be based on outdated information. For example, a person desiring to invest in the stock market is at a severe disadvantage if decisions are made based on week-old or even day-old data.
>
> *Accurate*—correct. Managers must be able to rely on the accuracy of the information provided to them. Incorrect data probably will cause bad decisions to be made.
>
> *Concise*—essential data only. A manager can absorb only so much information during any one period. Subsequently, managers must limit information to only the most necessary.
>
> *Relevant*—information that the manager needs to know. Computers can provide managers with volumes of information. However, because only a small portion of data available is actually useful in a given situation, it is important to single out only the most relevant data to analyze.
>
> *Complete*—all the information needed. Having no information is sometimes better than having partial data. A manager could draw false conclusions when basing decisions on incomplete information. The absence of even one of these characteristics reduces the effectiveness of the MIS and complicates the decision-making process.

▨ THE MIS AT DIFFERENT ORGANIZATIONAL LEVELS

Managers at each organizational level make unique demands on the MIS. Top-level managers often need information with which to make far-reaching decisions—usually they require extensive information relating to the external environment. For example, top-level managers at J.P. Stevens need to know about government legislation, economic trends and forecasts, and competitors' activities. On the other hand, J.P. Stevens's lower-level managers depend primarily on internal data. These managers typically need information on functional areas such as inventory reorder points and the number of workers to be assigned to a specific project. Top-level managers usually will want only product data that are summarized, perhaps by quarter. Lower-level managers are more likely to need production data on a daily or even hourly basis. Thus, each level of management benefits from information available from the MIS, but from different perspectives.

A successful MIS program will provide managers with up-to-date information in a usable form.
(Courtesy of International Business Machines Corporation)

Whether used by top-, mid-, or lower-level managers, a successful MIS must produce several types of output related to business operations, such as the following:

Routine reports. Business data summarized on a scheduled basis are referred to as routine reports. For example, weekly and monthly production reports may be sent to the general manager, whereas quarterly reports may be forwarded to upper-level managers.

Exception reports. Exception reports highlight major variations requiring management's attention. An example of this type of report is the quality-exception report, completed when the number of defects increases beyond a predetermined maximum.

On-demand reports. An on-demand report is information provided in response to a specific request. The number of defects created by each worker in the plant is an example of an on-demand report that management could request.

Forecasts. A forecast reports the results of applying predictive models to specific situations. Managers may need to forecast the number and types of employees needed to satisfy projected demand for a firm's product.

■ CREATING THE MIS

Managers must carefully consider the four recommended steps in designing an MIS that will provide the above-mentioned kinds of output and also conform to the MIS criteria discussed earlier (see Figure 22.2). These steps are not separate and distinct—considerable overlapping exists among each of them. The development of an MIS is not merely a matter of properly designing the system. Without a major commitment from top management, it is virtually impossible for an MIS to become smooth-functioning and operational.

Study the Present System

In assessing the existing information system, the following questions might be asked: (1) What is the present flow of information? (2) How is the information used? (3) How valuable is this information in terms of decision making? At one stage in his career, Wayne Mondy was a team member in charge of developing one of the first integrated state highway information systems. Detailed analysis

FIGURE 22.2 ■
Creating the MIS

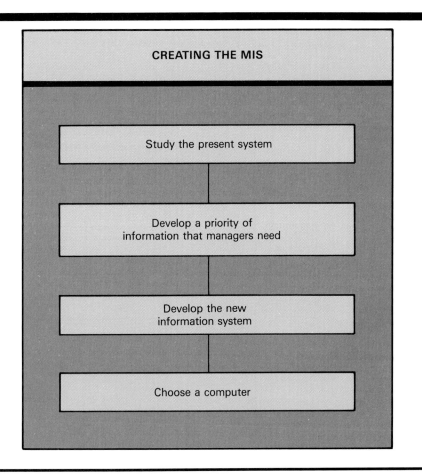

was done of all discernible information flows and uses. One of the agencies involved was the state highway patrol. In conversations with local troop members, Wayne discovered that the weekly report to headquarters caused special difficulty. For each troop (there were thirteen), it took one officer about four hours to prepare the report. Wayne went to headquarters to determine how the data were used in decision making. He found that the reports were neatly filed by a secretary, and the data were never used. When one of the reports was not submitted on time, however, the secretary was directed to prepare a letter of reprimand to the unit commander. Identifying this kind of deficiency is the reason for asking the third question above.

Develop a Priority of Information That Managers Need

Once the current system is thoroughly understood, it is used to develop a priority of information that managers need. There is certain information a manager must have if proper decisions are to be made, but some is merely nice to have, not critical to the manager's job performance. The MIS design must ensure provision of high-priority information, and data lower on the priority list should be generated only if their benefits exceed the costs of producing them. The weekly report described above should not have had the priority it was accorded.

The proposed approach to prioritizing information needs is to have individual managers develop their own priority lists and to integrate them into a list for the

F I G U R E   22.3   ■■■   Highway Safety Information System entire organization. Certain departments may discover that the information they identify as top priority will be far down the organization's list. The needs of the entire organization must be the controlling factor.

Develop the New Information System

The organization's information-needs priority list should govern the design of the new MIS. A system of required reports should be developed and diagrammed—treating the whole organization as a unit allows the elimination of duplicated information. At a certain point on the priority list, the information is not worth the cost of providing it and should not be included.

After thoroughly studying the existing highway information system discussed above, and setting priorities, Mondy prepared the diagram in Figure 22.3 to show how the system should function. The summary diagram was supported by many detailed reports and procedures. As can be seen, there are several types of necessary input data. For output, the system provides various types of information for both administration and operations. All departments are tied together. Data that comes in from one department of the state can provide the information used in another department. If a person has a car wreck and is given a ticket, this information not only is used by law enforcement agencies but also forms a data base to identify high-accident locations. When the MIS is properly designed, the important information an organization needs in the decision-making process is available.

Choose a Computer

Today it is reasonable to assume that the MIS for most organizations will make use of a computer. Because of computers' ever-expanding use, it is becoming increasingly important for a manager to be computer literate. Managers need not be data-processing experts, just as they need not be skilled accountants. Of course, managers need some accounting knowledge to understand and interpret financial reports, and they also need to know what computers can and cannot do, enough to make good decisions regarding their use. Computers certainly should not be feared—their presence is far too pervasive and their usefulness far too great.

If a computer is needed to provide accurate, timely, and useful information, the computer chosen should provide the best capability of processing the data that management needs as accurately and currently as possible. Because there are many types of computers and the capabilities of different types vary, one must review the possibilities and select the most beneficial. Before choosing a computer, some managers consult a systems analyst to evaluate the choices with regard to how they can improve the management system.

■■ TYPES OF COMPUTERS

The first commercially available computer was introduced over thirty-five years ago, and at that time the cost of processing data was extremely high. Since that

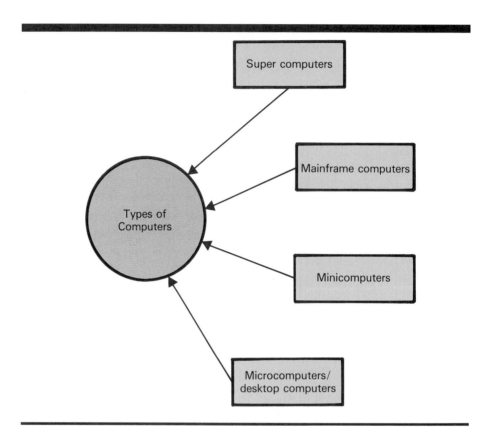

time, extraordinary reductions have been made in that cost. In fact, a tremendous reduction in the cost of data processing is currently being experienced, and much more is anticipated in the future. In effect, the result is much greater performance at a substantially reduced cost. Traditionally, computers have been classified as super, mainframes, minis, and micros, as described briefly in the following sections (see Figure 22.4).

Super Computers

At the upper end of the spectrum are computers costing millions of dollars and capable of handling vast amounts of data. Included in this category are the Cray and the CYBER computer. Depending on its configuration, the Cray may sell for up to $29 million. It requires specially constructed subflooring to support its weight and, in addition, needs special pumping to carry the fluorocarbon fluid that cools it. Included in the purchase price is the cost of two full-time engineers to maintain it for the life of the system.

As might be expected, the demand for super computers has been relatively small. However, it is expected to increase in the next few years. Applications for such computers include work with nuclear physics, meteorology, and the military. But because of their cost and the availability of more applicable systems, super computers are not expected to be used extensively in the typical management information system.

Mainframe Computers

Most of the data-processing work for large organizations is done on mainframe computers. Typical cost of a mainframe system ranges from over $400,000 to over $1 million. Mainframes such as those used at J.P. Stevens are normally housed in special rooms and are maintained by data-processing specialists. A data-processing manager is typically in charge of various computer specialists, such as systems analysts, programmers, and machine operators, who support the system. J.P. Stevens employed 100 programmers to develop and maintain its systems. IBM's share of the mainframe market is 70 percent.[4] Some of the other most recognizable manufacturers of mainframes include Digital Equipment Corporation (DEC) and Control Data Corporation. Because mainframes can support large networks of individual terminals and remote job-entry locations, most large firms and many government agencies are equipped with them. Simulation, design, engineering, and applications requiring large data bases are well within the capabilities of mainframe computers. Because of the computing capabilities of mainframes, a high percentage of management information systems are supported by such computers.

Minicomputers

Between the mainframe computer and the microcomputer is the minicomputer. The mainframe market is slipping about 7 percent annually, and as the mainframe market subsides, the minicomputer market is expected to expand.[5] These medium-sized computers are smaller, slower, and less expensive than mainframes and do not require special power hookups or environmental controls. Typical cost for a mini ranges from $20,000 to $40,000. Minis are usually supplemented by a large number of terminals and other peripheral devices. A prime advantage of minicomputers is the ability to enlarge the system to meet the needs of a growing organization. Minis were developed because they could meet particular needs at significantly lower costs than could large mainframes at locations in the organization where processing requirements are the greatest.

Microcomputers/Desktop Computers

Of the four categories of computers discussed, the micro operates at the slowest speed. However, this disadvantage is offset by the ease of operation and low cost. Microcomputers are not just for small businesses—large corporations use thousands of them. Because of their flexibility, micros simplify many aspects of management. The microcomputer, called a PC (for personal computer), can be a stand-alone tool, able to show financial trends, answer "what if" questions, and even keep the executive's calendar. Some managers who previously wrote memoranda in longhand now zip them out on the keyboard. Micros may interact with the mainframe to give executives access to corporate data bases or sophisticated programs. At J.P. Stevens, many managers used PCs that were tied to the firm's mainframes.

The main computing component of the micro is located on an integrated circuit or chip. Microcomputers are capable of acquiring data, taking measurements, and controlling all kinds of processes in ways that greatly simplify

BUSINESS
BRIEFS

INSIDE BUSINESS

Advances in Microcomputer Technology

MICROCOMPUTERS ARE GAINING widespread favor in research and development laboratories, on the shop floors, and in office management operations, as well as in the executive suite. Advances in the area of microcomputer technology can significantly impact productivity and are therefore extremely important to more and more employees. Compaq Computers continually strives to leapfrog new developments by IBM. Mr. Rod Canton, co-founder, president, and CEO, was eager to discuss Compaq's latest accomplishments in the area of desktop computers and portable computers. In his review of the competitive situation that exists in the computer industry, he discussed Compaq's development of the highest performance desktop computer in the world and the most powerful and highest-capacity portable in the world. He also provides a view of the future of portable computers and desktop computers. Canton also characterizes the pace of technological change in the industry, including aspects such as chip technology, storage areas, and obsolescence. Canton's insights came into full view when he was interviewed by the CNN business news team of Kandel, Cassidy, and Schuch.

manufacturing and production. They can be used in remote locations such as offshore oil-well platforms. They also work well in adverse environments such as on ships and airplanes. Micros can automatically change the settings of valves and other control devices in response to changes in physical conditions like pressures and temperatures. Industrial robots often depend on microcomputers to help them do factory assembly operations formerly too complex for mechanization.

Many engineering firms today specialize in computer-aided design and computer-aided manufacturing (CAD/CAM). These computer systems permit designers and engineers to develop a product, test it, and then program the equipment that makes it. The cost of CAD/CAM has been greatly reduced through the use of powerful microcomputers, some of which even small engineering and machine shops can afford. Because of their application to every stage of the product-development cycle, microcomputers have made major contributions toward meeting the productivity challenge.

In every kind of organization and at every level, microcomputers simplify the job of administration. Traditional office paperwork is created and processed with the help of computers. Because microcomputers can communicate with one another, many written reports and other documentation have been eliminated. Word processing software is available to assist in entering, arranging, correcting, retrieving, and printing all types of business information and correspondence. It is obvious that microcomputers are gaining widespread favor in research and development laboratories, on the shop floors, and in office management operation, as well as in the executive suite.

■ POSSIBLE INFORMATION SUBSYSTEMS FOR MANAGERS

Various means by which management uses information subsystems are discussed below. They are called subsystems because, taken separately, they do not constitute a management information system. In addition, some firms may have only one or perhaps two of these subsystems.

Accounting Information System

The processing of accounting data is traditionally the first area to receive much attention. It is through the use of these accounting information systems that managers receive much of their control information. Accuracy and speed is stressed in the processing of profit-and-loss information, taxes, and a multitude of other accounting-related activities. Subsets of a typical accounting system include accounts payable, payroll, accounts receivable, sales and invoices, inventory control, and financial reporting.

Office Management Systems

Only a few years ago, the typical office management system revolved around filing cabinets, letters being dictated to secretaries, who then typed and mailed them, and telephone messages being placed on the manager's desk to be answered at a later time. The potential for totally restructuring the office management system is now a reality. Managers may now sit in front of their desktop computers and send messages to other company employees at distant points through electronic mail.

Word processing has had a major impact on the modern management office system. Copies of correspondences that once filled a multitude of filing cabinets can now be conveniently stored on small floppy disks for rapid retrieval at a later date. Corrections, additions, and deletions can now be quickly accomplished without requiring a secretary to retype the document each time a change is made. Many managers have learned the ease with which they themselves can learn word processing. Often they find it much easier to type up correspondence themselves than to delegate this duty to others in the organization.

In addition, computer firms have introduced the concept of the desktop publishing work station. The software used for that purpose permits an office to turn out brochures and reports that look professionally printed.[6] The impact of these and other forms of modern technology is changing forever the way offices are run.

Manufacturing Systems

Not long ago managers at an automobile assembly plant supervised long lines of workers attaching parts to each unfinished car as it passed separate work stations. Managers and workers using computer terminals can now determine the exact equipment configuration of each car as it passes by. The manufacturing process of production scheduling, inventory control, design, equipment control, and cost accounting is tied together through the use of computers. Computers now provide even small firms with the capability to use modern production control and scheduling methods.

A computer innovation referred to as a VAN, or value-added network, has been developed in Japan. VANs link manufacturers with their customers and suppliers; through the VAN system, products can be automatically shipped from factory to retailers when inventory levels become low, helping to maintain inventory at a minimum level and thereby accomplishing considerable cost savings.[7]

The latest technique for improving the manufacturing process is statistical quality control, or SQC. Basically, SQC gauges the performance of the manufacturing process by carefully monitoring changes in whatever is being produced. The goal is to detect potential problems before they result in off-quality products, then pinpoint the reason for deviation and adjust the process to make the process more stable.[8]

Marketing Systems

The purpose of marketing is to ensure that the proper product is offered to the customer at the right price and location and with the correct amount of promotion. In the past, the complexity of this task was often overwhelming. Tying together a marketing system consisting of product analysis and development, marketing research, place analysis, price analysis, promotional analysis, and sales was often a difficult task without the benefits of the computer. Through computerized marketing systems, information is made available to the marketing manager concerning such vital areas as product profitability and advertising effectiveness.

Human Resource Information System

Whereas the accounting system was typically the first to be installed in a firm, the human resource information system (HRIS) was often the last. Firms are now realizing that a properly developed HRIS can provide tremendous benefits. Figure 22.5 presents an overview of a human resource information system that was prepared for one organization. Note that numerous types of input data are necessary—information from many sources. Through the HRIS, considerable output data become available, which may have far-reaching value ranging from human resource planning to operational uses. The HRIS permits all personnel areas to be tied together into an information system. Data from several input sources are integrated to provide needed output data. Information critical to the firm's personnel decision-making process is readily available when the system is properly designed; for instance, many firms are now studying historical trends to determine the best opportunity for securing qualified applicants. In addition, because of the major impact that government legislation has had on firms, it would be extremely difficult to comply, were it not for these modern HRISs. As the human component of the firm gains greater importance, it is likely that we will see continued growth of the HRIS in the future.

One firm that has pioneered the development of human resource information systems is Information Science Incorporated (InSci). Founded in 1965, InSci was the first company to engage in the commercial development of computer-based human resource information systems. InSci's comprehensive concept of human

FIGURE 22.5 ■■ A Human Resource Information System

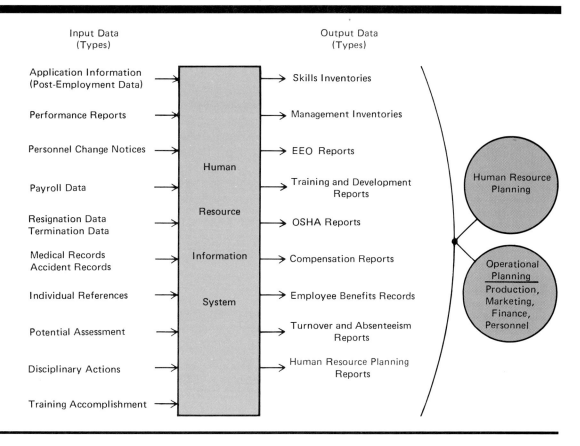

resource management consists of personnel, payroll, pension, health claims, flexible compensation, and decision support systems.

One of the components of the InSci system is its ability to provide management with information to assist in planning for the future. Information available from the HRIS may be obtained through either "hard copy" or data display screens. When data display screens are used, files may be updated rapidly. These CRTs may be placed at critical areas in the firm to provide instant access to personnel information for individuals with a need to know. Human resource decision-making information is available virtually immediately through these systems.

■■ THE MANAGEMENT INFORMATION SYSTEM

The discussion above focused on specific types of information subsystems. These systems were described as being separate and distinct from one another. A true MIS has the capability to integrate these various subsystems in order to provide managers at all levels with better decision-making capabilities. For example, information from the HRIS may provide the manager with knowledge relating to the feasibility of plant expansion in relation to specific personnel requirements. The accounting system may be consulted to determine if this anticipated plant expansion will be cost effective. Rather than each system acting as a separate entity, all are tied together in the MIS to give management that extra edge in making decisions.

In previous chapters, the basic functions of management, planning, organizing, influencing, and controlling, were identified. The purpose of a truly effective and useful management information system is to help accomplish these functions, and each of the subsystems mentioned above may assist in that. When integrated into a total management information system, the power of the information available for decision making is greatly enhanced.

▀▀ COMPUTER ADVANCEMENTS AFFECTING PRODUCTIVITY

New developments in computer hardware and software occur virtually every day. These developments have the potential to enhance productivity. In manufacturing, fixing the manufacturing system, not its products, is now seen as the primary key to better quality and enhanced productivity. Fixing the manufacturing system means upgrading quality through better management techniques, applying flexible work rules and just-in-time inventory, and assuring quality control through the use of appropriate technology.[9] Leading U.S. companies are beginning to learn that by integrating multiskilled, highly trained workers and computer-driven technology, they can realize remarkable gains in productivity.[10] Although it is impossible to foresee all the new uses for computers, the only certainty is that managers must be alert to these innovations. Failure to keep informed of such trends in this rapidly changing world threatens an organization's competitive position and even its survival. Some of the more important trends are discussed below.

Videotext

Videotext
The remote display on a CRT of information from computer files and data bases.

The remote display on a CRT of information from computer files and data bases is referred to as **videotext.** The growth of videotext is likely to be dramatic in the future, and it is expected to change the way many firms do business. For instance, in some cities banking at home is already possible. In other areas, customers are allowed to order merchandise from television displays. Even some major newspapers are planning to transmit their contents to videotext subscribers.

Teleconferencing

Teleconferencing
A method of conducting or participating in discussions by telephone or videophone.

Partly because of the high cost of business travel, in terms of both time and money, teleconferencing is becoming increasingly popular. **Teleconferencing** is a method of conducting or participating in discussions by telephone or videophone. One or more of the participants in a teleconference may be able to view the others as they speak. Teleconferencing may become a major means of not only improving managerial communication and productivity but also of lowering the cost of those improvements.

Voice Mail

Voice mail
Spoken messages transmitted electronically and stored for delivery to the recipient at a later time.

Voice mail is spoken messages transmitted electronically and stored for delivery to the recipient at a later time. When a voice mail system is used, an individual gains access by dialing a special number and providing a password and user-identification number. The user may then listen to any new messages, replay old messages, eliminate messages, and/or record messages for others. J.P. Stevens and Company extensively uses voice mail. Managers can place confidential information into the system and know the message will be received in the exact manner that it was sent.

Word Processing

Word processing
A computer application that creates and edits written material.

A computer application that creates and edits written material is referred to as **word processing.** Probably the most popular application of microcomputers is in the area of word processing. As previously discussed, productivity must be measured in terms of both quality and quantity of output. Word processing allows for the editing of virtually all forms of manuscripts and correspondence. Inserting a new paragraph at the beginning of a ten-page manuscript no longer requires retyping the entire document as it once did, which cuts down on the need for support staff. Managers have found that they, too, can use word processing—the manager merely types out the memo, edits on the screen, and with a few easily learned commands, prints out the memo. Word processing has become one of the most significant communication-enhancement tools of the current age.

Spreadsheet Programs

Until recently, the tools of financial managers included a paper pad, a calculator, a pencil, and an eraser. A modern version of these tools can be found in a spreadsheet program that provides a column-row matrix on which numbers or words can be entered and stored and calculations performed on that new data. The major advantage of a spreadsheet program resides with its ability to answer "what if" questions quickly and accurately. Grid cells can be quickly modified to determine what effect these changes would have on the entire model. Spreadsheet analysis is particularly beneficial in the planning process. Applications of spreadsheet programs include budget preparation, sales forecasting, inventory planning, profit planning, and financial projections.

Decision Support Systems

Thus far the discussion has centered on an ideal management information system where users are supplied with all the information they need when they need it. Such a utopian situation has not yet arrived for most companies, and often data-processing departments are backed up with demands for urgently needed information. To offset such occurrences, many managers have acquired their own

Decision support system (DSS)
An information system that allows users to interact directly with a computer so they can get answers quickly.

microcomputers and software. An alternative is a **decision support system (DSS)**, which is an information system that allows users to interact directly with a computer so they can get answers quickly. A DSS lets managers call up a menu of available programs. Normally DSSs are sophisticated data base systems capable of retrieving, displaying, and processing information. Graphics, simulation, modeling, and quantitative analysis are also typically available through decision support systems.

Data Base Management

The various subsystems commonly developed are for accounting, office management, manufacturing, marketing, and human resources. Often these programs are considered separate and distinct, which results in a tremendous amount of redundant data. For example, the accounting system would normally contain names and social security numbers of all employees, and so would the personnel files. The purpose of data base management is to reduce redundancies as much as possible; the term thus refers to the integration of the various information subsystems in order to reduce the duplication of information.

Robotic Systems

Robot
An automatically controlled machine that can perform mechanical tasks.

The use of robots in industry is increasing at a dramatic pace. A **robot** is an automatically controlled machine that can perform mechanical tasks. To date, robotic systems have had the greatest impact on the automobile, steel, and aerospace industries. General Motors has been a leader in using robotics and plans to have about 14,000 industrial robots in operation by 1990. Other automakers are following suit, because robots have thus far promoted high product quality and uniformity, as well as increases in production efficiencies. When IBM introduced its PC Convertible in 1986, it made the first computer

Data base management attempts to integrate the various information subsystems that are needed by an organization. (Courtesy of Air Products and Chemicals, Inc.)

built entirely by computers. The PC was assembled, tested, packaged, and shipped without a human touching a single component.[11]

Advanced robotics have touch sensors (allowing them to "feel") and optical scanners (allowing them to "see"). Some robots "learn" new patterns of movement by being led only once through an operating cycle. For example, a certain robotized paint sprayer will paint a series of identical automobiles after an experienced painter sets the controls.

Costs of robotic systems vary widely, ranging from under $8,000 to more than $170,000. Even costs approaching the high end are easy to justify, because robots can work around the clock and demand no fringe benefits or extra compensation. Because modern robots are electronically controlled, they can be made to generate data for management reports and for diagnostic purposes, another very attractive feature.

Artificial Intelligence

The successes in computer technology during the 1950s led many to believe that it might be possible to develop computers that "think." Although debate continues as to whether this has or even can come about, researchers continue to work, as they have been working for more than two decades, toward this end. **Artificial intelligence (AI)** is the field of information technology that attempts to simulate human cognitive processes, such as learning, reasoning, problem solving, and natural language communication. A leader in the field is Artificial Intelligence Corporation of Waltham, Massachusetts. That company markets software that allows users to question the computer in ordinary English, by typing queries into the system. If the computer does not understand one of the words used, it will tell the user, ask for a definition, and add the new word to its vocabulary. Thus, the computer can "learn," just as can the robot we described earlier.

In terms of human thinking, reasoning is perhaps a step beyond learning, and a number of systems currently in use simulate human reasoning processes.

Artificial intelligence (AI) The field of information technology that attempts to simulate human cognitive processes, such as learning, reasoning, problem solving, and natural language communication.

ETHICAL DILEMMA

YOU HAVE RECENTLY accepted a job with an aggressive manufacturer of microcomputers. The firm has just recently entered the marketplace. Microcomputer manufacturers are engaged in intense competition. Each tries to become the first to introduce software packages that utilize English rather than computer language and are thus easier to use for the average consumer. Your former employer is rumored to be the leader in this area of software development. When you were hired, you were led to believe that your selection was based on your management potential. On the Monday morning beginning the third week on the new job, you receive the following memo from the president: "Please meet with me tomorrow at 8:15 for the purpose of discussing the developments your former employer has made in microcomputer software." You can provide the information, or you can refuse to provide the information and possibly jeopardize your career.
What would you do?

At Stanford University, a computer-directed analyzer diagnoses certain blood infections. SRI International employs a system called "Prospector," which reads seismographic information and identifies possible mineral deposits. Of course, computers do not actually reason in the way that we normally think of the term, but many of the tasks that require reasoning on the part of humans can be done by computers.

A related area of AI research concerning communication in ordinary English, as mentioned above, includes voice synthesizers and speech recognition programs. Voice synthesizers create a voice output from computers. Speech recognition programs translate voice inputs into language the machine understands. Voice synthesizers have already received wide usage, notably at grocery-store check-out counters where a voice announces the price as the checker sweeps the product across an optical scanning device. Voice recognition, on the other hand, has proven more difficult to develop. Although a number of systems accept voice commands, the vocabularies are limited. The technology is still advancing, and as these issues are resolved, voice recognition will become increasingly popular. Artificial intelligence is a truly exciting field that promises great benefits in terms of productivity and quality of life enhancement.

Computer Graphics

"A picture is worth a thousand words." Managers already can use computer programs to produce various kinds of graphs and charts in both black and white and glowing color. Through computer graphics, visual relationships among several pieces of data can be seen immediately.

Telecommuting

Telecommuting
When workers are able to remain at home and perform their work over data lines tied to a computer as if they were at the office.

Many firms have turned to telecommuting as a way of solving particular personnel needs. When workers are able to remain at home and perform their work over data lines tied to a computer as if they were at the office, the procedure is called **telecommuting.** Telecommuting is not for everyone, but certain workers such as writers, reservation agents, researchers, and computer programmers can easily adapt to this style of work. Telecommuters do not confront the long drives to and from work. Also, handicapped people who cannot easily go to a centralized workplace find telecommuting a good alternative.

Although it has many positive aspects, managers often have difficulty coping with the concept of telecommuting in practice. The question they often ask is, "How do I supervise a person that I never see?" Some workers dislike telecommuting because they enjoy the friendly association of co-workers. At Pacific Bell, a systematic procedure exists for selecting both the types of jobs and the types of people to benefit from telecommuting. In spite of the potential difficulties associated with telecommuting, it has been estimated that approximately 10 million people will be using telecommuting by the end of the decade.

Voice Recognition

The traditional way for a person to communicate with a computer has always been through programming. A manager could tell by the written program if a programmer did not communicate in the desired manner. The trend today is voice recognition, a rapidly developing new use of computers. Programs are now being designed that accept voice input to control their operations. As yet, managers cannot carry on full-fledged conversations, but there is reason to believe that this capability will occur in the near future.

In word processing, the use of voice recognition has progressed beyond the developmental phase. Rather than keyboard in textual material, the user speaks directly to the computer, and the words appear on the screen. Many managers resist using a keyboard, a resistance we expect will diminish when they see the actual words they use appearing instantly on the screen. People skilled in dictating should find the transition to voice recognition relatively easy.

Program Generators

Program generators
Programs that have been designed to write other programs.

Program generators are programs that have been designed to write other programs. Still in its infancy, the program generator is expected to have a major impact on management informational support systems in the future. Often a data-processing department gets bogged down with the demands placed on it by users. A report that is needed today may not be available for weeks, because the programmer does not have the time to complete the job. It is expected that when program generators are used, managers will receive much faster turnaround of their informational needs and at lower costs. Data-processing departments will likely require fewer programmers to accomplish the same tasks. The entire field of programming as we know it today is expected to be affected as program generators achieve greater sophistication in the future.

SUMMARY

A management information system (MIS) is any organized approach for obtaining relevant and timely information on which to base management decisions. An effective MIS typically employs computers and other sophisticated technologies. It draws information from various internal functional areas such as marketing and finance and integrates this information with that of the external environment. Both internal and external information is needed, and it should be timely, accurate, and complete. If not, effectiveness is reduced, complicating the decision-making process.

Managers at each organizational level make unique demands on the MIS. Top-level managers need to make far-reaching decisions that usually require extensive information relating to the external environment. Lower-level managers depend primarily on internal data. In designing the MIS, all managers must carefully consider four recommended steps: study the present system, develop a priority of information needed, develop the new information system, and choose a computer, either a super, a mainframe, a mini, or a micro. Management also uses various information subsystems, including accounting, manufacturing, and human resource management. A true MIS integrates these in order to provide managers at all levels with better decision-making capabilities.

New developments in computer hardware and software occur virtually every day: for example, videotext, teleconferencing, voice mail, and word processing.

A spreadsheet program provides a column-row matrix on which numbers or words can be entered and stored and calculations performed on that new data. A decision support system (DSS) allows users to interact directly with a computer and get answers quickly. Data base management reduces redundancies. Robots perform mechanical tasks. Artificial intelligence (AI) attempts to simulate human cognitive processes such as learning, reasoning, problem solving, and natural language communication. Other developments include computer graphics, telecommuting, voice recognition in word processing, and program generators, programs designed to write other programs.

REVIEW QUESTIONS

1. Define a management information system. What are the information needs of a firm?
2. What are the basic characteristics required of the MIS?
3. Briefly describe the type of reports that an effective MIS should produce.
4. List and briefly describe the steps involved in designing the MIS.
5. Distinguish among the following general types of computers:
   a. Super computers
   b. Mainframe computers
   c. Minicomputers
   d. Microcomputers
6. List and briefly describe the various information subsystems available to managers.
7. List and briefly describe the new developments in computer hardware and software that can be used to enhance productivity.

KEY TERMS

management information system (MIS)
videotext
teleconferencing

voice mail
word processing
decision support system (DSS)
robot

artificial intelligence (AI)
telecommuting
program generators

DAVID McNEIL SPEAKS BEFORE THE DATA PROCESSING MANAGEMENT ASSOCIATION, HOUSTON, TEXAS

MY NAME IS DAVID McNEIL. I am CEO of the McNeil Company, which I founded in 1957. The company is involved in three businesses. We have a medical division, Procare, which offers extended care to the elderly through four facilities similar to nursing homes. Procare also operates two pharmacies. The second business is toys. We have seven leased toy stores in malls. Our third and biggest operation is shoes. I run ten shoe stores, mostly in malls, and twelve shoe departments in department stores. Judy Mondy, your program chair, asked me to tell you about my experience with computers.

When I bought the medical division five years ago, it had its own IBM "Baby 36" computer system. John Seeger, the previous owner and still the president of Procare, is something of a "computer whiz." So I asked him to help computerize Shoes and Toys and gave him a free rein about how to do it. Two years and $400,000 later, we had a Prime computer in the main office with point-of-sale terminals in all our stores. The system cranked out daily, weekly, and monthly reports on every topic imaginable. Procare was never hooked into the Prime since it already had a good system.

The year before last, Procare got into financial trouble and John had to start spending all his time trying to get it back on track. However, his systems analyst, who had been with Procare for years, helped the people in Medical and Shoes when he could. Prime had no local office, but quickly sent a maintenance person by plane when we called and was able to diagnose some problems through a modem hookup. Still, the system stayed down quite a bit after John went back to Procare.

I soon realized that the stacks of computer paper on all my managers' desks were not being used. I don't know much about computers but I do know how much useless paperwork costs. So I began to eliminate reports, waiting for someone to yell. No one ever yelled. Before long the Prime was just being used for payroll, accounts receivable and payable, and general ledger. The point-of-sale terminals are still connected to the Prime, which costs a lot in phone charges, but the terminals are just used as cash registers. It is a good thing my managers kept their manual reporting and accounting system as a backup to the computer. We have all agreed that it will be a long time before we spend that much money and time again without knowing what we are doing.

QUESTIONS

1. Was McNeil's computerization effort "doomed from the start"? Why or why not?
2. What alternatives concerning his MIS did McNeil have after Procare got into financial trouble? What should he have done?

THE MIS AT FORT STEEL PRODUCTS

"I DO NOT KNOW how we managed before we got our computer," said Martha Tolpin. Martha is the owner of Fort Steel Products, Inc., in Fort Collins, Colorado. Fort makes a line of metal patio furniture that is marketed through lawn and garden stores and furniture stores in the Southwest. Selling is mainly by telephone. Each Fort salesperson has an interactive terminal that provides up-to-date information on inventory levels, prices and costs of items, shipping availability and costs, customer credit status, and so forth. Of course, the system also performs all the usual accounting functions such as payroll, accounts payable, and general ledger. Martha gets a single weekly report, which gives her summarized information for the week, the previous quarter, and the year to date.

Martha had decided early that computers represented the "wave of the future" but shopped around several years before deciding on a system for Fort. In the meantime she became competent on an IBM PC she had bought, using it for word processing and for some spreadsheet calculations.

One of many computer salespeople who called on Fort over the years was Ivan Pierson. Pierson was with Darkar, a consulting firm in New Orleans. After hearing Pierson's presentation and checking with several of his clients, Martha purchased a complete hardware and software package from Darkar. The system was designed especially for small manufacturers and cost $73,000, including fifty hours free programming and maintenance time. The initial price also included a three-day course on the system for Fort's head bookkeeper and a clerk. Martha knew that she could have bought the hardware locally for about $12,000. Spending the extra $60,000 or so just for software and support was a difficult decision.

Because she was "intrigued" with computers, as she put it, Martha went to New Orleans to sit through the course with her two employees. While she was in New Orleans, Pierson and his boss treated Martha to a Cajun dinner at K-Paul's Kitchen (owned by world-famous chef Paul Prudhomme) and a tour of Bourbon Street and the French Quarter.

During the two years since the system was installed, Martha has continued the friendship. She has recommended Darkar to several acquaintances, two of whom have made purchases. Martha also was instrumental in promoting the Darkar system through the southwest division of the American Association of Manufacturers, a trade association to which Fort belongs. Martha received no commission on the sales, but Darkar has improved the basic system markedly since she bought hers, and Pierson has ensured that each improvement was installed at Fort at no charge. In fact, says Martha, "I have not gotten any bill at all from Darkar in over a year."

QUESTIONS

1. Did Martha pay too much for her system? Justify your answer.
2. Discuss the human aspects of the case.

EXPERIENTIAL EXERCISE

After studying this text, students should have a much better appreciation of what type of work managers are involved in. In this exercise, participants will attempt to develop a profile of what attributes a manager should possess. Knowledge gained throughout the semester should be used in identifying necessary attributes.

Participants will have a copy of Exhibits 1, 2, and 3. The attributes listed in Exhibit 1 may be more or less important for a manager. Participants will rank order this list by assigning the letter "A" to the five (5) attributes that you think are the most important for a manager to have. Assign a "B" to the five (5) attributes you think second most important; "C" to the five (5) attributes third most important; and "D" to the five (5) attributes you feel are least important. Definitions of each of these attributes are listed in Exhibit 2. You will have *ten minutes* for this activity.

After doing your individual rankings of these attributes, all students, *except 6 individuals,* will be placed into either *Group 1* or *Group 2*. The six individuals not assigned to Groups 1 or 2 will make up the *Review Committee.* These individuals will sit together and reach a consensus on the attribute rankings. *Groups 1* and *2* will also review the individual rankings of each of its members, discuss them, and then agree on a group ranking for the attributes listed. Exhibit 3, a Group Summary Sheet, is provided for this purpose. You will have *fifteen* minutes for this activity.

After the completion of this exercise, the debriefing will begin by asking both groups, "What are the top five qualities needed by managers? Why?"

Then, ask members of the Review Committee, "Which group identified the most appropriate top five qualities needed by managers? Why?"

Next, ask both groups, "What were the least important qualities needed by managers? Why?

Then, ask members of the Review Committee, "Which group identified the most appropriate, least important qualities needed by managers? Why?"

The result of this exercise should be a realistic profile of what attributes a manager should possess to be effective.

NOTES

1. This case is a composite of a number of published accounts, among them: "Voice Mail Boosts Sales, Management Efficiency," *Textile World,* May 1986, 77–78; Harvard Business School ("J.P. Stevens & Co., Inc."), HBS Case Services case number 9–184–022, rev. November 1984); Larry Ward, "The J.P. Stevens MIS" (student paper at Bentley College, January 1987); and J.P. Stevens and Company, *Annual Report* (various years).
2. John Rossant and Wendy Zeller, "How Chrysler's $30,000 Sports Car Got Sideswiped," *Business Week,* 23 January 1989, 68.

3. "Breathing Room for U.S. Chipmakers," Fortune, 7 July 1986, 10.
4. Geoff Lewis, Anne R. Field, John J. Keller, and John W. Verity, "Big Changes At Big Blue," *Business Week*, 15 February 1988, 93.
5. Lewis, et al., "Big Changes," 93.
6. "The Passion Is Back at Apple Computer," *Fortune*, 19 January 1987, 8.
7. Joel Dreyfuss, "Networking: Japan's Latest Computer Craze," *Fortune*, 7 July 1986, 94.
8. Otis Port, "The Push for Quality," *Business Week*, 8 June 1987, 132.
9. Port, "Push for Quality," 132.
10. John Hoerr, "Getting Man and Machines to Live Happily Ever After," *Business Week*, 20 April 1987, 61.
11. Bill Saporito, "IBMs No-Hands Assembly Line," *Fortune* 15 (September 1986): 105.

REFERENCES

Aldersey-Williams, Hugh, and David Hunter. "Robots Head for the Farm." *Business Week* (8 September 1986): 66–67.

Atchinson, Sandra D. "These Top Executives Work Where They Play." *Business Week* (October 1986): 132–134.

Attaran, Mohsen, and Hossein Bidgoli. "Developing an Effective Manufacturing Decision Support System." *Business* (October–December 1986): 9–16.

Betts, Mitch. "Arming the Data Center for Corporate Warfare." *Computerworld* 22 (9 May 1988): 88.

Bowen, William. "The Puny Payoff from Office Computers." *Fortune* 113 (26 May 1986): 20–24.

Bylinsky, Gene. "A Breakthrough in Automating the Assembly Line." *Fortune* (26 May 1986): 64–66.

Dolan, Shimon, and Sharon Tziner. "Implementing Computer-Based Automation in the Office: A Study of Experienced Stress." *Organizational Behavior Management* 9 (April 1988): 183–187.

Field, Anne R., and Catherine L. Harris. "The Information Business." *Business Week* (25 August 1986): 82–90.

Fisher, Jane A. "Forging a Link Between Technology and Training." *Personnel* 63 (April 1986): 13–16.

Gregory, Gene. "The Japanese Enterprise: Sources of Competitive Strength." *Business and Society* 24 (Spring 1985): 13–21.

Halloway, Clark, and Herbert H. Hand. "Who's Running the Store? Artificial Intelligence!!!" *Business Horizons* 31 (March–April 1988): 70–76.

Hamilton, Rosemary. "Facing, Welcoming, Implementing Change." *Computerworld* 22 (19 September 1988): 95–96.

Hatcher, Larry, and Timothy L. Ross. "Gainsharing Plans—How Managers Evaluate Them." *Business* (October–December 1986): 30–37.

Hutchins, Dexter. "Having a Hard Time with Just-In-Time." *Fortune* (9 June 1986): 64–66.

Katcher, Philip, and Randy Allen. "Computerize Your Operation for Profit." *Automotive Marketing* 17 (Spring 1988): 66–73.

Keller, John J., Pete Engardio, Kenneth Dreyfack, and Russell Mitchell. "The Rewiring of America." *Business Week* (15 September 1986): 188–196.

Kline, Randall R. "Introducing New Technology." *Journal of Systems Management* (September 1986): 12–15.

Litton, Moneca. "Reducing the Risk." *Executive Female* 11 (March–April 1988): 11.

McCartney, Laton. "Brainstorming Problems with the Computer." *Dun's Business Month* 129 (January 1987): 71–72.

Morris, Richard M., III. "Management Control and Decision Support Systems—An Overview." *Industrial Management* 28 (January–February, 1988): 8–15.

Newport, John Paul, Jr. "A Growing Gap in Software." *Fortune* 113 (28 April 1986): 132–142.

Nolan, Richard L., Douglas W. Brockway, and Charles N. Tuller. "Ten Principles Transform I-S Operation into Information Utility." *Data Management* 26 (January 1988): 18–23.

Ogilvis, John R., Michael F. Pohlen, and Louise H. Jones. "Organizational Information Processing and Productivity Improvement." *National Productivity Review* 7 (Summer 1988): 229–237.

O'Reilly, Bryan. "Making Computers Snoop-Proof." *Fortune* 113 (17 March 1986): 65.

Port, Otis. "Teaching a Computer to Read Your Handwriting." *Business Week* (25 August 1986): 94.

Port, Otis, and John W. Wilson. "They're Here: Computers That Think." *Business Week* (26 January 1986): 94–98.

Rothman, Matt, and Emily T. Smith. "The Leading Edge of 'White-Collar Robotics.' " *Business Week* (10 February 1986): 94–95.

Simmons, LeRoy F., and Laurette Poules. "DSS: The Successful Implementation of a Mathematical Programming Model for Strategic Planning." *Computers & Operations Research* 15 (February 1988): 1–5.

Siwolor, Sana. "Computer Aid for Computer-Aided Design." *Business Week* (11 August 1986): 69.

Smith, Emily T. "Computers That See the Forest, Not Just the Trees." *Business Week* (15 December 1986): 100.

———. "This Chip Could Teach Evelyn Wood a Thing or Two." *Business Week* (3 November 1986): 140.

Sussman, Susan. "Corporations Urged to Improve How They Organize Information." *PC Week* 1 (17 March 1987): 1–2.

Tracy, Eleanor Johnson. "Storing Computer Data Far from the Office." *Fortune* 113 (31 March 1986): 66–67.

Verney, Thomas P., Charles J. Hollen, and George Rogol. "HR Planning for Robots in the Work Place." *Personnel* 63 (February 1986): 8–9.

Whiteside, David E., and Anne R. Field. "Artificial Intelligence Finally Hits the Desktop." *Business Week* (9 June 1986): 68–70.

JOHN MEYER'S BIG opportunity had finally arrived. In September 1989 he was appointed plant manager at his company's tubular products facility near Memphis, Tennessee. The plant employed 175 workers at that time and was responsible for rolling stainless steel strip into tubing, welding up the seam, and drawing it down to various shapes and wall thicknesses. The process was a moderately complex one, most of it done by heavy machines. The workers, all hired from the local area, required only one or two weeks of training.

John had been with his employer, Tennco Manufacturing Corporation, for ten years, having joined the company as an engineer just out of college. He had worked at several Tennco plants, first as a draftsman, then as a design engineer, and most recently as plant engineer at a Tennco chemical plant in Texas. The tubing plant was far different from anywhere John had worked before, but he was confident that the job of managing was about the same regardless of the organization or management level.

WORK FORCE

At John's previous job, most workers were highly trained technicians, most of whom had at least some college. Here the rank and file were generally young and unskilled. There was a larger percentage of blacks and far more women workers than John had seen at his previous plants. In discussions with the personnel director, John had learned that employee turnover averaged about 50 percent a year. Almost none of the workers and few of the supervisors had been with Tennco for more than five years.

The work force was not unionized, but an organizing drive the year before had almost succeeded. When John took the job as plant manager, he was told by the company president, "The Memphis plant hasn't lived up to our expectations. That's why you're being sent down there. Any major reversals—if the plant goes union, for example—and we'll have no choice but to go out of the tubing business."

MANAGEMENT TEAM

John had reviewed the personnel records of each of his immediate subordinates and had questioned his predecessor about them. During the first few days on the job, he met with each of them individually. His purposes were to try to get to know them better, to learn about any problems they had, and to set the right tone for future relationships.

The personnel director was a twenty-eight-year-old college graduate accountant. He had moved into the personnel job because he "wanted to work with people" and because the previous personnel director had quit unexpectedly and no one else wanted the job. There were only two clerks who worked in personnel. During their conversation, the personnel director complained to John, "I've never had any authority around here. I'm really just a glorified record-keeper. The production manager does most of the hiring and firing."

The chief accountant, who was also responsible for financial planning and quality control, was on temporary assignment from the home office in Knoxville. He seemed to John to be very competent, but John knew that he would have to move back to his regular job as soon as a replacement could be found. There were three clerks in the bookkeeping department.

The production manager was the only "old salt" at the plant. He had been with Tennco for twenty-five years, the last fifteen at Memphis. He told John that although he didn't have a college degree, he knew more about this business than anybody else in the company. "I learned manufacturing in the school of hard knocks," he said, "and when you learn there it stays with you."

In discussions with each of the managers, John explained what he expected of them. "Our purpose here is to make as much standard quality, stainless steel tubing as we can at the lowest possible cost" is the way he put it. "Each manager should focus on helping me to accomplish that goal." John got no argument from anyone except the production manager, who simply said, "There is only so much you can do with the kind of lazy hoodlums you can hire for $4 an hour." John let that comment pass, but it was disturbing to him.

A TRUSTY SECRETARY

John felt that the most positive aspect of his new job was his secretary, Anne Bourne. Anne, nearly fifty, had retired from the U.S. civil service at a nearby navy base and had good typing and shorthand skills. After a few days, Anne asked if she could talk frankly with John. Assured that she could, Anne confided, "I really want to see this plant do well. For many of the people around here, it's the best job they could get, and they really need it. But you have your work cut out for you." John asked, "What do you see as the major problem?" Anne replied, "I don't know that there is any one major problem. This is the only tubing plant Tennco has, and I'm not sure they place much importance on it. I don't know what it will take to change that, but I want you to know that I'll do everything in my power to help you do it."

SUPPORT FROM THE TOP

At the end of that first week on the job, John called his boss, Noah Livingston. After the usual pleasantries, John said, "Mr. Livingston, I think I'm going to have to make some major changes down here, and some of our people are going to be pretty upset." "What kind of changes are you talking about?" asked Mr. Livingston. "Well,"

said John, "for one thing, I think I may have to hire a new production manager and let Sam go. Also, we're going to have to start paying decent wages here so we can get people with a higher skill level and keep them longer." Mr. Livingston answered, "Well, John, you know what your budget is, and you're much closer to that situation than I am. All I'm asking you to do is make it work. Whatever you need from me, except more money, you'll get. I've watched you for a long time and I have great confidence in your ability. Don't let me down. But more important than that, don't let yourself down." As John hung up the phone, he had the uneasy feeling that he was out on a limb and everybody around him had a saw.

QUESTIONS

1. What management function should John pay most attention to first? Justify your answer.
2. Do you agree with John that management is the same regardless of organization or management level? Why or why not?
3. What environmental forces are likely to affect John in his new job? What should be his attitude toward people and things outside the plant?
4. Should John terminate the production manager? Defend your answer.

PARMA CYCLE COMPANY of Parma, Ohio, a Cleveland suburb, is one of only three firms in the United States that actually manufacture complete bicycles. Most of Parma's competitors import parts from other countries and simply assemble the bicycles here. In 1989, Parma Cycle employed about 800 workers, mainly machine operators and assemblers. The main factory is laid out, coincidentally, like a bicycle wheel, with component manufacturing departments representing the tire and spokes and assembly being done in the factory's center, representing the hub.

Parma Cycle makes a line of bicycles that it markets under the Parma name; however, most of their bicycles are purchased by large national retailers and marketed under those retailers' house names. A few bicycles are exported to Europe and South America, but Parma has found it difficult to compete with Japanese and Italian bicycle manufacturers.

Jesse Heard is the personnel director. He has been with Parma Cycle for twenty-three years. His first job was as a painter, when painting was done with a hand-held spray gun. He was later promoted to supervisor and worked in several departments at the plant. Because the company paid for college tuition and fees, as well as books, to encourage supervisors to advance their education, Jesse went to college. In 1975, he received the bachelor's degree in personnel administration from Case Western University in Cleveland. Jesse was immediately promoted to a job in the personnel department and three years later became the personnel director.

Parma's work force is unionized; employee recruitment is done primarily through referrals from current workers. Selection is based on personal interviews, evaluation of job-related application forms, and, for certain jobs, a basic skills test conducted by the supervisor. The supervisor makes the final hiring decision. Workers must join the union before the end of a three-month probationary period. Over the years, the union, a member of the National Association of Machinists, has won wages and benefits about average for the Cleveland area.

In general, the working environment at Parma Cycle has been good. The company has a relatively flat organizational structure with few levels of managers (see the accompanying organizational chart).

In May 1985, the Equal Employment Opportunity Commission (EEOC) received a complaint about employment practices at Parma. It was alleged that while the proportion of blacks in the Cleveland area approached 25 percent, only 8 percent of the Parma Cycle work force was black. Further, the complaint alleged, there were only two black managers above the level of supervisor.

Jesse Heard felt that the company was doing everything it should with regard to equal opportunity. The firm had an affirmative action plan and a practice of encouraging managers to employ blacks and other minority group members, as well as women. In fact, Jesse's efforts to encourage the employment of protected group members had provoked some managers to complain to the company president. The complaint was withdrawn in 1986 after a visit from an EEOC investigator.

One morning in late 1988, Gene Wilson, the corporate planner at Parma, visited Jesse. Gene was ecstatic. He had just received word that the board of directors had approved a new southern plant, in Clarksdale, Mississippi. "I really appreciate your help on this, Jesse," he said. "Without the research you did on the personnel needs for the new plant, I don't think that it would have been approved." "We still have a long way to go," said Jesse. "There is no doubt that we can construct the building and install the machinery. But getting skilled workers in Clarksdale may not be so easy." "Well," said Gene, "the results of the labor survey that you did there last year indicate that we'll be able to get by. Anyway, some of the people here at Parma will surely agree to transfer." "When is the new plant scheduled to open?" asked Jesse. Gene replied, "The building will be finished in February 1989. The machinery will be in by

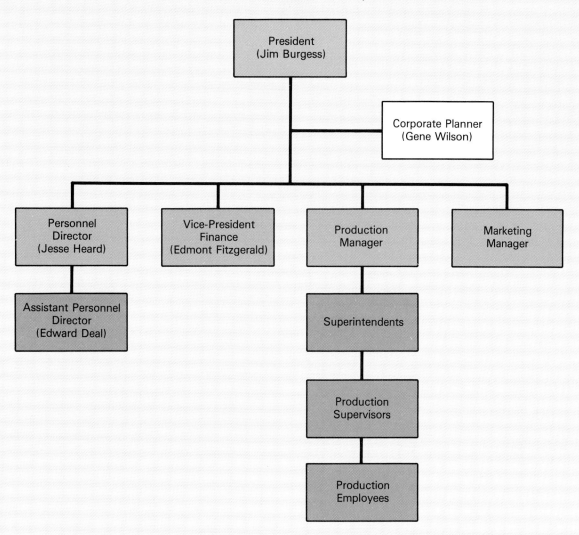

May. The goal is to be in production by September 1989." "Gosh," said Jesse, "I had better get to work."

A few minutes later, back in his office, Jesse considered what the future held at Parma Cycle. The company had been located at Parma, Ohio, a Cleveland suburb, since its founding. It had grown over the years to become the nation's fourth largest bicycle manufacturer. The decision to open the Clarksdale, Mississippi, plant had been made in hopes of achieving decreased production costs because of lower wages. Although no one ever came right out and said it, it was assumed that the southern plant would be non-union. The elimination of union work rules was expected to be a benefit.

The state of Mississippi had offered a ten-year exemption from all property taxes, a significant advantage because tax rates for Cleveland-area industries were extremely high. Jesse was pleased that he had been involved in the discussions from the time that the new plant was first suggested. Even with the advanced preparation he had done, he knew that the coming months would be extremely difficult for him and his staff.

At that moment, Jesse's assistant, Edward Deal, walked in with a bundle of papers. "Hi, Ed," said Jesse, "I'm glad you're here. The Clarksdale plant is definitely on the way, and you and I need to get our act together." "That's great," said Edward. "It is quite a coincidence, too, because I had just been going over this stack of job descriptions, identifying which ones we might eliminate as we scale back at this plant." Jesse said, "Remember, Ed, we are not going to cut back very much here. Some jobs will be deleted and others added. But out of the 800 positions here, I'll bet that not more than forty will be actually eliminated." "So, what you are saying is that we basically have to staff the plant with people we hire from the Clarksdale area?" Edward asked. Jesse replied, "No, Ed, we will have some people here who are willing to transfer even though their jobs are not being eliminated. We will then replace them with others we hire in the Cleveland area. Most of the workers at Clarksdale, though, will be recruited from that area."

Ed asked, "What about the management team?" "Well," said Jesse, "I think the boss already knows who the main people will be down there. They are managers we currently have on board, plus a fellow we located at a defunct three-wheeler plant in Mound Bayou, Mississippi."

"What will be that plant's relationship to this one?" asked Ed. Jesse replied, "The plant manager there will work directly for Mr. Burgess [the president]. But personnel, marketing, and finance will be centralized, with just a supervisor and a couple of clerks for each function in Clarksdale."

QUESTIONS
1. Draw an organizational chart for Parma Cycle as it will exist after the new plant is open. Classify the organization in at least two ways and explain your classifications.
2. Explain the part the informal organization might play in determining who is willing to transfer to the southern plant.
3. Discuss how you believe Parma Cycle should staff the new plant.

THROUGHOUT THE 1980s, Lincoln Electric Company has remained the world's largest manufacturer of welding machines and electrodes. It has 2,600 employees in two U.S. factories near Cleveland, Ohio, and approximately 600 in three factories located in other countries. Lincoln's market share is estimated at 40 percent of the U.S. market for arc welding equipment and supplies.

A HISTORICAL SKETCH

In 1895, after being "frozen out" of the depression-ravaged Elliott-Lincoln Company, John C. Lincoln obtained his second patent and began to manufacture an improved motor. He began business with $200 he had earned redesigning a motor for young Herbert Henry Dow, who later founded Dow Chemical Company.

In 1906, Lincoln incorporated and moved from a one-room, fourth-floor factory to a new three-story building erected in East Cleveland. He expanded his work force to thirty, and sales grew to over $50,000 a year. But John Lincoln preferred being an engineer and inventor, rather than a manager, and so it was left to another Lincoln to manage the company through its years of success.

In 1907, after a bout with typhoid fever forced him out of Ohio State in his senior year, James F. Lincoln, John's younger brother, joined the fledgling company. In 1914, with the company still small and determined to improve its financial condition, he became the active head of the firm, with the titles of general manager and vice-president. John Lincoln remained president of the company for some years, but he became more involved in other business ventures and in his work as an inventor.

One of James Lincoln's early actions as head of the firm was to ask employees to elect representatives to a committee to advise him on company operations. The advisory board has met with the chief executive officer twice monthly since that time. The first year the advisory board was in existence, working hours were reduced from fifty-five per week—then standard—to fifty hours a week. In 1915, the company gave each employee a paid-up life insurance policy. In 1918, an employee bonus plan was attempted. The plan was not continued, although the idea was to resurface later and become the backbone of the Lincoln Management System.

The Lincoln Electric Employees' Association was formed in 1919 to provide health benefits and social activities. This organization continues today and has assumed several additional functions over the years. By 1923, a piecework pay system was in effect, employees got a two-week paid vacation each year, and wages were adjusted for changes in the Consumer Price Index. Approximately 30 percent of Lincoln's stock was set aside for key employees in 1914 when James F. Lincoln became general manager, and a stock purchase plan for all employees was begun in 1925.

The board of directors voted to start a suggestion system in 1929. The program is still in effect, but cash awards, a part of the early program, were discontinued several years ago. Now, suggestions are rewarded by additional performance appraisal "points," which affect year-end bonuses. The legendary Lincoln bonus plan was proposed by the advisory board and accepted on a trial basis by James Lincoln in 1934. The first annual bonus amounted to about 25 percent of wages. There has been a bonus every year since then. The bonus plan has been a cornerstone of the Lincoln Management System, and recent bonuses have approximated annual wages.

James F. Lincoln died in 1965, and there was some concern, even among employees, that the Lincoln system would fall into disarray, that profits would decline, and that year-end bonuses might be discontinued. Quite the contrary, in 1982, seventeen years after Lincoln's death, the company appeared stronger than ever and remains so today. Each year since 1965, except for the recession years 1982 and 1983, has seen higher profits and bonuses. Employee morale and productivity remain high; employee turnover is almost nonexistent except for retirements, and Lincoln's market share is stable.

COMPANY PHILOSOPHY

James F. Lincoln was the son of a Congregational minister, and Christian principles were at the center of his business philosophy. While Christian principles have served as important guidelines for business operations, there is no indication that the company has attempted to evangelize its employees or customers—or the general public, for that matter. The current board chairman, Mr. Irrgang, and the president, Mr. Willis, do not even mention the Christian gospel in their recent speeches and interviews. The company motto, "The actual is limited, the possible is immense" is prominently displayed, but there is no display of religious slogans, and there is no company chapel.

Attitude toward the Customer

James Lincoln saw the customer's needs as the raison d'être for every company. "When any company has achieved success so that it is attractive as an investment," he wrote, "all money usually needed for expansion is supplied by the customer in retained earnings. It is obvious that the customer's interests, not the stockholder's, should come first." In 1964 he said, "Care should be taken . . . not to rivet attention on profit. Between 'How much do I get?' and 'How do I make this better, cheaper, more useful?' the difference is fundamental and decisive." Lincoln's goal, often stated, is "to build a better and better product at a lower and lower price." It is obvious, James Lincoln said, "that the customer's interests should be the first goal of industry."

Attitude toward Stockholders

Stockholders are given last priority at Lincoln. This is a continuation of James Lincoln's philosophy: "The last group to be considered is the stockholders who own stock because they think it will be more profitable than investing money in any other way." Concerning division of the largess produced by incentive management, Lincoln writes, "The absentee stockholders also will get their share, even if undeserved, out of the greatly increased profit that the efficiency produces."

Attitude toward Unionism

There has never been a serious effort to organize Lincoln employees. While James Lincoln criticized the labor movement for "selfishly attempting to better its position at the expense of the people it must serve," he still had kind words for union members. He excused abuses of union power as "the natural reactions of human beings to the abuses to which management has subjected them." Lincoln's idea of the correct relationship between workers and managers is shown by this comment: "Labor and management are properly not warring camps; they are parts of one organization in which they must and should cooperate fully and happily."

Beliefs and Assumptions about Employees

If fulfilling customer needs is the desired goal of business, then employee performance and productivity are the means by which this goal can best be achieved. It is the Lincoln attitude toward employees, reflected in the following quotations:

The greatest fear of the worker, which is the same as the greatest fear of the industrialist in operating a company, is lack of income. . . . The industrial manager is very conscious of his company's need of uninterrupted income. He is completely oblivious, evidently, of the fact that the worker has the same need.

He is just as eager as any manager is to be part of a team that is properly organized and working for the advancement of our economy. . . . He has no desire to make profits for those who do not hold up their end in production, as is true of absentee stockholders and inactive people in the company.

If money is to be used as an incentive, the program must provide that what is paid to the worker is what he has earned. The earnings of each must be in accordance with accomplishment.

Status is of great importance in all human relationships. The greatest incentive that money has, usually, is that it is a symbol of success. . . . The resulting status is the real incentive. . . . Money alone can be an incentive to the miser only.

There must be complete honesty and understanding between the hourly worker and management if high efficiency is to be obtained.

George E. Willis, president, dispels the impression that Lincoln management is "soft" management. "We care about one another around here, but we are quite autocratic. When managers tell workers to do something, they expect it to be done."

ORGANIZATIONAL STRUCTURE

Lincoln has never had a formal organization chart. The objective of this policy is to ensure maximum flexibility. An open-door policy is practiced throughout the company, and personnel are encouraged to take problems to the person most capable of resolving them. Perhaps because of the quality and enthusiasm of the Lincoln work force, routine supervision is almost nonexistent. A typical production foreman, for example, supervises as many as 100 workers, a span of control that does not allow for more than infrequent worker–supervisor interaction. Position titles and traditional flows of authority do imply something of an organization structure, however. For example, the vice-president, sales, and the vice-president, electrode division, report to the president, as do various staff assistants such as the personnel director and the director of purchasing. From such implied relationships, it has been determined that production workers have two or, at most, three levels of supervision between themselves and the president.

PERSONNEL POLICIES
Recruitment and Selection

Every job opening at Lincoln is advertised internally on company bulletin boards, and any employee can apply for any job so advertised. External hiring is done only for entry-level positions. Selection for these jobs is done on the basis of personal interviews—there is no aptitude or psychological testing. Out of about 3,500 applicants recently interviewed by the personnel department, fewer than 300 were hired. Final selection is made by the supervisor who has the job opening.

Job Security and Compensation

After one year, employees are guaranteed thirty hours per week and promised that they will not be discharged except for misconduct. There has been no layoff at Lincoln since 1949.

Insofar as possible, base wage rates are translated into piece rates. Practically all production workers and many others—for example, some forklift truck drivers—are paid by piece rate. Once established, piece rates are never changed unless a substantive change in the way a job is done results from a source other than the worker doing the job. In December of each year, a portion of annual profits is distributed to employees as bonuses. Incentive bonuses since 1934 have

averaged about the same as annual wages and somewhat more than after-tax profits. Even for the recession years 1982 and 1983, bonuses averaged over $10,000 each year. Afterward, bonuses returned to historic levels of over $15,000.

Training and Education

Production workers are given a short period of on-the-job training and then placed on a piecework pay system. Lincoln does not pay for off-site education. The idea behind this policy is that, since everyone cannot take advantage of such a program, it is unfair to expend company funds for an advantage to which there is unequal access. Sales personnel are given on-the-job training in the plant, followed by a period of work and training at one of the regional sales offices.

Fringe Benefits and Executive Perquisites

A medical plan and a company-paid retirement program have been in effect for many years. A plant cafeteria, operated on a break-even basis, serves meals at about 60 percent of usual costs. An employee association, to which the company does not contribute, provides disability insurance and organizes social and athletic activities. An employee stock ownership program, instituted in about 1925, and regular stock purchases have resulted in employee ownership of about 50 percent of Lincoln's stock.

As to executive perquisites, there are none—crowded, austere offices, no executive washrooms or lunchrooms, and no reserved parking spaces. Even the company president pays for his own meals and eats in the cafeteria.

FINANCIAL MANAGEMENT

James F. Lincoln felt strongly that financing for company growth should come from within the company—through initial cash investment by the founders, through retention of earnings, and through stock purchases by those who work in the firm. The company uses a minimum of debt in its capital structure. There is no borrowing at all, with the debt being limited to current payables. Even the new $20,000,000 plant in Mentor, Ohio, was financed totally from earnings.

The unusual pricing policy at Lincoln is succinctly stated by President Willis: " . . . at all times price on the basis of cost and at all times keep pressure on our costs." This policy resulted in Lincoln's price for the most popular welding electrode then in use going from 16 cents a pound in 1929 to 4.7 cents in 1938. More recently the SA-200 welder, Lincoln's largest-selling portable machine, decreased in price during much of recent history. According to Dr. C. Jackson Grayson of the American Productivity Center in Houston, Texas, Lincoln's prices in general have increased only one fifth as fast as the Consumer Price Index since 1934. This has resulted in a welding products market in which Lincoln is the undisputed price leader for the products it manufactures. Not even the major Japanese manufacturers, such as Nippon Steel for welding electrodes and Osaka Transformer for welding machines, have been able to penetrate this market.

WORKER PERFORMANCE AND ATTITUDES

Exceptional worker performance at Lincoln is a matter of record. The typical Lincoln employee earns about twice as much as other factory workers in the Cleveland area. Yet the labor cost per sales dollar at Lincoln, currently 23.5 cents, is well below industry averages.

Annual sales per Lincoln production employee is approximately $157,000. An observer at the factory quickly sees why this figure is so high. Each worker is proceeding busily and thoughtfully about his task. There is no idle chatter. Most workers take no coffee breaks. Many operate several machines and make a substantial component unaided. The supervisors, some with as many as 100 subordinates, are busy with planning and record-keeping duties with hardly a glance at the people they supervise. The manufacturing procedures appear efficient—no unnecessary steps, no wasted motions, no wasted materials. Finished components move smoothly to subsequent work on hand.

Worker turnover at Lincoln is practically nonexistent, except for retirements and departures by new employees.

In an effort to gain greater insight into company practices and the attitudes and perceptions of employees, a series of interviews were conducted. The following are excerpts from interviews with employees at Lincoln by the casewriter.

Ed Sanderson, a twenty-three-year-old high school graduate who had been with Lincoln for four years as a machine operator.

Q. Roughly, what were your earnings last year including your bonus?

A. $37,000.

Q. What have you done with the money since you have been here?

A. Well, we've lived pretty well and we've bought a condominium.

Q. Have you paid for the condo?

A. No, but I could!

Q. Are you paid on a piece-rate basis?

A. My gang is. There are nine of us who make the bare electrodes, and the whole gang gets paid on how many electrodes we make.

Q. Why do you think Lincoln employees produce more than workers in other plants?

A. That's the way the company is set up. The more you put out, the more you are going to make.

Q. Do you think it's the piece rate and bonus together?

A. I don't think people would work here if they didn't know that they would be rewarded at the end of the year.

Q. Do you think Lincoln employees will ever join a union?

A. No! We don't have a union shop and I don't think I could work in a union shop.

Betty Stewart, a fifty-two-year-old high school graduate, with Lincoln for thirteen year, who was working as a cost accounting clerk.

Q. What jobs have you held here besides the one you have now?

A. I worked in payroll for a while and then came into cost accounting.

Q. How much did you earn last year?

A. Roughly $20,000, but I was off several weeks because of back surgery.

Q. You weren't paid while you were off for back surgery?

A. No.

Q. Did the Employees' Association help out?

A. Yes. The company doesn't furnish that, though. We pay $6 a month into the Employees' Association. I think my check from them was $105.00 a week.

Q. How did you get your job at Lincoln?

A. I was bored silly where I was working, and I heard that Lincoln kept their people busy. So I applied and got the job.

Roger Lewis, twenty-three-year-old Purdue graduate in mechanical engineering, who has been in the Lincoln sales program for fifteen months.

Q. How did you get your job at Lincoln?

A. I saw that Lincoln was interviewing on campus at Purdue and I went by. I later came to Cleveland for a plant tour and was offered the job.

Q. Do you think Lincoln salesmen work harder than those in other companies?

A. Yes. I don't think there are many salesmen for other companies who are putting in fifty- to sixty-hour weeks. Everybody here works harder. You can go out in the plant or you can go upstairs and there's nobody sitting around.

Q. Why do you think Lincoln employees have such high productivity?

A. Piecework has a lot to do with it. Lincoln is smaller than many plants, too; you can stand in one place and see the materials come in one side and product go out the other. You feel a part of the company. The chance to get ahead is important, too. They have a strict policy of promoting from within; you know you have a chance. I think in a lot of other places you may not get as fair a shake as you do here. The sales offices are on a smaller scale, too. I like that. I tell someone that we have two people in the Baltimore office and they say, "You've got to be kidding." It's smaller and more personal. Pay is the most important thing. I have heard that this is the highest-paying factory in the world.

Joe Trahan, fifty-eight-year-old high school graduate, who had been with Lincoln thirty-nine years and was employed as a working supervisor in the tool room.

Q. Roughly, what was your pay last year and how much was your bonus?

A. Around $55,000; salary, bonus, stock dividends. My bonus was about $23,000.

Q. What do you think of the executives at Lincoln?

A. They're really top-notch.

Q. Why do you think you produce more than people in similar jobs?

A. We are on the incentive system. Everything we do we try to improve to make a better product with a minimum of outlay. We try to improve the bonus.

Q. Tell me something about Mr. James Lincoln, who died in 1965.

A. You are talking about Jimmy, Sr. He always strolled through the shop in his shirtsleeves. Big fellow. Always looked distinguished. Gray hair. Friendly sort of guy. I was a member of the advisory board one year. He was there each time.

QUESTIONS

1. Describe Lincoln Electric's management philosophy, especially with regard to the motivation and leadership of the firm's work force.
2. The typical Lincoln employee earns about twice as much as other factory workers, yet labor costs are well below industry averages. How can this be explained?
3. What are the major factors contributing to the high employee productivity at Lincoln Electric? Discuss.
4. What can other companies learn from Lincoln Electric's experience? Why haven't other firms applied the Lincoln philosophy and approach?
5. Would you want to work for Lincoln Electric? Explain your response.

REFERENCES

Lincoln, James F. *Incentive Management.* Cleveland, Ohio: Lincoln Electric Company, 1951.

Lincoln, James F. *A New Approach to Industrial Economics.* New York: Devin-Adair Company, 1961.

Sharplin, Arthur. "Lincoln Electric's Unique Policies." *Personnel Administrator* (June 1983): 70–76.

ON AUGUST 26, 1982, Manville Corporation, formerly Johns-Manville, filed for protection under Chapter 11 of the bankruptcy law. In 1987, Manville was still struggling to emerge from Chapter 11 protection. The company's bankruptcy climaxed an eight-year history during which Manville had grown to one of the largest, most prestigious U.S. industrial corporations.

The founder of what was to become Manville Corporation, Henry Ward Johns, built a sizable fortune in the late 1800s mining asbestos and inventing new uses for it. He died in 1898 of "dust pthisis pneumonitis," now called asbestosis. By the 1930s, it was clear that the problem of breathing asbestos dust was serious. Nearly fifty years later, a federal appeals court concluded, "The unpalatable facts are that in the twenties and thirties the hazards of working with asbestos were recognized." By 1930, however, Manville was the largest producer of asbestos, and new uses were being found for the product every year. It was eventually used in most automobiles, school buses, hospitals, schools, factories, and commercial facilities. Asbestos filled the bill anywhere a fireproof and permanent fibrous material was needed.

Manville successfully defended lawsuits brought by asbestos victims beginning in the 1920s. In 1934 Manville's chief lawyer wrote, "[It] is only within a comparatively recent time that asbestosis has been recognized by the medical and scientific professions as a disease—in fact [this has been] one of our principal defenses."

Manville opposed publication of information about asbestos dangers during 1934. A Manville executive wrote in 1934, "I quite agree that our interests are best served by having asbestosis receive the minimum of publicity." He was writing to another asbestos industry executive about a letter from the editor of *Asbestos,* an industry trade journal. The editor had written, "Always you have requested that for obvious reasons, we publish nothing, and, naturally your wishes have been respected."

In 1950, Manville's chief physician reported to top management that all but four of 708 asbestos workers he had studied had evidence of lung damage. Of the seven who had the most severe conditions, the physician wrote, "The fibrosis of this disease is irreversible and permanent. . . . It is felt that [they] should not be told of [their] condition so that [they] can live and work in peace and the company can benefit from [their] many years experience." Efforts were made during the 1950s to clean the air breathed by Manville workers, but the dangers to users and installers of asbestos products were concealed. The physician mentioned above later told of his unsuccessful efforts to have warning labels placed on asbestos products in the early 1950s.

Until an extensive study in 1964 resulted in public awareness of the problem, Manville placed no warnings on the thousands of tons of asbestos fiber it distributed worldwide. Even after 1964, the Manville label simply stated, "Inhalation of asbestos in excessive quantities over long periods of time may be harmful." With increasing public attention, however, substitute products began to be found, and asbestos use declined precipitously after about 1975.

Asbestos had always been very profitable for Manville. It became even more profitable as competitors left the industry on discovering the disaster they had helped to create. In 1976, although asbestos fiber constituted only 12 percent of Manville's sales, it accounted for 51 percent of operating profit. As asbestos use in the United States declined by one half, and as thousands of asbestos victims began filing increasingly successful lawsuits, Manville management tried to diversify into other products. Manville bought dozens of small companies and eventually purchased the huge Olinkraft Corporation, a paper company in West Monroe, Louisiana. Nothing worked. With an entrenched and elderly management team, and with the easy profits from asbestos rapidly disappearing, Manville was unable to keep net income from collapsing. Inflation-corrected earnings declined steadily from 1978 onward, to a $223 million loss in 1982.

By 1982, potential asbestos liabilities were estimated by Manville to exceed $2 billion and by others to be many times that. Through legal maneuvering, the company was able to delay payment of practically all of the asbestos judgments. The Chapter 11 filing in August 1982 stopped the asbestos lawsuits.

As receivables flowed in and debt no longer had to be paid, the company received over $300 million in extra cash. The bankruptcy filing also secured for Manville top managers a few more years of respectability, extensive corporate benefits, and half-million-dollar annual salaries.

More than 15,000 asbestos victims and their families waited for the cumbersome Chapter 11 process to end, although most admitted that their claims were unlikely to be paid anyway. And each month, hundreds more discovered that they had asbestosis or, worse, mesothelioma, a rapidly growing and always fatal cancer caused by asbestos.

Manville's unrepentant lawyer-chief executive, J.A. McKinney, who had been with the company for over thirty years, disclaimed responsibility. He wrote, "There has been no cover-up. . . . Your corporation has acted honorably." In late 1983, the company began an extensive public relations and lobbying effort aimed at getting government to protect Manville and help pay for the asbestos injuries. Then Manville filed its proposed reorganization plan with the bankruptcy court. The plan provided for a surviving corporation, Manville II, which would keep the assets of the old company but be immune from asbestos lawsuits.

QUESTIONS
1. Why do you believe Manville executives chose to suppress publicity about asbestosis? Defend or oppose their action.
2. Discuss the ethics involved in J.A. McKinney's statement that the corporation has acted honorably. Should Manville have been allowed to seek protection under the U.S. bankruptcy code? Why or why not?

Glossary

A

ABC inventory method
The classification of inventory items for control purposes into three categories according to unit costs and number of items kept on hand.

Acceptance sampling
The inspection of a portion of the output or input of a process to determine acceptability.

Accountability
Any means of ensuring that the person who is supposed to do a task actually performs it and does so correctly.

Action planning
The establishment of performance objectives and standards for individuals.

Activity ratios
Ratios that measure how efficiently the firm is utilizing its resources.

Activity trap
The tendency described by George Odiorne of some managers and employees to become so enmeshed in carrying out activities that they lose sight of the reasons for what they are doing.

Administrative model
A model that is descriptive and provides a framework for comprehending the nature of the process that decision makers actually use when selecting among various alternatives.

Affective conflict
Intragroup conflict that is based on emotional responses to a situation.

Affirmative action
Performance required to ensure that applicants are employed, and that employees are treated appropriately during employment, without regard to race, creed, color, or national origin.

Alternatives
Choices that the decision maker has to decide on.

Analyzer strategy
A strategy that attempts to maintain a stable business while innovating on the fringe.

Artificial intelligence (AI)
The field of information technology that attempts to simulate human cognitive processes, such as learning, reasoning, problem solving, and natural language communication.

Attainable-ideal norm
A norm that describes behavior where approval occurs for increasing amounts of behavior until an attainable goal is reached, then, further goal-oriented behavior lacks value.

Attribution
Determining the cause of a situation.

Authority
The right to decide, to direct others to take action, or to perform certain duties in achieving organizational goals.

Autocratic leader
A person who tells subordinates what to do, and expects to be obeyed without question.

B

Backward integration
A company's taking control of any of the sources of its inputs, including raw materials and labor.

Biosocial development
Involves the different developmental stages that influence an individual's behavior and attitudes at work.

Body language
A nonverbal method of communication in which physical actions such as motion, gestures, and facial expressions convey thoughts and emotions.

Boundary spanners
Individuals who serve the roles of information processor and representative for an organization or its subunits to others outside the unit's boundary.

Brainstorming
An idea-generating technique wherein a number of persons present alternatives without regard to questions of feasibility or practicality.

Budget
A statement of planned allocation of resources expressed in financial or numerical terms.

Bureaucracy
A prototype form of organization that emphasizes order, system, rationality, uniformity, and consistency.

Burnout
A state of fatigue or frustration, which stems from devotion to a cause, way of life, or relationship that did not provide the expected reward.

Business ethics
The application of ethical principles to business relationships and activities.

Business-level strategic planning
The process concerned with how to compete; it takes place within the strategic business units.

C

Capital budget
A statement of planned expenditures of funds for facilities and equipment.

Career
Individually perceived sequence of attitudes and behaviors associated with work-related experiences and activities over the span of a person's life.

Career management
A formalized approach to ensure that employees have opportunities to maximize their potential.

Carrying costs
Expenses associated with maintaining and storing the products before they are sold or used.

Centrality
The degree to which the activities of the position are linked and important to those of other individuals or subunits.

Centralization
The degree to which authority is retained by higher-level managers within an organization rather than being delegated.

Chain of command
The line along which authority flows from the top of the organization to any individual.

Change agent
The person who is responsible for ensuring that the planned change in OD is properly implemented.

Change sequence
The sequence of events that is needed to bring about change in an organization.

Closure
The tendency to form a complete mental image out of incomplete data among related stimuli.

Coalescing
The process of individuals or groups combining their resources to pursue common goals and objectives.

Coalitions
Informal groups that form to influence the goals, policies, and allocation of resources in groups.

Coercive power
Power derived from the ability to punish or to recommend punishment.

Cohesiveness
The degree of attraction that the group has for each of its members.

Committee
A group of people assigned to work together to do something not included in their regular jobs.

Communication channels
Means by which information is transmitted.

Communication networks
The flow of messages between and among people in organizations.

Communication
The transfer of information, ideas, understanding, or feelings between people.

Compensation
Includes all rewards individuals receive as a result of their employment.

Concentric diversification
The development of businesses related to the firm's current businesses.

Conceptual skill
The ability to comprehend abstract or general ideas and apply them to specific situations.

Conflict
Antagonism or opposition between or among persons.

Conglomerate diversification
The development of businesses unrelated to the firm's current businesses.

Consideration
The extent to which leaders have relationships with subordinates characterized by mutual trust, respect, and consideration of employees' ideas and feelings.

Contact chart
A diagram showing various individuals in the organization and the numbers of interactions they have with others.

Contingency planning
The development of different plans to be placed in effect if certain events occur.

Contingency theory
A management theory that refers to a manager's ability to adapt to meet particular circumstances and restraints a firm may encounter.

Control tolerances
Specifications of how much deviation will be permitted before corrective action is taken.

Control chart
A graphic record of how closely samples of a product or service conform to standards over time.

Controlling
The process of comparing actual performance with standards and taking any necessary corrective action.

Co-opting
A method of increasing power and creating alliances in which individuals or groups whose support is needed are absorbed into another group.

Coordination
The process of ensuring that persons who perform interdependent activities work together in a way that contributes to overall goal attainment.

Corporate culture
The system of shared values, beliefs, and habits within an organization that interacts with the formal structure to produce behavioral norms.

Corporate-level strategic planning
The process of defining the overall character and purpose of the organization, the businesses it will enter and leave, and how resources will be distributed among those businesses.

Cost leadership strategy
A strategy in which the organization aggressively seeks efficient facilities, pursues cost reductions, and uses tight cost controls to produce products more efficiently than competitors.

Critical path method (CPM)
A planning and control technique that involves the display of a complex project as a network, with one time estimate used for each step in the project.

Creativity
The ability to generate ideas that are both innovative and functional.

D

Decision making
The process of generating and evaluating alternatives and making choices among them.

Decision risk
Exposure to the probability that an incorrect decision will have an adverse effect on the organization.

Decision support system (DSS)
An information system that allows users to interact directly with a computer so they can get answers quickly.

Defender strategy
A strategy that seeks to maintain current market share by holding on to current customers.

Delegation
The process of assigning responsibility along with the needed authority.

Delphi technique
A formal procedure for obtaining consensus among a number of experts through the use of a series of questionnaires.

Democratic leader
A person who tries to do what the majority of subordinates desire.

Departmentation
The process of grouping related work activities into manageable units.

Differentiation strategy
A strategy that involves an attempt to distinguish the firm's products or services from others in the industry.

Disciplinary action
Action taken to correct unacceptable behavior.

Discipline without punishment
A process whereby a worker is given time off with pay when discipline is suggested to determine if he or she really wants to follow the rules and continue working for the company.

Discipline
The state of employee self-control and orderly conduct present within an organization.

Diversification
Increasing the variety of products or services made or sold.

Dominant cultures
Those cultures that express the shared views of the majority of the organization's members.

E

Economic order quantity (EOQ)
A procedure for balancing ordering costs and carrying costs so as to minimize total inventory costs.

Effectiveness
The degree to which the process produces the intended outputs.

Efficiency
The proportional relationship between the quality and quantity of inputs, and the quality and quantity of outputs produced.

Empathy
The ability to identify with the various feelings and thoughts of another person.

Employee assistance programs
Systematic efforts to help employees cope with problems that interfere with their productive ability on the job and their personal happiness.

Employment requisition
A form issued to activate the recruitment process; it typically includes such information as the job title, starting date, pay scale, and a brief summary of principal duties.

Equity theory
A theory which assumes that people assess their performance and attitudes by comparing both their contribution to work and the benefits they derive from it to the contributions and benefits of a "comparison other" whom the person selects–who in reality may be like or unlike the person.

Ethics
The discipline dealing with what is good and bad, or right and wrong, or with moral duty and obligation.

Expectancy
When participants anticipate certain behaviors from other participants.

Executive Orders (EOs)
Directives issued by the president that have the force and effect of laws enacted by Congress.

Expectancy theory
An approach to motivation that attempts to explain behavior in terms of an individual's goals and choices and the expectations of achieving these goals.

External environment
Those factors that affect a firm from outside the organization's boundaries.

Externalizers
Individuals who believe that others control their lives.

Extrinsic motivation
Motivation by factors outside the job itself, such as pay, job title, or tenure.

Extroverted person
An individual who is outgoing, often aggressive, and dominant.

F

Feeling-type individuals
Individuals who are aware of other people and their feelings, like harmony, need occasional praise, dislike telling people unpleasant things, tend to be sympathetic, and relate well to most people.

Focus strategy
A strategy in which the organization concentrates on a specific regional market, product line, or buyer group.

Formal communication channels
Communication channels that are officially recognized by the organization.

Forward integration
Integration toward the final users of a company's product or service.

Function
A type of work activity that can be identified and distinguished from other work.

Functional authority
This is the right of staff specialists to issue orders in their own names in designated areas.

Functional authority organization
A modification of the line and staff organization whereby staff departments are given authority over line personnel in narrow areas of specialization.

Functional-level strategic planning
The process of determining policies and procedures for relatively narrow areas of activity that are critical to the success of the organization.

G

Gatekeepers
Individuals in positions that allow them to screen information and control access to it.

Grapevine
The informal means by which information is transmitted in an organization.

Grievance procedure
A systematic process that permits employees to complain about matters affecting them.

Group structure process
The interpersonal interactions needed to accompany and accomplish task activities.

Group
Two or more people having a unifying relationship, such as common goals or physical proximity.

Groupthink
A mode of thinking with a norm of concurrence-seeking behavior.

H

Halo effect
Refers to an individual's using a general impression of a person to evaluate that individual's specific behaviors or attitudes.

Hawthorne effect
The influence of behavioral researchers on the people they study.

Health
Refers to the employees' freedom from illness and their general physical and mental well-being.

Horizontal conflict
Conflict that exists between employees or departments at the same level.

Horizontal differentiation
The process of forming additional units at the same level in the organization.

Horizontal integration
Buying or taking control of competitors at the same level in the production and marketing process.

Host country
The country in which resides the operational unit of the multinational corporation.

Human resources planning
The process of systematically reviewing personnel requirements to ensure that the required number of employees with the required skills are available when they are needed.

Human skill
The ability to understand, motivate, and get along with other people.

Hypothesis
A tentative statement of the nature of the relationship that exists between a cause and an effect, which provides an explanation of the cause that brought about the observed effect.

I

Individual or self-oriented roles
Roles that focus on satisfying an individual's needs; such role behaviors frequently distract the group from effective functioning through individual dominance in the group.

Influencing
The process of determining or affecting the behavior of others.

Informal communication channels
Ways of transmitting information within an organization that bypass formal channels.

Informal organization
The set of evolving relationships and patterns of human interaction within an organization that are not officially prescribed.

Informal group
Two or more persons associated with one another in ways not prescribed by the formal organization.

Information filtering
The process by which a message is altered through the elimination of certain data as the communication moves up from person to person in the organization.

Information overload
A condition that exists when an individual is presented with too much information in too short a time.

Initiating structure
The extent to which leaders establish goals and structure their roles and the roles of subordinates toward the attainment of the goals.

Integration
The unified control of a number of successive or similar operations.

Inter-role conflict
Conflict that occurs when the expectations associated with different roles come into conflict.

Intergroup conflict
Conflict that takes place between groups.

Internal environment
The organization's continuing purpose or reason for being.

Internalizers
Individuals who feel that they control their own lives and actions.

Interorganizational conflict
Conflict that exists between organizations that are interdependent with the same suppliers, customers, competitors, and governmental agencies, among others.

Interpersonal conflict
Conflict that results when two individuals disagree about issues, actions, or goals.

Intersender conflict
Conflict that occurs when different people with whom the role holder interacts have different expectations of him or her.

Intrapersonal conflict
Conflict that exists when an individual must choose between incompatible goals.

Intrasender conflict
Conflict that occurs when one person sends a role holder conflicting or inconsistent expectations.

Intrinsic motivation
Motivation by factors within the job, such as creativity, autonomy, and responsibility.

Introverted person
An individual who is shy and withdrawn.

Intuitive-type individuals
Individuals who like solving new problems, dislike doing the same

thing over and over again, jump to conclusions, are impatient with routine details, and dislike taking time for precision.

Inventory
Refers to the goods or materials available for use by a business.

Iron law of responsibility
In the long run, those who do not use power in a manner in which society considers responsible will tend to lose it.

J

Jargon
A special language that group members use in their daily interaction.

Job analysis
The systematic process of determining the skills and knowledge required for performing jobs in the organization.

Job description
A document that provides information regarding the tasks, duties, and responsibilities of the job.

Job enrichment
Refers to basic changes in the content and level of responsibility of a job so as to provide greater challenge to the worker.

Job sharing
Involves the filling of a job by two or more part-time employees, each working part of a regular work week and sharing the benefits of one full-time worker.

Job specification
A statement of the minimum acceptable qualifications that a person should possess to perform a particular job.

Just-in-time inventory method
The practice of having inputs to the production process delivered precisely when they are needed, thereby assigning the responsibility for keeping inventories to a minimum to suppliers.

L

Laissez-faire leader
A person who is uninvolved in the work of the unit.

Leadership continuum
The graphical representation developed by Robert Tannenbaum and Warren H. Schmidt showing the trade-off between a manager's use of authority and the freedom that subordinates experience as leadership style varies from boss centered to subordinate centered.

Leadership
Getting others to do what the leader wants them to do.

Learning
The acquisition of skills, knowledge, abilities, and attitudes through patterned actions and practice.

Leased employees
Individuals provided by an outside firm at a fixed hourly rate, similar to a rental fee, often for extended periods.

Legitimate power
Power that is derived from the position or job individuals hold in an organization.

Leverage ratios
Ratios that measure whether a firm has effectively used outside financing.

Line and staff organizations
Organizations that have direct, vertical relationships between different levels and also specialists responsible for advising and assisting other managers.

Line-staff conflict
Conflict that occurs over resources or the involvement of staff people in line decisions.

Line departments
Departments directly involved in accomplishing the primary purpose of the organization.

Line organizations
Those organizations that have only direct, vertical relationships between different levels within the firm. They include only line departments.

Liquidity ratios
Ratios that measure a firm's ability to meet its current obligations.

M

Machiavellianism
The extent to which an individual has a tendency to manipulate others.

Maintenance or group-building roles
Roles that direct the group toward positive member interaction and interpersonal behavior.

Management information system (MIS)
Any organized approach for obtaining relevant and timely information on which to base management decisions.

Management by objectives (MBO)
A philosophy of management that emphasizes the setting of agreed-on objectives by superior and subordinate managers and the use of these objectives as the primary bases of motivation, evaluation, and control efforts.

Management development programs
Formal efforts to improve the skills and attitudes of present and prospective managers.

Management
The process of getting things done through the efforts of other people.

Managerial Grid ®
A two-dimensional matrix developed by Robert Blake and Jane Mouton that shows concern for people on the vertical axis and concern for production on the horizontal axis.

Matrix organization
A permanent organization designed to achieve specific results by using teams of specialists from different functional areas within the organization.

Mechanistic organization
An organization that emphasizes relatively less flexible and more stable organizational structures.

Middle managers
Managers above the supervisory level but subordinate to the firm's most senior executives.

Mission
The organization's continuing purpose or reason for being.

Model
An abstraction of a real-world situation.

Motivation
The willingness to put forth effort in the pursuit of organizational goals.

Multinational company (MNC)
An organization that conducts a large part of its business outside the country in which it is headquartered and has a significant percentage of physical facilities and employees in other countries.

N

Networking
The cultivating of relationships with the right people for the purpose of obtaining power.

Noise
Anything that interferes with or disrupts the accurate transmission and/or reception of messages.

Nominal grouping
An approach to decision making that involves idea generation by group members, group interaction only to clarify ideas, member rankings of ideas presented, and alternative selection by summing ranks.

Nonroutine decisions
Decisions that are designed to deal with unusual problems or situations.

Norm
A standard of behavior expected of informal group members.

O

Objectives
The desired end results of any activity.

Obsolescence
The failure to maintain up-to-date knowledge in a career field.

Organizational constituency
Any identifiable group that organizational managers either have or acknowledge a responsibility to represent.

Ombudsperson
A complaint officer with access to top management who hears employee complaints, investigates, and sometimes recommends appropriate action.

Open-door policy
An established guideline that allows workers to bypass immediate supervisors concerning substantive matters without fear of reprisal.

Open system
An organization or assemblage of things that affects and is affected by outside events.

Operating budget
A statement of the planned income and expenses of a business or subunit.

Ordering costs
Administrative, clerical, and other expenses incurred in initially obtaining inventory items and placing them in storage.

Organic organizations
Organizations that have flexible organizational designs and can adjust rapidly to change.

Organization
Two or more people working together in a coordinated manner to achieve group results.

Organizational development
A planned and systematic attempt to change the organization, typically to a more behavioral environment.

Organizational mission
The organization's continuing purposes—in short, what is to be accomplished for whom.

Organizational behavior
The field of study that analyzes individuals, groups, and structure to determine the effect they have on behavior within an organization.

Organizational mirror
Describes a set of activities in which a particular organizational group, the host group, gets feedback from representatives of several other organizational groups about how it is perceived and regarded.

Organizational strategists
Individuals who spend a large portion of their time on matters of vital or far-ranging importance to the organization as a whole.

Organizational stakeholder
An individual or group whose interests are affected by organizational activities.

Organizational structure
The formal relationships among groups and individuals in the organization.

Organizing
The process of prescribing formal relationships among people and resources to accomplish goals.

Orientation
The process of introducing new employees to the job, the company, and other employees.

P

Parent country
The country in which the headquarters of the multinational corporation is located.

Participative leader
A person who involves subordinates in decision making but may retain the final authority.

Path-goal theory
The proposition that managers can facilitate job performance by showing employees how their performance directly affects their receiving desired rewards.

Payoff relationship
Evaluating alternatives in terms of their potential benefits or costs.

Perception set
A fixed tendency to interpret information in a certain way.

Perception
The understanding or view people have of things in the world around them.

Performance Appraisal
A formal system that provides a periodic review and evaluation of an individual's job performance.

Peripheral norms
Norms that guide behaviors that are important, but not essential, to the performance of the organization's goals or mission.

Person-role conflict
Conflict that occurs when the activities expected of a role holder violate the individual's values and morals.

Personal power
Power based on the contacts individuals have developed over time that allow them to influence the behavior of others.

Personality
Consists of a wide range of motives, emotions, values, interests, attitudes, and competencies regarding an individual.

PERT (Program Evaluation and Review Technique)
A planning and control technique that involves the display of a complex project as a network of events and activities with three time estimates used to calculate the expected time for each activity.

Pivotal norms
Norms that guide behavior essential to the core mission of the organization.

Planning
The process of determining in advance what should be accomplished and how it should be realized.

Plans
Statements of how objectives are to be accomplished.

Policy
A predetermined guide established to provide direction in decision making.

Political action committees
Tax-favored organizations formed by special interest groups representing U.S. industries to accept contributions and influence governmental action favoring those industries.

Politics
A network of interactions by which power is acquired, transferred, and exercised on others.

Pooled interdependence
Groups that rely on each other only because they belong to the same parent organization.

Portfolio strategy
The process of determining how an SBU will compete in a particular line of business. Specifically it pertains to the mix of business units and product lines that fit together in a logical way to provide maximum competitive advantage for the corporation.

Position power
Power that results from one's official place in an organization.

Positive reinforcement
Also known as *operant conditioning* or *behavior modification,* involves repeatedly pairing desired behaviors or outcomes with positive reinforcement, rewards, or feedback.

Preferred-value norm
A norm that describes behavior where either too much or too little of the behavior receives disapproval from group members.

Preliminary interviews
Interviews used to eliminate the obviously unqualified applicants.

Primary groups
Relatively small groups, characterized by relatively close associations among members.

Proactive response
The anticipation of what is occurring in the external environment and making decisions based on these conclusions.

Problem content
The environment in which the problem exists, along with the decision maker's knowledge of that environment, and the environment that will exist after a choice is made.

Procedure
A series of steps for the accomplishment of some specific project or endeavor.

Product life cycle
The pattern of sales volume that all products follow and that includes the stages of introduction, growth, maturity, and decline.

Productive power
Power that occurs when a job-holder has open channels to resources.

Productivity
A measure of the relationship between inputs (labor, capital, natural resources, energy, and so forth) and the quality and quantity of outputs (goods and services).

Profitability ratios
Ratios that measure the overall operating efficiency and profitability of the firm.

Program generators
Programs that have been designed to write other programs.

Power
The potential or actual ability to influence others in a desired direction.

Progressive discipline
A disciplinary-action approach designed to ensure that the minimum penalty appropriate to the offense is imposed.

Project organization
A temporary organization designed to achieve specific results by using teams of specialists from different functional areas within the organization.

Projection
An emotional biasing of perceptions.

Prospector strategy
A strategy involving innovation, by seeking out new opportunities, taking risks, and expanding.

Q
Quality
The degree of excellence of a product or service.

R
Rate-busters
Individuals who produce more than the level acceptable to the leaders.

Rational-economic model
A model that outlines how decisions should be made rather than describes how decisions actually are made.

Reactive response
The action by managers based on forces impacting the firm from the external environment.

Reciprocal interdependence
Groups where the operations of each precede and act as prerequisites to the functioning of the other.

Recruitment
The process of attracting individuals–in sufficient numbers and with appropriate qualifications–and encouraging them to apply for jobs with the organization.

Reinforcement theory
The idea that human behavior can be explained in terms of the previous positive or negative outcomes of that behavior.

Responsibility
An obligation to perform work activities.

Retrenchment
The reduction of the size or scope of a firm's activities.

Robot
An automatically controlled machine that can perform mechanical tasks.

Role ambiguity
A role holder who lacks sufficient information to perform the activities associated with that individual's role.

Role overload
A more complex form of conflict that occurs when the expectations sent to a role holder are compatible, but their performance exceeds the amount of time available to the person for performing the expected activities.

Role
The total pattern of expected behavior of an individual.

Rule
A specific and detailed guide to action set up to direct or restrict action to a fairly narrow manner.

S

Safety
The protection of employees from injuries due to work-related accidents.

Satisficing
Occurs when an alternative is selected that meets minimum rather than optimum standards of acceptance.

Scalar principle
The philosophy that authority and responsibility should flow from top management downward in a clear, unbroken line.

Scientific method
A formal way of doing research that comprises observation of events, hypothesis formulation, experimentation, and acceptance or rejection of hypotheses.

Scientific management
The name given to the principles and practices that grew out of the work of Frederick Taylor and his followers and that are characterized by concern for efficiency and systematization in management.

Secondary groups
Groups that are larger and less intimate than primary groups.

Selection
The process of identifying those recruited individuals who will best be able to assist the firm in achieving organizational goals.

Self-fulfilling prophecy
The idea that the manager's positive or negative expectations will have significant influence on employee motivation and performance.

Sensation-type individuals
Individuals who dislike new problems unless there are standard ways to solve them, like an established routine, must usually work all the way through to reach a conclusion, show patience with routine details, and tend to be good at precise work.

Sensitivity training
An organizational development (OD) technique that uses leaderless discussion groups.

Sequential interdependence
Occurs when one group's operations precede and act as prerequisites for the second group's.

Social contract
The set of rules and assumptions about behavior patterns among the various elements of society.

Social leader
Individuals who ''maintain'' the group and help it develop cohesiveness and collaboration by encouraging group members' involvement.

Social responsibility
The implied, enforced, or felt obligation of managers, acting in their official capacities, to serve or protect the interests of groups other than themselves.

Social audit
Measuring the degree to which firms contribute to the welfare of various elements of society and to that of society as a whole.

Sociotechnical school
A school of management thought which is based on the premise that managers could exclude neither technology (representing organizational structure) nor work groups (reflecting human relations) when trying to understand a work system.

Source
The person who has an idea or message to communicate to another person or persons.

Span of management
The number of people a manager can effectively supervise.

Span of management (control)
The number of direct subordinates reporting to any manager.

Specialization of labor
The division of a complex job into simpler tasks so that one person or group may carry out only identical or related activities.

Staff departments
Provide line people with advice and assistance in specialized areas.

Standard operating procedures (SOP)
The stable body of procedures, written and unwritten, that govern an organization.

Standards
Established levels of quality or quantity used to guide performance.

Standing plans
Plans that remain roughly the same for long periods of time.

Staffing
The formal process of ensuring that the organization has qualified workers available at all levels to meet its short- and long-term business objectives.

States of nature
Refers to the various situations that could occur and the probability of each of these situations happening.

Statistical process control
A procedure that gauges the performance of the manufacturing process by carefully monitoring changes in whatever is being produced.

Status symbol
A visible, external sign of one's social position.

Stereotyping
The situation when an individual attributes behaviors or attitudes to a person on the basis of the group or category to which that person belongs.

Stockholders
The owners of a corporation.

Strategic planning
The determination of overall organizational purposes and objectives and how they are to be achieved.

Strategic planning staff specialists
Specialists who assist and advise managers in strategic planning.

Strategic control points
Critical points selected for monitoring in the process of producing goods or services.

Strategic business unit
Any part of a business organization that is treated separately for strategic planning purposes.

Stress audit
An audit that helps identify the symptoms and causes of stress.

Stress
The body's reaction to any demand made on it.

Strong culture
An organization's dominant culture that is widely and ardently held by members of the organization.

Subcultures
Cultures characteristic of various subunits within an organization.

Substantive conflict
Intragroup conflict that is based on intellectual disagreement among group members.

Supervisory managers
Persons who directly oversee the efforts of those who actually perform the work.

Survey feedback method
The method of basing organizational change efforts on the systematic collection and measurement of subordinate attitudes by anonymous questionnaires.

Synergism
The cooperative action of two or more persons working together to accomplish more than they could working separately.

Systems approach
The viewing of any organization or entity as an arrangement of inter-related parts that interact in ways that can be specified and to some extent predicted.

T

Tactical plans
Plans designed to implement or carry out the strategic plans of top management.

Task activity
The steps used to perform a task, not including the procedures and materials required to accomplish it.

Task leader
Individuals who help the group achieve its goals by clarifying and summarizing member comments and focusing the group's tasks.

Task or functional groups
Groups that are determined by prescribed job requirements.

Task roles
Roles that focus on task or goal accomplishment.

Team building
A conscious effort to develop effective work groups throughout the organization.

Technical skill
The ability to use specific knowledge, methods, and techniques in performing work.

Telecommuting
Workers are able to remain at home and perform their work over data lines tied to a computer as if they were at the office.

Teleconferencing
A method of conducting or participating in discussions by telephone or videophone.

Theory Y
A view of management by which a manager believes people are capable of being responsible and mature.

Theory X
The traditional view of management that suggests that managers are required to coerce, control, or threaten employees in order to motivate them.

Thinking-type individuals
Individuals who are unemotional and uninterested in people's feelings, like analysis and putting things into logical order, are able to reprimand people and fire them when necessary, may seem hard-hearted, and tend to relate well only to other thinking types.

Timing
The determination of when a message should be communicated.

Top managers
The organization's most senior executives.

Trait approach to leadership
The evaluation and selection of leaders based on their physical, mental, and psychological characteristics.

Transactional analysis (TA)
A training and development method that considers the three ego states of Parent, Adult, and Child in helping people understand interpersonal relations.

Transactions
The exchange of resources, such as budgeted funds, support services, products, and information, between two work units.

Transformational leader
A person who has the ability to take an organization through a major strategic change such as revitalization.

Transformation processes
Key organizational components that change inputs into outputs.

Tunnel vision
Occurs when people have mental blinders, such as individual biases, that can restrict the search for an adequate solution to a relatively narrow range of alternatives.

Type I ethics
The strength of the relationship between what an individual or an organization believes to be moral and correct and what available sources of guidance suggest is morally correct.

Type A individuals
Individuals who tend to feel very competitive, be prompt for appointments, do things quickly, and always feel rushed.

Type B individuals
Individuals who tend to be more relaxed, take one thing at a time, and express their feelings.

Type II ethics
The strength of the relationship between what one believes and how one behaves.

U

Unattainable-ideal norm
A norm that describes behavior where ''more is better.''

Union
A group of employees who have joined together for the purpose of dealing with their employer.

Unity of command principle
The belief that each person should answer to only one immediate superior; each employee has only one boss.

V

Vertical conflict
Conflict that exists between supervisor and subordinates, who may disagree about the best way to accomplish a task.

Vertical differentiation
The process of creating additional levels in the organization.

Videotext
The remote display on a CRT of information from computer files and data bases.

Voice mail
Spoken messages transmitted electronically and stored for delivery to the recipient at a later time.

W

Word processing
A computer application that creates and edits written material.

Worker participation
The process of involving workers in the decision-making process.

Name Index

Company Index

Subject Index